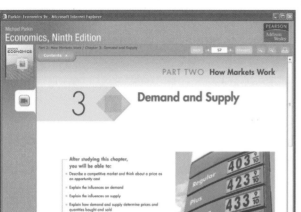

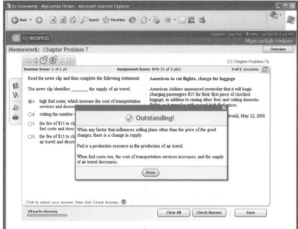

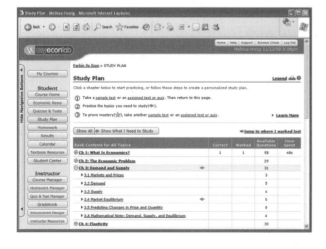

The full eText and a demo of MyEconLab are available at www.myeconlab.com

MyEconLab is an online assessment system that gives students the tools they need to learn from their mistakes — right at the moment they are struggling.

Online problem sets

In the Ninth Edition, all of the Review Quizzes and end-of-chapter problems and applications can be assigned and completed online. In addition, each chapter provides two pre-loaded Sample Tests so students can self-assess their understanding of the material.

Study Plan with targeted tutorial help

A Study Plan is generated from each student's results on Sample Tests and instructor assignments. Students see which topics they have mastered — and, more importantly, which need remediation. The Study Plan links to additional practice problems and tutorial help such as guided solutions and animated graphs. Flashcards and live tutoring are also available.

Hands-off course management, with options for customization

Instructors choose how much or how little energy they want to spend setting up the course, and they reap the benefits of online automatic grading. Students' results are tracked in MyEconLab's powerful online Gradebook.

ECONOMICS

NINTH EDITION

MICHAEL PARKIN
University of Western Ontario

Addison-Wesley
Boston San Francisco New York
London Toronto Sydney Tokyo Singapore Madrid
Mexico City Munich Paris Cape Town Hong Kong Montreal

Publisher	Denise Clinton
Editor in Chief	Donna Battista
Senior Acquisitions Editor	Adrienne D'Ambrosio
Development Editor	Deepa Chungi
Managing Editor	Nancy Fenton
Photo Researcher	Beth Anderson
Production Coordinator	Alison Eusden
Director of Media	Susan Schoenberg
Content Lead for MyEconLab	Douglas Ruby
Senior Media Producer	Melissa Honig
Executive Marketing Manager	Roxanne McCarley
Rights and Permissions Advisor	Shannon Barbe
Senior Manufacturing Buyer	Carol Melville
Copyeditor	Catherine Baum
Cover Design	Joyce Wells
Technical Illustrator	Richard Parkin
Text Design, Project Management and Page Make-up	Elm Street Publishing Services

Origami cover art folded by Michael G. LaFosse from handmade paper made by Richard L. Alexander, Origamido, Inc.

Photo credits appear on page C-1, which constitutes a continuation of the copyright page.

Library of Congress Cataloging-in-Publication Data
Parkin, Michael, 1939–
　　Economics/Michael Parkin. — 9th ed.
　　　　p. cm.
　　Includes index.
　　ISBN 0-321-58949-1; 978-0-321-58949-1 (alk. paper)
　　1. Economics.　　I. Title.
　　HB171.5.P313　　2008
　　330—dc22

1 2 3 4 5 6 7 8 10—CRK—12 11 10 09 08

Addison-Wesley
is an imprint of

PEARSON

www.pearsonhighered.com

ISBN 10: 0-321-58949-1
ISBN 13: 978-0-321-58949-1

TO

ROBIN

Michael Parkin received his training as an economist at the Universities of Leicester and Essex in England. Currently in the Department of Economics at the University of Western Ontario, Canada, Professor Parkin has held faculty appointments at Brown University, the University of Manchester, the University of Essex, and Bond University. He is a past president of the Canadian Economics Association and has served on the editorial boards of the *American Economic Review* and the *Journal of Monetary Economics* and as managing editor of the *Canadian Journal of Economics*. Professor Parkin's research on macroeconomics, monetary economics, and international economics has resulted in over 160 publications in journals and edited volumes, including the *American Economic Review*, the *Journal of Political Economy*, the *Review of Economic Studies*, the *Journal of Monetary Economics*, and the *Journal of Money, Credit and Banking*. He became most visible to the public with his work on inflation that discredited the use of wage and price controls. Michael Parkin also spearheaded the movement toward European monetary union. Professor Parkin is an experienced and dedicated teacher of introductory economics.

BRIEF
CONTENTS

PREFACE

Historic is a big word. Yet it accurately describes the economic events and policy responses that followed the subprime mortgage crisis of August 2007. Economics moved from the business report to the front page as fear gripped producers, consumers, financial institutions, and governments. The unimaginable repeat of a Great Depression gradually became imaginable as house prices plunged, credit markets froze, financial institutions failed, governments (both in the United States and around the world) mounted massive bailouts and rescues, the Fed made loans and bought debts of a quality that central banks don't normally touch, and the prices of items from gasoline and food to stocks and currencies fluctuated wildly.

Even the *idea* that the market is an efficient mechanism for allocating scarce resources came into question as some political leaders trumpeted the end of capitalism and the dawn of a new economic order in which tighter regulation reigned in unfettered greed.

Rarely do teachers of economics have such a rich feast on which to draw. And rarely are the principles of economics more surely needed to provide the solid foundation on which to think about economic events and navigate the turbulence of economic life.

Although thinking like an economist can bring a clearer perspective to and deeper understanding of today's events, students don't find the economic way of thinking easy or natural. *Economics* seeks to put clarity and understanding in the grasp of the student through its careful and vivid exploration of the tension between self interest and the social interest, the role and power of incentives—of opportunity cost and marginal benefit—and demonstrating the possibility that markets supplemented by other mechanisms, might allocate resources efficiently.

Parkin students begin to think about issues the way real economists do and learn how to explore difficult policy problems and make more informed decisions in their own economic lives.

The Ninth Edition Revision

The ninth edition of *Economics* retains all of the improvements achieved from its predecessors, with its thorough and detailed presentation of the principles of economics, its emphasis on real-world examples and applications, its development of critical thinking skills, its diagrams renowned for pedagogy and precision, and its path-breaking technology.

This comprehensive revision also incorporates and responds to the suggestions for improvements made by reviewers and users, in both the broad architecture of the text and chapter-by-chapter.

Current issues organize each chapter. News stories about today's major economic events tie each chapter together, from new chapter-opening vignettes to end-of-chapter problems and online practice. Students learn to use economic tools to analyze their own daily decisions and recent real-world events and issues.

Each chapter includes a discussion of a critical issue of our time, to demonstrate how economic theory can be applied to explore a particular debate or question. Issues of central importance include:

- Gains and tensions from globalization, the rise of Asia, and the changing structure of the global economy in Chapters 2, 7, and 23
- High and rising cost of food in Chapters 2 and 3
- Fluctuations in gas and oil prices and the effects of high gas prices on auto sales in Chapters 3, 4, and 18
- Changing patterns of consumption in the information age in Chapter 8
- Climate change in Chapter 16
- Efficient use of natural resources and today's tragedies of the commons in Chapter 17
- Fed and government rescues and bailouts in Chapters 24 and 31
- Financial instability of 2008 in Chapters 24, 27, and 31
- Currency fluctuations in Chapters 25 and 26
- Recession of 2008–2009 in Chapters 27, 28, 29, and 30
- Real-world examples and applications appear in the body of each chapter and in the end-of-chapter problems and applications. Each chapter has approximately 10 new additional problems tied to current news and events. All of these problems have parallel questions in MyEconLab.

Questions that appear daily in MyEconLab in the *Economics in the News* are also available in MyEconLab for assignment as homework, quizzes, or tests.

Highlights of the Micro Revision

In addition to being thoroughly updated and revised to include the topics and features just described, the microeconomics chapters feature the following seven major changes:

1. ***Global Markets in Action*** (Chapter 7): This new chapter explains the sources and effects of international trade, its winners and losers, and the effects of trade protection (tariffs and import quotas) on economic welfare. The chapter applies the tools of demand and supply, consumer and producer surplus, and deadweight loss explained in two earlier chapters. Offshore outsourcing and the ongoing failure of the Doha negotiations feature in this chapter.

2. ***Utility and Demand*** (Chapter 8): Extensively revised and reorganized, this chapter provides a more intuitive and less graphical analysis of utility maximization. Changes in consumer choices in the market for recorded music, in which digital downloads have almost driven out CDs, illustrate the predictions of marginal utility theory. The chapter includes an explanation of behavioral economics and neuroeconomics. (Material on the budget line found in the previous edition is omitted from this chapter but can be found in the first part of Chapter 9, an alternative chapter on indifference curves.)

3. ***Monopoly*** (Chapter 13): The final section of this chapter now covers the regulation of natural monopoly, which was previously found in a separate chapter. This change enables monopoly regulation to be covered when the material on unregulated monopoly and its inefficiency is fresh in the student's mind.

4. ***Monopolistic Competition*** (Chapter 14): In the ninth edition, this market type has its own full-chapter treatment. High selling costs are illustrated with the breakdown of the price of a pair of running shoes between manufacturing and selling. An example focused on cell phones illustrates product differentiation.

5. ***Oligopoly*** (Chapter 15): This market type also has its own chapter and is expanded to include a section

on antitrust law. As with the change in the monopoly chapter, this change enables antitrust law to be studied when the coverage of cartels and the temptation to fix prices is still in the student's mind.

6. ***Externalities*** (Chapter 16): This ninth edition chapter focuses on climate change and the economic debate it engenders, as we feature these topics at several points as the major example of a negative externality and the alternative ways of dealing with it.

7. ***Uncertainty and Information*** (Chapter 20): This chapter contains a heavily revised explanation of the "lemon" problem and trading risk in credit and insurance markets. The dramatic changes in the price of risk during the subprime crisis illustrate the working of the market for risky loans.

Highlights of the Macro Revision

The thoroughly updated coverage of macroeconomics is now organized in four parts: *monitoring the trends and fluctuations, understanding the trends, understanding the fluctuations,* and *macroeconomic policy.* The introductory chapter of previous editions is now redistributed across the other chapters as needed. The content of the previous edition's chapter on the classical model is distributed between the economic growth chapter and a new chapter on financial markets. In addition to these organizational changes, the macroeconomics chapters feature the following seven major revisions.

1. ***Measuring GDP and Economic Growth*** (Chapter 21): This chapter now includes a description and discussion of the recent history of real GDP growth and fluctuations found in the previous edition's introductory macro chapter. The explanation of the real GDP calculation has been simplified, and the current chain-dollar method of real GDP calculation is presented in a new Math Note at the end of the chapter.

2. ***Monitoring Jobs and Inflation*** (Chapter 22): This substantially revised chapter has a simplified coverage of the anatomy and types of unemployment but a more comprehensive explanation of the sources of unemployment. As today's unemployment is compared with that of the Great Depression, the empirical relationship between cyclical unemployment and the output gap is more clearly illustrated. The measurement of the price level and inflation is motivated with a discussion of inflation and why it is a problem. The

chapter also includes new material on alternative price indexes including the personal consumption expenditure deflator as well as the concept of core inflation. The chapter now concludes with a brief section on the general use of real variables in macroeconomics.

3. **Economic Growth** (Chapter 23): The process of economic growth now begins with an explanation of what determines potential GDP (adapted from the previous edition's classical model chapter), which is followed by an explanation of what makes potential GDP grow. The sources of labor productivity growth are thoroughly explored.

4. **Finance, Saving, and Investment** (Chapter 24): New to the ninth edition, this chapter provides a thorough and extensive explanation of financial markets and institutions and their role in providing the funds for investment, an engine of economic growth. The circular flow model of Chapter 21 is extended to include the flows in the market for loanable funds that finance investment. The chapter explains the role of government in the market for loanable funds and explains crowding out and the role of debt and the government budget deficit. The chapter also includes a discussion of borrowing and lending in the global loanable funds market. The credit crisis of 2008 is a central example used to illustrate the working of this vital macroeconomic market.

5. **Money, the Price Level, and Inflation** (Chapter 25): This chapter is heavily revised to simplify the explanation of the money creation process. A Math Note at the end of the chapter provides a more comprehensive analysis of this process. The explanation of the role and functions of the Federal Reserve includes coverage of the Fed's role in the 2008 credit crisis.

6. **Aggregate Supply and Aggregate Demand** (Chapter 27): This chapter is a streamlined version of the previous edition's content, but with a new and more detailed explanation and illustration of the U.S. business cycle. The added clarity and focus of this chapter reflects the tone and goals of the ninth edition.

7. **Fiscal Policy** (Chapter 30) and **Monetary Policy** (Chapter 31): These chapters are revised to incorporate the dramatic policy responses to the ongoing slowdown and increasingly likely recession of 2008–2009.

Features to Enhance Teaching and Learning

Chapter Openers

Each chapter opens with a student-friendly vignette that raises questions to motivate the student and focus the chapter. This chapter-opening story is woven into the main body of the chapter and is explored in the *Reading Between the Lines* feature that ends each chapter.

Chapter Objectives

A list of learning objectives enables students to see exactly where the chapter is going and to set their goals before they begin the chapter.

Key Terms

Highlighted terms simplify the student's task of learning the vocabulary of economics. Each highlighted term appears in an end-of-chapter list with page numbers, in an end-of-book glossary with page numbers, boldfaced in the index, in the Web glossary, and in the Web Flash Cards.

Diagrams That Show the Action

Through the past eight editions, this book has set new standards of clarity in its diagrams; the ninth edition continues to uphold this tradition. My goal has always been to show "where the economic action is." The diagrams in this book continue to generate an enormously positive response, which confirms my view that graphical analysis is the most powerful tool available for teaching and learning economics.

Because many students find graphs hard to work with, I have developed the entire art program with the study and review needs of the student in mind.

The diagrams feature:

- Original curves consistently shown in blue
- Shifted curves, equilibrium points, and other important features highlighted in red
- Color-blended arrows to suggest movement
- Graphs paired with data tables
- Diagrams labeled with boxed notes
- Extended captions that make each diagram and its caption a self-contained object for study and review.

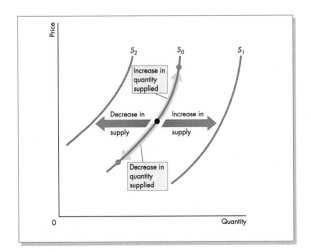

In-Text Review Quizzes

A review quiz at the end of most major sections enables students to determine whether a topic needs further study before moving on. This feature includes a reference to the appropriate MyEconLab study plan to help students further test their understanding.

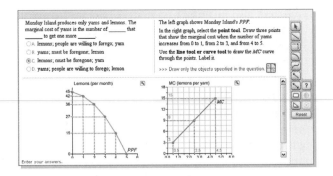

Reading Between the Lines

In *Reading Between the Lines*, which appears at the end of each chapter, students apply the tools they have just learned by analyzing an article from a newspaper or news Web site. Each article sheds additional light on the questions first raised in the Chapter Opener.

Questions about the article also appear with the end-of-chapter problems and applications.

End-of-Chapter Study Material

Each chapter closes with a concise summary organized by major topics, lists of key terms, figures and tables (all with page references), problems and applications. These learning tools provide students with a summary for review and exam preparation.

News-Based End-of-Chapter Questions

Each chapter's problems and applications section now includes an additional set of news-based real-world problems that are new to the ninth edition. All of the problems and applications are also available for self-assessment or assignment as a homework, quiz, or test in MyEconLab.

Interviews with Economists

Each major part of the text closes with a summary feature that includes an interview with a leading economist whose research and expertise correlates to what the student has just learned. These interviews explore the background, education, and research these prominent economics have conducted, as well as advice for those who want to continue the study of economics. New interviewees in this ninth edition are Susan Athey of Harvard University, and Stephanie Schmitt-Grohe and Richard Clarida, both of Columbia University.

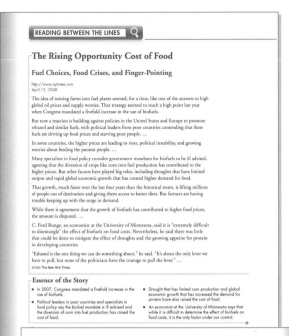

21. After you have studied *Reading Between the Lines* on pp. 46–47, answer the following questions:

21. After you have studied *Reading Between the Lines* on pp. 46–47, answer the following questions:
    a. How has an Act of the United States Congress increased U.S. production of corn?
    b. Why would you expect an increase in the quantity of corn produced to raise the opportunity cost of corn?
    c. Why did the cost of producing corn increase in the rest of the world?
    d. Is it possible that the increased quantity of corn produced, despite the higher cost of production, moves the United States closer to allocative efficiency?

For the Instructor

This book enables you to achieve three objectives in your principles course:

- Focus on the economic way of thinking
- Explain the issues and problems of our time
- Choose your own course structure

Focus on the Economic Way of Thinking

As an instructor, you know how hard it is to encourage a student to think like an economist. But that is your goal. Consistent with this goal, the text focuses on and repeatedly uses the central ideas: choice; tradeoff; opportunity cost; the margin; incentives; the gains from voluntary exchange; the forces of demand, supply, and equilibrium; the pursuit of economic rent; the tension between self-interest and the social interest; and the scope and limitations of government actions.

Explain the Issues of Our Global Economy

Students must *use* the central ideas and tools if they are to begin to *understand* them. There is no better way to motivate students than by using the tools of economics to explain the issues that confront today's world. Issues such as globalization and the emergence of China and India as major economic forces; the mortgage crisis, the recent bankruptcy, absorption or federally funded bailout of American banks, stock market fluctuations, the new economy with new near-monopolies such as eBay and Google; the widening income gap between rich and poor; the reallocation of resources toward counterterrorism; the disappearing tropical rain forests and the challenge that this tragedy of the commons creates; the challenge of managing the world's water resources; the looming debt that arises from our newly emerged federal budget deficit; our vast and rising international deficit and debt; and the tumbling value of the dollar on the foreign exchange market.

Flexible Structure

You have preferences for how you want to teach your course. I have organized this book to enable you to do so. The flexibility chart and alternative sequences table that appear on pages xxi–xxiii demonstrate this book's flexibility. Whether you want to teach a traditional course that blends theory and policy or focuses on current policy issues, *Economics* gives you the choice.

Supplemental Resources

Instructor's Manuals We have streamlined and reorganized the Instructor's Manual to reflect the focus and intuition of the ninth edition. Two separate Instructor's Manuals—one for *Microeconomics* and one for *Macroeconomics*—written by Kelly Blanchard of Purdue University and Jeffrey Reynolds of Northern Illinois University, integrate the teaching and learning package and serve as a guide to all the supplements.

Each chapter contains:

- A chapter overview.
- A list of what's new in the ninth edition.
- *Lecture Notes* Ready-to-use lecture notes from each chapter enable a new user of Parkin to walk into a classroom armed to deliver a polished lecture. The lecture notes provide an outline of the chapter; concise statements of key material; alternate tables and figures, key terms, definitions, and boxes that highlight key concepts, provide an interesting anecdote, or suggest how to handle a difficult idea; additional discussion questions; additional problems; and the solutions to these problems. The chapter outline and teaching suggestions sections are keyed to the PowerPoint® lecture notes.
- *Worksheets* Another innovative feature of the Instructor's Manual is a set of Worksheets prepared by Patricia Kuzyk of Washington State University. These Worksheets ask students to contemplate real-world problems that illustrate economic principles. Examples include showing the effect of the catastrophic events of 9/11 using a marginal cost/marginal benefit diagram, and calculating the effects of funding Social Security for the huge number of baby-boomer retirees. Instructors can assign these as in-class group projects or as homework. There is a Worksheet for every chapter of the book.

Solutions Manual For ease of use and instructor reference, a comprehensive solutions manual provides instructors with solutions to the Review Quizzes and the end-of-chapter problems. The Solutions Manual is available in hard copy and electronically on the Instructor's Resource Center CD-ROM, and in the instructor's resources section of MyEconLab, and on the Instructor's Resource Center.

Test Banks Six separate Test Banks—three for *Microeconomics* and three for *Macroeconomics*—with nearly 13,000 questions, provide multiple-choice, true-false, numerical, fill-in-the-blank, short-answer, and essay questions.

Mark Rush of the University of Florida reviewed and edited all existing questions to ensure their clarity and consistency with the ninth edition and incorporated new questions into the thousands of existing Test Bank questions. Written by Constantin Ogloblin of Georgia Southern University, Nora Underwood of the University of Central Florida and Jeffrey Reynolds, these problems follow the style and format of the end-of chapter text problems and provide the instructor with a whole new set of testing opportunities and/or homework assignments. Additionally, end-of-part tests contain questions that cover all the chapters in the part and feature integrative questions that span more than one chapter.

New News-based Problems The ninth edition includes a set of problems in each chapter that are based directly on current events, newspaper stories or magazine articles. Written by Karen Gebhardt of Colorado State University and Carol Dole of Jacksonville University, these questions link the real world to concepts students have learned in class. With these news-based questions, instructors will be able to showcase how economics exists in the world outside the classroom.

The Test Banks are available in hard copy and electronically on the Instructor's Resource Center CD-ROM, in the instructor's resources section of MyEconLab, and on the Instructor's Resource Center.

PowerPoint® Resources Robin Bade and I have developed a full-color Microsoft® PowerPoint Lecture Presentation for each chapter that includes all the figures and tables from the text, animated graphs, and speaking notes. The lecture notes in the Instructor's Manual and the slide outlines are correlated, and the speaking notes are based on the Instructor's Manual teaching suggestions. A separate set of PowerPoint files containing large-scale versions of all the text's figures (most of them animated) and tables (some of which are animated) are also available. The presentations can be used electronically in the classroom or can be printed to create hard copy transparency masters. This item is available for Macintosh® and Windows®.

Clicker-Ready PowerPoint Resources This edition features the addition of clicker-ready PowerPoint slides for the Personal Response System you use. Each chapter of the text includes ten multiple-choice questions that test important concepts. Instructors can assign these as in-class assignments or review quizzes.

Instructor's Resource Center CD-ROM Fully compatible with Windows® and Macintosh®, this CD-ROM contains electronic files of every instructor supplement for the ninth edition. Files included are: Microsoft® Word and Adobe® PDF files of the Instructor's Manual, Test Bank and Solutions Manual; complete PowerPoint slides; and the Computerized TestGen® Test Bank. Add this useful resource to your exam copy bookbag, or locate your local Pearson Education sales representative at **www.pearsonhighered.educator** to request a copy.

Computerized Testbank Component Fully networkable, it is available for Windows and Macintosh. TestGen's graphical interface enables instructors to view, edit, and add questions; transfer questions to tests; and print different forms of tests. Tests can be formatted with varying fonts and styles, margins, and headers and footers, as in any word-processing document. Search and sort features let the instructor quickly locate questions and arrange them in a preferred order. QuizMaster, working with your school's computer network, automatically grades the exams, stores the results on disk, and allows the instructor to view or print a variety of reports.

Instructors can download supplements from a secure, instructor-only source via the Pearson Higher Education Instructor Resource Center Web page (www.pearsonhighered.com/irc).

Study Guide The ninth edition Study Guide by Mark Rush is carefully coordinated with the text, MyEconLab, and the Test Banks. Each chapter of the Study Guide contains:

- Key concepts
- Helpful hints
- True/false/uncertain questions
- Multiple-choice questions
- Short-answer questions
- Common questions or misconceptions that the student explains as if he or she were the teacher
- Each part allows students to test their cumulative understanding with questions that go across chapters and work a sample midterm examination.

MyEconLab MyEconLab creates a perfect pedagogical loop that provides not only text-specific assessment and practice problems, but also tutorial support to make sure students learn from their mistakes.

At the core of MyEconLab are the following features:

Auto-graded Tests and Assignments MyEconLab comes with two preloaded Sample tests for each chapter so students can self-assess their understanding of the material. Instructors can assign these Sample Tests or create assignments using end-of-chapter problems and applications, Test Bank questions, or their own custom exercises.

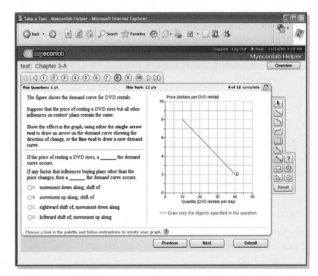

Study Plan A Study Plan is generated from each student's results on Sample Tests and instructor assignments. Students can clearly see which topics they have mastered—and, more importantly, which they need to work on. The Study Plan consists of material from the in-text Review Quizzes and end-of-chapter Problems and Applications. The Study Plan links to additional practice problems and tutorial help on those topics.

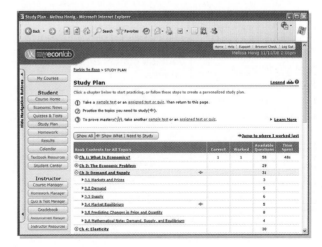

Unlimited Practice Many Study Plan and instructor-assigned exercises contain algorithmically generated values to ensure that students get as much practice as they need. Every problem links students to learning resources that further reinforce concepts they need to master.

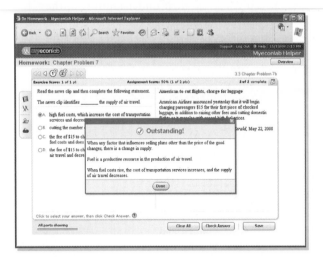

Learning Resources Each practice problem contains a link to the eText page that discusses the concept being applied. Students also have access to guided solutions, animated graphs, audio narrative, flashcards, and live tutoring.

Economics in the News Daily news updates during the school year are available in MyEconLab. Most days the author posts two links to relevant news articles from

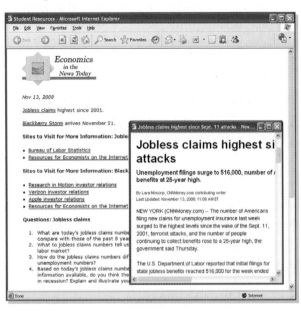

the day's headlines. One link directs students to a microeconomics article, and the other directs students to a macroeconomics article. Each article is accompanied by additional links, discussion questions, and a reference to relevant chapters in the textbook. An archive of *Economics in the News* articles and questions is also available.

New to the ninth edition are instructor-assignable *Economics in the News* questions in MyEconLab. These news analysis questions are updated routinely to ensure the latest news and news analysis problems are available for assignment.

Economics Videos and Assignable Questions Featuring abcNEWS Economics videos featuring ABC news enliven your course with short news clips featuring real-world issues. These 10 videos, available in MyEconLab, feature news footage and commentary by economists. Questions and problems for each video clip are available for assignment in MyEconLab.

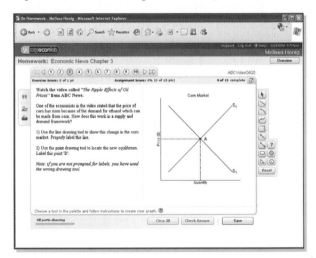

Pearson Tutoring Services powered by SMARTHINKING A subscription to MyEconLab includes complimentary access to Pearson Tutor Services, powered by SMARTHINKING Inc. Highly qualified tutors use whiteboard technology and feedback tools to help students understand and master the major concepts of economics. Students can receive real-time, one-on-one instruction, submit questions for a response within 24 hours, and view archives of past sessions.

Special Editions

Economist.com Edition The premier online source of economic news analysis, Economist.com provides your students with insight and opinion on current economic events. Through an agreement between Addison-Wesley and *The Economist*, your students can receive a low-cost subscription to this premium Web site for 12 weeks, including the complete text of the current issue of *The Economist* and access to *The Economist's* searchable archives. Other features include Web-only weekly articles, news feeds with current world and business news, and stock market and currency data. Professors who adopt this special edition will receive a complimentary one-year subscription to Economist.com.

The Wall Street Journal Edition Addison-Wesley is also pleased to provide your students with access to *The Wall Street Journal*, the most respected and trusted daily source for information on business and economics. For a small additional charge, Addison-Wesley offers your students a subscription to *The Wall Street Journal* and WSJ.com. A 15-week subscription is available. Adopting professors will receive a complimentary one-year subscription to *The Wall Street Journal* as well as access to WSJ.com.

Financial Times Edition Featuring international news and analysis from FT journalists in more than 50 countries, the *Financial Times* will provide your students with insights and perspectives on economic developments around the world. The Financial Times Edition provides your students with a 15-week subscription to one of the world's leading business publications. Adopting professors will receive a complimentary one-year subscription to the *Financial Times* as well as access to FT.com.

Pearson Choices

With ever-increasing demand on time and resources, today's college faculty and students want greater value, innovation, and flexibility in products designed to meet teaching and learning goals. We've responded to that need by creating Pearson Choices, a unique program that allows faculty and students to choose from a range of text and media formats that match their teaching and learning styles and students' budgets.

Books à la Carte Plus Edition For the student who wants a more flexible portable text, there is a three-hole punched version of *Economics*. Students who use this version can take only what they need to class, incorporate their own notes, and save money. This version is packaged with a laminated study card and comes with access to MyEconLab.

CourseSmart CourseSmart's mission is to improve teaching and learning through the availability of a lower-cost alternative to the traditional textbook, in a reliable Web application. For additional information, log onto www.coursesmart.com

Standalone Access to MyEconLab and the Complete eText Students may purchase access to MyEconLab, which includes online access to the complete, searchable eText, online at www.myeconlab.com or through the campus bookstore.

MyEconLab Students may purchase access to MyEconLab's assessment and learning resources. Partial access to the eText is included, which links practice problems to relevant sections of the text. Go to www.myeconlab.com for more information.

Print Upgrade to the à la Carte Edition from within MyEconLab Students may purchase an upgrade to the à la carte edition of *Economics* at any point following their online purchase of MyEconLab.

Pearson Custom Business Resources The Pearson Custom Database offers instructors the option of building their own book by selecting just the chapters they want and ordering them to fit their syllabus. Professors can also select chapters of the accompanying Study Guide as well as readings from Miller/Benjamin/North's *The Economics of Public Issues* and Miller/Benjamin's *The Economics of Macro Issues*. For additional information contact your Pearson representative.

◆ Acknowledgments

I thank my current and former colleagues and friends at the University of Western Ontario who have taught me so much. They are Jim Davies, Jeremy Greenwood, Ig Horstmann, Peter Howitt, Greg Huffman, David Laidler, Phil Reny, Chris Robinson, John Whalley, and Ron Wonnacott. I also thank Doug McTaggart and Christopher Findlay, co-authors of the Australian edition, and Melanie Powell and Kent Matthews, co-authors of the European edition. Suggestions arising from their adaptations of earlier editions have been helpful to me in preparing this edition.

I thank the several thousand students whom I have been privileged to teach. The instant response that comes from the look of puzzlement or enlightenment has taught me how to teach economics.

It is a special joy to thank the many outstanding editors, media specialists, and others at Addison-Wesley who contributed to the concerted publishing effort that brought this edition to completion. Denise Clinton, Publisher, has played a major role in the evolution of this text since its third edition, and her insights and ideas can still be found in this new edition. Donna Battista, Editor-in-Chief for Economics and Finance, is hugely inspiring and has provided overall direction to the project. As ever, Adrienne D'Ambrosio, Senior Acquisitions Editor for Economics and my sponsoring editor, played a major role in shaping this revision and the many outstanding supplements that accompany it. Adrienne brings intelligence and insight to her work and is the unchallengeable pre-eminent economics editor. Deepa Chungi, Development Editor, brought a fresh eye to the development process, obtained outstanding reviews from equally outstanding reviewers, digested and summarized the reviews, and made many solid suggestions as she diligently worked through the drafts of this edition. Nancy Fenton, Managing Editor, managed the entire production and design effort with her usual skill, played a major role in envisioning and implementing the cover design, and coped fearlessly with a tight production schedule. Susan Schoenberg, Director of Media, directed the development of MyEconLab; Doug Ruby, Content Lead for MyEconLab, managed a complex and thorough reviewing process for the content of MyEconLab; and Melissa Honig, Senior Media Producer ensured that all our media assets were correctly assembled. Roxanne McCarley, Executive Marketing Manager, provided inspired marketing strategy and direction. Catherine Baum provided a careful, consistent, and intelligent copy edit and accuracy check. Joyce Wells designed the cover and package and yet again surpassed the challenge of ensuring that we meet the highest design standards. Joe Vetere provided endless technical help with the text and art files. And Heather Johnson with the other members of an outstanding editorial and production team at Elm Street including Debbie Kubiak kept the project on track on an impossibly tight schedule. I thank all of these wonderful people. It has been inspiring to work with them and to share in creating what I believe is a truly outstanding educational tool.

I thank Luke Armstrong of Lee College for providing the news-based applications that appear at the end of each chapter. Luke has been using this type of material with his students and has now shared his talent with a wider audience.

I thank our talented ninth edition supplements authors—Jeff Reynolds, Kelly Blanchard, Pat Kuzyk, Nora Underwood, Constantin Ogloblin, Carol Dole, and Karen Gebhardt.

I especially thank Mark Rush, who yet again played a crucial role in creating another edition of this text and package. Mark has been a constant source of good advice and good humor.

I thank the many exceptional reviewers who have shared their insights through the various editions of this book. Their contribution has been invaluable.

I thank the people who work directly with me. Jeannie Gillmore provided outstanding research assistance on many topics, including the *Reading Between the Lines* news articles. Richard Parkin created the electronic art files and offered many ideas that improved the figures in this book. And Laurel Davies managed an ever-growing and ever more complex MyEconLab database.

As with the previous editions, this one owes an enormous debt to Robin Bade. I dedicate this book to her and again thank her for her work. I could not have written this book without the tireless and unselfish help she has given me. My thanks to her are unbounded.

Classroom experience will test the value of this book. I would appreciate hearing from instructors and students about how I can continue to improve it in future editions.

Michael Parkin
London, Ontario, Canada
michael.parkin@uwo.ca

Reviewers

Eric Abrams, Hawaii Pacific University

Christopher Adams, Federal Trade Commission

Tajudeen Adenekan, Bronx Community College

Syed Ahmed, Cameron University

Frank Albritton, Seminole Community College

Milton Alderfer, Miami-Dade Community College

William Aldridge, Shelton State Community College

Donald L. Alexander, Western Michigan University

Terence Alexander, Iowa State University

Stuart Allen, University of North Carolina, Greensboro

Sam Allgood, University of Nebraska, Lincoln

Neil Alper, Northeastern University

Alan Anderson, Fordham University

Lisa R. Anderson, College of William and Mary

Jeff Ankrom, Wittenberg University

Fatma Antar, Manchester Community Technical College

Kofi Apraku, University of North Carolina, Asheville

Moshen Bahmani-Oskooee, University of Wisconsin, Milwaukee

Donald Balch, University of South Carolina

Mehmet Balcilar, Wayne State University

Paul Ballantyne, University of Colorado

Sue Bartlett, University of South Florida

Jose Juan Bautista, Xavier University of Louisiana

Valerie R. Bencivenga, University of Texas, Austin

Ben Bernanke, Chairman of Federal Reserve

Radha Bhattacharya, California State University, Fullerton

Margot Biery, Tarrant County College, South

John Bittorowitz, Ball State University

David Black, University of Toledo

Kelly Blanchard, Purdue University

S. Brock Blomberg, Claremont McKenna College

William T. Bogart, Case Western Reserve University

Giacomo Bonanno, University of California, Davis

Tan Khay Boon, Nanyard Technological University

Sunne Brandmeyer, University of South Florida

Audie Brewton, Northeastern Illinois University

Baird Brock, Central Missouri State University

Byron Brown, Michigan State University

Jeffrey Buser, Columbus State Community College

Alison Butler, Florida International University

Tania Carbiener, Southern Methodist University

Kevin Carey, American University

Kathleen A. Carroll, University of Maryland, Baltimore County

Michael Carter, University of Massachusetts, Lowell

Edward Castronova, California State University, Fullerton

Francis Chan, Fullerton College

Ming Chang, Dartmouth College

Subir Chakrabarti, Indiana University-Purdue University

Joni Charles, Texas State University

Adhip Chaudhuri, Georgetown University

Gopal Chengalath, Texas Tech University

Daniel Christiansen, Albion College

Kenneth Christianson, Binghamton University

John J. Clark, Community College of Allegheny County, Allegheny Campus

Cindy Clement, University of Maryland

Meredith Clement, Dartmouth College

Michael B. Cohn, U. S. Merchant Marine Academy

Robert Collinge, University of Texas, San Antonio

Carol Condon, Kean University

Doug Conway, Mesa Community College

Larry Cook, University of Toledo

Bobby Corcoran, retired, Middle Tennessee State University

Kevin Cotter, Wayne State University

James Peery Cover, University of Alabama, Tuscaloosa

Erik Craft, University of Richmond

Eleanor D. Craig, University of Delaware

Jim Craven, Clark College

Jeremy Cripps, American University of Kuwait

Elizabeth Crowell, University of Michigan, Dearborn

Stephen Cullenberg, University of California, Riverside

David Culp, Slippery Rock University

Norman V. Cure, Macomb Community College

Dan Dabney, University of Texas, Austin

Andrew Dane, Angelo State University

Joseph Daniels, Marquette University

Gregory DeFreitas, Hofstra University

David Denslow, University of Florida

Mark Dickie, University of Central Florida

James Dietz, California State University, Fullerton

Carol Dole, State University of West Georgia

Ronald Dorf, Inver Hills Community College

John Dorsey, University of Maryland, College Park

Eric Drabkin, Hawaii Pacific University

Amrik Singh Dua, Mt. San Antonio College

Thomas Duchesneau, University of Maine, Orono

Lucia Dunn, Ohio State University

Donald Dutkowsky, Syracuse University

John Edgren, Eastern Michigan University

David J. Eger, Alpena Community College

Harry Ellis, Jr., University of North Texas

Ibrahim Elsaify, Goldey-Beacom College

Kenneth G. Elzinga, University of Virginia

Patrick Emerson, Oregon State University

Tisha Emerson, Baylor University

Monica Escaleras, Florida Atlantic University

Antonina Espiritu, Hawaii Pacific University

Gwen Eudey, University of Pennsylvania

Barry Falk, Iowa State University

M. Fazeli, Hofstra University

Philip Fincher, Louisiana Tech University

F. Firoozi, University of Texas, San Antonio

Nancy Folbre, University of Massachusetts, Amherst

Kenneth Fong, Temasek Polytechnic (Singapore)

Steven Francis, Holy Cross College

David Franck, University of North Carolina, Charlotte

Mark Frank, Sam Houston State University

Roger Frantz, San Diego State University

Mark Frascatore, Clarkson University

Alwyn Fraser, Atlantic Union College

Marc Fusaro, East Carolina University

James Gale, Michigan Technological University

Susan Gale, New York University

Roy Gardner, Indiana University

Eugene Gentzel, Pensacola Junior College

Kirk Gifford, Brigham Young University, Idaho

Scott Gilbert, Southern Illinois University, Carbondale

Andrew Gill, California State University, Fullerton

Robert Giller, Virginia Polytechnic Institute and State University

Robert Gillette, University of Kentucky

James N. Giordano, Villanova University

Maria Giuili, Diablo College

Susan Glanz, St. John's University

Robert Gordon, San Diego State University

Richard Gosselin, Houston Community College

John Graham, Rutgers University

John Griffen, Worcester Polytechnic Institute

Wayne Grove, Syracuse University

Robert Guell, Indiana State University

Jamie Haag, Pacific University, Oregon

Gail Heyne Hafer, Lindenwood University

Rik W. Hafer, Southern Illinois University, Edwardsville

Daniel Hagen, Western Washington University

David R. Hakes, University of Northern Iowa

Craig Hakkio, Federal Reserve Bank, Kansas City

Bridget Gleeson Hanna, Rochester Institute of Technology

Ann Hansen, Westminster College

Seid Hassan, Murray State University

Jonathan Haughton, Suffolk University

Randall Haydon, Wichita State University

Denise Hazlett, Whitman College

Julia Heath, University of Memphis

Jac Heckelman, Wake Forest University

Jolien A. Helsel, Kent State University

James Henderson, Baylor University

Doug Herman, Georgetown University

Jill Boylston Herndon, University of Florida

Gus Herring, Brookhaven College

John Herrmann, Rutgers University

John M. Hill, Delgado Community College

Jonathan Hill, Florida International University

Lewis Hill, Texas Tech University

Steve Hoagland, University of Akron

Tom Hoerger, Fellow, Research Triangle Institute

Calvin Hoerneman, Delta College

George Hoffer, Virginia Commonwealth University

Dennis L. Hoffman, Arizona State University

Paul Hohenberg, Rensselaer Polytechnic Institute

Jim H. Holcomb, University of Texas, El Paso

Harry Holzer, Georgetown University

Linda Hooks, Washington and Lee University

Jim Horner, Cameron University

Djehane Hosni, University of Central Florida

Harold Hotelling, Jr., Lawrence Technical University

Calvin Hoy, County College of Morris

Ing-Wei Huang, Assumption University, Thailand

Julie Hunsaker, Wayne State University

Beth Ingram, University of Iowa

Jayvanth Ishwaran, Stephen F. Austin State University

Michael Jacobs, Lehman College

S. Hussain Ali Jafri, Tarleton State University

Dennis Jansen, Texas A&M University

Barbara John, University of Dayton

Barry Jones, Binghamton University

Garrett Jones, Southern Florida University

Frederick Jungman, Northwestern Oklahoma State University

Paul Junk, University of Minnesota, Duluth

Leo Kahane, California State University, Hayward

Veronica Kalich, Baldwin-Wallace College

John Kane, State University of New York, Oswego

Eungmin Kang, St. Cloud State University

Arthur Kartman, San Diego State University

Gurmit Kaur, Universiti Teknologi (Malaysia)

Louise Keely, University of Wisconsin, Madison

Manfred W. Keil, Claremont McKenna College

Elizabeth Sawyer Kelly, University of Wisconsin, Madison

Rose Kilburn, Modesto Junior College

Robert Kirk, Indiana University-Purdue University, Indianapolis

Norman Kleinberg, City University of New York, Baruch College

Robert Kleinhenz, California State University, Fullerton

John Krantz, University of Utah

Joseph Kreitzer, University of St. Thomas

Patricia Kuzyk, Washington State University

David Lages, Southwest Missouri State University

W. J. Lane, University of New Orleans

Leonard Lardaro, University of Rhode Island

Kathryn Larson, Elon College

Luther D. Lawson, University of North Carolina, Wilmington

Elroy M. Leach, Chicago State University

Jim Lee, Texas A & M, Corpus Christi

Sang Lee, Southeastern Louisiana University

Robert Lemke, Florida International University

Mary Lesser, Iona College

Jay Levin, Wayne State University

Arik Levinson, University of Wisconsin, Madison

Tony Lima, California State University, Hayward

William Lord, University of Maryland, Baltimore County

Nancy Lutz, Virginia Polytechnic Institute and State University

Brian Lynch, Lakeland Community College

Murugappa Madhavan, San Diego State University

K. T. Magnusson, Salt Lake Community College

Svitlana Maksymenko, University of Pittsburgh

Mark Maier, Glendale Community College

Jean Mangan, Staffordshire University Business School

Denton Marks, University of Wisconsin, Whitewater

Michael Marlow, California Polytechnic State University

Akbar Marvasti, University of Houston

Wolfgang Mayer, University of Cincinnati

John McArthur, Wofford College

Amy McCormick, Mary Baldwin College

Russel McCullough, Iowa State University

Gerald McDougall, Wichita State University

Stephen McGary, Brigham Young University-Idaho

Richard D. McGrath, Armstrong Atlantic State University

Richard McIntyre, University of Rhode Island

John McLeod, Georgia Institute of Technology

Mark McLeod, Virginia Polytechnic Institute and State University

B. Starr McMullen, Oregon State University

Mary Ruth McRae, Appalachian State University

Kimberly Merritt, Cameron University

Charles Meyer, Iowa State University

Peter Mieszkowski, Rice University

John Mijares, University of North Carolina, Asheville

Richard A. Miller, Wesleyan University

Judith W. Mills, Southern Connecticut State University

Glen Mitchell, Nassau Community College

Jeannette C. Mitchell, Rochester Institute of Technology

Khan Mohabbat, Northern Illinois University

Bagher Modjtahedi, University of California, Davis

W. Douglas Morgan, University of California, Santa Barbara

William Morgan, University of Wyoming

James Morley, Washington University in St. Louis

William Mosher, Clark University

Joanne Moss, San Francisco State University

Nivedita Mukherji, Oakland University

Francis Mummery, Fullerton College

Edward Murphy, Southwest Texas State University

Kevin J. Murphy, Oakland University

Kathryn Nantz, Fairfield University

William S. Neilson, Texas A&M University

Bart C. Nemmers, University of Nebraska, Lincoln

Melinda Nish, Orange Coast College

Anthony O'Brien, Lehigh University

Norman Obst, Michigan State University

Constantin Ogloblin, Georgia Southern University

Mary Olson, Tulane University

Terry Olson, Truman State University

James B. O'Neill, University of Delaware

Farley Ordovensky, University of the Pacific

Z. Edward O'Relley, North Dakota State University

Donald Oswald, California State University, Bakersfield

Jan Palmer, Ohio University

Michael Palumbo, Chief, Federal Reserve Board

Chris Papageorgiou, Louisiana State University

G. Hossein Parandvash, Western Oregon State College

Randall Parker, East Carolina University

Robert Parks, Washington University

David Pate, St. John Fisher College

James E. Payne, Illinois State University

Donald Pearson, Eastern Michigan University

Steven Peterson, University of Idaho

Mary Anne Pettit, Southern Illinois University, Edwardsville

William A. Phillips, University of Southern Maine

Dennis Placone, Clemson University

Charles Plot, California Institute of Technology, Pasadena

Mannie Poen, Houston Community College

Kathleen Possai, Wayne State University

Ulrika Praski-Stahlgren, University College in Gavle-Sandviken, Sweden

Edward Price, Oklahoma State University

Rula Qalyoubi, University of Wisconsin, Eau Claire

K. A. Quartey, Talladega College

Herman Quirmbach, Iowa State University

Jeffrey R. Racine, University of South Florida

Peter Rangazas, Indiana University-Purdue University, Indianapolis

Vaman Rao, Western Illinois University

Laura Razzolini, University of Mississippi

Rob Rebelein, University of Cincinnati

J. David Reed, Bowling Green State University

Robert H. Renshaw, Northern Illinois University

Javier Reyes, University of Arkansas

Jeff Reynolds, Northern Illinois University

Rupert Rhodd, Florida Atlantic University

W. Gregory Rhodus, Bentley College

Jennifer Rice, Indiana University, Bloomington

John Robertson, Paducah Community College

Malcolm Robinson, University of North Carolina, Greensboro

Richard Roehl, University of Michigan, Dearborn

Carol Rogers, Georgetown University

William Rogers, University of Northern Colorado

Thomas Romans, State University of New York, Buffalo
David R. Ross, Bryn Mawr College
Thomas Ross, Baldwin Wallace College
Robert J. Rossana, Wayne State University
Jeffrey Rous, University of North Texas
Rochelle Ruffer, Youngstown State University
Mark Rush, University of Florida
Allen R. Sanderson, University of Chicago
Gary Santoni, Ball State University
John Saussy, Harrisburg Area Community College
Don Schlagenhauf, Florida State University
David Schlow, Pennsylvania State University
Paul Schmitt, St. Clair County Community College
Jeremy Schwartz, Hampden-Sydney College
Martin Sefton, University of Nottingham
James Self, Indiana University
Esther-Mirjam Sent, University of Notre Dame
Rod Shadbegian, University of Massachusetts, Dartmouth
Gerald Shilling, Eastfield College
Dorothy R. Siden, Salem State College
Mark Siegler, California State University at Sacramento
Scott Simkins, North Carolina Agricultural and Technical State University
Chuck Skoro, Boise State University
Phil Smith, DeKalb College
William Doyle Smith, University of Texas, El Paso
Sarah Stafford, College of William and Mary
Rebecca Stein, University of Pennsylvania
Frank Steindl, Oklahoma State University
Jeffrey Stewart, New York University
Allan Stone, Southwest Missouri State University
Courtenay Stone, Ball State University
Paul Storer, Western Washington University
Richard W. Stratton, University of Akron
Mark Strazicich, Ohio State University, Newark
Michael Stroup, Stephen F. Austin State University
Robert Stuart, Rutgers University
Della Lee Sue, Marist College
Abdulhamid Sukar, Cameron University
Terry Sutton, Southeast Missouri State University
Gilbert Suzawa, University of Rhode Island
David Swaine, Andrews University
Jason Taylor, Central Michigan University
Mark Thoma, University of Oregon
Janet Thomas, Bentley College
Kiril Tochkov, SUNY at Binghamton
Kay Unger, University of Montana

Anthony Uremovic, Joliet Junior College
David Vaughn, City University, Washington
Don Waldman, Colgate University
Francis Wambalaba, Portland State University
Rob Wassmer, California State University, Sacramento
Paul A. Weinstein, University of Maryland, College Park
Lee Weissert, St. Vincent College
Robert Whaples, Wake Forest University
David Wharton, Washington College
Mark Wheeler, Western Michigan University
Charles H. Whiteman, University of Iowa
Sandra Williamson, University of Pittsburgh
Brenda Wilson, Brookhaven Community College
Larry Wimmer, Brigham Young University
Mark Witte, Northwestern University
Willard E. Witte, Indiana University
Mark Wohar, University of Nebraska, Omaha
Laura Wolff, Southern Illinois University, Edwardsville
Cheonsik Woo, Vice President, Korea Development Institute
Douglas Wooley, Radford University
Arthur G. Woolf, University of Vermont
John T. Young, Riverside Community College
Michael Youngblood, Rock Valley College
Peter Zaleski, Villanova University
Jason Zimmerman, South Dakota State University
David Zucker, Martha Stewart Living Omnimedia

Supplements Authors

Sue Bartlett, University of South Florida
Kelly Blanchard, Purdue University
James Cobbe, Florida State University
Carol Dole, Jacksonville University
Karen Gebhardt, Colorado State University
John Graham, Rutgers University
Jill Herndon, University of Florida
Patricia Kuzyk, Washington State University
Sang Lee, Southeastern Louisiana University
James Morley, Washington University in St. Louis
William Mosher, Clark University
Constantin Ogloblin, Georgia Southern University
Edward Price, Oklahoma State University
Jeff Reynolds, Northern Illinois University
Mark Rush, University of Florida
Michael Stroup, Stephen F. Austin State University
Della Lee Sue, Marist College
Nora Underwood, University of Central Florida

FLEXIBILITY
BY CHAPTER

FOUR ALTERNATIVE
MICRO SEQUENCES

THREE ALTERNATIVE
MACRO SEQUENCES

TABLE OF

CONTENTS

2

The Economic Problem

After studying this chapter, you will be able to:

- Define the production possibilities frontier and calculate opportunity cost

- Distinguish between production possibilities and preferences and describe an efficient allocation of resources

- Explain how current production choices expand future production possibilities

- Explain how specialization and trade expand our production possibilities

- Describe the economic institutions that coordinate decisions

Why does food cost much more today than it did a few years ago? One reason is that we now use part of our corn crop to produce ethanol, a clean biofuel substitute for gasoline. Another reason is that drought in some parts of the world has decreased global grain production. In this chapter, you will study an economic model—the production possibilities frontier—and you will learn why ethanol production and drought have increased the cost of producing food. You will also learn how to assess whether it is a good idea to increase corn production to produce fuel; how we can expand our production possibilities; and how we gain by trading with others.

At the end of the chapter, in *Reading Between the Lines*, we'll apply what you've learned to understanding why ethanol production is raising the cost of food.

Production Possibilities and Opportunity Cost

Every working day, in mines, factories, shops, and offices and on farms and construction sites across the United States, 138 million people produce a vast variety of goods and services valued at $50 billion. But the quantities of goods and services that we can produce are limited both by our available resources and by technology. And if we want to increase our production of one good, we must decrease our production of something else—we face a tradeoff. You are going to learn about the production possibilities frontier, which describes the limit to what we can produce and provides a neat way of thinking about and illustrating the idea of a tradeoff.

The **production possibilities frontier** (*PPF*) is the boundary between those combinations of goods and services that can be produced and those that cannot. To illustrate the *PPF*, we focus on two goods at a time and hold the quantities produced of all the other goods and services constant. That is, we look at a *model* economy in which everything remains the same except for the production of the two goods we are considering.

Let's look at the production possibilities frontier for cola and pizza, which stand for *any* pair of goods or services.

Production Possibilities Frontier

The *production possibilities frontier* for cola and pizza shows the limits to the production of these two goods, given the total resources and technology available to produce them. Figure 2.1 shows this production possibilities frontier. The table lists some combinations of the quantities of pizza and cola that can be produced in a month given the resources available. The figure graphs these combinations. The *x*-axis shows the quantity of pizzas produced, and the *y*-axis shows the quantity of cola produced.

The *PPF* illustrates *scarcity* because we cannot attain the points outside the frontier. These points describe wants that can't be satisfied. We can produce at any point *inside* the *PPF* or *on* the *PPF*. These points are attainable. Suppose that in a typical month, we produce 4 million pizzas and 5 million cans of cola. Figure 2.1 shows this combination as point *E* and as possibility *E* in the table. The figure

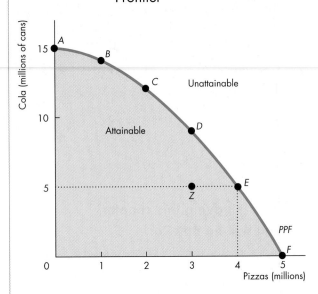

FIGURE 2.1   Production Possibilities Frontier

Possibility	Pizzas (millions)		Cola (millions of cans)
A	0	and	15
B	1	and	14
C	2	and	12
D	3	and	9
E	4	and	5
F	5	and	0

The table lists six production possibilities for cola and pizzas. Row *A* tells us that if we produce no pizza, the maximum quantity of cola we can produce is 15 million cans. Points *A, B, C, D, E,* and *F* in the figure represent the rows of the table. The curve passing through these points is the production possibilities frontier (*PPF*).

The *PPF* separates the attainable from the unattainable. Production is possible at any point *inside* the orange area or *on* the frontier. Points outside the frontier are unattainable. Points inside the frontier, such as point *Z*, are inefficient because resources are wasted or misallocated. At such points, it is possible to use the available resources to produce more of either or both goods.

myeconlab   animation

also shows other production possibilities. For example, we might stop producing pizza and move all the people who produce it into producing cola. Point *A* in the figure and possibility *A* in the table show this case. The quantity of cola produced increases to 15 million cans, and pizza production dries up. Alternatively, we might close the cola factories and switch all the resources into producing pizza. In this situation, we produce 5 million pizzas. Point *F* in the figure and possibility *F* in the table show this case.

Production Efficiency

We achieve **production efficiency** if we produce goods and services at the lowest possible cost. This outcome occurs at all the points *on* the *PPF.* At points *inside* the *PPF,* production is inefficient because we are giving up more than necessary of one good to produce a given quantity of the other good.

For example, at point *Z* in Fig. 2.1, we produce 3 million pizzas and 5 million cans of cola. But we could produce 3 million pizzas and 9 million cans of cola. Our pizzas cost more cola than necessary. We can get them for a lower cost. Only when we produce *on* the *PPF* do we incur the lowest possible cost of production.

Production is *inefficient* inside the *PPF* because resources are either *unused* or *misallocated* or both.

Resources are *unused* when they are idle but could be working. For example, we might leave some of the factories idle or some workers unemployed.

Resources are *misallocated* when they are assigned to tasks for which they are not the best match. For example, we might assign skilled pizza chefs to work in a cola factory and skilled cola producers to work in a pizza shop. We could get more pizzas *and* more cola from these same workers if we reassigned them to the tasks that more closely match their skills.

Tradeoff Along the *PPF*

Every choice *along* the *PPF* involves a *tradeoff.* On the *PPF* in Fig. 2.1, we trade off cola for pizzas.

Tradeoffs arise in every imaginable real-world situation, and you reviewed several of them in Chapter 1. At any given point in time, we have a fixed amount of labor, land, capital, and entrepreneurship. By using our available technologies, we can employ these resources to produce goods and services, but we are limited in what we can produce. This limit defines a

boundary between what we can attain and what we cannot attain. This boundary is the real-world's production possibilities frontier, and it defines the tradeoffs that we must make. On our real-world *PPF,* we can produce more of any one good or service only if we produce less of some other goods or services.

When doctors want to spend more on AIDS and cancer research, they face a tradeoff: more medical research for less of some other things. When Congress wants to spend more on education and health care, it faces a tradeoff: more education and health care for less national defense or less private spending (because of higher taxes). When an environmental group argues for less logging, it is suggesting a tradeoff: greater conservation of endangered wildlife for less paper. When you want to study more, you face a tradeoff: more study time for less leisure or sleep.

All tradeoffs involve a cost—an opportunity cost.

Opportunity Cost

The **opportunity cost** of an action is the highest-valued alternative forgone. The *PPF* makes this idea precise and enables us to calculate opportunity cost. Along the *PPF,* there are only two goods, so there is only one alternative forgone: some quantity of the other good. Given our current resources and technology, we can produce more pizzas only if we produce less cola. The opportunity cost of producing an additional pizza is the cola we *must* forgo. Similarly, the opportunity cost of producing an additional can of cola is the quantity of pizza we must forgo.

In Fig. 2.1, if we move from point *C* to point *D,* we get 1 million more pizzas but 3 million fewer cans of cola. The additional 1 million pizzas *cost* 3 million cans of cola. One pizza costs 3 cans of cola.

We can also work out the opportunity cost of moving in the opposite direction. In Fig. 2.1, if we move from point *D* to point *C,* the quantity of cola produced increases by 3 million cans and the quantity of pizzas produced decreases by 1 million. So if we choose point *C* over point *D,* the additional 3 million cans of cola *cost* 1 million pizzas. One can of cola costs 1/3 of a pizza.

Opportunity Cost Is a Ratio Opportunity cost is a ratio. It is the decrease in the quantity produced of one good divided by the increase in the quantity produced of another good as we move along the production possibilities frontier.

Because opportunity cost is a ratio, the opportunity cost of producing an additional can of cola is equal to the *inverse* of the opportunity cost of producing an additional pizza. Check this proposition by returning to the calculations we've just worked through. When we move along the *PPF* from *C* to *D*, the opportunity cost of a pizza is 3 cans of cola. The inverse of 3 is 1/3. If we decrease the production of pizza and increase the production of cola by moving from *D* to *C*, the opportunity cost of a can of cola must be 1/3 of a pizza. That is exactly the number that we calculated for the move from *D* to *C*.

Increasing Opportunity Cost The opportunity cost of a pizza increases as the quantity of pizzas produced increases. The outward-bowed shape of the *PPF* reflects increasing opportunity cost. When we produce a large quantity of cola and a small quantity of pizza—between points *A* and *B* in Fig. 2.1—the frontier has a gentle slope. An increase in the quantity of pizzas costs a small decrease in the quantity of cola—the opportunity cost of a pizza is a small quantity of cola.

When we produce a large quantity of pizza and a small quantity of cola—between points *E* and *F* in Fig. 2.1—the frontier is steep. A given increase in the quantity of pizzas *costs* a large decrease in the quantity of cola, so the opportunity cost of a pizza is a large quantity of cola.

The *PPF* is bowed outward because resources are not all equally productive in all activities. People with many years of experience working for PepsiCo are good at producing cola but not very good at making pizzas. So if we move some of these people from PepsiCo to Domino's, we get a small increase in the quantity of pizzas but a large decrease in the quantity of cola.

Similarly, people who have spent years working at Domino's are good at producing pizzas, but they have no idea how to produce cola. So if we move some of these people from Domino's to PepsiCo, we get a small increase in the quantity of cola but a large decrease in the quantity of pizzas. The more of either good we try to produce, the less productive are the additional resources we use to produce that good and the larger is the opportunity cost of a unit of that good.

Increasing Opportunity Cost
Opportunity Cost on the Farm

Sanders Wright, a homesick Mississippi native, is growing cotton in Iowa. But the growing season is short and commercial success unlikely. Cotton does not grow well in Iowa, but corn does. A farm with irrigation can produce 300 bushels of corn per acre—twice the U.S. average.

Ronnie Gerik, a Texas cotton farmer, has started to grow corn. But Ronnie doesn't have irrigation and instead relies on rainfall. That's not a problem for cotton, which just needs a few soakings a season. But it's a big problem for corn, which needs an inch of water a week. Also, corn can't take the heat like cotton, and if the temperature rises too much, Ronnie will be lucky to get 100 bushels an acre.

An Iowa corn farmer gives up almost no cotton to produce his 300 bushels of corn per acre—corn has a low opportunity cost. But Ronnie Gerick gives up a huge amount of cotton to produce his 100 bushels of corn per acre. By switching some land from cotton to corn, Ronnie has increased the production of corn, but the additional corn has a high opportunity cost.

"Deere worker makes 'cotton pickin' miracle happen," WCFCourier.com; and "Farmers stampede to corn," *USA Today*.

Review Quiz

1 How does the production possibilities frontier illustrate scarcity?
2 How does the production possibilities frontier illustrate production efficiency?
3 How does the production possibilities frontier show that every choice involves a tradeoff?
4 How does the production possibilities frontier illustrate opportunity cost?
5 Why is opportunity cost a ratio?
6 Why does the *PPF* for most goods bow outward so that opportunity cost increases as the quantity produced of a good increases?

 Work Study Plan 2.1 and get instant feedback.

We've seen that what we can produce is limited by the production possibilities frontier. We've also seen that production on the *PPF* is efficient. But we can produce many different quantities on the *PPF*. How do we choose among them? How do we know which point on the *PPF* is the best one?

Using Resources Efficiently

We achieve *production efficiency* at every point on the *PPF*. But which point is best? The answer is the point on the *PPF* at which goods and services are produced in the quantities that provide the greatest possible benefit. When goods and services are produced at the lowest possible cost and in the quantities that provide the greatest possible benefit, we have achieved **allocative efficiency.**

The questions that we raised when we reviewed the five big issues in Chapter 1 are questions about allocative efficiency. To answer such questions, we must measure and compare costs and benefits.

The *PPF* and Marginal Cost

The **marginal cost** of a good is the opportunity cost of producing one more unit of it. We calculate marginal cost from the slope of the *PPF*. As the quantity of pizzas produced increases, the *PPF* gets steeper and the marginal cost of a pizza increases. Figure 2.2 illustrates the calculation of the marginal cost of a pizza.

Begin by finding the opportunity cost of pizza in blocks of 1 million pizzas. The cost of the first million pizzas is 1 million cans of cola; the cost of the second million pizzas is 2 million cans of cola; the cost of the third million pizzas is 3 million cans of cola, and so on. The bars in part (a) illustrate these calculations.

The bars in part (b) show the cost of an average pizza in each of the 1 million pizza blocks. Focus on the third million pizzas—the move from *C* to *D* in part (a). Over this range, because 1 million pizzas cost 3 million cans of cola, one of these pizzas, on average, costs 3 cans of cola—the height of the bar in part (b).

Next, find the opportunity cost of each additional pizza—the marginal cost of a pizza. The marginal cost of a pizza increases as the quantity of pizzas produced increases. The marginal cost at point *C* is less than it is at point *D*. On the average over the range from *C* to *D*, the marginal cost of a pizza is 3 cans of cola. But it exactly equals 3 cans of cola only in the middle of the range between *C* and *D*.

The red dot in part (b) indicates that the marginal cost of a pizza is 3 cans of cola when 2.5 million pizzas are produced. Each black dot in part (b) is interpreted in the same way. The red curve that passes through these dots, labeled *MC*, is the marginal cost curve. It shows the marginal cost of a pizza at each quantity of pizzas as we move along the *PPF*.

FIGURE 2.2   The *PPF* and Marginal Cost

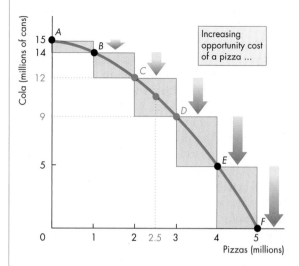

(a) PPF and opportunity cost

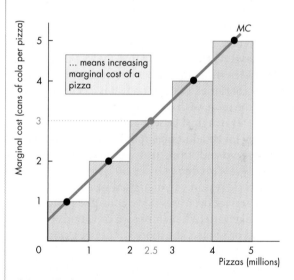

(b) Marginal cost

Marginal cost is calculated from the slope of the *PPF*. As the quantity of pizzas produced increases, the *PPF* gets steeper and the marginal cost of a pizza increases. The bars in part (a) show the opportunity cost of pizza in blocks of 1 million pizzas. The bars in part (b) show the cost of an average pizza in each of these 1 million blocks. The red curve, *MC*, shows the marginal cost of a pizza at each point along the *PPF*. This curve passes through the center of each of the bars in part (b).

myeconlab animation

Preferences and Marginal Benefit

Look around your classroom and notice the wide variety of shirts, pants, and shoes that you and your fellow students are wearing today. Why is there such a huge variety? Why don't you all wear the same styles and colors? The answer lies in what economists call preferences. **Preferences** are a description of a person's likes and dislikes.

You've seen that we have a concrete way of describing the limits to production: the *PPF*. We need a similarly concrete way of describing preferences. To describe preferences, economists use the concept of marginal benefit. The **marginal benefit** from a good or service is the benefit received from consuming one more unit of it.

We measure the marginal benefit from a good or service by the most that people are *willing to pay* for an additional unit of it. The idea is that you are willing to pay less for a good than it is worth to you but you are not willing to pay more than it is worth. So the most you are willing to pay for something measures its marginal benefit.

Economists illustrate preferences using the **marginal benefit curve**, which is a curve that shows the relationship between the marginal benefit from a good and the quantity consumed of that good. It is a general principle that the more we have of any good or service, the smaller is its marginal benefit and the less we are willing to pay for an additional unit of it. This tendency is so widespread and strong that we call it a principle—the *principle of decreasing marginal benefit.*

The basic reason why marginal benefit from a good or service decreases as we consume more of it is that we like variety. The more we consume of any one good or service, the more we tire of it and would prefer to switch to something else.

Think about your willingness to pay for a pizza. If pizza is hard to come by and you can buy only a few slices a year, you might be willing to pay a high price to get an additional slice. But if pizza is all you've eaten for the past few days, you are willing to pay almost nothing for another slice.

You've learned to think about cost as opportunity cost, not as a dollar cost. You can think about marginal benefit and willingness to pay in the same way. The marginal benefit, measured by what you are willing to pay for something, is the quantity of other goods and services that you are willing to forgo. Let's continue with the example of cola and pizza and illustrate preferences this way.

FIGURE 2.3   Preferences and the Marginal Benefit Curve

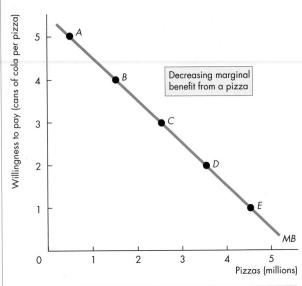

Possibility	Pizzas (millions)	Willingness to pay (cans of cola per pizza)
A	0.5	5
B	1.5	4
C	2.5	3
D	3.5	2
E	4.5	1

The smaller the quantity of pizzas produced, the more cola people are willing to give up for an additional pizza. If pizza production is 0.5 million, people are willing to pay 5 cans of cola per pizza. But if pizza production is 4.5 million, people are willing to pay only 1 can of cola per pizza. Willingness to pay measures marginal benefit. A universal feature of people's preferences is that marginal benefit decreases.

 animation

Figure 2.3 illustrates preferences as the willingness to pay for pizza in terms of cola. In row *A*, pizza production is 0.5 million, and at that quantity, people are willing to pay 5 cans of cola per pizza. As the quantity of pizzas produced increases, the amount that people are willing to pay for a pizza falls. When pizza production is 4.5 million, people are willing to pay only 1 can of cola per pizza.

Let's now use the concepts of marginal cost and marginal benefit to describe allocative efficiency.

FIGURE 2.4   Efficient Use of Resources

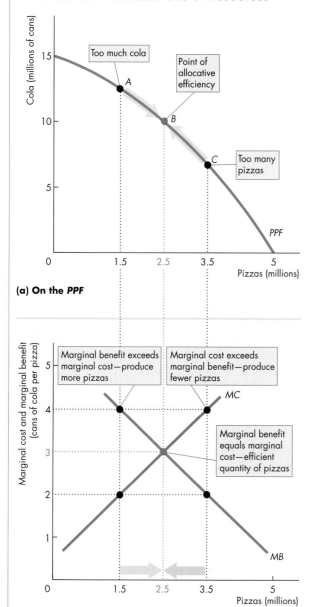

(a) On the PPF

(b) Marginal benefit equals marginal cost

The greater the quantity of pizzas produced, the smaller is the marginal benefit (MB) from pizza—the less cola people are willing to give up to get an additional pizza. But the greater the quantity of pizzas produced, the greater is the marginal cost (MC) of a pizza—the more cola people must give up to get an additional pizza. When marginal benefit equals marginal cost, resources are being used efficiently.

 animation

Allocative Efficiency

At *any* point on the *PPF*, we cannot produce more of one good without giving up some other good. At the *best* point on the *PPF*, we cannot produce more of one good without giving up some other good that provides greater benefit. We are producing at the point of allocative efficiency—the point on the *PPF* that we prefer above all other points.

Suppose in Fig. 2.4, we produce 1.5 million pizzas. The marginal cost of a pizza is 2 cans of cola, and the marginal benefit from a pizza is 4 cans of cola. Because someone values an additional pizza more highly than it costs to produce, we can get more value from our resources by moving some of them out of producing cola and into producing pizza.

Now suppose we produce 3.5 million pizzas. The marginal cost of a pizza is now 4 cans of cola, but the marginal benefit from a pizza is only 2 cans of cola. Because the additional pizza costs more to produce than anyone thinks it is worth, we can get more value from our resources by moving some of them away from producing pizza and into producing cola.

Suppose we produce 2.5 million pizzas. Marginal cost and marginal benefit are now equal at 3 cans of cola. This allocation of resources between pizza and cola is efficient. If more pizzas are produced, the forgone cola is worth more than the additional pizzas. If fewer pizzas are produced, the forgone pizzas are worth more than the additional cola.

Review Quiz

1 What is marginal cost? How is it measured?
2 What is marginal benefit? How is it measured?
3 How does the marginal benefit from a good change as the quantity produced of that good increases?
4 What is allocative efficiency and how does it relate to the production possibilities frontier?
5 What conditions must be satisfied if resources are used efficiently?

myeconlab Work Study Plan 2.2 and get instant feedback.

You now understand the limits to production and the conditions under which resources are used efficiently. Your next task is to study the expansion of production possibilities.

Economic Growth

During the past 30 years, production per person in the United States has doubled. Such an expansion of production is called **economic growth**. Economic growth increases our *standard of living*, but it doesn't overcome scarcity and avoid opportunity cost. To make our economy grow, we face a tradeoff—the faster we make production grow, the greater is the opportunity cost of economic growth.

The Cost of Economic Growth

Economic growth comes from technological change and capital accumulation. **Technological change** is the development of new goods and of better ways of producing goods and services. **Capital accumulation** is the growth of capital resources, including *human capital*.

Because of technological change and capital accumulation, we have an enormous quantity of cars that provide us with more transportation than was available when we had only horses and carriages; we have satellites that provide global communications on a much larger scale than that available with the earlier cable technology. But if we use our resources to develop new technologies and produce capital, we must decrease our production of consumption goods and services. New technologies and new capital have an opportunity cost. Let's look at this opportunity cost.

Instead of studying the *PPF* of pizza and cola, we'll hold the quantity of cola produced constant and examine the *PPF* for pizzas and pizza ovens. Figure 2.5 shows this *PPF* as the blue curve *ABC*. If we devote no resources to producing pizza ovens, we produce at point *A*. If we produce 3 million pizzas, we can produce 6 pizza ovens at point *B*. If we produce no pizza, we can produce 10 ovens at point *C*.

The amount by which our production possibilities expand depends on the resources we devote to technological change and capital accumulation. If we devote no resources to this activity (point *A*), our *PPF* remains at *ABC*—the blue curve in Fig. 2.5. If we cut the current production of pizza and produce 6 ovens (point *B*), then in the future, we'll have more capital and our *PPF* will rotate outward to the position shown by the red curve. The fewer resources we use for producing pizza and the more resources we use for producing ovens, the greater is the future expansion of our production possibilities.

FIGURE 2.5   Economic Growth

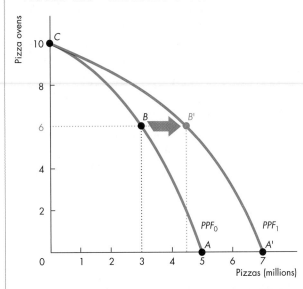

PPF_0 shows the limits to the production of pizza and pizza ovens, with the production of all other goods and services remaining the same. If we devote no resources to producing pizza ovens and produce 5 million pizzas, our production possibilities will remain the same PPF_0. But if we decrease pizza production to 3 million and produce 6 ovens, at point *B*, our production possibilities expand. After one period, the *PPF* rotates outward to PPF_1 and we can produce at point *B'*, a point outside the original PPF_0. We can rotate the *PPF* outward, but we cannot avoid opportunity cost. The opportunity cost of producing more pizzas in the future is fewer pizzas today.

myeconlab   animation

Economic growth is not free. To make it happen, we use more resources to produce new ovens and fewer resources to produce pizzas. In Fig. 2.5, we move from *A* to *B*. There is no free lunch. The opportunity cost of more pizzas in the future is fewer pizzas today. Also, economic growth is no magic formula for abolishing scarcity. On the new production possibilities frontier, we continue to face a tradeoff and opportunity cost.

The ideas about economic growth that we have explored in the setting of the pizza industry also apply to nations. Hong Kong and the United States provide an interesting case study.

Economic Growth
Hong Kong Catching Up to the United States

In 1968, the production possibilities per person in the United States were more than four times those in Hong Kong (see the figure). The United States devotes one fifth of its resources to accumulating capital and in 1968 was at point *A* on its *PPF*. Hong Kong devotes one third of its resources to accumulating capital and in 1968, Hong Kong was at point *A* on its *PPF*.

Since 1968, both countries have experienced economic growth, but because Hong Kong devotes a bigger fraction of its resources to accumulating capital, its production possibilities have expanded more quickly.

By 2008, production possibilities per person in Hong Kong had reached 94 percent of those in the United States. If Hong Kong continues to devote more resources to accumulating capital than we do (at point *B* on its 2008 *PPF*), it will continue to grow more rapidly. But if Hong Kong decreases capital accumulation (moving to point *D* on its 2008 *PPF*), then its rate of economic growth will slow.

Hong Kong is typical of the fast-growing Asian economies, which include Taiwan, Thailand, South Korea, and China. Production possibilities expand in these countries by between 5 and almost 10 percent a year.

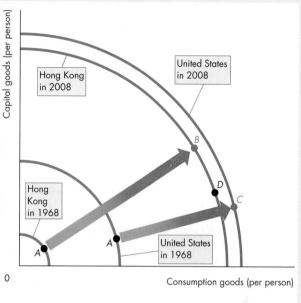

Economic Growth in the United States and Hong Kong

If such high economic growth rates are maintained, these other Asian countries will continue to close the gap between themselves and the United States, as Hong Kong is doing.

A Nation's Economic Growth

The experiences of the United States and Hong Kong make a striking example of the effects of our choices about consumption and capital goods on the rate of economic growth.

If a nation devotes all its factors of production to producing consumption goods and services and none to advancing technology and accumulating capital, its production possibilities in the future will be the same as they are today.

To expand production possibilities in the future, a nation must devote fewer resources to producing consumption goods and services and some resources to accumulating capital and developing new technologies. As production possibilities expand, consumption in the future can increase. The decrease in today's consumption is the opportunity cost of tomorrow's increase in consumption.

Review Quiz

1 What generates economic growth?
2 How does economic growth influence the production possibilities frontier?
3 What is the opportunity cost of economic growth?
4 Why has Hong Kong experienced faster economic growth than the United States?
5 Does economic growth overcome scarcity?

 Work Study Plan 2.3 and get instant feedback.

Next, we're going to study another way in which we expand our production possibilities—the amazing fact that *both* buyers and sellers gain from specialization and trade.

◆ Gains from Trade

People can produce for themselves all the goods and services that they consume, or they can produce one good or a few goods and trade with others. Producing only one good or a few goods is called *specialization*. We are going to learn how people gain by specializing in the production of the good in which they have a *comparative advantage* and trading with others.

Comparative Advantage and Absolute Advantage

A person has a **comparative advantage** in an activity if that person can perform the activity at a lower opportunity cost than anyone else. Differences in opportunity costs arise from differences in individual abilities and from differences in the characteristics of other resources.

No one excels at everything. One person is an outstanding pitcher but a poor catcher; another person is a brilliant lawyer but a poor teacher. In almost all human endeavors, what one person does easily, someone else finds difficult. The same applies to land and capital. One plot of land is fertile but has no mineral deposits; another plot of land has outstanding views but is infertile. One machine has great precision but is difficult to operate; another is fast but often breaks down.

Although no one excels at everything, some people excel and can outperform others in a large number of activities—perhaps even in all activities. A person who is more productive than others has an **absolute advantage**.

Absolute advantage involves comparing productivities—production per hour—whereas comparative advantage involves comparing opportunity costs.

Notice that a person who has an absolute advantage does not have a *comparative* advantage in every activity. John Grisham is a better lawyer and a better author of fast-paced thrillers than most people. He has an absolute advantage in these two activities. But compared to others, he is a better writer than lawyer, so his *comparative* advantage is in writing.

Because ability and resources vary from one person to another, people have different opportunity costs of producing various goods. These differences in opportunity cost are the source of comparative advantage.

Let's explore the idea of comparative advantage by looking at two smoothie bars: one operated by Liz and the other operated by Joe.

Liz's Smoothie Bar Liz produces smoothies and salads. In Liz's high-tech bar, she can turn out either a smoothie or a salad every 2 minutes—see Table 2.1. If Liz spends all her time making smoothies, she can produce 30 an hour. And if she spends all her time making salads, she can also produce 30 an hour. If she splits her time equally between the two, she can produce 15 smoothies and 15 salads an hour. For each additional smoothie Liz produces, she must decrease her production of salads by one, and for each additional salad she produces, she must decrease her production of smoothies by one. So

> Liz's opportunity cost of producing 1 smoothie is 1 salad,

and

> Liz's opportunity cost of producing 1 salad is 1 smoothie.

Liz's customers buy smoothies and salads in equal quantities, so she splits her time equally between the two items and produces 15 smoothies and 15 salads an hour.

Joe's Smoothie Bar Joe also produces smoothies and salads, but his bar is smaller than Liz's. Also, Joe has only one blender, and it's a slow, old machine. Even if Joe uses all his resources to produce smoothies, he can produce only 6 an hour—see Table 2.2. But Joe is good at making salads, so if he uses all his resources to make salads, he can produce 30 an hour.

Joe's ability to make smoothies and salads is the same regardless of how he splits an hour between the two tasks. He can make a salad in 2 minutes or a smoothie in 10 minutes. For each additional smoothie

---

TABLE 2.1 Liz's Production Possibilities

Item	Minutes to produce 1	Quantity per hour
Smoothies	2	30
Salads	2	30

TABLE 2.2   Joe's Production Possibilities

Item	Minutes to produce 1	Quantity per hour
Smoothies	10	6
Salads	2	30

Joe produces, he must decrease his production of salads by 5. And for each additional salad he produces, he must decrease his production of smoothies by 1/5 of a smoothie. So

> Joe's opportunity cost of producing 1 smoothie is 5 salads,

and

> Joe's opportunity cost of producing 1 salad is 1/5 of a smoothie.

Joe's customers, like Liz's, buy smoothies and salads in equal quantities. So Joe spends 50 minutes of each hour making smoothies and 10 minutes of each hour making salads. With this division of his time, Joe produces 5 smoothies and 5 salads an hour.

Liz's Absolute Advantage   Table 2.3(a) summarizes the production of Liz and Joe. You can see that Liz is three times as productive as Joe—her 15 smoothies and salads an hour are three times Joe's 5. Liz has an absolute advantage over Joe in producing both smoothies and salads. But Liz has a comparative advantage in only one of the activities.

Liz's Comparative Advantage   In which of the two activities does Liz have a comparative advantage? Recall that comparative advantage is a situation in which one person's opportunity cost of producing a good is lower than another person's opportunity cost of producing that same good. Liz has a comparative advantage in producing smoothies. Her opportunity cost of a smoothie is 1 salad, whereas Joe's opportunity cost of a smoothie is 5 salads.

Joe's Comparative Advantage   If Liz has a comparative advantage in producing smoothies, Joe must have a comparative advantage in producing salads. Joe's opportunity cost of a salad is 1/5 of a smoothie, whereas Liz's opportunity cost of a salad is 1 smoothie.

Achieving the Gains from Trade

Liz and Joe run into each other one evening in a singles bar. After a few minutes of getting acquainted, Liz tells Joe about her amazing smoothie business. Her only problem, she tells Joe, is that she would like to produce more because potential customers leave when her lines get too long.

Joe isn't sure whether to risk spoiling his chances by telling Liz about his own struggling business. But he takes the risk. When he explains to Liz that he spends 50 minutes of every hour making 5 smoothies and 10 minutes making 5 salads, Liz's eyes pop. "Have I got a deal for you!" she exclaims.

Here's the deal that Liz sketches on a table napkin. Joe stops making smoothies and allocates all his time to producing salads. And Liz stops making salads and allocates all her time to producing smoothies. That is, they both specialize in producing the good in which they have a comparative advantage. Together they produce 30 smoothies and 30 salads—see Table 2.3(b).

TABLE 2.3   Liz and Joe Gain from Trade

(a) Before trade	Liz	Joe
Smoothies	15	5
Salads	15	5

(b) Specialization	Liz	Joe
Smoothies	30	0
Salads	0	30

(c) Trade	Liz	Joe
Smoothies	sell 10	buy 10
Salads	buy 20	sell 20

(d) After trade	Liz	Joe
Smoothies	20	10
Salads	20	10

(e) Gains from trade	Liz	Joe
Smoothies	+5	+5
Salads	+5	+5

They then trade. Liz sells Joe 10 smoothies and Joe sells Liz 20 salads—the price of a smoothie is 2 salads—see Table 2.3(c).

After the trade, Joe has 10 salads—the 30 he produces minus the 20 he sells to Liz. He also has the 10 smoothies that he buys from Liz. So Joe now has increased the quantities of smoothies and salads that he can sell—see Table 2.3(d).

Liz has 20 smoothies—the 30 she produces minus the 10 she sells to Joe. She also has the 20 salads that she buys from Joe. Liz has increased the quantities of smoothies and salads that she can sell—see Table 2.3(d). Liz and Joe both gain 5 smoothies and 5 salads an hour—see Table 2.3(e).

To illustrate her idea, Liz grabs a fresh napkin and draws the graphs in Fig. 2.6. The blue *PPF* in part (a) shows Joe's production possibilities. Before trade, he is producing 5 smoothies and 5 salads an hour at point *A*.

The blue *PPF* in part (b) shows Liz's production possibilities. Before trade, she is producing 15 smoothies and 15 salads an hour at point *A*.

Liz's proposal is that they each specialize in producing the good in which they have a comparative advantage. Joe produces 30 salads and no smoothies at point *B* on his *PPF*. Liz produces 30 smoothies and no salads at point *B* on her *PPF*.

Liz and Joe then trade smoothies and salads at a price of 2 salads per smoothie or 1/2 a smoothie per salad. Joe gets smoothies for 2 salads each, which is less than the 5 salads it costs him to produce a smoothie. Liz gets salads for 1/2 a smoothie each, which is less than the 1 smoothie that it costs her to produce a salad.

With trade, Joe has 10 smoothies and 10 salads at point *C*—a gain of 5 smoothies and 5 salads. Joe moves to a point *outside* his *PPF*.

FIGURE 2.6 The Gains from Trade

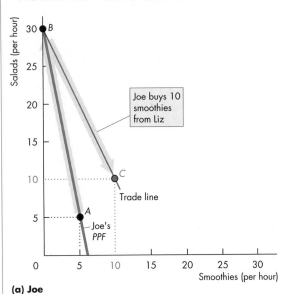
(a) Joe

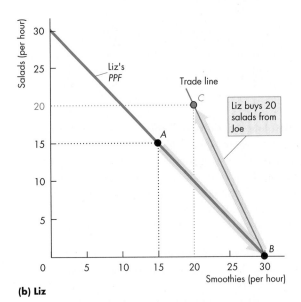
(b) Liz

Joe initially produces at point *A* on his *PPF* in part (a), and Liz initially produces at point *A* on her *PPF* in part (b). Joe's opportunity cost of producing a salad is less than Liz's, so Joe has a comparative advantage in producing salads. Liz's opportunity cost of producing a smoothie is less than Joe's, so Liz has a comparative advantage in producing smoothies. If Joe specializes in making salads, he produces 30 salads and no smoothies at point *B* on his *PPF*. If Liz specializes in making smoothies, she produces 30 smoothies and no salads at point *B* on her *PPF*. They exchange salads for smoothies along the red "Trade line." Liz buys salads from Joe for less than her opportunity cost of producing them. Joe buys smoothies from Liz for less than his opportunity cost of producing them. Each goes to point *C*—a point outside his or her *PPF*. Both Joe and Liz increase production by 5 smoothies and 5 salads with no change in resources.

With trade, Liz has 20 smoothies and 20 salads at point *C*—a gain of 5 smoothies and 5 salads. Liz moves to a point *outside* her *PPF.*

Despite Liz's absolute advantage in producing smoothies and salads, both Liz and Joe gain from specializing—producing the good in which they have a comparative advantage—and trading.

The gains that we achieve from international trade are similar to those achieved by Joe and Liz in this example. When Americans buy T-shirts from China and when China buys Boeing aircraft from the United States, both countries gain. We get our shirts at a lower cost than that at which we can produce them, and China gets its aircraft at a lower cost than that at which it can produce them.

Dynamic Comparative Advantage

At any given point in time, the resources and technologies available determine the comparative advantages that individuals and nations have. But just by repeatedly producing a particular good or service, people become more productive in that activity, a phenomenon called **learning-by-doing**. Learning-by-doing is the basis of *dynamic* comparative advantage. **Dynamic comparative advantage** is a comparative advantage that a person (or country) has acquired by specializing in an activity and becoming the lowest-cost producer as a result of learning-by-doing.

Singapore, for example, pursued dynamic comparative advantage when it decided to begin a biotechnology industry in which it initially didn't have a comparative advantage.

Review Quiz

1 What gives a person a comparative advantage?
2 Distinguish between comparative advantage and absolute advantage.
3 Why do people specialize and trade?
4 What are the gains from specialization and trade?
5 What is the source of the gains from trade?
6 How does dynamic comparative advantage arise?

 Work Study Plan 2.4 and get instant feedback.

Economic Coordination

People gain by specializing in the production of those goods and services in which they have a comparative advantage and then trading with each other. Liz and Joe, whose production of salads and smoothies we studied earlier in this chapter, can get together and make a deal that enables them to enjoy the gains from specialization and trade. But for billions of individuals to specialize and produce millions of different goods and services, their choices must somehow be coordinated.

Two competing economic coordination systems have been used: central economic planning and decentralized markets.

Central economic planning might appear to be the best system because it can express national priorities. But when this system was tried, as it was for 60 years in Russia and for 30 years in China, it was a miserable failure. Today, these and most other previously planned economies are adopting a decentralized market system.

To make decentralized coordination work, four complementary social institutions that have evolved over many centuries are needed. They are

- Firms
- Markets
- Property rights
- Money

Firms

A **firm** is an economic unit that hires factors of production and organizes those factors to produce and sell goods and services. Examples of firms are your local gas station, Wal-Mart, and General Motors.

Firms coordinate a huge amount of economic activity. For example, Wal-Mart buys or rents large buildings, equips them with storage shelves and checkout lanes, and hires labor. Wal-Mart directs the labor and decides what goods to buy and sell.

But Wal-Mart doesn't produce the goods that it sells. It could do so. Wal-Mart could own and coordinate the production of all the things that it sells in its stores. It could also produce all the raw materials that are used to produce the things that it sells. But Sam Walton would not have become one of the wealthiest people in the world if he had followed that path. The reason is that if a firm gets too big, it can't keep track of all the information that is needed to coordinate its activities. It is more efficient for firms to specialize (just as Liz and Joe did) and trade with each other. This trade between firms takes place in markets.

Markets

In ordinary speech, the word *market* means a place where people buy and sell goods such as fish, meat, fruits, and vegetables. In economics, a *market* has a more general meaning. A **market** is any arrangement that enables buyers and sellers to get information and to do business with each other. An example is the market in which oil is bought and sold—the world oil market. The world oil market is not a place. It is the network of oil producers, oil users, wholesalers, and brokers who buy and sell oil. In the world oil market, decision makers do not meet physically. They make deals by telephone, fax, and direct computer link.

Markets have evolved because they facilitate trade. Without organized markets, we would miss out on a substantial part of the potential gains from trade. Enterprising individuals and firms, each pursuing their own self-interest, have profited from making markets—standing ready to buy or sell the items in which they specialize. But markets can work only when property rights exist.

Property Rights

The social arrangements that govern the ownership, use, and disposal of anything that people value are called **property rights**. *Real property* includes land and buildings—the things we call property in ordinary speech—and durable goods such as plant and equipment. *Financial property* includes stocks and bonds and money in the bank. *Intellectual property* is the intangible product of creative effort. This type of property includes books, music, computer programs, and inventions of all kinds and is protected by copyrights and patents.

Where property rights are enforced, people have the incentive to specialize and produce the goods in which they have a comparative advantage. Where people can steal the production of others, resources are devoted not to production but to protecting possessions. Without property rights, we would still be hunting and gathering like our Stone Age ancestors.

Money

Money is any commodity or token that is generally acceptable as a means of payment. Liz and Joe didn't use money in the example above. They exchanged salads and smoothies. In principle, trade in markets can exchange any item for any other item. But you can perhaps imagine how complicated life would be if we exchanged goods for other goods. The "invention" of money makes trading in markets much more efficient.

Circular Flows Through Markets

Figure 2.7 shows the flows that result from the choices that households and firms make. Households specialize and choose the quantities of labor, land, capital, and entrepreneurial services to sell or rent to firms. Firms choose the quantities of factors of production to hire. These (red) flows go through the *factor markets*. Households choose the quantities of goods and services to buy, and firms choose the quantities to produce. These (red) flows go through the *goods markets*. Households receive incomes and make expenditures on goods and services (the green flows).

How do markets coordinate all these decisions?

Coordinating Decisions

Markets coordinate decisions through price adjustments. To see how, think about your local market for hamburgers. Suppose that too few hamburgers are available and some people who want to buy hamburgers are not able to do so. To make buying and selling plans the same, either more hamburgers must be offered for sale or buyers must scale down their appetites (or both). A rise in the price of a hamburger produces this outcome. A higher price encourages producers to offer more hamburgers for sale. It also encourages some people to change their lunch plans. Fewer people buy hamburgers, and more buy hot dogs. More hamburgers (and more hot dogs) are offered for sale.

Alternatively, suppose that more hamburgers are available than people want to buy. In this case, to make the choices of buyers and sellers compatible, more hamburgers must be bought or fewer hamburgers must be offered for sale (or both). A fall in the price of a hamburger achieves this outcome. A lower price encourages firms to produce a smaller quantity of hamburgers. It also encourages people to buy more hamburgers.

FIGURE 2.7   Circular Flows in the Market Economy

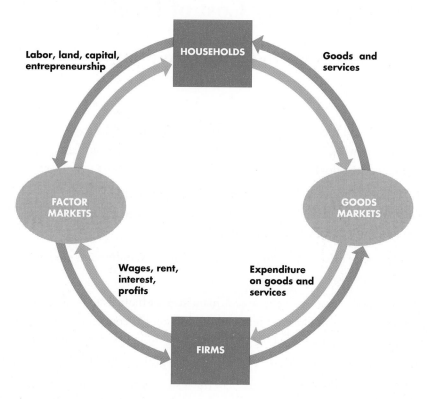

Households and firms make economic choices and markets coordinate these choices.

Households choose the quantities of labor, land, capital, and entrepreneurial services to sell or rent to firms in exchange for wages, rent, interest, and profit. Households also choose how to spend their incomes on the various types of goods and services available.

Firms choose the quantities of factors of production to hire and the quantities of goods and services to produce.

Goods markets and factor markets coordinate these choices of households and firms.

The counterclockwise red flows are real flows—the flow of factors of production from households to firms and the flow of goods and services from firms to households.

The clockwise green flows are the payments for the red flows. They are the flow of incomes from firms to households and the flow of expenditure on goods and services from households to firms.

myeconlab animation

Review Quiz

1 Why are social institutions such as firms, markets, property rights, and money necessary?
2 What are the main functions of markets?
3 What are the flows in the market economy that go from firms to households and the flows from households to firms?

myeconlab Work Study Plan 2.5 and get instant feedback.

◆ You have now begun to see how economists approach economic questions. Scarcity, choice, and divergent opportunity costs explain why we specialize and trade and why firms, markets, property rights, and money have developed. You can see all around you the lessons you've learned in this chapter. *Reading Between the Lines* on pp. 46–47 provides an opportunity to apply the *PPF* model to deepen your understanding of the reasons for the increase in the cost of food associated with the increase in corn production.

The Rising Opportunity Cost of Food

Fuel Choices, Food Crises, and Finger-Pointing

http://www.nytimes.com
April 15, 2008

The idea of turning farms into fuel plants seemed, for a time, like one of the answers to high global oil prices and supply worries. That strategy seemed to reach a high point last year when Congress mandated a fivefold increase in the use of biofuels.

But now a reaction is building against policies in the United States and Europe to promote ethanol and similar fuels, with political leaders from poor countries contending that these fuels are driving up food prices and starving poor people. …

In some countries, the higher prices are leading to riots, political instability, and growing worries about feeding the poorest people. …

Many specialists in food policy consider government mandates for biofuels to be ill advised, agreeing that the diversion of crops like corn into fuel production has contributed to the higher prices. But other factors have played big roles, including droughts that have limited output and rapid global economic growth that has created higher demand for food.

That growth, much faster over the last four years than the historical norm, is lifting millions of people out of destitution and giving them access to better diets. But farmers are having trouble keeping up with the surge in demand.

While there is agreement that the growth of biofuels has contributed to higher food prices, the amount is disputed. …

C. Ford Runge, an economist at the University of Minnesota, said it is "extremely difficult to disentangle" the effect of biofuels on food costs. Nevertheless, he said there was little that could be done to mitigate the effect of droughts and the growing appetite for protein in developing countries.

"Ethanol is the one thing we can do something about," he said. "It's about the only lever we have to pull, but none of the politicians have the courage to pull the lever." …

Essence of the Story

- In 2007, Congress mandated a fivefold increase in the use of biofuels.

- Political leaders in poor countries and specialists in food policy say the biofuel mandate is ill advised and the diversion of corn into fuel production has raised the cost of food.

- Drought that has limited corn production and global economic growth that has increased the demand for protein have also raised the cost of food.

- An economist at the University of Minnesota says that while it is difficult to determine the effect of biofuels on food costs, it is the only factor under our control.

Economic Analysis

- Ethanol is made from corn in the United States, so biofuel and food compete to use the same resources.

- To produce more ethanol and meet the Congress's mandate, farmers increased the number of acres devoted to corn production.

- In 2008, the amount of land devoted to corn production increased by 20 percent in the United States and by 2 percent in the rest of the world.

- Figure 1 shows the U.S. production possibilities frontier, *PPF*, for corn and other goods and services.

- The increase in the production of corn is illustrated by a movement along the *PPF* in Fig. 1 from point *A* in 2007 to point *B* in 2008.

- In moving from point *A* to point *B*, the United States incurs a higher opportunity cost of producing corn, indicated by the greater slope of the *PPF* at point *B*.

- In other regions of the world, despite the fact that more land was devoted to corn production, the amount of corn produced didn't change.

- The reason is that droughts in South America and Eastern Europe lowered the crop yield per acre in those regions.

- Figure 2 shows the rest of the world's *PPF* for corn and other goods and services in 2007 and 2008.

- The increase in the amount of land devoted to producing corn is illustrated by a movement along the PPF_{07}.

- With a decrease in the crop yield, production possibilities decreased and the *PPF* rotated inward.

- The rotation from PPF_{07} to PPF_{08} illustrates this decrease in production possibilities.

- The opportunity cost of producing corn in the rest of the world increased for two reasons: the movement along its *PPF* and the inward rotation of the *PPF*.

- With a higher opportunity cost of producing corn, the cost of both biofuel and food increases.

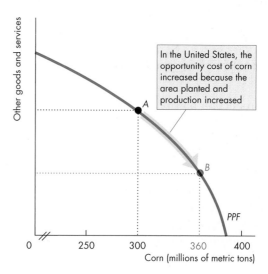

Figure 1 U.S. *PPF*

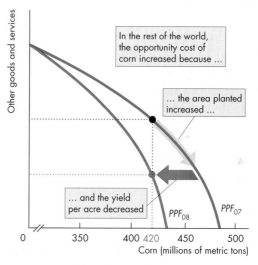

Figure 2 Rest of the World *PPF*

SUMMARY ◆

Key Points

Production Possibilities and Opportunity Cost
(pp. 32–34)

- The production possibilities frontier, *PPF*, is the boundary between production levels that are attainable and those that are not attainable when all the available resources are used to their limit.
- Production efficiency occurs at points on the *PPF*.
- Along the *PPF*, the opportunity cost of producing more of one good is the amount of the other good that must be given up.
- The opportunity cost of all goods increases as the production of the good increases.

Using Resources Efficiently (pp. 35–37)

- Allocative efficiency occurs when goods and services are produced at the least possible cost and in the quantities that bring the greatest possible benefit.
- The marginal cost of a good is the opportunity cost of producing one more unit of it.
- The marginal benefit from a good is the benefit received from consuming one more unit of it, measured by the willingness to pay for it.
- The marginal benefit of a good decreases as the amount of the good available increases.
- Resources are used efficiently when the marginal cost of each good is equal to its marginal benefit.

Economic Growth (pp. 38–39)

- Economic growth, which is the expansion of production possibilities, results from capital accumulation and technological change.
- The opportunity cost of economic growth is forgone current consumption.

Gains from Trade (pp. 40–43)

- A person has a comparative advantage in producing a good if that person can produce the good at a lower opportunity cost than everyone else.
- People gain by specializing in the activity in which they have a comparative advantage and trading with others.
- Dynamic comparative advantage arises from learning-by-doing.

Economic Coordination (pp. 43–45)

- Firms coordinate a large amount of economic activity, but there is a limit to the efficient size of a firm.
- Markets coordinate the economic choices of people and firms.
- Markets can work efficiently only when property rights exist.
- Money makes trading in markets more efficient.

Key Figures

Key Terms

PROBLEMS and APPLICATIONS ◆

 Work problems 1–11 in Chapter 2 Study Plan and get instant feedback.
Work problems 12–21 as Homework, a Quiz, or a Test if assigned by your instructor.

1. Brazil produces ethanol from sugar, and the land used to grow sugar can be used to grow food crops. Suppose that Brazil's production possibilities for ethanol and food crops are as follows

Ethanol (barrels per day)		Food crops (tons per day)
70	and	0
64	and	1
54	and	2
40	and	3
22	and	4
0	and	5

   a. Draw a graph of Brazil's *PPF* and explain how your graph illustrates scarcity.
   b. If Brazil produces 40 barrels of ethanol a day, how much food must it produce if it achieves production efficiency?
   c. Why does Brazil face a tradeoff on its *PPF*?
   d. If Brazil increases its production of ethanol from 40 barrels per day to 54 barrels per day, what is the opportunity cost of the additional ethanol?
   e. If Brazil increases its production of food crops from 2 tons per day to 3 tons per day, what is the opportunity cost of the additional food?
   f. What is the relationship between your answers to d and e?
   g. Does Brazil face an increasing opportunity cost of ethanol? What feature of the *PPF* that you've drawn illustrates increasing opportunity cost?

2. Define marginal cost and use the information provided in the table in problem 1 to calculate the marginal cost of producing a ton of food when the quantity produced is 2.5 tons per day.

3. Define marginal benefit, explain how it is measured, and explain why the information provided in the table in problem 1 does not enable you to calculate the marginal benefit of food.

4. Distinguish between *production efficiency* and *allocative efficiency*. Explain why many production possibilities achieve production efficiency but only one achieves allocative efficiency.

5. Harry enjoys tennis but wants a high grade in his economics course. The figure shows the limits to what he can achieve: It is Harry's *PPF* for these two "goods."

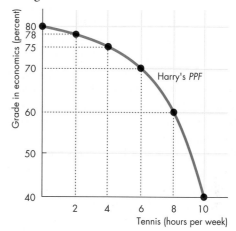

The following figure shows Harry's *MB* curve for tennis.

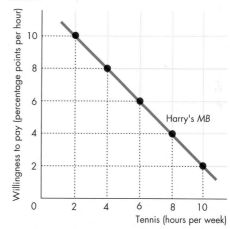

   a. What is Harry's marginal cost of tennis if he plays for (i) 3 hours a week; (ii) 5 hours a week; and (iii) 7 hours a week?
   b. If Harry uses his time to achieve allocative efficiency, what is his economics grade and how many hours of tennis does he play?
   c. Explain why Harry would be worse off getting a grade higher than your answer to b.
   d. If Harry becomes a tennis superstar with big earnings from tennis, what happens to his *PPF*, *MB* curve, and efficient time allocation?

e. If Harry suddenly finds high grades in economics easier to attain, what happens to his *PPF*, *MB* curve, and efficient time allocation?

6. A farm grows wheat and produces pork. The marginal cost of producing each of these products increases as more of it is produced.
   a. Make a graph that illustrates the farm's *PPF*.
   b. The farm adopts a new technology that allows it to use fewer resources to fatten pigs. Use your graph to illustrate the impact of the new technology on the farm's *PPF*.
   c. With the farm using the new technology described in b, has the opportunity cost of producing a ton of wheat increased, decreased, or remained the same? Explain and illustrate your answer.
   d. Is the farm more efficient with the new technology than it was with the old one? Why?

7. In an hour, Sue can produce 40 caps or 4 jackets and Tessa can produce 80 caps or 4 jackets.
   a. Calculate Sue's opportunity cost of producing a cap.
   b. Calculate Tessa's opportunity cost of producing a cap.
   c. Who has a comparative advantage in producing caps?
   d. If Sue and Tessa specialize in producing the good in which each of them has a comparative advantage, and they trade 1 jacket for 15 caps, who gains from the specialization and trade?

8. Suppose that Tessa buys a new machine for making jackets that enables her to make 20 jackets an hour. (She can still make only 80 caps per hour.)
   a. Who now has a comparative advantage in producing jackets?
   b. Can Sue and Tessa still gain from trade?
   c. Would Sue and Tessa still be willing to trade 1 jacket for 15 caps? Explain your answer.

9. "America's baby-boomers are embracing tea for its health benefits," said *The Economist* (July 8, 2005, p. 65). The article went on to say: "Even though the climate is suitable, tea-growing [in the United States] is simply too costly, since the process is labor-intensive and resists automation." Using this information:
   a. Sketch a *PPF* for the production of tea and other goods and services in India.
   b. Sketch a *PPF* for the production of tea and other goods and services in the United States.
   c. Sketch a marginal cost curve for the production of tea in India.
   d. Sketch a marginal cost curve for the production of tea in the United States.
   e. Sketch the marginal benefit curve for tea in the United States before and after the baby-boomers began to appreciate the health benefits of tea.
   f. Explain why the United States does not produce tea and instead imports it from India.
   g. Explain how the quantity of tea that achieves allocative efficiency has changed.
   h. Does the change in preferences toward tea affect the opportunity cost of producing tea?

10. Brazil produces ethanol from sugar at a cost of 83 cents per gallon. The United States produces ethanol from corn at a cost of $1.14 per gallon. Sugar grown on one acre of land produces twice the quantity of ethanol as the corn grown on an acre. The United States imports 5 percent of its ethanol consumption and produces the rest itself. Since 2003, U.S. ethanol production has more than doubled and U.S. corn production has increased by 45 percent.
    a. Does Brazil or the United States have a comparative advantage in producing ethanol?
    b. Do you expect the opportunity cost of producing ethanol in the United States to have increased since 2003? Explain why.
    c. Sketch the *PPF* for ethanol and other goods and services for the United States.
    d. Sketch the *PPF* for ethanol and other goods and services for Brazil.
    e. Sketch a figure similar to Fig. 2.6 on p. 42 to show how both the United States and Brazil can gain from specialization and trade.
    f. Do you think the United States has achieved production efficiency in its manufacture of ethanol? Explain why or why not.
    g. Do you think the United States has achieved allocative efficiency in its manufacture of ethanol? Explain why or why not.

11. For 50 years, Cuba has had a centrally planned economy in which the government makes the big decisions on how resources will be allocated. Why would you expect Cuba's production possibilities (per person) to be smaller than those of the United States? What are the social institutions that help the U.S. economy achieve allocative efficiency that Cuba might lack?

12. Suppose that Yucatan's production possibilities are

Food (pounds per month)		Sunscreen (gallons per month)
300	and	0
200	and	50
100	and	100
0	and	150

a. Draw a graph of Yucatan's *PPF* and explain how your graph illustrates a tradeoff.

b. If Yucatan produces 150 pounds of food per month, how much sunscreen must it produce if it achieves production efficiency?

c. What is Yucatan's opportunity cost of producing 1 pound of food?

d. What is Yucatan's opportunity cost of producing 1 gallon of sunscreen?

e. What is the relationship between your answers to c and d?

f. Does Yucatan face an increasing opportunity cost of food? What feature of a *PPF* illustrates increasing opportunity cost and why does the *PPF* that you have drawn not have this feature?

13. What is the marginal cost of a pound of food in Yucatan in problem 12 when the quantity produced is 150 pounds per day? What is special about the marginal cost of food in Yucatan?

14. In Yucatan, which has the production possibilities shown in the table in problem 12, preferences are described by the following table.

Sunscreen (gallons per month)	Willingness to pay (pounds of food per gallon)
25	3
75	2
125	1

a. What is the marginal benefit from sunscreen and how it is measured?

b. What information provided in the table above and the table in problem 12 do we need to be able to calculate the marginal benefit from sunscreen in Yucatan?

c. Draw a graph of Yucatan's marginal benefit from sunscreen.

15. "Dr. Arata Kochi, the World Health Organization malaria chief, ... [says that] eradication is counterproductive. With enough money, he said, current tools like nets, medicines and DDT could drive down malaria cases 90 percent.

'But eliminating the last 10 percent is a tremendous task and very expensive,' Dr. Kochi said. 'Even places like South Africa should think twice before taking this path.'"

The New York Times, March 4, 2008

a. Is Dr. Kochi talking about *production efficiency* or *allocative efficiency* or both?

b. Make a graph with the percentage of malaria cases eliminated on the *x*-axis and the marginal cost and marginal benefit of driving down malaria cases on the *y*-axis. On your graph:
(i) Draw a marginal cost curve that is consistent with Dr. Kochi's opinion reported in the news article.
(ii) Draw a marginal benefit curve that is consistent with Dr. Kochi's opinion reported in the news article.
(iii) Identify the quantity of malaria eradicated that achieves allocative efficiency.

16. Capital accumulation and technological change bring economic growth, which means that the *PPF* keeps shifting outward: Production that was unattainable yesterday becomes attainable today; and production that is unattainable today will become attainable tomorrow. Why doesn't this process of economic growth mean that scarcity is being defeated and will one day be gone?

17. "Inexpensive broadband access has done far more for online video than enable the success of services like YouTube and iTunes. By unchaining video watchers from their TV sets, it has opened the floodgates to a generation of TV producers for whom the Internet is their native medium."

The New York Times, December 2, 2007

a. How has inexpensive broadband changed the production possibilities of video entertainment and other goods and services?

b. Sketch a *PPF* for video entertainment and other goods and services before broadband.

c. Show how the arrival of inexpensive broadband has changed the *PPF*.

d. Sketch a marginal benefit curve for video entertainment.

e. Show how opening the "floodgates to a generation of TV producers for whom the Internet is their native medium" might have changed the marginal benefit from video entertainment.

f. Explain how the quantity of video entertainment that achieves allocative efficiency has changed.

18. Kim can produce 40 pies an hour or 400 cookies an hour. Liam can produce 100 pies an hour or 200 cookies an hour.
    a. Calculate Kim's opportunity cost of producing a pie.
    b. Calculate Liam's opportunity cost of producing a pie.
    c. Who has a comparative advantage in producing pies?
    d. If Kim and Liam spend 30 minutes of each hour producing pies and 30 minutes producing cookies, how many pies and cookies does each of them produce?
    e. Suppose that Kim and Liam increase the time they spend producing the good in which they have a comparative advantage by 15 minutes. What will be the increase in the total number of pies and cookies they produce?
    f. What is the highest price of a pie at which Kim and Liam would agree to trade pies and cookies?
    g. If Kim and Liam specialize and trade, what are the gains from trade?

19. Before the Civil War, the South traded with the North and with England. The South sold cotton and bought manufactured goods and food. During the war, one of President Lincoln's first actions was to blockade the ports, which prevented this trade. The South had to increase its production of munitions and food.
    a. In what did the South have a comparative advantage?
    b. Draw a graph to illustrate production, consumption, and trade in the South before the Civil War.
    c. Was the South consuming inside, on, or outside its *PPF*? Explain your answer.
    d. Draw a graph to show the effects of the Civil War on consumption and production in the South.
    e. Did the Civil War change any opportunity costs in the South? Did the opportunity cost of everything rise? Did any items cost less?
    f. Illustrate your answer to e with appropriate graphs.

20. "A two-time N.B.A. All-Star, Barron Davis has quietly been moonlighting as a [movie] producer since 2005, when he and a high school buddy, Cash Warren, formed a production company called Verso Entertainment.

    In January, Verso's first feature-length effort, "Made in America," a gang-life documentary directed by Stacy Peralta, had its premiere to good reviews at Sundance Film Festival and is being courted by distributors."

    The New York Times, February 24, 2008
    a. Does Barron Davis have an *absolute* advantage in basketball and movie directing and is this the reason for his success in both activities?
    b. Does Barron Davis have a comparative advantage in basketball or movie directing or both and is this the reason for his success in both activities?
    c. Sketch a *PPF* between playing basketball and producing other goods and services for Barron Davis and for yourself.
    d. How do you (and people like you) and Barron Davis (and people like him) gain from specialization and trade?

21. After you have studied *Reading Between the Lines* on pp. 46–47, answer the following questions:
    a. How has an Act of the United States Congress increased U.S. production of corn?
    b. Why would you expect an increase in the quantity of corn produced to raise the opportunity cost of corn?
    c. Why did the cost of producing corn increase in the rest of the world?
    d. Is it possible that the increased quantity of corn produced, despite the higher cost of production, moves the United States closer to allocative efficiency?

22. Use the links on MyEconLab (Textbook Resources, Chapter 2, Weblinks) to obtain data on the tuition and other costs of enrolling in the MBA program at a school that interests you.
    a. Draw a *PPF* that shows the tradeoff that you would face if you decided to enroll in the MBA program.
    b. Do you think your marginal benefit of an MBA exceeds your marginal cost?
    c. Based on your answer to b, do you plan to enroll in an MBA program? Is your answer to this question consistent with using your time to achieve your self-interest?

3 ◆ Demand and Supply

After studying this chapter, you will be able to:

- Describe a competitive market and think about a price as an opportunity cost

- Explain the influences on demand

- Explain the influences on supply

- Explain how demand and supply determine prices and quantities bought and sold

- Use the demand and supply model to make predictions about changes in prices and quantities

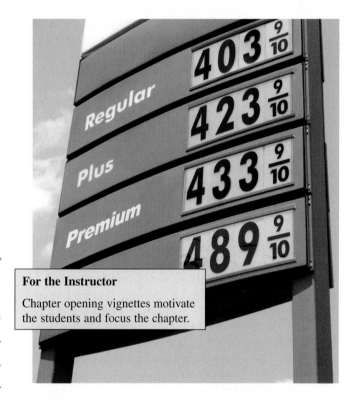

What makes the prices of oil and gasoline double in just one year? Will these prices keep on rising? Are the oil companies taking advantage of people? This chapter enables you to answer these and similar questions about prices—prices that rise, prices that fall, and prices that fluctuate.

You already know that economics is about the choices people make to cope with scarcity and how those choices respond to incentives. Prices act as incentives. You're going to see how people respond to prices and how prices get determined by demand and supply. The demand and supply model that you study in this chapter is the main tool of economics. It

helps us to answer the big economic question: What, how, and for whom goods and services are produced?

At the end of the chapter, in *Reading Between the Lines*, we'll apply the model to market for gasoline and explain why the price increased so sharply in 2008.

◆ Markets and Prices

When you need a new pair of running shoes, want a bagel and a latte, plan to upgrade your cell phone, or need to fly home for Thanksgiving, you must find a place where people sell those items or offer those services. The place in which you find them is a *market*. You learned in Chapter 2 (p. 44) that a market is any arrangement that enables buyers and sellers to get information and to do business with each other.

A market has two sides: buyers and sellers. There are markets for *goods* such as apples and hiking boots, for *services* such as haircuts and tennis lessons, for *resources* such as computer programmers and earthmovers, and for other manufactured *inputs* such as memory chips and auto parts. There are also markets for money such as Japanese yen and for financial securities such as Yahoo! stock. Only our imagination limits what can be traded in markets.

Some markets are physical places where buyers and sellers meet and where an auctioneer or a broker helps to determine the prices. Examples of this type of market are the New York Stock Exchange and the wholesale fish, meat, and produce markets.

Some markets are groups of people spread around the world who never meet and know little about each other but are connected through the Internet or by telephone and fax. Examples are the e-commerce markets and the currency markets.

But most markets are unorganized collections of buyers and sellers. You do most of your trading in this type of market. An example is the market for basketball shoes. The buyers in this $3 billion-a-year market are the 45 million Americans who play basketball (or who want to make a fashion statement). The sellers are the tens of thousands of retail sports equipment and footwear stores. Each buyer can visit several different stores, and each seller knows that the buyer has a choice of stores.

Markets vary in the intensity of competition that buyers and sellers face. In this chapter, we're going to study a **competitive market**—a market that has many buyers and many sellers, so no single buyer or seller can influence the price.

Producers offer items for sale only if the price is high enough to cover their opportunity cost. And consumers respond to changing opportunity cost by seeking cheaper alternatives to expensive items.

We are going to study how people respond to *prices* and the forces that determine prices. But to pursue these tasks, we need to understand the relationship between a price and an opportunity cost.

In everyday life, the *price* of an object is the number of dollars that must be given up in exchange for it. Economists refer to this price as the **money price**.

The *opportunity cost* of an action is the highest-valued alternative forgone. If, when you buy a cup of coffee, the highest-valued thing you forgo is some gum, then the opportunity cost of the coffee is the *quantity* of gum forgone. We can calculate the quantity of gum forgone from the money prices of the coffee and the gum.

If the money price of coffee is $1 a cup and the money price of gum is 50¢ a pack, then the opportunity cost of one cup of coffee is two packs of gum. To calculate this opportunity cost, we divide the price of a cup of coffee by the price of a pack of gum and find the *ratio* of one price to the other. The ratio of one price to another is called a **relative price**, and a *relative price is an opportunity cost.*

We can express the relative price of coffee in terms of gum or any other good. The normal way of expressing a relative price is in terms of a "basket" of all goods and services. To calculate this relative price, we divide the money price of a good by the money price of a "basket" of all goods (called a *price index*). The resulting relative price tells us the opportunity cost of the good in terms of how much of the "basket" we must give up to buy it.

The demand and supply model that we are about to study determines *relative prices,* and the word "price" means *relative* price. When we predict that a price will fall, we do not mean that its *money* price will fall—although it mig[...] price will fall. That is, its [...] average price of other goo[...]

> **For the Instructor**
>
> Review quizzes close each major section. All of the review quiz problems are in MyEconLab.

Review Quiz ◆

1 What is the distinction between a money price and a relative price?

2 Explain why a relative price is an opportunity cost.

3 Think of examples of goods whose relative price has risen or fallen by a large amount.

 Work Study Plan 3.1 and get instant feedback.

Let's begin our study of demand and supply, starting with demand.

◆ Demand

If you demand something, then you

1. Want it,
2. Can afford it, and
3. Plan to buy it.

Wants are the unlimited desires or wishes that people have for goods and services. How many times have you thought that you would like something "if only you could afford it" or "if it weren't so expensive"? Scarcity guarantees that many—perhaps most—of our wants will never be satisfied. Demand reflects a decision about which wants to satisfy.

The **quantity demanded** of a good or service is the amount that consumers plan to buy during a given time period at a particular price. The quantity demanded is not necessarily the same as the quantity actually bought. Sometimes the quantity demanded exceeds the amount of goods available, so the quantity bought is less than the quantity demanded.

The quantity demanded is measured as an amount per unit of time. For example, suppose that you buy one cup of coffee a day. The quantity of coffee that you demand can be expressed as 1 cup per day, 7 cups per week, or 365 cups per year.

Many factors influence buying plans, and one of them is the price. We look first at the relationship between the quantity demanded of a good and its price. To study this relationship, we keep all other influences on buying plans the same and we ask: How, other things remaining the same, does the quantity demanded of a good change as its price changes?

The law of demand provides the answer.

The Law of Demand

The **law of demand** states

> Other things remaining the same, the higher the price of a good, the smaller is the quantity demanded; and the lower the price of a good, the greater is the quantity demanded.

Why does a higher price reduce the quantity demanded? For two reasons:

- Substitution effect
- Income effect

Substitution Effect When the price of a good rises, other things remaining the same, its *relative* price—its opportunity cost—rises. Although each good is unique, it has *substitutes*—other goods that can be used in its place. As the opportunity cost of a good rises, the incentive to economize on its use and switch to a substitute becomes stronger.

Income Effect When a price rises, other things remaining the same, the price rises *relative* to income. Faced with a higher price and an unchanged income, people cannot afford to buy all the things they previously bought. They must decrease the quantities demanded of at least some goods and services. Normally, the good whose price has increased will be one of the goods that people buy less of.

To see the substitution effect and the income effect at work, think about the effects of a change in the price of an energy bar. Several different goods are substitutes for an energy bar. For example, an energy drink could be consumed instead of an energy bar.

Suppose that an energy bar initially sells for $3 and then its price falls to $1.50. People now substitute energy bars for energy drinks—the substitution effect. And with a budget that now has some slack from the lower price of an energy bar, people buy even more energy bars—the income effect. The quantity of energy bars demanded increases for these two reasons.

Now suppose that an energy bar initially sells for $3 and then the price doubles to $6. People now buy fewer energy bars and more energy drinks—the substitution effect. And faced with a tighter budget, people buy even fewer energy bars—the income effect. The quantity of energy bars demanded decreases for these two reasons.

Demand Curve and Demand Schedule

You are now about to study one of the two most used curves in economics: the demand curve. And you are going to encounter one of the most critical distinctions: the distinction between *demand* and *quantity demanded.*

The term **demand** refers to the entire relationship between the price of a good and the quantity demanded of that good. Demand is illustrated by the demand curve and the demand schedule. The term *quantity demanded* refers to a point on a demand curve—the quantity demanded at a particular price.

Figure 3.1 shows the demand curve for energy bars. A **demand curve** shows the relationship between the quantity demanded of a good and its price when all other influences on consumers' planned purchases remain the same.

The table in Fig. 3.1 is the demand schedule for energy bars. A *demand schedule* lists the quantities demanded at each price when all the other influences on consumers' planned purchases remain the same. For example, if the price of a bar is 50¢, the quantity demanded is 22 million a week. If the price is $2.50, the quantity demanded is 5 million a week. The other rows of the table show the quantities demanded at prices of $1.00, $1.50, and $2.00.

We graph the demand schedule as a demand curve with the quantity demanded on the *x*-axis and the price on the *y*-axis. The points on the demand curve labeled *A* through *E* correspond to the rows of the demand schedule. For example, point *A* on the graph shows a quantity demanded of 22 million energy bars a week at a price of 50¢ a bar.

Willingness and Ability to Pay Another way of looking at the demand curve is as a willingness-and-ability-to-pay curve. The willingness and ability to pay is a measure of *marginal benefit*.

If a small quantity is available, the highest price that someone is willing and able to pay for one more unit is high. But as the quantity available increases, the marginal benefit of each additional unit falls and the highest price that someone is willing and able to pay also falls along the demand curve.

In Fig. 3.1, if only 5 million energy bars are available each week, the highest price that someone is willing to pay for the 5 millionth bar is $2.50. But if 22 million energy bars are available each week, someone is willing to pay 50¢ for the last bar bought.

A Change in Demand

When any factor that influences buying plans other than the price of the good changes, there is a **change in demand**. Figure 3.2 illustrates an increase in demand. When demand increases, the demand curve shifts rightward and the quantity demanded at each price is greater. For example, at $2.50 a bar, the quantity demanded on the original (blue) demand curve is 5 million energy bars a week. On the new (red) demand curve, at $2.50 a bar, the quantity demanded is 15 million bars a week. Look closely at the numbers in the table and check that the quantity demanded at each price is greater.

FIGURE 3.1   The Demand Curve

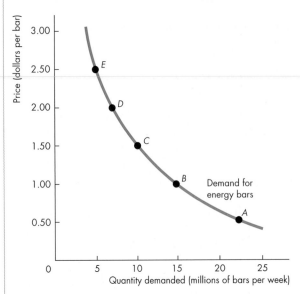

	Price (dollars per bar)	Quantity demanded (millions of bars per week)
A	0.50	22
B	1.00	15
C	1.50	10
D	2.00	7
E	2.50	5

The table shows a demand schedule for energy bars. At a price of 50¢ a bar, 22 million bars a week are demanded; at a price of $1.50 a bar, 10 million bars a week are demanded. The demand curve shows the relationship between quantity demanded and price, other things remaining the same. The demand curve slopes downward: As the price decreases, the quantity demanded increases.

The demand curve can be read in two ways. For a given price, the demand curve tells us the quantity that people plan to buy. For example, at a price of $1.50 a bar, people plan to buy 10 million bars a week. For a given quantity, the demand curve tells us the maximum price that consumers are willing and able to pay for the last bar available. For example, the maximum price that consumers will pay for the 15 millionth bar is $1.00.

FIGURE 3.2 An Increase in Demand

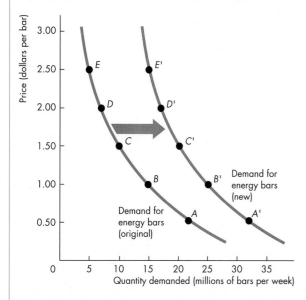

	Original demand schedule Original income			New demand schedule New higher income	
	Price (dollars per bar)	Quantity demanded (millions of bars per week)		Price (dollars per bar)	Quantity demanded (millions of bars per week)
A	0.50	22	A'	0.50	32
B	1.00	15	B'	1.00	25
C	1.50	10	C'	1.50	20
D	2.00	7	D'	2.00	17
E	2.50	5	E'	2.50	15

A change in any influence on buyers' plans other than the price of the good itself results in a new demand schedule and a shift of the demand curve. A change in income changes the demand for energy bars. At a price of $1.50 a bar, 10 million bars a week are demanded at the original income (row C of the table) and 20 million bars a week are demanded at the new higher income (row C'). A rise in income increases the demand for energy bars. The demand curve shifts *rightward*, as shown by the shift arrow and the resulting red curve.

myeconlab   animation

Six main factors bring changes in demand. They are changes in

- The prices of related goods
- Expected future prices
- Income
- Expected future income and credit
- Population
- Preferences

Prices of Related Goods The quantity of energy bars that consumers plan to buy depends in part on the prices of substitutes for energy bars. A **substitute** is a good that can be used in place of another good. For example, a bus ride is a substitute for a train ride; a hamburger is a substitute for a hot dog; and an energy drink is a substitute for an energy bar. If the price of a substitute for an energy bar rises, people buy less of the substitute and more energy bars. For example, if the price of an energy drink rises, people buy fewer energy drinks and more energy bars. The demand for energy bars increases.

The quantity of energy bars that people plan to buy also depends on the prices of complements with energy bars. A **complement** is a good that is used in conjunction with another good. Hamburgers and fries are complements, and so are energy bars and exercise. If the price of an hour at the gym falls, people buy more gym time *and more* energy bars.

Expected Future Prices If the price of a good is expected to rise in the future and if the good can be stored, the opportunity cost of obtaining the good for future use is lower today than it will be when the price has increased. So people retime their purchases—they substitute over time. They buy more of the good now before its price is expected to rise (and less afterward), so the demand for the good today increases.

For example, suppose that a Florida frost damages the season's orange crop. You expect the price of orange juice to rise, so you fill your freezer with enough frozen juice to get you through the next six months. Your current demand for frozen orange juice has increased, and your future demand has decreased.

Similarly, if the price of a good is expected to fall in the future, the opportunity cost of buying the good today is high relative to what it is expected to be in the future. So again, people retime their purchases. They buy less of the good now before its price falls, so the demand for the good decreases today and increases in the future.

Computer prices are constantly falling, and this fact poses a dilemma. Will you buy a new computer now, in time for the start of the school year, or will you wait until the price has fallen some more? Because people expect computer prices to keep falling, the current demand for computers is less (and the future demand is greater) than it otherwise would be.

Income Consumers' income influences demand. When income increases, consumers buy more of most goods; and when income decreases, consumers buy less of most goods. Although an increase in income leads to an increase in the demand for *most* goods, it does not lead to an increase in the demand for *all* goods. A **normal good** is one for which demand increases as income increases. An **inferior good** is one for which demand decreases as income increases. As incomes increase, the demand for air travel (a normal good) increases and the demand for long-distance bus trips (an inferior good) decreases.

Expected Future Income and Credit When income is expected to increase in the future, or when credit is easy to obtain, demand might increase now. For example, a salesperson gets the news that she will receive a big bonus at the end of the year, so she goes into debt and buys a new car right now.

Population Demand also depends on the size and the age structure of the population. The larger the population, the greater is the demand for all goods and services; the smaller the population, the smaller is the demand for all goods and services.

For example, the demand for parking spaces or movies or just about anything that you can imagine is much greater in New York City (population 7.5 million) than it is in Boise, Idaho (population 150,000).

Also, the larger the proportion of the population in a given age group, the greater is the demand for the goods and services used by that age group.

For example, during the 1990s, a decrease in the college-age population decreased the demand for college places. During those same years, the number of Americans aged 85 years and over increased by more than 1 million. As a result, the demand for nursing home services increased.

TABLE 3.1 The Demand for Energy Bars

The Law of Demand

The quantity of energy bars demanded

Decreases if:	Increases if:
■ The price of an energy bar rises	■ The price of an energy bar falls

Changes in Demand

The demand for energy bars

Decreases if:	Increases if:
■ The price of a substitute falls	■ The price of a substitute rises
■ The price of a complement rises	■ The price of a complement falls
■ The price of an energy bar is expected to fall	■ The price of an energy bar is expected to rise
■ Income falls*	■ Income rises*
■ Expected future income falls or credit becomes harder to get	■ Expected future income rises or credit becomes easier to get
■ The population decreases	■ The population increases

*An energy bar is a normal good.

Preferences Demand depends on preferences. *Preferences* determine the value that people place on each good and service. Preferences depend on such things as the weather, information, and fashion. For example, greater health and fitness awareness has shifted preferences in favor of energy bars, so the demand for energy bars has increased.

Table 3.1 summarizes the influences on demand and the direction of those influences.

A Change in the Quantity Demanded Versus a Change in Demand

Changes in the influences on buyers' plans bring either a change in the quantity demanded or a change in demand. Equivalently, they bring either a movement along the demand curve or a shift of the demand curve. The distinction between a change in the quantity demanded and a change in demand is

the same as t...
demand curv...

A point o...
demanded at...
the demand c...
demanded. The entire demand curve shows demand. So a shift of the demand curve shows a *change in demand*. Figure 3.3 illustrates these distinctions.

Movement Along the Demand Curve If the price of the good changes but no other influence on buying plans changes, we illustrate the effect as a movement along the demand curve.

A fall in the price of a good increases the quantity demanded of it. In Fig. 3.3, we illustrate the effect of a fall in price as a movement down along the demand curve D_0.

A rise in the price of a good decreases the quantity demanded of it. In Fig. 3.3, we illustrate the effect of a rise in price as a movement up along the demand curve D_0.

A Shift of the Demand Curve If the price of a good remains constant but some other influence on buyers' plans changes, there is a change in demand for that good. We illustrate a change in demand as a shift of the demand curve. For example, if more people work out at the gym, consumers buy more energy bars regardless of the price of a bar. That is what a rightward shift of the demand curve shows—more energy bars are demanded at each price.

In Fig. 3.3, there is a *change in demand* and the demand curve shifts when any influence on buyers' plans changes, other than the price of the good. Demand *increases* and the demand curve *shifts rightward* (to the red demand curve D_1) if the price of a substitute rises, the price of a complement falls, the expected future price of the good rises, income increases (for a normal good), expected future income or credit increases, or the population increases. Demand *decreases* and the demand curve *shifts leftward* (to the red demand curve D_2) if the price of a substitute falls, the price of a complement rises, the expected future price of the good falls, income decreases (for a normal good), expected future income or credit decreases, or the population decreases. (For an inferior good, the effects of changes in income are in the opposite direction to those described above.)

FIGURE 3.3 A Change in the Quantity Demanded Versus a Change in Demand

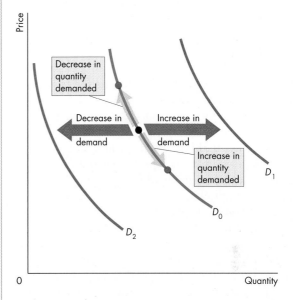

When the price of the good changes, there is a movement along the demand curve and *a change in the quantity demanded*, shown by the blue arrows on demand curve D_0. When any other influence on buyers' plans changes, there is a shift of the demand curve and a *change in demand*. An increase in demand shifts the demand curve rightward (from D_0 to D_1). A decrease in demand shifts the demand curve leftward (from D_0 to D_2).

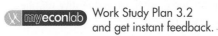 animation

Review Quiz

1 Define the quantity demanded of a good or service.
2 What is the law of demand and how do we illustrate it?
3 What does the demand curve tell us about the price that consumers are willing to pay?
4 List all the influences on buying plans that change demand, and for each influence, say whether it increases or decreases demand.
5 Why does demand not change when the price of a good changes with no change in the other influences on buying plans?

myeconlab Work Study Plan 3.2 and get instant feedback.

◆ Supply

If a firm supplies a good or service, the firm

1. Has the resources and technology to produce it,
2. Can profit from producing it, and
3. Plans to produce it and sell it.

A supply is more than just having the *resources* and the *technology* to produce something. *Resources and technology* are the constraints that limit what is possible.

Many useful things can be produced, but they are not produced unless it is profitable to do so. Supply reflects a decision about which technologically feasible items to produce.

The **quantity supplied** of a good or service is the amount that producers plan to sell during a given time period at a particular price. The quantity supplied is not necessarily the same amount as the quantity actually sold. Sometimes the quantity supplied is greater than the quantity demanded, so the quantity sold is less than the quantity supplied.

Like the quantity demanded, the quantity supplied is measured as an amount per unit of time. For example, suppose that GM produces 1,000 cars a day. The quantity of cars supplied by GM can be expressed as 1,000 a day, 7,000 a week, or 365,000 a year. Without the time dimension, we cannot tell whether a particular quantity is large or small.

Many factors influence selling plans, and again one of them is the price of the good. We look first at the relationship between the quantity supplied of a good and its price. Just as we did when we studied demand, to isolate the relationship between the quantity supplied of a good and its price, we keep all other influences on selling plans the same and ask: How does the quantity supplied of a good change as its price changes when other things remain the same?

The law of supply provides the answer.

The Law of Supply

The **law of supply** states:

> Other things remaining the same, the higher the
> price of a good, the greater is the quantity supplied;
> and the lower the price of a good, the smaller is the
> quantity supplied.

Why does a higher price increase the quantity supplied? It is because *marginal cost increases*. As the quantity produced of any good increases, the marginal cost of producing the good increases. (You can refresh your memory of increasing marginal cost in Chapter 2, p. 35.)

It is never worth producing a good if the price received for the good does not at least cover the marginal cost of producing it. When the price of a good rises, other things remaining the same, producers are willing to incur a higher marginal cost, so they increase production. The higher price brings forth an increase in the quantity supplied.

Let's now illustrate the law of supply with a supply curve and a supply schedule.

Supply Curve and Supply Schedule

You are now going to study the second of the two most used curves in economics: the supply curve. And you're going to learn about the critical distinction between *supply* and *quantity supplied*.

The term **supply** refers to the entire relationship between the price of a good and the quantity supplied of it. Supply is illustrated by the supply curve and the supply schedule. The term *quantity supplied* refers to a point on a supply curve—the quantity supplied at a particular price.

Figure 3.4 shows the supply curve of energy bars. A **supply curve** shows the relationship between the quantity supplied of a good and its price when all other influences on producers' planned sales remain the same. The supply curve is a graph of a supply schedule.

The table in Fig. 3.4 sets out the supply schedule for energy bars. A *supply schedule* lists the quantities supplied at each price when all the other influences on producers' planned sales remain the same. For example, if the price of a bar is 50¢, the quantity supplied is zero—in row *A* of the table. If the price of a bar is $1.00, the quantity supplied is 6 million energy bars a week—in row *B*. The other rows of the table show the quantities supplied at prices of $1.50, $2.00, and $2.50.

To make a supply curve, we graph the quantity supplied on the *x*-axis and the price on the *y*-axis, just as in the case of the demand curve. The points on the supply curve labeled *A* through *E* correspond to the rows of the supply schedule. For example, point *A* on the graph shows a quantity supplied of zero at a price of 50¢ an energy bar.

FIGURE 3.4   The Supply Curve

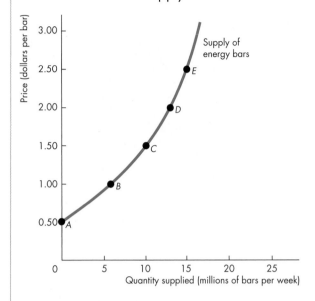

	Price (dollars per bar)	Quantity supplied (millions of bars per week)
A	0.50	0
B	1.00	6
C	1.50	10
D	2.00	13
E	2.50	15

The table shows the supply schedule of energy bars. For example, at a price of $1.00, 6 million bars a week are supplied; at a price of $2.50, 15 million bars a week are supplied. The supply curve shows the relationship between the quantity supplied and the price, other things remaining the same. The supply curve slopes upward: As the price of a good increases, the quantity supplied increases.

A supply curve can be read in two ways. For a given price, the supply curve tells us the quantity that producers plan to sell at that price. For example, at a price of $1.50 a bar, producers are willing to sell 10 million bars a week. For a given quantity, the supply curve tells us the minimum price at which producers are willing to sell one more bar. For example, if 15 million bars are produced each week, the lowest price at which a producer is willing to sell the 15 millionth bar is $2.50.

myeconlab animation

Minimum Supply Price   The supply curve can be interpreted as a minimum-supply-price curve—a curve that shows the lowest price at which someone is willing to sell. This lowest price is the *marginal cost*.

If a small quantity is produced, the lowest price at which someone is willing to sell one more unit is low. But as the quantity produced increases, the marginal cost of each additional unit rises, so the lowest price at which someone is willing to sell rises along the supply curve.

In Fig. 3.4, if 15 million bars are produced each week, the lowest price at which someone is willing to sell the 15 millionth bar is $2.50. But if 10 million bars are produced each week, someone is willing to accept $1.50 for the last bar produced.

A Change in Supply

When any factor that influences selling plans other than the price of the good changes, there is a **change in supply**. Six main factors bring changes in supply. They are changes in

- The prices of factors of production
- The prices of related goods produced
- Expected future prices
- The number of suppliers
- Technology
- The state of nature

Prices of Factors of Production   The prices of the factors of production used to produce a good influence its supply. To see this influence, think about the supply curve as a minimum-supply-price curve. If the price of a factor of production rises, the lowest price that a producer is willing to accept for that good rises, so supply decreases. For example, during 2008, as the price of jet fuel increased, the supply of air travel decreased. Similarly, a rise in the minimum wage decreases the supply of hamburgers.

Prices of Related Goods Produced   The prices of related goods that firms produce influence supply. For example, if the price of energy gel rises, firms switch production from bars to gel. The supply of energy bars decreases. Energy bars and energy gel are *substitutes in production*—goods that can be produced by using the same resources. If the price of beef rises, the supply of cowhide increases. Beef and cowhide are *complements in production*—goods that must be produced together.

Expected Future Prices If the price of a good is expected to rise, the return from selling the good in the future is higher than it is today. So supply decreases today and increases in the future.

The Number of Suppliers The larger the number of firms that produce a good, the greater is the supply of the good. And as firms enter an industry, the supply in that industry increases. As firms leave an industry, the supply in that industry decreases.

Technology The term "technology" is used broadly to mean the way that factors of production are used to produce a good. A technology change occurs when a new method is discovered that lowers the cost of producing a good. For example, new methods used in the factories that produce computer chips have lowered the cost and increased the supply of chips.

The State of Nature The state of nature includes all the natural forces that influence production. It includes the state of the weather and, more broadly, the natural environment. Good weather can increase the supply of many agricultural products and bad weather can decrease their supply. Extreme natural events such as earthquakes, tornadoes, and hurricanes can also influence supply.

Figure 3.5 illustrates an increase in supply. When supply increases, the supply curve shifts rightward and the quantity supplied at each price is larger. For example, at $1.00 per bar, on the original (blue) supply curve, the quantity supplied is 6 million bars a week. On the new (red) supply curve, the quantity supplied is 15 million bars a week. Look closely at the numbers in the table in Fig. 3.5 and check that the quantity supplied is larger at each price.

Table 3.2 summarizes the influences on supply and the directions of those influences.

A Change in the Quantity Supplied Versus a Change in Supply

Changes in the influences on producers' planned sales bring either a change in the quantity supplied or a change in supply. Equivalently, they bring either a movement along the supply curve or a shift of the supply curve.

A point on the supply curve shows the quantity supplied at a given price. A movement along the supply curve shows a **change in the quantity supplied**. The entire supply curve shows supply. A shift of the supply curve shows a *change in supply*.

FIGURE 3.5   An Increase in Supply

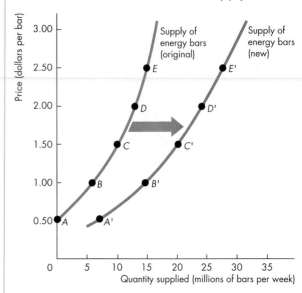

Original supply schedule Old technology			New supply schedule New technology		
	Price (dollars per bar)	Quantity supplied (millions of bars per week)		Price (dollars per bar)	Quantity supplied (millions of bars per week)
A	0.50	0	A'	0.50	7
B	1.00	6	B'	1.00	15
C	1.50	10	C'	1.50	20
D	2.00	13	D'	2.00	25
E	2.50	15	E'	2.50	27

A change in any influence on sellers' plans other than the price of the good itself results in a new supply schedule and a shift of the supply curve. For example, a new, cost-saving technology for producing energy bars changes the supply of energy bars. At a price of $1.50 a bar, 10 million bars a week are supplied when producers use the old technology (row C of the table) and 20 million energy bars a week are supplied when producers use the new technology (row C'). An advance in technology *increases* the supply of energy bars. The supply curve shifts *rightward*, as shown by the shift arrow and the resulting red curve.

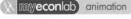 animation

Figure 3.6 illustrates and summarizes these distinctions. If the price of the good falls and other things remain the same, the quantity supplied of that good decreases and there is a movement down along the supply curve S_0. If the price of the good rises and other things remain the same, the quantity supplied increases and there is a movement up along the supply curve S_0. When any other influence on selling plans changes, the supply curve shifts and there is a *change in supply*. If supply increases, the supply curve shifts rightward to S_1. If supply decreases, the supply curve shifts leftward to S_2.

TABLE 3.2   The Supply of Energy Bars

The Law of Supply

The quantity of energy bars supplied

Decreases if:	Increases if:
■ The price of an energy bar falls	■ The price of an energy bar rises

Changes in Supply

The supply of energy bars

Decreases if:	Increases if:
■ The price of a factor of production used to produce energy bars rises	■ The price of a factor of production used to produce energy bars falls
■ The price of a substitute in production rises	■ The price of a substitute in production falls
■ The price of a complement in production falls	■ The price of a complement in production rises
■ The price of an energy bar is expected to rise	■ The price of an energy bar is expected to fall
■ The number of suppliers of bars decreases	■ The number of suppliers of bars increases
■ A technology change decreases energy bar production	■ A technology change increases energy bar production
■ A natural event decreases energy bar production	■ A natural event increases energy bar production

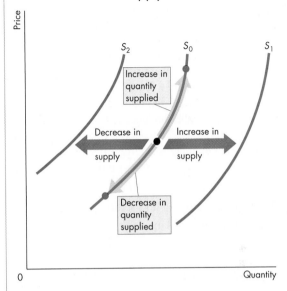

FIGURE 3.6   A Change in the Quantity Supplied Versus a Change in Supply

When the price of the good changes, there is a movement along the supply curve and *a change in the quantity supplied,* shown by the blue arrows on supply curve S_0. When any other influence on selling plans changes, there is a shift of the supply curve and a *change in supply.* An increase in supply shifts the supply curve rightward (from S_0 to S_1), and a decrease in supply shifts the supply curve leftward (from S_0 to S_2).

myeconlab   animation

Review Quiz

1 Define the quantity supplied of a good or service.
2 What is the law of supply and how do we illustrate it?
3 What does the supply curve tell us about the producer's minimum supply price?
4 List all the influences on selling plans, and for each influence, say whether it changes supply.
5 What happens to the quantity of cell phones supplied and the supply of cell phones if the price of a cell phone falls?

myeconlab   Work Study Plan 3.3 and get instant feedback.

Now we're going to combine demand and supply and see how prices and quantities are determined.

Market Equilibrium

We have seen that when the price of a good rises, the quantity demanded *decreases* and the quantity supplied *increases*. We are now going to see how the price adjusts to coordinate the plans of buyers and sellers and achieve an equilibrium in the market.

An *equilibrium* is a situation in which opposing forces balance each other. Equilibrium in a market occurs when the price balances the plans of buyers and sellers. The **equilibrium price** is the price at which the quantity demanded equals the quantity supplied. The **equilibrium quantity** is the quantity bought and sold at the equilibrium price. A market moves toward its equilibrium because

- Price regulates buying and selling plans.
- Price adjusts when plans don't match.

Price as a Regulator

The price of a good regulates the quantities demanded and supplied. If the price is too high, the quantity supplied exceeds the quantity demanded. If the price is too low, the quantity demanded exceeds the quantity supplied. There is one price at which the quantity demanded equals the quantity supplied. Let's work out what that price is.

Figure 3.7 shows the market for energy bars. The table shows the demand schedule (from Fig. 3.1) and the supply schedule (from Fig. 3.4). If the price of a bar is 50¢, the quantity demanded is 22 million bars a week but no bars are supplied. There is a shortage of 22 million bars a week. This shortage is shown in the final column of the table. At a price of $1.00 a bar, there is still a shortage but only of 9 million bars a week. If the price of a bar is $2.50, the quantity supplied is 15 million bars a week but the quantity demanded is only 5 million. There is a surplus of 10 million bars a week. The one price at which there is neither a shortage nor a surplus is $1.50 a bar. At that price, the quantity demanded is equal to the quantity supplied: 10 million bars a week. The equilibrium price is $1.50 a bar, and the equilibrium quantity is 10 million bars a week.

Figure 3.7 shows that the demand curve and the supply curve intersect at the equilibrium price of $1.50 a bar. At each price *above* $1.50 a bar, there is a surplus of bars. For example, at $2.00 a bar, the surplus is 6

FIGURE 3.7   Equilibrium

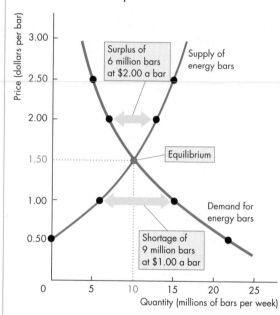

Price (dollars per bar)	Quantity demanded	Quantity supplied	Shortage (–) or surplus (+)
	(millions of bars per week)		
0.50	22	0	–22
1.00	15	6	–9
1.50	10	10	0
2.00	7	13	+6
2.50	5	15	+10

The table lists the quantity dem[...] plied as well as the shortage o[...] price. If the price is $1.00 a b[...] are demanded and 6 million are supplied. There is a shortage of 9 million bars a week, and the price rises.

If the price is $2.00 a bar, 7 million bars a week are demanded and 13 million are supplied. There is a surplus of 6 million bars a week, and the price falls.

If the price is $1.50 a bar, 10 million bars a week are demanded and 10 million bars are supplied. There is neither a shortage nor a surplus. Neither buyers nor sellers have an incentive to change the price. The price at which the quantity demanded equals the quantity supplied is the equilibrium price. And 10 million bars a week is the equilibrium quantity.

> **For the Instructor**
>
> For added clarity, many graphs are paired with data tables.

myeconlab   animation

million bars a week, as shown by the blue arrow. At each price *below* $1.50 a bar, there is a shortage of bars. For example, at $1.00 a bar, the shortage is 9 million bars a week, as shown by the red arrow.

Price Adjustments

You've seen that if the price is below equilibrium, there is a shortage and that if the price is above equilibrium, there is a surplus. But can we count on the price to change and eliminate a shortage or a surplus? We can, because such price changes are beneficial to both buyers and sellers. Let's see why the price changes when there is a shortage or a surplus.

A Shortage Forces the Price Up Suppose the price of an energy bar is $1. Consumers plan to buy 15 million bars a week, and producers plan to sell 6 million bars a week. Consumers can't force producers to sell more than they plan, so the quantity that is actually offered for sale is 6 million bars a week. In this situation, powerful forces operate to increase the price and move it toward the equilibrium price. Some producers, noticing lines of unsatisfied consumers, raise the price. Some producers increase their output. As producers push the price up, the price rises toward its equilibrium. The rising price reduces the shortage because it decreases the quantity demanded and increases the quantity supplied. When the price has increased to the point at which there is no longer a shortage, the forces moving the price stop operating and the price comes to rest at its equilibrium.

A Surplus Forces the Price Down Suppose the price of a bar is $2. Producers plan to sell 13 million bars a week, and consumers plan to buy 7 million bars a week. Producers cannot force consumers to buy more than they plan, so the quantity that is actually bought is 7 million bars a week. In this situation, powerful forces operate to lower the price and move it toward the equilibrium price. Some producers, unable to sell the quantities of energy bars they planned to sell, cut their prices. In addition, some producers scale back production. As producers cut the price, the price falls toward its equilibrium. The falling price decreases the surplus because it increases the quantity demanded and decreases the quantity supplied. When the price has fallen to the point at which there is no longer a surplus, the forces moving the price stop operating and the price comes to rest at its equilibrium.

The Best Deal Available for Buyers and Sellers

When the price is below equilibrium, it is forced upward. Why don't buyers resist the increase and refuse to buy at the higher price? Because they value the good more highly than the current price and they can't satisfy their demand at the current price. In some markets—for example, the markets that operate on eBay—the buyers might even be the ones who force the price up by offering to pay a higher price.

When the price is above equilibrium, it is bid downward. Why don't sellers resist this decrease and refuse to sell at the lower price? Because their minimum supply price is below the current price and they cannot sell all they would like to at the current price. Normally, it is the sellers who force the price down by offering lower prices to gain market share.

At the price at which the quantity demanded and the quantity supplied are equal, neither buyers nor sellers can do business at a better price. Buyers pay the highest price they are willing to pay for the last unit bought, and sellers receive the lowest price at which they are willing to supply the last unit sold.

When people freely make offers to buy and sell and when demanders try to buy at the lowest possible price and suppliers try to sell at the highest possible price, the price at which trade takes place is the equilibrium price—the price at which the quantity demanded equals the quantity supplied. The price coordinates the plans of buyers and sellers, and no one has an incentive to change it.

Review Quiz

1 What is the equilibrium price of a good or service?
2 Over what range of prices does a shortage arise?
3 Over what range of prices does a surplus arise?
4 What happens to the price when there is a shortage?
5 What happens to the price when there is a surplus?
6 Why is the price at which the quantity demanded equals the quantity supplied the equilibrium price?
7 Why is the equilibrium price the best deal available for both buyers and sellers?

myeconlab Work Study Plan 3.4 and get instant feedback.

Predicting Changes in Price and Quantity

The demand and supply model that we have just studied provides us with a powerful way of analyzing influences on prices and the quantities bought and sold. According to the model, a change in price stems from a change in demand, a change in supply, or a change in both demand and supply. Let's look first at the effects of a change in demand.

An Increase in Demand

When more and more people join health clubs, the demand for energy bars increases. The table in Fig. 3.8 shows the original and new demand schedules for energy bars (the same as those in Fig. 3.2) as well as the supply schedule of energy bars.

When demand increases, there is a shortage at the original equilibrium price of $1.50 a bar. To eliminate the shortage, the price must rise. The price that makes the quantity demanded and quantity supplied equal again is $2.50 a bar. At this price, 15 million bars are bought and sold each week. When demand increases, both the price and the quantity increase.

Figure 3.8 shows these changes. The figure shows the original demand for and supply of energy bars. The original equilibrium price is $1.50 an energy bar, and the quantity is 10 million energy bars a week. When demand increases, the demand curve shifts rightward. The equilibrium price rises to $2.50 an energy bar, and the quantity supplied increases to 15 million energy bars a week, as highlighted in the figure. There is an *increase in the quantity supplied* but *no change in supply*—a movement along, but no shift of, the supply curve.

A Decrease in Demand

We can reverse this change in demand. Start at a price of $2.50 a bar with 15 million energy bars a week being bought and sold, and then work out what happens if demand decreases to its original level. Such a decrease in demand might arise if people switch to energy gel (a substitute for energy bars). The decrease in demand shifts the demand curve leftward. The equilibrium price falls to $1.50 a bar, and the equilibrium quantity decreases to 10 million bars a week.

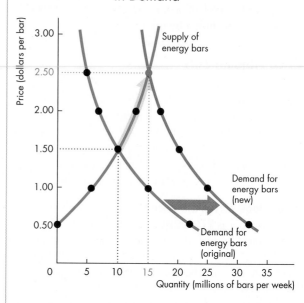

FIGURE 3.8 The Effects of a Change in Demand

Price (dollars per bar)	Quantity demanded (millions of bars per week)		Quantity supplied (millions of bars per week)
	Original	New	
0.50	22	32	0
1.00	15	25	6
1.50	**10**	20	**10**
2.00	7	17	13
2.50	5	15	15

Initially, the demand for energy bars is the blue demand curve. The equilibrium price is $1.50 a bar, and the equilibrium quantity is 10 million bars a week. When more health-conscious people do more exercise, the demand for energy bars increases and the demand curve shifts rightward to become the red curve.

At $1.50 a bar, there is now a shortage of 10 million bars a week. The price of a bar rises to a new equilibrium of $2.50. As the price rises to $2.50, the quantity supplied increases—shown by the blue arrow on the supply curve—to the new equilibrium quantity of 15 million bars a week. Following an increase in demand, the quantity supplied increases but supply does not change—the supply curve does not shift.

myeconlab animation

We can now make our first two predictions:

1. When demand increases, both the price and the quantity increase.
2. When demand decreases, both the price and the quantity decrease.

An Increase in Supply

When Nestlé (the producer of PowerBar) and other energy bar producers switch to a new cost-saving technology, the supply of energy bars increases. Figure 3.9 shows the new supply schedule (the same one that was shown in Fig. 3.5). What are the new equilibrium price and quantity? The price falls to $1.00 a bar, and the quantity increases to 15 million bars a week. You can see why by looking at the quantities demanded and supplied at the old price of $1.50 a bar. The quantity supplied at that price is 20 million bars a week, and there is a surplus of bars. The price falls. Only when the price is $1.00 a bar does the quantity supplied equal the quantity demanded.

Figure 3.9 illustrates the effect of an increase in supply. It shows the demand curve for energy bars and the original and new supply curves. The initial equilibrium price is $1.50 a bar, and the quantity is 10 million bars a week. When supply increases, the supply curve shifts rightward. The equilibrium price falls to $1.00 a bar, and the quantity demanded increases to 15 million bars a week, highlighted in the figure. There is an *increase in the quantity demanded* but *no change in demand*—a movement along, but no shift of, the demand curve.

A Decrease in Supply

Start out at a price of $1.00 a bar with 15 million bars a week being bought and sold. Then suppose that the cost of labor or raw materials rises and the supply of energy bars decreases. The decrease in supply shifts the supply curve leftward. The equilibrium price rises to $1.50 a bar, and the equilibrium quantity decreases to 10 million bars a week.

We can now make two more predictions:

1. When supply increases, the quantity increases and the price falls.
2. When supply decreases, the quantity decreases and the price rises.

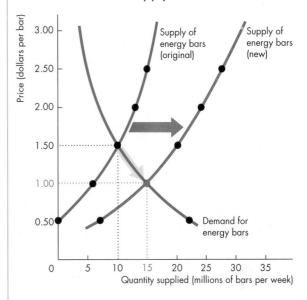

FIGURE 3.9   The Effects of a Change in Supply

Price (dollars per bar)	Quantity demanded (millions of bars per week)	Quantity supplied (millions of bars per week)	
		Original	New
0.50	22	0	7
1.00	15	6	15
1.50	**10**	**10**	20
2.00	7	13	25
2.50	5	15	27

Initially, the supply of energy bars is shown by the blue supply curve. The equilibrium price is $1.50 a bar, and the equilibrium quantity is 10 million bars a week. When the new cost-saving technology is adopted, the supply of energy bars increases and the supply curve shifts rightward to become the red curve.

At $1.50 a bar, there is now a surplus of 10 million bars a week. The price of an energy bar falls to a new equilibrium of $1.00 a bar. As the price falls to $1.00, the quantity demanded increases—shown by the blue arrow on the demand curve—to the new equilibrium quantity of 15 million bars a week. Following an increase in supply, the quantity demanded increases but demand does not change—the demand curve does not shift.

myeconlab   animation

How Markets Interact to Reallocate Resources

Fuel, Food, and Fertilizer

The demand and supply model provides insights into all competitive markets. Here, we'll apply what you've learned to the markets for

- Crude oil
- Corn
- Fertilizers

Crude Oil

Crude oil is like the life-blood of the global economy. It is used to fuel our cars, airplanes, trains, and buses, to generate electricity, and to produce a wide range of plastics. When the price of crude oil rises, the cost of transportation, power, and materials all increase.

In 2006, the price of a barrel of oil was $50. In 2008, the price had reached $135. While the price of oil has been rising, the quantity of oil produced and consumed has barely changed. Since 2006, the world has produced a steady 85 million barrels of oil a day.

Who or what has been raising the price of oil? Is it the fault of greedy oil producers?

Oil producers might be greedy, and some of them might be big enough to withhold supply and raise the price, but it wouldn't be in their self-interest to do so. The higher price would bring forth a greater quantity supplied from other producers and the profit of the one limiting supply would fall.

Producers could try to cooperate and jointly withhold supply. The Organization of Petroleum Exporting Countries, OPEC, is such a group of suppliers. But OPEC doesn't control the world supply and its members self-interests are to produce the quantities that give them the maximum attainable profit.

So even though the global oil market has some big players, they don't fix the price. Instead, the actions of thousands of buyers and sellers and the forces of demand and supply determine the price of oil. So how have demand and supply changed?

Because the price has increased with an unchanged quantity, demand must have increased and supply must have decreased.

Demand has increased for two reasons. First, world production, particularly in China and India, is

expanding at a rapid [rate. The production] of electricity, gasoli[ne, and other] goods has increased the demand for oil.

Second, the rapid expansion of production in China, India, and other developing economies is expected to continue. So the demand for oil is expected to keep increasing at a rapid rate. As the demand for oil keeps increasing, the price of oil will keep rising *and be expected* to keep rising.

A higher expected future price increases demand yet further. It also decreases supply because producers know they can get a greater return from their oil by leaving it in the ground and selling it in a later year.

So an *expected* rise in price brings both an increase in demand and a decrease in supply, which in turn brings an *actual* rise in price.

Because an expected price rise brings an actual price rise, it is possible for expectations to create a process called a **speculative bubble**. In a speculative bubble, the price rises purely because it is expected to rise and events reinforce the expectation. No one knows whether the world oil market was in a bubble in 2008, but bubbles always burst, so we will eventually know.

Figure 1 illustrates the events that we've just described and summarizes the forces at work on demand and supply in the world market for oil.

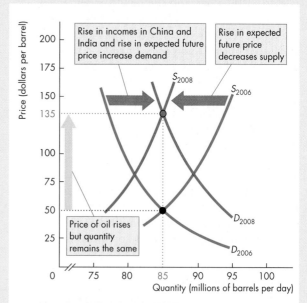

Figure 1 The Market for Crude Oil

Corn

Corn is used as food, animal feed, and a source of ethanol. Global corn production increased during the past few years, but the price also increased.

The story of the production and price of corn, like the story of the price of oil, begins in China and India. Greater production and higher incomes in these countries have increased the demand for corn.

Some of the increase in demand is for corn as food. But more of the increase is for corn as cattle feed, driven by an increased demand for beef—it takes 7 pounds of corn to produce 1 pound of beef.

In addition, mandated targets for ethanol production (see Chapter 2, pp. 34 and 46–47) have increased the demand for corn as a source of biofuel.

While the demand for corn has increased, the supply has decreased. Drought in several parts of the world cut production and decreased supply. Higher fertilizer prices increased the cost of growing corn, which also decreased supply.

So the demand for corn increased and the supply of corn decreased. This combination of changes in demand and supply raised the price of corn. Also, the increase in demand was greater than the decrease in supply, so the quantity of corn increased.

Figure 2 provides a summary of the events that we've just described in the market for corn.

Fertilizers

Nitrogen, potassium, and potash are not on your daily shopping list, but you consume them many times each day. They are the reason why our farms are so productive. And like the prices of oil and corn, the prices of fertilizers have gone skyward.

The increase in the global production of corn and other grains as food and sources of biofuels has increased the demand for fertilizers.

All fertilizers are costly to produce and use energy-intensive processes. Nitrogen is particularly energy intensive and uses natural gas. Potash is made from deposits of chloride and sodium chloride that are found 900 meters or deeper underground, and energy is required to bring the material to the surface and more energy is used to separate the chemicals and turn them into fertilizer.

All energy sources are substitutes, so the rise in the price of oil has increased the prices of all other energy sources. Consequently, the energy cost of producing fertilizers has risen. This higher cost of production has decreased the supply of fertilizers.

The increase in demand and the decrease in supply combine to raise the price. The increase in demand has been greater than the decrease in supply, so the quantity of fertilizer has increased. Figure 3 illustrates the market for fertilizers.

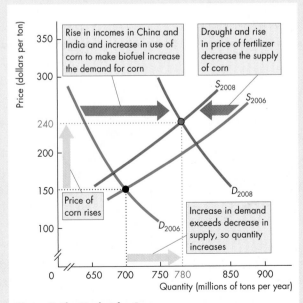

Figure 2 **The Market for Corn**

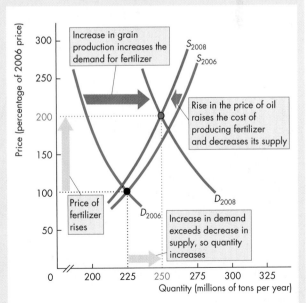

Figure 3 **The Market for Fertilizer**

FIGURE 3.10   The Effects of All the Possible Changes in Demand and Supply

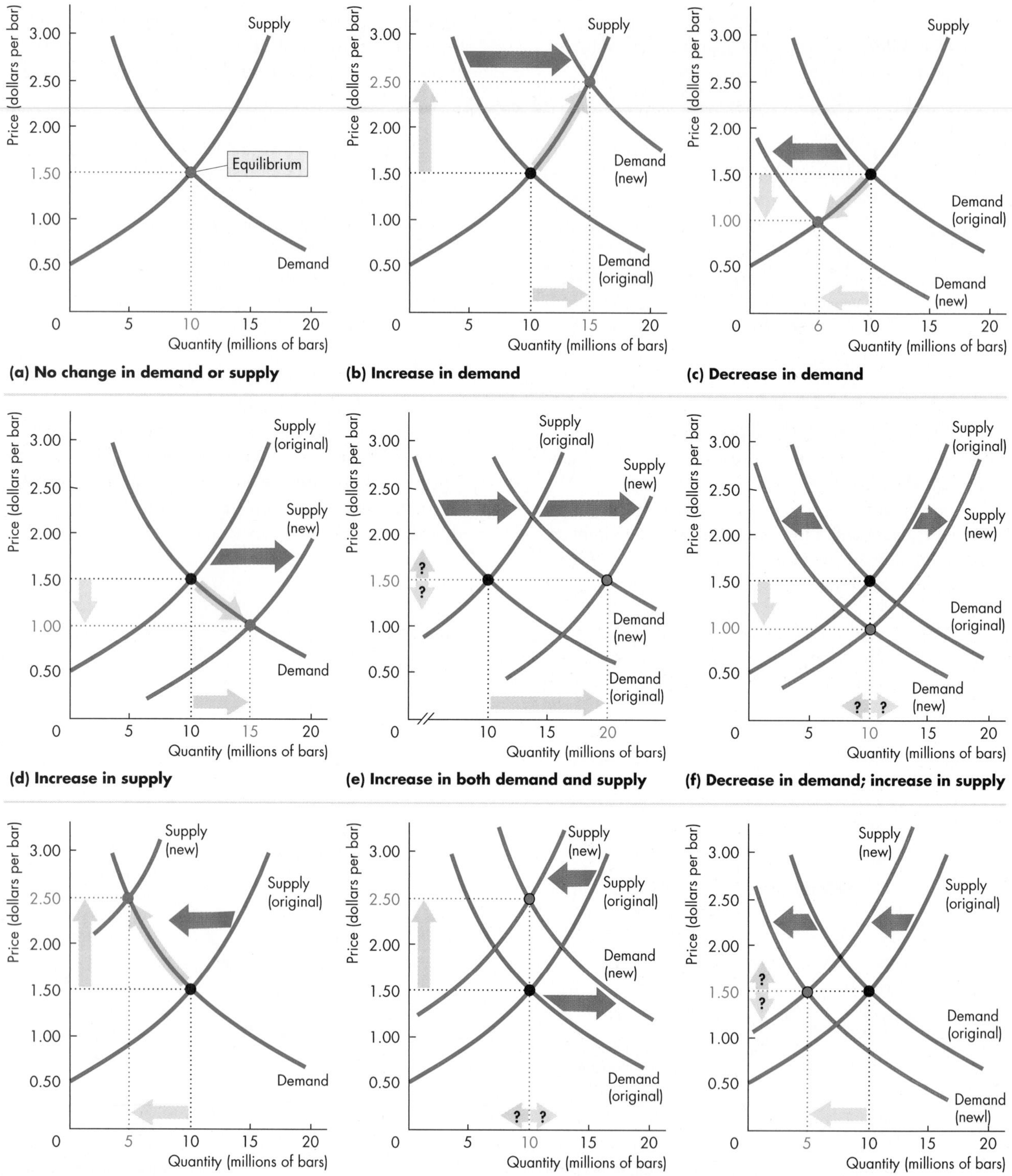

(a) No change in demand or supply
(b) Increase in demand
(c) Decrease in demand
(d) Increase in supply
(e) Increase in both demand and supply
(f) Decrease in demand; increase in supply
(g) Decrease in supply
(h) Increase in demand; decrease in supply
(i) Decrease in both demand and supply

myeconlab animation

All the Possible Changes in Demand and Supply

Figure 3.10 brings together and summarizes the effects of all the possible changes in demand and supply. With what you've learned about the effects of a change in *either* demand or supply, you can predict what happens if *both* demand and supply change together. Let's begin by reviewing what you already know.

Change in Demand with No Change in Supply The first row of Fig. 3.10, parts (a), (b), and (c), summarizes the effects of a change in demand with no change in supply. In part (a), with no change in either demand or supply, neither the price nor the quantity changes. With an *increase* in demand and no change in supply in part (b), both the price and quantity increase. And with a *decrease* in demand and no change in supply in part (c), both the price and the quantity decrease.

Change in Supply with No Change in Demand The first column of Fig. 3.10, parts (a), (d), and (g), summarizes the effects of a change in supply with no change in demand. With an *increase* in supply and no change in demand in part (d), the price falls and quantity increases. And with a *decrease* in supply and no change in demand in part (g), the price rises and the quantity decreases.

Increase in Both Demand and Supply You've seen that an increase in demand raises the price and increases the quantity. And you've seen that an increase in supply lowers the price and increases the quantity. Fig. 3.10(e) combines these two changes. Because either an increase in demand or an increase in supply increases the quantity, the quantity also increases when both demand and supply increase. But the effect on the price is uncertain. An increase in demand raises the price and an increase in supply lowers the price, so we can't say whether the price will rise or fall when both demand and supply increase. We need to know the magnitudes of the changes in demand and supply to predict the effects on price. In the example in Fig. 3.10(e), the price does not change. But notice that if demand increases by slightly more than the amount shown in the figure, the price will rise. And if supply increases by slightly more than the amount shown in the figure, the price will fall.

Decrease in Both Demand and Supply Figure 3.10(i) shows the case in which demand and supply *both decrease*. For the same reasons as those we've just reviewed, when both demand and supply decrease, the quantity decreases, and again the direction of the price change is uncertain.

Decrease in Demand and Increase in Supply You've seen that a decrease in demand lowers the price and decreases the quantity. And you've seen that an increase in supply lowers the price and increases the quantity. Fig. 3.10(f) combines these two changes. Both the decrease in demand and the increase in supply lower the price, so the price falls. But a decrease in demand decreases the quantity and an increase in supply increases the quantity, so we can't predict the direction in which the quantity will change unless we know the magnitudes of the changes in demand and supply. In the example in Fig. 3.10(f), the quantity does not change. But notice that if demand decreases by slightly more than the amount shown in the figure, the quantity will decrease. And if supply increases by slightly more than the amount shown in the figure, the quantity will increase.

Increase in Demand and Decrease in Supply Figure 3.10(h) shows the case in which demand increases and supply decreases. Now, the price rises, and again the direction of the quantity change is uncertain.

Review Quiz

What is the effect on the price of an MP3 player (such as an iPod) and the quantity of MP3 players if
1 The price of a PC falls or the price of an MP3 download rises? (Draw the diagrams!)
2 More firms produce MP3 players or electronics workers' wages rise? (Draw the diagrams!)
3 Any two of the events in questions 1 and 2 occur together? (Draw the diagrams!)

myeconlab Work these problems in Study Plan 3.5 and get instant feedback.

Now that you understand the demand and supply model and the predictions that it makes, try to get into the habit of using the model in your everyday life. To see how you might use the model, take a look at *Reading Between the Lines* on pp. 76–77, which uses the tools of demand and supply to explain the rising price of gasoline in 2008.

Demand and Supply: The Price of Gasoline

Record Gas Prices Squeeze Drivers

Americans feel the pinch as retail gasoline hits all-time high of $3.51 a gallon

CNN Money
April 22, 2008

NEW YORK (AP)—Cabbies here complain their take-home pay is thinner than it used to be. Trucking companies across the country are making drivers slow down to conserve fuel. Filling station owners plead that really, really, the skyrocketing prices aren't their fault. …

With gas prices now averaging $3.51 a gallon nationwide, … more and more Americans who have to drive are weighing the need for each and every trip. … Some would-be drivers are considering less energy-dependent alternatives simply for money's sake.

In Los Angeles, for example, fiction writer Brian Edwards sold his gas-guzzling Ford truck and now relies on his skateboard or the bus to get around. Sharon Cooper of Chicago, meanwhile, said she is planning to buy a bicycle to use on her 2 1/2-mile commute to work. …

"It's hell," said legal aide Zebib Yemane, … "When going downhill, I used to step on the gas. Now I don't." …

"Bottom line, we can't afford it no more, man. It's too much," Bak Zoumane said as he filled up his yellow cab at a BP station in midtown New York. The West African immigrant said his next car will likely be a hybrid so he won't have to pay so much at the pump.

Gasoline prices typically rise in the spring as stations switch over to pricier summer-grade fuel and demand picks up as more travelers take to the road.

But this year prices are rising even faster than normal, experts say, because of the massive jump in benchmark crude prices, which spiked to a record $117.76 a barrel Monday. …

Essence of the Story

- The retail price of gasoline hit a record high of $3.51 a gallon in April 2008.

- Gas station owners said the high prices weren't their fault.

- Drivers weighed the need for each trip and conserved energy by slowing down, easing off the gas when going down hill, or switching to hybrid vehicles.

- Some people found alternative means of transportation that include the bus, a bicycle, or even a skateboard.

- The switch to summer-grade fuel and a seasonal increase in travel normally raise the price of gasoline in the spring.

- In 2008, gas prices rose faster than normal because of a large rise in the price of crude oil, which reached $118 a barrel.

Economic Analysis

- In April 2007, the average price of gasoline was $2.75 a gallon and 9.3 million barrels of gasoline were consumed on average each day.

- Figure 1 shows the market for gasoline in April 2007. The demand curve is D, the supply curve is S_{2007}, and the market equilibrium is at 9.3 million barrels a day and $2.75 a gallon.

- Two main factors influenced the demand for gasoline in the year to April 2008.

- Slightly higher incomes increased demand and the gradual move toward hybrid vehicles and the increased use of ethanol decreased demand.

- The combined effects of these two factors left the demand for gasoline the same in 2008 as it had been in 2007.

- The price of crude oil was the biggest influence on the market for gasoline during 2007 and 2008.

- Between April 2007 and April 2008, the price of crude oil increased from $65 a barrel to $118 a barrel.

- The rise in the price of crude oil raised the cost of producing gasoline and decreased the supply of gasoline.

- Figure 2 shows what had happened in the market for gasoline by April 2008.

- Demand remained unchanged, but supply decreased from S_{2007} to S_{2008}.

- Because demand was unchanged and supply decreased, the price increased and the quantity decreased.

- The equilibrium price increased from $2.75 a gallon to $3.51 a gallon and the equilibrium quantity decreased from 9.3 million barrels a day to 9.2 million barrels a day.

- You can see the effects of drivers conserving gasoline, switching to hybrid vehicles, and finding alternative means of transportation that include the bus, a bicycle, or even a skateboard.

- This analysis of the market for gasoline emphasizes the distinction between a change in demand and a *change in the quantity demanded* and a change in supply and a *change in the quantity supplied.*

- In this example, there is a change in supply, no change in demand, and a change in the quantity demanded.

- Supply decreases—the supply curve shifts leftward.

- The demand curve does not shift, but as the price of gasoline rises, the quantity of gasoline demanded decreases in a movement along the demand curve D.

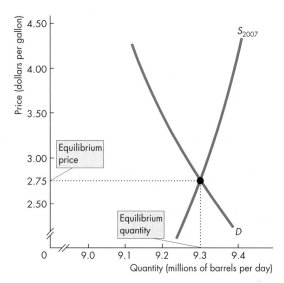

Figure 1 The gasoline market in 2007

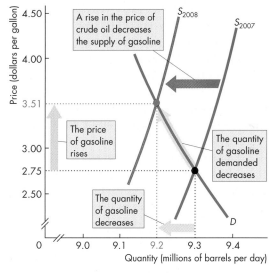

Figure 2 The gasoline market in 2008

MATHEMATICAL NOTE

Demand, Supply, and Equilibrium

Demand Curve

The law of demand says that as the price of a good or service falls, the quantity demanded of that good or service increases. We can illustrate the law of demand by drawing a graph of the demand curve or writing down an equation. When the demand curve is a straight line, the following equation describes it:

$$P = a - bQ_D,$$

where P is the price and Q_D is the quantity demanded. The a and b are positive constants.

The demand equation tells us three things:

1. The price at which no one is willing to buy the good (Q_D is zero). That is, if the price is a, then the quantity demanded is zero. You can see the price a in Figure 1. It is the price at which the demand curve hits the y-axis—what we call the demand curve's "intercept on the y-axis."

2. As the price falls, the quantity demanded increases. If Q_D is a positive number, then the price P must be less than a. And as Q_D gets larger, the price P becomes smaller. That is, as the quantity increases, the maximum price that buyers are willing to pay for the last unit of the good falls.

3. The constant b tells us how fast the maximum price that someone is willing to pay for the good falls as the quantity increases. That is, the constant b tells us about the steepness of the demand curve. The equation tells us that the slope of the demand curve is $-b$.

Supply Curve

The law of supply says that as the price of a good or service rises, the quantity supplied of that good or service increases. We can illustrate the law of supply by drawing a graph of the supply curve or writing down an equation. When the supply curve is a straight line, the following equation describes it:

$$P = c + dQ_S,$$

where P is the price and Q_S is the quantity supplied. The c and d are positive constants.

The supply equation tells us three things:

1. The price at which sellers are not willing to supply the good (Q_S is zero). That is, if the price is c, then no one is willing to sell the good. You can see the price c in Figure 2. It is the price at which the supply curve hits the y-axis—what we call the supply curve's "intercept on the y-axis."

2. As the price rises, the quantity supplied increases. If Q_S is a positive number, then the price P must be greater than c. And as Q_S increases, the price P becomes larger. That is, as the quantity increases, the minimum price that sellers are willing to accept for the last unit rises.

3. The constant d tells us how fast the minimum price at which someone is willing to sell the good rises as the quantity increases. That is, the constant d tells us about the steepness of the supply curve. The equation tells us that the slope of the supply curve is d.

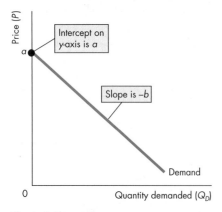

Figure 1 Demand curve

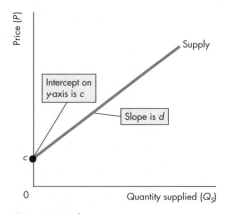

Figure 2 Supply curve

Market Equilibrium

Demand and supply determine market equilibrium. Figure 3 shows the equilibrium price (P^*) and equilibrium quantity (Q^*) at the intersection of the demand curve and the supply curve.

We can use the equations to find the equilibrium price and equilibrium quantity. The price of a good adjusts until the quantity demanded Q_D equals the quantity supplied Q_S. So at the equilibrium price (P^*) and equilibrium quantity (Q^*),

$$Q_D = Q_S = Q^*.$$

To find the equilibrium price and equilibrium quantity, substitute Q^* for Q_D in the demand equation and Q^* for Q_S in the supply equation. Then the price is the equilibrium price (P^*), which gives

$$P^* = a - bQ^*$$
$$P^* = c + dQ^*.$$

Notice that

$$a - bQ^* = c + dQ^*.$$

Now solve for Q^*:

$$a - c = bQ^* + dQ^*$$
$$a - c = (b + d)Q^*$$
$$Q^* = \frac{a - c}{b + d}.$$

To find the equilibrium price, (P^*), substitute for Q^* in either the demand equation or the supply equation.

Using the demand equation, we have

$$P^* = a - b\left(\frac{a - c}{b + d}\right)$$
$$P^* = \frac{a(b + d) - b(a - c)}{b + d}$$
$$P^* = \frac{ad + bc}{b + d}.$$

Alternatively, using the supply equation, we have

$$P^* = c + d\left(\frac{a - c}{b + d}\right)$$
$$P^* = \frac{c(b + d) + d(a - c)}{b + d}$$
$$P^* = \frac{ad + bc}{b + d}.$$

An Example

The demand for ice-cream cones is

$$P = 800 - 2Q_D.$$

The supply of ice-cream cones is

$$P = 200 + 1Q_S.$$

The price of a cone is expressed in cents, and the quantities are expressed in cones per day.

To find the equilibrium price (P^*) and equilibrium quantity (Q^*), substitute Q^* for Q_D and Q_S and P^* for P. That is,

$$P^* = 800 - 2Q^*$$
$$P^* = 200 + 1Q^*.$$

Now solve for Q^*:

$$800 - 2Q^* = 200 + 1Q^*$$
$$600 = 3Q^*$$
$$Q^* = 200.$$

And

$$P^* = 800 - 2(200)$$
$$= 400.$$

The equilibrium price is \$4 a cone, and the equilibrium quantity is 200 cones per day.

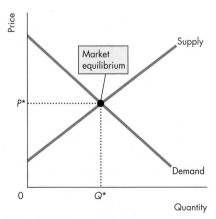

Figure 3 Market equilibrium

SUMMARY ◆

Key Points

Markets and Prices (p. 58)

- A competitive market is one that has so many buyers and sellers that no single buyer or seller can influence the price.
- Opportunity cost is a relative price.
- Demand and supply determine relative prices.

Demand (pp. 59–63)

- Demand is the relationship between the quantity demanded of a good and its price when all other influences on buying plans remain the same.
- The higher the price of a good, other things remaining the same, the smaller is the quantity demanded—the law of demand.
- Demand depends on the prices of related goods (substitutes and complements), expected future prices, income, expected future income and credit, population, and preferences.

Supply (pp. 64–67)

- Supply is the relationship between the quantity supplied of a good and its price when all other influences on selling plans remain the same.
- The higher the price of a good, other things remaining the same, the greater is the quantity supplied—the law of supply.

- Supply depends on the prices of resources used to produce a good, the prices of related goods produced, expected future prices, the number of suppliers, technology, and the state of nature.

Market Equilibrium (pp. 68–69)

- At the equilibrium price, the quantity demanded equals the quantity supplied.
- At any price above equilibrium, there is a surplus and the price falls.
- At any price below equilibrium, there is a shortage and the price rises.

Predicting Changes in Price and Quantity (pp. 70–75)

- An increase in demand brings a rise in the price and an increase in the quantity supplied. A decrease in demand brings a fall in the price and a decrease in the quantity supplied.
- An increase in supply brings a fall in the price and an increase in the quantity demanded. A decrease in supply brings a rise in the price and a decrease in the quantity demanded.
- An increase in demand and an increase in supply bring an increased quantity but an uncertain price change. An increase in demand and a decrease in supply bring a higher price but an uncertain change in quantity.

Key Figures

Key Terms

PROBLEMS and APPLICATIONS ◆

 Work problems 1–13 in Chapter 3 Study Plan and get instant feedback.
Work problems 16–28 as Homework, a Quiz, or a Test if assigned by your instructor.

1. William Gregg owned a mill in South Carolina. In December 1862, he placed a notice in the *Edgehill Advertiser* announcing his willingness to exchange cloth for food and other items. Here is an extract:

   1 yard of cloth for 1 pound of bacon
   2 yards of cloth for 1 pound of butter
   4 yards of cloth for 1 pound of wool
   8 yards of cloth for 1 bushel of salt

   a. What is the relative price of butter in terms of wool?

   b. If the money price of bacon was 20¢ a pound, what do you predict was the money price of butter?

   c. If the money price of bacon was 20¢ a pound and the money price of salt was $2.00 a bushel, do you think anyone would accept Mr. Gregg's offer of cloth for salt?

2. The price of food increased during the past year.

   a. Explain why the law of demand applies to food just as it does to all other goods and services.

   b. Explain how the substitution effect influences food purchases and provide some examples of substitutions that people might make when the price of food rises and other things remain the same.

   c. Explain how the income effect influences food purchases and provide some examples of the income effect that might occur when the price of food rises and other things remain the same.

3. Place the following goods and services into pairs of likely substitutes and into pairs of likely complements. (You may use an item in more than one pair.) The goods and services are

   coal, oil, natural gas, wheat, corn, rye, pasta, pizza, sausage, skateboard, roller blades, video game, laptop, iPod, cell phone, text message, email, phone call, voice mail

4. During 2008, the average income in China increased by 10 percent. Compared to 2007, how do you expect the following would change:

   a. The demand f[...]

   b. The demand f[...]

5. In January 2007[...] $2.38 a gallon. [...] increased to $3.[...] were no changes[...] tion, or any othe[...] How would you expect the rise in the price of gasoline to affect

   a. The demand for gasoline? Explain your answer.

   b. The quantity of gasoline demanded? Explain your answer.

6. In 2008, the price of corn increased by 35 percent and some cotton farmers in Texas stopped growing cotton and started to grow corn.

   a. Does this fact illustrate the law of demand or the law of supply? Explain your answer.

   b. Why would a cotton farmer grow corn?

7. **American to Cut Flights, Charge for Luggage**

   American Airlines announced yesterday that it will begin charging passengers $15 for their first piece of checked luggage, in addition to raising other fees and cutting domestic flights as it grapples with record-high fuel prices.

   Boston Herald, May 22, 2008

   a. How does this news clip illustrate a change in supply? Explain your answer.

   b What is the influence on supply identified in the news clip? Explain your answer.

   c. Explain how supply changes.

8. **Oil Soars to New Record Over $135**

   The price of oil hit a record high above $135 a barrel on Thursday—more than twice what it cost a year ago ... OPEC has so far blamed price rises on speculators and says there is no shortage of oil.

   BBC News, May 22, 2008

   a. Explain how the price of oil can rise even though there is no shortage of oil.

   b If a shortage of oil does occur, what does that imply about price adjustments and the role of price as a regulator in the market for oil?

   c If OPEC is correct, what factors might have

changed demand and/or supply and shifted the demand curve and/or the supply curve to cause the price to rise?

9. "As more people buy computers, the demand for Internet service increases and the price of Internet service decreases. The fall in the price of Internet service decreases the supply of Internet service." Is this statement true or false? Explain.

10. The following events occur one at a time:
    (i) The price of crude oil rises.
    (ii) The price of a car rises.
    (iii) All speed limits on highways are abolished.
    (iv) Robots cut car production costs.

    Which of these events will increase or decrease (state which occurs)
    a. The demand for gasoline?
    b. The supply of gasoline?
    c. The quantity of gasoline demanded?
    d. The quantity of gasoline supplied?

11. The demand and supply schedules for gum are

Price (cents per pack)	Quantity demanded (millions of packs a week)	Quantity supplied (millions of packs a week)
20	180	60
40	140	100
60	100	140
80	60	180
100	20	220

    a. Draw a graph of the gum market, label the axes and the curves, and mark in the equilibrium price and quantity.
    b. Suppose that the price of gum is 70¢ a pack. Describe the situation in the gum market and explain how the price adjusts.
    c. Suppose that the price of gum is 30¢ a pack. Describe the situation in the gum market and explain how the price adjusts.
    d. A fire destroys some factories that produce gum and the quantity of gum supplied decreases by 40 million packs a week at each price. Explain what happens in the market for gum and illustrate the changes on your graph.
    e. If at the time the fire occurs in d, there is an increase in the teenage population, which increases the quantity of gum demanded by 40 million packs a week at each price, what are the new equilibrium price and quantity of gum? Illustrate these changes in your graph.

12. **Eurostar Boosted by Da Vinci Code**
    Eurostar, the train service linking London to Paris ... , said on Wednesday first-half sales rose 6 per cent, boosted by devotees of the blockbuster Da Vinci movie.
    CNN, July 26, 2006
    a. Explain how Da Vinci Code fans helped to raise Eurostar's sales.
    b. CNN commented on the "fierce competition from budget airlines." Explain the effect of this competition on Eurostar's sales.
    c. What markets in Paris do you think these fans influenced? Explain the influence on three markets.

13. **Of Gambling, Grannies, and Good Sense**
    Nevada has the fastest growing elderly population of any state. ... Las Vegas has ... plenty of jobs for the over 50s.
    The Economist, July 26, 2006
    Explain how grannies have influenced the
    a. Demand side of some Las Vegas markets.
    b. Supply side of other Las Vegas markets.

14. Use the link on MyEconLab (Textbook Resources, Chapter 3, Web Links) to obtain data on the prices and quantities of bananas in 1985 and 2002.
    a. Make a graph to illustrate the market for bananas in 1985 and 2002.
    b. On the graph, show the changes in demand and supply and the changes in the quantity demanded and the quantity supplied that are consistent with the price and quantity data.
    c. Why do you think the demand for and supply of bananas changed?

15. Use the link on MyEconLab (Textbook Resources, Chapter 3, Web Links) to obtain data on the price of oil since 2000.
    a. Describe how the price of oil changed.
    b. Use a demand-supply graph to explain what happens to the price when supply increases or decreases and demand is unchanged.
    c. What do you predict would happen to the price of oil if a new drilling technology permitted deeper ocean sources to be used?
    d. What do you predict would happen to the price of oil if a clean and safe nuclear technology were developed?
    e. How does a higher price of oil influence the market for ethanol?
    f. How does an increase in the supply of ethanol influence the market for oil?

16. What features of the world market for crude oil make it a competitive market?

17. The money price of a textbook is $90 and the money price of the Wii game *Super Mario Galaxy* is $45.
    a. What is the opportunity cost of a textbook in terms of the Wii game?
    b. What is the relative price of the Wii game in terms of textbooks?

18. The price of gasoline has increased during the past year.
    a. Explain why the law of demand applies to gasoline just as it does to all other goods and services.
    b. Explain how the substitution effect influences gasoline purchases and provide some examples of substitutions that people might make when the price of gasoline rises and other things remain the same.
    c. Explain how the income effect influences gasoline purchases and provide some examples of the income effects that might occur when the price of gasoline rises and other things remain the same.

19. Classify the following pairs of goods and services as substitutes, complements, substitutes in production, or complements in production.
    a. Bottled water and health club memberships
    b. French fries and baked potatoes
    c. Leather purses and leather shoes
    d. SUVs and pickup trucks
    e. Diet coke and regular coke
    f. Low-fat milk and cream

20. Think about the demand for the three popular game consoles: XBox, PS3, and Wii. Explain the effect the following event on the demand for XBox games and the quantity of XBox games demanded, other things remaining the same.
    a. The price of an XBox falls.
    b. The prices of a PS3 and a Wii fall.
    c. The number of people writing and producing XBox games increases.
    d. Consumers' incomes increase.
    e. Programmers who write code for XBox games become more costly to hire.
    f. The price of an XBox game is expected to fall.
    g. A new game console comes onto the market, which is a close substitute for XBox.

21. In 2008, as the prices of homes fell across the United States, the number of homes offered for sale decreased.
    a. Does this fact illustrate the law of demand or the law of supply? Explain your answer.
    b. Why would home owners hold off trying to sell?

22. **G.M. Cuts Production for Quarter**

    General Motors cut its fourth-quarter production schedule by 10 percent on Tuesday as a tightening credit market caused sales at the Ford Motor Company, Chrysler and even Toyota to decline in August. … Bob Carter, group vice president for Toyota Motor Sales USA, said … dealerships were still seeing fewer potential customers browsing the lots.

    The New York Times, September 5, 2007

    Explain whether this news clip illustrates
    a. A change in supply
    b. A change in the quantity supplied
    c. A change in demand
    d. A change in the quantity demanded

23. The figure illustrates the market for pizza.

    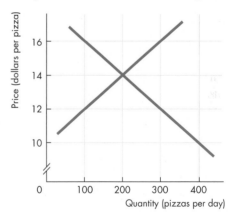

    a. Label the curves. Which curve shows the willingness to pay for a pizza?
    b. If the price of a pizza is $16, is there a shortage or a surplus and does the price rise or fall?
    c. Sellers want to receive the highest possible price, so why would they be willing to accept less than $16 a pizza?
    d. If the price of a pizza is $12, is there a shortage or a surplus and does the price rise or fall?
    e. Buyers want to pay the lowest possible price, so why would they be willing to pay more than $12 for a pizza?

24. **Plenty of "For Sale" Signs but Actual Sales Lagging**

    Like spring flowers, the "For Sale" signs are sprouting in front yards all over the country. But anxious sellers are facing the most brutal environment in decades, with a slumping economy, falling home prices, and rising mortgage foreclosures.

    The New York Times, May 26, 2008

    a. Describe the changes in demand and supply in the market for homes in the United States.

    b. Is there a surplus of homes?

    c. What does the information in the news clip imply about price adjustments and the role of price as a regulator in the market for homes?

25. **'Popcorn Movie' Experience Gets Pricier**

    … cinemas are raising … prices. … Demand for field corn, used for animal feed, … corn syrup and … ethanol, has caused its price to explode. That's caused some farmers to shift from popcorn to easier-to-grow field corn, cutting supply and pushing its price higher, too. …

    USA Today, May 24, 2008

    Explain and illustrate graphically the events described in the news clip in the markets for

    a. Popcorn.

    b. Viewing movies in the theater.

26. The table sets out the demand and supply schedules for potato chips.

Price (cents per bag)	Quantity demanded (millions of bags per week)	Quantity supplied (millions of bags per week)
50	160	130
60	150	140
70	140	150
80	130	160
90	120	170
100	110	180

    a. Draw a graph of the potato chip market and mark in the equilibrium price and quantity.

    b. If the price is 60¢ a bag, is there a shortage or a surplus, and how does the price adjust?

    c. If a new dip increases the quantity of potato chips that people want to buy by 30 million bags per week at each price, how does the demand and/or supply of chips change?

    d. If a new dip has the effect described in c, how does the price and quantity of chips change?

    e. If a virus destroys potato crops and the quantity of potato chips produced decreases by 40 million bags a week at each price, how does the supply of chips change?

    f. If the virus that destroys the potato crops in e hits just as the new dip in c comes onto the market, how does the price and quantity of chips change?

27. **Sony's Blu-Ray Wins High-Definition War**

    Toshiba Corp. yesterday raised the white flag in the war over the next-generation home movie format, announcing the end of its HD DVD business in a victory for Sony Corp.'s Blu-ray technology. The move could finally jump-start a high-definition home DVD market that has been hamstrung as consumers waited on the sidelines for the battle to play out in a fight reminiscent of the VHS-Betamax videotape war of the 1980s.

    The Washington Times, February 20, 2008

    How would you expect the end of Toshiba's HD DVD format to influence

    a. The price of a used Toshiba player on eBay? Would the outcome that you predict result from a change in demand or a change in supply or both, and in which directions?

    b. The price of a Blu-ray player?

    c. The demand for Blu-ray format movies?

    d. The supply of Blu-ray format movies?

    e. The price of Blu-ray format movies?

    f. The quantity of Blu-ray format movies?

28. After you have studied *Reading Between the Lines* on pp. 76–77, answer the following questions:

    a. How high did the retail price of gasoline go in April 2008?

    b. What substitutions did drivers make to decrease the quantity of gasoline demanded?

    c. Why would the switch to summer-grade fuel and the seasonal increase in travel normally raise the price of gasoline in the spring?

    d. What were the two main factors that influenced the demand for gasoline in 2008 and how did they change demand?

    e. What was the main influence on the supply of gasoline during 2007 and 2008 and how did supply change?

    f. How did the combination of the factors you have noted in d and e influence the price and quantity of gasoline?

    g. Was the change in quantity a change in the quantity demanded or a change in the quantity supplied?

5 ◆ Efficiency and Equity

After studying this chapter, you will be able to:

■ Describe the alternative methods of allocating scarce resources

■ Explain the connection between demand and marginal benefit and define consumer surplus

■ Explain the connection between supply and marginal cost and define producer surplus

■ Explain the conditions under which markets are efficient and inefficient

■ Explain the main ideas about fairness and evaluate claims that markets result in unfair outcomes

Every time you pour a glass of water or order a pizza, you express your view about how scarce resources should be used and you make choices in your *self-interest*. Markets coordinate your choices along with those of everyone else. But do markets do a good job? Do they allocate resources between water, pizza, and everything else efficiently?

The market economy generates huge income inequality. You can afford to buy a bottle of fresh spring water, while a student in India must make the best of dirty well water or expensive water from a tanker. Is this situation fair?

The *social interest* has the two dimensions that we've just discussed: efficiency and fairness (or equity). So our central question in this chapter is: Do markets operate in the social interest? At the end of the chapter, in *Reading Between the Lines*, we return to the issue of the use of the water resources. Do we use markets and other arrangements that allocate scarce water efficiently and fairly?

Resource Allocation Methods

The goal of this chapter is to evaluate the ability of markets to allocate resources efficiently and fairly. But to see whether the market does a good job, we must compare it with its alternatives. Resources are scarce, so they must be allocated somehow. And trading in markets is just one of several alternative methods.

Resources might be allocated by

- Market price
- Command
- Majority rule
- Contest
- First-come, first-served
- Lottery
- Personal characteristics
- Force

Let's briefly examine each method.

Market Price

When a market price allocates a scarce resource, the people who are willing and able to pay that price get the resource. Two kinds of people decide not to pay the market price: those who can afford to pay but choose not to buy and those who are too poor and simply can't afford to buy.

For many goods and services, distinguishing between those who choose not to buy and those who can't afford to buy doesn't matter. But for a few items, it does matter. For example, poor people can't afford to pay school fees and doctors' fees. Because poor people can't afford items that most people consider to be essential, these items are usually allocated by one of the other methods.

Command

A **command system** allocates resources by the order (command) of someone in authority. In the U.S. economy, the command system is used extensively inside firms and government departments. For example, if you have a job, most likely someone tells you what to do. Your labor is allocated to specific tasks by a command.

A command system works well in organizations in which the lines of authority and responsibility are

clear and it is easy to monitor the activities being performed. But a command system works badly when the range of activities to be monitored is large and when it is easy for people to fool those in authority. The system works so badly in North Korea, where it is used extensively in place of markets, that it fails even to deliver an adequate supply of food.

Majority Rule

Majority rule allocates resources in the way that a majority of voters choose. Societies use majority rule to elect representative governments that make some of the biggest decisions. For example, majority rule decides the tax rates that end up allocating scarce resources between private use and public use. And majority rule decides how tax dollars are allocated among competing uses such as education and health care.

Majority rule works well when the decisions being made affect large numbers of people and self-interest must be suppressed to use resources most effectively.

Contest

A contest allocates resources to a winner (or a group of winners). Sporting events use this method. Tiger Woods competes with other golfers, and the winner gets the biggest payoff. But contests are more general than those in a sports arena, though we don't normally call them contests. For example, Bill Gates won a contest to provide the world's personal computer operating system.

Contests do a good job when the efforts of the "players" are hard to monitor and reward directly. When a manager offers everyone in the company the opportunity to win a big prize, people are motivated to work hard and try to become the winner. Only a few people end up with a big prize, but many people work harder in the process of trying to win. The total output produced by the workers is much greater than it would be without the contest.

First-Come, First-Served

A first-come, first-served method allocates resources to those who are first in line. Many casual restaurants won't accept reservations. They use first-come, first-served to allocate their scarce tables. Highway space is allocated in this way too: the first to arrive at the on-ramp gets the road space. If too many vehicles enter the highway, the speed slows and people wait in line for some space to become available.

First-come, first-served works best when, as in the above examples, a scarce resource can serve just one user at a time in a sequence. By serving the user who arrives first, this method minimizes the time spent waiting for the resource to become free.

Lottery

Lotteries allocate resources to those who pick the winning number, draw the lucky cards, or come up lucky on some other gaming system. State lotteries and casinos reallocate millions of dollars worth of goods and services every year.

But lotteries are more widespread than jackpots and roulette wheels in casinos. They are used to allocate landing slots to airlines at some airports and have been used to allocate fishing rights and the electromagnetic spectrum used by cell phones.

Lotteries work best when there is no effective way to distinguish among potential users of a scarce resource.

Personal Characteristics

When resources are allocated on the basis of personal characteristics, people with the "right" characteristics get the resources. Some of the resources that matter most to you are allocated in this way. For example, you will choose a marriage partner on the basis of personal characteristics. But this method is also used in unacceptable ways. Allocating the best jobs to white, Anglo-Saxon males and discriminating against visible minorities and women is an example.

Force

Force plays a crucial role, for both good and ill, in allocating scarce resources. Let's start with the ill.

War, the use of military force by one nation against another, has played an enormous role historically in allocating resources. The economic supremacy of European settlers in the Americas and Australia owes much to the use of this method.

Theft, the taking of the property of others without their consent, also plays a large role. Both large-scale organized crime and small-scale petty crime collectively allocate billions of dollars worth of resources annually.

But force plays a crucial positive role in allocating resources. It provides the state with an effective method of transferring wealth from the rich to the poor, and it provides the legal framework in which voluntary exchange in markets takes place.

A legal system is the foundation on which our market economy functions. Without courts to enforce contracts, it would not be possible to do business. But the courts could not enforce contracts without the ability to apply force if necessary. The state provides the ultimate force that enables the courts to do their work.

More broadly, the force of the state is essential to uphold the principle of the rule of law. This principle is the bedrock of civilized economic (and social and political) life. With the rule of law upheld, people can go about their daily economic lives with the assurance that their property will be protected—that they can sue for violations against their property (and be sued if they violate the property of others).

Free from the burden of protecting their property and confident in the knowledge that those with whom they trade will honor their agreements, people can get on with focusing on the activity at which they have a comparative advantage and trading for mutual gain.

Review Quiz

1 Why do we need methods of allocating scarce resources?
2 Describe the alternative methods of allocating scarce resources.
3 Provide an example of each allocation method that illustrates when it works well.
4 Provide an example of each allocation method that illustrates when it works badly.

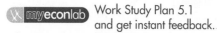 Work Study Plan 5.1 and get instant feedback.

In the next sections, we're going to see how a market can achieve an efficient use of resources, examine the obstacles to efficiency, and see how sometimes an alternative method might improve on the market. After looking at efficiency, we'll turn our attention to the more difficult issue of fairness.

Demand and Marginal Benefit

Resources are allocated efficiently when they are used in the ways that people value most highly. This outcome occurs when marginal benefit equals marginal cost (Chapter 2, pp. 35–37). So to determine whether a competitive market is efficient, we need to see whether, at the market equilibrium quantity, marginal benefit equals marginal cost. We begin by seeing how market demand reflects marginal benefit.

Demand, Willingness to Pay, and Value

In everyday life, we talk about "getting value for money." When we use this expression, we are distinguishing between *value* and *price*. Value is what we get, and price is what we pay.

The value of one more unit of a good or service is its marginal benefit. And we measure marginal benefit by the maximum price that is willingly paid for another unit of the good or service. But willingness to pay determines demand. *A demand curve is a marginal benefit curve.*

In Fig. 5.1(a), Lisa is willing to pay $1 for the 30th slice of pizza and $1 is her marginal benefit from that slice. In Fig. 5.1(b), Nick is willing to pay $1 for the 10th slice of pizza and $1 is his marginal benefit from that slice. But at what quantity is the market willing to pay $1 for the marginal slice? The answer is provided by the *market demand curve*.

Individual Demand and Market Demand

The relationship between the price of a good and the quantity demanded by one person is called *individual demand*. And the relationship between the price of a good and the quantity demanded by all buyers is called *market demand*.

The market demand curve is the horizontal sum of the individual demand curves and is formed by adding the quantities demanded by all the individuals at each price.

Figure 5.1(c) illustrates the market demand for pizza if Lisa and Nick are the only people in the market. Lisa's demand curve in part (a) and Nick's demand curve in part (b) sum horizontally to the market demand curve in part (c).

FIGURE 5.1   Individual Demand, Market Demand, and Marginal Social Benefit

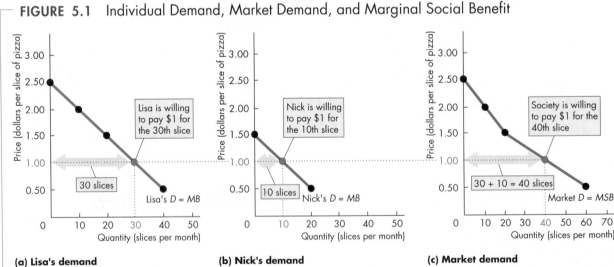

(a) Lisa's demand   **(b) Nick's demand**   **(c) Market demand**

At a price of $1 a slice, the quantity demanded by Lisa is 30 slices and the quantity demanded by Nick is 10 slices, so the quantity demanded by the market is 40 slices. Lisa's demand curve in part (a) and Nick's demand curve in part (b) sum horizontally to the market demand curve in part (c). The market demand curve is the marginal social benefit (*MSB*) curve.

myeconlab animation

At a price of $1 a slice, Lisa demands 30 slices and Nick demands 10 slices, so the market quantity demanded at $1 a slice is 40 slices.

From the market demand curve, we see that the economy is willing to pay $1 for 40 slices a day. *The market demand curve is the marginal social benefit (MSB) curve.*

Although we're measuring the price in dollars, think of the price as telling us the number of *dollars' worth of other goods and services willingly forgone* to obtain one more slice of pizza.

Consumer Surplus

We don't always have to pay what we are willing to pay. We get a bargain. When people buy something for less than it is worth to them, they receive a consumer surplus. A **consumer surplus** is the value (or marginal benefit) of a good minus the price paid for it, summed over the quantity bought.

Figure 5.2(a) shows Lisa's consumer surplus from pizza when the price is $1 a slice. At this price, she buys 30 slices a month because the 30th slice is worth exactly $1 to her. But Lisa is willing to pay $2 for the 10th slice, so her marginal benefit from this slice is

$1 more than she pays for it—she receives a surplus of $1 on the 10th slice.

Lisa's consumer surplus is the sum of the surpluses on *all of the slices she buys*. This sum is the area of the green triangle—the area below the demand curve and above the market price line. The area of this triangle is equal to its base (30 slices) multiplied by its height ($1.50) divided by 2, which is $22.50. The area of the blue rectangle in Fig. 5.2(a) shows what Lisa pays for 30 slices of pizza.

Figure 5.2(b) shows Nick's consumer surplus, and part (c) shows the consumer surplus for the market. The consumer surplus for the market is the sum of the consumer surpluses of Lisa and Nick.

All goods and services, like pizza, have decreasing marginal benefit, so people receive more benefit from their consumption than the amount they pay.

Review Quiz

1 How do we measure the value or marginal benefit of a good or service?

2 What is consumer surplus? How is it measured?

 Work Study Plan 5.2 and get instant feedback.

FIGURE 5.2 Demand and Consumer Surplus

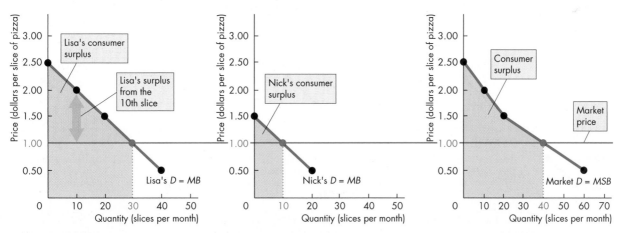

(a) Lisa's consumer surplus   **(b) Nick's consumer surplus**   **(c) Market consumer surplus**

Lisa is willing to pay $2.00 for her 10th slice of pizza in part (a). At a market price of $1 a slice, Lisa receives a surplus of $1 on the 10th slice. The green triangle shows her consumer surplus on the 30 slices she buys at $1 a slice.

The green triangle in part (b) shows Nick's consumer surplus on the 10 slices that he buys at $1 a slice. The green area in part (c) shows the consumer surplus for the market. The blue rectangles show the amounts spent on pizza.

 animation

Supply and Marginal Cost

We are now going to see how market supply reflects marginal cost. This section closely parallels the related ideas about market demand and marginal benefit that you've just studied. Firms are in business to make a profit. To do so, they must sell their output for a price that exceeds the cost of production. Let's investigate the relationship between cost and price.

Supply, Cost, and Minimum Supply-Price

Firms make a profit when they receive more from the sale of a good or service than the cost of producing it. Just as consumers distinguish between value and price, so producers distinguish between cost and price. Cost is what a producer gives up, and price is what a producer receives.

The cost of producing one more unit of a good or service is its marginal cost. Marginal cost is the minimum price that producers must receive to induce them to offer one more unit of a good or service for sale. But the minimum supply-price determines supply. *A supply curve is a marginal cost curve.*

In Fig. 5.3(a), Max is willing to produce the 100th pizza for $15, his marginal cost of that pizza. In Fig. 5.3(b), Mario is willing to produce the 50th pizza for $15, his marginal cost of that pizza. But what quantity is this market willing to produce for $15 a pizza? The answer is provided by the *market supply curve.*

Individual Supply and Market Supply

The relationship between the price of a good and the quantity supplied by one producer is called *individual supply*. And the relationship between the price of a good and the quantity supplied by all producers is called *market supply*.

> The market supply curve is the horizontal sum of the individual supply curves and is formed by adding the quantities supplied by all the producers at each price.

Figure 5.3(c) illustrates the market supply if Max and Mario are the only producers of pizzas. Max's supply curve in part (a) and Mario's supply curve in part (b) sum horizontally to the market supply curve in part (c).

FIGURE 5.3 Individual Supply, Market Supply, and Marginal Social Cost

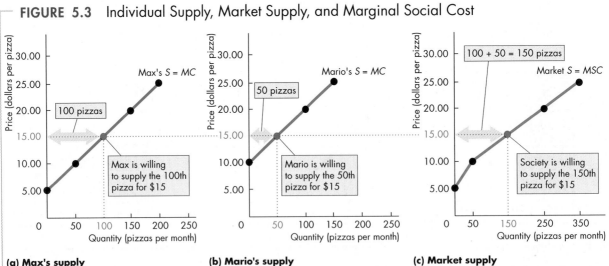

(a) Max's supply

(b) Mario's supply

(c) Market supply

At a price of $15 a pizza, the quantity supplied by Max is 100 pizzas and the quantity supplied by Mario is 50 pizzas, so the quantity supplied by the market is 150 pizzas.

Max's supply curve in part (a) and Mario's supply curve in part (b) sum horizontally to the market supply curve in part (c). The market supply curve is the marginal social cost (MSC) curve.

At a price of $15 a pizza, Max supplies 100 pizzas and Mario supplies 50 pizzas, so the quantity supplied by the market at $15 a pizza is 150 pizzas.

So from the market supply curve, we see that the market is willing to supply 150 pizzas a month for $15 each. *The market supply curve is the marginal social cost (MSC) curve.*

Again, although we're measuring price in dollars, think of the price as telling us the number of *dollars' worth of other goods and services that must be forgone* to produce one more pizza.

Producer Surplus

When price exceeds marginal cost, the firm receives a producer surplus. A **producer surplus** is the price received for a good minus its minimum supply-price (or marginal cost), summed over the quantity sold.

Figure 5.4(a) shows Max's producer surplus from pizza when the price is $15 a pizza. At this price, he sells 100 pizzas a month because the 100th pizza costs him $15 to produce. But Max is willing to produce the 50th pizza for his marginal cost, which is $10, so he receives a surplus of $5 on this pizza.

Max's producer surplus is the sum of the surpluses on pizzas he sells. This sum is the area of the blue tri-

angle—the area below the market price and above the supply curve. The area of this triangle is equal to its base (100) multiplied by its height ($10) divided by 2, which is $500.

The red area in Fig. 5.4(a) below the supply curve shows what it costs Max to produce 100 pizzas.

The area of the blue triangle in Fig. 5.4(b) shows Mario's producer surplus and the blue area in Fig. 5.4(c) shows the producer surplus for the market. The producer surplus for the market is the sum of the producer surpluses of Max and Mario.

Review Quiz

1 What is the relationship between the marginal cost, minimum supply-price, and supply?
2 What is producer surplus? How is it measured?

 Work Study Plan 5.3 and get instant feedback.

Consumer surplus and producer surplus can be used to measure the efficiency of a market. Let's see how we can use these concepts to study the efficiency of a competitive market.

FIGURE 5.4 Supply and Producer Surplus

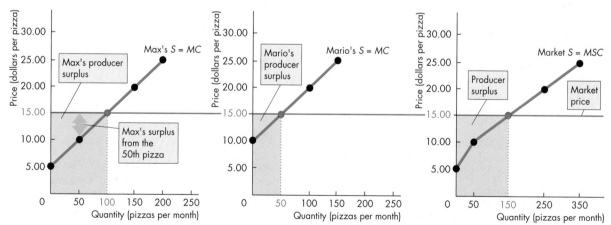

(a) Max's producer surplus

(b) Mario's producer surplus

(c) Market producer surplus

Max is willing to produce the 50th pizza for $10 in part (a). At a market price of $15 a pizza, Max gets a surplus of $5 on the 50th pizza. The blue triangle shows his producer surplus on the 100 pizzas he sells at $15 each. The

blue triangle in part (b) shows Mario's producer surplus on the 50 pizzas that he sells at $15 each. The blue area in part (c) shows producer surplus for the market. The red areas show the cost of producing the pizzas sold.

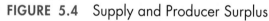 animation

◆ Is the Competitive Market Efficient?

Figure 5.5(a) shows the market for pizza. The market forces that you studied in Chapter 3 (pp. 68–69) pull the pizza market to its equilibrium price of $15 a pizza and equilibrium quantity of 10,000 pizzas a day. Buyers enjoy a consumer surplus (green area) and sellers enjoy a producer surplus (blue area), but is this competitive equilibrium efficient?

Efficiency of Competitive Equilibrium

You've seen that the demand curve tells us the marginal benefit from a pizza. If the only people who benefit from pizza are the people who buy it, then the demand curve for pizzas measures the marginal benefit to the entire society from pizza. We call the marginal benefit to the entire society, marginal *social* benefit, *MSB*. In this case, the demand curve is also the *MSB* curve.

You've also seen that the supply curve tells us the marginal cost of a pizza. If the only people who bear the cost of pizza are the people who produce it, then the supply curve of pizzas measures the marginal cost of a pizza to the entire society. We call the marginal cost to the entire society, marginal *social* cost, *MSC*. In this case, the supply curve is also the *MSC* curve.

So where the demand curve and the supply curve intersect in part (a), marginal social benefit equals marginal social cost in part (b). This condition delivers an efficient use of resources for the entire society.

If production is less than 10,000 pizzas a day, the marginal pizza is valued more highly than it costs to produce. If production exceeds 10,000 pizzas a day, the marginal pizza costs more to produce than the value that consumers place on it. Only when 10,000 pizzas a day are produced is the marginal pizza worth exactly what it costs.

The competitive market pushes the quantity of pizzas produced to its efficient level of 10,000 a day. If production is less than 10,000 pizzas a day, a shortage raises the price, which increases production. If production exceeds 10,000 pizzas a day, a surplus of pizzas lowers the price, which decreases production. So a competitive pizza market is efficient.

When the efficient quantity is produced, *total surplus* (the sum of consumer surplus and producer surplus) is maximized. Buyers and sellers acting in their self-interest end up promoting the social interest.

FIGURE 5.5   An Efficient Market for Pizza

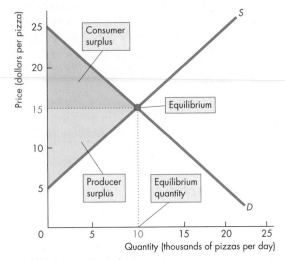

(a) Equilibrium and surpluses

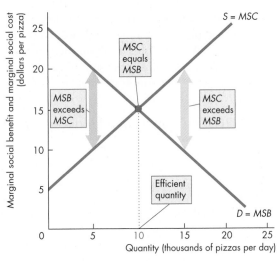

(b) Efficiency

Competitive equilibrium in part (a) occurs when the quantity demanded equals the quantity supplied. Consumer surplus is the area under the demand curve and above the market price (the green triangle). Producer surplus is the area above the supply curve and below the market price (the blue triangle). Resources are used efficiently in part (b) when marginal social benefit, *MSB*, equals marginal social cost, *MSC*.

The efficient quantity in part (b) is the same as the equilibrium quantity in part (a). The competitive pizza market produces the efficient quantity of pizzas.

Markets At Work
The Invisible Hand

Writing in his *Wealth of Nations* in 1776, Adam Smith was the first to suggest that competitive markets send resources to the uses in which they have the highest value (see p. 53). Smith believed that each participant in a competitive market is "led by an invisible hand to promote an end [the efficient use of resources] which was no part of his intention."

You can see the invisible hand at work in the cartoon and in the world today.

Umbrella for Sale The cold drinks vendor has cold drinks and shade and he has a marginal cost and a minimum supply-price of each. The reader on the park bench has a marginal benefit and willingness to pay for each. The reader's marginal benefit from shade exceeds the vendor's marginal cost; but the vendor's marginal cost of a cold drink exceeds the reader's marginal benefit. They trade the umbrella. The vendor gets a producer surplus from selling the shade for more than its marginal cost, and the reader gets a consumer surplus from buying the shade for less than its marginal benefit. Both are better off and the umbrella has moved to its highest-valued use.

The Invisible Hand at Work Today The market economy relentlessly performs the activity illustrated in the cartoon to achieve an efficient allocation of resources.

A Florida frost cuts the supply of oranges. With fewer oranges available, the marginal social benefit increases. A shortage of oranges raises their price, so the market allocates the smaller quantity available to the people who value them most highly.

A new technology cuts the cost of producing a computer. With a lower production cost, the supply of computers increases and the price of a computer falls. The lower price encourages an increase in the quantity demanded of this now less-costly tool. The marginal

social benefit from a computer is brought to equality with its marginal social cost.

In both the oranges and computer examples, market forces persistently bring marginal social cost and marginal social benefit to equality, allocate scarce resources efficiently, and maximize total surplus (consumer surplus plus producer surplus).

Underproduction and Overproduction

Inefficiency can occur because either too little of an item is produced (underproduction) or too much is produced (overproduction).

Underproduction In Fig. 5.6(a), the quantity of pizzas produced is 5,000 a day. At this quantity, consumers are willing to pay $20 for a pizza that costs only $10 to produce. By producing only 5,000 pizzas a day, total surplus is smaller than its maximum possible level. The quantity produced is inefficient—there is underproduction.

We measure the scale of inefficiency by **deadweight loss**, which is the decrease in total surplus that results

FIGURE 5.6 Underproduction and Overproduction

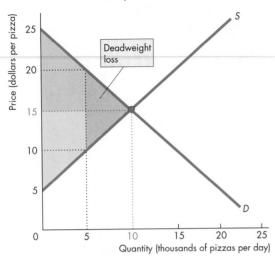

(a) Underproduction

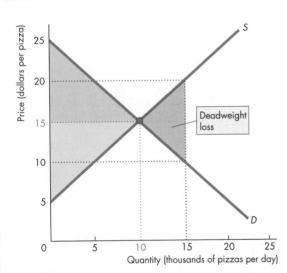

(b) Overproduction

If pizza production is 5,000 a day in part (a), total surplus (shown by the green and blue areas) is smaller than its maximum level by the amount of the deadweight loss (shown by the gray triangle). At all production levels below 10,000 pizzas a day, the benefit from one more pizza exceeds its cost.

If pizza production is 15,000 a day in part (b), total surplus is also smaller than its maximum level by the amount of the deadweight loss. At all production levels in excess of 10,000 pizzas a day, the cost of one more pizza exceeds its benefit.

myeconlab animation

from an inefficient level of production. The gray triangle in Fig. 5.6(a) shows the deadweight loss.

Overproduction In Fig. 5.6(b), the quantity of pizzas produced is 15,000 a day. At this quantity, consumers are willing to pay only $10 for a pizza that costs $20 to produce. By producing the 15,000th pizza, $10 of resources are wasted. Again, the gray triangle shows the deadweight loss, which reduces the total surplus to less than its maximum.

The deadweight loss is borne by the entire society: It is a social loss.

Obstacles to Efficiency

The obstacles to efficiency that bring underproduction or overproduction are

- Price and quantity regulations
- Taxes and subsidies
- Externalities
- Public goods and common resources
- Monopoly
- High transactions costs

Price and Quantity Regulations *Price regulations* that put a cap on the rent a landlord is permitted to charge and laws that require employers to pay a minimum wage sometimes block the price adjustments that balance the quantity demanded and the quantity supplied and lead to underproduction. *Quantity regulations* that limit the amount that a farm is permitted to produce also lead to underproduction.

Taxes and Subsidies *Taxes* increase the prices paid by buyers and lower the prices received by sellers. So taxes decrease the quantity produced and lead to underproduction. *Subsidies*, which are payments by the government to producers, decrease the prices paid by buyers and increase the prices received by sellers. So subsidies increase the quantity produced and lead to overproduction.

Externalities An *externality* is a cost or a benefit that affects someone other than the seller or the buyer. An *external cost* arises when an electric utility burns coal and emits carbon dioxide. The utility doesn't consider the cost of climate change when it decides how much power to produce. The result is overproduction. An *external benefit* arises when an apartment owner installs a smoke detector and decreases her neighbor's fire risk. She doesn't consider the benefit to her neighbor when she decides how many detectors to install. The result is underproduction.

Public Goods and Common Resources A *public good* is a good or service that is consumed simultaneously by everyone even if they don't pay for it. National defense is an example. Competitive markets would underproduce national defense because it is in each person's interest to free ride on everyone else and avoid paying for her or his share of such a good.

A *common resource* is owned by no one but available to be used by everyone. Atlantic salmon is an example. It is in everyone's self-interest to ignore the costs they impose on others when they decide how much of a common resource to use. The result is that the resource is overused.

Monopoly A *monopoly* is a firm that is the sole provider of a good or service. Local water supply and cable television are supplied by firms that are monopolies. The monopoly's self-interest is to maximize its profit. Because the monopoly has no competitors, it can set the price to achieve its self-interested goal. To achieve its goal, a monopoly produces too little and charges too high a price. It leads to underproduction.

High Transactions Costs Stroll around a shopping mall and observe the retail markets in which you participate. You'll see that these markets employ enormous quantities of scarce labor and capital resources. It is costly to operate any market. Economists call the opportunity costs of making trades in a market **transactions costs**.

To use market price as the allocator of scarce resources, it must be worth bearing the opportunity cost of establishing a market. Some markets are just too costly to operate. For example, when you want to play tennis on your local "free" court, you don't pay a market price for your slot on the court. You hang around until the court becomes vacant, and you "pay" with your waiting time. When transactions costs are high, the market might underproduce.

You now know the conditions under which resource allocation is efficient. You've seen how a competitive market can be efficient, and you've seen some obstacles to efficiency. Can alternative allocation methods improve on the market?

Alternatives to the Market

When a market is inefficient, can one of the alternative nonmarket methods that we described at the beginning of this chapter do a better job? Sometimes it can.

Often, majority rule might be used in an attempt to improve the allocation of resources. But majority rule has its own shortcomings. A group that pursues the self-interest of its members can become the majority. For example, a price or quantity regulation that creates inefficiency is almost always the result of a self-interested group becoming the majority and imposing costs on the minority. Also, with majority rule, votes must be translated into actions by bureaucrats who have their own agendas based on their self-interest.

Managers in firms issue commands and avoid the transactions costs that they would incur if they went to a market every time they needed a job done.

First-come, first-served works best in some situations. Think about the scene at a busy ATM. Instead of waiting in line people might trade places at a "market" price. But someone would need to ensure that trades were honored. At a busy ATM, first-come, first-served is the most efficient arrangement.

There is no one efficient mechanism that allocates all resources efficiently. But markets, when supplemented by other mechanisms such as majority rule, command systems, and first-come, first-served, do an amazingly good job.

Review Quiz

1 Do competitive markets use resources efficiently? Explain why or why not.
2 What is deadweight loss and under what conditions does it occur?
3 What are the obstacles to achieving an efficient allocation of resources in the market economy?

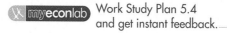 Work Study Plan 5.4 and get instant feedback.

Is an efficient allocation of resources also a fair allocation? Does the competitive market provide people with fair incomes for their work? Do people always pay a fair price for the things they buy? Don't we need the government to step into some competitive markets to prevent the price from rising too high or falling too low? Let's now study these questions.

Is the Competitive Market Fair?

When a natural disaster strikes, such as a severe winter storm or a hurricane, the prices of many essential items jump. The reason prices jump is that the demand and willingness to pay for these items has increased, but the supply has not changed. So the higher prices achieve an efficient allocation of scarce resources. News reports of these price hikes almost never talk about efficiency. Instead, they talk about equity or fairness. The claim that is often made is that it is unfair for profit-seeking dealers to cheat the victims of natural disaster.

Similarly, when low-skilled people work for a wage that is below what most would regard as a "living wage," the media and politicians talk of employers taking unfair advantage of their workers.

How do we decide whether something is fair or unfair? You know when you *think* something is unfair. But how do you *know?* What are the *principles* of fairness?

Philosophers have tried for centuries to answer this question. Economists have offered their answers too. But before we look at the proposed answers, you should know that there is no universally agreed upon answer.

Economists agree about efficiency. That is, they agree that it makes sense to make the economic pie as large as possible and to produce it at the lowest possible cost. But they do not agree about equity. That is, they do not agree about what are fair shares of the economic pie for all the people who make it. The reason is that ideas about fairness are not exclusively economic ideas. They touch on politics, ethics, and religion. Nevertheless, economists have thought about these issues and have a contribution to make. Let's examine the views of economists on this topic.

To think about fairness, think of economic life as a game—a serious game. All ideas about fairness can be divided into two broad groups. They are

- It's not fair if the *result* isn't fair.
- It's not fair if the *rules* aren't fair.

It's Not Fair If the *Result* Isn't Fair

The earliest efforts to establish a principle of fairness were based on the view that the result is what matters. The general idea was that it is unfair if people's incomes are too unequal. For example, it is

unfair that a bank president earns millions of dollars a year while a bank teller earns only thousands of dollars. It is unfair that a store owner makes a larger profit and her customers pay higher prices in the aftermath of a winter storm.

During the nineteenth century, economists thought they had made the incredible discovery: Efficiency requires equality of incomes. To make the economic pie as large as possible, it must be cut into equal pieces, one for each person. This idea turns out to be wrong. But there is a lesson in the reason that it is wrong, so this idea is worth a closer look.

Utilitarianism The nineteenth century idea that only equality brings efficiency is called *utilitarianism*. **Utilitarianism** is a principle that states that we should strive to achieve "the greatest happiness for the greatest number." The people who developed this idea were known as utilitarians. They included the most eminent thinkers, such as Jeremy Bentham and John Stuart Mill.

Utilitarians argued that to achieve "the greatest happiness for the greatest number," income must be transferred from the rich to the poor up to the point of complete equality—to the point at which there are no rich and no poor.

They reasoned in the following way: First, everyone has the same basic wants and a similar capacity to enjoy life. Second, the greater a person's income, the smaller is the marginal benefit of a dollar. The millionth dollar spent by a rich person brings a smaller marginal benefit to that person than the marginal benefit that the thousandth dollar spent brings to a poorer person. So by transferring a dollar from the millionaire to the poorer person, more is gained than is lost. The two people added together are better off.

Figure 5.7 illustrates this utilitarian idea. Tom and Jerry have the same marginal benefit curve, *MB*. (Marginal benefit is measured on the same scale of 1 to 3 for both Tom and Jerry.) Tom is at point *A*. He earns $5,000 a year, and his marginal benefit from a dollar is 3 units. Jerry is at point *B*. He earns $45,000 a year, and his marginal benefit from a dollar is 1 unit. If a dollar is transferred from Jerry to Tom, Jerry loses 1 unit of marginal benefit and Tom gains 3 units. So together, Tom and Jerry are better off—they are sharing the economic pie more efficiently. If a second dollar is transferred, the same thing happens: Tom gains more than Jerry loses. And the same is true for every dollar transferred until they both reach point *C*. At point *C*, Tom and Jerry have $25,000

FIGURE 5.7 Utilitarian Fairness

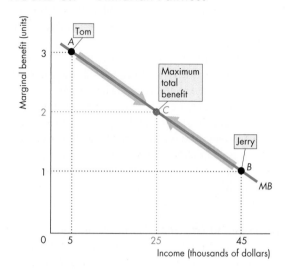

Tom earns $5,000 and has 3 units of marginal benefit at point *A*. Jerry earns $45,000 and has 1 unit of marginal benefit at point *B*. If income is transferred from Jerry to Tom, Jerry's loss is less than Tom's gain. Only when each of them has $25,000 and 2 units of marginal benefit (at point *C*) can the sum of their total benefit increase no further.

each and a marginal benefit of 2 units. Now they are sharing the economic pie in the most efficient way. It brings the greatest happiness to Tom and Jerry.

The Big Tradeoff One big problem with the utilitarian ideal of complete equality is that it ignores the costs of making income transfers. Recognizing the costs of making income transfers leads to what is called the **big tradeoff**, which is a tradeoff between efficiency and fairness.

The big tradeoff is based on the following facts. Income can be transferred from people with high incomes to people with low incomes only by taxing the high incomes. Taxing people's income from employment makes them work less. It results in the quantity of labor being less than the efficient quantity. Taxing people's income from capital makes them save less. It results in the quantity of capital being less than the efficient quantity. With smaller quantities of both labor and capital, the quantity of goods and services produced is less than the efficient quantity. The economic pie shrinks.

The tradeoff is between the size of the economic pie and the degree of equality with which it is shared. The greater the amount of income redistribution through income taxes, the greater is the inefficiency—the smaller is the economic pie.

There is a second source of inefficiency. A dollar taken from a rich person does not end up as a dollar in the hands of a poorer person. Some of the dollar is spent on administration of the tax and transfer system. The cost of tax-collecting agencies, such as the IRS, and welfare-administering agencies, such as the Health Care Financing Administration, which administers Medicaid and Medicare, must be paid with some of the taxes collected. Also, taxpayers hire accountants, auditors, and lawyers to help them ensure that they pay the correct amount of taxes. These activities use skilled labor and capital resources that could otherwise be used to produce goods and services that people value.

When all these costs are taken into account, taking a dollar from a rich person does not give a dollar to a poor person. It is possible that with high taxes, people with low incomes might end up being worse off. Suppose, for example, that highly taxed entrepreneurs decide to work less hard and shut down some of their businesses. Low-income workers get fired and must seek other, perhaps even lower-paid, work.

Today, because of the big tradeoff, no one says that fairness requires equality of incomes.

Make the Poorest as Well Off as Possible A new solution to the big tradeoff problem was proposed by philosopher John Rawls in a classic book entitled *A Theory of Justice*, published in 1971. Rawls says that, taking all the costs of income transfers into account, the fair distribution of the economic pie is the one that makes the poorest person as well off as possible. The incomes of rich people should be taxed, and after paying the costs of administering the tax and transfer system, what is left should be transferred to the poor. But the taxes must not be so high that they make the economic pie shrink to the point at which the poorest person ends up with a smaller piece. A bigger share of a smaller pie can be less than a smaller share of a bigger pie. The goal is to make the piece enjoyed by the poorest person as big as possible. Most likely, this piece will not be an equal share.

The "fair results" idea requires a change in the results after the game is over. Some economists say that these changes are themselves unfair and propose a different way of thinking about fairness.

It's Not Fair If the *Rules* Aren't Fair

The idea that it's not fair if the rules aren't fair is based on a fundamental principle that seems to be hardwired into the human brain: the symmetry principle. The **symmetry principle** is the requirement that people in similar situations be treated similarly. It is the moral principle that lies at the center of all the big religions and that says, in some form or other, "Behave toward other people in the way you expect them to behave toward you."

In economic life, this principle translates into *equality of opportunity*. But equality of opportunity to do what? This question is answered by the philosopher Robert Nozick in a book entitled *Anarchy, State, and Utopia*, published in 1974.

Nozick argues that the idea of fairness as an outcome or result cannot work and that fairness must be based on the fairness of the rules. He suggests that fairness obeys two rules:

1. The state must enforce laws that establish and protect private property.
2. Private property may be transferred from one person to another only by voluntary exchange.

The first rule says that everything that is valuable must be owned by individuals and that the state must ensure that theft is prevented. The second rule says that the only legitimate way a person can acquire property is to buy it in exchange for something else that the person owns. If these rules, which are the only fair rules, are followed, then the result is fair. It doesn't matter how unequally the economic pie is shared, provided that the pie is made by people, each one of whom voluntarily provides services in exchange for the share of the pie offered in compensation.

These rules satisfy the symmetry principle. If these rules are not followed, the symmetry principle is broken. You can see these facts by imagining a world in which the laws are not followed.

First, suppose that some resources or goods are not owned. They are common property. Then everyone is free to participate in a grab to use them. The strongest will prevail. But when the strongest prevails, the strongest effectively *owns* the resources or goods in question and prevents others from enjoying them.

Second, suppose that we do not insist on voluntary exchange for transferring ownership of resources from one person to another. The alternative is *involuntary* transfer. In simple language, the alternative is theft.

Both of these situations violate the symmetry principle. Only the strong acquire what they want. The weak end up with only the resources and goods that the strong don't want.

In a majority rule political system, the strong are those in the majority or those with enough resources to influence opinion and achieve a majority.

In contrast, if the two rules of fairness are followed, everyone, strong and weak, is treated in a similar way. Everyone is free to use their resources and human skills to create things that are valued by themselves and others and to exchange the fruits of their efforts with each other. This set of arrangements is the only one that obeys the symmetry principle.

Fairness and Efficiency If private property rights are enforced and if voluntary exchange takes place in a competitive market, resources will be allocated efficiently if there are no

1. Price and quantity regulations
2. Taxes and subsidies
3. Externalities
4. Public goods and common resources
5. Monopolies
6. High transactions costs

And according to the Nozick rules, the resulting distribution of income and wealth will be fair. Let's study an example to check the claim that if resources are allocated efficiently, they are also allocated fairly.

Case Study: A Water Shortage in a Natural Disaster

An earthquake has broken the pipes that deliver drinking water to a city. Bottled water is available, but there is no tap water. What is the fair way to allocate the bottled water?

Market Price Suppose that if the water is allocated by market price, the price jumps to $8 a bottle—five times its normal price. At this price, the people who own water can make a large profit by selling it. People who are willing and able to pay $8 a bottle get the water. And because most people can't afford the $8 price, they end up either without water or consuming just a few drops a day.

You can see that the water is being used efficiently. There is a fixed amount available, some people are willing to pay $8 to get a bottle, and the water goes to those people. The people who own and sell water receive a large producer surplus and total surplus is maximized.

In the rules view, the outcome is fair. No one is denied the water they are willing to pay for. In the results view, the outcome would most likely be regarded as unfair. The lucky owners of water make a killing, and the poorest end up the thirstiest.

Nonmarket Methods Suppose that by a majority vote, the citizens decide that the government will buy all the water, pay for it with a tax, and use one of the nonmarket methods to allocate the water to the citizens. The possibilities now are

Command Someone decides who is the most deserving and needy. Perhaps everyone is given an equal share. Or perhaps government officials and their families end up with most of the water.

Contest Bottles of water are prizes that go to those who are best at a particular contest.

First-come, first-served Water goes to the first off the mark or to those who place the lowest value on their time and can afford to wait in line.

Lottery Water goes to those in luck.

Personal characteristics Water goes to those with the "right" characteristics. Perhaps the old, the young, or pregnant women get the water.

Except by chance, none of these methods delivers an allocation of water that is either fair or efficient. It is unfair in the rules view because the tax involves involuntary transfers of resources among citizens. And it is unfair in the results view because the poorest don't end up being made as well off as possible.

The allocation is inefficient for two reasons. First, resources have been used to operate the allocation scheme. Second, some people are willing to pay for more water than the quantity they have been allocated and others have been allocated more water than they are willing to pay for.

The second source of inefficiency can be overcome if, after the nonmarket allocation, people are permitted to trade water at its market price. Those who value the water they have at less than the market price sell, and people who are willing to pay the market price to obtain more water buy. Those who value the water most highly are the ones who consume it.

Market Price with Taxes Another approach is to allocate the scarce water using the market price but then to alter the redistribution of buying power by taxing the sellers and providing benefits to the poor.

Suppose water owners are taxed on each bottle sold and the revenue from these taxes is given to the poorest people. People are then free, starting from this new distribution of buying power, to trade water at the market price.

Because the owners of water are taxed on what they sell, they have a weaker incentive to offer water for sale and the supply decreases. The equilibrium price rises to more than $8 a bottle. There is now a deadweight loss in the market for water—similar to the loss that arises from underproduction on pp. 115–116. (We study the effects of a tax and show its inefficiency in Chapter 6 on pp. 135–140.)

So the tax is inefficient. In the rules view, the tax is also unfair because it forces the owners of water to make a transfer to others. In the results view, the outcome might be regarded as being fair.

This brief case study illustrates the complexity of ideas about fairness. Economists have a clear criterion of efficiency but no comparably clear criterion of fairness. Most economists regard Nozick as being too extreme and want a fair tax system. But there is no consensus about what a fair tax system looks like.

Review Quiz

1 What are the two big approaches to thinking about fairness?
2 What is the utilitarian idea of fairness and what is wrong with it?
3 Explain the big tradeoff. What idea of fairness has been developed to deal with it?
4 What is the idea of fairness based on fair rules?

myeconlab Work Study Plan 5.5 and get instant feedback.

You've now studied the two biggest issues that run through the whole of economics: efficiency and equity, or fairness. In the next chapter, we study some sources of inefficiency and unfairness. At many points throughout this book—and in your life—you will return to and use the ideas about efficiency and fairness that you've learned in this chapter. *Reading Between the Lines* on pp. 122–123 looks at an example of an inefficiency in our economy today.

Is Water Use Efficient?

India Digs Deeper, but Wells Are Drying Up, and a Farming Crisis Looms

http://www.nytimes.com
September 30, 2006

… Across India, where most people still live off the land, the chief source of irrigation is groundwater, at least for those who can afford to pump it.

Indian law has virtually no restrictions on who can pump groundwater, how much and for what purpose. Anyone, it seems, can—and does—extract water as long as it is under his or her patch of land. That could apply to homeowner, farmer or industry. …

"We forgot that water is a costly item," lamented K. P. Singh, regional director of the Central Groundwater Board, in his office in the city of Jaipur. "Our feeling about proper, judicious use of water vanished."

… On a parched, hot morning … a train pulled into the railway station at a village called Peeplee Ka Bas. Here, the wells have run dry and the water table fallen so low that it is too salty even to irrigate the fields.

The train came bearing precious cargo: 15 tankers loaded with nearly 120,000 gallons of clean, sweet drinking water.

The water regularly travels more than 150 miles, taking nearly two days, by pipeline and then by rail, so that the residents of a small neighboring town can fill their buckets with water for 15 minutes every 48 hours.

It is a logistically complicated, absurdly expensive proposition. Bringing the water here costs the state about a penny a gallon; the state charges the consumer a monthly flat rate of 58 cents for about 5,300 gallons, absorbing the loss. …

Essence of the Story

- In India, groundwater is the chief source of irrigation.
- Indian law has few restrictions on who can pump groundwater.
- A regional director of the Central Groundwater Board laments that Indians are behaving as if water were a free resource.
- Where the wells have run dry, water is delivered by pipeline and then by train.
- Water is rationed by permitting residents to fill their buckets with water for 15 minutes every 48 hours.
- Transporting water costs 1 cent per gallon, but consumers pay about 11 cents per 1,000 gallons.

Economic Analysis

- Water is one of the world's most vital resources, and it is used inefficiently.

- Markets in water are not competitive. They are controlled by governments or private producers, and they do not work like the competitive markets that deliver an efficient use of resources.

- The major problem in achieving an efficient use of water is to get it from the places where it is most abundant to the places in which it has the most valuable uses.

- Some places have too little water, and some have too much.

- The news article tells us that the owners of land that has groundwater under it pump the water and sell it and pay little attention to the fact that they will pump the well dry.

- Figure 1 illustrates this situation. The curve D shows the demand for water and its marginal social benefit MSB. The curve S shows the supply of water and its marginal social cost MSC.

- Ignoring the high marginal social cost, land owners produce W_A gallons a day, which is greater than the efficient quantity. Farmers are willing to pay B, which is less than the marginal social cost C but enough to earn the land owner a profit.

- A deadweight loss arises from overproduction.

- Figure 2 shows the situation in places where the wells have run dry.

- A limited quantity of water, W_B, is transported in, and each consumer is restricted to the quantity that can be put into a bucket in 15 minutes every 48 hours.

- Consumers are willing to pay B per gallon, which is much more than the marginal social cost C.

- The green area shows the consumer surplus, and the red rectangle shows the cost of the water, which is paid by the government and borne by the taxpayers.

- A deadweight loss arises from underproduction.

- The situation in India is replicated in thousands of places around the world.

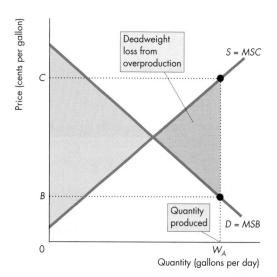

Figure 1 Overproduction where wells are not dry

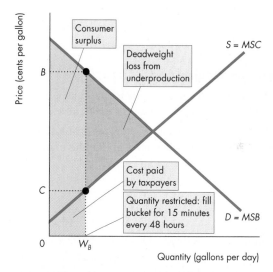

Figure 2 Underproduction where wells run dry

123

SUMMARY ◆

Key Points

Resource Allocation Methods (pp. 108–109)

- Because resources are scarce, some mechanism must allocate them.
- The alternative allocation methods are market price; command; majority rule; contest; first-come, first-served; lottery; personal characteristics; and force.

Demand and Marginal Benefit (pp. 110–111)

- The maximum price willingly paid is marginal benefit, so a demand curve is also a marginal benefit curve.
- The market demand curve is the horizontal sum of the individual demand curves and is the marginal social benefit curve.
- Value is what people are *willing to* pay; price is what people *must* pay.
- Consumer surplus equals value minus price, summed over the quantity bought.

Supply and Marginal Cost (pp. 112–113)

- The minimum supply-price is marginal cost, so a supply curve is also a marginal cost curve.
- The market supply curve is the horizontal sum of the individual supply curves and is the marginal social cost curve.

- Cost is what producers pay; price is what producers receive.
- Producer surplus equals price minus marginal cost, summed over the quantity sold.

Is the Competitive Market Efficient? (pp. 114–117)

- In a competitive equilibrium, marginal social benefit equals marginal social cost and resource allocation is efficient.
- Buyers and sellers acting in their self-interest end up promoting the social interest.
- The sum of consumer surplus and producer surplus is maximized.
- Producing less than or more than the efficient quantity creates deadweight loss.
- Price and quantity regulations; taxes and subsidies; externalities; public goods and common resources; monopoly; and high transactions costs can lead to underproduction or overproduction and create inefficiency.

Is the Competitive Market Fair? (pp. 118–121)

- Ideas about fairness can be divided into two groups: fair *results* and fair *rules*.
- Fair-results ideas require income transfers from the rich to the poor.
- Fair-rules ideas require property rights and voluntary exchange.

Key Figures

Key Terms

PROBLEMS and APPLICATIONS

 Work problems 1–9 in Chapter 5 Study Plan and get instant feedback.
Work problems 10–16 as Homework, a Quiz, or a Test if assigned by your instructor.

1. At Chez Panisse, the restaurant in Berkeley that is credited with having created California cuisine, reservations are essential. At Mandarin Dynasty, a restaurant near the University of California San Diego, reservations are recommended. At Eli Cannon's, a restaurant in Middletown, Connecticut, reservations are not accepted.
    a. Describe the method of allocating scarce table resources at these three restaurants.
    b. Why do you think restaurants have different reservations policies?
    c. Why might each restaurant be using an efficient allocation method?
    d. Why do you think restaurants don't use the market price to allocate their tables?
2. The table provides information on the demand schedules for train travel for Ann, Beth, and Cy, who are the only buyers in the market.

Price	Quantity demanded (miles)		
(dollars per mile)	Ann	Beth	Cy
3	30	25	20
4	25	20	15
5	20	15	10
6	15	10	5
7	10	5	0
8	5	0	0
9	0	0	0

    a. Construct the market demand schedule.
    b. What are the maximum prices that Ann, Beth, and Cy are willing to pay to travel 20 miles? Why?
    c. What is the marginal social benefit when the total distance travelled is 60 miles?
    d. What is the marginal private benefit for each person when they travel a total distance of 60 miles and how many miles does each of the people travel?
    e. What is each traveler's consumer surplus when the price is $4 a mile?
    f. What is the market consumer surplus when the price is $4 a mile?

3. **eBay Saves Billions for Bidders**
    If you think you would save money by bidding on eBay auctions, you would likely be right. ... Two associate professors ... calculate the difference between the actual purchase price paid for auction items and the top price bidders stated they were willing to pay ... and the Maryland researchers found it averaged at least $4 per auction.
    Information Week, January 28, 2008
    a. What method is used to allocate goods on eBay?
    b. How do eBay auctions influence consumer surplus?
4. The table provides information on the supply schedules of hot air balloon rides by Xavier, Yasmin, and Zack, who are the only sellers in the market.

Price	Quantity supplied (rides per week)		
(dollars per ride)	Xavier	Yasmin	Zack
100	30	25	20
90	25	20	15
80	20	15	10
70	15	10	5
60	10	5	0
50	5	0	0
40	0	0	0

    a. Construct the market supply schedule.
    b. What are the minimum prices that Xavier, Yasmin, and Zack are willing to accept to supply 20 rides? Why?
    c. What is the marginal social cost when the total number of rides is 30?
    d. What is the marginal cost for each supplier when the total number of rides is 30 and how many rides does each of the firms supply?
    e. What is each firm's producer surplus when the price is $70 a ride?
    f. What is the market producer surplus when the price is $70 a ride?
5. Based on the information provided in the news clip in problem 3,

a. Can an eBay auction give the seller a surplus?

b. Draw a graph to illustrate an eBay auction and show the consumer surplus and producer surplus that it generates.

6. The figure illustrates the market for cell phones.

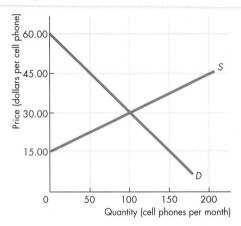

a. What are the equilibrium price and equilibrium quantity of cell phones?

b. Shade in and label the consumer surplus and the producer surplus.

c. Shade in and label the cost of producing the cell phones sold.

d. Calculate total surplus.

e. What is the efficient quantity of cell phones?

7. The table gives the demand and supply schedules for sunscreen.

Price (dollars per bottle)	Quantity demanded (bottles per day)	Quantity supplied (bottles per day)
0	400	0
5	300	100
10	200	200
15	100	300
20	0	400

Sunscreen factories are required to limit production to 100 bottles a day.

a. What is the maximum price that consumers are willing to pay for the 100th bottle?

b. What is the minimum price that producers are willing to accept for the 100th bottle?

c. Describe the situation in this market.

d. How can the 100 bottles be allocated to beachgoers? Which possible methods would be fair and which would be unfair?

8. **Wii Sells Out Across Japan**

… Japan finally came in for its share of Wii madness this weekend. … However, given the large amount of interest in the console—which Nintendo has flogged with a TV-ad blitz for the past two months—demand is expected to be much higher than supply. … Yodobashi Camera was selling Wii games on a first-come, first-served basis, so eager customers showed up early so as not to miss out on their favorite titles. [But] customers who tried to get in the … line after 6 or 7 a.m. were turned away. … [and] many could be spotted rushing off to the smaller Akihabara stores that were holding raffles to decide who got a Wii.

Gamespot News, December 1, 2006

a. Why was the quantity demanded of Wii expected to exceed the quantity supplied?

b. Did Nintendo produce the efficient quantity of Wii? Explain.

c. Can you think of reasons why Nintendo might want to underproduce and leave the market with fewer Wii than people want to buy?

d. What are the two methods of resource allocation described in the news clip?

e. Is either method of allocating Wii efficient?

f. What do you think some of the people who managed to buy a Wii did with it?

g. Explain which is the fairer method of allocating the Wii: the market price or the two methods described in the news clip.

9. **"Two Buck Chuck" Wine Cult**

It's the California wine with the cult following. "Charles Shaw is known in local circles as "Two Buck Chuck," … the $1.99 nectar of the gods that is sinfully cheap and good. … A full year after flooding the market largely on the West Coast, it's still being sold by the case to wine lovers who can't get enough. … It's an overabundance of grapes that's made Charles Shaw cheap to bottle—an estimated 5 million cases so far.

CBS, June 2, 2003

a. Explain how the Invisible Hand has worked in the market for this California wine.

b. How has "Two Buck Chuck" influenced consumer surplus from wine?

c. How has "Two Buck Chuck" influenced producer surplus for its producer and for the producers of other wines?

10. The table gives the supply schedules for jet-ski rides by three owners: Rick, Sam, and Tom, the only suppliers of jet-ski rides.

Price (dollars per ride)	Quantity supplied (rides per day)		
	Rick	Sam	Tom
10.00	0	0	0
12.50	5	0	0
15.00	10	5	0
17.50	15	10	5
20.00	20	15	10

a. What is each owner's minimum supply-price of 10 rides a day?

b. Which owner has the largest producer surplus when the price of a ride is $17.50? Explain.

c. What is the marginal social cost of producing 45 rides a day?

d. Construct the market supply schedule of jet-ski rides.

11. The table gives the demand and supply schedules for sandwiches.

Price (dollars per sandwich)	Quantity demanded	Quantity supplied
	(sandwiches per hour)	
0	300	0
1	250	50
2	200	100
3	150	150
4	100	200
5	50	250
6	0	300

a. What is the maximum price that consumers are willing to pay for the 200th sandwich?

b. What is the minimum price that producers are willing to accept for the 200th sandwich?

c. Are 200 sandwiches a day less than or greater than the efficient quantity?

d. If sandwich makers produce 200 a day, what is the deadweight loss?

e. If the sandwich market is efficient, what is the consumer surplus, what is the producer surplus, and what is the total surplus?

f. If the demand for sandwiches increases and sandwich makers produce the efficient quantity, what happens to producer surplus and deadweight loss?

12. **The Right Price for Digital Music: Why 99 cents per Song is Too Much, and Too Little**

Apple's 99-cents-for-everything model isn't perfect. Isn't 99 cents too much to pay for music that appeals to just a few people? What we need is a system that will continue to pack the corporate coffers yet be fair to music lovers. The solution: a real-time commodities market that combines aspects of Apple's iTunes, Nasdaq, the Chicago Mercantile Exchange, Priceline, and eBay. … Songs would be priced strictly on demand. The more people who download [a particular song] … the higher the price [of that song] will go. … The fewer people who buy a [particular] song, the lower the price [of that song] goes. … In essence, this is a pure free-market solution—the market alone would determine price.

Slate, December 5, 2005

Assume that the marginal social cost of downloading a song from the iTunes Store is zero. (This assumption means that the cost of operating the iTunes Store doesn't change if people download more songs.)

a. Draw a graph of the market for downloadable music with a price of 99 cents for everything. On your graph, show consumer surplus and producer surplus.

b. With a price of 99 cents for everything, is the market efficient or inefficient? If it is inefficient, show the deadweight loss on your graph.

c. If the pricing scheme described in the news clip were adopted, how would consumer surplus, producer surplus, and the deadweight loss change?

d. If the pricing scheme described in the news clip were adopted, would the market be efficient or inefficient? Explain.

e. Is the pricing scheme described in the news clip a "pure free-market solution"? Explain.

13. **Was Katie Holmes' Marathon Entrance Unfair?**

Runners in the recent New York Marathon have been asking why Katie Holmes was admitted to the race when 60,000 hopefuls were denied. … Holmes was admitted to the race as a VIP. She was not given a spot through a lottery system, or for running in one of the 26 sanctioned New York Marathon charities … or even for having a competitive running time. The minimum qualifying run time for a woman runner is 3 hours and 23 minutes. Katie completed the marathon in 5 hours, 29 minutes and 58 seconds.

MSNBC, November 9, 2007

a. By what allocation method did Holmes obtain entrance to the marathon?

b. Evaluate the "fairness" of Holmes being admitted to the marathon.

14. **MYTH: Price-Gouging Is Bad**

Mississippi Attorney General Jim Hood announced a crackdown on gougers after Hurricane Katrina. John Shepperson was one of the "gougers" authorities arrested. Shepperson and his family live in Kentucky. They watched news reports about Katrina and learned that people desperately needed things. Shepperson thought he could help and make some money, too, so he bought 19 generators. He and his family then rented a U-Haul and drove 600 miles to an area of Mississippi that was left without power in the wake of the hurricane. He offered to sell his generators for twice what he had paid for them, and people were eager to buy. Police confiscated his generators, though, and Shepperson was jailed for four days for price-gouging.

ABC News, May 12, 2006

a. Explain how the invisible hand (Shepperson) actually reduced deadweight loss in the market for generators following Katrina.

b. Evaluate the "fairness" of Shepperson's actions.

15. After you have studied *Reading Between the Lines* on pp. 122–123, answer the following questions:

a. What is the major problem in achieving an efficient use of the world's water?

b. If there were a global market in water, like there is in oil, how do you think the market would work?

c. Would a free world market in water achieve an efficient use of the world's water resources? Explain why or why not.

d. Would a free world market in water achieve a fair use of the world's water resources? Explain why or why not and be clear about the concept of fairness that you are using.

16. **Fight over Water Rates; Escondido Farmers Say Increase would Put Them out of Business**

The city is considering significant increases in water rates for agriculture, which historically has paid less than residential and business users. ... [S]ince 1993, water rates have gone up more than 90 percent for residential customers while agricultural users ... have seen increases of only about 50 percent, ...

The San Diego Union-Tribune, June 14, 2006

a. Do you think that the allocation of water among San Diego agricultural and residential users is likely to be efficient? Explain your answer.

b. If agricultural users pay a higher price for water, will the allocation of resources become more efficient?

c. If agricultural users pay a higher price for water, what will happen to consumer surplus and producer surplus from water?

d. Is the difference in price paid by agricultural and residential users fair?

17. Use the link on MyEconLab (Chapter Resources, Chapter 5, Web links) to visit the Web site of Health Action International and read the article by Catrin Schulte-Hillen entitled "Study concerning the availability and price of AZT." Then answer the following questions and explain your answers using the concepts of marginal benefit, marginal cost, price, consumer surplus, and producer surplus.

a. What is the range of retail prices of AZT across the countries covered by the study?

b. What, if anything, do you think could be done to increase the quantity of AZT and decrease its price?

c. Canadian online pharmacies sell AZT to Americans for a price below the U.S. price. Does this practice increase or decrease consumer surplus, producer surplus, and deadweight loss from AZT in the United States?

7 Global Markets in Action

After studying this chapter, you will be able to:

- Explain how markets work with international trade
- Identify the gains from international trade and its winners and losers
- Explain the effects of international trade barriers
- Explain and evaluate arguments used to justify restricting international trade

iPods, Wii games, and Nike shoes are just three of the items you might buy that are not produced in the United States. In fact, most of the goods that you buy are produced abroad, often in Asia, and transported here in container ships or cargo jets. And it's not just goods produced abroad that you buy—it is services too. When you make a technical support call, most likely you'll be talking with someone in India, or to a voice recognition system that was programmed in India. Satellites or fiber cables will carry your conversation along with huge amounts of other voice messages, video images, and data.

All these activities are part of the globalization process that is having a profound effect on our lives. Globalization is controversial and generates heated debate. Many Americans want to know how we can compete with people whose wages are a fraction of our own.

Why do we go to such lengths to trade and communicate with others in faraway places? You will find some answers in this chapter. And in *Reading Between the Lines* at the end of the chapter, you can apply what you've learned and examine the effects of a tariff on shoes—not designer shoes, but lower-priced and children's shoes.

153

◆ How Global Markets Work

Because we trade with people in other countries, the goods and services that we can buy and consume are not limited by what we can produce. The goods and services that we buy from other countries are our **imports**; and the goods and services that we sell to people in other countries are our **exports**.

International Trade Today

Global trade today is enormous. In 2008, global exports and imports were $35 trillion, which is more than half of the value of global production. The United States is the world's largest international trader and accounts for 10 percent of world exports and 15 percent of world imports. Germany and China, which rank 2 and 3 behind the United States, lag by a large margin.

In 2008, total U.S. exports were $1.8 trillion, which is about 13 percent of the value of U.S. production. Total U.S. imports were $2.5 trillion, which is about 18 percent of total expenditure in the United States.

We trade both goods and services. In 2008, exports of services were about 30 percent of total exports and imports of services were about 16 percent of total imports.

What Drives International Trade?

Comparative advantage is the fundamental force that drives international trade. Comparative advantage (see Chapter 2, p. 40) is a situation in which a person can perform an activity or produce a good or service at a lower opportunity cost than anyone else. This same idea applies to nations. We can define *national comparative advantage* as a situation in which a nation can perform an activity or produce a good or service at a lower opportunity cost than any other nation.

The opportunity cost of producing a T-shirt is lower in China than in the United States, so China has a comparative advantage in producing T-shirts. The opportunity cost of producing an airplane is lower in the United States than in China, so the United States has a comparative advantage in producing airplanes.

You saw in Chapter 2 how Liz and Joe reap gains from trade by specializing in the production of the good at which they have a comparative advantage and trading. Both are better off.

Items Most Traded by the United States
Trading Services for Oil

The figure shows the five largest exports and imports for the United States. Services top the list of exports and oil is the largest import by a large margin.

The services that we export are banking, insurance, business consulting, and other private services. Airplanes are the largest category of goods that we export.

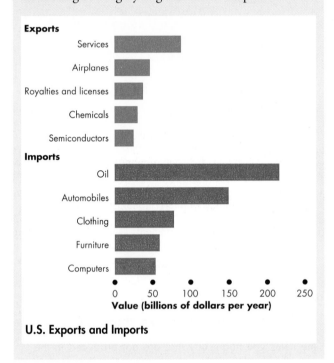

U.S. Exports and Imports

This same principle applies to trade among nations. Because China has a comparative advantage at producing T-shirts and the United States has a comparative advantage at producing airplanes, the people of both countries can gain from specialization and trade. China can buy airplanes from the United States at a lower opportunity cost than that at which Chinese firms can produce them. And Americans can buy T-shirts from China for a lower opportunity cost than that at which U.S. firms can produce them. Also, through international trade, Chinese producers can get higher prices for their T-shirts and Boeing can sell airplanes for a higher price. Both countries gain from international trade.

Let's now illustrate the gains from trade that we've just described by studying demand and supply in the global markets for T-shirts and airplanes.

Why the United States Imports T-Shirts

The United States imports T-shirts because the rest of the world has a comparative advantage in producing T-shirts. Figure 7.1 illustrates how this comparative advantage generates international trade and how trade affects the price of a T-shirt and the quantities produced and bought.

The demand curve D_{US} and the supply curve S_{US} show the demand and supply in the U.S. domestic market only. The demand curve tells us the quantity of T-shirts that Americans are willing to buy at various prices. The supply curve tells us the quantity of T-shirts that U.S. garment makers are willing to sell at various prices—that is, the quantity supplied at each price when all T-shirts sold in the United States are produced in the United States.

Figure 7.1(a) shows what the U.S. T-shirt market would be like with no international trade. The price of a shirt would be $8 and 40 million shirts a year would be produced by U.S. garment makers and bought by U.S. consumers.

Figure 7.1(b) shows the market for T-shirts with international trade. Now the price of a T-shirt is determined in the world market, not the U.S. domestic market. The world price is less than $8 a T-shirt, which means that the rest of the world has a comparative advantage in producing T-shirts. The world price line shows the world price at $5 a shirt.

The U.S demand curve, D_{US}, tells us that at $5 a shirt, Americans buy 60 million shirts a year. The U.S. supply curve, S_{US}, tells us that at $5 a shirt, U.S. garment makers produce 20 million T-shirts a year. To buy 60 million T-shirts when only 20 million are produced in the United States, we must import T-shirts from the rest of the world. The quantity of T-shirts imported is 40 million a year.

FIGURE 7.1   A Market With Imports

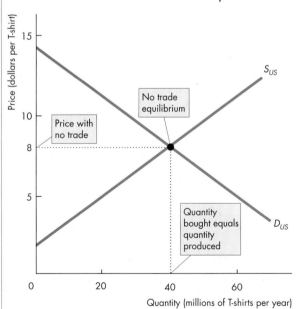

(a) Equilibrium with no international trade

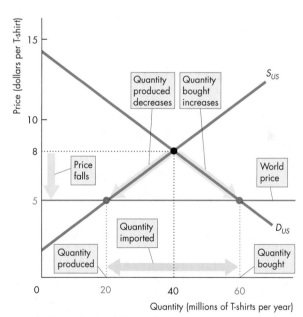

(b) Equilibrium in a market with imports

Part (a) shows the U.S. market for T-shirts with no international trade. The U.S. domestic demand curve D_{US} and U.S. domestic supply curve S_{US} determine the price of a T-shirt at $8 and the quantity of T- shirts produced and bought in the United States at 40 million a year.

Part (b) shows the U.S. market for T-shirts with interna-

tional trade. World demand and world supply determine the world price, which is $5 per T-shirt. The price in the U.S. market falls to $5 a shirt. U.S. purchases of T-shirts increases to 60 million a year, and U.S. production of T-shirts decreases to 20 million a year. The United States imports 40 million T-shirts a year.

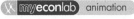

Why the United States Exports Airplanes

Figure 7.2 illustrates international trade in airplanes. The demand curve D_{US} and the supply curve S_{US} show the demand and supply in the U.S. domestic market only. The demand curve tells us the quantity of airplanes that U.S. airlines are willing to buy at various prices. The supply curve tells us the quantity of airplanes that U.S. aircraft makers are willing to sell at various prices.

Figure 7.2(a) shows what the U.S. airplane market would be like with no international trade. The price of an airplane would be $100 million and 400 airplanes a year would be produced by U.S. aircraft makers and bought by U.S. airlines.

Figure 7.2(b) shows the U.S. airplane market with international trade. Now the price of an airplane is determined in the world market and the world price is higher than $100 million, which means that the United States has a comparative advantage in produc-

ing airplanes. The world price line shows the world price at $150 million.

The U.S. demand curve, D_{US}, tells us that at $150 million an airplane, U.S. airlines buy 200 airplanes a year. The U.S. supply curve, S_{US}, tells us that at $150 million an airplane, U.S. aircraft makers produce 700 airplanes a year. The quantity produced in the United States (700 a year) minus the quantity purchased by U.S. airlines (200 a year) is the quantity of airplanes exported, which is 500 airplanes a year.

Review Quiz

1 Describe the situation in the market for a good or service that the United States imports.
2 Describe the situation in the market for a good or service that the United States exports.

myeconlab Work Study Plan 7.1 and get instant feedback.

FIGURE 7.2   A Market With Exports

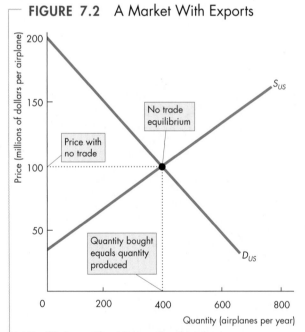

(a) Equilibrium without international trade

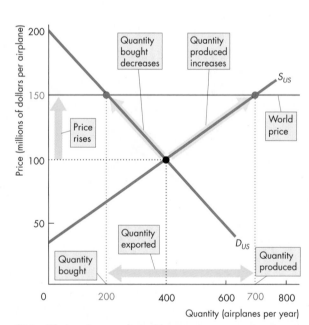

(b) Equilibrium in a market with exports

In part (a), the U.S. market with no international trade, the U.S. domestic demand curve D_{US} and the U.S. domestic supply curve S_{US} determine the price of an airplane at $100 million and 400 airplanes are produced and bought each year.

In part (b), the U.S. market with international trade,

world demand and world supply determine the world price, which is $150 million per airplane. The price in the U.S. market rises. U.S. airplane production increases to 700 a year, and U.S. purchases of airplanes decrease to 200 a year. The United States exports 500 airplanes a year.

myeconlab animation

Winners, Losers, and the Net Gain from Trade

International trade has winners but it also has losers. That's why you often hear people complaining about international competition. We're now going to see who wins and who loses from international trade. You will then be able to understand who complains about international competition and why. You will learn why we hear producers complaining about cheap foreign imports. You will also see why we never hear consumers of imported goods and services complaining and why we never hear exporters complaining except when they want greater access to foreign markets.

Gains and Losses from Imports

We measure the gains and losses from imports by examining their effect on consumer surplus, producer surplus, and total surplus. The winners are those whose surplus increases and the losers are those whose surplus decreases.

Figure 7.3(a) shows what consumer surplus and producer surplus would be with no international trade in T-shirts. U.S. domestic demand, D_{US}, and U.S. domestic supply, S_{US}, determine the price and quantity. The green area shows consumer surplus and the blue area shows producer surplus. Total surplus is the sum of consumer surplus and producer surplus.

Figure 7.3(b) shows how these surpluses change when the U.S. market opens to imports. The U.S. price falls to the world price. The quantity bought increases to the quantity demanded at the world price and consumer surplus expands from A to the larger green area $A + B + D$. The quantity produced in the United States decreases to the quantity supplied at the world price and producer surplus shrinks to the smaller blue area C.

Part of the gain in consumer surplus, the area B, is a loss of producer surplus—a redistribution of total surplus. But the other part of the increase in consumer

FIGURE 7.3 Gains and Losses in a Market With Imports

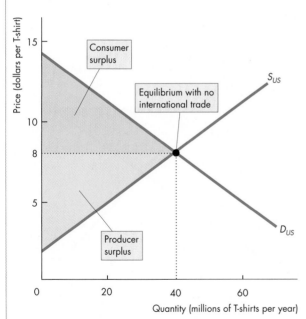

(a) Consumer surplus and producer surplus with no international trade

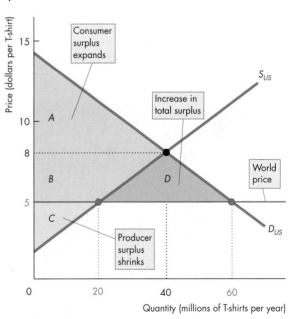

(b) Gains and losses from imports

In part (a), with no international trade, the green area shows the consumer surplus and the blue area shows the producer surplus.

In part (b), with international trade, the price falls to the world price of $5 a shirt. Consumer surplus expands to area $A + B + D$. Producer surplus shrinks to area C. Area B is a transfer of surplus from producers to consumers. Area D is an increase in total surplus—the gain from imports.

surplus, the area D, is a net gain. This increase in total surplus results from the lower price and increased purchases and is the gain from imports.

Gains and Losses from Exports

We measure the gains and losses from exports just like we measured those from imports, by their effect on consumer surplus, producer surplus, and total surplus.

Figure 7.4(a) shows what the consumer surplus and producer surplus would be with no international trade. Domestic demand, D_{US}, and domestic supply, S_{US}, determine the price and quantity. The green area shows consumer surplus and the blue area shows producer surplus. The two surpluses sum to total surplus.

Figure 7.4(b) shows how the consumer surplus and producer surplus change when the good is exported. The price rises to the world price. The quantity bought decreases to the quantity demanded at the world price and the consumer surplus shrinks to the green area A. The quantity produced increases

to the quantity supplied at the world price and the producer surplus expands from the blue area C to the larger blue area $B + C + D$.

Part of the gain of producer surplus, the area B, is a loss in consumer surplus—a redistribution of the total surplus. But the other part of the increase in producer surplus, the area D, is a net gain. This increase in total surplus results from the higher price and increased production and is the gain from exports.

Review Quiz

1 How is the gain from imports distributed between consumers and domestic producers?
2 How is the gain from exports distributed between consumers and domestic producers?
3 Why is the net gain from international trade positive?

FIGURE 7.4   Gains and Losses in a Market With Exports

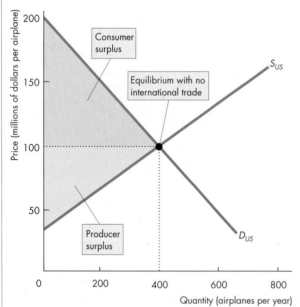

(a) Consumer surplus and producer surplus with no international trade

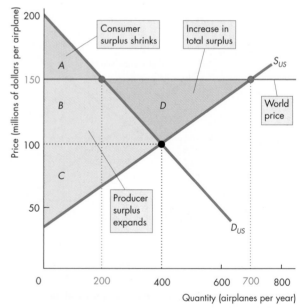

(b) Gains and losses from exports

In part (a), the U.S. market with no international trade, the green area shows the consumer surplus and the blue area shows the producer surplus. In part (b), the U.S. market with international trade, the price rises to the world price.

Consumer surplus shrinks to area A. Producer surplus expands to area $B + C + D$. Area B is a transfer of surplus from consumers to producers. Area D is an increase in total surplus—the gain from exports.

◆ International Trade Restrictions

Governments use four sets of tools to influence international trade and protect domestic industries from foreign competition. They are

- Tariffs
- Import quotas
- Other import barriers
- Export subsidies

Tariffs

A **tariff** is a tax on a good that is imposed by the importing country when an imported good crosses its international boundary. For example, the government of India imposes a 100 percent tariff on wine imported from California. So when an Indian imports a $10 bottle of Californian wine, he pays the Indian government a $10 import duty.

The temptation for governments to impose tariffs is a strong one. First, they provide revenue to the government. Second, they enable the government to satisfy the self-interest of the people who earn their incomes in the import-competing industries. But as you will see, tariffs and other restrictions on free international trade decrease the gains from trade and are not in the social interest. Let's see why.

The Effects of a Tariff To see the effects of a tariff, let's return to the example in which the United States imports T-shirts. With free trade, the T-shirts are imported and sold at the world price. Then, under pressure from U.S. garment makers, the U.S. government imposes a tariff on imported T-shirts. Buyers of T-shirts must now pay the world price plus the tariff. Several consequences follow and Fig. 7.5 illustrates them.

Figure 7.5(a) shows the situation with free international trade. The United States produces 20 million

FIGURE 7.5   The Effects of a Tariff

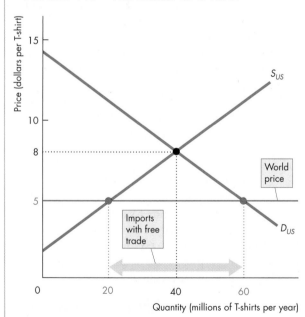

(a) Free trade

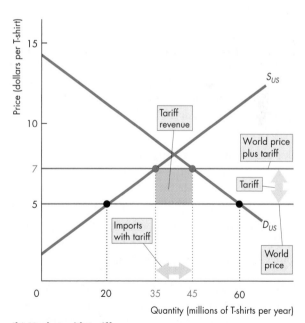

(b) Market with tariff

The world price of a T-shirt is $5. With free trade in part (a), Americans buy 60 million T-shirts a year. U.S. garment makers produce 20 million T-shirts a year and the United States imports 40 million a year.

With a tariff of $2 per T-shirt in part (b), the price in

the U.S. market rises to $7 a T-shirt. U.S. production increases, U.S. purchases decrease, and the quantity imported decreases. The U.S. government collects a tariff revenue of $2 on each T-shirt imported, which is shown by the purple rectangle.

T-shirts a year and imports 40 million a year at the world price of $5 a shirt. Figure 7.5(b) shows what happens with a tariff set at $2 per T-shirt. The following changes occur in the market for T-shirts:

- The price of a T-shirt in the United States rises by $2.
- The quantity of T-shirts bought in the United States decreases.
- The quantity of T-shirts produced in the United States increases.
- The quantity of T-shirts imported into the United States decreases.
- The U.S. government collects a tariff revenue.

Rise in Price of a T-Shirt To buy a T-shirt, Americans must pay the world price plus the tariff, so the price of a T-shirt rises by $2 to $7. Figure 7.5(b) shows the new domestic price line, which lies $2 above the world price line.

Decrease in Purchases The higher price of a T-shirt brings a decrease in the quantity demanded along the demand curve. Figure 7.5(b) shows the decrease from 60 million T-shirts a year at $5 a shirt to 45 million a year at $7 a shirt.

Increase in Domestic Production The higher price of a T-shirt stimulates domestic production, and U.S. garment makers increase the quantity supplied along the supply curve. Figure 7.5(b) shows the increase from 20 million T-shirts at $5 a shirt to 35 million a year at $7 a shirt.

Decrease in Imports T-shirt imports decrease by 30 million, from 40 million to 10 million a year. Both the decrease in purchases and the increase in domestic production contribute to this decrease in imports.

Tariff Revenue The government's tariff revenue is $20 million—$2 per shirt on 10 million imported shirts—shown by the purple rectangle.

Winners, Losers, and the Social Loss from a Tariff A tariff on an imported good creates winners and losers and a social loss. When the U.S. government imposes a tariff on an imported good,

- U.S. consumers of the good lose.
- U.S. producers of the good gain.
- U.S. consumers lose more than U.S. producers gain.
- Society loses: a deadweight loss arises.

U.S. Consumers of the Good Lose Because the price of a T-shirt in the United States rises, the quantity of T-shirts demanded decreases. The combination of a higher price and smaller quantity bought decreases consumer surplus—the loss to U.S. consumers that arises from a tariff.

U.S. Producers of the Good Gain Because the price of an imported T-shirt rises by the amount of the tariff, U.S. T-shirt producers are now able to sell their T-shirts for the world price plus the tariff. At the higher price, the quantity of T-shirts supplied by U.S. producers increases. The combination of a higher price and larger quantity produced increases producer surplus—the gain to U.S. producers from the tariff.

U.S. Consumers Lose More Than U.S. Producers Gain Consumer surplus decreases for four reasons: Some becomes producer surplus, some is lost in a higher cost of production (domestic producers have higher costs than foreign producers), some is lost because imports decrease, and some goes to the government as tariff revenue. Figure 7.6 shows these sources of lost consumer surplus.

Figure 7.6(a) shows the consumer surplus and producer surplus with free international trade in T-shirts. Figure 7.6(b) shows the consumer surplus and producer surplus with a $2 tariff on imported T-shirts. By comparing Fig. 7.6(b) with Fig. 7.6(a), you can see how a tariff changes these surpluses.

Consumer surplus—the green area—shrinks. The decrease in consumer surplus is made up of four parts. First, some of the consumer surplus is transferred to producers. The blue area *B* represents this loss (and gain of producer surplus). Second, part of the consumer surplus is lost in the higher cost of domestic production. The gray area *C* shows this loss. Third, some of the consumer surplus is transferred to the government. The purple area *D* shows this loss (and gain of government revenue). Fourth, some of the consumer surplus is lost because imports decrease. The gray area *E* shows this loss.

Society Loses: A Deadweight Loss Arises Some of the loss of consumer surplus is transferred to producers and some is transferred to the government and spent on government programs that people value. But the increase in production cost and the loss from decreased imports is transferred to no one: It is a social loss—a deadweight loss. The gray areas labeled *C* and *E* represent this deadweight loss. Total surplus decreases by the area *C* + *E*.

FIGURE 7.6 The Winners and Losers from a Tariff

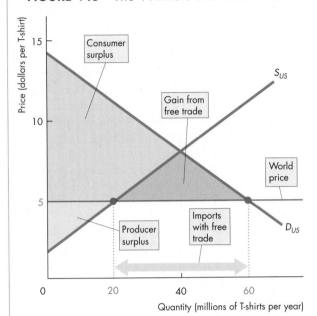

(a) Free trade

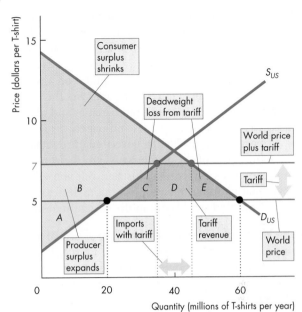

(b) Market with tariff

The world price of a T-shirt is $5. In part (a), with free trade, the United States imports 40 million T-shirts. Consumer surplus, producer surplus, and the gains from free trade are as large as possible.

In part (b), a tariff of $2 per T-shirt raises the U.S. price

of a T-shirt to $7. The quantity imported decreases. Consumer surplus shrinks by the areas B, C, D, and E. Producer surplus expands by area B. The government's tariff revenue is area D, and the tariff creates a deadweight loss equal to the area $C + E$.

myeconlab animation

U.S. Tariffs
Almost Gone

The Smoot-Hawley Act, which was passed in 1930, took U.S. tariffs to a peak average rate of 20 percent in 1933. (One third of imports was subject to a 60 percent tariff.) The **General Agreement on Tariffs and Trade (GATT)**, was established in 1947. Since then tariffs have fallen in a series of negotiating rounds, the most significant of which are identified in the figure. Tariffs are now as low as they have ever been but import quotas and other trade barriers persist.

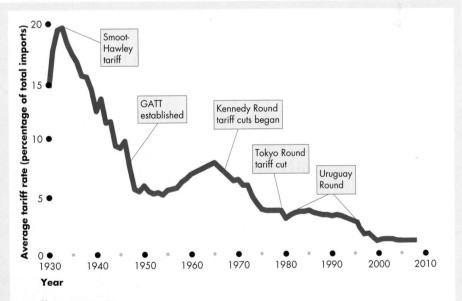

Tariffs: 1930–2008

Sources of data: U.S. Bureau of the Census, *Historical Statistics of the United States, Colonial Times to 1970,* Bicentennial Edition, Part 1 (Washington, D.C., 1975); Series U-212: updated from *Statistical Abstract of the United States:* various editions.

Import Quotas

We now look at the second tool for restricting trade: import quotas. An **import quota** is a restriction that limits the maximum quantity of a good that may be imported in a given period.

Most countries impose import quotas on a wide range of items. The United States imposes them on food products such as sugar and bananas and manufactured goods such as textiles and paper.

Import quotas enable the government to satisfy the self-interest of the people who earn their incomes in the import-competing industries. But you will discover that like a tariff, an import quota decreases the gains from trade and is not in the social interest.

The Effects of an Import Quota The effects of an import quota are similar to those of a tariff. The price rises, the quantity bought decreases, and the quantity produced in the United States increases. Figure 7.7 illustrates the effects.

Figure 7.7(a) shows the situation with free international trade. Figure 7.7(b) shows what happens with an import quota of 10 million T-shirts a year. The U.S. supply curve of T-shirts becomes the domestic supply curve, S_{US}, plus the quantity that the import quota permits. So the supply curve becomes S_{US} + *quota*. The price of a T-shirt rises to $7, the quantity of T-shirts bought in the United States decreases to 45 million a year, the quantity of T-shirts produced in the United States increases to 35 million a year, and the quantity of T-shirts imported into the United States decreases to the quota quantity of 10 million a year. All the effects of this quota are identical to the effects of a $2 per shirt tariff, as you can check in Fig. 7.6(b).

Winners, Losers, and the Social Loss from an Import Quota An import quota creates winners and losers that are similar to those of a tariff but with an interesting difference.

FIGURE 7.7 The Effects of an Import Quota

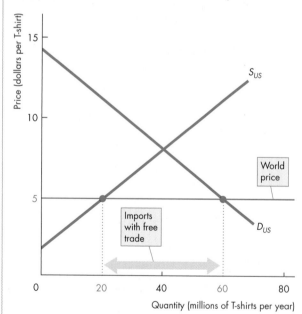

(a) Free trade

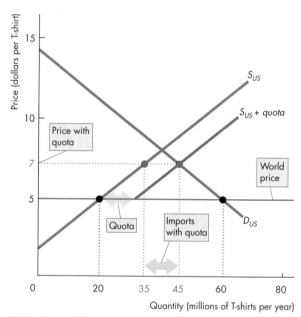

(b) Market with import quota

With free international trade, in part (a), Americans buy 60 million T-shirts at the world price. The United States produces 20 million T-shirts and imports 40 million a year. With an import quota of 10 million T-shirts a year, in part (b),

the supply of T-shirts in the United States is shown by the curve S_{US} + *quota*. The price in the United States rises to $7 a T-shirt. U.S. production increases, U.S. purchases decrease, and the quantity of T-shirts imported decreases.

When the government imposes an import quota,

- U.S. consumers of the good lose.
- U.S. producers of the good gain.
- Importers of the good gain.
- Society loses: a deadweight loss arises.

Figure 7.8 shows these gains and losses from a quota. By comparing Fig. 7.8(b) with a quota and Fig. 7.8(a) with free trade, you can see how an import quota of 10 million T-shirts a year changes the consumer and producer surpluses.

Consumer surplus—the green area—shrinks. This decrease is the loss to consumers from the import quota. The decrease in consumer surplus is made up of four parts. First, some of the consumer surplus is transferred to producers. The blue area *B* represents this loss of consumer surplus (and gain of producer surplus). Second, part of the consumer surplus is lost because the domestic cost of production is higher

than the world price. The gray area *C* represents this loss. Third, part of the consumer surplus is transferred to importers who buy T-shirts for $5 (the world price) and sell them for $7 (the U.S. domestic price). The two blue areas *D* represent this loss of consumer surplus and profit for importers. Fourth, part of the consumer surplus is lost because imports decrease. The gray area *E* represents this loss.

The losses of consumer surplus from the higher cost of production and the decrease in imports is a social loss—a deadweight loss. The gray areas labeled *C* and *E* represent this deadweight loss. Total surplus decreases by the area *C* + *E*.

You can now see the one difference between a quota and a tariff. A tariff brings in revenue for the government while a quota brings a profit for the importers. All the other effects are the same, provided the quota is set at the same quantity of imports that results from the tariff.

FIGURE 7.8   The Winners and Losers from an Import Quota

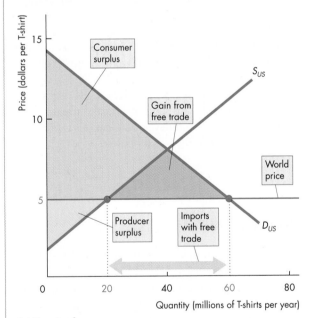

(a) Free trade

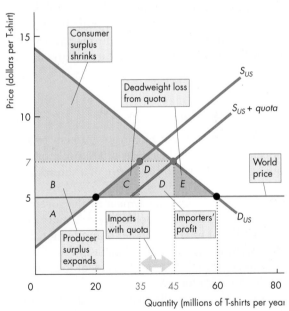

(b) Market with import quota

The world price of a T-shirt is $5. In part (a), with free trade, the United States produces 20 million T-shirts a year and imports 40 million T-shirts. Consumer surplus, producer surplus, and the gain from free international trade (darker green area) are as large as possible.

In part (b), the import quota raises the price of a T-shirt to $7. The quantity imported decreases. Consumer surplus shrinks by the areas *B*, *C*, *D*, and *E*. Producer surplus expands by area *B*. Importers' profit is the two areas *D*, and the quota creates a deadweight loss equal to *C* + *E*.

Other Import Barriers

Two sets of policies that influence imports are

- Health, safety, and regulation barriers
- Voluntary export restraints

Health, Safety, and Regulation Barriers Thousands of detailed health, safety, and other regulations restrict international trade. For example, U.S. food imports are examined by the Food and Drug Administration to determine whether the food is "pure, wholesome, safe to eat, and produced under sanitary conditions." The discovery of BSE (mad cow disease) in just one U.S. cow in 2003 was enough to close down international trade in U.S. beef. The European Union bans imports of most genetically modified foods, such as U.S.-produced soybeans. Although regulations of the type we've just described are not designed to limit international trade, they have that effect.

Voluntary Export Restraints A *voluntary export restraint* is like a quota allocated to a foreign exporter of a good. This type of trade barrier isn't common. It was initially used during the 1980s when Japan voluntarily limited its exports of car parts to the United States.

Export Subsidies

A *subsidy* is a payment by the government to a producer. You studied the effects of a subsidy on the quantity produced and the price of a subsidized farm product in Chapter 6, pp. 142–143.

An *export subsidy* is a payment by the government to the producer of an exported good. Export subsidies are illegal under a number of international agreements, including the North American Free Trade Agreement (NAFTA), and the rules of the World Trade Organization (WTO).

Although export subsidies are illegal, the subsidies that the U.S. and European Union governments pay to farmers end up increasing domestic production, some of which gets exported. These exports of subsidized farm products make it harder for producers in other countries, notably in Africa and Central and South America, to compete in global markets. Export subsidies bring gains to domestic producers, but they result in inefficient underproduction in the rest of the world and create a deadweight loss.

Failure in Doha
Self-Interest Beats the Social Interest

The **World Trade Organization (WTO)** is an international body established by the world's major trading nations for the purpose of supervising international trade and lowering the barriers to trade.

In 2001, at a meeting of trade ministers from all the WTO member-countries held in Doha, Qatar, an agreement was made to begin negotiations to lower tariff barriers and quotas that restrict international trade in farm products and services. These negotiations are called the **Doha Development Agenda** or the **Doha Round**.

In the period since 2001, thousands of hours of conferences in Cancún in 2003, Geneva in 2004, and Hong Kong in 2005, and ongoing meetings at WTO headquarters in Geneva, costing millions of taxpayers' dollars, have made disappointing progress.

Rich nations, led by the United States, the European Union, and Japan, want greater access to the markets of developing nations in exchange for allowing those nations greater access to the rich world's markets, especially for farm products.

Developing nations, led by Brazil, China, India, and South Africa, want access to the farm product markets of the rich world, but they also want to protect their infant industries.

With two incompatible positions, these negotiations are stalled and show no signs of a breakthrough. The self-interest of rich and developing nations is preventing the achievement of the social interest.

Review Quiz

1 What are the tools that a country can use to restrict international trade?
2 Explain the effects of a tariff on domestic production, the quantity bought, and the price.
3 Explain who gains and who loses from a tariff and why the losses exceed the gains.
4 Explain the effects of an import quota on domestic production, consumption, and price.
5 Explain who gains and who loses from an import quota and why the losses exceed the gains.

myeconlab Work Study Plan 7.3 and get instant feedback.

The Case Against Protection

For as long as nations and international trade have existed, people have debated whether a country is better off with free international trade or with protection from foreign competition. The debate continues, but for most economists, a verdict has been delivered and is the one you have just seen. Free trade promotes prosperity for all countries; protection is inefficient. We've seen the most powerful case for free trade—it brings gains for consumers that exceed any losses incurred by producers, so there is a net gain for society.

But there is a broader range of issues in the free trade versus protection debate. Let's review these issues.

Two classical arguments for restricting international trade are

- The infant-industry argument
- The dumping argument

The Infant-Industry Argument

The **infant-industry argument** for protection is that it is necessary to protect a new industry to enable it to grow into a mature industry that can compete in world markets. The argument is based on the idea of *dynamic comparative advantage*, which can arise from *learning-by-doing* (see Chapter 2, p. 43).

Learning-by-doing, a powerful engine of productivity growth, and on-the-job experience can change comparative advantage. But these facts do not justify protection.

First, the infant-industry argument is valid only if the benefits of learning-by-doing *not only* accrue to the owners and workers of the firms in the infant industry but also *spill over* to other industries and parts of the economy. For example, there are huge productivity gains from learning-by-doing in the manufacture of aircraft.

But almost all of these gains benefit the stockholders and workers of Boeing and other aircraft producers. Because the people making the decisions, bearing the risk, and doing the work are the ones who benefit, they take the dynamic gains into account when they decide on the scale of their activities. In this case, almost no benefits spill over to other parts of the economy, so there is no need for government assistance to achieve an efficient outcome.

Second, even if the case is made for protecting an infant industry, it is more efficient to do so by giving the firms in the industry a subsidy, which is financed out of taxes. Such a subsidy would encourage the industry to mature and to compete with efficient world producers and keep the price faced by consumers at the world price.

The Dumping Argument

Dumping occurs when a foreign firm sells its exports at a lower price than its cost of production. Dumping might be used by a firm that wants to gain a global monopoly. In this case, the foreign firm sells its output at a price below its cost to drive domestic firms out of business. When the domestic firms have gone, the foreign firm takes advantage of its monopoly position and charges a higher price for its product. Dumping is illegal under the rules of the WTO and is usually regarded as a justification for temporary tariffs, which are called *countervailing duties*.

But there are powerful reasons to resist the dumping argument for protection. First, it is virtually impossible to detect dumping because it is hard to determine a firm's costs. As a result, the test for dumping is whether a firm's export price is below its domestic price. But this test is a weak one because it can be rational for a firm to charge a low price in a market in which the quantity demanded is highly sensitive to price and a higher price in a market in which demand is less price-sensitive.

Second, it is hard to think of a good that is produced by a *global* monopoly. So even if all the domestic firms in some industry were driven out of business, it would always be possible to find alternative foreign sources of supply and to buy the good at a price determined in a competitive market.

Third, if a good or service were a truly global monopoly, the best way of dealing with it would be by regulation—just as in the case of domestic monopolies (see Chapter 13, pp. 313–315). Such regulation would require international cooperation.

The two arguments for protection that we've just examined have an element of credibility. The counterarguments are in general stronger, however, so these arguments do not make the case for protection. But they are not the only arguments that you might encounter. There are many other new arguments against globalization and for protection. The most common ones are that protection

- Saves jobs
- Allows us to compete with cheap foreign labor
- Penalizes lax environmental standards
- Prevents rich countries from exploiting developing countries

Saves Jobs

First, free trade does cost some jobs, but it also creates other jobs. It brings about a global rationalization of labor and allocates labor resources to their highest-valued activities. International trade in textiles has cost tens of thousands of jobs in the United States as textile mills and other factories closed. But tens of thousands of jobs have been created in other countries as textile mills opened. And tens of thousands of U.S. workers got better-paying jobs than as textile workers because U.S. export industries expanded and created new jobs. More jobs have been created than destroyed.

Although protection does save particular jobs, it does so at a high cost. For example, until 2005, U.S. textile jobs were protected by an international agreement called the Multifiber Arrangement. The U.S. International Trade Commission (ITC) has estimated that because of import quotas, 72,000 jobs existed in the textile industry that would otherwise have disappeared and that the annual clothing expenditure in the United States was $15.9 billion ($160 per family) higher than it would have been with free trade. Equivalently, the ITC estimated that each textile job saved cost $221,000 a year.

Imports don't only destroy jobs. They create jobs for retailers that sell imported goods and for firms that service those goods. Imports also create jobs by creating incomes in the rest of the world, some of which are spent on U.S.-made goods and services.

Allows Us to Compete with Cheap Foreign Labor

With the removal of tariffs on trade between the United States and Mexico, people said we would hear a "giant sucking sound" as jobs rushed to Mexico. Let's see what's wrong with this view.

The labor cost of a unit of output equals the wage rate divided by labor productivity. For example, if a U.S. autoworker earns $30 an hour and produces 15 units of output an hour, the average labor cost of a unit of output is $2. If a Mexican auto assembly worker earns $3 an hour and produces 1 unit of output an hour, the average labor cost of a unit of output is $3. Other things remaining the same, the higher a worker's productivity, the higher is the worker's wage rate. High-wage workers have high productivity; low-wage workers have low productivity.

Although high-wage U.S. workers are more productive, on average, than low-wage Mexican workers, there are differences across industries. U.S. labor is relatively more productive in some activities than in others. For example, the productivity of U.S. workers in producing movies, financial services, and customized computer chips is relatively higher than their productivity in the production of metals and some standardized machine parts. The activities in which U.S. workers are relatively more productive than their Mexican counterparts are those in which the United States has a *comparative advantage*. By engaging in free trade, increasing our production and exports of the goods and services in which we have a comparative advantage and decreasing our production and increasing our imports of the goods and services in which our trading partners have a comparative advantage, we can make ourselves and the citizens of other countries better off.

Penalizes Lax Environmental Standards

Another argument for protection is that many poorer countries, such as China and Mexico, do not have the same environmental policies that we have and, because they are willing to pollute and we are not, we cannot compete with them without tariffs. So if poorer countries want free trade with the richer and "greener" countries, they must raise their environmental standards.

This argument for protection is weak. First, a poor country cannot afford to be as concerned about its environmental standard as a rich country can. Today, some of the worst pollution of air and water is found in China, Mexico, and the former communist countries of Eastern Europe. But only a few decades ago, London and Los Angeles led the pollution league table. The best hope for cleaner air in Beijing and Mexico City is rapid income growth. And free trade contributes to that growth. As incomes in developing countries grow, they will have the *means* to match their desires to improve their environment. Second, a poor country may have a comparative advantage at doing "dirty" work, which helps it to raise its income and at the same time enables the global economy to achieve higher environmental standards than would otherwise be possible.

Prevents Rich Countries from Exploiting Developing Countries

Another argument for protection is that international trade must be restricted to prevent the people of the rich industrial world from exploiting the poorer people of the developing countries and forcing them to work for slave wages.

Child labor and near-slave labor are serious problems that are rightly condemned. But by trading with poor countries, we increase the demand for the goods that these countries produce and, more significantly, we increase the demand for their labor. When the demand for labor in developing countries increases, the wage rate also increases. So, rather than exploiting people in developing countries, trade can improve their opportunities and increase their incomes.

The arguments for protection that we've reviewed leave free-trade unscathed. But a new phenomenon is at work in our economy: *offshore outsourcing*. Surely we need protection from this new source of foreign competition. Let's investigate.

Offshore Outsourcing

Citibank, the Bank of America, Apple Computer, Nike, Wal-Mart: What do these U.S. icons have in common? They all send jobs that could be done in America to China, India, Thailand, or even Canada—they are offshoring. What exactly is offshoring?

What Is Offshoring? A firm in United States can obtain the things that it sells in any of four ways:
1. Hire American labor and produce in America.
2. Hire foreign labor and produce in other countries.
3. Buy finished goods, components, or services from other firms in the United States.
4. Buy finished goods, components, or services from other firms in other countries.

Activities 3 and 4 are **outsourcing**, and activities 2 and 4 are **offshoring**. Activity 4 is **offshore outsourcing**. Notice that offshoring includes activities that take place inside U.S. firms. If a U.S. firm opens its own facilities in another country, then it is offshoring.

Offshoring has been going on for hundreds of years,

but it expanded rapidly and became a source of concern during the 1990s as many U.S. firms moved information technology services and general office services such as finance, accounting, and human resources management overseas.

Why Did Offshoring of Services Boom During the 1990s? The gains from specialization and trade that you saw in the previous section must be large enough to make it worth incurring the costs of communication and transportation. If the cost of producing a T-shirt in China isn't lower than the cost of producing the T-shirt in the United States by more than the cost of transporting the shirt from China to America, then it is more efficient to produce shirts in the United States and avoid the transport costs.

The same considerations apply to trade in services. If services are to be produced offshore, then the cost of delivering those services must be low enough to leave the buyer with an overall lower cost. Before the 1990s, the cost of communicating across large distances was too high to make the offshoring of business services efficient. But during the 1990s, when satellites, fiber-optic cables, and computers cut the cost of a phone call between America and India to less than a dollar an hour, a huge base of offshore resources became competitive with similar resources in the United States.

What Are the Benefits of Offshoring? Offshoring brings gains from trade identical to those of any other type of trade. We could easily change the names of the items traded from T-shirts and airplanes (the examples in the previous sections of this chapter) to banking services and call center services (or any other pair of services). An American bank might export banking services to Indian firms, and Indians might provide call center services to U.S. firms. This type of trade would benefit both Americans and Indians provided the United States has a comparative advantage in banking services and India has a comparative advantage in call center services.

Comparative advantages like these emerged during the 1990s. India has the world's largest educated English-speaking population and is located in a time zone half a day ahead of the U.S. east coast and midway between Asia and Europe, which facilitates 24/7 operations. When the cost of communicating with a worker in India was several dollars a minute, as it was before the 1990s, tapping these vast resources was just too costly. But at today's cost of a long-distance telephone call or Internet connection, resources in India can be used to produce services in the United States at a lower cost than those services can be produced by using resources located in the United States. And with the incomes that Indians earn from exporting services, some of the services (and goods) that Indians buy are produced in the United States.

Why Is Offshoring a Concern? Despite the gain from specialization and trade that offshoring brings, many people believe that it also brings costs that eat up the gains. Why?

A major reason is that offshoring is taking jobs in services. The loss of manufacturing jobs to other countries has been going on for decades, but the U.S. service sector has always expanded by enough to create new jobs to replace the lost manufacturing jobs. Now that service jobs are also going overseas, the fear is that there will not be enough jobs for Americans. This fear is misplaced.

Some service jobs are going overseas, while others are expanding at home. The United States imports call center services, but it exports education, health care, legal, financial, and a host of other types of services. Jobs in these sectors are expanding and will continue to expand.

The exact number of jobs that have moved to lower-cost offshore locations is not known, and estimates vary. But even the highest estimate is a tiny number compared to the normal rate of job creation.

Winners and Losers Gains from trade do not bring gains for every single person. Americans, on average, gain from offshore outsourcing, but some people lose. The losers are those who have invested in the human capital to do a specific job that has now gone offshore.

Unemployment benefits provide short-term temporary relief for these displaced workers. But the long-term solution requires retraining and the acquisition of new skills.

Beyond providing short-term relief through unemployment benefits, there is a large role for government in the provision of education and training to enable the labor force of the twenty-first century to be capable of ongoing learning and rapid retooling to take on new jobs that today we can't foresee.

Schools, colleges, and universities will expand and get better at doing their jobs of producing a highly educated and flexible labor force.

Avoiding Trade Wars

We have reviewed the arguments commonly heard in favor of protection and the counterarguments against it. There is one counterargument to protection that is general and quite overwhelming: Protection invites retaliation and can trigger a trade war.

The best example of a trade war occurred during the Great Depression of the 1930s when the United States introduced the Smoot-Hawley tariff. Country after country retaliated with its own tariff, and in a short period, world trade had almost disappeared. The costs to all countries were large and led to a renewed international resolve to avoid such self-defeating moves in the future. The costs also led to the creation of GATT and are the impetus behind current attempts to liberalize trade.

Why Is International Trade Restricted?

Why, despite all the arguments against protection, is trade restricted? There are two key reasons:

■ Tariff revenue
■ Rent seeking

Tariff Revenue Government revenue is costly to collect. In developed countries such as the United States, a well-organized tax collection system is in place that can generate billions of dollars of income tax and sales tax revenues. This tax collection system is made possible by the fact that most economic transactions are done by firms that must keep properly audited financial records. Without such records, revenue collection agencies (the Internal Revenue Service in the United States) would be severely hampered in their work. Even with audited financial accounts, some potential tax revenue is lost. Nonetheless, for industrialized countries, the income tax and sales taxes are the major sources of revenue and tariffs play a very small role.

But governments in developing countries have a difficult time collecting taxes from their citizens. Much economic activity takes place in an informal economy with few financial records, so only a small amount of revenue is collected from income taxes and sales taxes. The one area in which economic transactions are well recorded and audited is international trade. So this activity is an attractive base for tax collection in these countries and is used much more extensively than it is in developed countries.

Rent Seeking Rent seeking is the major reason why international trade is restricted. **Rent seeking** is lobbying for special treatment by the government to create economic profit or to divert consumer surplus or producer surplus away from others. Free trade increases consumption possibilities *on average*, but not everyone shares in the gain and some people even lose. Free trade brings benefits to some and imposes costs on others, with total benefits exceeding total costs. The uneven distribution of costs and benefits is the principal obstacle to achieving more liberal international trade.

Returning to the example of trade in T-shirts and airplanes, the benefits from free trade accrue to all the producers of airplanes and to those producers of T-shirts that do not bear the costs of adjusting to a smaller garment industry. These costs are transition costs, not permanent costs. The costs of moving to free trade are borne by the garment producers and their employees who must become producers of other goods and services in which the United States has a comparative advantage.

The number of winners from free trade is large. But because the gains are spread thinly over a large number of people, the gain per person is small. The winners could organize and become a political force lobbying for free trade. But political activity is costly. It uses time and other scarce resources and the gains per person are too small to make the cost of political activity worth bearing.

In contrast, the number of losers from free trade is small, but the loss per person is large. Because the loss per person is large, the people who lose *are* willing to incur considerable expense to lobby against free trade.

Both the winners and losers weigh benefits and costs. Those who gain from free trade weigh the benefits it brings against the cost of achieving it. Those who lose from free trade and gain from protection weigh the benefit of protection against the cost of maintaining it. The protectionists undertake a larger quantity of political lobbying than the free traders.

Compensating Losers

If, in total, the gains from free international trade exceed the losses, why don't those who gain compensate those who lose so that everyone is in favor of free trade?

Some compensation does take place. When Congress approved the North American Free Trade

Agreement, (NAFTA), with Canada and Mexico, it set up a $56 million fund to support and retrain workers who lost their jobs as a result of the new trade agreement. During NAFTA's first six months, only 5,000 workers applied for benefits under this scheme. The losers from international trade are also compensated indirectly through the normal unemployment compensation arrangements. But only limited attempts are made to compensate those who lose.

The main reason why full compensation is not attempted is that the costs of identifying all the losers and estimating the value of their losses would be enormous. Also, it would never be clear whether a person who has fallen on hard times is suffering because of free trade or for other reasons that might be largely under her or his control. Furthermore, some people who look like losers at one point in time might, in fact, end up gaining. The young autoworker who loses his job in Michigan and becomes a computer assembly worker in Minneapolis resents the loss of work and the need to move. But a year later, looking back on events, he counts himself fortunate.

Because we do not, in general, compensate the losers from free international trade, protectionism is a popular and permanent feature of our national economic and political life.

Review Quiz

1 What are the infant industry and dumping arguments for protection? Are they correct?
2 Can protection save jobs and the environment and prevent workers in developing countries from being exploited?
3 What is offshore outsourcing? Who benefits from it and who loses?
4 What are the main reasons for imposing a tariff?
5 Why don't the winners from free trade win the political argument?

myeconlab Work Study Plan 7.4 and get instant feedback.

◆ We end this chapter on global markets in action in *Reading Between the Lines* on pp. 170–171. It applies what you've learned by looking at the effects of a tariff on U.S. imports of children's shoes and who gains from passage of the Affordable Footwear Act.

A Worn-Out Tariff

Affordable Footwear Act Takes A Step Forward

just-style.com
20 June 2008

Legislation to eliminate import tariffs on about 60% of all shoes sold in the United States has reached another landmark on its way to final passage, a U.S. trade group said yesterday (19 June).

The Affordable Footwear Act (HR 3934/ S 2372) has now garnered support from one-third of the members of the US House of Representatives according, to the American Apparel & Footwear Association (AAFA).

The legislation aims to abolish old-fashioned import duties known collectively as the "shoe tax" on certain lower to moderately priced footwear and all children's shoes.

These types of shoes typically carry the highest rate of duty—up to 67.5%—despite being the lowest priced, with the shoe tax ultimately contributing to as much as 40% of the retail price.

"With 99% of all footwear sold in the United States imported, the shoe tax has worn out its purpose and remains as an unavoidable, harmful tax on something everyone must buy—shoes," said Kevin M. Burke, president and CEO of the American Apparel & Footwear Association (AAFA).

"The footwear industry unanimously agrees that this bill will not harm domestic footwear manufacturers, while granting significant tax relief to hard-working U.S. families at a time they need it most."

© 2008 just-style.com.

Essence of the Story

- Of the footwear sold in the United States, 99 percent is imported.

- Lower-priced shoes and children's shoes—60 percent of shoes sold—bear an import duty of up to 67.5 percent, which translates to 40 percent of the retail price.

- The Affordable Footwear Act seeks to abolish this tariff.

- The footwear industry agrees that it will not be harmed by removing the tariff.

Economic Analysis

- In the 1920s, most footwear sold in the United States was also produced in the United States.

- Lower-priced shoes produced in Mexico, Brazil, and Italy began to compete with U.S.-produced shoes and the shoemakers turned to Congress for protection.

- Congress met the shoemakers' demands by introducing a tariff on imported shoes.

- When the tariff was introduced, its effects were similar to those explained on pp. 159–161 and illustrated in Fig. 7.6 on p. 161.

- U.S. shoe producers enjoyed an increase in producer surplus, but the price of shoes increased, consumer surplus decreased, and a deadweight loss was incurred.

- During the 1990s, as the cost of producing shoes in Asia tumbled, even with the shoe tariff, U.S. shoe producers could not compete with foreign producers and the U.S. shoe industry all but disappeared.

- Today, no lower-priced or children's shoes are produced in the United States. They are all imported.

- With no domestic supply and no producer surplus, the only effects of the shoe tariff are to generate a small amount of revenue for the government, decrease consumer surplus, and bring deadweight loss.

- Figure 1 illustrates the situation in the market for lower-priced and children's shoes.

- The U.S. demand curve is D_{US}. There is no U.S. supply curve at the price shown in the figure. (There is a U.S. supply but at prices higher than those shown in the figure).

- The world price is $20 a pair and this price would be the U.S. price in the absence of the tariff.

- The tariff is $8 a pair and the U.S. price including the tariff is $28 a pair.

- The purple rectangle illustrates the tariff revenue, the green triangle is the consumer surplus, and the gray triangle is the deadweight loss.

- Figure 2 shows how consumer surplus expands with efficient free trade in shoes.

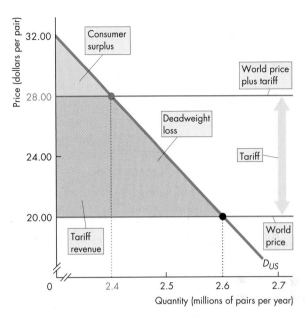

Figure 1 The shoe market with a tariff

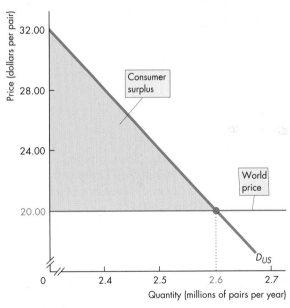

Figure 2 The shoe market without a tariff

SUMMARY ◆

Key Points

How Global Markets Work (pp. 154–156)

■ Comparative advantage drives international trade.

■ If the world price of a good is lower than the domestic price, the rest of the world has a comparative advantage in producing that good and the domestic country gains by producing less, consuming more, and importing the good.

■ If the world price of a good is higher than the domestic price, the domestic country has a comparative advantage in producing that good and gains by producing more, consuming less, and exporting the good.

Winners, Losers, and the Net Gain from Trade (pp. 157–158)

■ Compared to a no-trade situation, in a market with imports, consumer surplus is larger, producer surplus is smaller, and total surplus is larger with free international trade.

■ Compared to a no-trade situation, in a market with exports, consumer surplus is smaller, producer surplus is larger, and total surplus is larger with free international trade.

International Trade Restrictions (pp. 159–164)

■ Countries restrict international trade by imposing tariffs, import quotas, and other import barriers.

■ Trade restrictions raise the domestic price of imported goods, lower the quantity imported, decrease consumer surplus, increase producer surplus, and create a deadweight loss.

The Case Against Protection (pp. 165–169)

■ Arguments that protection is necessary for infant industries and to prevent dumping are weak.

■ Arguments that protection saves jobs, allows us to compete with cheap foreign labor, is needed to penalize lax environmental standards, and prevents exploitation of developing countries are flawed.

■ Offshore outsourcing is just a new way of reaping gains from trade and does not justify protection.

■ Trade restrictions are popular because protection brings a small loss per person to a large number of people and a large gain per person to a small number of people. Those who gain have a stronger political voice than those who lose and it is too costly to identify and compensate losers.

Key Figures

Key Terms

PROBLEMS and APPLICATIONS

Work problems 1–10 in Chapter 7 Study Plan and get instant feedback.
Work problems 11–22 as Homework, a Quiz, or a Test if assigned by your instructor.

1. Wholesalers of roses (the firms that supply your local flower shop with roses for Valentine's Day) buy and sell roses in containers that hold 120 stems. The table provides information about the wholesale market for roses in the United States. The demand schedule is the wholesalers' demand and the supply schedule is the U.S. rose growers' supply.

Price (dollars per container)	Quantity demanded	Quantity supplied
	(millions of containers per year)	
100	15	0
125	12	2
150	9	4
175	6	6
200	3	8
225	0	10

Wholesalers can buy roses at auction in Aalsmeer, Holland, for $125 per container.
a. Without international trade, what would be the price of a container of roses and how many containers of roses a year would be bought and sold in the United States?
b. At the price in your answer to a, does the United States or the rest of the world have a comparative advantage in producing roses?
c. If U.S. wholesalers buy roses at the lowest possible price, how many do they buy from U.S. growers and how many do they import?
d. Draw a graph to illustrate the U.S. wholesale market for roses. Show the equilibrium in that market with no international trade and the equilibrium with free trade. Mark the quantity of roses produced in the United States, the quantity imported, and the total quantity bought.

2. **Underwater Oil Discovery to Transform Brazil into a Major Exporter**

A huge underwater oil field discovered late last year has the potential to transform South America's largest country into a sizable exporter. … Just a decade ago the notion that Brazil would become self-sufficient in energy, let alone emerge as an exporter, seemed far-fetched. … Petrobras was formed five decades ago largely as a trading company to import oil to support Brazil's growing economy. … Yet two years ago … Brazil reached its long-sought goal of energy self-sufficiency. …
International Herald Tribune, January 11, 2008
a. Describe Brazil's comparative advantage in producing oil and explain why its comparative advantage has changed.
b. Draw a graph to illustrate the Brazilian market for oil and explain why Brazil was an importer of oil until a few years ago.
c. Draw a graph to illustrate the Brazilian market for oil and explain why Brazil may become an exporter of oil in the near future.

3. Use the information on the U.S. wholesale market for roses in problem 1 to
a. Explain who gains and who loses from free international trade in roses compared to a situation in which Americans buy only roses grown in the United States.
b. Draw a graph to illustrate the gains and losses from free trade.
c. Calculate the gain from international trade.

4. **Postcard: Bangalore. Hearts Set on Joining the Global Economy, Indian IT Workers are Brushing up on Their Interpersonal Skills**

The huge number of Indian workers staffing the world's tech firms and call centers … possess cutting-edge technical knowledge, [but] their interpersonal and communication skills lag far behind. … Enter Bangalore's finishing schools.
Time, May 5, 2008
a. What comparative advantages does this news clip identify?
b. Using the information in this news clip, what services do you predict Bangalore (India) exports and what services do you predict it imports?
c. Who will gain and who will lose from the international trade that you described in your answer to b?

5. **Steel Tariffs Appear to Have Backfired on Bush**
President Bush set aside his free-trade principles last year and imposed heavy tariffs on imported steel to help out struggling mills in Pennsylvania

and West Virginia, two states crucial for his reelection. … Some economists say the tariffs may have cost more jobs than they saved, by driving up costs for automakers and other steel users. …

The Washington Post, September 19, 2003

a. Explain how a high tariff on steel imports can help domestic steel producers.

b. Explain how a high tariff on steel imports can harm steel users.

c. Draw a graph of the U.S. market for steel to show how a high tariff on steel imports

 i. Helps U.S. steel producers.

 ii. Harms U.S. steel users.

 iii. Creates a deadweight loss.

6. Use the information on the U.S. wholesale market for roses in problem 1.

a. If the United States puts a tariff of $25 per container on imports of roses, what happens to the U.S. price of roses, the quantity of roses bought, the quantity produced in the United States, and the quantity imported?

b. Who gains and who loses from this tariff?

c. Draw a graph to illustrate the gains and losses from the tariff and on the graph identify the gains and losses, the tariff revenue, and the deadweight loss.

7. Use the information on the U.S. wholesale market for roses in problem 1.

a. If the United States puts an import quota on roses of 5 million containers, what happens to the U.S. price of roses, the quantity of roses bought, the quantity produced in the United States, and the quantity imported?

b. Who gains and who loses from this quota?

c. Draw a graph to illustrate the gains and losses from the import quota and on the graph identify the gains and losses, the importers' profit, and the deadweight loss.

8. **Car Sales Go Up as Prices Tumble**

Car affordability [in Australia] is now at its best in 20 years, fueling a surge in sales as prices tumble. … [In 2000, Australia cut the tariff to 15 percent and] on January 1, 2005, the tariff on imported vehicles fell from 15 percent to 10 percent.

Courier Mail, February 26, 2005

a. Explain who gains and who loses from the lower tariff on imported cars.

b. Draw a graph to show how the price of a car, the quantity bought, the quantity produced in Australia, and imports of cars changed.

9. **Chinese Tire Maker Rejects U.S. Charge of Defects**

… regulators in the United States ordered the recall of more than 450,000 faulty tires . … The Chinese company that produced the tires … disputed the allegations Tuesday and hinted that the recall might be an effort by foreign competitors to hamper the company's exports to the United States. … Mounting scrutiny of Chinese-made goods has become a source of new trade frictions between the United States and China and fueled worries among regulators, corporations, and consumers about the risks associated with many products imported from China. …

International Herald Tribune, June 26, 2007

a. What does the information in the news clip imply about the comparative advantage of producing tires in the United States and China?

b. Could product quality be a valid argument against free trade?

c. How would the product-quality argument against free trade be open to abuse by domestic producers of the imported good?

10. **Why the World Can't Afford Food**

As [food] stocks dwindled, some countries placed export restrictions on food to protect their own supplies. This in turn drove up prices, punishing countries—especially poor ones—that depend on imports for much of their food.

Time, May 19, 2008

a. What are the benefits to a country from importing food?

b. What costs might arise from relying on imported food?

c. If a country restricts food exports, what effect does this restriction have in that country on

 i.   The price of food?

 ii. The quantity of food produced?

 iii. The quantity of food consumed?

 iv. The quantity of food exported?

d. Draw a graph of the market for food in a country that exports food. On the graph show how the price of food and the quantities of food consumed, produced, and exported change when food exports are restricted.

11. Suppose that the world price of sugar is 10 cents a pound, the United States does not trade internationally, and the equilibrium price of sugar in the United States is 20 cents a pound. The United States then begins to trade internationally.
    a. How does the price of sugar in the United States change?
    b. Do U.S. consumers buy more or less sugar?
    c. Do U.S. sugar growers produce more or less sugar?
    d. Does the United States export or import sugar and why?

12. Suppose that the world price of steel is $100 a ton, India does not trade internationally, and the equilibrium price of steel in India is $60 a ton. India then begins to trade internationally.
    a. How does the price of steel in India change?
    b. How does the quantity of steel produced in India change?
    c. How does the quantity of steel bought by India change?
    d. Does India export or import steel and why?

13. A semiconductor is a key component in your laptop, cell phone, and iPod. The table provides information about the market for semiconductors in the United States.

Price (dollars per unit)	Quantity demanded (billions of units per year)	Quantity supplied (billions of units per year)
10	25	0
12	20	20
14	15	40
16	10	60
18	5	80
20	0	100

Producers of semiconductors can get $18 a unit on the world market.
    a. With no international trade, what would be the price of a semiconductor and how many semiconductors a year would be bought and sold in the United States?
    b. At the price in your answer to a, does the United States have a comparative advantage in producing semiconductors?
    c. If U.S. producers of semiconductors sell at the highest possible price, how many do they sell in the United States and how many do they export?

14. **South Korea to Resume U.S. Beef Imports**
    South Korea will open its market to most U.S. beef. … South Korea banned imports of U.S. beef in 2003 amid concerns over a case of mad cow disease in the United States. The ban closed what was then the third-largest market for U.S. beef exporters. …
    CNN, May 29, 2008
    a. Which country, South Korea or the United States, has a comparative advantage in producing beef? What fact in the news clip did you use to answer this question?
    b. Explain how South Korea's import ban on U.S. beef affected beef producers and consumers in South Korea.
    c. Draw a graph of the market for beef in South Korea to illustrate your answer to b. Identify the changes in consumer surplus, producer surplus, and deadweight loss.
    d. Assuming that South Korea is the only importer of U.S. beef, explain how South Korea's import ban on U.S. beef affected beef producers and consumers in the United States.
    e. Draw a graph of the market for beef in the United States to illustrate your answer to d. Identify the changes in consumer surplus, producer surplus, and deadweight loss.

15. **Act Now, Eat Later**
    … looming hunger crisis in poor countries … has its roots in … misguided policy in the U.S. and Europe of subsidizing the diversion of food crops to produce biofuels like corn-based ethanol … [That is,] doling out subsidies to put the world's dinner into the gas tank.
    Time, May 5, 2008
    a. What is the effect on the world price of corn of the increased use of corn to produce ethanol in the United States and Europe?
    b. How does the change in the world price of corn affect the quantity of corn produced in a poor developing country with a comparative advantage in producing corn, the quantity it consumes, and the quantity that it either exports or imports?
    c. Draw a graph of the market for corn in a poor developing country to illustrate your answer to b. Identify the changes in consumer surplus, producer surplus, and deadweight loss.

16. Before 1995, trade between the United States and Mexico was subject to tariffs. In 1995, Mexico joined NAFTA and all U.S. and Mexican tariffs are gradually being removed.

    a. Explain how the price that U.S. consumers pay for goods from Mexico and the quantity of U.S. imports from Mexico have changed. Who are the winners and who are the losers from this free trade?

    b. Explain how the quantity of U.S. exports to Mexico and the U.S. government's tariff revenue from trade with Mexico have changed.

    c. Suppose that in 2008, tomato growers in Florida lobby the U.S. government to impose an import quota on Mexican tomatoes. Explain who in the United States would gain and who would lose from such a quota.

17. Suppose that in response to huge job losses in the U.S. textile industry, Congress imposes a 100 percent tariff on imports of textiles from China.

    a. Explain how the tariff on textiles will change the price that U.S. buyers pay for textiles, the quantity of textiles imported, and the quantity of textiles produced in the United States.

    b. Explain how the U.S. and Chinese gains from trade will change. Who in the United States will lose and who will gain?

18. With free trade between Australia and the United States, Australia would export beef to the United States. But the United States imposes an import quota on Australian beef.

    a. Explain how this quota influences the price that U.S. consumers pay for beef, the quantity of beef produced in the United States, and the U.S. and the Australian gains from trade.

    b. Explain who in the United States gains from the quota on beef imports and who loses.

19. **Aid May Grow for Laid-Off Workers**

    … the expansion of the Trade Adjustment Assistance (TAA) program would begin to reweave the social safety net for the 21st century, as advances permit more industries to take advantage of cheap foreign labor—even for skilled, white-collar work. By providing special compensation to more of globalization's losers and retraining them for stable jobs at home, … an expanded program could begin to ease the resentment and insecurity arising from the new economy.

    The Washington Post, July 23, 2007

    a. Why does the United States engage in international trade if it causes U.S. workers to lose their jobs?

    b. Explain how an expansion of the Trade Adjustment Assistance will make it easier for the United States to move toward freer international trade.

20. Study *Reading Between the Lines* on pp. 170–171 and answer the following questions.

    a. Who will gain and who will lose if the tariff is abolished?

    b. If Congress imposed an import quota on shoes, who would gain and who would lose?

21. **Trading Up**

    … the cost of protecting jobs in uncompetitive sectors through tariffs is foolishly high. …
    The Federal Reserve Bank of Dallas reported in 2002 that saving a job in the sugar industry cost American consumers $826,000 in higher prices a year, saving a dairy industry job cost $685,000 per year, and saving a job in the manufacturing of women's handbags cost $263,000.

    The New York Times, June 26, 2006

    a. What are the arguments for saving the jobs mentioned in this news clip?

    b. Explain why these arguments are faulty.

    c. Is there any merit to saving these jobs?

22. **Vows of New Aid to the Poor Leave the Poor Unimpressed**

    … the United States, the European Union, and Japan [plan] to eliminate duties and [import] quotas on almost all goods from up to 50 of the world's poor nations. … The proposal for duty-free, quota-free treatment is so divisive among developing countries that even some negotiators … are saying that the plan must be broadened.

    The New York Times, December 15, 2005

    a. Why do the United States, the European Union, and Japan want to eliminate trade barriers on imports from only the poorest countries?

    b. Who will win from the elimination of these trade barriers? Who will lose?

    c. Why is the plan divisive among developing countries?

8  Utility and Demand

After studying this chapter, you will be able to:

■ Describe preferences using the concept of utility, distinguish between total utility and marginal utility, and explain the marginal utility theory of consumer choice

■ Use marginal utility theory to predict the effects of changes in prices and incomes and to explain the paradox of value

■ Describe some new ways of explaining consumer choices

You want Coldplay's latest hit album, *Viva la Vida*,
and you want the Justin Timberlake and Madonna single, *Four Minutes*. Will you download the album and the single? Or will you buy two CDs? Or will you buy the album on a CD and download the single? What determines our choices as buyers of recorded music? And how much better off are we because we can download a song for 99 cents?

You know that diamonds are expensive and water is cheap. Doesn't that seem odd? Why do we place a higher value on useless diamonds than on essential-to-life water? You can think of many other examples of this paradox. For example, paramedics who save people's lives get paid a tiny fraction of what a National Hockey League player earns. Do we really place less value on the people who take care of the injured and the sick than we place on those who provide us with entertaining hockey games? *Reading Between the Lines* answers this question.

The theory of consumer choice that you're going to study in this chapter answers questions like the ones we've just posed. The main purpose of this theory is to explain the law of demand and the influences on buying plans. To explain the theory, we will study the choices of Lisa, a student who loves movies and has a thirst for soda. But the theory explains all choices including your choices in the market for recorded music as well as the paradox that the prices of water and diamonds are so out of proportion with their benefits.

181

Maximizing Utility

Your income and the prices that you face limit your consumption choices. You can buy only the things that you can afford. But you still have lots of choices. Of all the alternative combinations of goods and services that you can afford, what will you buy?

The economist's answer to this question is that you will buy the goods and services that maximize your utility. **Utility** is the benefit or satisfaction that a person gets from the consumption of goods and services. To understand how people's choices maximize utility, we distinguish between two concepts:

- Total utility
- Marginal utility

Total Utility

Total utility is the total benefit that a person gets from the consumption of all the different goods and services. Total utility depends on the level of consumption—more consumption generally gives more total utility.

To make the concept of total utility more concrete, think about the choices of Lisa, a student who spends all her income on two goods: movies and soda. We tell Lisa that we want to measure her utility from these two goods. We can use any scale that we wish to measure utility and give her two starting points: (1) we will call the total utility from no movies and no soda zero utility; and (2) we will call the total utility she gets from seeing 1 movie a month 50 units.

We then ask Lisa to tell us, using the same scale, how much she would like 2 movies, and more, up to 10 a month. We also ask her to tell us, on the same scale, how much she would like 1 case of soda a month, 2 cases, and more, up to 10 cases a month.

In Table 8.1, the columns headed "Total utility" show Lisa's answers. Looking at those numbers, you can say quite a lot about how much Lisa likes soda and movies. She says that 1 case of soda gives her 75 units of utility—50 percent more than the utility that she gets from seeing 1 movie.

But you can also see that her total utility from soda climbs more slowly than her total utility from movies. By the time she is buying 9 cases of soda and seeing 9 movies a month, she gets almost the same utility from each good. And at 10 of each, she gets

TABLE 8.1   Lisa's Utility from Movies and Soda

Movies			Soda		
Quantity (per month)	Total utility	Marginal utility	Cases (per month)	Total utility	Marginal utility
0	0		0	0	
		 50			 75
1	50		1	75	
		 40			 48
2	90		2	123	
		 32			 36
3	122		3	159	
		 28			 24
4	150		4	183	
		 26			 22
5	176		5	205	
		 24			 20
6	200		6	225	
		 22			 13
7	222		7	238	
		 20			 10
8	242		8	248	
		 17			 7
9	259		9	255	
		 16			 5
10	275		10	260	

more total utility from movies (275 units) than she gets from soda (260 units).

Marginal Utility

Marginal utility is the change in total utility that results from a one-unit increase in the quantity of a good consumed.

In Table 8.1, the columns headed "Marginal utility" show Lisa's marginal utility from movies and soda. You can see that if Lisa increases the soda she buys from 1 to 2 cases a month, her total utility from soda increases from 75 units to 123 units. For Lisa, the marginal utility from the second case each month is 48 units (123 − 75).

The marginal utility numbers appear midway between the quantities of soda because it is the *change* in the quantity she buys from 1 to 2 cases that produces the marginal utility of 48 units.

Marginal utility is *positive,* but it *diminishes* as the quantity consumed of a good increases.

Positive Marginal Utility All the things that people enjoy and want more of have a positive marginal utility. Some objects and activities can generate negative marginal utility—and lower total utility. Two examples are hard labor and polluted air. But the goods and services that people value and that we are thinking about here all have positive marginal utility: total utility increases as the quantity consumed increases.

Diminishing Marginal Utility As Lisa sees more movies, her total utility from movies increases but her marginal utility from movies decreases. Similarly, as she consumes more soda, her total utility from soda increases but her marginal utility from soda decreases.

The tendency for marginal utility to decrease as the consumption of a good increases is so general and universal that we give it the status of a *principle*—the principle of **diminishing marginal utility**.

You can see Lisa's diminishing marginal utility by calculating a few numbers. Her marginal utility from soda decreases from 75 units from the first case to 48 units from the second case and to 36 units from the third. Her marginal utility from movies decreases from 50 units for the first movie to 40 units for the second and 32 units for the third. Lisa's marginal utility diminishes as she buys more of each good.

You can confirm that the principle of diminishing marginal utility applies to your own utility by thinking about the following two situations: In one, you've been studying all through the day and evening, and you've been too busy finishing an assignment to go shopping. A friend drops by with a can of soda. The utility you get from that soda is the marginal utility from one can. In the second situation, you've been on a soda binge. You've been working on an assignment all day but you've guzzled ten cans of soda while doing so, and are now totally wired. You are happy enough to have one more can, but the thrill that you get from it is not very large. It is the marginal utility from the nineteenth can in a day.

Graphing Lisa's Utility Schedules

Figure 8.1(a) illustrates Lisa's total utility from soda. The more soda Lisa consumes in a month, the more total utility she gets. Her total utility curve slopes upward.

Figure 8.1(b) illustrates Lisa's marginal utility from soda. It is a graph of the marginal utility numbers in Table 8.1. This graph shows Lisa's diminishing marginal utility from soda. Her marginal utility curve slopes downward as she consumes more soda.

We've now described Lisa's preferences. Our next task is to see how she chooses what to consume to maximize her utility.

FIGURE 8.1 Total Utility and Marginal Utility

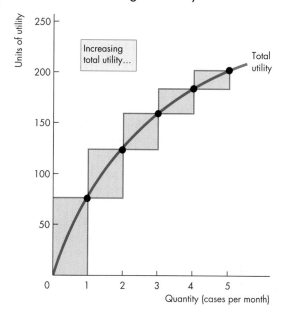

(a) Total utility

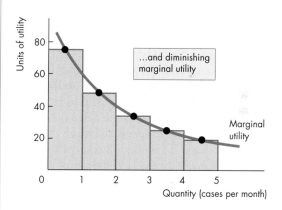

(b) Marginal utility

The figure graphs Lisa's total utility and marginal utility from soda based on the numbers for the first 5 cases of soda a month in Table 8.1. Part (a) shows that her total utility increases as her consumption of soda increases—increasing total utility. The bars along the total utility curve show the extra total utility from each additional case of soda—marginal utility. Part (b) shows that Lisa's marginal utility from soda diminishes as her consumption of soda increases—diminishing marginal utility. The bars that measure marginal utility get shorter as soda consumption increases.

myeconlab animation

The Utility-Maximizing Choice

Suppose that Lisa earns $40 a month and she spends it all on movies and soda. The prices that she faces are $8 for a movie and $4 for a case of soda.

Lisa's most direct way of finding the quantities of movies and soda that maximize her utility is to make a spreadsheet like Table 8.2.

The rows of the table show the combinations of movies and soda that Lisa can afford and that exhaust her $40 income. She can afford smaller quantities of movies and soda than those in the table, but smaller quantities don't maximize her utility. Why? Because her marginal utilities of movies and soda are positive, so the more of each that she buys, the more total utility she gets.

Table 8.2 shows the total utility that Lisa gets from the just-affordable quantities of movies and soda. The middle column adds the total utility from movies to the total utility from soda. This number, the total utility from movies *and* soda, is what Lisa wants to maximize.

In row *A*, Lisa watches no movies and buys 10 cases of soda. She gets no utility from movies and 260 units of utility from soda. Her total utility from movies and soda (the center column) is 260 units.

In row *C*, highlighted in the table, Lisa sees 2 movies and buys 6 cases of soda. She gets 90 units of utility from movies and 225 units of utility from soda. Her total utility from movies and soda is 315 units. This combination of movies and soda maximizes Lisa's total utility. This is the best Lisa can do, when she has only $40 to spend and given the prices of movies and cases. If Lisa buys 8 cases of soda, she can see only 1 movie. She gets 298 units of total utility, 17 less than the maximum attainable. If she sees 3 movies, she can buy only 4 cases of soda. She gets 305 units of total utility, 10 less than the maximum attainable.

We've just described Lisa's consumer equilibrium. A **consumer equilibrium** is a situation in which a consumer has allocated all of his or her available income in the way that maximizes his or her total utility, given the prices of goods and services. Lisa's consumer equilibrium is 2 movies and 6 cases of soda.

To find Lisa's consumer equilibrium, we measured her *total* utility from all the affordable combinations of movies and soda. But a simpler way of finding a consumer equilibrium uses the idea that choices are made at the margin—an idea that you first met in Chapter 1. Let's look at this approach.

TABLE 8.2 Lisa's Utility-Maximizing Combinations

	Movies $8		Total utility from movies and soda	Soda $4	
	Quantity (per month)	Total utility		Total utility	Cases (per month)
A	0	0	260	260	10
B	1	50	298	248	8
C	2	90	315	225	6
D	3	122	305	183	4
E	4	150	273	123	2
F	5	176	176	0	0

Choosing at the Margin

A consumer's total utility is maximized by following the rule:

- Spend all the available income
- Equalize the marginal utility per dollar for all goods

Spend All the Available Income Because more consumption brings more utility, only those choices that exhaust income can maximize utility. For Lisa, combinations of movies and soda that leave her with money to spend don't give her as much total utility as those that spend her entire income of $40 a month.

Equalize Marginal Utility per Dollar We've defined marginal utility as the increase in total utility from consuming *one more unit* of a good. **Marginal utility per dollar** is the marginal utility from a good obtained by spending *one more dollar* on that good.

The distinction between these two marginal concepts is clearest for a good that is infinitely divisible, such as gasoline. You can buy gasoline by the smallest fraction of a gallon and literally choose to spend one more or one less dollar at the pump. When you buy a movie ticket or a case of soda, you must spend your dollars in bigger lumps. But the principles that apply at the gas pump also apply at the movie house and the convenience store.

Let's see how this marginal approach works.

The Basic Idea The basic idea behind the utility maximizing rule is to move dollars from good *A* to good *B* if doing so increases the utility from good *A* by more than it decreases the utility from good *B*. Such a utility-increasing move is possible if the marginal utility per dollar from good *A* exceeds that from good *B*.

But buying more of good *A* decreases its marginal utility. And buying less of good *B* increases its marginal utility. So by moving dollars from good *A* to good *B*, total utility rises, but the gap between the marginal utilities per dollar gets smaller.

So long as a gap exists—so long as the marginal utility per dollar from good *A* exceeds that from good *B*, total utility can be increased by spending more on *A* and less on *B*. But when enough dollars have been moved from *B* to *A* to make the two marginal utilities per dollar equal, total utility cannot be increased further. Utility is maximized.

Lisa's Marginal Calculation Let's apply the basic idea to Lisa. To calculate Lisa's marginal utility per dollar, we divide her marginal utility numbers for each quantity of each good by the price of the good. Table 8.3 shows these calculations for Lisa. The rows of the table are affordable combinations of movies and soda.

Too Few Movies and Too Much Soda In row *B*, Lisa sees 1 movie a month and consumes 8 cases of soda a month. Her marginal utility from seeing 1 movie a month is 50 units. Because the price of a movie is $8, Lisa's marginal utility per dollar from movies is 50 units divided by $8, or 6.25 units of utility per dollar.

Lisa's marginal utility from soda when she consumes 8 cases of soda a month is 10 units. Because the price of soda is $4 a case, Lisa's marginal utility per dollar from soda is 10 units divided by $4, or 2.50 units of utility per dollar.

When Lisa consumes 1 movie and 8 cases of soda a month, her marginal utility per dollar from movies *exceeds* her marginal utility per dollar from soda. If Lisa spent an extra dollar on movies and a dollar less on soda, her total utility would increase. She would get 6.25 units from the extra dollar spent on movies and lose 2.50 units from the dollar less spent on soda. Her total utility would increase by 3.75 units (6.25 – 2.50).

But if Lisa sees more movies and consumes less soda, her marginal utility from movies falls and her marginal utility from soda rises.

TABLE 8.3 Equalizing Marginal Utilities per Dollar

	Movies ($8 each)			Soda ($4 per case)		
	Quantity	Marginal utility	Marginal utility per dollar	Cases	Marginal utility	Marginal utility per dollar
A	0	0		10	5	1.25
B	1	50	6.25	8	10	2.50
C	2	40	5.00	6	20	5.00
D	3	32	4.00	4	24	6.00
E	4	28	3.50	2	48	12.00
F	5	26	3.25	0	0	

Too Many Movies and Too Little Soda In row *D*, Lisa sees 3 movies a month and consumes 4 cases of soda. Her marginal utility from seeing the third movie a month is 32 units. At a price of $8 a movie, Lisa's marginal utility per dollar from movies is 32 units divided by $8, or 4 units of utility per dollar.

Lisa's marginal utility from soda when she buys 4 cases a month is 24 units. At a price of $4 a case, Lisa's marginal utility per dollar from soda is 24 units divided by $4, or 6 units of utility per dollar.

When Lisa sees 3 movies and consumes 4 cases of soda a month, her marginal utility from soda *exceeds* her marginal utility from movies. If Lisa spent an extra dollar on soda and a dollar less on movies, her total utility would increase. She would get 6 units from the extra dollar spent on soda and she lose 4 units from the dollar less spent on movies. Her total utility would increase by 2 units (6 – 4).

But if Lisa sees fewer movies and consumes more soda, her marginal utility from movies rises and her marginal utility from soda falls.

Utility-Maximizing Movies and Soda In Table 8.3, if Lisa moves from row *B* to row *C*, she increases the movies she sees from 1 to 2 a month and she decreases the soda she consumes from 8 to 6 cases a month. Her marginal utility per dollar from movies falls to 5 and her marginal utility per dollar from soda rises to 5.

Similarly, if Lisa moves from row *D* to row *C*, she

decreases the movies she sees from 3 to 2 a month and she increases the soda she consumes from 4 to 6 cases a month. Her marginal utility per dollar from movies rises to 5 and her marginal utility per dollar from soda falls to 5.

At this combination of movies and soda, Lisa is maximizing her utility. If she spent an extra dollar on movies and a dollar less on soda, or an extra dollar on soda and a dollar less on movies, her total utility would not change.

The Power of Marginal Analysis

The method we've just used to find Lisa's utility-maximizing choice of movies and soda is an example of the power of marginal analysis. Lisa doesn't need a computer and a spreadsheet program to maximize utility. She can achieve this goal by comparing the marginal gain from having more of one good with the marginal loss from having less of another good.

The rule that she follows is simple: If the marginal utility per dollar from movies exceeds the marginal utility per dollar from soda, see more movies and buy less soda; if the marginal utility per dollar from soda exceeds the marginal utility per dollar from movies, buy more soda and see fewer movies.

More generally, if the marginal gain from an action exceeds the marginal loss, take the action. You will meet this principle time and again in your study of economics, and you will find yourself using it when you make your own economic choices, especially when you must make big decisions.

Units of Utility In maximizing total utility by making the marginal utility per dollar equal for all goods, the units in which utility is measured do not matter. Any arbitrary units will work. In this respect, utility is like temperature. Predictions about the freezing point of water don't depend on the temperature scale; and predictions about a household's consumption choice don't depend on the units of utility.

When we introduced the idea of utility, we arbitrarily chose 50 units as Lisa's total utility from 1 movie. But we could have given her any number. And as you're now about to discover, we didn't even need to ask Lisa to tell us her preferences. We can figure out Lisa's preferences for ourselves by observing what she buys at various prices. To see how, we need to use a bit of math.

Call the marginal utility from movies MU_M and the price of a movie P_M. Then the marginal utility per dollar from movies is

$$MU_M/P_M.$$

Call the marginal utility from soda MU_S and the price of a case of soda P_S. Then the marginal utility per dollar from soda is

$$MU_S/P_S.$$

When Lisa maximizes utility,

$$MU_S/P_S = MU_M/P_M.$$

Multiply both sides of this equation by P_S to obtain

$$MU_S = MU_M \times P_S/P_M.$$

This equation says that the marginal utility from soda, MU_S, is equal to the marginal utility from movies, MU_M, multiplied by the ratio of the price of soda, P_S, to the price of a movie, P_M.

For Lisa, when $P_M = \$8$ and $P_S = \$4$ we observe that in a month she goes to the movies twice and buys 6 cases of soda. So we know that her MU_S from 6 cases of soda equals her MU_M from 2 movies multiplied by \$4/\$8 or 0.5. If we call MU_M from the second movie 40, then MU_S from the sixth case of soda is 20. If we observe enough prices and quantities, we can construct an entire utility schedule for an arbitrary starting value.

Review Quiz

1 What is utility and how do we use the concept of utility to describe a consumer's preferences?
2 What is the distinction between total utility and marginal utility?
3 What is the key assumption about marginal utility?
4 What two conditions are met when a consumer is maximizing utility?
5 Explain why equalizing the marginal utility per dollar from each good maximizes utility.

 Work Study Plan 8.1 and get instant feedback.

Predictions of Marginal Utility Theory

We're now going to use marginal utility theory to make some predictions. You will see that marginal utility theory predicts the law of demand. The theory also predicts that a fall in the price of a substitute of a good decreases the demand for the good and that for a normal good, a rise in income increases demand. All these effects, which in Chapter 3 we simply assumed, are predictions of marginal utility theory.

To derive these predictions, we will study the effects of three events:

- A fall in the price of a movie
- A rise in the price of soda
- A rise in income

A Fall in the Price of a Movie

With the price of a movie at $8 and the price of soda at $4, Lisa is maximizing utility by seeing 2 movies and buying 6 cases of soda each month. Then, with no change in her $40 income and no change in the price of soda, the price of a movie falls from $8 to $4. How does Lisa change her buying plans?

Finding the New Quantities of Movies and Soda

You can find the effect of a fall in the price of a movie on the quantities of movies and soda that Lisa buys in a three-step calculation.

1. Determine the just-affordable combinations of movies and soda at the new prices.
2. Calculate the new marginal utilities per dollar from the good whose price has changed.
3. Determine the quantities of movies and soda that make their marginal utilities per dollar equal.

Affordable Combinations The lower price of a movie means that Lisa can afford more movies or more soda. Table 8.4 shows her new affordable combinations. In row *A*, if she continues to see 2 movies a month, she can now afford 8 cases of soda and in row *B*, if she continues to buy 6 cases of soda, she can now afford 4 movies. Lisa can afford any of the combinations shown in the rows of Table 8.4.

The next step is to find her new marginal utilities per dollar from movies.

New Marginal Utilities per Dollar from Movies A person's preferences don't change just because a price has changed. With no change in her preferences, Lisa's marginal utilities in Table 8.4 are the same as those in Table 8.1. But because the price of a movie has changed, the marginal utility *per dollar* from movies changes. In fact, with a halving of the price from $8 to $4, the marginal utility per dollar from movies has doubled.

The numbers in Table 8.4 show Lisa's marginal utility per dollar from movies for each quantity of movies. The table also shows Lisa's marginal utility from soda for each quantity.

Equalizing the Marginal Utilities per Dollar You can see that if Lisa continues to see 2 movies a month (row *A*), her marginal utility per dollar from movies is 10 units and if Lisa continues to buy 6 cases of soda (row *B*), her marginal utility per dollar from soda is only 5 units. Lisa is buying too much soda and too few movies. If she spends a dollar more on movies and a dollar less on soda, her total utility increases by 5 units (10 – 5).

You can also see that if Lisa continues to buy 6 cases of soda and sees 4 movies (row *B*), her marginal

TABLE 8.4 How a Change in the Price of Movies Affects Lisa's Choices

	Movies ($4 each)			Soda ($4 per case)		
	Quantity	Marginal utility	Marginal utility per dollar	Cases	Marginal utility	Marginal utility per dollar
	0	0		10	5	1.25
	1	50	12.50	9	7	1.75
A	2	40	**10.00**	8	10	2.50
	3	32	8.00	7	13	3.25
B	4	28	7.00	**6**	20	**5.00**
	5	26	6.50	5	22	5.50
C	6	24	6.00	4	24	6.00
	7	22	5.50	3	36	9.00
	8	20	5.00	2	48	12.00
	9	17	4.25	1	75	18.75
	10	16	4.00	0	0	

utility per dollar from movies is 7 units and her marginal utility per dollar from soda is only 5 units. Lisa is still buying too much soda and seeing too few movies. If she spends a dollar more on movies and a dollar less on soda, her total utility increases by 2 units (7 – 5).

But if Lisa sees 6 movies and buys 4 cases of soda a month (row C), her marginal utility per dollar from movies (6 units) equals her marginal utility per dollar from soda. If Lisa moves from this allocation of her budget, her total utility decreases. She is maximizing utility.

Lisa's increased purchases of movies results from a substitution effect—she substitutes the now lower-priced movies for soda—and an income effect—she can afford more movies.

A Change in the Quantity Demanded Lisa's increase in the quantity of movies that she sees is a change in the quantity demanded. It is the change in the quantity of movies that she plans to see each month when the price of a movie changes and all other influences on buying plans remain the same. We illustrate a change in the quantity demanded by a movement along a demand curve.

Figure 8.2(a) shows Lisa's demand curve for movies. When the price of a movie is $8, Lisa sees 2 movies a month. And when the price of a movie falls to $4, she sees 6 movies a month. Lisa moves downward along her demand curve for movies.

The demand curve traces the quantities that maximize utility at each price, with all other influences remaining the same. You can also see that utility-maximizing choices generate a downward-sloping demand curve. Utility maximization with diminishing marginal utility implies the law of demand.

A Change in Demand Lisa's decrease in the quantity of soda that she buys is the change in the quantity of soda that she plans to buy each month at a given price of soda when the price of a movie changes. It is a change in her demand for soda. We illustrate a change in demand by a shift of a demand curve.

Figure 8.2(b) shows Lisa's demand for soda. The price of soda is fixed at $4 a case. When the price of a movie is $8, Lisa buys 6 cases of soda on demand curve D_0. When the price of a movie falls to $4, Lisa buys 4 cases of soda on demand curve D_1. The fall in the price of a movie decreases Lisa's demand for soda. Her demand curve for soda shifts leftward. For Lisa, soda and movies are substitutes.

FIGURE 8.2   A Fall in the Price of a Movie

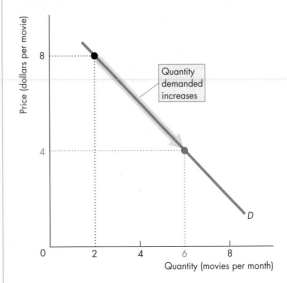

(a) Demand for movies

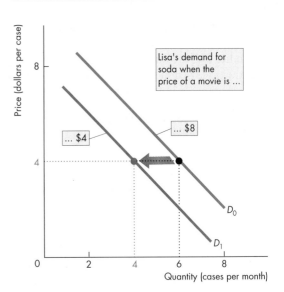

(b) Demand for soda

When the price of a movie falls and the price of soda remains the same, the quantity of movies demanded by Lisa increases, and in part (a), Lisa moves along her demand curve for movies. Also, when the price of a movie falls, Lisa's demand for soda decreases, and in part (b), her demand curve for soda shifts leftward. For Lisa, soda and movies are substitutes.

myeconlab   animation

A Rise in the Price of Soda

Now suppose that with the price of a movie at $4, the price of soda rises from $4 to $8 a case. How does this price change influence Lisa's buying plans? We find the answer by repeating the three-step calculation with the new price of soda.

Table 8.5 shows Lisa's new affordable combinations. In row *A*, if she continues to buy 4 cases of soda a month she can afford to see only 2 movies; and in row *B*, if she continues to see 6 movies a month, she can afford only 2 cases of soda.

Table 8.5 show Lisa's marginal utility per dollar from soda for each quantity of soda when the price is $8 a case. The table also shows Lisa's marginal utility per dollar from movies for each quantity.

If Lisa continues to buy 4 cases of soda a month (row *A*), her marginal utility per dollar from soda is 3. But she must cut her movies to 2 a month, which gives her 12 units of utility per dollar from movies. Lisa is buying too much soda and too few movies. If she spends a dollar less on soda and a dollar more on movies, her utility increases by 9 units (12 − 3) .

But if Lisa sees 6 movies a month and cuts her soda back to 2 cases (row *B*), her marginal utility per dollar from movies (6 units) equals her marginal utility per dollar from soda. She is maximizing utility.

Lisa's decreased purchases of soda results from an income effect—she can afford fewer cases and she buys fewer cases. But she continues to buy the same quantity of movies.

Lisa's Demand for Soda Now that we've calculated the effect of a change in the price of soda on Lisa's buying plans, we have found two points on her demand curve for soda: When the price of soda is $4 a case, Lisa buys 4 cases a month; and when the price rises to $8 a case, she buys 2 cases a month.

Figure 8.3 shows these points on Lisa's demand curve for soda. It also shows the change in the quantity of soda demanded when the price of soda rises and all other influences on Lisa's buying plans remain the same.

In this particular case, Lisa continues to buy the same quantity of movies. This outcome does not always occur. It is a consequence of Lisa's utility schedule. With different marginal utilities, she might have decreased or increased the quantity of movies that she sees when the price of soda changes.

You've seen that marginal utility theory predicts the law of demand—the way in which the quantity demanded of a good changes when its price changes. Next we'll see how marginal utility theory predicts the effect of a change in income on demand.

TABLE 8.5   How a Change in the Price of Soda Affects Lisa's Choices

	Movies ($4 each)			Soda ($8 per case)		
	Quantity	Marginal utility	Marginal utility per dollar	Cases	Marginal utility	Marginal utility per dollar
	0	0		5	22	2.75
A	2	40	12.00	**4**	24	**3.00**
	4	28	7.00	3	36	4.50
B	6	24	6.00	2	48	6.00
	8	20	5.00	1	75	9.38
	10	16	4.00	0	0	

FIGURE 8.3   A Rise in the Price of Soda

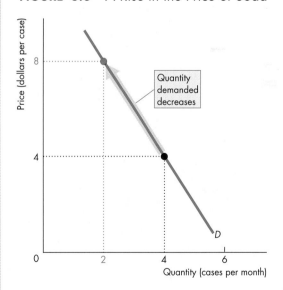

When the price of soda rises and the price of a movie and Lisa's income remain the same, the quantity of soda demanded by Lisa decreases. Lisa moves along her demand curve for soda.

myeconlab animation

A Rise in Income

Suppose that Lisa's income increases from $40 to $56 a month and that the price of a movie is $4 and the price of a case of soda is $4. With these prices and with an income of $40 a month, Lisa sees 6 movies and buys 4 cases of soda a month (Table 8.4). How does the increase in Lisa's income from $40 to $56 change her buying plans?

Table 8.6 shows the calculations needed to answer this question. If Lisa continues to see 6 movies a month, she can now afford to buy 8 cases of soda (row A); and if she continues to buy 4 cases of soda, she can now afford to see 10 movies (row C).

In row A, Lisa's marginal utility per dollar from movies is greater than her marginal utility per dollar from soda. She is buying too much soda and too few movies. In row C, Lisa's marginal utility per dollar from movies is less than her marginal utility per dollar from soda. She is buying too little soda and too many movies. But in row B, when Lisa sees 8 movies a month and buys 6 cases of soda, her marginal utility per dollar from movies equals that from soda. She is maximizing utility.

Figure 8.4 shows the effects of the rise in Lisa's income on her demand curves for movies and soda. The price of each good is $4. When Lisa's income

rises to $56 a month, she sees 2 more movies and buys 2 more cases of soda. Her demand curves for both movies and soda shift rightward—her demand for both movies and soda increases. With a larger income, the consumer always buys more of a *normal* good. For Lisa, movies and soda are normal goods.

TABLE 8.6   Lisa's Choices with an Income of $56 a Month

	Movies ($4 each)			Soda ($4 per case)		
	Quantity	Marginal utility	Marginal utility per dollar	Cases	Marginal utility	Marginal utility per dollar
	4	28	7.00	10	5	1.25
	5	26	6.50	9	7	1.75
A	6	24	**6.00**	8	10	2.50
	7	22	5.50	7	13	3.25
B	8	20	5.00	6	20	5.00
	9	17	4.25	5	22	5.50
C	10	16	4.00	**4**	24	**6.00**

FIGURE 8.4   The Effects of a Rise in Income

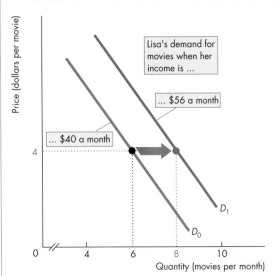

(a) Demand for movies

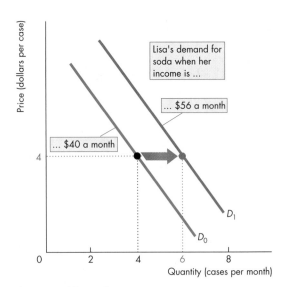

(b) Demand for soda

When Lisa's income increases, her demand for movies and her demand for soda increase. Lisa's demand curves for movies, in part (a), and for soda, in part (b), shift rightward. For Lisa, movies and soda are normal goods.

The Paradox of Value

The price of water is low and the price of a diamond is high, but water is essential to life while diamonds are used mostly just for decoration. How can valuable water be so cheap while a relatively useless diamond is so expensive? This so-called *paradox of value* has puzzled philosophers for centuries. Not until the theory of marginal utility had been developed could anyone give a satisfactory answer.

The Paradox Resolved The paradox is resolved by distinguishing between *total* utility and *marginal* utility. The total utility that we get from water is enormous. But remember, the more we consume of something, the smaller is its marginal utility.

We use so much water that its marginal utility—the benefit we get from one more glass of water or another 30 seconds in the shower—diminishes to a small value.

Diamonds, on the other hand, have a small total utility relative to water, but because we buy few diamonds, they have a high marginal utility.

When a household has maximized its total utility, it has allocated its income in the way that makes the marginal utility per dollar equal for all goods. That is, the marginal utility from a good divided by the price of the good is equal for all goods.

This equality of marginal utilities per dollar holds true for diamonds and water: Diamonds have a high price and a high marginal utility. Water has a low price and a low marginal utility. When the high marginal utility from diamonds is divided by the high price of a diamond, the result is a number that equals the low marginal utility from water divided by the low price of water. The marginal utility per dollar is the same for diamonds and water.

Value and Consumer Surplus Another way to think about the paradox of value and illustrate how it is resolved uses *consumer surplus*. Figure 8.5 explains the paradox of value by using this idea. The supply of water in part (a) is perfectly elastic at price P_W, so the quantity of water consumed is Q_W and the consumer surplus from water is the large green area. The supply of diamonds in part (b) is perfectly inelastic at the quantity Q_D, so the price of a diamond is P_D and the consumer surplus from diamonds is the small green area. Water is cheap but brings a large consumer surplus, while diamonds are expensive but bring a small consumer surplus.

FIGURE 8.5   The Paradox of Value

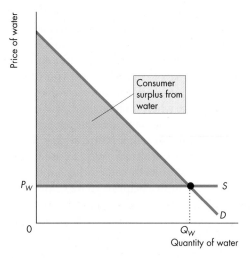

(a) Water

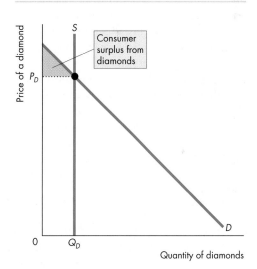

(b) Diamonds

Part (a) shows the demand for and supply of water. Supply is perfectly elastic at the price P_W. At this price, the quantity of water consumed is Q_W and consumer surplus is the large green triangle. Part (b) shows the demand for and supply of diamonds. Supply is perfectly inelastic at the quantity Q_D. At this quantity, the price of a diamond is P_D and consumer surplus is the small green triangle. Water is valuable—has a large consumer surplus—but cheap. Diamonds are less valuable than water—have a smaller consumer surplus—but are expensive.

myeconlab   animation

Temperature: An Analogy

Utility is similar to temperature. Both are abstract concepts, and both have units of measurement that are arbitrary. You can't *observe* temperature. You can observe water turning to steam if it is hot enough or turning to ice if it is cold enough. And you can construct an instrument—a thermometer—that can help you to predict when such changes will occur. We call the scale on the thermometer *temperature* and we call the units of temperature *degrees*. But these degree units are arbitrary. We can use Celsius units or Fahrenheit units or some other units.

The concept of utility helps us to make predictions about consumption choices in much the same way that the concept of temperature helps us to make predictions about physical phenomena.

Admittedly, marginal utility theory does not enable us to predict how buying plans change with the same precision that a thermometer enables us to predict when water will turn to ice or steam. But the theory provides important insights into buying plans and has some powerful implications. It helps us to understand why people buy more of a good or service when its price falls and why people buy more of most goods when their incomes increase. It also resolves the paradox of value.

We're going to end this chapter by looking at some new ways of studying individual economic choices and consumer behavior.

Review Quiz

1 When the price of a good falls and the prices of other goods and a consumer's income remain the same, what happens to the consumption of the good whose price has fallen and to the consumption of other goods?

2 Elaborate on your answer to the previous question by using demand curves. For which good does demand change and for which good does the quantity demanded change?

3 If a consumer's income increases and if all goods are normal goods, how does the quantity bought of each good change?

4 What is the paradox of value and how is the paradox resolved?

5 What are the similarities between utility and temperature?

myeconlab   Work Study Plan 8.2
and get instant feedback.

Maximizing Utility in Markets for Recorded Music

Downloads Versus Discs

In 2007, Americans spent $10 billion on recorded music, down from $14 billion in 2000. But the combined quantity of discs and downloads bought increased from 1 billion in 2000 to 1.8 billion in 2007 and the average price of a unit of recorded music fell from $14 to $5.50.

The average price fell because the mix of formats bought changed dramatically. In 2000, we bought 1 billion CDs; in 2007, we bought only 0.5 billion CDs and downloaded 1.3 billion music files.

Figure 1 shows the longer history of the changing formats of recorded music.

The music that we buy isn't just one good—it is several goods. Singles and albums are different goods; downloads and discs are different goods; and downloads to a computer and downloads to a cell phone are different goods. There are five major categories (excluding DVDs and cassettes) and the table shows the quantities of each that we bought in 2007.

Format	Singles	Albums
	(millions in 2007)	
Disc	3	500
Download	800	40
Mobile	400	–

Source of data: Recording Industry Association of America.

Most people buy all their music in digital form, but many still buy physical CDs and some people buy both downloads and CDs.

We get utility from the singles and albums that we buy, and the more songs and albums we have, the more utility we get. But our marginal utility from songs and albums decreases as the quantity that we own increases.

We also get utility from convenience. A song that we can buy with a mouse click and play with the spin of a wheel is more convenient both to buy and to use than a song on a CD. The convenience of songs downloaded over the Internet means that, song for song, we get more utility from songs in this format than we get from physical CDs.

But most albums are still played at home on a CD player. So for most people, a physical CD is a more convenient medium for delivering an album. Album

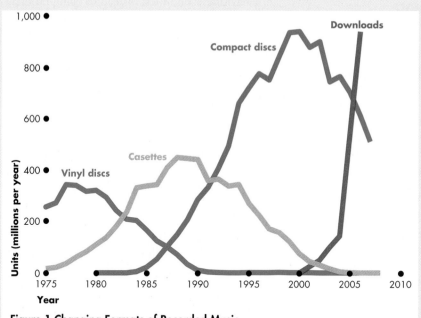

Figure 1 Changing Formats of Recorded Music

Source of data: www.swivel.com.

In the 1970s, recorded music came on vinyl discs. Cassettes gradually replaced vinyl, then compact discs gradually replaced cassettes, and today, digital files downloaded to computers and mobile devices are replacing physical CDs.

for album, people on average get more utility from a CD than from a download.

When we decide how many singles and albums to download and how many to buy on CD, we compare the marginal utility per dollar from each type of music in each format. We make the marginal utility per dollar from each type of music in each format equal, as the equations below show.

The market for single downloads has created an enormous consumer surplus. The table shows that the quantity of single downloads demanded at 99 cents each was 800 million in 2007, and the quantity of singles on a disc demanded at $4.75 a disc was 3 million in 2007. If we assume that $4.75 is the most that anyone would pay for a single download (probably an underestimate), the demand curve for single downloads is that shown in Fig. 2.

With the price of a single download at $0.99, consumer surplus (the area of the green triangle) is $1.5 billion.

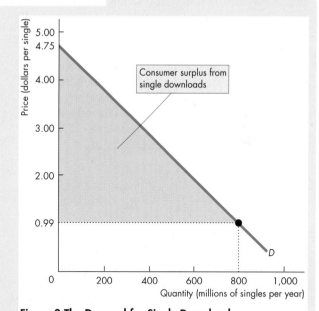

Figure 2 The Demand for Single Downloads

$$\frac{MU_{single\ downloads}}{P_{single\ downloads}} = \frac{MU_{album\ downloads}}{P_{album\ downloads}} = \frac{MU_{physical\ singles}}{P_{physical\ singles}} = \frac{MU_{physical\ albums}}{P_{physical\ albums}} = \frac{MU_{mobile}}{P_{mobile}}$$

$$\frac{MU_{single\ downloads}}{\$0.99} = \frac{MU_{album\ downloads}}{\$10} = \frac{MU_{physical\ singles}}{\$4.75} = \frac{MU_{physical\ albums}}{\$15} = \frac{MU_{mobile}}{\$2.50}$$

◆ New Ways of Explaining Consumer Choices

When William Stanley Jevons developed marginal utility theory in the 1860s, he would have loved to look inside people's brains and "see" their utility. But he believed that the human brain was the ultimate black box that could never be observed directly. For Jevons, and for most economists today, the purpose of marginal utility theory is to explain our *actions*, not what goes on inside our brains.

Economics has developed over the past 150 years with little help from and paying little attention to advances being made in psychology. Both economics and psychology seek to explain human behavior, but they have developed different ways of attacking the challenge.

A few researchers *have* paid attention to the potential payoff from exploring economic problems by using the tools of psychology. These researchers, some economists and some psychologists, think that marginal utility theory is based on a view of how people make choices that attributes too much to reason and rationality. They propose an alternative approach based on the methods of psychology.

Other researchers, some economists and some neuroscientists, are using new tools to look inside the human brain and open up Jevons' "black box."

This section provides a very brief introduction to these new and exciting areas of economics. We'll explore the two related research agendas:

- Behavioral economics
- Neuroeconomics

Behavioral Economics

Behavioral economics studies the ways in which limits on the human brain's ability to compute and implement rational decisions influences economic behavior—both the decisions that people make and the consequences of those decisions for the way markets work.

Behavioral economics starts with observed behavior. It looks for anomalies—choices that do not seem to be rational. It then tries to account for the anomalies by using ideas developed by psychologists that emphasize features of the human brain that limit rational choice.

In behavioral economics, instead of being rational utility maximizers, people are assumed to have three impediments that prevent rational choice: bounded rationality, bounded willpower, and bounded self-interest.

Bounded Rationality Bounded rationality is rationality that is limited by the computing power of the human brain. We can't always work out the rational choice.

For Lisa, choosing between movies and soda, it seems unlikely that she would have much trouble figuring out what to buy. But toss Lisa some uncertainty and the task becomes harder. She's read the reviews of "Mamma Mia!" on Fandango, but does she really want to see that movie? How much marginal utility will it give her? Faced with uncertainty, people might use rules of thumb, listen to the views of others, and make decisions based on gut instinct rather than on rational calculation.

Bounded Willpower Bounded willpower is the less-than-perfect willpower that prevents us from making a decision that we know, at the time of implementing the decision, we will later regret.

Lisa might be feeling particularly thirsty when she passes a soda vending machine. Under Lisa's rational utility-maximizing plan, she buys her soda at the discount store, where she gets it for the lowest possible price. Lisa has already bought her soda for this month, but it is at home. Spending $1 on a can now means giving up a movie later this month.

Lisa's rational choice is to ignore the temporary thirst and stick to her plan. But she might not possess the will power to do so—sometimes she will and sometimes she won't.

Bounded Self-Interest Bounded self-interest is the limited self-interest that results in sometimes suppressing our own interests to help others.

A hurricane hits the Florida coast and Lisa, feeling sorry for the victims, donates $10 to a fund-raiser. She now has only $30 to spend on movies and soda this month. The quantities that she buys are not, according to her utility schedule, the ones that maximize her utility.

The main applications of behavioral economics are in two areas: finance, where uncertainty is a key factor in decision making, and savings, where the future is a key factor.

But one behavior observed by behavioral economists is more general and might affect your choices. It is called the endowment effect.

The Endowment Effect The endowment effect is the tendency for people to value something more highly simply because they own it. If you have allocated your income to maximize utility, the price you are willing to pay for a coffee mug should be the same as the price you would be willing to accept to give up an identical coffee mug that you own.

In experiments, students seem to display the endowment effect: The price they are willing to pay for a coffee mug is less than the price they would be willing to accept to give up an identical coffee mug that they own. Behavioral economists say that this behavior contradicts marginal utility theory.

Neuroeconomics

Neuroeconomics is the study of the activity of the human brain when a person makes an economic decision. The discipline uses the observational tools and ideas of neuroscience to better understand economic decisions.

Neuroeconomics is an experimental discipline. In an experiment, a person makes an economic decision and the electrical or chemical activity of the person's brain is observed and recorded using the same type of equipment that neurosurgeons use to diagnose brain disorders.

The observations provide information about which regions of the brain are active at different points in the process of making an economic decision.

It has been observed that some economic decisions generate activity in the area of the brain (called the prefrontal cortex) where we store memories, analyze data, and anticipate the consequences of our actions. If people make rational utility-maximizing decisions, it is in this region of the brain that the decision occurs.

But some economic decisions generate activity in the region of the brain (called the hippocampus) where we store memories of anxiety and fear. Decisions that are influenced by activity in this part of the brain might be non-rational and driven by fear or panic.

Neuroeconomists are also able to observe the amount of a brain hormone (called dopamine), the quantity of which increases in response to pleasurable events and decreases in response to disappointing events. These observations might one day enable neuroeconomists to actually measure utility and shine a bright light inside what was once believed to be the ultimate black box.

Controversy

The new ways of studying consumer choice that we've briefly described here are being used more widely to study business decisions and decisions in financial markets, and this type of research is surely going to become more popular.

But behavioral economics and neuroeconomics generate controversy. Most economists hold the view of Jevons that the goal of economics is to explain the decisions that we observe people make, and not to explain what goes on inside people's heads.

Also, most economists would prefer to probe apparent anomalies more deeply and figure out why they are not anomalies after all.

Finally, economists point to the power of marginal utility theory and its ability to explain consumer choice and demand as well as resolve the paradox of value.

Review Quiz

1 Define behavioral economics.
2 What are the three limitations on human rationality that behavioral economics emphasizes?
3 Define neuroeconomics.
4 What do behavioral economics and neuroeconomics seek to achieve?

 Work Study Plan 8.3 and get instant feedback.

◆ You have now completed your study of the marginal utility theory and some new ideas about how people make economic choices. You can see marginal utility theory in action once again in *Reading Between the Lines* on pp. 196–197, where it is used to explain why paramedics who save people's lives earn so much less than hockey players who merely provide entertainment.

A Paradox of Value: Paramedics and Hockey Players

Salaries, Strong Recruitment Ease Area Paramedic Shortage

April 4, 2008

To curb a critical shortage, fire departments across the Washington region have pursued paramedics like star athletes in recent years, enticing them with signing bonuses, handsome salaries and the promise of fast-track career paths.

Montgomery County hired a marketing expert and launched a national recruiting drive, reaching out in particular to women and minorities. Fairfax County offered top starting salaries, now totaling about $57,000—as much as 50 percent higher than some other local jurisdictions, though Fairfax paramedics generally work longer hours. ...

Ducks Give Perry $26.6 Million Deal

July 2, 2008

The Ducks' first free-agent signing might also be their last, their biggest and their most expected.

Within the first hour of the NHL's free agency period, Corey Perry signed a five-year, $26.625 million contract that will keep the 23-year-old in Anaheim until 2013. Both parties had expressed an interest in completing the deal for several months but it wasn't possible until Tuesday, when the Ducks had enough room for long-term contracts under the salary cap.

"I really wanted to stay in Anaheim," Perry said. "It's home now and I didn't want to leave here. It's a great place to play hockey and it just shows how well the organization is run."

Including an $8 million signing bonus spread over its duration, the contract will pay Perry $4.5 million in 2008–09, then $6.5 million, $5.375 million, $5.375 million and $4.875 million, respectively, over the final four years. ...

Essence of the Stories

- In Washington, the starting salary for a paramedic is $57,000 per year.
- Corey Perry has a 5-year contract with the Anaheim Ducks that will earn him $26.6 million.

Economic Analysis

- If resources are used efficiently, the marginal utility per dollar from the services of a paramedic, MU_P/P_P, equals the marginal utility per dollar from the services of a hockey player, MU_H/P_H. That is,

$$\frac{MU_P}{P_P} = \frac{MU_H}{P_H}.$$

- A paramedic in Washington earns $57,000 a year, but the national average paramedic wage is $27,000 a year.

- Corey Perry earns $26.6 million over 5 years, or $5.32 million a year on average.

- If we put these numbers into the above formula, we get

$$\frac{MU_P}{\$27,000} = \frac{MU_H}{\$5,320,000}.$$

Equivalently,

$$\frac{MU_H}{MU_P} = 197.$$

- Is the marginal utility from Corey Perry's services really 197 times that from the paramedic's services?

- The answer is no. A paramedic might serve about 8 people a day, or perhaps 2,000 in a year; a hockey player like Corey Perry serves millions of people a year.

- If a paramedic serves 2,000 people a year, then the price of a paramedic's service per customer served is $27,000/2,000, which equals $13.50.

- If Corey Perry serves 1,000,000 people a year, then the price of Corey Perry's service per customer served is $5,320,000/1,000,000, which equals $5.32.

- Using these prices of the services per customer, a paramedic is worth 2.5 times as much as a hockey player—the marginal utility from the services of a paramedic is 2.5 times that from a hockey player.

- Figure 1 shows the market for paramedics. The equilibrium quantity is 200,000 workers, and the average wage rate is $27,000 a year.

- Figure 2 shows the market for professional hockey players. The equilibrium quantity is 500 players and the aver-

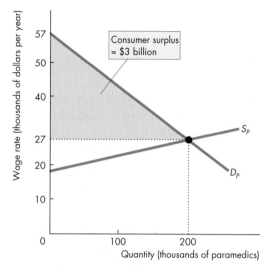

Figure 1 The value of paramedics

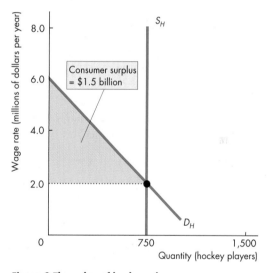

Figure 2 The value of hockey players

age wage rate is $4,000,000 a year. (Corey Perry earns more than the average player.)

- Not only is the marginal utility from a paramedic greater than that from a hockey player, but paramedics also create a greater consumer surplus.

197

SUMMARY

Key Points

Maximizing Utility (pp. 182–186)

- A household's preferences can be described by a utility schedule that lists the total utility and marginal utility derived from various quantities of goods and services consumed.
- The principle of diminishing marginal utility is that the marginal utility from a good or service decreases as consumption of the good or service increases.
- Total utility is maximized when all the available income is spent and when the marginal utility per dollar from all goods is equal.
- If the marginal utility per dollar for good *A* exceeds that for good *B*, total utility increases if the quantity purchased of good *A* increases and the quantity purchased of good *B* decreases.

Predictions of Marginal Utility Theory (pp. 187–193)

- Marginal utility theory predicts the law of demand. That is, other things remaining the same, the higher the price of a good, the smaller is the quantity demanded of that good.
- Marginal utility theory also predicts that, other things remaining the same, the larger the consumer's income, the larger is the quantity demanded of a normal good.
- Marginal utility theory resolves the paradox of value.
- Total value is *total* utility or consumer surplus. But price is related to *marginal* utility.
- Water, which we consume in large amounts, has a high total utility and a large consumer surplus, but the price of water is low and the marginal utility from water is low.
- Diamonds, which we buy in small quantities, have a low total utility and a small consumer surplus, but the price of a diamond is high and the marginal utility from diamonds is high.

New Ways of Explaining Consumer Choices (pp. 194–195)

- Behavioral economics studies limits on the ability of the human brain to compute and implement rational decisions.
- Bounded rationality, bounded willpower, and bounded self-interest are believed to explain some choices.
- Neuroeconomics uses the ideas and tools of neuroscience to study the effects of economic events and choices inside the human brain.

Key Figures

Figure 8.1   Total Utility and Marginal Utility, 183
Figure 8.2   A Fall in the Price of a Movie, 188
Figure 8.3   A Rise in the Price of Soda, 189
Figure 8.4   The Effects of a Rise in Income, 190
Figure 8.5   The Paradox of Value, 191

Key Terms

Behavioral economics, 194
Consumer equilibrium, 184
Diminishing marginal utility, 183
Marginal utility, 182
Marginal utility per dollar, 184
Neuroeconomics, 195
Total utility, 182
Utility, 182

PROBLEMS and APPLICATIONS

myeconlab Work problems 1–10 in Chapter 8 Study Plan and get instant feedback.
Work problems 11–21 as Homework, a Quiz, or a Test if assigned by your instructor.

1. Max enjoys windsurfing and snorkeling. The table shows the total utility he gets from each activity.

Hours per day	Total utility from windsurfing	Total utility from snorkeling
1	120	40
2	220	76
3	300	106
4	360	128
5	396	140
6	412	150
7	422	158

   a. Find Max's marginal utility from windsurfing at each number of hours per day.
   b. Find Max's marginal utility from snorkeling at each number of hours per day.
   c. Do Max's marginal utility from windsurfing and from snorkeling obey the principle of diminishing marginal utility?
   d. Which does Max enjoy more: his 6th hour of windsurfing or his 6th hour of snorkeling?

2. Max in problem 1 has $35 a day to spend, and he can spend as much time as he likes on his leisure pursuits. Windsurfing equipment rents for $10 an hour, and snorkeling equipment rents for $5 an hour.
   a. Make a table that shows the various combinations of hours spent windsurfing and snorkeling that Max can afford.
   b. In your table, add two columns and list Max's marginal utility per dollar from windsurfing and from snorkeling.
   c. How long does Max spend windsurfing and how long does he spend snorkeling to maximize his total utility?
   d. If compared to c, Max spent a dollar more on windsurfing and a dollar less on snorkeling, by how much would his total utility change?
   e. If compared to c, Max spent a dollar less on windsurfing and a dollar more on snorkeling, by how much would his total utility change?
   f. Explain why, if Max equalized the marginal utility per hour from windsurfing and from snorkeling, he would *not* maximize his utility.

3. Max in problems 1 and 2 is offered a special deal on windsurfing equipment: a rental rate of $5 an hour. His income remains at $35 a day and the rental price of snorkeling equipment remains at $5 an hour.
   a. Make a table that shows the new combinations of hours spent windsurfing and snorkeling that Max can afford.
   b. In your table, list Max's marginal utilities per dollar from windsurfing and snorkeling.
   c. How many hours does Max now spend windsurfing and how many hours does he spend snorkeling?

4. Given the information about Max in problems 1, 2, and 3,
   a. Find two points on Max's demand curve for rented windsurfing equipment.
   b. Draw Max's demand curve for rented windsurfing equipment.
   c. Is Max's demand for renting windsurfing equipment elastic or inelastic?

5. Max, with the utility schedules in problem 1, gets an increase in income from $35 to $55 a day. Windsurfing equipment rents for $10 an hour, and snorkeling equipment rents for $5 an hour. Show the effect of the increase in Max's income on Max's demand curve for
   a. Rented windsurfing equipment, and explain whether, for Max, windsurfing equipment is a normal good or an inferior good.
   b. Rented snorkeling equipment, and explain whether, for Max, snorkeling equipment is a normal good or an inferior good.

6. **Schools Get a Lesson in Lunch Line Economics**
   Sharp rises in the cost of milk, grain, and fresh fruits and vegetables are hitting cafeterias across the country, forcing cash-strapped schools to raise prices or pinch pennies by serving more economical dishes. ... Fairfax schools, for instance, serve oranges—14 cents each—instead of grapes, which are a quarter a serving.
   The Washington Post, April 14, 2008
   Assume that a Fairfax school has a $14 daily fruit budget.
   a. How many oranges a day can the school afford to serve if it serves no grapes?

b. How many servings of grapes can the school afford each day if it serves no oranges?

c. If the school provides 50 oranges a day and maximizes utility, how many servings of grapes does it provide?

d. If the marginal utility from an orange is 14 units of utility, what is the marginal utility from a serving of grapes?

7. **Can Money Buy Happiness?**

"Whoever said money can't buy happiness isn't spending it right."... You know that there must be some connection between money and happiness. If there weren't, you'd be less likely to stay late at work (or even come in at all). ... "Once you get basic human needs met, a lot more money doesn't make a lot more happiness." ... Going from earning less than $20,000 a year to making more than $50,000 makes you twice as likely to be happy, yet the payoff for then surpassing $90,000 is slight.

CNN, July 18, 2006

a. What does the fundamental assumption of marginal utility theory suggest about the connection between money and happiness?

b. Explain why this article is consistent with marginal utility theory.

8. **Eating Away the Innings in Baseball's Cheap Seats**

Baseball and gluttony, two of America's favorite pastimes, are merging in a controversial trend taking hold at Major League Baseball stadiums across the nation: all-you-can-eat seats. ... Some fans try to "set personal records" during their first game in the section. By their second or third time in such seats ... they eat like they normally would at a game.

USA Today, March 6, 2008

a. What conflict might exist between utility-maximization and setting "personal records" for eating?

b. What does the fact that fans eat less at subsequent games indicate about what happens to the marginal utility from ballpark food as the quantity consumed increases?

c. How can setting personal records for eating be reconciled with marginal utility theory?

d. Which ideas of behavioral economics are consistent with the information in the news clip?

9. **Compared to Other Liquids, Gasoline is Cheap**

Think a $4 gallon of gas is expensive? Consider the prices of these other fluids that people buy every day without complaint. ...

Gatorade, 20 oz @ $1.59	= $10.17 per gallon ...
Wite-Out, 7 oz @ $1.39	= $25.42 per gallon ...
HP Ink Cartridge, 16 ml @ $18	= $4,294.58 per gallon

The New York Times, May 27, 2008

a. What does marginal utility theory predict about the marginal utility per dollar from gasoline, Gatorade, Wite-Out, and printer ink?

b. What do the prices per gallon reported in this news clip tell you about the marginal utility from a gallon of gasoline, Gatorade, Wite-Out, and printer ink?

c. What do the prices per unit reported in this news clip tell you about the marginal utility from a gallon of gasoline, a 20 oz bottle of Gatorade, a 7 oz bottle of Wite-Out, and a cartridge of printer ink?

d. How can the paradox of value be used to explain why the fluids listed in the news clip might be less valuable than gasoline, yet far more expensive?

10. **Exclusive Status: It's in The Bag; $52,500 Purses. 24 Worldwide. 1 in Washington.**

Forget your Coach purse. Put away your Kate Spade. Even Hermes's famous Birkin bag seems positively discount.

The Louis Vuitton Tribute Patchwork is this summer's ultimate status bag, ringing in at $52,500. And it is arriving in Washington. ...

The company ... [is] offering only five for sale in North America and 24 worldwide. ...

The Washington Post, August 21, 2007

a. Use marginal utility theory to explain the facts reported in the news clip.

b. If Louis Vuitton offered 500 Tribute Patchwork bags in North America and 2,400 worldwide, what do you predict would happen to the price that buyers would be willing to pay and what would happen to the consumer surplus?

c. If the Tribute Patchwork bag is copied and thousands are sold illegally, what do you predict would happen to the price that buyers would be willing to pay for a genuine bag and what would happen to the consumer surplus?

11. Cindy enjoys golf and tennis. The table shows the marginal utility she gets from each activity.

Hours per month	Marginal utility from golf	Marginal utility from tennis
1	80	40
2	60	36
3	40	30
4	30	20
5	20	10
6	10	5
7	6	2

Cindy has $70 a month to spend, and she can spend as much time as she likes on her leisure pursuits. The price of an hour of golf is $10, and the price of an hour of tennis is $5.

a. Make a table that shows the various combinations of hours spent playing golf and tennis that Cindy can afford.

b. In your table, add two columns and list Cindy's marginal utility per dollar from golf and from tennis.

c. How long does Cindy spend playing golf and how long does she spend playing tennis to maximize her utility?

d. Compared to c, if Cindy spent a dollar more on golf and a dollar less on tennis, by how much would her total utility change?

e. Compared to c, if Cindy spent a dollar less on golf and a dollar more on tennis, by how much would her total utility change?

f. Explain why, if Cindy equalized the marginal utility per hour of golf and tennis, she would *not* maximize her utility.

12. Cindy's tennis club raises its price of an hour of tennis to $10. The price of golf and Cindy's income remain the same.

a. Make a table that shows the combinations of hours spent playing golf and tennis that Cindy can now afford.

b. In your table, list Cindy's marginal utility per dollar from golf and from tennis.

c. How many hours does Cindy now spend playing golf and how many hours does she spend playing tennis?

13. Given the information in problems 11 and 12,

a. Find two points on Cindy's demand curve for tennis.

b. Draw Cindy's demand curve for tennis.

c. Is Cindy's demand for tennis elastic or inelastic?

d. Explain how Cindy's demand for golf changed when the price of an hour of tennis increased.

e. What is Cindy's cross elasticity of demand for golf with respect to the price of tennis?

f. Are tennis and golf substitutes or complements for Cindy?

14. Cindy, with the utility schedules in problem 11, loses her math tutoring job and her income falls to $35 a month. With golf at $10 an hour and tennis at $5 an hour, how does the decrease in Cindy's income change her demand for

a. Golf, and explain whether, for Cindy, golf is a normal good or an inferior good.

b. Tennis, and explain whether, for Cindy, tennis is a normal good or an inferior good.

15. Cindy in problem 11 takes a Club Med vacation, the cost of which includes unlimited sports activities. With no extra charge for golf and tennis, Cindy allocates a total of 4 hours a day to these activities.

a. How many hours does Cindy play golf and how many hours does she play tennis?

b. What is Cindy's marginal utility from golf and from tennis?

c. Why does Cindy equalize the marginal utilities rather than the marginal utility per dollar from golf and from tennis?

16. Ben spends $50 a year on 2 bunches of flowers and $50 a year on 10,000 gallons of tap water. Ben is maximizing utility and his marginal utility from water is 0.5 unit per gallon.

a. Are flowers or water more valuable to Ben?

b. Explain how Ben's expenditure on flowers and water illustrates the paradox of value.

17. **Blu-Ray Format Expected to Dominate, but When?**

Blu-ray stomped HD DVD to become the standard format for high-definition movie discs, but years may pass before it can claim victory over the good old DVD. ... "The group that bought $2,000, 40-inch TVs are the ones that will lead the charge. ... Everyone else will come along when the price comes down."... Blu-ray machine prices are starting to drop. Wal-Mart Stores Inc. began stocking a $298 Magnavox model. ...

That's cheaper than most alternatives but a hefty price hike from a typical $50 DVD player.

CNN, June 2, 2008

a. What does marginal utility theory predict about the marginal utility from a Magnavox Blu-ray machine compared to the marginal utility from a typical DVD player?

b. What will have to happen to the marginal utility from a Blu-ray machine before it is able to "claim victory over the good old DVD"?

18. **Five Signs You Have Too Much Money**

Some people think bottled water is a fool's drink. I'm not among them, but when a bottle of water costs $38, it's hard not to see their point. The drink of choice these days among image-conscious status seekers and high-end tee-totalers in L.A. is Bling H2O... it's not the water that accounts for the cost. ... Much of the $38 is due to the "limited edition" bottle decked out in Swarovski crystals.

CNN, January 17, 2006

a. Assuming that the price of a bottle of Bling H2O is $38 in all the major cities in the United States, what might its popularity in Los Angeles reveal about consumers' incomes or consumers' preferences in Los Angeles relative to other U.S. cities?

b. Why might the marginal utility from a bottle of Bling H2O decrease more rapidly than the marginal utility from ordinary bottled water?

19. **How To Buy Happiness. Cheap**

Sure, in any given country at any given point in time, the rich tend to be a bit happier than the poor. But across-the-board increases in living standards don't seem to make people any happier. Disposable income for the average American has grown about 80% since 1972, but the percentage describing themselves as "very happy" (roughly a third) has barely budged over the years. ... As living standards increase, most of us respond by raising our own standards. Things that once seemed luxuries now seem necessities. ... As a result, we're working harder than ever to buy stuff that satisfies us less and less.

CNN, October 1, 2004

a. According to this news clip, how do wide-spread increases in living standards influence total utility?

b. What does the news clip imply about how the total utility from consumption changes over time?

c. What does the news clip imply about how the marginal utility from consumption changes over time?

20. **Putting a Price on Human Life**

What's a healthy human life worth? According to Stanford and University of Pennsylvania Researchers, about $129,000. Using Medicare records on treatment costs for kidney dialysis as a benchmark, the authors tried to pinpoint the threshold beyond which ensuring another "quality" year of life was no longer financially worthwhile. The study comes amid debate over whether Medicare should start rationing health care on a cost-effectiveness basis. ...

Time, June 9, 2008

a. Why might it be necessary for Medicare to ration health care according to treatment that is "financially worthwhile" as opposed to providing as much treatment as is needed by a patient, regardless of costs?

b. What conflict might exist between a person's valuation of his or her own life and the rest of society's valuation of that person's life?

c. How does the potential conflict between self-interest and the social interest complicate setting a financial threshold for Medicare treatments?

21. Study *Reading Between the Lines* (pp. 196–197).

a. If a wave of natural disasters put paramedics in the news and a large number of people decide to try to get jobs as paramedics, what happens to
    i. The marginal utility of the services of a paramedic?
    ii. Consumer surplus in the market for the services of paramedics?

b. If television advertising revenues during hockey games double, what happens to
    i. The marginal utility of the services of a hockey player?
    ii. Consumer surplus in the market for the services of hockey players?

11 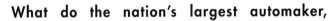 Output and Costs

After studying this chapter, you will be able to:

- Distinguish between the short run and the long run

- Explain the relationship between a firm's output and labor employed in the short run

- Explain the relationship between a firm's output and costs in the short run and derive a firm's short-run cost curves

- Explain the relationship between a firm's output and costs in the long run and derive a firm's long-run average cost curve

What do the nation's largest automaker, General Motors, a big electricity supplier in Pennsylvania, PennPower, and a small (fictional) producer of knitwear, Campus Sweaters, have in common? Like every firm, they must decide how much to produce, how many people to employ, and how much and what type of capital equipment to use. How do firms make these decisions?

GM and the other automakers in the United States could produce more cars than they can sell. Why do automakers have expensive equipment lying around that isn't fully used?

PennPower and the other electric utilities in the United States use technologies that contribute to climate change and global warming. Why don't they make more use of clean solar and wind technologies?

We are going to answer these questions in this chapter.

To explain the basic ideas as clearly as possible, we are going to focus on the economic decisions of Campus Sweaters, Inc. Studying the way Cindy copes with her firm's economic problems will give us a clear view of the problems faced by all firms. We'll then apply what we learn in this chapter to the real-world costs of producing cars and electricity. In *Reading Between the Lines*, we'll look at the effects of changing technologies that aim to lower the cost of clean electricity.

251

◆ Decision Time Frames

People who operate firms make many decisions, and all of their decisions are aimed at achieving one overriding goal: maximum attainable profit. But not all decisions are equally critical. Some decisions are big ones. Once made, they are costly (or impossible) to reverse. If such a decision turns out to be incorrect, it might lead to the failure of the firm. Other decisions are small. They are easily changed. If one of these decisions turns out to be incorrect, the firm can change its actions and survive.

The biggest decision that an entrepreneur makes is in what industry to establish a firm. For most entrepreneurs, their background knowledge and interests drive this decision. But the decision also depends on profit prospects—on the expectation that total revenue will exceed total cost.

Cindy has already decided to set up Campus Sweaters. She has also decided the most effective method of organizing the firm. But she has not decided the quantity to produce, the factors of production to hire, or the price to charge for sweaters.

Decisions about the quantity to produce and the price to charge depend on the type of market in which the firm operates. Perfect competition, monopolistic competition, oligopoly, and monopoly all confront the firm with their own special problems. But decisions about *how* to produce a given output do not depend on the type of market in which the firm operates. *All* types of firms in *all* types of markets make similar decisions about how to produce.

The actions that a firm can take to influence the relationship between output and cost depend on how soon the firm wants to act. A firm that plans to change its output rate tomorrow has fewer options than one that plans to change its output rate six months or six years from now.

To study the relationship between a firm's output decision and its costs, we distinguish between two decision time frames:

- The short run
- The long run

The Short Run

The **short run** is a time frame in which the quantity of at least one factor of production is fixed. For most firms, capital, land, and entrepreneurship are fixed factors of production and labor is the variable factor of production. We call the fixed factors of production the firm's *plant*: In the short run, a firm's plant is fixed.

For Campus Sweaters, the fixed plant is its factory building and its knitting machines. For an electric power utility, the fixed plant is its buildings, generators, computers, and control systems.

To increase output in the short run, a firm must increase the quantity of a variable factor of production, which is usually labor. So to produce more output, Campus Sweaters must hire more labor and operate its knitting machines for more hours a day. Similarly, an electric power utility must hire more labor and operate its generators for more hours a day.

Short-run decisions are easily reversed. The firm can increase or decrease its output in the short run by increasing or decreasing the amount of labor it hires.

The Long Run

The **long run** is a time frame in which the quantities of *all* factors of production can be varied. That is, the long run is a period in which the firm can change its *plant*.

To increase output in the long run, a firm can change its plant as well as the quantity of labor it hires. Campus Sweaters can decide whether to install more knitting machines, use a new type of machine, reorganize its management, or hire more labor. Long-run decisions are *not* easily reversed. Once a plant decision is made, the firm usually must live with it for some time. To emphasize this fact, we call the past expenditure on a plant that has no resale value a **sunk cost**. A sunk cost is irrelevant to the firm's current decisions. The only costs that influence its current decisions are the short-run cost of changing its labor inputs and the long-run cost of changing its plant.

Review Quiz ◆

1 Distinguish between the short run and the long run.

2 Why is a sunk cost irrelevant to a firm's current decisions?

 Work Study Plan 11.1 and get instant feedback.

We're going to study costs in the short run and the long run. We begin with the short run and describe a firm's technology constraint.

Short-Run Technology Constraint

To increase output in the short run, a firm must increase the quantity of labor employed. We describe the relationship between output and the quantity of labor employed by using three related concepts:

1. Total product
2. Marginal product
3. Average product

These product concepts can be illustrated either by product schedules or by product curves. Let's look first at the product schedules.

Product Schedules

Table 11.1 shows some data that describe Campus Sweaters' total product, marginal product, and average product. The numbers tell us how the quantity of sweaters increases as Campus Sweaters employs more workers. The numbers also tell us about the productivity of the labor that Campus Sweaters employs.

Focus first on the columns headed "Labor" and "Total product." **Total product** is the maximum output that a given quantity of labor can produce. You can see from the numbers in these columns that as Campus Sweaters employs more labor, total product increases. For example, when 1 worker is employed, total product is 4 sweaters a day, and when 2 workers are employed, total product is 10 sweaters a day. Each increase in employment increases total product.

The **marginal product** of labor is the increase in total product that results from a one-unit increase in the quantity of labor employed, with all other inputs remaining the same. For example, in Table 11.1, when Campus Sweaters increases employment from 2 to 3 workers and does not change its capital, the marginal product of the third worker is 3 sweaters—total product increases from 10 to 13 sweaters.

Average product tells how productive workers are on average. The **average product** of labor is equal to total product divided by the quantity of labor employed. For example, in Table 11.1, the average product of 3 workers is 4.33 sweaters per worker—13 sweaters a day divided by 3 workers.

If you look closely at the numbers in Table 11.1, you can see some patterns. As Campus Sweaters hires

TABLE 11.1 Total Product, Marginal Product, and Average Product

	Labor (workers per day)	Total product (sweaters per day)	Marginal product (sweaters per additional worker)	Average product (sweaters per worker)
A	0	0		
			4	
B	1	4		4.00
			6	
C	2	10		5.00
			3	
D	3	13		4.33
			2	
E	4	15		3.75
			1	
F	5	16		3.20

Total product is the total amount produced. Marginal product is the change in total product that results from a one-unit increase in labor. For example, when labor increases from 2 to 3 workers a day (row C to row D), total product increases from 10 to 13 sweaters a day. The marginal product of going from 2 to 3 workers is 3 sweaters. Average product is total product divided by the quantity of labor employed. For example, the average product of 3 workers is 4.33 sweaters per worker (13 sweaters a day divided by 3 workers).

more labor, marginal product increases initially, and then begins to decrease. For example, marginal product increases from 4 sweaters a day for the first worker to 6 sweaters a day for the second worker and then decreases to 3 sweaters a day for the third worker. Average product also increases at first and then decreases. You can see the relationships between the quantity of labor hired and the three product concepts more clearly by looking at the product curves.

Product Curves

The product curves are graphs of the relationships between employment and the three product concepts you've just studied. They show how total product, marginal product, and average product change as employment changes. They also show the relationships among the three concepts. Let's look at the product curves.

Total Product Curve

Figure 11.1 shows Campus Sweaters' total product curve, *TP*, which is a graph of the total product schedule. Points *A* through *F* correspond to rows *A* through *F* in Table 11.1. To graph the entire total product curve, we vary labor by hours rather than whole days.

Notice the shape of the total product curve. As employment increases from zero to 1 worker a day, the curve becomes steeper. Then, as employment increases to 3, 4, and 5 workers a day, the curve becomes less steep.

The total product curve is similar to the *production possibilities frontier* (explained in Chapter 2). It separates the attainable output levels from those that are unattainable. All the points that lie above the curve are unattainable. Points that lie below the curve, in the orange area, are attainable, but they are inefficient—they use more labor than is necessary to produce a given output. Only the points *on* the total product curve are technologically efficient.

FIGURE 11.1   Total Product Curve

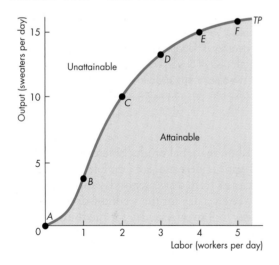

The total product curve, *TP*, is based on the data in Table 11.1. The total product curve shows how the quantity of sweaters produced changes as the quantity of labor employed changes. For example, 2 workers can produce 10 sweaters a day (point *C*). Points *A* through *F* on the curve correspond to the rows of Table 11.1. The total product curve separates attainable outputs from unattainable outputs. Points below the *TP* curve are inefficient.

 animation

Marginal Product Curve

Figure 11.2 shows Campus Sweaters' marginal product of labor. Part (a) reproduces the total product curve from Fig. 11.1 and part (b) shows the marginal product curve, *MP*.

In part (a), the orange bars illustrate the marginal product of labor. The height of a bar measures marginal product. Marginal product is also measured by the slope of the total product curve. Recall that the slope of a curve is the change in the value of the variable measured on the *y*-axis—output—divided by the change in the variable measured on the *x*-axis—labor—as we move along the curve. A one-unit increase in labor, from 2 to 3 workers, increases output from 10 to 13 sweaters, so the slope from point *C* to point *D* is 3 sweaters per additional worker, the same as the marginal product we've just calculated.

Again varying the amount of labor in the smallest units possible, we can draw the marginal product curve shown in Fig. 11.2(b). The *height* of this curve measures the *slope* of the total product curve at a point. Part (a) shows that an increase in employment from 2 to 3 workers increases output from 10 to 13 sweaters (an increase of 3). The increase in output of 3 sweaters appears on the *y*-axis of part (b) as the marginal product of going from 2 to 3 workers. We plot that marginal product at the midpoint between 2 and 3 workers. Notice that the marginal product shown in Fig. 11.2(b) reaches a peak at 1.5 workers, and at that point, marginal product is 6 sweaters per additional worker. The peak occurs at 1.5 workers because the total product curve is steepest when employment increases from 1 worker to 2 workers.

The total product and marginal product curves differ across firms and types of goods. GM's product curves are different from those of PennPower, whose curves in turn are different from those of Campus Sweaters. But the shapes of the product curves are similar because almost every production process has two features:

- Increasing marginal returns initially
- Diminishing marginal returns eventually

Increasing Marginal Returns Increasing marginal returns occur when the marginal product of an additional worker exceeds the marginal product of the previous worker. Increasing marginal returns arise from increased specialization and division of labor in the production process.

FIGURE 11.2 Total Product and Marginal Product

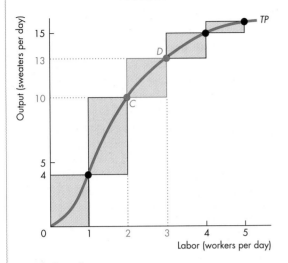

(a) Total product

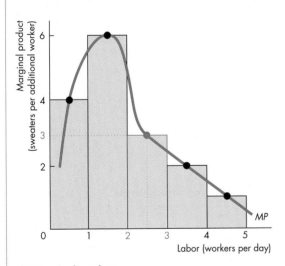

(b) Marginal product

Marginal product is illustrated by the orange bars. For example, when labor increases from 2 to 3 workers a day, marginal product is the orange bar whose height is 3 sweaters. (Marginal product is shown midway between the quantities of labor to emphasize that marginal product results from *changing* the quantity of labor.) The steeper the slope of the total product curve (*TP*) in part (a), the larger is marginal product (*MP*) in part (b). Marginal product increases to a maximum (in this example when 1.5 workers a day are employed) and then declines—diminishing marginal product.

myeconlab animation

For example, if Campus Sweaters employs one worker, that person must learn all the aspects of sweater production: running the knitting machines, fixing breakdowns, packaging and mailing sweaters, buying and checking the type and color of the wool. All these tasks must be performed by that one person.

If Campus Sweaters hires a second person, the two workers can specialize in different parts of the production process and can produce more than twice as much as one worker. The marginal product of the second worker is greater than the marginal product of the first worker. Marginal returns are increasing.

Diminishing Marginal Returns Most production processes experience increasing marginal returns initially, but all production processes eventually reach a point of *diminishing* marginal returns. **Diminishing marginal returns** occur when the marginal product of an additional worker is less than the marginal product of the previous worker.

Diminishing marginal returns arise from the fact that more and more workers are using the same capital and working in the same space. As more workers are added, there is less and less for the additional workers to do that is productive. For example, if Campus Sweaters hires a third worker, output increases but not by as much as it did when it hired the second worker. In this case, after two workers are hired, all the gains from specialization and the division of labor have been exhausted. By hiring a third worker, the factory produces more sweaters, but the equipment is being operated closer to its limits. There are even times when the third worker has nothing to do because the machines are running without the need for further attention. Hiring more and more workers continues to increase output but by successively smaller amounts. Marginal returns are diminishing. This phenomenon is such a pervasive one that it is called a "law"—the law of diminishing returns. The **law of diminishing returns** states that

As a firm uses more of a variable factor of production, with a given quantity of the fixed factor of production, the marginal product of the variable factor eventually diminishes.

You are going to return to the law of diminishing returns when we study a firm's costs. But before we do that, let's look at the average product of labor and the average product curve.

Average Product Curve

Figure 11.3 illustrates Campus Sweaters' average product of labor and shows the relationship between average product and marginal product. Points *B* through *F* on the average product curve *AP* correspond to those same rows in Table 11.1. Average product increases from 1 to 2 workers (its maximum value at point *C*) but then decreases as yet more workers are employed. Notice also that average product is largest when average product and marginal product are equal. That is, the marginal product curve cuts the average product curve at the point of maximum average product. For the number of workers at which marginal product exceeds average product, average product is *increasing*. For the number of workers at which marginal product is less than average product, average product is *decreasing*.

The relationship between the average product and marginal product is a general feature of the relationship between the average and marginal values of any variable—even your grades.

FIGURE 11.3   Average Product

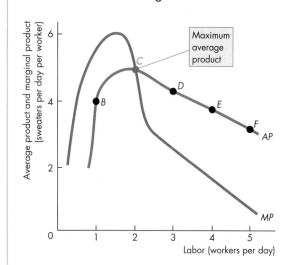

The figure shows the average product of labor and the connection between average product and marginal product. With 1 worker, marginal product exceeds average product, so average product is increasing. With 2 workers, marginal product equals average product, so average product is at its maximum. With more than 2 workers, marginal product is less than average product, so average product is decreasing.

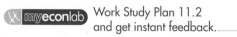 animation

Marginal Grades and Average Grades
How to Pull Up Your Average

Do you want to pull up your average grade? Then make sure that your next test is better than your current average! Your next test is your marginal test. If your marginal grade exceeds your average grade (like Economics in the graph), your average will rise. If your marginal grade equals your average grade (like English in the graph), your average won't change. If your marginal grade is below your average grade (like History in the figure), your average will fall.

The relationship between your marginal and average grades is exactly the same as that between marginal product and average product.

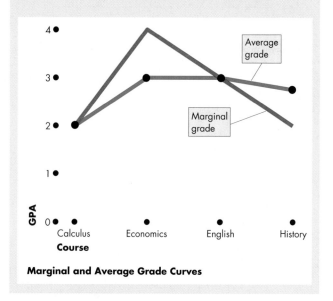

Marginal and Average Grade Curves

Review Quiz

1 Explain how the marginal product of labor and the average product of labor change as the quantity of labor employed increases (a) initially and (b) eventually.
2 What is the law of diminishing returns? Why does marginal product eventually diminish?
3 Explain the relationship between marginal product and average product.

myeconlab Work Study Plan 11.2 and get instant feedback.

Campus Sweaters' product curves influence its costs, as you are now going to see.

Short-Run Cost

To produce more output in the short run, a firm must employ more labor, which means that it must increase its costs. We describe the relationship between output and cost by using three cost concepts:

- Total cost
- Marginal cost
- Average cost

Total Cost

A firm's **total cost** (*TC*) is the cost of *all* the factors of production it uses. We separate total cost into total *fixed* cost and total *variable* cost.

Total fixed cost (*TFC*) is the cost of the firm's fixed factors. For Campus Sweaters, total fixed cost includes the cost of renting knitting machines and *normal profit*, which is the opportunity cost of Cindy's entrepreneurship (see Chapter 10, p. 229). The quantities of fixed factors don't change as output changes, so total fixed cost is the same at all outputs.

Total variable cost (*TVC*) is the cost of the firm's variable factors. For Campus Sweaters, labor is the variable factor, so this component of cost is its wage bill. Total variable cost changes as output changes.

Total cost is the sum of total fixed cost and total variable cost. That is,

$$TC = TFC + TVC.$$

The table in Fig. 11.4 shows total costs. Campus Sweaters rents one knitting machine for $25 a day, so its *TFC* is $25. To produce sweaters, the firm hires labor, which costs $25 a day. *TVC* is the number of workers multiplied by $25. For example, to produce 13 sweaters a day, in row *D*, the firm hires 3 workers and *TVC* is $75. *TC* is the sum of *TFC* and *TVC*, so to produce 13 sweaters a day, *TC* is $100. Check the calculations in the other rows of the table.

Figure 11.4 shows Campus Sweaters' total cost curves, which graph total cost against output. The green *TFC* curve is horizontal because total fixed cost ($25 a day) does not change when output changes. The purple *TVC* curve and the blue *TC* curve both slope upward because to increase output, more labor must be employed, which increases total variable cost. Total fixed cost equals the vertical distance between the *TVC* and *TC* curves.

Let's now look at a firm's marginal cost.

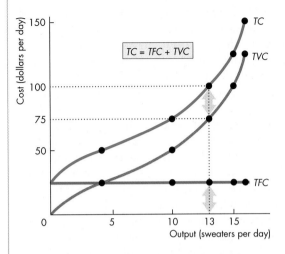

FIGURE 11.4   Total Cost Curves

Labor (workers per day)	Output (sweaters per day)	Total fixed cost (*TFC*)	Total variable cost (*TVC*)	Total cost (*TC*)
		(dollars per day)		
A 0	0	25	0	25
B 1	4	25	25	50
C 2	10	25	50	75
D 3	**13**	**25**	**75**	**100**
E 4	15	25	100	125
F 5	16	25	125	150

Campus Sweaters rents a knitting machine for $25 a day, so this cost is the firm's total fixed cost. The firm hires workers at a wage rate of $25 a day, and this cost is its total variable cost. For example, in row *D*, Campus Sweaters employs 3 workers and its total variable cost is 3 × $25, which equals $75. Total cost is the sum of total fixed cost and total variable cost. For example, when Campus Sweaters employs 3 workers, total cost is $100—total fixed cost of $25 plus total variable cost of $75.

The graph shows Campus Sweaters' total cost curves. Total fixed cost is constant—the *TFC* curve is a horizontal line. Total variable cost increases as output increases, so the *TVC* curve and the *TC* curve increase as output increases. The vertical distance between the *TC* curve and the *TVC* curve equals total fixed cost, as illustrated by the two arrows.

Marginal Cost

Figure 11.4 shows that total variable cost and total cost increase at a decreasing rate at small outputs but eventually, as output increases, total variable cost and total cost increase at an increasing rate. To understand this pattern in the change in total cost as output increases, we need to use the concept of *marginal cost*.

A firm's **marginal cost** is the increase in total cost that results from a one-unit increase in output. We calculate marginal cost as the increase in total cost divided by the increase in output. The table in Fig. 11.5 shows this calculation. When, for example, output increases from 10 sweaters to 13 sweaters, total cost increases from $75 to $100. The change in output is 3 sweaters, and the change in total cost is $25. The marginal cost of one of those 3 sweaters is ($25 ÷ 3), which equals $8.33.

Figure 11.5 graphs the marginal cost data in the table as the red marginal cost curve, *MC*. This curve is U-shaped because when Campus Sweaters hires a second worker, marginal cost decreases, but when it hires a third, a fourth, and a fifth worker, marginal cost successively increases.

At small outputs, marginal cost decreases as output increases because of greater specialization and the division of labor, but as output increases further, marginal cost eventually increases because of the *law of diminishing returns*. The law of diminishing returns means that the output produced by each additional worker is successively smaller. To produce an additional unit of output, ever more workers are required, and the cost of producing the additional unit of output—marginal cost—must eventually increase.

Marginal cost tells us how total cost changes as output increases. The final cost concept tells us what it costs, on average, to produce a unit of output. Let's now look at Campus Sweaters' average costs.

Average Cost

Three average costs of production are

1. Average fixed cost
2. Average variable cost
3. Average total cost

Average fixed cost (*AFC*) is total fixed cost per unit of output. **Average variable cost** (*AVC*) is total variable cost per unit of output. **Average total cost** (*ATC*) is total cost per unit of output. The average cost con-

cepts are calculated from the total cost concepts as follows:

$$TC = TFV + TVC.$$

Divide each total cost term by the quantity produced, Q, to get

$$\frac{TC}{Q} = \frac{TFC}{Q} + \frac{TVC}{Q},$$

or

$$ATC = AFC + AVC.$$

The table in Fig. 11.5 shows the calculation of average total cost. For example, in row C, output is 10 sweaters. Average fixed cost is ($25 ÷ 10), which equals $2.50, average variable cost is ($50 ÷ 10), which equals $5.00, and average total cost is ($75 ÷ 10), which equals $7.50. Note that average total cost is equal to average fixed cost ($2.50) plus average variable cost ($5.00).

Figure 11.5 shows the average cost curves. The green average fixed cost curve (*AFC*) slopes downward. As output increases, the same constant total fixed cost is spread over a larger output. The blue average total cost curve (*ATC*) and the purple average variable cost curve (*AVC*) are U-shaped. The vertical distance between the average total cost and average variable cost curves is equal to average fixed cost—as indicated by the two arrows. That distance shrinks as output increases because average fixed cost declines with increasing output.

Marginal Cost and Average Cost

The marginal cost curve (*MC*) intersects the average variable cost curve and the average total cost curve *at their minimum points*. When marginal cost is less than average cost, average cost is decreasing, and when marginal cost exceeds average cost, average cost is increasing. This relationship holds for both the *ATC* curve and the *AVC* curve. It is another example of the relationship you saw in Fig. 11.3 for average product and marginal product and in your average and marginal grades.

Why the Average Total Cost Curve Is U-Shaped

Average total cost is the sum of average fixed cost and average variable cost, so the shape of the *ATC* curve

FIGURE 11.5   Marginal Cost and Average Costs

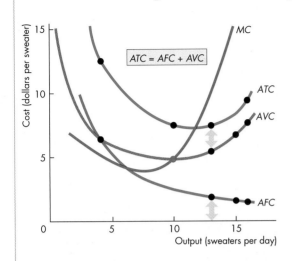

Marginal cost is calculated as the change in total cost divided by the change in output. When output increases from 4 to 10 sweaters, an increase of 6 sweaters, total cost increases by $25. Marginal cost is $25 ÷ 6, which is $4.17.

Each average cost concept is calculated by dividing the related total cost by output. When 10 sweaters are produced, AFC is $2.50 ($25 ÷ 10), AVC is $5 ($50 ÷ 10), and ATC is $7.50 ($75 ÷ 10).

The graph shows that the MC curve is U-shaped and intersects the AVC curve and the ATC curve at their minimum points. Average fixed cost curve (AFC) is downward sloping. The ATC curve and AVC curve are U-shaped. The vertical distance between the ATC curve and the AVC curve is equal to average fixed cost, as illustrated by the two arrows.

	Labor (workers per day)	Output (sweaters per day)	Total fixed cost (TFC)	Total variable cost (TVC)	Total cost (TC)	Marginal cost (MC) (dollars per additional sweater)	Average fixed cost (AFC)	Average variable cost (AVC)	Average total cost (ATC)
			(dollars per day)				(dollars per sweater)		
A	0	0	25	0	25		—	—	—
						.... 6.25			
B	1	4	25	25	50		6.25	6.25	12.50
						.... 4.17			
C	2	10	25	50	75		2.50	5.00	7.50
						.... 8.33			
D	3	13	25	75	100		1.92	5.77	7.69
						.......12.50			
E	4	15	25	100	125		1.67	6.67	8.33
						.......25.00			
F	5	16	25	125	150		1.56	7.81	9.38

myeconlab animation

combines the shapes of the *AFC* and *AVC* curves. The U shape of the *ATC* curve arises from the influence of two opposing forces:

1. Spreading total fixed cost over a larger output
2. Eventually diminishing returns

When output increases, the firm spreads its total fixed cost over a larger output and so its average fixed cost decreases—its *AFC* curve slopes downward.

Diminishing returns means that as output increases, ever-larger amounts of labor are needed to produce an additional unit of output. So as output increases, average variable cost decreases initially but

eventually increases, and the *AVC* curve slopes upward. The *AVC* curve is U shaped.

The shape of the *ATC* curve combines these two effects. Initially, as output increases, both average fixed cost and average variable cost decrease, so average total cost decreases. The *ATC* curve slopes downward.

But as output increases further and diminishing returns set in, average variable cost starts to increase. With average fixed cost decreasing more quickly than average variable cost is increasing, the *ATC* curve continues to slope downward. Eventually, average variable cost starts to increase more quickly than average fixed cost decreases, so average total cost starts to increase. The *ATC* curve slopes upward.

Cost Curves and Product Curves

The technology that a firm uses determines its costs. Figure 11.6 shows the links between the firm's product curves and its cost curves. The upper graph shows the average product curve, *AP*, and the marginal product curve, *MP*—like those in Fig. 11.3. The lower graph shows the average variable cost curve, *AVC*, and the marginal cost curve, *MC*—like those in Fig. 11.5.

As labor increases up to 1.5 workers a day (upper graph), output increases to 6.5 sweaters a day (lower graph). Marginal product and average product rise and marginal cost and average variable cost fall. At the point of maximum marginal product, marginal cost is at a minimum.

As labor increases to 2 workers a day, (upper graph) output increases to 10 sweaters a day (lower graph). Marginal product falls and marginal cost rises, but average product continues to rise and average variable cost continues to fall. At the point of maximum average product, average variable cost is at a minimum. As labor increases further, output increases. Average product diminishes and average variable cost increases.

Shifts in the Cost Curves

The position of a firm's short-run cost curves depends on two factors:

- Technology
- Prices of factors of production

Technology A technological change that increases productivity increases the marginal product and average product of labor. With a better technology, the same factors of production can produce more output, so the technological advance lowers the costs of production and shifts the cost curves downward.

For example, advances in robot production techniques have increased productivity in the automobile industry. As a result, the product curves of Chrysler, Ford, and GM have shifted upward and their cost curves have shifted downward. But the relationships between their product curves and cost curves have not changed. The curves are still linked in the way shown in Fig. 11.6.

Often, as in the case of robots producing cars, a technological advance results in a firm using more capital, a fixed factor, and less labor, a variable factor.

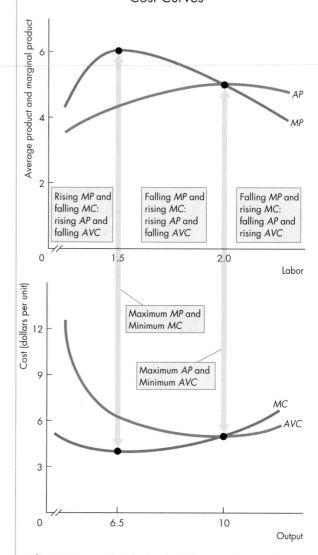

FIGURE 11.6 Product Curves and Cost Curves

A firm's *MP* curve is linked to its *MC* curve. If, as the firm increases its labor from 0 to 1.5 workers a day, the firm's marginal product rises, its marginal cost falls. If marginal product is at a maximum, marginal cost is at a minimum. If, as the firm hires more labor, its marginal product diminishes, its marginal cost rises.

A firm's *AP* curve is linked to its *AVC* curve. If, as the firm increases its labor to 2 workers a day, its average product rises, its average variable cost falls. If average product is at a maximum, average variable cost is at a minimum. If, as the firm hires more labor, its average product diminishes, its average variable cost rises.

TABLE 11.2   A Compact Glossary of Costs

Term	Symbol	Definition	Equation
Fixed cost		Cost that is independent of the output level; cost of a fixed factor of production	
Variable cost		Cost that varies with the output level; cost of a variable factor of production	
Total fixed cost	TFC	Cost of the fixed factors of production	
Total variable cost	TVC	Cost of the variable factors of production	
Total cost	TC	Cost of all factors of production	$TC = TFC + TVC$
Output (total product)	TP	Total quantity produced (output Q)	
Marginal cost	MC	Change in total cost resulting from a one-unit increase in total product	$MC = \Delta TC \div \Delta Q$
Average fixed cost	AFC	Total fixed cost per unit of output	$AFC = TFC \div Q$
Average variable cost	AVC	Total variable cost per unit of output	$AVC = TVC \div Q$
Average total cost	ATC	Total cost per unit of output	$ATC = AFC + AVC$

Another example is the use of ATMs by banks to dispense cash. ATMs, which are fixed capital, have replaced tellers, which are variable labor. Such a technological change decreases total cost but increases fixed costs and decreases variable cost. This change in the mix of fixed cost and variable cost means that at small outputs, average total cost might increase, while at large outputs, average total cost decreases.

Prices of Factors of Production An increase in the price of a factor of production increases the firm's costs and shifts its cost curves. But how the curves shift depends on which factor price changes.

An increase in rent or some other component of *fixed* cost shifts the *TFC* and *AFC* curves upward and shifts the *TC curve* upward but leaves the *AVC* and *TVC* curves and the *MC* curve unchanged. For example, if the interest expense paid by a trucking company increases, the fixed cost of transportation services increases.

An increase in wages, gasoline, or another component of *variable* cost shifts the *TVC* and *AVC* curves upward and shifts the *MC* curve upward but leaves the *AFC* and *TFC* curves unchanged. For example, if

truck drivers' wages or the price of gasoline increases, the variable cost and marginal cost of transportation services increase.

You've now completed your study of short-run costs. All the concepts that you've met are summarized in a compact glossary in Table 11.2.

Review Quiz

1 What relationships do a firm's short-run cost curves show?
2 How does marginal cost change as output increases (a) initially and (b) eventually?
3 What does the law of diminishing returns imply for the shape of the marginal cost curve?
4 What is the shape of the *AFC* curve and why does it have this shape?
5 What are the shapes of the *AVC* curve and the *ATC* curve and why do they have these shapes?

myeconlab   Work Study Plan 11.3 and get instant feedback.

Long-Run Cost

We are now going to study the firm's long-run costs. In the long run, a firm can vary both the quantity of labor and the quantity of capital, so in the long run, all the firm's costs are variable.

The behavior of long-run cost depends on the firm's *production function*, which is the relationship between the maximum output attainable and the quantities of both labor and capital.

The Production Function

Table 11.3 shows Campus Sweaters' production function. The table lists total product schedules for four different quantities of capital. The quantity of capital identifies the plant size. The numbers for plant 1 are for a factory with 1 knitting machine—the case we've just studied. The other three plants have 2, 3, and 4 machines. If Campus Sweaters uses plant 2 with 2 knitting machines, the various amounts of labor can produce the outputs shown in the second column of the table. The other two columns show the outputs of yet larger quantities of capital. Each column of the table could be graphed as a total product curve for each plant.

Diminishing Returns Diminishing returns occur with each of the four plant sizes as the quantity of labor increases. You can check that fact by calculating the marginal product of labor in each of the plants with 2, 3, and 4 machines. With each plant size, as the firm increases the quantity of labor employed, the marginal product of labor (eventually) diminishes.

Diminishing Marginal Product of Capital
Diminishing returns also occur with each quantity of labor as the quantity of capital increases. You can check that fact by calculating the marginal product of capital at a given quantity of labor. The *marginal product of capital* is the change in total product divided by the change in capital when the quantity of labor is constant—equivalently, the change in output resulting from a one-unit increase in the quantity of capital. For example, if Campus Sweaters has 3 workers and increases its capital from 1 machine to 2 machines, output increases from 13 to 18 sweaters a day. The marginal product of the second machine is 5 sweaters a day. If the firm increases the number of

TABLE 11.3 The Production Function

Labor (workers per day)	Output (sweaters per day)			
	Plant 1	Plant 2	Plant 3	Plant 4
1	4	10	13	15
2	10	15	18	20
3	13	18	22	24
4	15	20	24	26
5	16	21	25	27
Knitting machines (number)	1	2	3	4

The table shows the total product data for four quantities of capital (plant sizes). The greater the plant size, the larger is the output produced by any given quantity of labor. But for a given plant size, the marginal product of labor diminishes as more labor is employed. For a given quantity of labor, the marginal product of capital diminishes as the quantity of capital used increases.

machines from 2 to 3, output increases from 18 to 22 sweaters a day. The marginal product of the third machine is 4 sweaters a day, down from 5 sweaters a day for the second machine.

Let's now see what the production function implies for long-run costs.

Short-Run Cost and Long-Run Cost

As before, Campus Sweaters can hire workers for $25 a day and rent knitting machines for $25 a day. Using these factor prices and the data in Table 11.3, we can calculate the average total cost and graph the *ATC* curves for factories with 1, 2, 3, and 4 knitting machines. We've already studied the costs of a factory with 1 machine in Figs. 11.4 and 11.5. In Fig. 11.7, the average total cost curve for that case is ATC_1. Figure 11.7 also shows the average total cost curve for a factory with 2 machines, ATC_2, with 3 machines, ATC_3, and with 4 machines, ATC_4.

You can see, in Fig. 11.7, that the plant size has a big effect on the firm's average total cost. Two things stand out:

FIGURE 11.7 Short-Run Costs of Four Different Plants

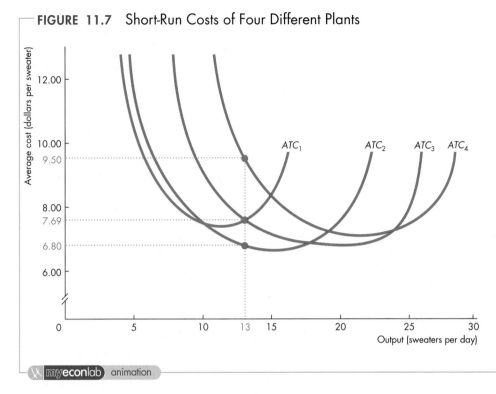

The figure shows short-run average total cost curves for four different quantities of capital at Campus Sweaters. The firm can produce 13 sweaters a day with 1 knitting machine on ATC_1 or with 3 knitting machines on ATC_3 for an average cost of $7.69 a sweater. The firm can produce 13 sweaters a day by using 2 machines on ATC_2 for $6.80 a sweater or by using 4 machines on ATC_4 for $9.50 a sweater.

If the firm produces 13 sweaters a day, the least-cost method of production, *the long-run method*, is with 2 machines on ATC_2.

1. Each short-run ATC curve is U-shaped.
2. For each short-run ATC curve, the larger the plant, the greater is the output at which average total cost is at a minimum.

Each short-run ATC curve is U-shaped because, as the quantity of labor increases, its marginal product initially increases and then diminishes. This pattern in the marginal product of labor, which we examined in some detail for the plant with 1 knitting machine on pp. 254–255, occurs at all plant sizes.

The minimum average total cost for a larger plant occurs at a greater output than it does for a smaller plant because the larger plant has a higher total fixed cost and therefore, for any given output, a higher average fixed cost.

Which short-run ATC curve a firm operates on depends on the plant it has. But in the long run, the firm can choose its plant and the plant it chooses is the one that enables it to produce its planned output at the lowest average total cost.

To see why, suppose that Campus Sweaters plans to produce 13 sweaters a day. In Fig. 11.7, with 1 machine, the average total cost curve is ATC_1 and the

average total cost of 13 sweaters a day is $7.69 a sweater. With 2 machines, on ATC_2, average total cost is $6.80 a sweater. With 3 machines, on ATC_3, average total cost is $7.69 a sweater, the same as with 1 machine. Finally, with 4 machines, on ATC_4, average total cost is $9.50 a sweater.

The economically efficient plant for producing a given output is the one that has the lowest average total cost. For Campus Sweaters, the economically efficient plant to use to produce 13 sweaters a day is the one with 2 machines.

In the long run, Cindy chooses the plant that minimizes average total cost. When a firm is producing a given output at the least possible cost, it is operating on its *long-run average cost curve.*

The **long-run average cost curve** is the relationship between the lowest attainable average total cost and output when the firm can change both the plant it uses and the quantity of labor it employs.

The long-run average cost curve is a planning curve. It tells the firm the plant and the quantity of labor to use at each output to minimize average cost. Once the firm chooses a plant, the firm operates on the short-run cost curves that apply to that plant.

The Long-Run Average Cost Curve

Figure 11.8 shows how a long-run average cost curve is derived. The long-run average cost curve *LRAC* consists of pieces of the four short-run *ATC* curves. For outputs up to 10 sweaters a day, average total cost is the lowest on ATC_1. For outputs between 10 and 18 sweaters a day, average total cost is the lowest on ATC_2. For outputs between 18 and 24 sweaters a day, average total cost is the lowest on ATC_3. And for outputs in excess of 24 sweaters a day, average total cost is the lowest on ATC_4. The piece of each *ATC* curve with the lowest average total cost is highlighted in dark blue in Fig. 11.8. This dark blue scallop-shaped curve made up of the pieces of the four *ATC* curves is the *LRAC* curve.

Economies and Diseconomies of Scale

Economies of scale are features of a firm's technology that make average total cost *fall* as output increases. When economies of scale are present, the *LRAC* curve slopes downward. In Fig. 11.8, Campus Sweaters has economies of scale for outputs up to 15 sweaters a day.

Greater specialization of both labor and capital is the main source of economies of scale. For example, if

GM produces 100 cars a week, each worker must perform many different tasks and the capital must be general-purpose machines and tools. But if GM produces 10,000 cars a week, each worker specializes in a small number of tasks, uses task-specific tools, and becomes highly proficient.

Diseconomies of scale are features of a firm's technology that make average total cost *rise* as output increases. When diseconomies of scale are present, the *LRAC* curve slopes upward. In Fig. 11.8, Campus Sweaters experiences diseconomies of scale at outputs greater than 15 sweaters a day.

The challenge of managing a large enterprise is the main source of diseconomies of scale.

Constant returns to scale are features of a firm's technology that keep average total cost constant as output increases. When constant returns to scale are present, the *LRAC* curve is horizontal.

Economies of Scale at Campus Sweaters The economies of scale and diseconomies of scale at Campus Sweaters arise from the firm's production function in Table 11.3. With 1 machine and 1 worker, the firm produces 4 sweaters a day. With 2 machines and 2 workers, total cost doubles but out-

---

FIGURE 11.8   Long-Run Average Cost Curve

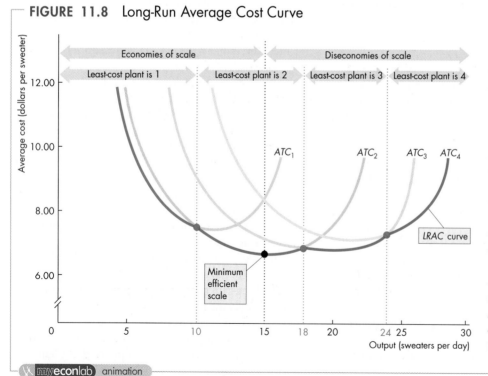

The long-run average cost curve traces the lowest attainable *ATC* when both labor and capital change. The green arrows highlight the output range over which each plant achieves the lowest *ATC*. Within each range, to change the quantity produced, the firm changes the quantity of labor it employs.

Along the *LRAC* curve, economies of scale occur if average cost falls as output increases; diseconomies of scale occur if average cost rises as output increases. Minimum efficient scale is the output at which average cost is lowest, 15 sweaters a day.

myeconlab   animation

Economies of Scale at an Auto Plant
Produce More to Cut Cost

Why do GM, Ford, and the other automakers have expensive equipment lying around that isn't fully used? You can answer this question with what you've learned in this chapter.

The basic answer is that auto production enjoys economies of scale. A larger output rate brings a lower long-run average cost—the firm's *LRAC* curve slopes downward.

An auto producer's average total cost curves look like those in the figure. To produce 20 vehicles an hour, the firm installs the plant with the short-run average total cost curve ATC_1. The average cost of producing a vehicle is $20,000.

Producing 20 vehicles an hour doesn't use the plant at its lowest possible average total cost. If the firm could sell enough cars for it to produce 40 vehicles an hour, the firm could use its current plant and produce at an average cost of $15,000 a vehicle.

But if the firm planned to produce 40 vehicles an hour, it would not stick with its current plant. The firm would install a bigger plant with the short-run average total cost curve ATC_2, and produce 40 vehicles an hour for $10,000 a car.

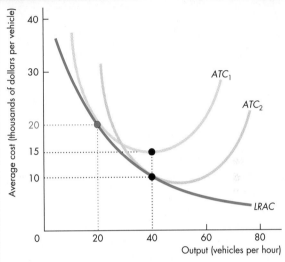

Automobile Plant Average Cost Curves

put more than doubles to 15 sweaters a day, so average cost decreases and Campus Sweaters experiences economies of scale. With 4 machines and 4 workers, total cost doubles again but output less than doubles to 26 sweaters a day, so average cost increases and the firm experiences diseconomies of scale.

Minimum Efficient Scale A firm's **minimum efficient scale** is the smallest output at which long-run average cost reaches its lowest level. At Campus Sweaters, the minimum efficient scale is 15 sweaters a day.

The minimum efficient scale plays a role in determining market structure. In a market in which the minimum efficient scale is small relative to market demand, the market has room for many firms, and the market is competitive. In a market in which the minimum efficient scale is large relative to market demand, only a small number of firms, and possibly only one firm, can make a profit and the market is either an oligopoly or monopoly. We will return to this idea in the next three chapters.

Review Quiz

1 What does a firm's production function show and how is it related to a total product curve?

2 Does the law of diminishing returns apply to capital as well as labor? Explain why or why not.

3 What does a firm's long-run average cost curve show? How is it related to the firm's short-run average cost curves?

4 What are economies of scale and diseconomies of scale? How do they arise? What do they imply for the shape of the long-run average cost curve?

5 What is a firm's minimum efficient scale?

myeconlab Work Study Plan 11.4 and get instant feedback.

Reading Between the Lines on pp. 266–267 applies what you've learned about a firm's cost curves. It looks at the cost curves for generating electricity using a variety of technologies and compares the total cost and marginal cost of traditional and new technologies.

Cutting the Cost of Clean Electricity

Start-Up: Affordable Solar PowerPossible in a Year

http://www.usatoday.com
April 29, 2008

A Silicon Valley start-up says it has developed technology that can deliver solar power in about a year at prices competitive with coal-fired electricity. ...

SUNRGI's "concentrated photovoltaic" system relies on lenses to magnify sunlight 2,000 times, letting it produce as much electricity as standard panels with a far smaller system. Craig Goodman, head of the National Energy Marketers Association, is expected to announce the breakthrough today. ...

Executives of the year-old company say they'll start producing solar panels by mid-2009 that will generate electricity for about 7 cents a kilowatt hour, including installation. That's roughly the price of cheap coal-fired electricity. ...

Solar power is acclaimed as free of greenhouse gas emissions and able to supply electricity midday when demand is highest. But its cost—20 cents to 30 cents a kilowatt hour—has inhibited broad adoption. Solar makes up less than 1% of U.S. power generation.

An armada of solar technology makers aim to drive solar's price to 10 to 18 cents a kilowatt hour by 2010, and 5 to 10 cents by 2015, at or below utility costs. ...

Essence of the Story

- A new Silicon Valley firm, SUNRGI, says it has developed technology that can deliver solar power for 7 cents a kilowatt hour.

- 7 cents a kilowatt hour is roughly the price of electricity produced by coal.

- Solar power on current technology costs 20 cents to 30 cents a kilowatt hour.

- A large number of solar technology makers aim to bring costs down to 10 to 18 cents a kilowatt hour by 2010 and to 5 to 10 cents by 2015.

Economic Analysis

- Figure 1 shows the average total cost (*ATC*) of producing electricity using seven alternative technologies.

- The cost differences come from differences in fuel and capital costs. Hydro, wind, and solar have zero fuel costs.

- Today's solar technology has the highest average total cost at 15 cents per kilowatt hour.

- The new SUNRGI technology slashes the average total cost of solar power, but the cost doesn't get it down to a level that competes with the other technologies.

- The news article says that SUNRGI's average total cost of 7 cents a kilowatt hour is "roughly the price of cheap coal-fired electricity."

- Figure 1 shows the average total cost of coal-generated electricity at 4 cents per kilowatt hour. Based on this (correct) cost, it appears that SUNRGI cannot compete with coal (if we ignore the emission costs of coal).

- Remember, though, that average total cost varies with the output rate. The costs in Fig. 1 are those for operating plants at their most efficient level—80 percent of maximum capacity. (The closer a plant operates to its theoretical maximum output, the higher are the maintenance costs and so the higher is the average total cost.)

- Figures 2 and 3 compare the *ATC* curves and *MC* curves for producing electricity by using coal and solar technologies.

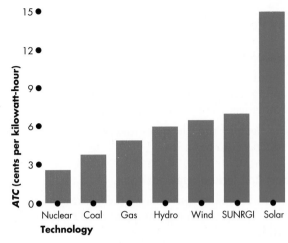

Figure 1 Average total costs compared

- In Fig. 2, the average total cost of electricity generated by coal has a minimum at 4 cents per kilowatt hour at 80 percent plant capacity.

- In Fig. 3, the average total cost of electricity generated by solar technology decreases as the plant is operated closer to capacity.

- The marginal cost of producing electricity by using coal eventually rises (Fig. 2), but the marginal cost of solar electricity is zero (Fig.3). All the costs for solar power are fixed costs.

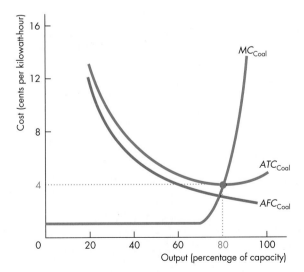

Figure 2 Cost curves for coal-generated electricity

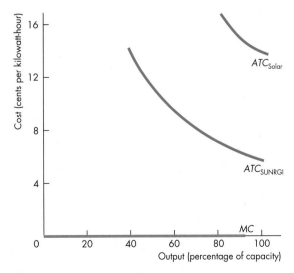

Figure 3 Cost curves for solar power

SUMMARY

Key Points

Decision Time Frames (p. 252)

- In the short run, the quantity of at least one factor of production is fixed and the quantities of the other factors of production can be varied.

- In the long run, the quantities of all factors of production can be varied.

Short-Run Technology Constraint (pp. 253–256)

- A total product curve shows the quantity a firm can produce with a given quantity of capital and different quantities of labor.

- Initially, the marginal product of labor increases as the quantity of labor increases, because of increased specialization and the division of labor.

- Eventually, marginal product diminishes because an increasing quantity of labor must share a fixed quantity of capital—the law of diminishing returns.

- Initially, average product increases as the quantity of labor increases, but eventually average product diminishes.

Short-Run Cost (pp. 257–261)

- As output increases, total fixed cost is constant, and total variable cost and total cost increase.

- As output increases, average fixed cost decreases and average variable cost, average total cost, and marginal cost decrease at low outputs and increase at high outputs. These cost curves are U-shaped.

Long-Run Cost (pp. 262–265)

- A firm has a set of short-run cost curves for each different plant. For each output, the firm has one least-cost plant. The larger the output, the larger is the plant that will minimize average total cost.

- The long-run average cost curve traces out the lowest attainable average total cost at each output when both capital and labor inputs can be varied.

- With economies of scale, the long-run average cost curve slopes downward. With diseconomies of scale, the long-run average cost curve slopes upward.

Key Figures and Table

Key Terms

PROBLEMS and APPLICATIONS ◆

myeconlab Work problems 1–11 in Chapter 11 Study Plan and get instant feedback.
Work problems 12–22 as Homework, a Quiz, or a Test if assigned by your instructor.

1. Which of the following news items involves a short-run decision and which involves a long-run decision? Explain.

   January 31, 2008: Starbucks will open 75 more stores abroad than originally predicted, for a total of 975.

   February 25, 2008: For three hours on Tuesday, Starbucks will shut down every single one of its 7,100 stores so that baristas can receive a refresher course.

   June 2, 2008: Starbucks replaces baristas with vending machines.

   July 18, 2008: Starbucks is closing 616 stores by the end of March.

2. The table sets out Sue's Surfboards' total product schedule.

Labor (workers per week)	Output (surfboards per week)
1	30
2	70
3	120
4	160
5	190
6	210
7	220

   a. Draw the total product curve.
   b. Calculate the average product of labor and draw the average product curve.
   c. Calculate the marginal product of labor and draw the marginal product curve.
   d. Over what output range does the firm enjoy the benefits of increased specialization and division of labor?
   e. Over what output range does the firm experience diminishing marginal product of labor?
   f. Over what output range does this firm experience an increasing average product of labor but a diminishing marginal product of labor?
   g. Explain how it is possible for a firm to experience simultaneously an increasing *average* product but a diminishing *marginal* product.

3. Sue's Surfboards, in problem 2, hires workers at $500 a week and its total fixed cost is $1,000 a week.

   a. Calculate total cost, total variable cost, and total fixed cost of each output in the table. Plot these points and sketch the short-run total cost curves passing through them.
   b. Calculate average total cost, average fixed cost, average variable cost, and marginal cost of each output in the table. Plot these points and sketch the short-run average and marginal cost curves passing through them.
   c. Illustrate the connection between Sue's *AP*, *MP*, *AVC*, and *MC* curves in graphs like those in Fig. 11.6.

4. Sue's Surfboards, in problems 2 and 3, rents a factory building and the rent is increased by $200 a week. If other things remain the same, how do Sue's Surfboards' short-run average cost curves and marginal cost curve change?

5. Workers at Sue's Surfboards, in problems 2 and 3, negotiate a wage increase of $100 a week for each worker. If other things remain the same, explain how Sue's Surfboards' short-run average cost curves and marginal cost curve change.

6. Sue's Surfboards, in problem 2, buys a second plant and the output produced by each worker increases by 50 percent. The total fixed cost of operating each plant is $1,000 a week. Each worker is paid $500 a week.

   a. Calculate the average total cost of producing 180 and 240 surfboards a week when Sue's Surfboards operates two plants. Graph these points and sketch the *ATC* curve.
   b. To produce 180 surfboards a week, is it efficient to operate one or two plants?
   c. To produce 160 surfboards a week, is it efficient for Sue's to operate one or two plants?

7. **Airlines Seek Out New Ways to Save on Fuel as Costs Soar**

   The financial pain of higher fuel prices is particularly acute for airlines because it is their single biggest expense. ... [Airlines] pump about 7,000 gallons into a Boeing 737 and as much as 60,000 gallons into the bigger 747 jet. ... Each generation of aircraft is more efficient. At Northwest, the Airbus A330 long-range jets use 38 percent less fuel than the DC-10s they replaced, while the Airbus A319 medium-range planes are 27 percent more efficient than DC-9s. ...

The New York Times, June 11, 2008

a. Is the price of fuel a fixed cost or a variable cost for an airline?

b. Explain how an increase in the price of fuel changes an airline's total costs, average costs, and marginal cost.

c. Draw a graph to show the effects of an increase in the price of fuel on an airline's *TFC*, *TVC*, *AFC*, *AVC*, and *MC* curves.

d. Explain how a technological advance that makes an airplane engine more fuel efficient changes an airline's total product, marginal product, and average product.

e. Draw a graph to illustrate the effects of a more fuel-efficient aircraft on an airline's *TP*, *MP*, and *AP* curves.

f. Explain how a technological advance that makes an airplane engine more fuel-efficient changes an airline's average variable cost, marginal cost, and average total cost.

g. Draw a graph to illustrate how a technological advance that makes an airplane engine more fuel efficient changes an airline's *AVC*, *MC*, and *ATC* curves.

8. The table shows the production function of Jackie's Canoe Rides.

Labor	Output (rides per day)			
(workers per day)	Plant 1	Plant 2	Plant 3	Plant 4
10	20	40	55	65
20	40	60	75	85
30	65	75	90	100
40	75	85	100	110
Canoes	10	20	30	40

Jackie's pays $100 a day for each canoe it rents and $50 a day for each canoe operator it hires.

a. Graph the *ATC* curves for Plant 1 and Plant 2.

b. On your graph in a, plot the *ATC* curves for Plant 3 and Plant 4.

c. On Jackie's *LRAC* curve, what is the average cost of producing 40, 75, and 85 rides a week?

d. What is Jackie's minimum efficient scale?

e. Explain how Jackie's uses its *LRAC* curve to decide how many canoes to rent.

f. Does Jackie's production function feature economies of scale or diseconomies of scale?

9. **Business Boot Camp**

At a footwear company called Caboots, sales rose from $160,000 in 2000 to $2.3 million in 2006. But in 2007 sales dipped to $1.5 million. Joey and Priscilla Sanchez, who run Caboots, blame the decline partly on a flood that damaged the firm's office and sapped morale.

Based on a *Fortune* article, *CNN*, April 23, 2008

If the Sanchezes are correct in their assumptions and the prices of footwear didn't change

a. Explain the effect of the flood on the total product curve and marginal product curve at Caboots.

b. Draw a graph to show the effect of the flood on the total product curve and marginal product curve at Caboots.

10. **No Need for Economies of Scale**

Illinois Tool Works Inc. might not seem like an incubator for innovation. The 93-year-old company manufactures a hodgepodge of mundane products, from automotive components and industrial fasteners to zip-strip closures for plastic bags ... and dedicates production lines and resources to high-volume products. A line will run only those three or four products. ... Runs are much longer and more efficient. By physically linking machines ... they are able to eliminate work in process and storage areas. ... All the material handling and indirect costs are reduced.

BusinessWeek, October 31, 2005

a. How would you expect "physically linking machines" to affect the firm's short-run product curves and short-run average cost curves?

b. Draw a graph to show your predicted effects of "physically linking machines" on the firm's short-run product curves and cost curves.

c. Explain how concentrating "production lines and resources to high-volume products" can influence long-run average cost as the output rate increases.

11. **Grain Prices Go the Way of the Oil Price**

Every morning millions of Americans confront the latest trend in commodities markets at their kitchen table. ... Rising prices for crops ... have begun to drive up the cost of breakfast.

The Economist, July 21, 2007

Explain how the rising price of crops affects the average total cost and marginal cost of producing breakfast cereals.

12. Coffee King Starbucks Raises Its Prices

Blame the sour news at Starbucks this week on soaring milk costs. … The wholesale price [of] milk is up nearly 70% in the 12 months. …"There's a lot of milk in those [Starbucks] lattes," notes John Glass, CIBC World Markets restaurant analyst.

USA Today, July 24, 2007

a. Is milk a fixed factor of production or a variable factor of production?

b. Describe how the increase in the price of milk changes Starbucks' short-run cost curves.

13. Bill's Bakery has a fire and Bill loses some of his cost data. The bits of paper that he recovers after the fire provide the information in the following table (all the cost numbers are dollars).

TP	AFC	AVC	ATC	MC
10	120	100	220	
				80
20	*A*	*B*	150	
				90
30	40	90	130	
				130
40	30	*C*	*D*	
				E
50	24	108	132	

Bill asks you to come to his rescue and provide the missing data in the five spaces identified as *A*, *B*, *C*, *D*, and *E*.

14. ProPainters hires students at $250 a week to paint houses. It leases equipment at $500 a week. The table sets out its total product schedule.

Labor (students)	Output (houses painted per week)
1	2
2	5
3	9
4	12
5	14
6	15

a. If ProPainters paints 12 houses a week, calculate its total cost, average total cost, and marginal cost

b. At what output is average total cost a minimum?

c. Explain why the gap between total cost and total variable cost is the same at all outputs.

15. ProPainters hires students at $250 a week to paint houses. It leases equipment at $500 a week. Suppose that ProPainters doubles the number of students it hires and doubles the amount of equipment it leases. ProPainters experiences diseconomies of scale.

a. Explain how the *ATC* curve with one unit of equipment differs from that when ProPainters uses double the amount of equipment.

b. Explain what might be the source of the diseconomies of scale that ProPainters experiences.

16. The table shows the production function of Bonnie's Balloon Rides.

Labor (workers per day)	Output (rides per day)			
	Plant 1	Plant 2	Plant 3	Plant 4
10	4	10	13	15
20	10	15	18	20
30	13	18	22	24
40	15	20	24	26
50	16	21	25	27
Balloons (number)	1	2	3	4

Bonnie's pays $500 a day for each balloon it rents and $25 a day for each balloon operator it hires.

a. Graph the *ATC* curves for Plant 1 and Plant 2.

b. On your graph in a, plot the *ATC* curves for Plant 3 and Plant 4.

c. On Bonnie's *LRAC* curve, what is the average cost of producing 18 rides and 15 rides a day?

d. Explain how Bonnie's uses its long-run average cost curve to decide how many balloons to rent.

17. A firm is producing at minimum average total cost with its current plant. Sketch the firm's short-run average total cost curve and long-run average cost curve for each of the following situations and explain, using the concepts of economies of scale and diseconomies of scale, the circumstances in which the firm

a. Can lower its average total cost by increasing its plant.

b. Can lower its average total cost by decreasing its plant.

c. Cannot lower its average total cost.

18. **Starbucks Unit Brews Up Self-Serve Espresso Bars**

    … automated, self-serve espresso kiosks are in grocery stores. … The machines, which grind their own beans, crank out lattes, … and drip coffees … take credit and debit cards, [and] cash. … Concordia Coffee, a small Bellevue coffee equipment maker, builds the self-serve kiosks and sells them to Coinstar for just under $40,000 per unit. Coinstar installs them … and provides maintenance. The kiosks use [Starbucks'] Seattle's Best Coffee. … The self-serve kiosks remove the labor costs of having a barista. … Store personnel handle refills of coffee beans and milk. …

    MSNBC, June 1, 2008

    a. What is Coinstar's total fixed cost of operating one self-serve kiosk?
    b. What are Coinstar's variable costs of providing coffee at a self-serve kiosk?
    c. Assume that a coffee machine operated by a barista costs less than $40,000. Explain how the fixed costs, variable costs, and total costs of barista-served and self-served coffee differ.
    d. Sketch the marginal cost and average cost curves implied by your answer to c.

19. **A Bakery on the Rise**

    Some 500 customers a day line up to buy Avalon's breads, scones, muffins, and coffee. … Staffing and management are worries. Avalon now employs 35 … [and] it will hire 15 more. … Payroll will climb by 30% to 40%. … As new CEO, Victor has quickly executed an ambitious agenda that includes the move to a larger space. … Avalon's costs will soar. … Its monthly rent, for example, will leap to $10,000, from $3,500.

    CNN, March 24, 2008

    a. Which of Avalon's decisions described in the news clip is a short-run decision and which is a long-run decision?
    b. Why is Avalon's long-run decision riskier than its short-run decision?
    c. By how much will Avalon's short-run decision increase its total variable cost?
    d. By how much will Avalon's long-run decision increase its monthly total fixed cost?
    e. Draw a graph to illustrate Avalon's short-run *ATC* curve before and after the events described in the news clip.

20. **Gap Will Focus on Smaller Scale Stores**

    Gap has too many stores that are 12,500 square feet … deemed too large. … "Stores are larger than we need." … The target size of stores should be 6,000 square feet to 10,000 square feet. In addition, the company plans to combine previously separate concept stores. Some Gap body, adult, maternity, baby and kids stores will be combined in one, rather than in separate spaces as they have been previously.

    CNN, June 10, 2008

    a. Thinking of a Gap store as a production plant, explain why Gap is making a decision to reduce the size of its stores.
    b. Is Gap's decision a long-run decision or a short-run decision? Explain.
    c. How might combining Gap's concept stores into one store help better take advantage of economies of scale?

21. **The Sunk-Cost Fallacy**

    You have good tickets to a basketball game an hour's drive away. There's a blizzard raging outside, and the game is being televised. You can sit warm and safe at home by a roaring fire and watch it on TV, or you can bundle up, dig out your car, and go to the game. What do you do?

    Slate, September 9, 2005

    a. What type of cost is your expenditure on tickets?
    b. Why is the cost of the ticket irrelevant to your current decision about whether to stay at home or go to the game?

22. Study *Reading Between the Lines* on pp. 266-267 and then answer the following questions.

    a. Sketch the *AFC*, *AVC*, and *ATC* curves for electricity production using seven technologies: (i) nuclear, (ii) coal, (iii) gas, (iv) hydro (v) wind, (vi) SUNRGI's new solar system, and (vii) today's solar technology.
    b. Sketch the marginal cost curves for electricity production using seven technologies: (i) nuclear, (ii) coal, (iii) gas, (iv) hydro, (v) wind, (vi) SUNRGI's new solar system, and (vii) today's solar technology.
    c. Given the cost differences among the different methods of generating electricity, why do you think we use more than one method? If we could use only one method, which would it be?

12 ◆ Perfect Competition

After studying this chapter, you will be able to:

- Define perfect competition

- Explain how a firm makes its output decision and why it sometimes shuts down temporarily and lays off its workers

- Explain how price and output are determined in a perfectly competitive market

- Explain why firms enter and leave a competitive market and the consequences of entry and exit

- Predict the effects of a change in demand and of a technological advance

- Explain why perfect competition is efficient

Airlines and producers of trucks, cars, and motor bikes are facing tough times: prices are being slashed to drive sales and profits are turning into losses. Airlines are cutting back on flights, charging to check bags, drink a soda, or use a blanket, and some are even going out of business. Vehicle production has been scaled back and workers have either been laid off temporarily or let go permanently.

Taking a longer view, astonishing transformations have occurred over the past decade. Today, at $600 for a powerful laptop, almost every student owns one. Fifteen years ago, at $6,000 for a heavy, slow portable computer, these machines were a rare sight on campus.

What forces are responsible for this diversity of performance of production, prices, and profits? What are the causes and consequences of firms entering or leaving a market? Why do firms sometimes stop producing and temporarily lay off their workers?

To study competitive markets, we are going to build a model of a market in which competition is as fierce and extreme as possible—more extreme than in the examples we've just considered. We call this situation "perfect competition." In *Reading Between the Lines* at the end of the chapter, we'll apply the model to the market for air transportation services and see how the effects of high fuel prices and a fall in demand are playing out in that market.

273

◆ What Is Perfect Competition?

The firms that you study in this chapter face the force of raw competition. We call this extreme form of competition perfect competition. **Perfect competition** is a market in which

- Many firms sell identical products to many buyers.
- There are no restrictions on entry into the market.
- Established firms have no advantage over new ones.
- Sellers and buyers are well informed about prices.

Farming, fishing, wood pulping and paper milling, the manufacture of paper cups and shopping bags, grocery retailing, photo finishing, lawn services, plumbing, painting, dry cleaning, and laundry services are all examples of highly competitive industries.

How Perfect Competition Arises

Perfect competition arises if the minimum efficient scale of a single producer is small relative to the market demand for the good or service. In this situation, there is room in the market for many firms. A firm's *minimum efficient scale* is the smallest output at which long-run average cost reaches its lowest level. (See Chapter 11, p. 265.)

In perfect competition, each firm produces a good that has no unique characteristics, so consumers don't care which firm's good they buy.

Price Takers

Firms in perfect competition are price takers. A **price taker** is a firm that cannot influence the market price because its production is an insignificant part of the total market.

Imagine that you are a wheat farmer in Kansas. You have a thousand acres planted—which sounds like a lot. But compared to the millions of acres in Colorado, Oklahoma, Texas, Nebraska, and the Dakotas, as well as the millions more in Canada, Argentina, Australia, and Ukraine, your thousand acres are a drop in the ocean. Nothing makes your wheat any better than any other farmer's, and all the buyers of wheat know the price at which they can do business.

If the market price of wheat is $4 a bushel, then that is the highest price you can get for your wheat. Ask for $4.10 and no one will buy from you. Offer it for $3.90 and you'll be sold out in a flash and have given away 10¢ a bushel. You take the market price.

Economic Profit and Revenue

A firm's goal is to maximize *economic profit*, which is equal to total revenue minus total cost. Total cost is the *opportunity cost* of production, which includes *normal profit*. (See Chapter 10, p. 228.)

A firm's **total revenue** equals the price of its output multiplied by the number of units of output sold (price × quantity). **Marginal revenue** is the change in total revenue that results from a one-unit increase in the quantity sold. Marginal revenue is calculated by dividing the change in total revenue by the change in the quantity sold.

Figure 12.1 illustrates these revenue concepts. In part (a), the market demand curve, D, and market supply curve, S, determine the market price. The market price is $25 a sweater. Campus Sweaters is one of the many producers of sweaters. So the best it can do is to sell its sweaters for $25 each.

Total Revenue Total revenue is equal to the price multiplied by the quantity sold. In the table in Fig. 12.1, if Campus Sweaters sells 9 sweaters, its total revenue is $225 (9 × $25).

Figure 12.1(b) shows the firm's total revenue curve (TR), which graphs the relationship between total revenue and the quantity sold. At point A on the TR curve, the firm sells 9 sweaters and has a total revenue of $225. Because each additional sweater sold brings in a constant amount—$25—the total revenue curve is an upward-sloping straight line.

Marginal Revenue Marginal revenue is the change in total revenue that results from a one-unit increase in quantity sold. In the table in Fig. 12.1, when the quantity sold increases from 8 to 9 sweaters, total revenue increases from $200 to $225, so marginal revenue is $25 a sweater.

Because the firm in perfect competition is a price taker, the change in total revenue that results from a one-unit increase in the quantity sold equals the market price. *In perfect competition, the firm's marginal revenue equals the market price.* Figure 12.1(c) shows the firm's marginal revenue curve (MR) as the horizontal line at the market price.

Demand for the Firm's Product The firm can sell any quantity it chooses at the market price. So the demand curve for the firm's product is a horizontal line at the market price, the same as the firm's marginal revenue curve.

FIGURE 12.1 Demand, Price, and Revenue in Perfect Competition

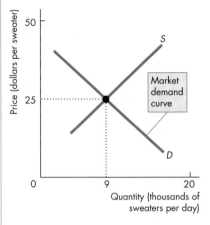

(a) Sweater market

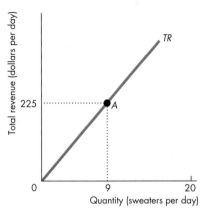

(b) Campus Sweaters total revenue

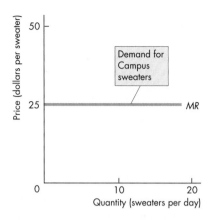

(c) Campus Sweaters marginal revenue

Quantity sold (Q) (sweaters per day)	Price (P) (dollars per sweater)	Total revenue (TR = P × Q) (dollars)	Marginal revenue (MR = ∆TR/∆Q) (dollars per additional sweater)
8	25	200	
			 25
9	25	225	
			 25
10	25	250	

In part (a), market demand and market supply determine the market price (and quantity). Part (b) shows the firm's total revenue curve (*TR*). Point *A* corresponds to the second row of the table—Campus Sweaters sells 9 sweaters at $25 a sweater, so total revenue is $225. Part (c) shows the firm's marginal revenue curve (*MR*). This curve is also the demand curve for the firm's sweaters. The demand for sweaters from Campus Sweaters is perfectly elastic at the market price of $25 a sweater.

myeconlab animation

A horizontal demand curve illustrates a perfectly elastic demand, so the demand for the firm's product is perfectly elastic. A sweater from Campus Sweaters is a *perfect substitute* for a sweater from any other factory. But the *market* demand for sweaters is *not* perfectly elastic: Its elasticity depends on the substitutability of sweaters for other goods and services.

The Firm's Decisions

The goal of the competitive firm is to maximize economic profit, given the constraints it faces. To achieve its goal, a firm must decide

1. How to produce at minimum cost
2. What quantity to produce
3. Whether to enter or exit a market

You've already seen how a firm makes the first decision. It does so by operating with the plant that minimizes long-run average cost—by being on its long-run average cost curve. We'll now see how the firm makes the other two decisions. We start by looking at the firm's output decision.

Review Quiz

1 Why is a firm in perfect competition a price taker?
2 In perfect competition, what is the relationship between the demand for the firm's output and the market demand?
3 In perfect competition, why is a firm's marginal revenue curve also the demand curve for the firm's output?
4 What decisions must a firm make to maximize profit?

myeconlab Work Study Plan 12.1 and get instant feedback.

◆ The Firm's Output Decision

A firm's cost curves (total cost, average cost, and marginal cost) describe the relationship between its output and costs (see pp. 257–261). A firm's revenue curves (total revenue and marginal revenue) describe the relationship between its output and revenue (p. 275). From the firm's cost curves and revenue curves, we can find the output that maximizes the firm's economic profit.

Figure 12.2 shows how to do this for Campus Sweaters. The table lists the firm's total revenue and total cost at different outputs, and part (a) of the figure shows the firm's total revenue curve, *TR*, and total cost curve, *TC*. These curves are graphs of the

numbers in the first three columns of the table.

Economic profit equals total revenue minus total cost. The fourth column of the table in Fig. 12.2 shows the economic profit made by Campus Sweaters, and part (b) of the figure graphs these numbers as its economic profit curve, *EP*.

Economic profit is maximized at an output of 9 sweaters a day. At this output, total revenue is $225 a day, total cost is $183 a day, and economic profit is $42 a day. No other output rate achieves a larger profit. At outputs of less than 4 sweaters and more than 12 sweaters a day, the firm incurs an economic loss. At either 4 or 12 sweaters a day, the firm makes zero economic profit, called a *break-even* point.

FIGURE 12.2 Total Revenue, Total Cost, and Economic Profit

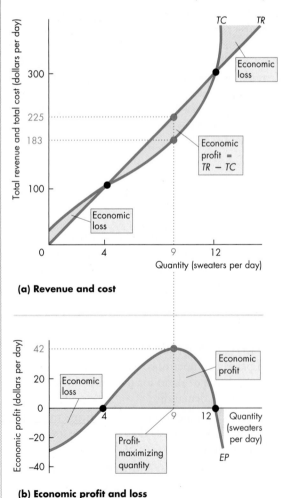

(a) Revenue and cost

(b) Economic profit and loss

Quantity (Q) (sweaters per day)	Total revenue (TR) (dollars)	Total cost (TC) (dollars)	Economic profit (TR – TC) (dollars)
0	0	22	–22
1	25	45	–20
2	50	66	–16
3	75	85	–10
4	100	100	0
5	125	114	11
6	150	126	24
7	175	141	34
8	200	160	40
9	**225**	**183**	**42**
10	250	210	40
11	275	245	30
12	300	300	0
13	325	360	–35

The table lists the total revenue, total cost, and economic profit of Campus Sweaters. Part (a) graphs the total revenue and total cost curves and part (b) graphs economic profit. Campus Sweaters makes maximum economic profit, $42 a day ($225 – $183), when it produces 9 sweaters a day. At outputs of 4 sweaters and 12 sweaters a day, Campus Sweaters makes zero economic profit—these are break-even points. At outputs less than 4 sweaters and greater than 12 sweaters a day, Campus Sweaters incurs an economic loss.

Marginal Analysis and the Supply Decision

Another way to find the profit-maximizing output is to use *marginal analysis*, which compares marginal revenue, *MR*, with marginal cost, *MC*. As output increases, marginal revenue is constant but marginal cost eventually increases.

If marginal revenue exceeds the firm's marginal cost ($MR > MC$), then the revenue from selling one more unit exceeds the cost of producing that unit and an increase in output will increase economic profit. If marginal revenue is less than marginal cost ($MR < MC$), then the revenue from selling one more unit is less than the cost of producing that unit and a decrease in output will increase economic profit. If marginal revenue equals marginal cost ($MR = MC$), then the revenue from selling one more unit equals the cost incurred to produce that unit. Economic profit is maximized and either an increase or a decrease in output decreases economic profit.

Figure 12.3 illustrates these propositions. If Campus Sweaters increases its output from 8 sweaters to 9 sweaters a day, marginal revenue ($25) exceeds marginal cost ($23), so by producing the 9th sweater economic profit increases by $2 from $40 to $42 a day. The blue area in the figure shows the increase in economic profit when the firm increases production from 8 to 9 sweaters per day.

If Campus Sweaters increases its output from 9 sweaters to 10 sweaters a day, marginal revenue ($25) is less than marginal cost ($27), so by producing the 10th sweater, economic profit decreases. The last column of the table shows that economic profit decreases from $42 to $40 a day. The red area in the figure shows the economic loss that arises from increasing production from 9 to 10 sweaters a day.

Campus Sweaters maximizes economic profit by producing 9 sweaters a day, the quantity at which marginal revenue equals marginal cost.

A firm's profit-maximizing output is its quantity supplied at the market price. The quantity supplied at a price of $25 a sweater is 9 sweaters a day. If the price were higher than $25 a sweater, the firm would increase production. If the price were lower than $25 a sweater, the firm would decrease production. These profit-maximizing responses to different market prices are the foundation of the law of supply:

Other things remaining the same, the higher the market price of a good, the greater is the quantity supplied of that good.

FIGURE 12.3   Profit-Maximizing Output

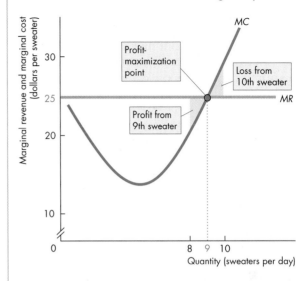

Quantity (Q) (sweaters per day)	Total revenue (TR) (dollars)	Marginal revenue (MR) (dollars per additional sweater)	Total cost (TC) (dollars)	Marginal cost (MC) (dollars per additional sweater)	Economic profit (TR − TC) (dollars)
7	175		141		34
		25		19	
8	200		160		40
		25		23	
9	225		183		42
		25		27	
10	250		210		40
		25		35	
11	275		245		30

The firm maximizes profit by producing the output at which marginal revenue equals marginal cost and marginal cost is increasing. The table and figure show that marginal cost equals marginal revenue and economic profit is maximized when Campus Sweaters produces 9 sweaters a day. The table shows that if Campus Sweaters increases output from 8 to 9 sweaters, marginal cost is $23, which is less than the marginal revenue of $25. If output increases from 9 to 10 sweaters, marginal cost is $27, which exceeds the marginal revenue of $25. If marginal revenue exceeds marginal cost, an increase in output increases economic profit. If marginal revenue is less than marginal cost, an increase in output decreases economic profit. If marginal revenue equals marginal cost, economic profit is maximized.

 myeconlab animation

Temporary Shutdown Decision

You've seen that a firm maximizes profit by producing the quantity at which marginal revenue (price) equals marginal cost. But suppose that at this quantity, price is less than average total cost. In this case, the firm incurs an economic loss. Maximum profit is a loss (a minimum loss). What does the firm do?

If the firm expects the loss to be permanent, it goes out of business. But if it expects the loss to be temporary, the firm must decide whether to shut down temporarily and produce no output, or to keep producing. To make this decision, the firm compares the loss from shutting down with the loss from producing and takes the action that minimizes its loss.

Loss Comparisons A firm's economic loss equals total fixed cost, *TFC*, plus total variable cost minus total revenue. Total variable cost equals average variable cost, *AVC* multiplied by the quantity produced, *Q*, and total revenue equals price, *P*, multiplied by the quantity *Q*. So

$$\text{Economic loss} = TFC + (AVC - P) \times Q.$$

If the firm shuts down, it produces no output ($Q = 0$). The firm has no variable costs and no revenue but it must pay its fixed costs, so its economic loss equals total fixed cost.

If the firm produces, then in addition to its fixed costs, it incurs variable costs. But it also receives revenue. Its economic loss equals total fixed cost—the loss when shut down—plus total variable cost minus total revenue. If total variable cost exceeds total revenue, this loss exceeds total fixed cost and the firm shuts down. Equivalently, if average variable cost exceeds price, this loss exceeds total fixed cost and the firm shuts down.

The Shutdown Point A firm's **shutdown point** is the price and quantity at which it is indifferent between producing and shutting down. The shutdown point occurs at the price and the quantity at which average variable cost is a minimum. At the shutdown point, the firm is minimizing its loss and its loss equals total fixed cost. If the price falls below minimum average variable cost, the firm shuts down temporarily and continues to incur a loss equal to total fixed cost. At prices above minimum average variable cost but below average total cost, the firm produces the loss minimizing output and incurs a loss, but a loss that is less than total fixed cost.

Figure 12.4 illustrates the firm's shutdown decision and the shutdown point that we've just described for Campus Sweaters.

The firm's average variable cost curve is *AVC* and the marginal cost curve is *MC*. Average variable cost has a minimum of $17 a sweater when output is 7 sweaters a day. The *MC* curve intersects the *AVC* curve at its minimum. (We explained this relationship between a marginal and average cost in Chapter 11; see pp. 258–259.)

The figure shows the marginal revenue curve *MR* when the price is $17 a sweater, a price equal to minimum average variable cost.

Marginal revenue equals marginal cost at 7 sweaters a day, so this quantity maximizes economic profit (minimizes economic loss). The *ATC* curve shows that the firm's average total cost of producing 7 sweaters a day is $20.14 a sweater. The firm incurs a loss equal to $3.14 a sweater on 7 sweaters a day, so its loss is $22 a day, which equals total fixed cost.

FIGURE 12.4 The Shutdown Decision

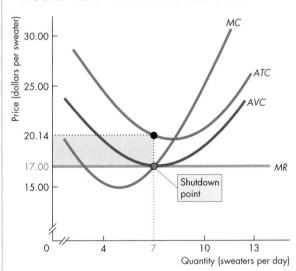

The shutdown point is at minimum average variable cost. At a price below minimum average variable cost, the firm shuts down and produces no output. At a price equal to minimum average variable cost, the firm is indifferent between shutting down and producing no output or producing the output at minimum average variable cost. Either way, the firm minimizes its economic loss and incurs a loss equal to total fixed cost.

myeconlab animation

The Firm's Supply Curve

A perfectly competitive firm's supply curve shows how its profit-maximizing output varies as the market price varies, other things remaining the same. The supply curve is derived from the firm's marginal cost curve and average variable cost curves. Figure 12.5 illustrates the derivation of the supply curve.

When the price *exceeds* minimum average variable cost (more than $17), the firm maximizes profit by producing the output at which marginal cost equals price. If the price rises, the firm increases its output—it moves up along its marginal cost curve.

When the price is *less than* minimum average variable cost (less than $17 a sweater), the firm maximizes profit by temporarily shutting down and producing no output. The firm produces zero output at all prices below minimum average variable cost.

When the price *equals* minimum average variable cost, the firm maximizes profit *either* by temporarily shutting down and producing no output *or* by producing the output at which average variable cost is a minimum—the shutdown point, T. The firm never produces a quantity between zero and the quantity at the shutdown point T (a quantity greater than zero and less than 7 sweaters a day).

The firm's supply curve in Fig. 12.5(b) runs along the y-axis from a price of zero to a price equal to minimum average variable cost, jumps to point T, and then, as the price rises above minimum average variable cost, follows the marginal cost curve.

Review Quiz

1 Why does a firm in perfect competition produce the quantity at which marginal cost equals price?
2 What is the lowest price at which a firm produces an output? Explain why.
3 What is the relationship between a firm's supply curve, its marginal cost curve, and its average variable cost curve?

 Work Study Plan 12.2 and get instant feedback.

So far, we have studied a single firm in isolation. We have seen that the firm's profit-maximizing decisions depend on the market price, which the firm takes as given. But how is the market price determined? Let's find out.

FIGURE 12.5 A Firm's Supply Curve

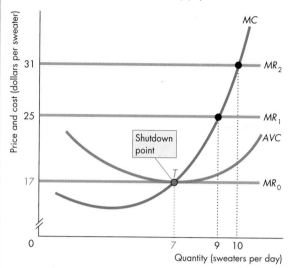

(a) Marginal cost and average variable cost

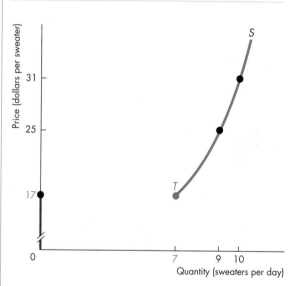

(b) Campus Sweaters short-run supply curve

Part (a) shows the firm's profit-maximizing output at various market prices. At $25 a sweater, it produces 9 sweaters, and at $17 a sweater, it produces 7 sweaters. At all prices below $17 a sweater, Campus Sweaters produces nothing. Its shutdown point is T. Part (b) shows the firm's supply curve—the quantity of sweaters it produces at each price. Its supply curve is made up of the marginal cost curve at all prices above minimum average variable cost and the vertical axis at all prices below minimum average variable cost.

myeconlab animation

Output, Price, and Profit in the Short Run

To determine the price and quantity in a perfectly competitive market, we need to know how market demand and market supply interact. We start by studying a perfectly competitive market in the short run. The short run is a situation in which the number of firms is fixed.

Market Supply in the Short Run

The **short-run market supply curve** shows the quantity supplied by all the firms in the market at each price when each firm's plant and the number of firms remain the same.

You've seen how an individual firm's supply curve is determined. The market supply curve is derived from the individual supply curves. The quantity supplied by the market at a given price is the sum of the quantities supplied by all the firms in the market at that price.

Figure 12.6 shows the supply curve for the competitive sweater market. In this example, the market consists of 1,000 firms exactly like Campus Sweaters. At each price, the quantity supplied by the market is 1,000 times the quantity supplied by a single firm.

The table in Fig. 12.6 shows the firm's and the market's supply schedules and how the market supply curve is constructed. At prices below $17 a sweater, every firm in the market shuts down; the quantity supplied by the market is zero. At $17 a sweater, each firm is indifferent between shutting down and producing nothing or operating and producing 7 sweaters a day. Some firms will shut down, and others will supply 7 sweaters a day. The quantity supplied by each firm is *either* 0 or 7 sweaters, and the quantity supplied by the market is *between* 0 (all firms shut down) and 7,000 (all firms produce 7 sweaters a day each).

The market supply curve is a graph of the market supply schedules and the points on the supply curve A through D represent the rows of the table.

To construct the market supply curve, we sum the quantities supplied by all the firms at each price. Each of the 1,000 firms in the market has a supply schedule like Campus Sweaters. At prices below $17 a sweater, the market supply curve runs along the *y*-axis. At $17 a sweater, the market supply curve is horizontal—supply is perfectly elastic. As the price

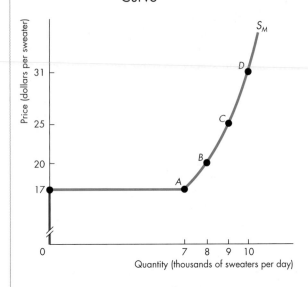

FIGURE 12.6   Short-Run Market Supply Curve

	Price (dollars per sweater)	Quantity supplied by Campus Sweaters (sweaters per day)	Quantity supplied by market (sweaters per day)
A	17	0 or 7	0 to 7,000
B	20	8	8,000
C	25	9	9,000
D	31	10	10,000

The market supply schedule is the sum of the supply schedules of all the individual firms. A market that consists of 1,000 identical firms has a supply schedule similar to that of one firm, but the quantity supplied by the market is 1,000 times as large as that of the one firm (see the table). The market supply curve is S_M. Points A, B, C, and D correspond to the rows of the table. At the shutdown price of $17 a sweater, each firm produces either 0 or 7 sweaters a day and the quantity supplied by the market is between 0 and 7,000 sweaters a day. The market supply is perfectly elastic at the shutdown price.

rises above $17 a sweater, each firm increases its quantity supplied and the quantity supplied by the market increases by 1,000 times that of one firm.

Short-Run Equilibrium

Market demand and short-run market supply determine the market price and market output. Figure 12.7(a) shows a short-run equilibrium. The short-run supply curve, S, is the same as S_M in Fig. 12.6. If the market demand curve is D_1, the market price is $20 a sweater. Each firm takes this price as given and produces its profit-maximizing output, which is 8 sweaters a day. Because the market has 1,000 identical firms, the market output is 8,000 sweaters a day.

A Change in Demand

Changes in demand bring changes to short-run market equilibrium. Figure 12.7 shows these changes.

If demand increases and the demand curve shifts rightward to D_2, the market price rises to $25 a sweater. At this price, each firm maximizes profit by increasing its output to 9 sweaters a day. The market output increases to 9,000 sweaters a day.

If demand decreases and the demand curve shifts leftward to D_3, the market price falls to $17. At this price, each firm maximizes profit by decreasing its output. If each firm produces 7 sweaters a day, the market output decreases to 7,000 sweaters a day.

If the demand curve shifts farther leftward than D_3, the market price remains at $17 a sweater because the market supply curve is horizontal at that price. Some firms continue to produce 7 sweaters a day, and others temporarily shut down. Firms are indifferent between these two activities, and whichever they choose, they incur an economic loss equal to total fixed cost. The number of firms continuing to produce is just enough to satisfy the market demand at a price of $17 a sweater.

Profits and Losses in the Short Run

In short-run equilibrium, although the firm produces the profit-maximizing output, it does not necessarily end up making an economic profit. It might do so, but it might alternatively break even or incur an economic loss. Economic profit (or loss) per sweater is price, P, minus average total cost, ATC. So economic profit (or loss) is $(P - ATC) \times Q$. If price

---

FIGURE 12.7 Short-Run Equilibrium

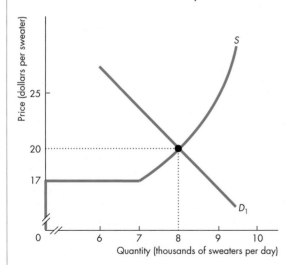

(a) Equilibrium

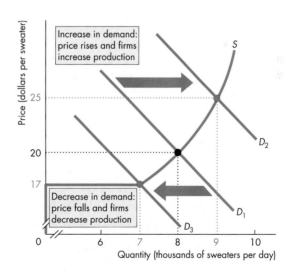

(b) Change in equilibrium

In part (a), the market supply curve is S and the market demand curve is D_1. The market price is $20 a sweater. At this price, each firm produces 8 sweaters a day and the market produces 8,000 sweaters a day.

In part (b), if the market demand increases to D_2, the

price rises to $25 a sweater. Each firm produces 9 sweaters a day and market output is 9,000 sweaters. If market demand decreases to D_3, the price falls to $17 a sweater and each firm decreases its output. If each firm produces 7 sweaters a day, the market output is 7,000 sweaters a day.

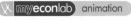

equals average total cost, a firm breaks even—the entrepreneur makes normal profit. If price exceeds average total cost, a firm makes an economic profit. If price is less than average total cost, a firm incurs an economic loss. Figure 12.8 shows these three possible short-run profit outcomes for Campus Sweaters that correspond to the three different levels of market demand that we've just examined.

Three Possible Short-Run Outcomes

Figure 12.8(a) corresponds to the situation in Fig. 12.7(a) where the market demand is D_1. The equilibrium price of a sweater is $20 and the firm produces 8 sweaters a day. Average total cost is $20 a sweater. Price equals average total cost (ATC), so the firm breaks even (makes zero economic profit).

Figure 12.8(b) corresponds to the situation in Fig. 12.7(b) where the market demand is D_2. The equilibrium price of a sweater is $25 and the firm produces 9 sweaters a day. Here, price exceeds average total cost, so the firm makes an economic profit. Its economic profit is $42 a day, which equals $4.67 per sweater ($25.00 – $20.33) multiplied by 9, the

profit-maximizing number of sweaters produced. The blue rectangle shows this economic profit. The height of that rectangle is profit per sweater, $4.67, and the length is the quantity of sweaters produced, 9 a day. So the area of the rectangle is economic profit of $42 a day.

Figure 12.8(c) corresponds to the situation in Fig. 12.7(b) where the market demand is D_3. The equilibrium price of a sweater is $17. Here, the price is less than average total cost, so the firm incurs an economic loss. Price and marginal revenue are $17 a sweater, and the profit-maximizing (in this case, loss-minimizing) output is 7 sweaters a day. Total revenue is $119 a day (7 × $17). Average total cost is $20.14 a sweater, so the economic loss is $3.14 per sweater ($20.14 – $17.00). This loss per sweater multiplied by the number of sweaters is $22. The red rectangle shows this economic loss. The height of that rectangle is economic loss per sweater, $3.14, and the length is the quantity of sweaters produced, 7 a day. So the area of the rectangle is the firm's economic loss of $22 a day. If the price dips below $17 a sweater, the firm temporarily shuts down and incurs an economic loss equal to total fixed cost.

FIGURE 12.8   Three Short-Run Outcomes for the Firm

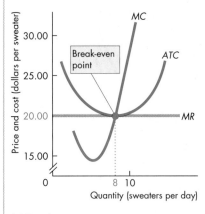

(a) Break even

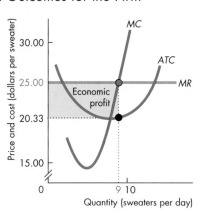

(b) Economic profit

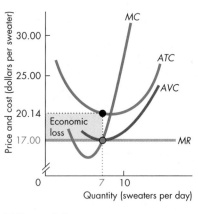

(c) Economic loss

In the short run, the firm might break even (make zero economic profit), make an economic profit, or incur an economic loss. In part (a), the price equals minimum average total cost. At the profit-maximizing output, the firm breaks even and makes zero economic profit. In part (b), the market price is $25 a sweater. At the profit-maximizing output,

the price exceeds average total cost and the firm makes an economic profit equal to the area of the blue rectangle. In part (c), the market price is $17 a sweater. At the profit-maximizing output, the price is below minimum average total cost and the firm incurs an economic loss equal to the area of the red rectangle.

Production Cutback and Temporary Shutdown

Drop in Demand for Bikes at Harley-Davidson

The high price of gasoline and anxiety about unemployment and future incomes brought a decrease in the demand for luxury goods including high-end motorcycles such as Harley-Davidsons.

Harley-Davidson's profit-maximizing response to the decrease in demand was to cut production and lay off workers. Some of the production cuts and lay-offs were temporary and some were permanent.

Harley-Davidson's bike production plant in York County, Pennsylvania, was temporarily shut down in the summer of 2008 because total revenue was insufficient to cover total variable cost.

The firm also permanently cut its workforce by 300 people. This permanent cut was like that at Campus Sweaters when the market demand for sweaters decreased from D_1 to D_3 in Fig. 12.7(b).

Review Quiz

1 How do we derive the short-run market supply curve in perfect competition?

2 In perfect competition, when market demand increases, explain how the price of the good and the output and profit of each firm changes in the short run.

3 In perfect competition, when market demand decreases, explain how the price of the good and the output and profit of each firm changes in the short run.

 Work Study Plan 12.3 and get instant feedback.

Output, Price, and Profit in the Long Run

In short-run equilibrium, a firm might make an economic profit, incur an economic loss, or break even. Although each of these three situations is a short-run equilibrium, only one of them is a long-run equilibrium. The reason is that in the long run, firms can enter or exit the market.

Entry and Exit

Entry occurs in a market when new firms come into the market and the number of firms increases. Exit occurs when existing firms leave a market and the number of firms decreases.

Firms respond to economic profit and economic loss by either entering or exiting a market. New firms enter a market in which existing firms are making an economic profit. Firms exit a market in which they are incurring an economic loss. Temporary economic profit and temporary economic loss don't trigger entry and exit. It's the prospect of persistent economic profit or loss that triggers entry and exit.

Entry and exit change the market supply, which influences the market price, the quantity produced by each firm, and its economic profit (or loss).

If firms enter a market, supply increases and the market supply curve shifts rightward. The increase in supply lowers the market price and eventually eliminates economic profit. When economic profit reaches zero, entry stops.

If firms exit a market, supply decreases and the market supply curve shifts leftward. The market price rises and economic loss decreases. Eventually, economic loss is eliminated and exit stops.

To summarize:

- New firms enter a market in which existing firms are making an economic profit.
- As new firms enter a market, the market price falls and the economic profit of each firm decreases.
- Firms exit a market in which they are incurring an economic loss.
- As firms leave a market, the market price rises and the economic loss incurred by the remaining firms decreases.
- Entry and exit stop when firms make zero economic profit.

A Closer Look at Entry

The sweater market has 800 firms with cost curves like those in Fig. 12.9(a). The market demand curve is D, the market supply curve is S_1, and the price is $25 a sweater in Fig. 12.9(b). Each firm produces 9 sweaters a day and makes an economic profit.

This economic profit is a signal for new firms to enter the market. As entry takes place, supply increases and the market supply curve shifts rightward toward S^*. As supply increases with no change in demand, the market price gradually falls from $25 to $20 a sweater. At this lower price, each firm makes zero economic profit and entry stops.

Entry results in an increase in market output, but each firm's output *decreases*. Because the price falls, each firm moves down its supply curve and produces less. Because the number of firms increases, the market produces more.

A Closer Look at Exit

Now, the sweater market has 1,200 firms with cost curves like those in Fig. 12.9(a). The market demand curve is D, the market supply curve is S_2, and the price is $17 a sweater in Fig. 12.9(b). Each firm produces 7 sweaters a day and incurs an economic loss.

This economic loss is a signal for firms to exit the market. As exit takes place, supply decreases and the market supply curve shifts leftward toward S^*. As supply decreases with no change in demand, the market price gradually rises from $17 to $20 a sweater. At this higher price, losses are eliminated, each firm makes zero economic profit, and exit stops.

Exit results in a decrease in market output, but each firm's output *increases*. Because the price rises, each firm moves up its supply curve and produces more. Because the number of firms decreases, the market produces less.

FIGURE 12.9   Entry, Exit, and Long-Run Equilibrium

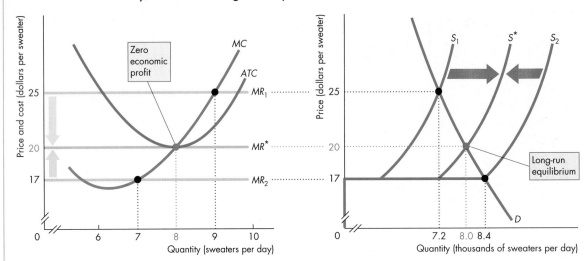

(a) Campus Sweaters

(b) The sweater market

Each firm has cost curves like those of Campus Sweaters in part (a). The market demand curve is D in part (b). When the market supply in part (b) is S_1, the price is $25 a sweater. In part (a), each firm produces 9 sweaters a day and makes an economic profit. Profit triggers the entry of new firms and as new firms enter, the market supply curve shifts rightward, from S_1 toward S^*. The price falls from $25 to $20 a sweater, and the quantity produced increases from 7,200 to 8,000 sweaters. Each firm's output decreases to 8

sweaters a day and economic profit is zero.
When the market supply is S_2, the price is $17 a sweater. In part (a), each firm produces 7 sweaters a day and incurs an economic loss. Loss triggers exit and as firms exit, the market supply curve shifts leftward, from S_2 toward S^*. The price rises from $17 to $20 a sweater, and the quantity produced decreases from 8,400 to 8,000 sweaters. Each firm's output increases from 7 to 8 sweaters a day and economic profit is zero.

myeconlab animation

Entry and Exit in Action
Personal Computers and Farm Machines

An example of entry and falling prices occurred during the 1980s and 1990s in the personal computer market. When IBM introduced its first PC in 1981, IBM had little competition. The price was $7,000 (about $16,850 in today's money) and IBM made a large economic profit selling the new machine.

Observing IBM's huge success, new firms such as Gateway, NEC, Dell, and a host of others entered the market with machines that were technologically identical to IBM's. In fact, they were so similar that they came to be called "clones." The massive wave of entry into the personal computer market increased the market supply and lowered the price. The economic profit for all firms decreased.

Today, a $400 computer is vastly more powerful than its 1981 ancestor that cost 42 times as much.

The same PC market that saw entry during the 1980s and 1990s has seen some exit more recently. In 2001, IBM, the firm that first launched the PC, announced that it was exiting the market. The intense competition from Gateway, NEC, Dell, and others that entered the market following IBM's lead has lowered the price and eliminated the economic profit. So IBM now concentrates on servers and other parts of the computer market.

IBM exited the PC market because it was incurring economic losses. Its exit decreased market supply and made it possible for the remaining firms in the market to make zero economic profit.

International Harvester, a manufacturer of farm equipment, provides another example of exit. For decades, people associated the name "International Harvester" with tractors, combines, and other farm machines. But International Harvester wasn't the only maker of farm equipment. The market became intensely competitive, and the firm began to incur economic losses. Now the firm has a new name, Navistar International, and it doesn't make tractors any more. After years of economic losses and shrinking revenues, it got out of the farm-machine business in 1985 and started to make trucks.

International Harvester exited because it was incurring an economic loss. Its exit decreased supply and made it possible for the remaining firms in the market to break even.

Long-Run Equilibrium

You've now seen how economic profit induces entry, which in turn eliminates the profit. You've also seen how economic loss induces exit, which in turn eliminates the loss.

When economic profit and economic loss have been eliminated and entry and exit have stopped, a competitive market is in *long-run equilibrium.*

You've seen how a competitive market adjusts toward its long-run equilibrium. But a competitive market is rarely *in* a state of long-run equilibrium. Instead, it is constantly and restlessly evolving toward long-run equilibrium. The reason is that the market is constantly bombarded with events that change the constraints that firms face.

Markets are constantly adjusting to keep up with changes in tastes, which change demand, and changes in technology, which change costs.

In the next sections, we're going to see how a competitive market reacts to changing tastes and technology and how it guides resources to their highest-valued use.

Review Quiz

1 What triggers entry in a competitive market? Describe the process that ends further entry.
2 What triggers exit in a competitive market? Describe the process that ends further exit.

 Work Study Plan 12.4 and get instant feedback.

Changing Tastes and Advancing Technology

Increased awareness of the health hazards of smoking has decreased the demand for tobacco products. The development of inexpensive automobile and air transportation during the 1990s decreased the demand for long-distance trains and buses. Solid-state electronics has decreased the demand for TV and radio repair. The development of good-quality inexpensive clothing has decreased the demand for sewing machines. What happens in a competitive market when there is a permanent decrease in the demand for its product?

Microwave food preparation has increased the demand for paper, glass, and plastic cooking utensils and for plastic wrap. The Internet has increased the demand for a personal computer and the widespread use of the computer has increased the demand for high-speed connections and music downloads. What happens in a competitive market when the demand for its output increases?

Advances in technology are constantly lowering the costs of production. New biotechnologies have dramatically lowered the costs of producing many food and pharmaceutical products. New electronic technologies have lowered the cost of producing just about every good and service. What happens in a competitive market for a good when technological change lowers its production costs?

Let's use the theory of perfect competition to answer these questions.

A Permanent Change in Demand

Figure 12.10(a) shows a competitive market that initially is in long-run equilibrium. The demand curve is D_0, the supply curve is S_0, the market price is P_0, and market output is Q_0. Figure 12.10(b) shows a single firm in this initial long-run equilibrium. The firm produces q_0 and makes zero economic profit.

Now suppose that demand decreases and the demand curve shifts leftward to D_1, as shown in Fig. 12.10(a). The market price falls to P_1, and the quantity supplied by the market decreases from Q_0 to Q_1 as the market moves down along its short-run supply curve S_0. Figure 12.10(b) shows the situation facing a firm. The market price is now below the firm's minimum average total cost, so the firm incurs an eco-

nomic loss. But to minimize its loss, the firm adjusts its output to keep marginal cost equal to price. At a price of P_1, each firm produces an output of q_1.

The market is now in short-run equilibrium but not long-run equilibrium. It is in short-run equilibrium because each firm is maximizing profit; it is not in long-run equilibrium because each firm is incurring an economic loss—its average total cost exceeds the price.

The economic loss is a signal for some firms to exit the market. As they do so, short-run market supply decreases and the market supply curve gradually shifts leftward. As market supply decreases, the price rises. At each higher price, a firm's profit-maximizing output is greater, so the firms remaining in the market increase their output as the price rises. Each firm moves up along its marginal cost or supply curve in Fig. 12.10(b). That is, as some firms exit the market, market output decreases but the output of the firms that remain in the market increases.

Eventually, enough firms have exited the market for the market supply curve to have shifted to S_1 in Fig. 12.10(a). The market price has returned to its original level, P_0. At this price, the firms remaining in the market produce q_0, the same quantity that they produced before the decrease in demand. Because firms are now making zero economic profit, no firm has an incentive to enter or exit the market. The market supply curve remains at S_1, and market output is Q_2. The market is again in long-run equilibrium.

The difference between the initial long-run equilibrium and the final long-run equilibrium is the number of firms in the market. A permanent decrease in demand has decreased the number of firms. Each firm remaining in the market produces the same output in the new long-run equilibrium as it did initially and makes zero economic profit. In the process of moving from the initial equilibrium to the new one, firms incur economic losses.

We've just worked out how a competitive market responds to a permanent *decrease* in demand. A permanent increase in demand triggers a similar response, except in the opposite direction. The increase in demand brings a higher price, economic profit, and entry. Entry increases market supply and eventually lowers the price to its original level and economic profit to zero.

The demand for Internet service increased permanently during the 1990s and huge profit opportunities arose in this market. The result was a massive rate

FIGURE 12.10   A Decrease in Demand

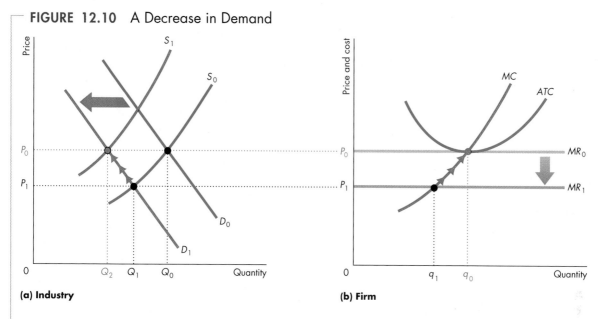

(a) Industry

(b) Firm

A market starts out in long-run competitive equilibrium. Part (a) shows the market demand curve D_0, the market supply curve S_0, the market price P_0, and the equilibrium quantity Q_0. Each firm sells its output at the price P_0, so its marginal revenue curve is MR_0 in part (b). Each firm produces q_0 and makes zero economic profit.

Market demand decreases permanently from D_0 to D_1 in part (a) and the market price falls to P_1. Each firm decreases its output to q_1 in part (b), and market output

decreases to Q_1 in part (a).

Firms now incur economic losses and some firms exit the market. As they do so, the market supply curve gradually shifts leftward, from S_0 toward S_1. This shift gradually raises the market price from P_1 back to P_0. While the price is below P_0, firms incur economic losses and some firms exit the market. Once the price has returned to P_0, each firm makes zero economic profit and has no incentive to exit. Each firm produces q_0, and market output is Q_2.

of entry of Internet service providers. The process of competition and change in the Internet service market is similar to what we have just studied but with an increase in demand rather than a decrease in demand.

We've now studied the effects of a permanent change in demand for a good. In doing so, we began and ended in a long-run equilibrium and examined the process that takes a market from one equilibrium to another. It is this process, not the equilibrium points, that describes the real world.

One feature of the predictions that we have just generated seems odd: In the long run, regardless of whether demand increases or decreases, the market price returns to its original level. Is this outcome inevitable? In fact, it is not. It is possible for the equilibrium market price in the long run to remain the same, rise, or fall.

External Economies and Diseconomies

The change in the long-run equilibrium price depends on external economies and external diseconomies. **External economies** are factors beyond the control of an individual firm that lower the firm's costs as the *market* output increases. **External diseconomies** are factors outside the control of a firm that raise the firm's costs as the *market* output increases. With no external economies or external diseconomies, a firm's costs remain constant as the market output changes.

Figure 12.11 illustrates these three cases and introduces a new supply concept: the long-run market supply curve.

A **long-run market supply curve** shows how the quantity supplied in a market varies as the market price varies after all the possible adjustments have been made, including changes in each firm's plant and the number of firms in the market.

Figure 12.11(a) shows the case we have just studied—no external economies or diseconomies. The long-run market supply curve (LS_A) is perfectly elastic. In this case, a permanent increase in demand from D_0 to D_1 has no effect on the price in the long run. The increase in demand brings a temporary increase in price to P_S and in the short run the quantity increases from Q_0 to Q_S. Entry increases short-run supply from S_0 to S_1, which lowers the price from P_S back to P_0 and increases the quantity to Q_1.

Figure 12.11(b) shows the case of external diseconomies. The long-run market supply curve (LS_B) slopes upward. A permanent increase in demand from D_0 to D_1 increases the price in both the short run and the long run. The increase in demand brings a temporary increase in price to P_S and in the short run the quantity increases from Q_0 to Q_S. Entry increases short-run supply from S_0 to S_2, which lowers the price from P_S to P_2 and increases the quantity to Q_2.

One source of external diseconomies is congestion. The airline market provides a good example. With bigger airline market output, congestion at both airports

and in the air increases, resulting in longer delays and extra waiting time for passengers and airplanes. These external diseconomies mean that as the output of air transportation services increases (in the absence of technological advances), average cost increases. As a result, the long-run market supply curve is upward sloping. A permanent increase in demand brings an increase in quantity and a rise in the price. (Markets with external diseconomies might nonetheless have a falling price because technological advances shift the long-run supply curve downward.)

Figure 12.11(c) shows the case of external economies. The long-run market supply curve (LS_C) slopes downward. A permanent increase in demand from D_0 to D_1 increases the price in the short run and lowers it in the long run. Again, the increase in demand brings a temporary increase in price to P_S and in the short run the quantity increases from Q_0 to Q_S. Entry increases short-run supply from S_0 to S_3, which lowers the price to P_3 and increases the quantity to Q_3.

An example of external economies is the growth of specialist support services for a market as it expands.

FIGURE 12.11 Long-Run Changes in Price and Quantity

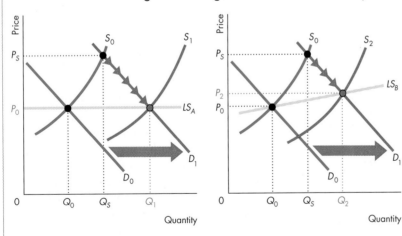
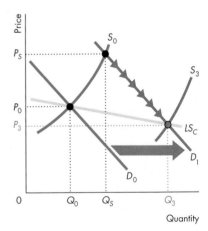

(a) Constant-cost industry   **(b) Increasing-cost industry**   **(c) Decreasing-cost industry**

Three possible changes in price and quantity occur in the long run. When demand increases from D_0 to D_1, entry occurs and the market supply curve shifts rightward from S_0 to S_1. In part (a), the long-run market supply curve, LS_A, is horizontal. The quantity increases from Q_0 to Q_1, and the price remains constant at P_0.

In part (b), the long-run market supply curve is LS_B; the price rises to P_2, and the quantity increases to Q_2. This case occurs in industries with external diseconomies. In part (c), the long-run market supply curve is LS_C; the price falls to P_3, and the quantity increases to Q_3. This case occurs in a market with external economies.

myeconlab animation

As farm output increased in the nineteenth and early twentieth centuries, the services available to farmers expanded. New firms specialized in the development and marketing of farm machinery and fertilizers. As a result, average farm costs decreased. Farms enjoyed the benefits of external economies. As a consequence, as the demand for farm products increased, the output increased but the price fell.

Over the long term, the prices of many goods and services have fallen, not because of external economies but because of technological change. Let's now study this influence on a competitive market.

Technological Change

Industries are constantly discovering lower-cost techniques of production. Most cost-saving production techniques cannot be implemented, however, without investing in new plant and equipment. As a consequence, it takes time for a technological advance to spread through a market. Some firms whose plants are on the verge of being replaced will be quick to adopt the new technology, while other firms whose plants have recently been replaced will continue to operate with an old technology until they can no longer cover their average variable cost. Once average variable cost cannot be covered, a firm will scrap even a relatively new plant (embodying an old technology) in favor of a plant with a new technology.

New technology allows firms to produce at a lower cost. As a result, as firms adopt a new technology, their cost curves shift downward. With lower costs, firms are willing to supply a given quantity at a lower price or, equivalently, they are willing to supply a larger quantity at a given price. In other words, market supply increases, and the market supply curve shifts rightward. With a given demand, the quantity produced increases and the price falls.

Two forces are at work in a market undergoing technological change. Firms that adopt the new technology make an economic profit, so there is entry by new-technology firms. Firms that stick with the old technology incur economic losses. They either exit the market or switch to the new technology.

As old-technology firms disappear and new-technology firms enter, the price falls and the quantity produced increases. Eventually, the market arrives at a long-run equilibrium in which all the firms use the new technology and make a zero economic profit. Because in the long run competition eliminates economic profit, technological change brings only tem-

porary gains to producers. But the lower prices and better products that technological advances bring are permanent gains for consumers.

The process that we've just described is one in which some firms experience economic profits and others experience economic losses. It is a period of dynamic change in a market. Some firms do well, and others do badly. Often, the process has a geographical dimension—the expanding new-technology firms bring prosperity to what was once the boondocks, and traditional industrial regions decline. Sometimes, the new-technology firms are in a foreign country, while the old-technology firms are in the domestic economy. The information revolution of the 1990s produced many examples of changes like these. Commercial banking, which was traditionally concentrated in New York, San Francisco, and other large cities now flourishes in Charlotte, North Carolina, which has become the nation's number three commercial banking city. Television shows and movies, traditionally made in Los Angeles and New York, are now made in large numbers in Orlando.

Technological advances are not confined to the information and entertainment industries. Even food production is undergoing a major technological change because of genetic engineering.

Review Quiz

1 Describe the course of events in a competitive market following a permanent decrease in demand. What happens to output, price, and economic profit in the short run and in the long run?

2 Describe the course of events in a competitive market following a permanent increase in demand. What happens to output, price, and economic profit in the short run and in the long run?

3 Describe the course of events in a competitive market following the adoption of a new technology. What happens to output, price, and economic profit in the short run and in the long run?

myeconlab Work Study Plan 12.5 and get instant feedback.

We've seen how a competitive market operates in the short run and the long run, but is a competitive market efficient?

Competition and Efficiency

A competitive market can achieve an efficient use of resources. You first studied efficiency in Chapter 2. Then in Chapter 5, using only the concepts of demand, supply, consumer surplus, and producer surplus, you saw how a competitive market achieves efficiency. Now that you have learned what lies behind the demand and supply curves of a competitive market, you can gain a deeper understanding of the efficiency of a competitive market.

Efficient Use of Resources

Recall that resource use is efficient when we produce the goods and services that people value most highly (see Chapter 2, p. 37 and Chapter 5, p. 110). If someone can become better off without anyone else becoming worse off, resources are *not* being used efficiently. For example, suppose we produce a computer that no one wants and no one will ever use and, at the same time, some people are clamoring for more video games. If we produce fewer computers and reallocate the unused resources to produce more video games, some people will become better off and no one will be worse off. So the initial resource allocation was inefficient.

In the more technical language that you have learned, resource use is efficient when marginal social benefit equals marginal social cost. In the computer and video games example, the marginal social benefit of a video game exceeds its marginal social cost; the marginal social cost of a computer exceeds its marginal social benefit. So by producing fewer computers and more video games, we move resources toward a higher-valued use.

Choices, Equilibrium, and Efficiency

We can use what you have learned about the decisions made by consumers and competitive firms and market equilibrium to describe an efficient use of resources.

Choices Consumers allocate their budgets to get the most value possible out of them. We derive a consumer's demand curve by finding how the best budget allocation changes as the price of a good changes. So consumers get the most value out of their resources at all points along their demand curves. If the people who consume a good or service are the only ones who benefit from it, then the market demand curve measures the benefit to the entire society and is the marginal social benefit curve.

Competitive firms produce the quantity that maximizes profit. We derive the firm's supply curve by finding the profit-maximizing quantity at each price. So firms get the most value out of their resources at all points along their supply curves. If the firms that produce a good or service bear all the costs of producing it, then the market supply curve measures the marginal cost to the entire society and the market supply curve is the marginal social cost curve.

Equilibrium and Efficiency Resources are used efficiently when marginal social benefit equals marginal social cost. Competitive equilibrium achieves this efficient outcome because for consumers, price equals marginal social benefit, and for producers, price equals marginal social cost.

The gains from trade are the sum of consumer surplus and producer surplus. The gains from trade for consumers are measured by *consumer surplus*, which is the area below the demand curve and above the price paid. (See Chapter 5, p. 111.) The gains from trade for producers are measured by *producer surplus*, which is the area above the supply curve and below the price received. (See Chapter 5, p. 113.) The total gains from trade are the sum of consumer surplus and producer surplus. When the market for a good or service is in equilibrium, the gains from trade are maximized.

Illustrating an Efficient Allocation Figure 12.12 illustrates the efficiency of perfect competition in long-run equilibrium. Part (a) shows the individual firm, and part (b) shows the market. The equilibrium market price is P^*. At that price, each firm makes zero economic profit and each firm has the plant that enables it to produce at the lowest possible average total cost. Consumers are as well off as possible because the good cannot be produced at a lower cost and the price equals that least possible cost.

In part (b), consumers get the most out of their resources at all points on the market demand curve, $D = MSB$. Consumer surplus is the green area. Producers get the most out of their resources at all points on the market supply curve, $S = MSC$. Producer surplus is the blue area. Resources are used efficiently at the quantity Q^* and price P^*. At this point, marginal social benefit equals marginal social

FIGURE 12.12   Efficiency of Perfect Competition

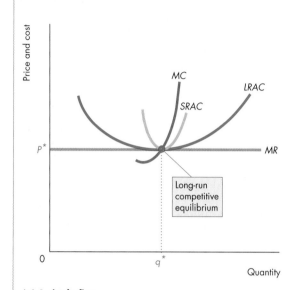

(a) A single firm

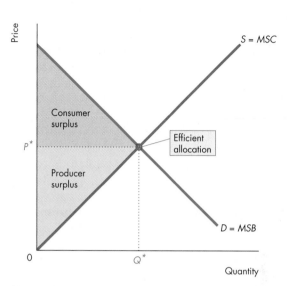

(b) A market

In part (a), a firm in perfect competition produces at the lowest possible long-run average total cost at q*. In part (b), consumers have made the best available choices and are on the market demand curve and firms are producing at

least cost and are on the market supply curve. With no external benefits or external costs, resources are used efficiently at the quantity Q* and the price P*. Perfect competition achieves an efficient use of resources.

myeconlab animation

cost, and total surplus (the sum of producer surplus and consumer surplus) is maximized.

When firms in perfect competition are away from long-run equilibrium, either entry or exit is taking place and the market is moving toward the situation depicted in Figure 12.12. But the market is still

efficient. As long as marginal social benefit (on the market demand curve) equals marginal social cost (on the market supply curve), the market is efficient. But it is only in long-run equilibrium that consumers pay the lowest possible price.

You've now completed your study of perfect competition. *Reading Between the Lines* on pp. 292–293 gives you an opportunity to use what you have learned to understand the recent exit of small airlines from the U.S. airline market.

Although many markets approximate the model of perfect competition, many do not. In Chapter 13, we study markets at the opposite extreme of market power: monopoly. Then we'll study markets that lie between perfect competition and monopoly. In Chapter 14, we study monopolistic competition and in Chapter 15 we study oligopoly. When you have completed this study, you'll have a tool kit that will enable you to understand the variety of real-world markets.

Review Quiz

1   State the conditions that must be met for resources to be allocated efficiently.

2   Describe the choices that consumers make and explain why consumers are efficient on the market demand curve.

3   Describe the choices that producers make and explain why producers are efficient on the market supply curve.

4   Explain why resources are used efficiently in a competitive market.

myeconlab   Work Study Plan 12.6 and get instant feedback.

Airlines Exit

Fuel Costs, Economy Down 3 Airlines

http://www.washingtontimes.com
April 9, 2008

The loss of three airlines in little more than a week is prompting warnings from financial analysts that the worst is not over for the industry or its passengers.

Rising fuel prices and a slow economy mean higher expenses but fewer passengers. ATA Airlines, Aloha Airlines and Skybus Airlines all succumbed recently to that fatal combination.

The next airline expected to go belly up is Champion Air, a Bloomington, Minn., charter service that operates 14 Boeing 727 aircraft.

"Unfortunately, our business model is no longer viable in a world of $110 oil, a struggling economy and rapidly changing demand for our services," Chief Executive Officer Lee Steele said in announcing the airline's planned May 31 closure. …

Airlines already are starting to raise prices to cover their higher fuel costs—a risky business move that could reduce demand for tickets.

High fuel costs leave them few choices, analysts said. …

Major carriers, like Northwest Airlines and Delta Air Lines, are stepping in to absorb some of the defunct airlines' routes. …

In a bankruptcy filing Monday in U.S. Bankruptcy Court for the District of Delaware, Skybus Chief Financial Officer Barry Barnard said his airline failed largely because of high fuel prices and a "recession" that reduced demand for flights.

Essence of the Story

- High fuel prices and lower demand have put three airlines (ATA Airlines, Aloha Airlines and Skybus Airlines) out of business.
- Champion Air, a Bloomington, Minn., airline is also expected to go out of business.
- Airlines are raising prices to cover their higher fuel costs.
- Higher prices will decrease the quantity of tickets sold.
- Major carriers (Northwest Airlines and Delta Air Lines) are filling the gaps left by the exit of the three airlines.

Economic Analysis

- The market for air travel is not *perfectly* competitive but it is highly competitive and the perfect competition model provides insights into that market.

- In 2008, airlines were being squeezed by rising costs and falling demand.

- Figure 1 shows an airline's cost and revenue curves.

- Initially an airline's average total cost curve is ATC_0 and its marginal cost curve is MC_0.

- Figure 2 shows the market for air transportation services.

- Initially the demand curve is D_0 and the supply curve is S_0. The equilibrium price is $100 a trip.

- Airlines face a marginal revenue curve, MR, in Fig. 1 and maximize profit by producing 50 trips per day. Economic profit is zero. The market is in long-run equilibrium.

- Two events disturb this long-run equilibrium: (1) In what the news article calls a "slow economy," incomes stop growing and people decide to cut back on their air travel plans; and (2) fuel costs rocket upward.

- The "slow economy" decreases the demand for air travel and the demand curve shifts leftward to D_1.

- The rise in fuel prices increases the airline's costs.

- The airline's average total cost shifts upward to ATC_1 and the marginal cost curve shifts upward to MC_1.

- The increase in marginal cost decreases supply and the market supply curve shifts leftward to S_1.

- The market comes to a new equilibrium. The quantity decreases but (in this example) the price doesn't change.

- The combination of no change in price and a rise in costs results in the airlines incurring an economic loss.

- As the loss persists, some airlines exit.

- When airlines exit (not shown in the figures), market supply decreases, the price rises, and the airlines remaining in the industry (like Northwest and Delta in the news article) increase production.

- Eventually, exit stops and the market returns to long-run equilibrium but at a higher price.

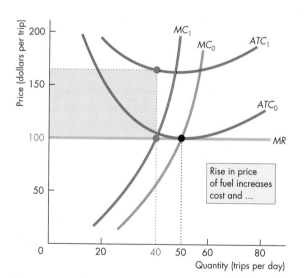

Figure 1 An airline's cost and revenue curves

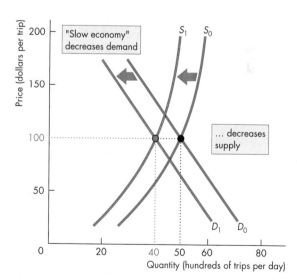

Figure 2 The market for air travel

SUMMARY

Key Points

What Is Perfect Competition? (pp. 274–275)

- In perfect competition, many firms sell identical products to many buyers; there are no restrictions on entry; and sellers and buyers are well informed about prices.
- A perfectly competitive firm is a price taker.
- A perfectly competitive firm's marginal revenue always equals the market price.

The Firm's Output Decision (pp. 276–279)

- The firm produces the output at which marginal revenue (price) equals marginal cost.
- In short-run equilibrium, a firm can make an economic profit, incur an economic loss, or break even.
- If price is less than minimum average variable cost, the firm temporarily shuts down.
- At prices below minimum average variable cost, a firm's supply curve runs along the y-axis; at prices above minimum average variable cost, a firm's supply curve is its marginal cost curve.

Output, Price, and Profit in the Short Run

(pp. 280–283)

- The market supply curve shows the sum of the quantities supplied by each firm at each price.
- Market demand and market supply determine price.
- A firm might make a positive economic profit, a zero economic profit, or incur an economic loss.

Output, Price, and Profit in the Long Run

(pp. 283–285)

- Economic profit induces entry and economic loss induces exit.
- Entry increases supply and lowers price and profit. Exit decreases supply and raises price and profit.
- In long-run equilibrium, economic profit is zero. There is no entry or exit.

Changing Tastes and Advancing Technology

(pp. 286–289)

- A permanent decrease in demand leads to a smaller market output and a smaller number of firms. A permanent increase in demand leads to a larger market output and a larger number of firms.
- The long-run effect of a change in demand on price depends on whether there are external economies (the price falls) or external diseconomies (the price rises) or neither (the price remains constant).
- New technologies increase supply and in the long run lower the price and increase the quantity.

Competition and Efficiency (pp. 290–291)

- Resources are used efficiently when we produce goods and services in the quantities that people value most highly.
- When there are no external benefits and external costs, perfect competition achieves an efficient allocation. In long-run equilibrium, consumers pay the lowest possible price and marginal social benefit equals marginal social cost.

Key Figures

Key Terms

PROBLEMS and APPLICATIONS

myeconlab Work problems 1–10 in Chapter 12 Study Plan and get instant feedback.
Work problems 11–18 as Homework, a Quiz, or a Test if assigned by your instructor.

1. Lin's fortune cookies are identical to the fortune cookies made by dozens of other firms, and there is free entry in the fortune cookie market. Buyers and sellers are well informed about prices.
   a. In what type of market does Lin's operate?
   b. What determines the price of fortune cookies?
   c. What determines Lin's marginal revenue of fortune cookies?
   d. If fortune cookies sell for $10 a box and Lin offers his cookies for sale at $10.50 a box, how many boxes does he sell?
   e. If fortune cookies sell for $10 a box and Lin offers his cookies for sale at $9.50 a box, how many boxes does he sell?
   f. What is the elasticity of demand for Lin's fortune cookies and how does it differ from the elasticity of the market demand for fortune cookies?

2. Pat's Pizza Kitchen is a price taker. Its costs are

Output (pizzas per hour)	Total cost (dollars per hour)
0	10
1	21
2	30
3	41
4	54
5	69

   a. Calculate Pat's profit-maximizing output and economic profit if the market price is
      (i) $14 a pizza.
      (ii) $12 a pizza.
      (iii) $10 a pizza.
   b. What is Pat's shutdown point and what is Pat's economic profit if it shuts down temporarily?
   c. Derive Pat's supply curve.
   d. At what price will firms with costs identical to Pat's exit the pizza market in the long run?
   e. At what price will firms with costs identical to Pat's enter the pizza market in the long run?

3. The market is perfectly competitive and there are 1,000 firms that produce paper. The table sets out the market demand schedule for paper.

Price (dollars per box)	Quantity demanded (thousands of boxes per week)
3.65	500
5.20	450
6.80	400
8.40	350
10.00	300
11.60	250
13.20	200

Each producer of paper has the following costs when it uses its least-cost plant:

Output (boxes per week)	Marginal cost (dollars per additional box)	Average variable cost	Average total cost
		(dollars per box)	
200	6.40	7.80	12.80
250	7.00	7.00	11.00
300	7.65	7.10	10.43
350	8.40	7.20	10.06
400	10.00	7.50	10.00
450	12.40	8.00	10.22
500	20.70	9.00	11.00

   a. What is the market price of paper?
   b. What is the market's output?
   c. What is the output produced by each firm?
   d. What is the economic profit made or economic loss incurred by each firm?
   e. Do firms have an incentive to enter or exit the paper market in the long run?
   f. What is the number of firms in the long run?
   g. What is the market price in the long run?
   h. What is the equilibrium quantity of paper produced in the long run?

4. **Never Pay Retail Again**
   Not only has scouring the Web for the best possible price become standard protocol before buying a big-ticket item, but more consumers are employing creative strategies for scoring hot deals. ... Comparison shopping, haggling and swapping discount codes are all becoming mainstream marks of savvy shoppers ... online shoppers can check a comparison service like Price Grabber before making a purchase. ...
   CNN, May 30, 2008

a. Explain the effect of the Internet on the degree of competition in the market.

b. Explain how the Internet influences market efficiency.

5. As the quality of computer monitors improves, more people are reading documents online rather than printing them out. The demand for paper permanently decreases and the demand schedule becomes

Price (dollars per box)	Quantity demanded (thousands of boxes per week)
2.95	500
4.13	450
5.30	400
6.48	350
7.65	300
8.83	250
10.00	200
11.18	150

If each firm producing paper has the costs set out in problem 3,

a. What is the market price, market output, and economic profit or loss of each firm?

b. What is the long-run equilibrium price, market output, and economic profit or loss of each firm?

c. Does this market experience external economies, external diseconomies, or constant cost? Illustrate by drawing the long-run supply curve.

6. **Fuel Prices Could Squeeze Cheap Flights**

Continental has eliminated service to airports big and small all across the nation. … The money-losing airline market is scrapping its least-fuel efficient flights in step with the dramatic increases in energy costs. … Airlines are having difficulty keeping prices low for flights … especially as fuel prices keep rising. … Airlines have continually raised—or tried to raise—fares this year to make up for the fuel costs. … American Airlines increased its fuel surcharge by $20 a roundtrip. American had raised fares just days earlier—an increase that was matched by Delta Air Lines Inc. and UAL Corp.'s United Airlines and Continental—but retracted the increase. … United said it would start charging $15 for the first checked bag. … This follows an earlier announcement from American, which plans to begin charging $15 for the first checked bag. …

CNN, June 12, 2008

a. Explain how an increase in fuel prices might cause an airline to change its output (number of flights) in the short run.

b. Draw a graph to show the increase in fuel prices on an airline's output in the short run.

c. Explain why an airline might incur an economic loss in the short run as fuel prices rise.

d. If some airlines decide to exit the market, explain how the economic profit or loss of the remaining airlines will change.

7. **Coors Brewing Expanding Plant**

Coors Brewing Co. of Golden will expand its Virginia packaging plant at a cost of $24 million. The addition will accommodate a new production line that will bottle mostly Coors Light. … It also will bottle beer faster. … Coors Brewing employs roughly 470 people at its Virginia plant. The expanded packaging line will add another eight jobs.

Denver Business Journal, January 6, 2006

a. How will Coors' expansion of a plant change the firm's marginal cost curve and short-run supply curve?

b. What does this expansion decision imply about the point on Coors' *LRAC* curve at which the firm was before the expansion?

c. If other breweries follow the lead of Coors, what will happen to the market price of beer?

d. How will the adjustment that you have described in c influence the economic profit of Coors and other beer producers?

8. In a perfectly competitive market in long-run equilibrium can

a. Consumer surplus be increased?

b. Producer surplus be increased?

c. A consumer become better off by making a substitution away from this market?

d. The average total cost be reduced?

9. Explain and illustrate graphically how the growing world population is influencing the world market for wheat and a representative individual wheat farmer.

10. Explain and illustrate graphically how the diaper service market has been affected by the decrease in the North American birth rate and the development of disposable diapers.

11. The market demand schedule for smoothies is

Price (dollars per smoothie)	Quantity demanded (smoothies per hour)
1.90	1,000
2.00	950
2.20	800
2.91	700
4.25	550
5.25	400
5.50	300

The market is perfectly competitive, and each firm has the following costs when it uses its least-cost plant:

Output (smoothies per hour)	Marginal cost (dollars per additional smoothie)	Average variable cost	Average total cost
		(dollars per smoothie)	
3	2.50	4.00	7.33
4	2.20	3.53	6.03
5	1.90	3.24	5.24
6	2.00	3.00	4.67
7	2.91	2.91	4.34
8	4.25	3.00	4.25
9	8.00	3.33	4.44

There are 100 smoothie sellers in the market.
  a. What is the market price of a smoothie?
  b. What is the market quantity of smoothies?
  c. How many smoothies does each firm sell?
  d. What is the economic profit made or economic loss incurred by each firm?
  e. Do firms enter or exit the market in the long run?
  f. What is the market price and the equilibrium quantity in the long run?

12. **Money in the Tank**

In Marietta, where the road hugs the Susquehanna River, a Rutter's Farm Store gas station stands on one side, a Sheetz gas station on the other. Kelly Bosley, who manages Rutter's, doesn't even have to look across the highway to know when Sheetz changes its price for a gallon of gas. When Sheetz raises prices, her own pumps are busy. When Sheetz lowers prices, she has not a car in sight. ... You think you feel helpless at the pump? Bosley makes a living selling gas—and even she has little control over what it costs.

The Mining Journal, May 24, 2008

  a. Describe the elasticity of demand that each of these gas stations faces.

  b. Why does each of these gas stations have so little control over the price of the gasoline they sell?
  c. How do these gas stations decide how much gasoline to make available for sale?

13. Quick Copy is one of many copy shops near campus. The figure shows Quick Copy's costs.

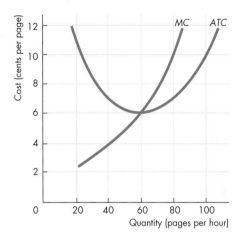

If the market price of copying a page is 10 cents, calculate Quick Copy's
  a. Marginal revenue.
  b. Profit-maximizing output.
  c. Economic profit.

14. **Cadillac Plant Shuts Down Temporarily, Future Uncertain**

Delta Truss in Cadillac [Michigan] is shutting down in what [its] parent company, Pro-Build, calls "temporarily discontinuing truss production." Workers fear this temporary shut down will become permanent. About 60 people work at Delta Truss when it's in peak season. Right now, about 20 people work there. ... A corporate letter ... says "we are anticipating resuming production at these plants when the spring business begins."

9&10 News, February 18, 2008

  a. Explain how the shutdown decision will affect Delta Truss' *TFC*, *TVC*, and *TC*.
  b. Under what conditions would this shutdown decision maximize Delta Truss' economic profit (or minimize its loss)?
  c. Under what conditions will Delta Truss start producing again?
  d. Under what conditions will Delta Truss make the shutdown permanent and exit the market?

15. **Exxon Mobil Selling All Its Gas Stations to Distributors**

Exxon Mobil Corp. said Thursday it's getting out of the retail gasoline business, following other major oil companies. … "As the highly competitive fuels marketing business in the U.S. continues to evolve, we believe this transition is the best way for Exxon Mobil to compete and grow in the future," said Ben Soraci, the director of Exxon Mobil's U.S. retail sales. Exxon Mobil is not alone among Big Oil exiting the retail gas business, a market where profits have gotten tougher as crude oil prices have risen. … Station owners say they're struggling to turn a profit on gas because while wholesale gasoline prices have risen sharply, … they've been unable to raise pump prices fast enough to keep pace.

Houston Chronicle, June 12, 2008

a. Is Exxon Mobil making a shutdown or exit decision in the retail gasoline market?

b. Under what conditions will this decision maximize Exxon Mobil's economic profit?

c. How might this decision by Exxon Mobil affect the economic profit made by other firms that sell retail gasoline?

16. **Another DVD Format, but This One Says It's Cheaper**

No sooner has the battle for the next-generation high definition DVD format ended, with Blu-ray triumphing over HD DVD, than a new contender has emerged. A new system … called HD VMD … is trying to find a niche. New Medium Enterprises, the London company behind HD VMD, says its system's quality is equal to Blu-ray's but it costs less. … While Blu-ray players typically cost more than $300, an HD VMD unit is priced at $199. … New Medium's price strategy will fail, said Andy Parsons, chairman of the Blu-ray Disc Association, … because it relies on a false assumption: Blu-ray technology will always be more expensive. "When you mass produce blue lasers in large quantities, hardware costs will absolutely come down," Mr. Parsons said. "I'm sure we'll eventually be able to charge $90 for a Blu-ray player."

The New York Times, March 10, 2008

a. Explain how technological change in Blu-ray production might support Mr. Parson's predictions of lower prices in the long-run and illustrate your explanation with a graph.

b. Even if Blu-ray prices do drop to $90 in the long run, why might the red-laser HD VMD still end up being less expensive at that time?

17. **Cell Phone Sales Hit 1 Billion Mark**

More than 1.15 billion mobile phones were sold worldwide in 2007, a 16 percent increase from the 990.9 million phones sold in 2006. … "Emerging markets, especially China and India, provided much of the growth as many people bought their first phone," Carolina Milanesi, research director for mobile devices at Gartner, said in a statement. "In mature markets, such as Japan and Western Europe, consumers' appetite for feature-laden phones was met with new models packed with TV tuners, global positioning satellite (GPS) functions, touch screens and high-resolution cameras."

CNET News, February 27, 2008

a. Explain the effects of the global increase in demand for cell phones on the market for cell phones and individual cell-phone producers in the short run.

b. Draw a graph to illustrate your explanation in a.

c. Explain the effects of the global increase in demand for cell phones on the market for cell phones in the long run.

d. What factors will determine whether the price of cell phones will rise, fall, or stay the same in the new long-run equilibrium?

18. Study *Reading Between the Lines* about the U.S. market for air travel on pp. 292–293, and then answer the following questions.

a. What are the features of the market for air travel that make it highly competitive?

b. If the fuel price increase had occurred with no decrease in demand, how would the outcome differ from that on p. 293?

c. Is the news article correct in its remark that it is risky for the airlines to raise prices because that move could reduce the demand for tickets? Explain your answer.

d. Explain how the market for air travel gets back to a long-run equilibrium.

e. Draw a graph to illustrate the market in the new long-run equilibrium.

f. Draw a graph of the cost and revenue curves of an airline to illustrate the situation in the new long-run equilibrium.

15

Oligopoly

After studying this chapter, you will be able to:

■ Define and identify oligopoly

■ Explain two traditional oligopoly models

■ Use game theory to explain how price and output are determined in oligopoly

■ Use game theory to explain other strategic decisions

■ Describe the antitrust laws that regulate oligopoly

An intense price war in the market for PCs has driven the price of a laptop below $1,000 and the price of a desktop below $500. A handful of firms—Dell, Hewlett-Packard, Lenovo, Acer, and Toshiba—account for more than one half of the global market. Each of these firms must pay close attention to what the other firms are doing

In some markets, there are only two firms. Computer chips are an example. The chips that drive most PCs are made by Intel and Advanced Micro Devices. How does competition between just two chip makers work?

When a small number of firms compete in a market, do they operate in the social interest, like firms in perfect competition?

Or do they restrict output to increase profit, like a monopoly?

The theories of perfect competition and monopoly don't predict the behavior of the firms we've just described. To understand how markets work when only a handful of firms compete, we need the richer models that are explained in this chapter. In *Reading Between the Lines* at the end of this chapter, we'll return to the market for personal computers and see how Dell and Hewlett-Packard slugged it out for dominance in that market.

◆ What Is Oligopoly?

Oligopoly, like monopolistic competition, lies between perfect competition and monopoly. The firms in oligopoly might produce an identical product and compete only on price, or they might produce a differentiated product and compete on price, product quality, and marketing. **Oligopoly** is a market structure in which

- Natural or legal barriers prevent the entry of new firms.
- A small number of firms compete.

Barriers to Entry

Natural or legal barriers to entry can create oligopoly. You saw in Chapter 13 how economies of scale and demand form a natural barrier to entry that can create a *natural monopoly*. These same factors can create a *natural oligopoly*.

Figure 15.1 illustrates two natural oligopolies. The demand curve, *D* (in both parts of the figure), shows the demand for taxi rides in a town. If the average

total cost curve of a taxi company is ATC_1 in part (a), the market is a natural **duopoly**—an oligopoly market with two firms. You can probably see some examples of duopoly where you live. Some cities have only two taxi companies, two car rental firms, two copy centers, or two college bookstores.

The lowest price at which the firm would remain in business is $10 a ride. At that price, the quantity of rides demanded is 60 a day, the quantity that can be provided by just two firms. There is no room in this market for three firms. But if there were only one firm, it would make an economic profit and a second firm would enter to take some of the business and economic profit.

If the average total cost curve of a taxi company is ATC_2 in part (b), the efficient scale of one firm is 20 rides a day. This market is large enough for three firms.

A legal oligopoly arises when a legal barrier to entry protects the small number of firms in a market. A city might license two taxi firms or two bus companies, for example, even though the combination of demand and economies of scale leaves room for more than two firms.

FIGURE 15.1   Natural Oligopoly

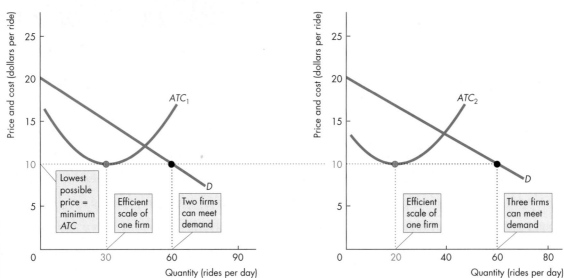

(a) Natural duopoly

(b) Natural oligopoly with three firms

The lowest possible price is $10 a ride, which is the minimum average total cost. When a firm produces 30 rides a day, the efficient scale, two firms can satisfy the market demand. This natural oligopoly has two firms—a natural duopoly.

When the efficient scale of one firm is 20 rides per day, three firms can satisfy the market demand at the lowest possible price. This natural oligopoly has three firms.

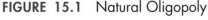 **myeconlab** animation

Small Number of Firms

Because barriers to entry exist, oligopoly consists of a small number of firms, each of which has a large share of the market. Such firms are interdependent, and they face a temptation to cooperate to increase their joint economic profit.

Interdependence With a small number of firms in a market, each firm's actions influence the profits of all the other firms. When Penny Stafford opened her coffee shop in Bellevue, Washington, a nearby Starbucks coffee shop took a hit. Within days, Starbucks began to attract Penny's customers with enticing offers and lower prices. Starbucks survived but Penny eventually went out of business. Penny Stafford and Starbucks were interdependent.

Temptation to Cooperate When a small number of firms share a market, they can increase their profits by forming a cartel and acting like a monopoly. A **cartel** is a group of firms acting together—colluding—to limit output, raise price, and increase economic profit. Cartels are illegal, but they do operate in some markets. But for reasons that you'll discover in this chapter, cartels tend to break down.

Examples of Oligopoly

The box below shows some examples of oligopoly. The dividing line between oligopoly and monopolistic competition is hard to pin down. As a practical matter, we identify oligopoly by looking at concentration ratios, the Herfindahl-Hirschman Index, and information about the geographical scope of the market and barriers to entry. The HHI that divides oligopoly from monopolistic competition is generally taken to be 1,000. An HHI below 1,000 is usually an example of monopolistic competition, and a market in which the HHI exceeds 1,000 is usually an example of oligopoly.

Review Quiz

1 What are the two distinguishing characteristics of oligopoly?
2 Why are firms in oligopoly interdependent?
3 Why do firms in oligopoly face a temptation to collude?
4 Can you think of some examples of oligopolies that you buy from?

 Work Study Plan 15.1 and get instant feedback.

Oligopoly Today
Near Duopoly in Batteries

These markets are oligopolies. Although in some of them, the number of firms (in parentheses) is large, the share of the market held by the 4 largest firms (the red bars) is close to 100 percent.

The most concentrated markets—cigarettes, glass bottles and jars, washing machines and dryers, and batteries, are dominated by just one or two firms.

If you want to buy an AAA battery for your TV remote or toothbrush, you'll find it hard to avoid buying a Duracell or an Energizer.

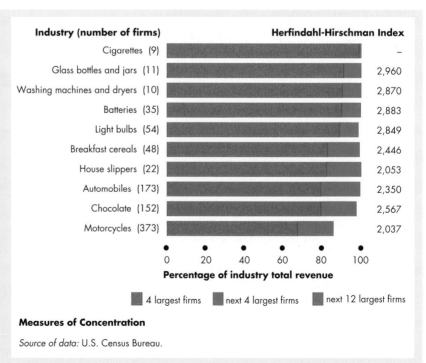

Measures of Concentration

Source of data: U.S. Census Bureau.

Two Traditional Oligopoly Models

Suppose you run one of three gas stations in a small town. You're trying to decide whether to cut your price. To make your decision, you must predict how the other firms will react and calculate the effects of those reactions on your profit. If you cut your price and your competitors don't cut theirs, you sell more and the other two firms sell less. But won't the other firms cut their prices too and make your profits fall? What will you do?

Several models have been developed to explain the prices and quantities in oligopoly markets. The models fall into two broad groups: traditional models and game theory models. We'll look at examples of both types, starting with two traditional models.

The Kinked Demand Curve Model

The kinked demand curve model of oligopoly is based on the assumption that each firm believes that if it raises its price, others will not follow, but if it cuts its price, other firms will cut theirs.

Figure 15.2 shows the demand curve (D) that a firm believes it faces. The demand curve has a kink at the current price, P, and quantity, Q. At prices above P, a small price rise brings a big decrease in the quantity sold. If one firm raises its price, other firms will hold their current price constant. The firm that raised its price will have the highest price and it will lose market share. At prices below P, even a large price cut brings only a small increase in the quantity sold. In this case, if one firm cuts its price, other firms will match the price cut. The firm that cuts its price will get no price advantage over its competitors.

The kink in the demand curve creates a break in the marginal revenue curve (MR). To maximize profit, the firm produces the quantity at which marginal cost equals marginal revenue. That quantity, Q, is where the marginal cost curve passes through the gap AB in the marginal revenue curve. If marginal cost fluctuates between A and B, like the marginal cost curves MC_0 and MC_1, the firm does not change its price or its output. Only if marginal cost fluctuates outside the range AB does the firm change its price and output. So the kinked demand curve model predicts that price and quantity are insensitive to small cost changes.

But this model has a problem. If marginal cost increases by enough to cause the firm to increase its price and if all firms experience the same increase in

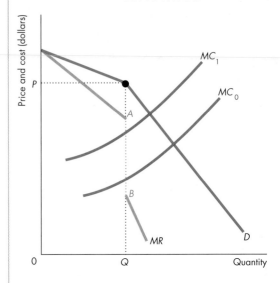

FIGURE 15.2   The Kinked Demand Curve Model

The price in an oligopoly market is P. Each firm believes it faces the demand curve D. At prices above P, a small price rise brings a big decrease in the quantity sold because other firms do not raise their prices. At prices below P, even a big price cut brings only a small increase in the quantity sold because other firms also cut their prices. Because the demand curve is kinked, the marginal revenue curve, MR, has a break AB. Profit is maximized by producing Q. The marginal cost curve passes through the break in the marginal revenue curve. Changes in marginal cost inside the range AB leave the price and quantity unchanged.

myeconlab   animation

marginal cost, they all increase their prices together. The firm's belief that others will not join it in a price rise is incorrect. A firm that bases its actions on beliefs that are wrong does not maximize profit and might even end up incurring an economic loss.

Dominant Firm Oligopoly

A second traditional model explains a dominant firm oligopoly, which arises when one firm—the dominant firm—has a big cost advantage over the other firms and produces a large part of the industry output. The dominant firm sets the market price and the other firms are price takers. Examples of dominant firm oligopoly are a large gasoline retailer or a big box store that dominates its local market.

FIGURE 15.3   A Dominant Firm Oligopoly

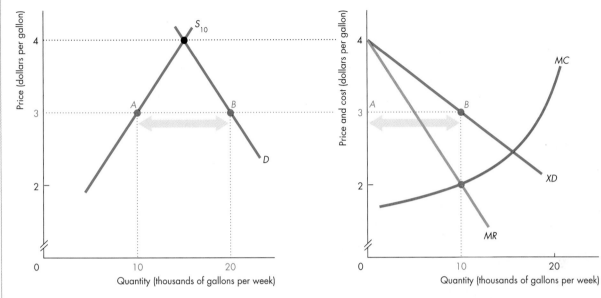

(a) Ten small firms and market demand

(b) Big-G's price and output decision

The demand curve for gas in a city is *D* in part (a). There are 10 small competitive firms that together have a supply curve of S_{10}. In addition, there is 1 large firm, Big-G, shown in part (b). Big-G faces the demand curve *XD*, determined as the market demand *D* minus the supply of the 10 small firms S_{10} —the demand that is not satisfied by the small firms. Big-G's mar-

ginal revenue curve is *MR* and its marginal cost curve is *MC*. Big-G sets its output to maximize profit by equating marginal cost and marginal revenue. This output is 10,000 gallons per week. The price at which Big-G can sell this quantity is $3 a gallon. The 10 small firms take this price, and each firm sells 1,000 gallons per week, point *A* in part (a).

myeconlab animation

To see how a dominant firm oligopoly works, suppose that 11 firms operate gas stations in a city. Big-G is the dominant firm. Figure 15.3 shows the market for gas in this city. In part (a), the demand curve *D* tells us the total quantity of gas demanded in the city at each price. The supply curve S_{10} is the supply curve of the 10 small firms. Part (b) shows the situation facing Big-G. Its marginal cost curve is *MC*. Big-G faces the demand curve *XD*, and its marginal revenue curve is *MR*. The demand curve *XD* shows the excess demand not met by the 10 small firms. For example, at a price of $3 a gallon, the quantity demanded is 20,000 gallons, the quantity supplied by the 10 small firms is 10,000 gallons, and the excess quantity demanded is 10,000 gallons, measured by the distance *AB* in both parts of the figure.

To maximize profit, Big-G operates like a monopoly. It sells 10,000 gallons a week, where its marginal revenue equals its marginal cost, for a price of $3 a gallon. The 10 small firms take the price of $3 a gal-

lon. They behave just like firms in perfect competition. The quantity of gas demanded in the entire city at $3 a gallon is 20,000 gallons, as shown in part (a). Of this amount, Big-G sells 10,000 gallons and the 10 small firms each sell 1,000 gallons.

Review Quiz

1   What does the kinked demand curve model predict and why must it sometimes make a prediction that contradicts its basic assumption?

2   Do you think a market with a dominant firm is in long-run equilibrium? Explain why or why not.

myeconlab   Work Study Plan 15.2 and get instant feedback.

The traditional models don't enable us to understand all oligopoly markets and we're now going to study some newer models based on game theory.

Oligopoly Games

Economists think about oligopoly as a game, and to study oligopoly markets they use a set of tools called game theory. **Game theory** is a tool for studying *strategic behavior*—behavior that takes into account the expected behavior of others and the recognition of mutual interdependence. Game theory was invented by John von Neumann in 1937 and extended by von Neumann and Oskar Morgenstern in 1944 (p. 369). Today, it is one of the major research fields in economics.

Game theory seeks to understand oligopoly as well as other forms of economic, political, social, and even biological rivalries by using a method of analysis specifically designed to understand games of all types, including the familiar games of everyday life (see Talking with Drew Fudenberg on pp. 370–372). We will begin our study of game theory and its application to the behavior of firms by thinking about familiar games.

What Is a Game?

What is a game? At first thought, the question seems silly. After all, there are many different games. There are ball games and parlor games, games of chance and games of skill. But what is it about all these different activities that make them games? What do all these games have in common? We're going to answer these questions by looking at a game called "the prisoners' dilemma." This game captures the essential features of many games, including oligopoly, and it gives a good illustration of how game theory works and how it generates predictions.

The Prisoners' Dilemma

Art and Bob have been caught red-handed stealing a car. Facing airtight cases, they will receive a sentence of two years each for their crime. During his interviews with the two prisoners, the district attorney begins to suspect that he has stumbled on the two people who were responsible for a multimillion-dollar bank robbery some months earlier. But this is just a suspicion. He has no evidence on which he can convict them of the greater crime unless he can get them to confess. But how can he extract a confession? The answer is by making the prisoners play a game. The district attorney makes the prisoners play the following game.

All games share four common features:

- Rules
- Strategies
- Payoffs
- Outcome

Rules Each prisoner (player) is placed in a separate room and cannot communicate with the other prisoner. Each is told that he is suspected of having carried out the bank robbery and that

If both of them confess to the larger crime, each will receive a sentence of 3 years for both crimes.

If he alone confesses and his accomplice does not, he will receive only a 1-year sentence while his accomplice will receive a 10-year sentence.

Strategies In game theory, **strategies** are all the possible actions of each player. Art and Bob each have two possible actions:

1. Confess to the bank robbery.
2. Deny having committed the bank robbery.

Because there are two players, each with two strategies, there are four possible outcomes:

1. Both confess.
2. Both deny.
3. Art confesses and Bob denies.
4. Bob confesses and Art denies.

Payoffs Each prisoner can work out his *payoff* in each of these situations, and we can tabulate the four possible payoffs for each of the prisoners in what is called a payoff matrix for the game. A **payoff matrix** is a table that shows the payoffs for every possible action by each player for every possible action by each other player.

Table 15.1 shows a payoff matrix for Art and Bob. The squares show the payoffs for each prisoner—the red triangle in each square shows Art's and the blue triangle shows Bob's. If both prisoners confess (top left), each gets a prison term of 3 years. If Bob confesses but Art denies (top right), Art gets a 10-year sentence and Bob gets a 1-year sentence. If Art confesses and Bob denies (bottom left), Art gets a 1-year sentence and Bob gets a 10-year sentence. Finally, if both of them deny (bottom right), neither can be convicted of the bank robbery charge but both are sentenced for the car theft—a 2-year sentence.

Outcome The choices of both players determine the outcome of the game. To predict that outcome, we use an equilibrium idea proposed by John Nash of Princeton University (who received the Nobel Prize for Economic Science in 1994 and was the subject of the 2001 movie *A Beautiful Mind*). In **Nash equilibrium**, player *A* takes the best possible action given the action of player *B* and player *B* takes the best possible action given the action of player *A*.

In the case of the prisoners' dilemma, the Nash equilibrium occurs when Art makes his best choice given Bob's choice and when Bob makes his best choice given Art's choice.

To find the Nash equilibrium, we compare all the possible outcomes associated with each choice and eliminate those that are dominated—that are not as good as some other choice. Let's find the Nash equilibrium for the prisoners' dilemma game.

Finding the Nash Equilibrium Look at the situation from Art's point of view. If Bob confesses (top row), Art's best action is to confess because in that case, he is sentenced to 3 years rather than 10 years. If Bob denies (bottom row), Art's best action is still to confess because in that case he receives 1 year rather than 2 years. So Art's best action is to confess.

Now look at the situation from Bob's point of view. If Art confesses (left column), Bob's best action is to confess because in that case, he is sentenced to 3 years rather than 10 years. If Art denies (right column), Bob's best action is still to confess because in that case, he receives 1 year rather than 2 years. So Bob's best action is to confess.

Because each player's best action is to confess, each does confess, each goes to jail for 3 years, and the district attorney has solved the bank robbery. This is the Nash equilibrium of the game.

The Dilemma Now that you have found the outcome to the prisoners' dilemma, you can better see the dilemma. The dilemma arises as each prisoner contemplates the consequences of denying. Each prisoner knows that if both of them deny, they will receive only a 2-year sentence for stealing the car. But neither has any way of knowing that his accomplice will deny. Each poses the following questions: Should I deny and rely on my accomplice to deny so that we will both get only 2 years? Or should I confess in the hope of getting just 1 year (provided that my accomplice denies) knowing that if my accomplice does confess,

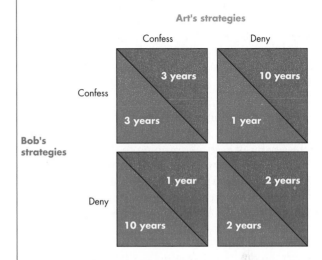

TABLE 15.1   Prisoners' Dilemma Payoff Matrix

	Art's strategies	
	Confess	Deny
Confess	3 years / 3 years	10 years / 1 year
Deny	1 year / 10 years	2 years / 2 years

Each square shows the payoffs for the two players, Art and Bob, for each possible pair of actions. In each square, the red triangle shows Art's payoff and the blue triangle shows Bob's. For example, if both confess, the payoffs are in the top left square. The equilibrium of the game is for both players to confess and each gets a 3-year sentence.

we will both get 3 years in prison? The dilemma leads to the equilibrium of the game.

A Bad Outcome For the prisoners, the equilibrium of the game, with each confessing, is not the best outcome. If neither of them confesses, each gets only 2 years for the lesser crime. Isn't there some way in which this better outcome can be achieved? It seems that there is not, because the players cannot communicate with each other. Each player can put himself in the other player's place, and so each player can figure out that there is a best strategy for each of them. The prisoners are indeed in a dilemma. Each knows that he can serve 2 years only if he can trust the other to deny. But each prisoner also knows that it is not in the best interest of the other to deny. So each prisoner knows that he must confess, thereby delivering a bad outcome for both.

The firms in an oligopoly are in a similar situation to Art and Bob in the prisoners' dilemma game. Let's see how we can use this game to understand oligopoly.

An Oligopoly Price-Fixing Game

We can use game theory and a game like the prisoners' dilemma to understand price fixing, price wars, and other aspects of the behavior of firms in oligopoly. We'll begin with a price-fixing game.

To understand price fixing, we're going to study the special case of duopoly—an oligopoly with two firms. Duopoly is easier to study than oligopoly with three or more firms, and it captures the essence of all oligopoly situations. Somehow, the two firms must share the market. And how they share it depends on the actions of each. We're going to describe the costs of the two firms and the market demand for the item they produce. We're then going to see how game theory helps us to predict the prices charged and the quantities produced by the two firms in a duopoly.

Cost and Demand Conditions Two firms, Trick and Gear, produce switchgears. They have identical costs. Figure 15.4(a) shows their average total cost curve (*ATC*) and marginal cost curve (*MC*). Figure 15.4(b) shows the market demand curve for switchgears (*D*). The two firms produce identical switchgears, so one firm's switchgear is a perfect substitute for the other's, and the market price of each firm's product is identical. The quantity demanded depends on that price—the higher the price, the smaller is the quantity demanded.

This industry is a natural duopoly. Two firms can produce this good at a lower cost than either one firm or three firms can. For each firm, average total cost is at its minimum when production is 3,000 units a week. When price equals minimum average total cost, the total quantity demanded is 6,000 units a week, and two firms can just produce that quantity.

Collusion We'll suppose that Trick and Gear enter into a collusive agreement. A **collusive agreement** is an agreement between two (or more) producers to form a cartel to restrict output, raise the price, and increase profits. Such an agreement is illegal in the United States and is undertaken in secret. The strategies that firms in a cartel can pursue are to

- Comply
- Cheat

A firm that complies carries out the agreement. A firm that cheats breaks the agreement to its own benefit and to the cost of the other firm.

Because each firm has two strategies, there are four possible combinations of actions for the firms:

1. Both firms comply.
2. Both firms cheat.
3. Trick complies and Gear cheats.
4. Gear complies and Trick cheats.

FIGURE 15.4 Costs and Demand

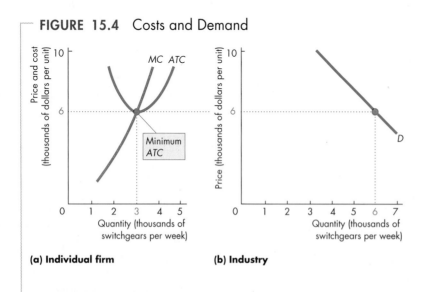

(a) Individual firm

(b) Industry

The average total cost curve for each firm is *ATC*, and the marginal cost curve is *MC* (part a). Minimum average total cost is $6,000 a unit, and it occurs at a production of 3,000 units a week.

Part (b) shows the market demand curve. At a price of $6,000, the quantity demanded is 6,000 units per week. The two firms can produce this output at the lowest possible average cost. If the market had one firm, it would be profitable for another to enter. If the market had three firms, one would exit. There is room for only two firms in this industry. It is a natural duopoly.

Colluding to Maximize Profits Let's work out the payoffs to the two firms if they collude to make the maximum profit for the cartel by acting like a monopoly. The calculations that the two firms perform are the same calculations that a monopoly performs. (You can refresh your memory of these calculations by looking at Chapter 13, pp. 304–305.) The only thing that the firms in duopoly must do beyond what a monopoly does is to agree on how much of the total output each of them will produce.

Figure 15.5 shows the price and quantity that maximize industry profit for the duopoly. Part (a) shows the situation for each firm, and part (b) shows the situation for the industry as a whole. The curve labeled MR is the industry marginal revenue curve. This marginal revenue curve is like that of a single-price monopoly (Chapter 13, p. 302). The curve labeled MC_I is the industry marginal cost curve if each firm produces the same quantity of output. This curve is constructed by adding together the outputs of the two firms at each level of marginal cost. Because the two firms are the same size, at each level of marginal cost, the industry output is twice the output of one firm. The curve MC_I in part (b) is twice as far to the right as the curve MC in part (a).

To maximize industry profit, the firms in the duopoly agree to restrict output to the rate that makes the industry marginal cost and marginal revenue equal. That output rate, as shown in part (b), is 4,000 units a week. The demand curve shows that the highest price for which the 4,000 switchgears can be sold is $9,000 each. Trick and Gear agree to charge this price.

To hold the price at $9,000 a unit, production must be 4,000 units a week. So Trick and Gear must agree on output rates for each of them that total 4,000 units a week. Let's suppose that they agree to split the market equally so that each firm produces 2,000 switchgears a week. Because the firms are identical, this division is the most likely.

The average total cost (ATC) of producing 2,000 switchgears a week is $8,000, so the profit per unit is $1,000 and economic profit is $2 million (2,000 units × $1,000 per unit). The economic profit of each firm is represented by the blue rectangle in Fig. 15.5(a).

We have just described one possible outcome for a duopoly game: The two firms collude to produce the monopoly profit-maximizing output and divide that output equally between themselves. From the industry point of view, this solution is identical to a monopoly. A duopoly that operates in this way is indistinguishable from a monopoly. The economic profit that is made by a monopoly is the maximum total profit that can be made by the duopoly when the firms collude.

But with price greater than marginal cost, either firm might think of trying to increase profit by cheating on the agreement and producing more than the agreed amount. Let's see what happens if one of the firms does cheat in this way.

FIGURE 15.5   Colluding to Make Monopoly Profits

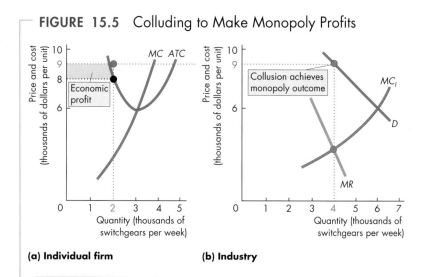

(a) Individual firm

(b) Industry

The industry marginal cost curve, MC_I in part (b), is the horizontal sum of the two firms' marginal cost curves, MC in part (a). The industry marginal revenue curve is MR. To maximize profit, the firms produce 4,000 units a week (the quantity at which marginal revenue equals marginal cost). They sell that output for $9,000 a unit. Each firm produces 2,000 units a week. Average total cost is $8,000 a unit, so each firm makes an economic profit of $2 million (blue rectangle)—2,000 units multiplied by $1,000 profit a unit.

myeconlab   animation

One Firm Cheats on a Collusive Agreement To set the stage for cheating on their agreement, Trick convinces Gear that demand has decreased and that it cannot sell 2,000 units a week. Trick tells Gear that it plans to cut its price so that it can sell the agreed 2,000 units each week. Because the two firms produce an identical product, Gear matches Trick's price cut but still produces only 2,000 units a week.

In fact, there has been no decrease in demand. Trick plans to increase output, which it knows will lower the price, and Trick wants to ensure that Gear's output remains at the agreed level.

Figure 15.6 illustrates the consequences of Trick's cheating. Part (a) shows Gear (the complier); part (b) shows Trick (the cheat); and part (c) shows the industry as a whole. Suppose that Trick increases output to 3,000 units a week. If Gear sticks to the agreement to produce only 2,000 units a week, total output is now 5,000 a week, and given demand in part (c), the price falls to $7,500 a unit.

Gear continues to produce 2,000 units a week at a cost of $8,000 a unit and incurs a loss of $500 a unit, or $1 million a week. This economic loss is shown by the red rectangle in part (a). Trick produces 3,000 units a week at an average total cost of $6,000 each. With a price of $7,500, Trick makes a profit of

$1,500 a unit and therefore an economic profit of $4.5 million. This economic profit is the blue rectangle in part (b).

We've now described a second possible outcome for the duopoly game: One of the firms cheats on the collusive agreement. In this case, the industry output is larger than the monopoly output and the industry price is lower than the monopoly price. The total economic profit made by the industry is also smaller than the monopoly's economic profit. Trick (the cheat) makes an economic profit of $4.5 million, and Gear (the complier) incurs an economic loss of $1 million. The industry makes an economic profit of $3.5 million. This industry profit is $0.5 million less than the economic profit that a monopoly would make. But the profit is distributed unevenly. Trick makes a bigger economic profit than it would under the collusive agreement, while Gear incurs an economic loss.

A similar outcome would arise if Gear cheated and Trick complied with the agreement. The industry profit and price would be the same, but in this case, Gear (the cheat) would make an economic profit of $4.5 million and Trick (the complier) would incur an economic loss of $1 million.

Let's next see what happens if both firms cheat.

FIGURE 15.6   One Firm Cheats

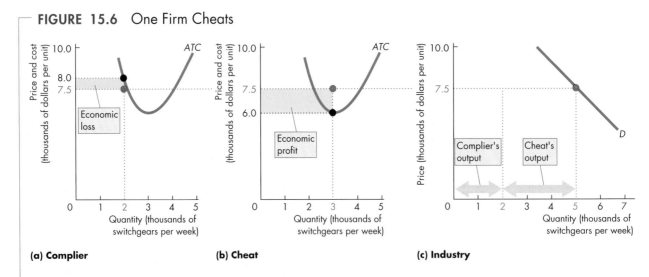

(a) Complier   **(b) Cheat**   **(c) Industry**

One firm, shown in part (a), complies with the agreement and produces 2,000 units. The other firm, shown in part (b), cheats on the agreement and increases its output to 3,000 units a week. Given the market demand curve, shown in part (c), and with a total production of 5,000 units a week,

the price falls to $7,500 a unit. At this price, the complier in part (a) incurs an economic loss of $1 million ($500 per unit × 2,000 units), shown by the red rectangle. In part (b), the cheat makes an economic profit of $4.5 million ($1,500 per unit × 3,000 units), shown by the blue rectangle.

Both Firms Cheat Suppose that both firms cheat and that each firm behaves like the cheating firm that we have just analyzed. Each tells the other that it is unable to sell its output at the going price and that it plans to cut its price. But because both firms cheat, each will propose a successively lower price. As long as price exceeds marginal cost, each firm has an incentive to increase its production—to cheat. Only when price equals marginal cost is there no further incentive to cheat. This situation arises when the price has reached $6,000. At this price, marginal cost equals price. Also, price equals minimum average total cost. At a price less than $6,000, each firm incurs an economic loss. At a price of $6,000, each firm covers all its costs and makes zero economic profit. Also, at a price of $6,000, each firm wants to produce 3,000 units a week, so the industry output is 6,000 units a week. Given the demand conditions, 6,000 units can be sold at a price of $6,000 each.

Figure 15.7 illustrates the situation just described. Each firm, in part (a), produces 3,000 units a week, and its average total cost is a minimum ($6,000 per unit). The market as a whole, in part (b), operates at the point at which the market demand curve (D) intersects the industry marginal cost curve (MC_I). Each firm has lowered its price and increased its output to try to gain an advantage over the other firm. Each has pushed this process as far as it can without incurring an economic loss.

We have now described a third possible outcome of this duopoly game: Both firms cheat. If both firms cheat on the collusive agreement, the output of each firm is 3,000 units a week and the price is $6,000 a unit. Each firm makes zero economic profit.

The Payoff Matrix Now that we have described the strategies and payoffs in the duopoly game, we can summarize the strategies and the payoffs in the form of the game's payoff matrix. Then we can find the Nash equilibrium.

Table 15.2 sets out the payoff matrix for this game. It is constructed in the same way as the payoff matrix for the prisoners' dilemma in Table 15.1. The squares show the payoffs for the two firms—Gear and Trick. In this case, the payoffs are profits. (For the prisoners' dilemma, the payoffs were losses.)

The table shows that if both firms cheat (top left), they achieve the perfectly competitive outcome—each firm makes zero economic profit. If both firms comply (bottom right), the industry makes the monopoly profit and each firm makes an economic profit of $2 million. The top right and bottom left squares show the payoff if one firm cheats while the other complies. The firm that cheats makes an economic profit of $4.5 million, and the one that complies incurs a loss of $1 million.

Nash Equilibrium in the Duopolists' Dilemma The duopolists have a dilemma like the prisoners' dilemma. Do they comply or cheat? To answer this question, we must find the Nash equilibrium.

FIGURE 15.7 Both Firms Cheat

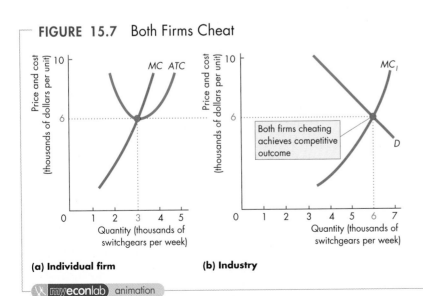

(a) Individual firm

(b) Industry

If both firms cheat by increasing production, the collusive agreement collapses. The limit to the collapse is the competitive equilibrium. Neither firm will cut its price below $6,000 (minimum average total cost) because to do so will result in losses. In part (a), each firm produces 3,000 units a week at an average total cost of $6,000. In part (b), with a total production of 6,000 units, the price falls to $6,000. Each firm now makes zero economic profit. This output and price are the ones that would prevail in a competitive industry.

myeconlab animation

TABLE 15.2   Duopoly Payoff Matrix

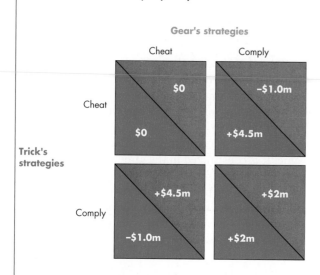

Each square shows the payoffs from a pair of actions. For example, if both firms comply with the collusive agreement, the payoffs are recorded in the bottom right square. The red triangle shows Gear's payoff, and the blue triangle shows Trick's. In Nash equilibrium, both firms cheat.

◆

Look at things from Gear's point of view. Gear reasons as follows: Suppose that Trick cheats. If I comply, I will incur an economic loss of $1 million. If I also cheat, I will make zero economic profit. Zero is better than *minus* $1 million, so I'm better off if I cheat. Now suppose Trick complies. If I cheat, I will make an economic profit of $4.5 million, and if I comply, I will make an economic profit of $2 million. A $4.5 million profit is better than a $2 million profit, so I'm better off if I cheat. So regardless of whether Trick cheats or complies, it pays Gear to cheat. Cheating is Gear's best strategy.

Trick comes to the same conclusion as Gear because the two firms face an identical situation. So both firms cheat. The Nash equilibrium of the duopoly game is that both firms cheat. And although the industry has only two firms, they charge the same price and produce the same quantity as those in a competitive industry. Also, as in perfect competition, each firm makes zero economic profit.

This conclusion is not general and will not always arise. We'll see why not by looking first at some other games that are like the prisoners' dilemma. Then we'll broaden the types of games we consider.

Other Oligopoly Games

Firms in oligopoly must decide whether to mount expensive advertising campaigns; whether to modify their product; whether to make their product more reliable and more durable; whether to price discriminate and, if so, among which groups of customers and to what degree; whether to undertake a large research and development (R&D) effort aimed at lowering production costs; and whether to enter or leave an industry.

All of these choices can be analyzed as games that are similar to the one that we've just studied. Let's look at one example: an R&D game.

An R&D Game
Procter & Gamble Versus Kimberly-Clark

Disposable diapers have been around for a bit more than 40 years. Procter & Gamble (which has a 40 percent market share with Pampers) and Kimberly-Clark (which has a 33 percent market share with Huggies) have always been the market leaders.

When the disposable diaper was first introduced, it had to be cost-effective in competition with reusable, laundered diapers. A costly research and development effort resulted in the development of machines that could make disposable diapers at a low enough cost to achieve that initial competitive edge. But new firms tried to get into the business and take market share away from the two industry leaders, and the industry leaders themselves battled each other to maintain or increase their own market shares.

During the early 1990s, Kimberly-Clark was the first to introduce Velcro closures. And in 1996, Procter & Gamble was the first to introduce "breathable" diapers.

The key to success in this industry (as in any other) is to design a product that people value highly relative to the cost of producing it. The firm that creates the most highly valued product and also develops the least-cost technology for producing it gains a competitive edge, undercutting the rest of the market, increasing its market share, and increasing its profit.

But the R&D that must be undertaken to improve product quality and cut cost is itself costly. So the cost of R&D must be deducted from the profit resulting from the increased market share that lower costs achieve. If no firm does R&D, every firm can be better off, but if one firm initiates the R&D activity, all must follow.

Table 15.3 illustrates the dilemma (with hypothetical numbers) for the R&D game that Kimberly-Clark and Procter & Gamble play. Each firm has two strategies: Spend $25 million a year on R&D or spend nothing on R&D. If neither firm spends on R&D, they make a joint profit of $100 million: $30 million for Kimberly-Clark and $70 million for Procter & Gamble (bottom right of the payoff matrix). If each firm conducts R&D, market shares are maintained but each firm's profit is lower by the amount spent on R&D (top left square of the payoff matrix). If Kimberly-Clark pays for R&D but Procter & Gamble does not, Kimberly-Clark gains a large part of Procter & Gamble's market. Kimberly-Clark profits, and Procter & Gamble loses (top right square of the payoff matrix). Finally, if Procter & Gamble conducts R&D and Kimberly-Clark does not, Procter & Gamble gains market share from Kimberly-Clark, increasing its profit, while Kimberly-Clark incurs a loss (bottom left square).

TABLE 15.3   Pampers Versus Huggies: An R&D Game

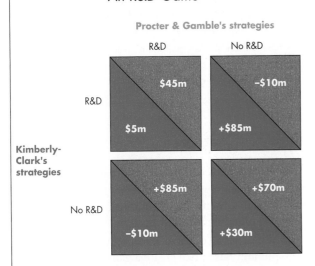

Procter & Gamble's strategies

	R&D	No R&D
R&D	$45m / $5m	−$10m / +$85m
No R&D	+$85m / −$10m	+$70m / +$30m

Kimberly-Clark's strategies

If both firms undertake R&D, their payoffs are those shown in the top left square. If neither firm undertakes R&D, their payoffs are in the bottom right square. When one firm undertakes R&D and the other one does not, their payoffs are in the top right and bottom left squares. The red triangle shows Procter & Gamble's payoff, and the blue triangle shows Kimberly-Clark's. The Nash equilibrium for this game is for both firms to undertake R&D. The structure of this game is the same as that of the prisoners' dilemma.

Confronted with the payoff matrix in Table 15.3, the two firms calculate their best strategies. Kimberly-Clark reasons as follows: If Procter & Gamble does not undertake R&D, we will make $85 million if we do and $30 million if we do not; so it pays us to conduct R&D. If Procter & Gamble conducts R&D, we will lose $10 million if we don't and make $5 million if we do. Again, R&D pays off. So conducting R&D is the best strategy for Kimberly-Clark. It pays, regardless of Procter & Gamble's decision.

Procter & Gamble reasons similarly: If Kimberly-Clark does not undertake R&D, we will make $70 million if we follow suit and $85 million if we conduct R&D. It therefore pays to conduct R&D. If Kimberly-Clark does undertake R&D, we will make $45 million by doing the same and lose $10 million by not doing R&D. Again, it pays us to conduct R&D. So for Procter & Gamble, R&D is also the best strategy.

Because R&D is the best strategy for both players, it is the Nash equilibrium. The outcome of this game is that both firms conduct R&D. They make less profit than they would if they could collude to achieve the cooperative outcome of no R&D.

The real-world situation has more players than Kimberly-Clark and Procter & Gamble. A large number of other firms share a small portion of the market, all of them ready to eat into the market share of Procter & Gamble and Kimberly-Clark. So the R&D efforts by these two firms not only serve the purpose of maintaining shares in their own battle but also help to keep barriers to entry high enough to preserve their joint market share.

The Disappearing Invisible Hand

All the games that we've studied are versions of the prisoners' dilemma. The essence of that game lies in the structure of its payoffs. The worst possible outcome for each player arises from cooperating when the other player cheats. The best possible outcome, for each player to cooperate, is not a Nash equilibrium because it is in neither player's *self-interest* to cooperate if the other one cooperates. It is this failure to achieve the best outcome for both players—the best social outcome if the two players are the entire economy—that led John Nash to claim (as he was portrayed as doing in the movie *A Beautiful Mind*) that he had challenged Adam Smith's idea that we are always guided, as if by an invisible hand, to promote the social interest when we are pursuing our self-interest.

A Game of Chicken

The Nash equilibrium for the prisoners' dilemma is called a **dominant strategy equilibrium**, which is an equilibrium in which the best strategy of each player is to cheat (confess) *regardless of the strategy of the other player.* Not all games have such an equilibrium, and one that doesn't is a game called "chicken."

In a graphic, if disturbing, version of this game, two cars race toward each other. The first driver to swerve and avoid a crash is "chicken." The payoffs are a big loss for both if no one "chickens," zero for the chicken, and a gain for the player who stays the course. If player 1 chickens, player 2's best strategy is to stay the course. And if player 1 stays the course, player 2's best strategy is to chicken.

For an economic form of this game, suppose the R&D that creates a new diaper technology results in information that cannot be kept secret or patented, so both firms benefit from the R&D of either firm. The chicken in this case is the firm that does the R&D.

Table 15.4 illustrates a payoff matrix for an R&D game of chicken between Kimberly-Clark and Procter & Gamble. Each firm has two strategies: Do the R&D (and "chicken") or do not do the R&D (and stand firm).

If neither "chickens," there is no R&D and each firm makes zero additional profit. If each firm conducts R&D—each "chickens"—each firm makes $5 million (the profit from the new technology minus the cost of the research). If one of the firms does the R&D, the payoffs are $1 million for the chicken and $10 million for the one who stands firm.

Confronted with the payoff matrix in Table 15.4, the two firms calculate their best strategies. Kimberly-Clark is better off doing R&D if Procter & Gamble does not undertake it. Procter & Gamble is better off doing R&D if Kimberly-Clark doesn't do it. There are two equilibrium outcomes: One firm does the R&D, but we can't predict which firm it will be.

You can see that it isn't a Nash equilibrium if no firm does the R&D because one firm would then be better off doing it. And you can see that it isn't a Nash equilibrium if both firms do the R&D because then one firm would be better off not doing it.

The firms could toss a coin or use some other random device to make a decision in this game. In some circumstances, such a strategy—called a mixed strategy—is actually better for both firms than choosing any of the strategies we've considered.

TABLE 15.4   An R&D Game of Chicken

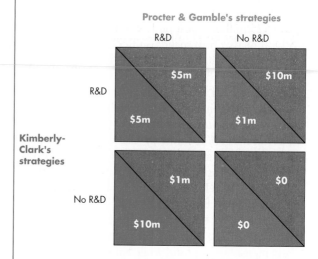

Procter & Gamble's strategies

Kimberly-Clark's strategies

If both firms undertake R&D, their payoffs are those shown in the top left square. If neither firm undertakes R&D, their payoffs are in the bottom right square. When one firm undertakes R&D and the other one does not, their payoffs are in the top right and bottom left squares. The red triangle shows Procter & Gamble's payoff, and the blue triangle shows Kimberly-Clark's. The equilibrium for this R&D game of chicken is for only one firm to undertake R&D. We cannot tell which firm will do the R&D and which will not.

Review Quiz

1 What are the common features of all games?
2 Describe the prisoners' dilemma game and explain why the Nash equilibrium delivers a bad outcome for both players.
3 Why does a collusive agreement to restrict output and raise price create a game like the prisoners' dilemma?
4 What creates an incentive for firms in a collusive agreement to cheat and increase production?
5 What is the equilibrium strategy for each firm in a duopolists' dilemma and why do the firms not succeed in colluding to raise the price and profits?
6 Describe two structures of payoffs for an R&D game and contrast the prisoners' dilemma and the chicken game.

myeconlab   Work Study Plan 15.3 and get instant feedback.

Repeated Games and Sequential Games

The games that we've studied are played just once. In contrast, many real-world games are played repeatedly. This feature of games turns out to enable real-world duopolists to cooperate, collude, and make a monopoly profit.

Another feature of the games that we've studied is that the players move simultaneously. But in many real-world situations, one player moves first and then the other moves—the play is sequential rather than simultaneous. This feature of real-world games creates a large number of possible outcomes.

We're now going to examine these two aspects of strategic decision-making.

A Repeated Duopoly Game

If two firms play a game repeatedly, one firm has the opportunity to penalize the other for previous "bad" behavior. If Gear cheats this week, perhaps Trick will cheat next week. Before Gear cheats this week, won't it consider the possibility that Trick will cheat next week? What is the equilibrium of this game?

Actually, there is more than one possibility. One is the Nash equilibrium that we have just analyzed. Both players cheat, and each makes zero economic profit forever. In such a situation, it will never pay one of the players to start complying unilaterally because to do so would result in a loss for that player and a profit for the other. But a **cooperative equilibrium** in which the players make and share the monopoly profit is possible.

A cooperative equilibrium might occur if cheating is punished. There are two extremes of punishment. The smallest penalty is called "tit for tat." A *tit-for-tat strategy* is one in which a player cooperates in the current period if the other player cooperated in the previous period, but cheats in the current period if the other player cheated in the previous period. The most severe form of punishment is called a trigger strategy. A *trigger strategy* is one in which a player cooperates if the other player cooperates but plays the Nash equilibrium strategy forever thereafter if the other player cheats.

In the duopoly game between Gear and Trick, a tit-for-tat strategy keeps both players cooperating and making monopoly profits. Let's see why with an example.

Table 15.5 shows the economic profit that Trick and Gear will make over a number of periods under two alternative sequences of events: colluding and cheating with a tit-for-tat response by the other firm.

If both firms stick to the collusive agreement in period 1, each makes an economic profit of $2 million. Suppose that Trick contemplates cheating in period 1. The cheating produces a quick $4.5 million economic profit and inflicts a $1 million economic loss on Gear. But a cheat in period 1 produces a response from Gear in period 2. If Trick wants to get back into a profit-making situation, it must return to the agreement in period 2 even though it knows that Gear will punish it for cheating in period 1. So in period 2, Gear punishes Trick and Trick cooperates. Gear now makes an economic profit of $4.5 million, and Trick incurs an economic loss of $1 million. Adding up the profits over two periods of play, Trick would have made more profit by cooperating—$4 million compared with $3.5 million.

What is true for Trick is also true for Gear. Because each firm makes a larger profit by sticking with the collusive agreement, both firms do so and the monopoly price, quantity, and profit prevail.

In reality, whether a cartel works like a one-play game or a repeated game depends primarily on the

TABLE 15.5   Cheating with Punishment

Period of play	Collude		Cheat with tit-for-tat	
	Trick's profit	Gear's profit	Trick's profit	Gear's profit
	(millions of dollars)		(millions of dollars)	
1	2	2	4.5	−1.0
2	2	2	−1.0	4.5
3	2	2	2.0	2.0
4	.	.	.	.

If duopolists repeatedly collude, each makes a profit of $2 million per period of play. If one player cheats in period 1, the other player plays a tit-for-tat strategy and cheats in period 2. The profit from cheating can be made for only one period and must be paid for in the next period by incurring a loss. Over two periods of play, the best that a duopolist can achieve by cheating is a profit of $3.5 million, compared to an economic profit of $4 million by colluding.

number of players and the ease of detecting and punishing cheating. The larger the number of players, the harder it is to maintain a cartel.

Games and Price Wars   A repeated duopoly game can help us understand real-world behavior and, in particular, price wars. Some price wars can be interpreted as the implementation of a tit-for-tat strategy. But the game is a bit more complicated than the one we've looked at because the players are uncertain about the demand for the product.

Playing a tit-for-tat strategy, firms have an incentive to stick to the monopoly price. But fluctuations in demand lead to fluctuations in the monopoly price, and sometimes, when the price changes, it might seem to one of the firms that the price has fallen because the other has cheated. In this case, a price war will break out. The price war will end only when each firm is satisfied that the other is ready to cooperate again. There will be cycles of price wars and the restoration of collusive agreements. Fluctuations in the world price of oil might be interpreted in this way.

Some price wars arise from the entry of a small number of firms into an industry that had previously been a monopoly. Although the industry has a small number of firms, the firms are in a prisoners' dilemma and they cannot impose effective penalties for price cutting. The behavior of prices and outputs in the computer chip industry during 1995 and 1996 can be explained in this way. Until 1995, the market for Pentium chips for IBM-compatible computers was dominated by one firm, Intel Corporation, which was able to make maximum economic profit by producing the quantity of chips at which marginal cost equaled marginal revenue. The price of Intel's chips was set to ensure that the quantity demanded equaled the quantity produced. Then in 1995 and 1996, with the entry of a small number of new firms, the industry became an oligopoly. If the firms had maintained Intel's price and shared the market, together they could have made economic profits equal to Intel's profit. But the firms were in a prisoners' dilemma, so prices fell toward the competitive level.

Let's now study a sequential game. There are many such games, and the one we'll examine is among the simplest. It has an interesting implication and it will give you the flavor of this type of game. The sequential game that we'll study is an entry game in a contestable market.

A Sequential Entry Game in a Contestable Market

If two firms play a sequential game, one firm makes a decision at the first stage of the game and the other makes a decision at the second stage.

We're going to study a sequential game in a **contestable market**—a market in which firms can enter and leave so easily that firms in the market face competition from *potential* entrants. Examples of contestable markets are routes served by airlines and by barge companies that operate on the major waterways. These markets are contestable because firms could enter if an opportunity for economic profit arose and could exit with no penalty if the opportunity for economic profit disappeared.

If the Herfindahl-Hirschman Index (p. 238) is used to determine the degree of competition, a contestable market appears to be uncompetitive. But a contestable market can behave as if it were perfectly competitive. To see why, let's look at an entry game for a contestable air route.

A Contestable Air Route   Agile Air is the only firm operating on a particular route. Demand and cost conditions are such that there is room for only one airline to operate. Wanabe Inc. is another airline that could offer services on the route.

We describe the structure of a sequential game by using a *game tree* like that in Fig. 15.8. At the first stage, Agile Air must set a price. Once the price is set and advertised, Agile can't change it. That is, once set, Agile's price is fixed and Agile can't react to Wanabe's entry decision. Agile can set its price at either the monopoly level or the competitive level.

At the second stage, Wanabe must decide whether to enter or to stay out. Customers have no loyalty (there are no frequent-flyer programs) and they buy from the lowest-price firm. So if Wanabe enters, it sets a price just below Agile's and takes all the business.

Figure 15.8 shows the payoffs from the various decisions (Agile's in the red triangles and Wanabe's in the blue triangles).

To decide on its price, Agile's CEO reasons as follows: Suppose that Agile sets the monopoly price. If Wanabe enters, it earns 90 (think of all payoff numbers as thousands of dollars). If Wanabe stays out, it earns nothing. So Wanabe will enter. In this case Agile will lose 50.

FIGURE 15.8   Agile Versus Wanabe: A Sequential Entry Game in a Contestable Market

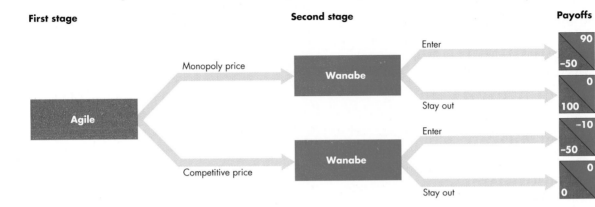

First stage	Second stage	Payoffs

If Agile sets the monopoly price, Wanabe makes 90 (thousand dollars) by entering and earns nothing by staying out. So if Agile sets the monopoly price, Wanabe enters.

If Agile sets the competitive price, Wanabe earns nothing if it stays out and incurs a loss if it enters. So if Agile sets the competitive price, Wanabe stays out.

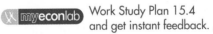 animation

Now suppose that Agile sets the competitive price. If Wanabe stays out, it earns nothing, and if it enters, it loses 10, so Wanabe will stay out. In this case, Agile will make zero economic profit.

Agile's best strategy is to set its price at the competitive level and make zero economic profit. The option of earning 100 by setting the monopoly price with Wanabe staying out is not available to Agile. If Agile sets the monopoly price, Wanabe enters, undercuts Agile, and takes all the business.

In this example, Agile sets its price at the competitive level and makes zero economic profit. A less costly strategy, called **limit pricing**, sets the price at the highest level that inflicts a loss on the entrant. Any loss is big enough to deter entry, so it is not always necessary to set the price as low as the competitive price. In the example of Agile and Wanabe, at the competitive price, Wanabe incurs a loss of 10 if it enters. A smaller loss would still keep Wanabe out.

This game is interesting because it points to the possibility of a monopoly behaving like a competitive industry and serving the social interest without regulation. But the result is not general and depends on one crucial feature of the setup of the game: At the second stage, Agile is locked in to the price set at the first stage.

If Agile could change its price in the second stage, it would want to set the monopoly price if Wanabe stayed out—100 with the monopoly price beats zero with the competitive price. But Wanabe can figure out

what Agile would do, so the price set at the first stage has no effect on Wanabe. Agile sets the monopoly price and Wanabe might either stay out or enter.

We've looked at two of the many possible repeated and sequential games, and you've seen how these types of games can provide insights into the complex forces that determine prices and profits.

Review Quiz

1 If a prisoners' dilemma game is played repeatedly, what punishment strategies might the players employ and how does playing the game repeatedly change the equilibrium?
2 If a market is contestable, how does the equilibrium differ from that of a monopoly?

myeconlab Work Study Plan 15.4 and get instant feedback.

So far, we've studied oligopoly with unregulated market power. Firms like Trick and Gear are free to collude to maximize their profit with no concern for the consumer or the law.

But when firms collude to achieve the monopoly outcome, they also have the same effects on efficiency and the social interest as monopoly. Profit is made at the expense of consumer surplus and a deadweight loss arises. Your next task is to see how U.S. antitrust law limits market power.

Antitrust Law

Antitrust law is the law that regulates oligopolies and prevents them from becoming monopolies or behaving like monopolies. Two government agencies cooperate to enforce the antitrust laws: the Federal Trade Commission and the Antitrust Division of the U.S. Department of Justice.

The Antitrust Laws

The two main antitrust laws are
- The Sherman Act, 1890
- The Clayton Act, 1914.

The Sherman Act The Sherman Act made it a felony to create or attempt to create a monopoly or a cartel.

During the 1880s, lawmakers and the general public were outraged and disgusted by the practices of some of the big-name leaders of American business. The actions of J.P. Morgan, John D. Rockefeller, and W.H. Vanderbilt led to them being called the "robber barons." It turns out that the most lurid stories of the actions of these great American capitalists were not of their creation of monopoly power to exploit consumers but of their actions to damage each other.

Nevertheless, monopolies that damaged the consumer interest did emerge. For example, John D. Rockefeller had a virtual monopoly in the market for oil.

Table 15.6 summarizes the two main provisions of the Sherman Act. Section 1 of the act is precise:

TABLE 15.6   The Sherman Act of 1890

Section 1:

Every contract, combination in the form of trust or otherwise, or conspiracy, in restraint of trade or commerce among the several States, or with foreign nations, is hereby declared to be illegal.

Section 2:

Every person who shall monopolize, or attempt to monopolize, or combine or conspire with any other person or persons, to monopolize any part of the trade or commerce among the several States, or with foreign nations, shall be deemed guilty of a felony.

Conspiring with others to restrict competition is illegal. But Section 2 is general and imprecise. Just what is an "attempt to monopolize"?

The Clayton Act The Clayton Act, which was passed in response to a wave of mergers that occurred at the beginning of the twentieth century, provided the answer to the question left dangling by the Sherman Act: It defined the "attempt to monopolize." The Clayton Act supplemented the Sherman Act and strengthened and clarified the antitrust law.

When Congress passed the Clayton Act, it also established the Federal Trade Commission, the federal agency charged with the task of preventing monopoly practices that damage the consumer interest.

Two amendments to the Clayton Act, the Robinson-Patman Act of 1936 and the Celler-Kefauver Act of 1950, outlaw specific practices and provided even greater precision to the antitrust law. Table 15.7 describes these practices and summarizes the main provisions of these three acts.

TABLE 15.7   The Clayton Act and Its Amendments

Clayton Act	1914
Robinson-Patman Act	1936
Celler-Kefauver Act	1950

These acts prohibit the following practices *only if* they substantially lessen competition or create monopoly:

1. Price discrimination
2. Contracts that require other goods to be bought from the same firm (called *tying arrangements*)
3. Contracts that require a firm to buy all its requirements of a particular item from a single firm (called *requirements contracts*)
4. Contracts that prevent a firm from selling competing items (called *exclusive dealing*)
5. Contracts that prevent a buyer from reselling a product outside a specified area (called *territorial confinement*)
6. Acquiring a competitor's shares or assets
7. Becoming a director of a competing firm

Price Fixing Always Illegal

Colluding to fix the price is *always* a violation of the antitrust law. If the Justice Department can prove the existence of a price fixing cartel, defendants can offer no acceptable excuse.

The predictions of the effects of price fixing that you saw in the previous sections of this chapter provide the reasons for the unqualified attitude toward price fixing. A duopoly cartel can maximize profit and behave like a monopoly. To achieve the monopoly outcome, the cartel restricts production and fixes the price at the monopoly level. The consumer suffers because consumer surplus shrinks. And the outcome is inefficient because a deadweight loss arises.

It is for these reasons that the law declares that all price fixing is illegal. No excuse can justify the practice.

Other antitrust practices are more controversial and generate debate among lawyers and economists. We'll examine three of these practices.

Three Antitrust Policy Debates

The three practices that we'll examine are

- Resale price maintenance
- Tying arrangements
- Predatory pricing

Resale Price Maintenance Most manufacturers sell their products to the final consumer indirectly through a wholesale and retail distribution system. **Resale price maintenance** occurs when a manufacturer agrees with a distributor on the price at which the product will be resold.

Resale price maintenance (also called vertical price fixing) *agreements* are illegal under the Sherman Act. But it isn't illegal for a manufacturer to refuse to supply a retailer who doesn't accept guidance on what the price should be.

Nor is it illegal to set a *minimum* retail price provided it is not anticompetitive. In 2007, the Supreme Court ruled that a handbag manufacturer could impose a minimum retail price on a Dallas store, Kay's Kloset. Since that ruling, many manufacturers have imposed minimum retail prices. The practice is judged on a case-by-case basis.

Does resale price maintenance create an inefficient or efficient use of resources? Economists can be found on both sides of this question.

Inefficient Resale Price Maintenance Resale price maintenance is inefficient if it enables dealers to charge the monopoly price. By setting and enforcing the resale price, the manufacturer might be able to achieve the monopoly price.

Efficient Resale Price Maintenance Resale price maintenance might be efficient if it enables a manufacturer to induce dealers to provide the efficient standard of service. Suppose that SilkySkin wants shops to demonstrate the use of its new unbelievable moisturizing cream in an inviting space. With resale price maintenance, SilkySkin can offer all the retailers the same incentive and compensation. Without resale price maintenance, a cut-price drug store might offer SilkySkin products at a low price. Buyers would then have an incentive to visit a high-price shop and get the product demonstrated and then buy from the low-price shop. The low-price shop would be a free rider (like the consumer of a public good in Chapter 17, p. xxx), and an inefficient level of service would be provided.

SilkySkin could pay a fee to retailers that provide good service and leave the resale price to be determined by the competitive forces of supply and demand. But it might be too costly for SilkySkin to monitor shops and ensure that they provided the desired level of service.

Tying Arrangements A **tying arrangement** is an agreement to sell one product only if the buyer agrees to buy another, different product. With tying, the only way the buyer can get the one product is to also buy the other product. Microsoft has been accused of tying Internet Explorer and Windows. Textbook publishers sometimes tie a Web site and a textbook and force students to buy both. (You can't buy the book you're now reading, new, without the Web site. But you can buy the Web site access without the book, so these products are not tied.)

Could textbook publishers make more money by tying a book and access to a Web site? The answer is sometimes but not always. Suppose that you and other students are willing to pay $80 for a book and $20 for access to a Web site. The publisher can sell these items separately for these prices or bundled for $100. The publisher does not gain from bundling.

But now suppose that you and only half of the students are willing to pay $80 for a book and $20 for a Web site and the other half of the students are willing to pay $80 for a Web site and $20 for a book. Now if the two items are sold separately, the publisher can charge $80 for the book and $80 for the Web site. Half the students buy the book but not the Web site, and the other half buy the Web site but not the book. But if the book and Web site are bundled for $100, everyone buys the bundle and the publisher makes an extra $20 per student. In this case, bundling has enabled the publisher to price discriminate.

There is no simple, clear-cut test of whether a firm is engaging in tying or whether, by doing so, it has increased its market power and profit and created inefficiency.

Predatory Pricing **Predatory pricing** is setting a low price to drive competitors out of business with the intention of setting a monopoly price when the competition has gone. John D. Rockefeller's Standard Oil Company was the first to be accused of this practice in the 1890s, and it has been claimed often in antitrust cases since then. Predatory pricing is an attempt to create a monopoly and as such it is illegal under Section 2 of the Sherman Act.

It is easy to see that predatory pricing is an idea, not a reality. Economists are skeptical that predatory pricing occurs. They point out that a firm that cuts its price below the profit-maximizing level loses during the low-price period. Even if it succeeds in driving its competitors out of business, new competitors will enter as soon as the price is increased, so any potential gain from a monopoly position is temporary. A high and certain loss is a poor exchange for a temporary and uncertain gain. No case of predatory pricing has been definitively found.

An Antitrust Showcase
The United States Versus Microsoft

In 1998, the Antitrust Division of the U.S. Department of Justice along with the Departments of Justice of a number of states charged Microsoft, the world's largest producer of software for personal computers, with violations of both sections of the Sherman Act.

A 78-day trial followed that pitched two prominent MIT economics professors against each other, Franklin Fisher for the government and Richard Schmalensee for Microsoft.

The Case Against Microsoft The claims against Microsoft were that it

- Possessed monopoly power
- Used predatory pricing and tying arrangements
- Used other anticompetitive practices

It was claimed that with 80 percent of the market for PC operating systems, Microsoft had excessive monopoly power. This monopoly power arose from two barriers to entry: economies of scale and network economies. Microsoft's average total cost falls as production increases (economies of scale) because the fixed cost of developing an operating system such as Windows is large while the marginal cost of producing one copy of Windows is small. Further, as the number of Windows users increases, the range of Windows applications expands (network economies), so a potential competitor would need to produce not only a competing operating system but also an entire range of supporting applications as well.

When Microsoft entered the Web browser market with its Internet Explorer, it offered the browser for a zero price. This price was viewed as predatory pricing. Microsoft integrated Internet Explorer with Windows so that anyone who uses this operating system would not need a separate browser such as Netscape Navigator. Microsoft's competitors claimed that this practice was an illegal tying arrangement.

Microsoft's Response Microsoft challenged all these claims. It said that Windows was vulnerable to competition from other operating systems such as Linux and Apple's Mac OS and that there was a permanent threat of competition from new entrants.

Microsoft claimed that integrating Internet Explorer with Windows provided a single, unified product of greater consumer value like a refrigerator with a chilled water dispenser or an automobile with a CD player.

The Outcome The court agreed that Microsoft was in violation of the Sherman Act and ordered that it be broken into two firms: an operating systems producer and an applications producer. Microsoft successfully appealed this order. In the final judgment, though, Microsoft was ordered to disclose to other software developers details of how its operating system works, so that they could compete effectively against Microsoft. In the summer of 2002, Microsoft began to comply with this order.

Mergers and Acquisitions

Mergers, which occur when two or more firms agree to combine to create one larger firm, and *acquisitions*, which occur when one firm buys another firm, are common events. Mergers occurred when Chrysler and the German auto producer Daimler-Benz combined to form DaimlerChrysler and when the Belgian beer producer InBev bought the U.S. brewing giant Anheuser-Busch and created a new combined company, Anheuser-Busch InBev. An acquisition occurred when Rupert Murdoch's News Corp bought Myspace.

The mergers and acquisitions that occur don't create a monopoly. But two (or more) firms might be tempted to try to merge so that they can gain market power and operate like a monopoly. If such a situation arises, the Federal Trade Commission (FTC) takes an interest in the move and stands ready to block the merger.

To determine which mergers it will examine and possibly block, the FTC uses guidelines, one of which is the Herfindahl-Hirschman Index (HHI) (see Chapter 10, pp. 238–239).

A market in which the HHI is less than 1,000 is regarded as competitive. An index between 1,000 and 1,800 indicates a moderately concentrated market, and a merger in this market that would increase the index by 100 points is challenged by the FTC. An index above 1,800 indicates a concentrated market, and a merger in this market that would increase the index by 50 points is challenged. You can see an application of these guidelines in the box below.

Review Quiz

1 What are the two main antitrust laws and when were they enacted?
2 When is price fixing not a violation of the antitrust laws?
3 What is an attempt to monopolize an industry?
4 What are resale price maintenance, tying arrangements, and predatory pricing?
5 Under what circumstances is a merger unlikely to be approved?

 Work Study Plan 15.5 and get instant feedback.

◆ Oligopoly is a market structure that you often encounter in your daily life. *Reading Between the Lines* on pp. 362–363 looks at a game played by Dell and HP in the market for personal computers.

Merger Guidelines
FTC Takes the Fizz out of Soda Mergers

The FTC used its HHI guidelines to block proposed mergers in the market for soft drinks. PepsiCo wanted to buy 7-Up and Coca-Cola wanted to buy Dr Pepper. The market for carbonated soft drinks is highly concentrated. Coca-Cola had a 39 percent share, PepsiCo had 28 percent, Dr Pepper was next with 7 percent, followed by 7-Up with 6 percent. One other producer, RJR, had a 5 percent market share. So the five largest firms in this market had an 85 percent market share.

The PepsiCo and 7-Up merger would have increased the HHI by more than 300 points. The Coca-Cola and Dr Pepper merger would have increased it by more than 500 points, and both mergers together would have increased the index by almost 800 points.

The FTC decided that increases in the HHI of these magnitudes were not in the social interest and blocked the mergers. The figure summarizes the HHI guideline and HHIs in the soft drinks market.

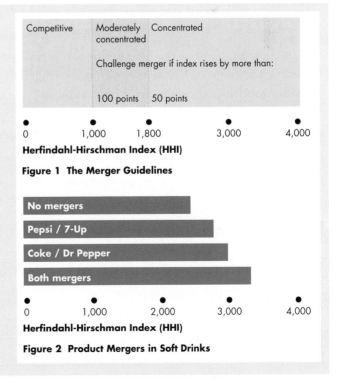

Figure 1 The Merger Guidelines

Figure 2 Product Mergers in Soft Drinks

Dell and HP in a Market Share Game

The Old Price-War Tactic May Not Faze Rivals Now

http://www.nytimes.com
May 13, 2006

Dell is sharply reducing prices on its computers.

The tactic is classic, straight out of the playbook that made the company the world's largest computer maker. As overall demand for personal computers slows, lower your prices. Profit margins will take a temporary hit, but the move would hurt competitors worse as you take market share and enjoy revenue growth for years to come.

Dell did it in 2000 and it worked beautifully. But after Dell rolled out the plan last month, knocking as much as $700 off a $1,200 Inspiron and $500 off a $1,079 Dimension desktop, many of the securities analysts who follow the company, based in Round Rock, Tex., said that this time around it could be folly. ...

What changed? ... More than anything else, Dell's competitors have changed. In particular, Hewlett-Packard is no longer the bloated and slow-moving company it was six years ago. ...

The most telling evidence of the new landscape for PCs was seen in statistics on worldwide shipments. While the industry grew 12.9 percent in the first three months of the year, ... Dell's shipments grew 10.2 percent. It was the first time since analysts began tracking Dell that its shipments grew more slowly than the industry's. Hewlett's shipments, meanwhile, grew 22.2 percent. ...

Inside Hewlett, however, there is a feeling that it can beat Dell without resorting to price wars. ... The company has started an ambitious marketing campaign to make that point with ads that proclaim, "the computer is personal again." ...

The campaign ... will feature celebrities and how they individualize their computers ... [HP] has added technology like QuickPlay, which lets a user view a DVD or listen to a CD without waiting for the laptop's operating system to boot up. The ads will say, "Don't boot. Play." ...

Essence of the Story

- Dell cut its prices in 2000 and increased its market share and revenue in the years that followed.

- In April 2006, Dell slashed its prices.

- Experts say the price cut will not work as well today.

- Hewlett-Packard (HP) is much stronger than it was six years ago.

- Total PC shipments increased by 12.9 percent in the first quarter of 2006: Dell's shipments increased by 10.2 percent, and HP's increased by 22.2 percent.

♦ HP says that it can beat Dell without a price cut. Instead it will launch a campaign to market PCs with new and improved features, such as one that plays DVDs and CDs without booting the operating system.

Economic Analysis

- The global PC market has many firms, but two firms dominate the market: Dell and Hewlett-Packard (HP).

- Figure 1 shows the shares in the global PC market. You can see that Dell and HP are the two biggest players but almost 50 percent of the market is served by small firms, each with less than 4 percent of the market.

- Table 1 shows the payoff matrix (millions of dollars of profit) for the game played by Dell and HP in 2000. (The numbers are hypothetical.)

- This game has a dominant strategy equilibrium similar to that for the duopoly game on p. 353.

- If HP cuts its price, Dell makes a larger profit by cutting its price (+$20m versus –$10m), and if HP holds its price constant, Dell again makes a larger profit by cutting its price (+$40m versus zero).

- So Dell's best strategy is to cut its price.

- If Dell cuts its price, HP makes a larger profit by cutting its price (+$5m versus –$20m), and if Dell holds its price constant, HP again makes a larger profit by cutting its price (+$10m versus zero).

- So HP's best strategy is to cut its price.

- Table 2 shows the payoffs from the game between Dell and HP in 2006.

- This game, too, has a dominant strategy equilibrium.

- If HP cuts its price, Dell makes a larger profit by cutting its price (+$10m versus –$10m), and if HP improves its marketing and design, Dell again makes a larger profit by cutting its price (+$5m versus –$20m).

- So Dell's best strategy is to cut its price.

- If Dell cuts its price, HP makes a larger profit by improving its marketing and design (+$20m versus +$10m), and if Dell holds its price constant, HP again makes a larger profit by improving its marketing and design (+$40m versus +$20m).

- So HP's best strategy is to improve its marketing and design.

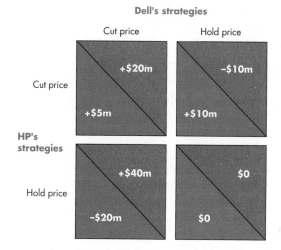

Table 1 The strategies and equilibrium in 2000

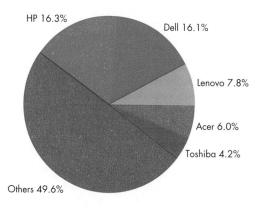

Figure 1 Market shares in the PC market in 2006

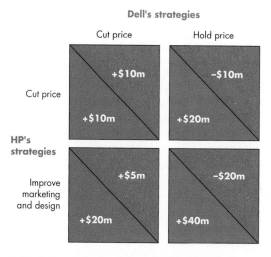

Table 2 The strategies and equilibrium in 2006

SUMMARY ◆

Key Points

What Is Oligopoly? (pp. 342–343)

- Oligopoly is a market in which a small number of firms compete.

Two Traditional Oligopoly Models (pp. 344–345)

- If rivals match price cuts but do not match price hikes, each firm faces a kinked demand curve.
- If one firm dominates a market, it acts like a monopoly and the small firms act as price takers.

Oligopoly Games (pp. 346–354)

- Oligopoly is studied by using game theory, which is a method of analyzing strategic behavior.
- In a prisoners' dilemma game, two prisoners acting in their own self-interest harm their joint interest.
- An oligopoly (duopoly) price-fixing game is a prisoners' dilemma in which the firms might collude or cheat.
- In Nash equilibrium, both firms cheat and output and price are the same as in perfect competition.
- Firms' decisions about advertising and R&D can be studied by using game theory.

Repeated Games and Sequential Games (pp. 355–357)

- In a repeated game, a punishment strategy can produce a cooperative equilibrium in which price and output are the same as in a monopoly.

- In a sequential contestable market game, a small number of firms can behave like firms in perfect competition.

Antitrust Law (pp. 358–361)

- The first antitrust law, the Sherman Act, was passed in 1890, and the law was strengthened in 1914 when the Clayton Act was passed and the Federal Trade Commission was created.
- All price-fixing agreements are violations of the Sherman Act, and no acceptable excuse exists.
- Resale price maintenance might be efficient if it enables a producer to ensure the efficient level of service by distributors.
- Tying arrangements can enable a monopoly to price discriminate and increase profit, but in many cases, tying would not increase profit.
- Predatory pricing is unlikely to occur because it brings losses and only temporary potential gains.
- The Federal Trade Commission uses guidelines such as the Herfindahl-Hirschman Index to determine which mergers to investigate and possibly block.

Key Figures and Tables

Key Terms

Antitrust law, 358
Cartel, 343
Collusive agreement, 348
Contestable market, 356
Cooperative equilibrium, 355
Dominant strategy equilibrium, 354
Duopoly, 342
Game theory, 346
Limit pricing, 357
Nash equilibrium, 347
Oligopoly, 342
Payoff matrix, 346
Predatory pricing, 360
Resale price maintenance, 359
Strategies, 346
Tying arrangement, 359

PROBLEMS and APPLICATIONS

 Work problems 1–11 in Chapter 15 Study Plan and get instant feedback.
Work problems 12–19 as Homework, a Quiz, or a Test if assigned by your instructor.

1. Two firms make most of the chips that power a PC: Intel and Advanced Micro Devices. What makes the market for PC chips a duopoly? Sketch the market demand curve and cost curves that describe the situation in this market and that prevent other firms from entering.

2. The price at which Wal-Mart can buy flat-panel TVs has fallen, and it is making a decision about whether to cut its selling price. Wal-Mart believes that if it cuts its price, all its competitors will cut their prices, but if it raises its price, none of its competitors will raise theirs.
   a. Draw a figure to illustrate the situation that Wal-Mart believes it faces in the market for flat-panel TVs.
   b. Do you predict that Wal-Mart will lower its price of a flat-panel TV? Explain and illustrate your answer.

3. Big Joe's Trucking has lower costs than the other 20 small truckers in the market. The market operates like a dominant firm oligopoly and is initially in equilibrium. Then the demand for trucking services increases. Explain the effects of the increase in demand on the price, output, and economic profit of
   a. Big Joe's.
   b. A typical small firm.

4. Consider a game with two players, who cannot communicate, and in which each player is asked a question. The players can answer the question honestly or lie. If both answer honestly, each receives $100. If one answers honestly and the other lies, the liar receives $500 and the honest player gets nothing. If both lie, then each receives $50.
   a. Describe the strategies and payoffs of this game.
   b. Construct the payoff matrix.
   c. What is the equilibrium of this game?
   d. Compare this game to the prisoners' dilemma. Are the two games similar or different? Explain.

5. Soapy Inc. and Suddies Inc. are the only producers of soap powder. They collude and agree to share the market equally. If neither firm cheats

on the agreement, each makes $1 million profit. If either firm cheats, the cheat makes a profit of $1.5 million, while the complier incurs a loss of $0.5 million. If both cheat, they break even. Neither firm can monitor the other's actions.
   a. What are the strategies in this game?
   b. Construct the payoff matrix for this game.
   c. What is the equilibrium of this game if it is played only once?
   d. Is the equilibrium a dominant strategy equilibrium? Explain.

6. If Soapy Inc. and Suddies Inc. repeatedly play the duopoly game that has the payoffs described in problem 5 on each round of play,
   a. What now are the strategies that each firm might adopt?
   b. Can the firms adopt a strategy that gives the game a cooperative equilibrium?
   c. Would one firm still be tempted to cheat in a cooperative equilibrium? Explain your answer.

7. **Oil City**
   In the late '90s, Reliance spent $6 billion and employed 75,000 workers to build a world-class oil refinery at Jamnagar, India. … Now Reliance is more than doubling the size of the facility, which … will claim the title of the world's biggest … with an output of 1.2 million gallons of gasoline per day, or about 5% of global capacity. … Reliance plans to aim Jamnagar's spigots westward, at the U.S. and Europe, where it's too expensive and politically difficult to build new refineries. …The bulked-up Jamnagar will be able to move markets: Singapore traders expect a drop in fuel prices as soon as it's going full tilt.
   Fortune, April 28, 2008
   a. Explain this news clip's claims that the global market for gasoline is not perfectly competitive.
   b. What barriers to entry might limit competition in this market and give a firm such as Reliance power to influence the market price?

8. **Congress Examines Giant Airline Merger**
   Congress Wednesday examined a proposed $3.1 billion merger that would create the world's

largest carrier as critics of the deal warned it could drive up the price of air travel. … [Committee Chairman James Oberstar] said the Delta-Northwest merger would discourage competition at major hubs, reduce service to customers and result in higher fares. Delta Chief Executive Officer Richard Anderson said that the merger would not limit competition because the carriers primarily serve different geographic regions. … About a dozen witnesses scheduled to testify before the House Subcommittee on Transportation and Infrastructure were likely to focus on whether a merger between Delta Air Lines and Northwest Airlines would benefit consumers by lowering prices through cost savings, or harm them by reducing competition.

CNN, May 14, 2008

a. Explain how this airline merger might increase air travel prices.
b. Explain how this airline merger might lower air travel production costs.
c. Explain how cost savings might get passed on to travelers and might boost producers profits. Which do you predict will happen from this airline merger and why?
d. Explain the guidelines that the Federal Trade Commission uses to evaluate mergers and why it might permit or block this merger.

9. **U.K. Price Cuts Seen for Apple's New iPhone**
AT&T is planning to sell the new iPhone this summer for around $200. … The new iPhone would be available later this month in the U.S. through Apple and AT&T. AT&T pricing strategy calls for a $200 subsidy for customers who sign two-year service contracts. …

The lower-priced phones in the U.S. … would help juice the iPhone's sales volume and give the telcos an attractive weapon to win new subscribers.

In the United States, AT&T says it pulls in an average of $95 a month from each iPhone customer, nearly twice the average monthly bill of its conventional cell phone user. AT&T has a revenue-sharing agreement with Apple that requires it to give Apple as much as 25% of its iPhone customers' monthly payments.

Subsidies are a widespread pricing practice in the United States and overseas. In exchange for a cheaper phone, customers are locked in to a car-

rier for a year or two. It's a small investment by the telcos for a large return. … After giving Apple its cut of the revenue, the remaining take for AT&T is between $70 and $75 a month per iPhone user, totaling more than $1,700 over the life of the two-year contract. …

Fortune, June 2, 2008

a. How does this arrangement between AT&T and Apple regarding the iPhone affect competition in the market for cell phone service?
b. Does this arrangement between AT&T and Apple regarding the iPhone violate U.S. antitrust laws? Explain.

10. **Starbucks Sued for Trying to Sink Competition**
An independent coffee shop owner filed a lawsuit against Starbucks Corp. Monday, charging the coffee house giant with using anti-competitive tactics to rid itself of competition. The suit … was filed … by Penny Stafford, owner of the Seattle-based Belvi Coffee and Tea Exchange Inc. The lawsuit contends that Starbucks exploited its monopoly power in the specialty retail coffee market through such predatory practices as offering to pay leases that exceeded market value if the building owner would refuse to allow competitors from occupying the same building. Stafford says Starbucks also used methods such as having employees offer free drink samples in front of her store to lure away customers, which she says ultimately forced her to close her store. … The suit contends the world's largest specialty coffee retailer also used other predatory tactics nationwide including offering to buy out competitors at below-market prices and threatening to open nearby stores if the offer is rejected.

CNN, September 26, 2006

a. Explain how Starbucks is alleged to have violated U.S. antitrust laws in Seattle.
b. Explain why it is unlikely that Starbucks might use predatory pricing to permanently drive out competition.
c. What information would you need that is not provided in the news clip to decide whether Starbucks had practiced predatory pricing?
d. Draw a graph of the situation facing Belvi Coffee and Tea Exchange Inc. when Penny Stafford closed the firm.

11. **Oil Trading Probe May Uncover Manipulation**

Amid soaring oil prices … the government Thursday announced a wide ranging probe into oil price manipulation. … The CFTC [Commodity Futures Trade Commission] is looking into … manipulation of the physical oil market … by commercial players who might literally withhold oil from the market in an attempt to drive prices higher.

The CFTC has found evidence of this in the past. … Haigh [a former economist at CFTC] thinks it's likely CFTC will find evidence of this again given that the agency has been investigating for six months and has now chosen to make it public. But he stressed that a single player acting alone would in all likelihood not have a huge influence on prices. "It's difficult to imagine a price run-up of $90 to $135 being done by one entity," he said.

CNN, May 30, 2008

a. What type of market does former CFTC economist Haigh imply best describes the U.S. oil market?

b. Is economist Haigh's comment consistent with the predictions of the kinked demand curve model of oligopoly? Explain.

c. Is economist Haigh's comment consistent with the predictions of the dominant firm oligopoly model? Explain.

d. Is economist Haigh's comment consistent with the predictions of any model of oligopoly? Explain.

12. Bud and Wise are the only two producers of aniseed beer, a New Age product designed to displace root beer. Bud and Wise are trying to figure out how much of this new beer to produce. They know that if they both limit production to 10,000 gallons a day, they will make the maximum attainable joint profit of $200,000 a day—$100,000 a day each. They also know that if either of them produces 20,000 gallons a day while the other produces 10,000 a day, the one that produces 20,000 gallons will make an economic profit of $150,000 and the one that sticks with 10,000 gallons will incur an economic loss of $50,000. Each also knows that if they both increase production to 20,000 gallons a day, they will both make zero economic profit.

a. Construct a payoff matrix for the game that Bud and Wise must play.

b. Find the Nash equilibrium of the game that Bud and Wise play.

c. What is the equilibrium of the game if Bud and Wise play it repeatedly?

13. **Gadgets for Sale … or Not**

How come some gadgets, like the iPod, cost the same no matter where you shop? … No, the answer isn't that Apple illegally manages prices. In reality, Steve Jobs and Co. use an accepted, if controversial, tactic, a retail strategy called minimum advertised price, to discourage resellers from discounting.

The minimum advertised price, or MAP, is the absolute lowest price retailers are allowed to advertise a product for. MAP is usually enforced through marketing subsidies offered by a manufacturer to its resellers. If a retailer keeps prices at or above the minimum advertised price, then a manufacturer like Apple will give them money to help advertise. If a store's price dips too low, on the other hand, the manufacturer can withdraw these advertising subsidies. …

Stable prices are important to the company, because it's a manufacturer and a retailer (both online and through its chain of Apple Stores). If Apple resellers dropped prices on iPods and iMacs—selling at or below cost to get customers in the door, or as a way to cross-sell stuff like software or iPod skins—they could squeeze the Apple Stores out of their own markets.

There is a downside to all that stability, however. By limiting how low sellers can go, MAP keeps prices artificially high (or at least higher than they might otherwise be with unfettered price competition).

Slate, December 22, 2006

a. Describe the practice of resale price maintenance that violates the Sherman Act.

b. Describe the MAP strategy used by iPod and explain how it differs from a resale price maintenance agreement that would violate the Sherman Act.

c. Why might the MAP strategy be against the consumer interest?

d. Why might the MAP strategy benefit the consumer?

e. What is the bottom line on the MAP strategy: does it benefit the consumer or only the producer?

14. **Asian Rice Exporters to Discuss Cartel**

Rice-exporting nations planned to discuss a proposed cartel to control the price of the staple food. … Rice exporters Thailand, Cambodia, Laos and Myanmar planned to meet Tuesday to discuss a proposal by Thailand, the world's largest rice exporter, that they form a cartel. Ahead of the meeting … the countries sought to assuage concerns that they might force up prices by limiting supplies.

Unlike the Organization of Petroleum Exporting Countries, the purpose of the rice cartel would be "to contribute to ensuring food stability, not just in an individual country but also to address food shortages in the region and the world," Cambodian Prime Minister Hun Sen said Monday.

"We shall not hoard (rice) and raise prices when there are shortages," Hun Sen said. The Philippines wasn't convinced.

"It is a bad idea. … It will create an oligopoly and it's against humanity," Edgardo Angara, chairman of the Philippine Senate's Committee on Agriculture, said Friday, adding that the cartel could price the grain out of reach for "millions and millions of people."

CNN, May 6, 2008

a. Assuming the rice-exporting nations become a profit-maximizing colluding oligopoly, explain how they would influence the global market for rice and the world price of rice.

b. Assuming the rice-exporting nations become a profit-maximizing colluding oligopoly, draw a graph to illustrate their influence on the global market for rice.

c. Even in the absence of international antitrust laws, why might it be difficult for this cartel to successfully collude? Use the ideas of game theory to explain.

15. **An Energy Drink with a Monster of a Stock**

The $5.7 billion energy-drink category, in which Monster holds the No. 2 position behind industry leader Red Bull, has slowed down as copycat brands jostle for shelf space—and the attention of teen consumers. … Over the past five years Red Bull's market share in dollar terms has gone from 91 percent to well under 50 percent … and much of that loss has been Monster's gain.

Fortune, December 25, 2006

a. Describe the structure of the energy-drink market. How has that structure changed over the past few years?

b. Explain the various difficulties Monster and Red Bull would have if they attempted to collude and charge monopoly prices for energy drinks.

16. Suppose that Firefox and Microsoft each develop their own versions of an amazing new Web browser that allows advertisers to target consumers with great precision. Also, the new browser is easier and more fun to use than existing browsers. Each firm is trying to decide whether to sell the browser or to give it away. What are the likely benefits from each action? Which action is likely to occur?

17. Why do Coca-Cola and PepsiCo spend huge amounts on advertising? Do they benefit? Does the consumer benefit? Explain your answer by constructing a game to illustrate the choices Coca-Cola and PepsiCo make.

18. Microsoft with Xbox 360, Nintendo with Wii, and Sony with PlayStation 3 are slugging it out in the market for the latest generation of video games consoles. Xbox 360 was the first to market; Wii has the lowest price; PS3 uses the most advanced technology and has the highest price.

a. Thinking of the competition among these firms in the market for consoles as a game, describe the firms' strategies concerning design, marketing, and price.

b. What, based on the information provided, turned out to be the equilibrium of the game?

c. Can you think of reasons why the three consoles are so different?

19. Study *Reading Between the Lines* on pp. 362–363 and then answer the following questions.

a. What were the strategies of Dell and HP in 2000 and in 2006?

b. Why, according to the news article, was Dell having a harder time in 2006 than it had in 2000?

c. Why wouldn't HP launch its new product and marketing campaign *and* cut its price?

d. What do you think Dell must do to restore its place as market leader?

e. How would you describe the global market for PCs? Is it an example of oligopoly or monopolistic competition?

16

Externalities

After studying this chapter, you will be able to:

- Explain how externalities arise

- Explain why negative externalities lead to inefficient over-production and how property rights, emission charges, marketable permits, and taxes can be used to achieve a more efficient outcome

- Explain why positive externalities lead to inefficient under-production and how public provision, subsidies, vouchers, and patents can increase economic efficiency

◆

We burn huge quantities of fossil fuels—coal, natural gas, and oil—that cause acid rain and global warming. We dump toxic waste into rivers, lakes, and oceans. These environmental issues are simultaneously everybody's problem and nobody's problem. How can we take account of the damage that we cause others every time we turn on our heating or air-conditioning systems?

Almost every day, we hear about a new discovery—in medicine, engineering, chemistry, physics, or even economics. The advance of knowledge seems boundless. Ever more people are learning more and more of what is already known. The stock of knowledge is increasing, apparently without limit. But are we spending enough on research and education? Do enough people remain in school for long enough?

In this chapter, we study the problems that arise because many of our actions affect other people, for good or ill, in ways that we do not take into account when we make our own economic choices. We will focus on two big areas—pollution and knowledge. In *Reading Between the Lines* at the end of the chapter, we look at the effects of a carbon tax designed to lower carbon emissions and address global warming.

Externalities in Our Lives

An **externality** is a *cost* or a *benefit* that arises from *production* and falls on someone other than the producer, or a *cost* or *benefit* that arises from *consumption* and falls on someone other than the consumer. We call an externality that imposes a cost a **negative externality**; and we call an externality that provides a benefit a **positive externality**.

We identify externalities as four types:

■ Negative production externalities
■ Negative consumption externalities
■ Positive production externalities
■ Positive consumption externalities

Negative Production Externalities

Congestion, pollution, and carbon emission are the sources of the most costly and widespread negative production externalities.

Congestion The Lincoln Tunnel, which connects New Jersey to Manhattan under the Hudson River, is 1.5 miles long. Yet it can take 2 hours to get through the tunnel in the worst traffic.

The costs of congestion are time costs and fuel costs. Drivers and their passengers spend extra hours

sitting in stalled traffic, burning additional fuel. Each rush-hour user of the Lincoln Tunnel imposes a cost on the other users. This cost is a negative production externality.

The economic analysis of externalities looks at alternative ways of dealing with problems such as the cost of congestion in the Lincoln Tunnel.

Pollution and Carbon Emission When you run your air-conditioning, use hot water, drive a car, take a trip by airplane, or even ride a bus or train, your action contributes to pollution and increases your carbon footprint.

Economic activity pollutes air, water, and land, and these individual areas of pollution interact through the *ecosystem*.

Air Pollution Sixty percent of our air pollution comes from road transportation and industrial processes. Only 20 percent arises from electric power generation. See the trends in U.S. air pollution since 1980 below.

A common belief is that air pollution is getting worse. In many developing countries, air pollution *is* getting worse. The rapid economic development of China has created a serious air quality problem for Beijing. During the 2008 Olympics, construction activity was halted and factories closed in an attempt

U.S. Air Pollution Trends
Cleaner and Safer

The figure shows the trends in the concentrations of six air pollutants. Lead has been almost eliminated from our air. Sulfur dioxide, carbon monoxide, and suspended particulates have been reduced to around a half of their 1980 levels. And even the more stubborn ozone and nitrogen dioxide have been reduced to around 70 percent of their 1980 levels.

These reductions in air pollution levels are even more impressive when they are seen against the trends in economic activity. Between 1980 and 2007, total production in the United States increased by 123 percent. During this same period, vehicle miles traveled increased by 90 percent, energy consumption increased by 82 percent, and the population increased by 35 percent. While all this economic activity was on the increase, air pollution from all sources *decreased* by more than 30 percent.

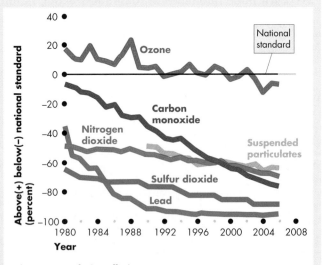

Six Sources of Air Pollution

Source of data: Latest Findings on National Air Quality: Status and Trends through 2006, United States Environmental Protection Agency, http://www.epa.gov/air/airtrends/2007/

to provide temporary relief from air that would endanger the health of athletes.

But air pollution in the world's richest countries is getting less severe for most substances. Air pollution in the United States has been on a downward trend for more than 30 years.

In contrast to the trends in air pollution, carbon emissions and emissions of other global warming gases such as methane are on the increase, and consequently the carbon dioxide concentration in the Earth's atmosphere is increasing at an unprecedented pace.

The costs of air pollution and carbon emission are high and widespread. Sulfur dioxide and nitrogen oxide emissions from coal-fired and oil-fired generators of electric utilities cause *acid rain*, which damages trees and crops. Airborne substances such as lead from leaded gasoline are believed to cause cancer and other life-threatening conditions. Depletion of the *ozone layer* exposes us to higher doses of cancer-causing ultraviolet rays from the sun. And most costly of all, the increased carbon concentration is bringing global warming and potentially extremely costly climate change.

Some technological changes to cut costs, lessen air pollution, and slow the carbon buildup are possible either now or with further research and development.

Road vehicles can be made "greener" with new fuels including ethanol, alcohol, natural gas, propane and butane, and hydrogen. Vehicles can also be powered by electricity or batteries. But whether this

Global Temperature and CO$_2$ Trends
The Greatest Market Failure?

British economist Nicholas Stern prepared a major report on global warming and climate change for the United Kingdom government and his report, the *Stern Review on the Economics of Climate Change* has attracted a great deal of attention. Stern calls climate change "the greatest market failure the world has ever seen." To avoid the risk of catastrophic damage from climate change, he says that greenhouse gas levels must be held at not more than 550 parts per million (ppm) of CO$_2$ (and its equivalent in other greenhouse gases). The level in 2007 was 430ppm but it is rising at more than 2ppm a year, so the world will reach the critical level by about 2070.

Global temperature and CO$_2$ trends are starkly opposite to those of U.S. air pollution, as the figure shows. Scientists debate the contribution of human economic activity to these trends but most say it is the major source. Although ice-core estimates show long swings in CO$_2$, there has never been a time when its concentration increased so rapidly.

To hold greenhouse gas levels at 550ppm, emissions need to be cut to 75 percent or less of their current levels by 2050 and eventually, cut to 20 percent of their current levels.

The cost of achieving these cuts is high. Stern's estimate is 1 percent of the value of global production. If this cost were to be met by the people who live in the rich countries, and realistically they are the only ones who could afford to pay, it would cost about $750 per person every year.

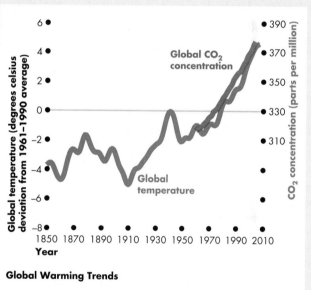

Global Warming Trends

Sources of data: Met Office Hadley Centre and Scripps Institution of Oceanography.

Some economists question Stern's assumptions and conclusions and argue that the cost of reducing emissions will be much lower if we go a bit more slowly and take advantage of future technological advances that will lower the cost of renewable energy sources—the sun, tide, and wind.

All economists agree that solving the global warming problem will require changes in the incentives that people face. The cost of carbon-emitting activities must rise and the cost of the search for new energy technologies must fall.

change lessens air pollution and carbon emissions depends on how electricity is produced.

Pollution-free electricity can be generated by harnessing wind power, solar power, tidal power, or geothermal power. Another alternative is nuclear power. This method is good for air pollution but creates a potential long-term problem for land and water pollution because there is no known entirely safe method of disposing of spent nuclear fuel.

Water Pollution The dumping of industrial waste and untreated sewage and the runoff from fertilizers pollute oceans, lakes, and rivers.

There are two main alternatives to polluting the waterways and oceans. One is the chemical processing of waste to render it inert or biodegradable. The other, in wide use for nuclear waste, is to use land sites for storage in secure containers.

Land Pollution Land pollution arises from dumping toxic waste products. Ordinary household garbage does not pose a pollution problem unless contaminants from dumped garbage seep into the water supply. Recycling is an apparently attractive alternative, but it requires an investment in new technologies to be effective. Incineration is a high-cost alternative to landfill, and it produces air pollution. Furthermore, these alternatives are not free, and they become efficient only when the cost of using landfill is high.

Negative Consumption Externalities

Negative consumption externalities are a source of irritation for most of us. Smoking tobacco in a confined space creates fumes that many people find unpleasant and that pose a health risk. Smoking creates a negative consumption externality. To deal with this externality, in many places and in almost all public places, smoking is banned. But banning smoking imposes a negative consumption externality on smokers! The majority imposes a cost on the minority—the smokers who would prefer to consume tobacco while dining or taking a plane trip.

Noisy parties and outdoor rock concerts are other examples of negative consumption externalities. They are also examples of the fact that a simple ban on an activity is not a solution. Banning noisy parties avoids the external cost on sleep-seeking neighbors, but it results in the sleepers imposing an external cost on the fun-seeking partygoers.

Permitting dandelions to grow in lawns, not picking up leaves in the fall, and allowing a dog to bark loudly or to foul a neighbor's lawn are other sources of negative consumption externalities.

Positive Production Externalities

If a honey farmer places beehives beside an orange grower's orchard, two positive production externalities arise. The honey farmer gets a positive production externality from the orange grower because the bees collect pollen and nectar from orange blossoms. And the orange grower gets a positive production externality because the bees pollinate the blossoms.

Positive Consumption Externalities

When you get a flu vaccination, you lower your risk of getting infected this winter. But if you avoid the flu, your neighbor who didn't get vaccinated has a better chance of avoiding it too. Flu vaccination generates positive consumption externalities.

When the owner of a historic building restores it, everyone who sees the building gets pleasure from it. Similarly, when someone erects a spectacular house—such as those built by Frank Lloyd Wright during the 1920s and 1930s—or another exciting building—such as the Chrysler Building and the Empire State Building in New York or the Wrigley Building in Chicago—an external consumption benefit flows to everyone who has an opportunity to view it. Education, which we examine in this chapter, is another example of this type of externality.

Review Quiz

1 What are the four types of externality?
2 Give an example of each type of externality that is different from the ones described above.
3 How are the externalities that you've described addressed, either by the market or by public policy?

 Work Study Plan 16.1 and get instant feedback.

We've described the four types of externalities and provided some examples of each. Pollution is the most important of the negative externalities and it is this example that we use to study the economics of external costs.

◆ Negative Externalities: Pollution

To study the economics of the negative externalities that arise from pollution, we distinguish between the private cost and the social cost of production.

Private Costs and Social Costs

A *private cost* of production is a cost that is borne by the producer of a good or service. *Marginal cost* is the cost of producing an *additional unit* of a good or service. So **marginal private cost** (*MC*) is the cost of producing an additional unit of a good or service that is borne by the producer of that good or service.

An *external cost* is a cost of producing a good or service that is *not* borne by the producer but borne by other people. A **marginal external cost** is the cost of producing an additional unit of a good or service that falls on people other than the producer.

Marginal social cost (*MSC*) is the marginal cost incurred by the producer and by everyone else on whom the cost falls—by society. It is the sum of marginal private cost and marginal external cost. That is,

$$MSC = MC + \text{Marginal external cost.}$$

We express costs in dollars, but we must always remember that a cost is an opportunity cost—something real, such as a clean river or clean air, is given up to get something.

Valuing an External Cost Economists use market prices to put a dollar value on the cost of pollution. For example, suppose that there are two similar rivers, one polluted and the other clean. Five hundred identical homes are built along the side of each river. The homes on the clean river rent for $2,500 a month, and those on the polluted river rent for $1,500 a month. If the pollution is the only detectable difference between the two rivers and the two locations, the rent decrease of $1,000 per month is the cost of the pollution. For the 500 homes on the polluted river, the external cost is $500,000 a month.

External Cost and Output Figure 16.1 shows an example of the relationship between output and cost in a chemical industry that pollutes. The marginal cost curve, *MC*, describes the marginal private cost borne by the firms that produce the chemical. Marginal cost increases as the quantity of chemical produced increases. If the firms dump waste into a

river, they impose an external cost that increases with the amount of the chemical produced. The marginal social cost curve, *MSC*, is the sum of marginal private cost and marginal external cost. For example, when output is 4,000 tons of chemical a month, marginal private cost is $100 a ton, marginal external cost is $125 a ton, and marginal social cost is $225 a ton.

In Fig. 16.1, when the quantity of chemical produced increases, the amount of pollution increases and the external cost of pollution increases.

Figure 16.1 shows the relationship between the quantity of chemical produced and the cost of the pollution it creates, but it doesn't tell us how much pollution gets created. That quantity depends on how the market for the chemical operates. First, we'll see what happens when the industry is free to pollute.

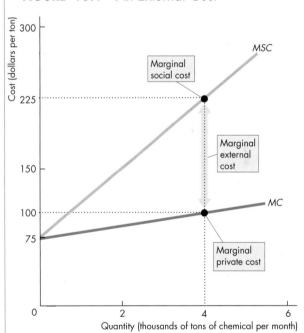

FIGURE 16.1   An External Cost

The *MC* curve shows the marginal private cost borne by the factories that produce a chemical. The *MSC* curve shows the sum of marginal private cost and marginal external cost. When output is 4,000 tons of chemical a month, marginal private cost is $100 a ton, marginal external cost is $125 a ton, and marginal social cost is $225 a ton.

myeconlab animation   ◆

Production and Pollution: How Much?

When an industry is unregulated, the amount of pollution it creates depends on the market equilibrium price and quantity of the good produced. In Fig. 16.2, the demand curve for a pollution-creating chemical is D. This curve also measures the marginal social benefit, MSB, of the chemical. The supply curve is S. This curve also measures the producers' marginal private cost, MC. The supply curve is the marginal private cost curve because when firms make their production and supply decisions, they consider only the costs that they will bear. Market equilibrium occurs at a price of $100 a ton and 4,000 tons of chemical a month.

This equilibrium is inefficient. You learned in Chapter 5 that the allocation of resources is efficient when marginal social benefit equals marginal social cost. But we must count all the costs—private and external—when we compare marginal social benefit and marginal social cost. So with an external cost, the allocation is efficient when marginal social benefit equals marginal *social* cost. This outcome occurs when the quantity of chemical produced is 2,000 tons a month. The unregulated market overproduces by 2,000 tons of chemical a month and creates a deadweight loss shown by the gray triangle.

How can the people who live by the polluted river get the chemical factories to decrease their output of chemical and create less pollution? If some method can be found to achieve this outcome, everyone—the owners of the chemical factories and the residents of the riverside homes—can gain. Let's explore some solutions.

Property Rights

Sometimes it is possible to reduce the inefficiency arising from an externality by establishing a property right where one does not currently exist. **Property rights** are legally established titles to the ownership, use, and disposal of factors of production and goods and services that are enforceable in the courts.

Suppose that the chemical factories own the river and the 500 homes alongside it. The rent that people are willing to pay depends on the amount of pollution. Using the earlier example, people are willing to pay $2,500 a month to live alongside a pollution-free river but only $1,500 a month to live with the pollution created by 4,000 tons of chemical a month. If the factories produce this quantity, they lose $1,000 a month for each home for a total of $500,000 a month.

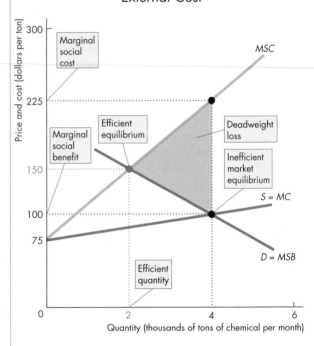

FIGURE 16.2   Inefficiency with an External Cost

The supply curve is the marginal private cost curve, $S = MC$. The demand curve is the marginal social benefit curve, $D = MSB$. Market equilibrium at a price of $100 a ton and 4,000 tons a month is inefficient because marginal social cost exceeds marginal social benefit. The efficient quantity is 2,000 tons a month. The gray triangle shows the deadweight loss created by the pollution externality.

myeconlab   animation

The chemical factories are now confronted with the cost of their pollution—forgone rent from the people who live by the river.

Figure 16.3 illustrates the outcome by using the same example as in Fig. 16.2. With property rights in place, the MC curve no longer measures all the costs that the factories face in producing the chemical. It excludes the pollution costs that they must now bear. The MSC curve now becomes the marginal private cost curve MC. All the costs fall on the factories, so the market supply curve is based on all the marginal costs and is the curve labeled $S = MC = MSC$.

Market equilibrium now occurs at a price of $150 a ton and 2,000 tons of chemical a month. This outcome is efficient. The factories still produce some pollution, but it is the efficient quantity.

FIGURE 16.3 Property Rights Achieve an Efficient Outcome

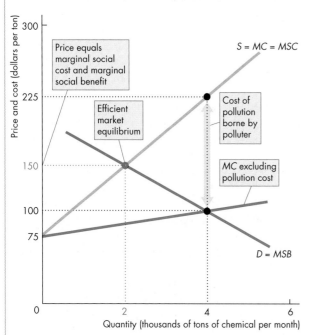

With property rights, the marginal cost curve that excludes pollution costs shows only part of the producers' marginal cost. The marginal private cost curve includes the cost of pollution, so the supply curve is $S = MC = MSC$. Market equilibrium is at a price of $150 a ton and 2,000 tons of chemical a month and is efficient because marginal social cost equals marginal social benefit. The efficient quantity of pollution is not zero.

 animation

The Coase Theorem

Does it matter how property rights are assigned? Does it matter whether the polluter or the victim of the pollution owns the resource that might be polluted? Until 1960, everyone thought that it did matter. But in 1960, Ronald Coase (see p. 413) had a remarkable insight, now called the Coase theorem.

The **Coase theorem** is the proposition that if property rights exist, if only a small number of parties are involved, and if transactions costs are low, then private transactions are efficient. There are no externalities because the transacting parties take all the costs and benefits into account. Furthermore, it doesn't matter who has the property rights.

Application of the Coase Theorem In the example that we've just studied, the factories own the river and the homes. Suppose that instead, the residents own their homes and the river. Now the factories must pay a fee to the homeowners for the right to dump their waste. The greater the quantity of waste dumped into the river, the more the factories must pay. So again, the factories face the opportunity cost of the pollution they create. The quantity of chemical produced and the amount of waste dumped are the same whoever owns the homes and the river. If the factories own them, they bear the cost of pollution because they receive a lower income from home rents. And if the residents own the homes and the river, the factories bear the cost of pollution because they must pay a fee to the homeowners. In both cases, the factories bear the cost of their pollution and dump the efficient amount of waste into the river.

The Coase solution works only when transactions costs are low. **Transactions costs** are the opportunity costs of conducting a transaction. For example, when you buy a house, you incur a series of transactions costs. You might pay a real estate agent to help you find the best place and a lawyer to run checks that assure you that the seller owns the property and that after you've paid for it, the ownership has been properly transferred to you.

In the example of the homes alongside a river, the transactions costs that are incurred by a small number of chemical factories and a few homeowners might be low enough to enable them to negotiate the deals that produce an efficient outcome. But in many situations, transactions costs are so high that it would be inefficient to incur them. In these situations, the Coase solution is not available.

Suppose, for example, that everyone owns the airspace above their homes up to, say, 10 miles. If someone pollutes your airspace, you can charge a fee. But to collect the fee, you must identify who is polluting your airspace and persuade them to pay you. Imagine the costs of negotiating and enforcing agreements with the 50 million people who live in your part of the United States (and perhaps in Canada or Mexico) and the several thousand factories that emit sulfur dioxide and create acid rain that falls on your property! In this situation, we use public choices to cope with externalities. But the transactions costs that block a market solution are real costs, so attempts by the government to deal with externalities offer no easy solution. Let's look at some of these attempts.

Government Actions in the Face of External Costs

The three main methods that governments use to cope with externalities are

- Taxes
- Emission charges
- Marketable permits

Taxes The government can use taxes as an incentive for producers to cut back on pollution. Taxes used in this way are called **Pigovian taxes**, in honor of Arthur Cecil Pigou, the British economist who first worked out this method of dealing with externalities during the 1920s.

By setting the tax equal to the marginal external cost, firms can be made to behave in the same way as they would if they bore the cost of the externality directly. To see how government actions can change market outcomes in the face of externalities, let's return to the example of the chemical factories and the river.

Assume that the government has assessed the marginal external cost accurately and imposes a tax on the factories that exactly equals this cost. Figure 16.4 illustrates the effects of this tax.

The demand curve and marginal social benefit curve, $D = MSB$, and the firms' marginal cost curve, MC, are the same as in Fig. 16.2. The pollution tax equals the marginal external cost of the pollution. We add this tax to the marginal private cost to find the market supply curve. This curve is the one labeled $S = MC + tax = MSC$. This curve is the market supply curve because it tells us the quantity supplied at each price given the firms' marginal cost and the tax they must pay. This curve is also the marginal social cost curve because the pollution tax has been set equal to the marginal external cost.

Demand and supply now determine the market equilibrium price at $150 a ton and a quantity of 2,000 tons of chemical a month. At this quantity of chemical production, the marginal social cost is $150 and the marginal social benefit is $150, so the outcome is efficient. The firms incur a marginal cost of $88 a ton and pay a tax of $62 a ton. The government collects tax revenue of $124,000 a month.

Emission Charges Emission charges are an alternative to a tax for confronting a polluter with the external cost of pollution. The government sets a price per unit of pollution. The more pollution a firm creates, the more it

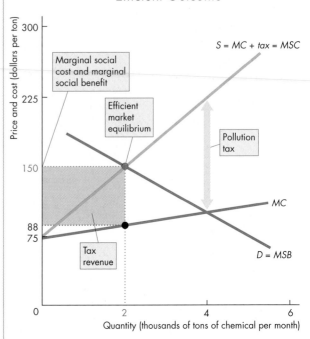

FIGURE 16.4 A Pollution Tax to Achieve an Efficient Outcome

A pollution tax is imposed equal to the marginal external cost of pollution. The supply curve becomes the marginal private cost curve, MC, plus the tax—$S = MC + tax$. Market equilibrium is at a price of $150 a ton and 2,000 tons of chemical a month and is efficient because marginal social cost equals marginal social benefit. The government collects a tax revenue shown by the purple rectangle.

myeconlab animation

pays in emission charges. This method of dealing with pollution externalities has been used only modestly in the United States but is common in Europe where, for example, France, Germany, and the Netherlands make water polluters pay a waste disposal charge.

To work out the emission charge that achieves efficiency, the government needs a lot of information about the polluting industry that, in practice, is rarely available.

Marketable Permits Instead of taxing or imposing emission charges on polluters, each potential polluter might be assigned a permitted pollution limit. Each firm knows its own costs and benefits of pollution, and making pollution limits marketable is a clever way of using this private information that is unknown to the government. The government issues each firm a permit to emit a certain amount of pollution, and firms can buy and sell these permits. Firms that have a low marginal cost of reducing pollution sell their permits, and firms that have a high marginal cost of reducing pollution buy permits. The market in permits determines the price at which firms trade permits. Each firm buys or sells permits until its marginal cost of pollution equals the market price of a permit.

This method of dealing with pollution provides an even stronger incentive than emission charges to find lower-polluting technologies because the price of a permit to pollute rises as the demand for permits increases.

The Market for Emission Permits in the United States

Trading in lead pollution permits became common during the 1980s, and this marketable permit program has been rated a success. It enabled lead to be virtually eliminated from the atmosphere of the United States (see p. 374). But this success might not easily translate to other situations because lead pollution has some special features. First, most lead pollution came from a single source: leaded gasoline. Second, lead in gasoline is easily monitored. Third, the objective of the program was clear: to eliminate lead in gasoline.

The Environmental Protection Agency is now considering using marketable permits to promote efficiency in the control of chlorofluorocarbons, the gases that are believed to damage the ozone layer.

Review Quiz

1 What is the distinction between private cost and social cost?

2 How does a negative externality prevent a competitive market from allocating resources efficiently?

3 How can a negative externality be eliminated by assigning property rights? How does this method of coping with an externality work?

4 How do taxes help us to cope with negative externalities? At what level must a pollution tax be set if it is to induce firms to produce the efficient quantity of pollution?

5 How do emission charges and marketable pollution permits work?

 Work Study Plan 16.2 and get instant feedback.

Positive Externalities: Knowledge

Knowledge comes from education and research. To study the economics of knowledge, we distinguish between private benefits and social benefits.

Private Benefits and Social Benefits

A *private benefit* is a benefit that the consumer of a good or service receives. *Marginal benefit* is the benefit from an *additional unit* of a good or service. So a **marginal private benefit** (MB) is the benefit from an additional unit of a good or service that the consumer of that good or service receives.

The *external benefit* from a good or service is the benefit that someone other than the consumer receives. A **marginal external benefit** is the benefit from an additional unit of a good or service that people other than the consumer enjoy.

Marginal social benefit (MSB) is the marginal benefit enjoyed by society—by the consumer of a good or service (marginal private benefit) plus the marginal benefit enjoyed by others (the marginal external benefit). That is,

$$MSB = MB + \text{Marginal external benefit.}$$

Figure 16.5 shows an example of the relationship between marginal private benefit, marginal external benefit, and marginal social benefit. The marginal benefit curve, MB, describes the marginal private benefit—such as expanded job opportunities and higher incomes—enjoyed by college graduates. Marginal private benefit decreases as the quantity of education increases.

But college graduates generate external benefits. On the average, they tend to be better citizens. Their crime rates are lower, and they are more tolerant of the views of others. A society with a large number of college graduates can support activities such as high-quality newspapers and television channels, music, theater, and other organized social activities.

In the example in Fig. 16.5, the marginal external benefit is $15,000 per student per year when 15 million students enroll in college. The marginal social benefit curve, MSB, is the sum of marginal private benefit and marginal external benefit. For example, when 15 million students a year enroll in college, the marginal private benefit is $10,000 per student and

FIGURE 16.5   An External Benefit

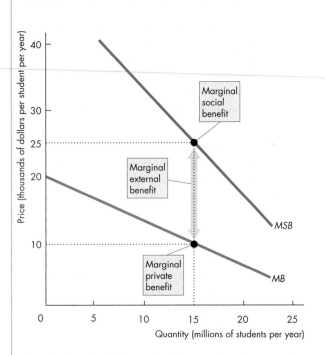

The *MB* curve shows the marginal private benefit enjoyed by the people who receive a college education. The *MSB* curve shows the sum of marginal private benefit and marginal external benefit. When 15 million students attend college, marginal private benefit is $10,000 per student, marginal external benefit is $15,000 per student, and marginal social benefit is $25,000 per student.

 animation

FIGURE 16.6   Inefficiency with an External Benefit

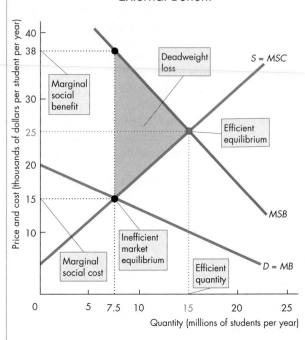

The market demand curve is the marginal private benefit curve, *D = MB*. The supply curve is the marginal social cost curve, *S = MSC*. Market equilibrium at a tuition of $15,000 a year and 7.5 million students is inefficient because marginal social benefit exceeds marginal social cost. The efficient quantity is 15 million students. A deadweight loss arises (gray triangle) because too few students enroll in college.

myeconlab animation

the marginal external benefit is $15,000 per student, so the marginal social benefit is $25,000 per student.

When people make schooling decisions, they ignore its external benefits and consider only its private benefits. So if education were provided by private schools that charged full-cost tuition, we would produce too few college graduates.

Figure 16.6 illustrates the underproduction that would exist if the government left education to the private market. The supply curve is the marginal social cost curve, *S = MSC*. The demand curve is the marginal private benefit curve, *D = MB*. Market equilibrium occurs at a tuition of $15,000 per student per year and 7.5 million students per year. At this equilibrium, marginal social benefit is $38,000 per student, which exceeds marginal social cost by $23,000. There are too few students in college. The efficient number is 15 million per year, where mar-

ginal social benefit equals marginal social cost. The gray triangle shows the deadweight loss.

Underproduction similar to that in Fig. 16.6 would occur in grade school and high school if public education was left to an unregulated market. When children learn basic reading, writing, and number skills, they receive the private benefit of increased earning power. But even these basic skills bring the external benefit of developing better citizens.

External benefits also arise from the discovery of new knowledge. When Isaac Newton worked out the formulas for calculating the rate of response of one variable to another—calculus—everyone was free to use his method. When a spreadsheet program called VisiCalc was invented, Lotus Corporation and Microsoft were free to copy the basic idea and create 1-2-3 and Excel. When the first shopping mall was built and found to be a successful way of arranging retailing, everyone was free to copy the idea, and malls sprouted like mushrooms.

Once someone has discovered a basic idea others can copy it. Because they do have to work to copy an idea, they face an opportunity cost, but they do not usually have to pay a fee for the idea. When people make decisions, they ignore the external benefits and consider only the private benefits.

When people make decisions about the amount of education or research to undertake, they balance the marginal private cost against the marginal private benefit. They ignore the external benefit. As a result, if we left education and research to unregulated market forces, we would get too little of these activities.

To get closer to producing the efficient quantity of a good or service that generates an external benefit, we make public choices, through governments, to modify the market outcome.

Government Actions in the Face of External Benefits

Four devices that governments can use to achieve a more efficient allocation of resources in the presence of external benefits are

- Public provision
- Private subsidies
- Vouchers
- Patents and copyrights

Public Provision Under **public provision**, a public authority that receives its revenue from the government produces the good or service. The education services produced by the public universities, colleges, and schools are examples of public provision.

Figure 16.7(a) shows how public provision might overcome the underproduction that arises in Fig. 16.6.

FIGURE 16.7 Public Provision or Private Subsidy to Achieve an Efficient Outcome

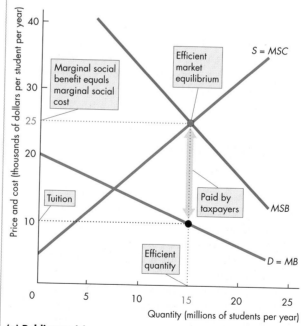

(a) Public provision

(b) Private subsidy

In part (a), marginal social benefit equals marginal social cost with 15 million students per year, the efficient quantity. Tuition is set at $10,000 per student equal to marginal private benefit. Taxpayers cover the other $15,000 of cost per student.

In part (b), with a subsidy of $15,000 per student, the supply curve is $S_1 = MSC - subsidy$. The equilibrium price is $10,000, and the market equilibrium is efficient with 15 million students per year. Marginal social benefit equals marginal social cost.

 animation

Public provision cannot lower the cost of production, so marginal social cost is the same as before. Marginal private benefit and marginal external benefit are also the same as before.

The efficient quantity occurs where marginal social benefit equals marginal social cost. In Fig. 16.7(a), this quantity is 15 million students. Tuition is set to ensure that the efficient number of students enrolls. That is, tuition is set equal to the marginal private benefit at the efficient quantity. In Fig. 16.7(a), tuition is $10,000 a year. The rest of the cost of the public university is borne by the taxpayers and, in this example, is $15,000 per student per year.

Private Subsidies A **subsidy** is a payment that the government makes to private producers. By making the subsidy depend on the level of output, the government can induce private decision makers to consider external benefits when they make their choices.

Figure 16.7(b) shows how a subsidy to private colleges works. In the absence of a subsidy, the market supply curve is $S_0 = MSC$. The demand curve is the marginal private benefit curve, $D = MB$. If the government provides a subsidy to colleges of $15,000 per student per year, we must subtract the subsidy from the colleges' marginal cost to find the new market supply curve. That curve is $S_1 = MSC - subsidy$. The market equilibrium is tuition of $10,000 a year and 15 million students a year. The marginal social cost of educating 15 million students is $25,000 and the marginal social benefit is $25,000. So with marginal social cost equal to marginal social benefit, the subsidy has achieved an efficient outcome. The tuition and the subsidy just cover the colleges' marginal cost.

Vouchers A **voucher** is a token that the government provides to households, which they can use to buy specified goods or services. Food stamps are examples of vouchers. The vouchers (stamps) can be spent only on food and are designed to improve the diet and health of extremely poor families.

School vouchers have been advocated as a means of improving the quality of education and are used in Washington D.C..

A school voucher allows parents to choose the school their children will attend and to use the voucher to pay part of the cost. The school cashes the vouchers to pay its bills. A voucher could be provided to a college student in a similar way, and although technically not a voucher, a federal Pell Grant has a similar effect.

FIGURE 16.8   Vouchers Achieve an Efficient Outcome

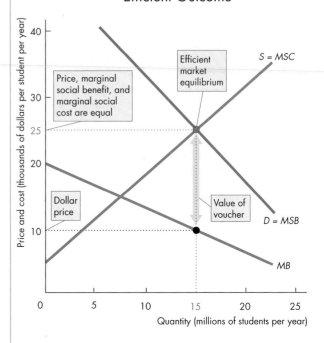

With vouchers, buyers are willing to pay *MB* plus the value of the voucher, so the demand curve becomes the marginal social benefit curve, *D = MSB*. Market equilibrium is efficient with 15 million students enrolled in college because price, marginal social benefit, and marginal social cost are equal. The tuition consists of the dollar price of $10,000 and a voucher valued at $15,000.

myeconlab   animation

Because vouchers can be spent only on a specified item, they increase the willingness to pay for that item and so increase the demand for it. Figure 16.8 shows how a voucher system works. The government provides a voucher per student equal to the marginal external benefit. Parents (or students) use these vouchers to supplement the dollars they pay for education. The marginal social benefit curve becomes the demand for college education, *D = MSB*. The market equilibrium occurs at a price of $25,000 per student per year, and 15 million students attend college. Each student pays $10,000 tuition, and schools collect an additional $15,000 per student from the voucher.

If the government estimates the value of the external benefit correctly and makes the value of the voucher equal the marginal external benefit, the outcome from the voucher scheme is efficient.

Marginal social cost equals marginal social benefit, and the deadweight loss is eliminated.

Vouchers are similar to subsidies, but their advocates say that they are more efficient than subsidies because the consumer can monitor school performance more effectively than the government can.

Patents and Copyrights Knowledge might be an exception to the principle of diminishing marginal benefit. Additional knowledge (about the right things) makes people more productive. And there seems to be no tendency for the additional productivity from additional knowledge to diminish.

For example, in just 15 years, advances in knowledge about microprocessors have given us a sequence of processor chips that has made our personal computers increasingly powerful. Each advance in knowledge about how to design and manufacture a processor chip has brought apparently ever larger increments in performance and productivity. Similarly, each advance in knowledge about how to design and build an airplane has brought apparently ever larger increments in performance: Orville and Wilbur Wright's 1903 Flyer was a one-seat plane that could hop a farmer's field. The Lockheed Constellation, designed in 1949, was an airplane that could fly 120 passengers from New York to London, but with two refueling stops in Newfoundland and Ireland. The latest version of the Boeing 747 can carry 400 people nonstop from Los Angeles to Sydney, Australia, or New York to Tokyo (flights of 7,500 miles that take 13 hours). Similar examples can be found in agriculture, biogenetics, communications, engineering, entertainment, and medicine.

One reason why the stock of knowledge increases without diminishing returns is the sheer number of different techniques that can in principle be tried. Paul Romer, an economist at Stanford University, explains this fact. "Suppose that to make a finished good, 20 different parts have to be attached to a frame, one at a time. A worker could proceed in numerical order, attaching part one first, then part two. … Or the worker could proceed in some other order, starting with part 10, then adding part seven. …With 20 parts, … there are [more] different sequences … than the total number of seconds that have elapsed since the big bang created the universe, so we can be confident that in all activities, only a very small fraction of the possible sequences have ever been tried."[1]

Think about all the processes, all the products, and all the different bits and pieces that go into each, and you can see that we have only begun to scratch the surface of what is possible.

Because knowledge is productive and generates external benefits, it is necessary to use public policies to ensure that those who develop new ideas have incentives to encourage an efficient level of effort. The main way of providing the right incentives uses the central idea of the Coase theorem and assigns property rights—called **intellectual property rights**—to creators. The legal device for establishing intellectual property rights is the patent or copyright. A **patent** or **copyright** is a government-sanctioned exclusive right granted to the inventor of a good, service, or productive process to produce, use, and sell the invention for a given number of years. A patent enables the developer of a new idea to prevent others from benefiting freely from an invention for a limited number of years.

Although patents encourage invention and innovation, they do so at an economic cost. While a patent is in place, its holder has a monopoly. And monopoly is another source of inefficiency (which is explained in Chapter 13). But without a patent, the effort to develop new goods, services, or processes is diminished and the flow of new inventions is slowed. So the efficient outcome is a compromise that balances the benefits of more inventions against the cost of temporary monopoly in newly invented activities.

Review Quiz

1 What is special about knowledge that creates external benefits?

2 How might governments use public provision, private subsidies, and vouchers to achieve an efficient amount of education?

3 How might governments use public provision, private subsidies, vouchers, and patents and copyrights to achieve an efficient amount of research and development?

 Work Study Plan 16.3 and get instant feedback.

◆ *Reading Between the Lines* on pp. 386–387 looks at the effects of a carbon tax and solar subsidy to reduce greenhouse gas emissions.

---

[1] Paul Romer, "Ideas and Things," in *The Future Surveyed*, supplement to *The Economist*, September 11, 1993, pp. 71–72.

Fighting Carbon Emissions with a Carbon Tax and Solar Subsidy

On Carbon, Tax and Don't Spend

http://www.nytimes.com
March 25, 2008

… a carbon tax isn't a new idea. Denmark, Finland, Norway and Sweden have had carbon taxes in place since the 1990s, but the tax has not led to large declines in emissions in most of these countries—in the case of Norway, emissions have actually increased by 43 percent per capita. …

The one country in which carbon taxes have led to a large decrease in emissions is Denmark, … What did Denmark do right? …

Denmark avoids the temptation to maximize the tax revenue by giving the proceeds back to industry, earmarking much of it to subsidize environmental innovation. Danish firms are pushed away from carbon and pulled into environmental innovation, and the country's economy isn't put at a competitive disadvantage. So this is lesson No. 1 from Denmark.

The second lesson is that the carbon tax worked in Denmark because it was easy for Danish firms to switch to cleaner fuels. Danish policy makers made huge investments in renewable energy and subsidized environmental innovation. Denmark back then was more reliant on coal than the other three countries were (but not more so than the United States is today), so when the tax gave companies a reason to leave coal and the investments in renewable energy gave them an easy way to do so, they switched. The key was providing easy substitutes. …

An increase in gasoline taxes … would … be the wrong policy. … Higher gas taxes would raise revenue but do little to curb pollution.

Instead, if we want to reduce carbon emissions, then we should follow Denmark's example: tax the industrial emission of carbon and return the revenue to industry through subsidies for research and investment in alternative energy sources, cleaner-burning fuel, carbon-capture technologies and other environmental innovations.

Essence of the Story

- Denmark, Finland, Norway and Sweden have had carbon taxes since the 1990s.

- Emissions increased in Norway, changed little in Finland and Sweden, and decreased in Denmark.

- Denmark used the carbon tax revenues to make it easy for power utilities to switch from coal.

- A gas tax increase in the United States would raise revenue but not curb pollution.

- The United States should follow Denmark's example.

Economic Analysis

- Figure 1 illustrates why, as the article states, a carbon tax on gasoline would do little to curb pollution.

- The demand for gasoline in the short run, D_{SR}, is inelastic. If the U.S. gas price was raised (by a carbon tax) to the European level, gasoline consumption would decrease by very little.

- The demand for gasoline in the long run, D_{LR}, is elastic, so consumption might fall to the European level eventually, but it would take many years.

- Figure 2 illustrates why a carbon tax that is spent on subsidies to clean fuel cuts pollution, as the article states.

- Figure 2(a) shows the costs of producing electricity using coal, which has an external cost: MSC exceeds MC. Figure 2(b) shows the cost using solar power, which has no external cost: $MC = MSC$.

- Assume that the marginal social cost of producing electricity equals the marginal benefit of electricity at 30 cents per kilowatt hour (kWh) and that the market price of electricity is also 30 cents per kWh.

- In part (a), a carbon tax equal to the marginal external cost raises the producer's marginal cost to equal the marginal social cost.

- With no subsidy for solar, a coal-fired power station continues to operate and produces 5 MWh.

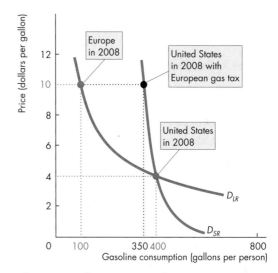

Figure 1 A carbon tax on gasoline

- But with a carbon tax and a solar subsidy, the marginal coal-fired power station shuts down and switches to solar power. As the article says, the subsidy makes fuel substitution easy for the producer.

- The combination of the tax and subsidy is *inefficient*. Electricity is now being produced by solar power at a marginal social cost of 50 cents per kWh instead of the efficient 30 cents per kWh using coal.

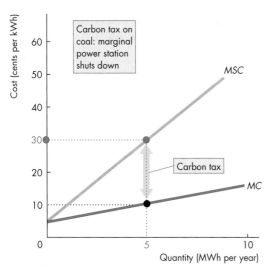

(a) Coal generation

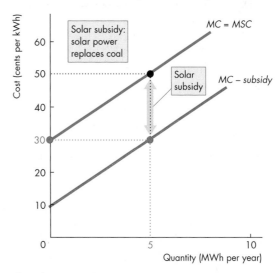

(b) Solar generation

Figure 2 Using carbon tax to subsidize alternative fuels

387

SUMMARY

Key Points

Externalities in Our Lives (p. 374–376)

- An externality can arise from either a production activity or a consumption activity.
- A negative externality imposes an external cost.
- A positive externality provides an external benefit.

Negative Externalities: Pollution (pp. 377–381)

- External costs are costs of production that fall on people other than the producer of a good or service. Marginal social cost equals marginal private cost plus marginal external cost.
- Producers take account only of marginal private cost and produce more than the efficient quantity when there is a marginal external cost.
- Sometimes it is possible to overcome a negative externality by assigning a property right.
- When property rights cannot be assigned, governments might overcome externalities by using taxes, emission charges, or marketable permits.

Positive Externalities: Knowledge (pp. 381–385)

- External benefits are benefits that are received by people other than the consumer of a good or service. Marginal social benefit equals marginal private benefit plus marginal external benefit.
- External benefits from education arise because better-educated people tend to be better citizens, commit fewer crimes, and support social activities.
- External benefits from research arise because once someone has worked out a basic idea, others can copy it.
- Vouchers or subsidies to schools or the provision of public education below cost can achieve a more efficient provision of education.
- Patents and copyrights create intellectual property rights and an incentive to innovate. But they do so by creating a temporary monopoly, the cost of which must be balanced against the benefit of more inventive activity.

Key Figures

Key Terms

PROBLEMS and APPLICATIONS

 Work problems 1–9 in Chapter 16 Study Plan and get instant feedback.
Work problems 10–18 as Homework, a Quiz, or a Test if assigned by your instructor.

1. Consider each of the following activities or events and say for each one whether it is an externality. If so, say whether it is a positive or negative production or consumption externality.
   - Airplanes take off from LaGuardia Airport during the U.S. Open tennis tournament, which is taking place nearby.
   - A sunset over the Pacific Ocean
   - An increase in the number of people who are studying for graduate degrees
   - A person wears strong perfume while attending an orchestra concert.
   - A homeowner plants an attractive garden in front of his house.
   - A person drives talking on a cell phone.
   - A bakery bakes bread.

2. The table provides information about costs and benefits that arise from the pesticide production that pollutes a lake used by a trout farmer.

Output of pesticide (tons per week)	Marginal cost	Marginal external cost	Marginal social benefit
		(dollars per ton)	
0	0	0	250
1	5	33	205
2	15	67	165
3	30	100	130
4	50	133	100
5	75	167	75
6	105	200	55
7	140	233	40

   a. If no one owns the lake and if there is no regulation of pollution, what is the quantity of pesticide produced and what is the marginal cost of pollution borne by the trout farmer?
   b. If the trout farm owns the lake, how much pesticide is produced and what does the pesticide producer pay the farmer per ton?
   c. If the pesticide producer owns the lake, and if a pollution-free lake rents for $1,000 a week, how much pesticide is produced and how much rent does the farmer pay the factory for the use of the lake?

   d. Compare the quantities of pesticide produced in b and c, and explain the relationship between these quantities.

3. Back at the pesticide plant and trout farm described in problem 2, suppose that no one owns the lake and that the government introduces a pollution tax.
   a. What is the tax per ton of pesticide produced that achieves an efficient outcome?
   b. Explain the connection between your answer to a and the answer to problem 2a.

4. Using the information provided in problem 2, suppose that no one owns the lake and that the government issues three marketable pollution permits, two to the farmer and one to the factory. Each permit allows the same amount of pollution of the lake, and the total amount of pollution is the efficient amount.
   a. What is the quantity of pesticide produced?
   b. What is the market price of a pollution permit? Who buys and who sells a permit?
   c. What is the connection between your answer and the answers to problems 2a and 3a?

5. The marginal cost of educating a student is $4,000 a year and is constant. The figure shows the marginal private benefit curve.

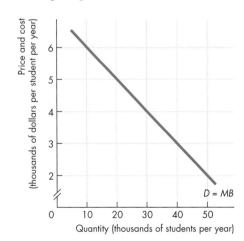

   a. With no government involvement and if the schools are competitive, how many students are enrolled and what is the tuition?

b. The external benefit from education is $2,000 per student per year and is constant. If the government provides the efficient amount of education, how many students will be accepted and what is the tuition?

6. **Bag Revolution**

[T]raditional plastic bags ... aren't biodegradable and often end up in the ocean. ... Americans consume roughly 110 billion bags annually. ... 28 cities in the U.S. have proposed laws restricting the use of plastic bags. ... But San Francisco now requires all retailers with revenue over $2 million to offer only compostable or reusable bags, and Seattle has proposed a 25-cent per-bag tax.

Fortune, May 12, 2008

a. Describe the externality that arises from plastic bags.
b. Draw a graph to illustrate how plastic bags create deadweight loss.
c. Explain the effects of Seattle's policy on the use of plastic bags.
d. Draw a graph to illustrate Seattle's policy and show the change in the deadweight loss that arises from this policy.
e. Explain why a complete ban on plastic bags might be inefficient.

7. **The Year in Medicine: Cell Phones**

Think you're safer because you talk on a hands-free cell phone while driving? Think again. Using either type of phone while trying to drive a car is roughly equivalent to driving with a blood-alcohol concentration ... high enough to get you arrested ... for driving under the influence. Folks who use hands-free cell phones in simulation trials also exhibited slower reaction times and took longer to hit the brakes than drivers who weren't otherwise distracted. Data from real-life driving tests show that cell-phone use rivals drowsy driving as a major cause of accidents.

Time, December 4, 2006

a. What negative externalities arise from using a cell phone while driving?
b. Explain why the market for cell-phone service creates a deadweight loss.
c. Draw a graph to illustrate how a deadweight loss arises from the use of cell phones.
d. Explain how government intervention might improve the efficiency of cell-phone use.

8. **D.C. Handgun Ban**

But it is not just D.C. that has experienced increases in murder and violent crime after guns are banned. Chicago also experienced an increase after its ban in 1982. Island nations supposedly present ideal environments for gun control because it is relatively easy for them to control their borders, but countries such as Great Britain, Ireland, and Jamaica have experienced large increases in murder and violent crime after gun bans. For example, after handguns were banned in 1997, the number of deaths and injuries from gun crime in England and Wales increased 340 percent in the seven years from 1998 to 2005. Passing a gun ban simply doesn't mean that we are going to get guns away from criminals. The real problem is that if it is the law-abiding good citizens who obey these laws and not the criminals, criminals have less to fear and crime can go up.

FOXNews, September 14, 2007

a. What external costs do handguns impose?
b. What external benefits do handguns bring?
c. If both negative and positive externalities arise from handguns, how can we determine whether gun ownership should be discouraged or encouraged or neither?

9. **My Child, My Choice**

Fully vaccinating all U.S. children born in a given year from birth to adolescence saves 33,000 lives, prevents 14 million infections and saves $10 billion in medical costs. Part of the reason is that vaccinations protect not only the kids that receive the shots but also those who can't receive them—such as newborns and cancer patients with suppressed immune systems. ... The higher the immunization rate in any population, the less likely that a pathogen will penetrate the group and find a susceptible person inside.

Time, June 2, 2008

a. Describe the private benefits and external benefits of vaccinations and explain why a private market for vaccinations would produce an inefficient outcome.
b. Draw a graph to illustrate a private market for vaccinations and show the deadweight loss.
c. Explain how government intervention could achieve an efficient quantity of vaccinations and draw a graph to illustrate this outcome.

10. The figure illustrates the unregulated market for a pesticide. When factories produce pesticide, they also create waste, which they dump into a lake on the outskirts of the town. The marginal external cost of the dumped waste is equal to the marginal private cost of producing the pesticide (that is, the marginal social cost of producing the pesticide is double the marginal private cost).

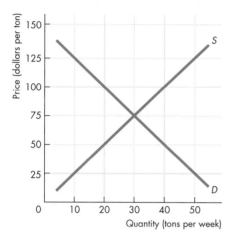

a. What is the quantity of pesticide produced if no one owns the lake and what is the efficient quantity of pesticide?

b. If the residents of the town own the lake, what is the quantity of pesticide produced and how much do residents of the town charge the factories to dump waste?

c. If the pesticide factories own the lake, how much pesticide is produced?

d. If no one owns the lake and the government levies a pollution tax, what is the tax that achieves the efficient outcome?

11. Betty and Anna work at the same office in Philadelphia. They both must attend a meeting in Pittsburgh, so they decide to drive to the meeting together. Betty is a cigarette smoker and her marginal benefit from smoking a package of cigarettes a day is $40. Cigarettes are $6 a pack. Anna dislikes cigarette smoke, and her marginal benefit from a smoke-free environment is $50 a day. What is the outcome if

a. Betty drives her car with Anna as a passenger?

b. Anna drives her car with Betty as a passenger?

12. The first two columns of the table show the demand schedule for electricity from a coal burning utility; the second and third columns show the utility's cost of producing electricity. The

Price (cents per kilowatt)	Quantity (kilowatts per day)	Marginal cost (cents per kilowatt)
4	500	10
8	400	8
12	300	6
16	200	4
20	100	2

marginal external cost of the pollution created is equal to the marginal cost.

a. With no pollution control, what is the quantity of electricity produced, the price of electricity, and the marginal external cost of the pollution generated?

b. With no pollution control, what is the marginal social cost of the electricity generated and the deadweight loss?

c. Suppose that the government levies a pollution tax, such that the utility produces the efficient quantity. What are the price of electricity, the tax, and the tax revenue per day?

13. Most nurses in the United States receive their education in community colleges. Mainly because of differences in class size, the cost of educating a nurse is about four times that of an average community college student. Community college budgets depend on the number of students and not on the subjects taught.

a. Explain why this funding arrangement might be expected to lead to an inefficiency in the number of nurses trained.

b. Suggest a better arrangement and explain how it would work.

14. **China Vows to Clean Up Polluted Lake**

… Officials in Jiangsu Province [announced] plans to spend 108.5 billion yuan, or $14.4 billion, for a cleanup of Lake Tai, the country's third-largest freshwater lake. The campaign would focus initially on eradicating the toxic algal bloom that choked the lake this spring and left more than two million people without drinking water. …

Lake Tai, known as China's ancient "land of rice and fish," is a legendary setting, once famous for its bounty of white shrimp, whitebait, and whitefish. But over time, an industrial buildup transformed the region. More than 2,800 chemical factories arose around the lake, and industrial dumping became a severe problem and, eventually, a crisis. …

"The pollution of Lake Tai has sounded the alarm for us," Mr. Wen [Prime Minister] said, "The problem has never been tackled at its root."

New York Times, October 27, 2007

a. What are the externalities included in this news clip?

b. What are the external costs associated with the pollution of Lake Tai?

c. What was the "alarm" that the pollution of Lake Tai sounded and why has the problem "never been tackled at its root"?

15. **Fast-Food Trash Be Gone!**

Some Oakland, Calif., residents are sick and tired of tripping over burger wrappers and soda cans, and the city is ready to do something about it. The Oakland City Council is proposing a tax on fast-food restaurants, gas station markets, liquor stores and convenience stores that serve take-out food or beverages. Councilwoman Jane Brunner, who wrote the legislation, estimates that the tax will raise approximately $237,000 a year, which would cover the cost of a clean-up crew and the initial purchase of trucks and equipment to keep the streets and sidewalks surrounding the city's schools litter-free. "Having a clean city affects everything," Brunner said.

CNN, February 6, 2006

a. What is the external cost associated with take-out food and beverages?

b. Draw a graph to illustrate and explain why the market for take-out food and beverages creates a deadweight loss.

c. Draw a graph to illustrate and explain how Oakland's policy might improve efficiency.

16. On April 7, 2008, MSNBC reported that:

Compact fluorescent light bulbs—the squiggly, coiled bulbs that generate light by heating gases in a glass tube—are generally considered to use more than 50 percent less energy and to last several times longer than incandescent bulbs. …

There is no disputing that overall, fluorescent bulbs save energy and reduce pollution in general. An average incandescent bulb lasts about 800 to 1,500 hours; a spiral fluorescent bulb can last as long as 10,000 hours. In just more than a year—since the beginning of 2007—9 million fluorescent bulbs have been purchased in California, preventing the release of 1.5 billion pounds of carbon dioxide compared with

traditional bulbs, according to the U.S. Environmental Protection Agency.

a. Relative to a traditional bulb, what is the external benefit associated with fluorescent bulbs?

b. Draw a graph to illustrate and explain why the market for fluorescent bulbs is inefficient.

c. Draw a graph to illustrate and explain how government actions might achieve an efficient outcome in the market for bulbs.

17. **Clean Green Flying Machine?**

… Aviation generates 2–3 percent of man-made emissions of carbon dioxide, the main greenhouse gas. … Most environmentalists think that the only solution is to make air travel more expensive, say through hefty fuel taxes. … But the airline industry [says it] produces far more benefits than ills—[contributing] 8 percent to global [output] by transporting tourists, business travelers, and cargo around the globe.

Economist.com, August 14, 2007

a. What are the externalities created by the airline industry?

b. Why will hefty fuel taxes encourage airlines to operate in the social interest?

18. After you have studied *Reading Between the Lines* on pp. 386–387, answer the following questions:

a. How does a carbon tax change the costs faced by the operator of a coal-fired power plant?

b. How does a solar subsidy change the costs faced by a solar power station?

c. Why might the operator of a coal-fired power station be influenced by a solar subsidy?

d. Why might the combination of a carbon tax and social subsidy lead to producing electricity at too high a marginal social cost?

e. Would it ever make sense to impose a carbon tax *and* pay a solar subsidy?

19. Use the link on MyEconlab (Textbook Resources, Chapter 16) and read the article about wind farms.

a. What types of externalities arise in the production of electricity using wind technologies?

b. Comparing the externalities from wind technologies with those from burning coal and oil, which are more costly?

c. How do you think the external costs of using wind technologies should be dealt with? Compare the alternative range of solutions considered in this chapter.

18 ◆ Markets for Factors of Production

After studying this chapter, you will be able to:

- Describe the anatomy of factor markets

- Explain how the value of marginal product determines the demand for a factor of production

- Explain how wage rates and employment are determined and how labor unions influence the labor market

- Explain how capital and land rental rates and natural resource prices are determined

You know that wage rates vary a lot. A server at McDonald's earns $8 an hour. Demetrio Luna, who spends his days in a small container suspended from the top of Houston's high-rise buildings cleaning windows, makes $12 an hour. Richard Seymour, who plays for the New England Patriots, collects a cool $25 million a year. Some differences in earnings might seem surprising. For example, your college football coach earns much more than your economics professor. What determines the wages that people earn?

The price of oil became a big issue in 2008 as new record highs were set. What determines the prices of the natural resources that we use to produce goods and services? Why do these prices fluctuate and sometimes seem to lose connection with the fundamentals of supply and value?

In this chapter, we study the markets for labor, capital, and natural resources and learn how their prices are determined. *In Reading Between the Lines* at the end of the chapter, we focus on the market for oil and look at the debate over whether it would be a good idea to try to increase the supply of oil by exploring the undersea resources off the U.S. coast.

417

The Anatomy of Factor Markets

The four factors of production are

- Labor
- Capital
- Land (natural resources)
- Entrepreneurship

Let's take a brief look at the anatomy of the markets in which these factors of production are traded.

Markets for Labor Services

Labor services are the physical and mental work effort that people supply to produce goods and services. A labor market is a collection of people and firms who trade labor services. The price of labor services is the wage rate.

Some labor services are traded day by day. These services are called *casual labor*. People who pick fruit and vegetables often just show up at a farm and take whatever work is available that day. But most labor services are traded on a contract, called a **job**.

Most labor markets have many buyers and many sellers and are competitive. In these labor markets, the wage rate is determined by supply and demand, just like the price is determined in any other competitive market.

In some labor markets, a labor union organizes labor, which introduces an element of monopoly on the supply-side of the labor market. In this type of labor market, a bargaining process between the union and the employer determines the wage rate.

We'll study both competitive labor markets and labor unions in this chapter.

Markets for Capital Services

Capital consists of the tools, instruments, machines, buildings, and other constructions that have been produced in the past and that businesses now use to produce goods and services. These physical objects are themselves goods—capital goods. Capital goods are traded in goods markets, just as bottled water and toothpaste are. The price of a dump truck, a capital good, is determined by supply and demand in the market for dump trucks. This market is not a market for capital services.

A market for *capital services* is a *rental market*—a market in which the services of capital are hired.

An example of a market for capital services is the vehicle rental market in which Avis, Budget, Hertz, U-Haul, and many other firms offer automobiles and trucks for hire. The price in a capital services market is a *rental rate*.

Most capital services are not traded in a market. Instead, a firm buys capital and uses it itself. The services of the capital that a firm owns and operates have an implicit price that arises from depreciation and interest costs (see Chapter 10, pp. 228–229). You can think of this price as the implicit rental rate of capital. Firms that buy capital and use it themselves are *implicitly* renting the capital to themselves.

Markets for Land Services and Natural Resources

Land consists of all the gifts of nature—natural resources. The market for land as a factor of production is the market for the *services of land*—the use of land. The price of the services of land is a rental rate.

Most natural resources, such as farm land, can be used repeatedly. But a few natural resources are nonrenewable. **Nonrenewable natural resources** are resources that can be used only once. Examples are oil, natural gas, and coal. The prices of nonrenewable natural resources are determined in global *commodity markets* and are called *commodity prices*.

Entrepreneurship

Entrepreneurial services are not traded in markets. Entrepreneurs receive the profit or bear the loss that results from their business decisions.

Review Quiz

1 What are the factors of production and their prices?
2 What is the distinction between capital and the services of capital?
3 What is the distinction between the price of capital equipment and the rental rate of capital?

myeconlab Work Study Plan 18.1 and get instant feedback.

The rest of this chapter explores the influences on the demand and supply of factors of production. We begin by studying the demand for a factor of production.

The Demand for a Factor of Production

The demand for a factor of production is a **derived demand**—it is derived from the demand for the goods and services that it is used to produce. You've seen, in Chapters 10 through 15, how a firm determines its profit-maximizing output. The quantities of factors of production demanded are a consequence of firms' output decisions. A firm hires the quantities of factors of production that maximize its profit.

To decide the quantity of a factor of production to hire, a firm compares the cost of hiring an additional unit of the factor with its value to the firm. The cost of hiring an additional unit of a factor of production is the *factor price*. The value to the firm of hiring one more unit of a factor of production is called the factor's value of marginal product. The **value of marginal product** equals the price of a unit of output multiplied by the marginal product of the factor of production.

To study the demand for a factor of production, we'll use labor as the example. But what you learn here about the demand for labor applies to the demand for all factors of production.

Value of Marginal Product

Table 18.1 shows you how to calculate the value of the marginal product of labor at Angelo's Bakery.

The first two columns show Angelo's total product schedule—the number of loaves per hour that each quantity of labor can produce. The third column shows the marginal product of labor—the change in total product that results from a one-unit increase in the quantity of labor employed. (See Chapter 11, pp. 253–256 for a refresher on product schedules.)

Angelo can sell bread at the going market price of $2 a loaf. Given this information, we can calculate the value of marginal product (fourth column). It equals price multiplied by marginal product. For example, the marginal product of hiring the second worker is 6 loaves an hour. Each loaf sold brings in $2, so the value of the marginal product of the second worker is $12 (6 loaves at $2 each).

A Firm's Demand for Labor

The value of the marginal product of labor tells us what an additional worker is worth to a firm. It tells us the revenue that the firm earns by hiring one more worker. The wage rate tells us what an additional worker costs a firm.

The value of the marginal product of labor and the wage rate together determine the quantity of labor demanded by a firm. Because the value of marginal product decreases as the quantity of labor employed increases, there is a simple rule for maximizing profit: Hire the quantity of labor at which the value of marginal product equals the wage rate.

If the value of marginal product of labor exceeds the wage rate, a firm can increase its profit by hiring

---

TABLE 18.1   Value of Marginal Product at Angelo's Bakery

	Quantity of labor (L) (workers)	Total product (TP) (loaves per hour)	Marginal product (MP = ΔTP/ΔL) (loaves per worker)	Value of marginal product (VMP = MP × P) (dollars per worker)
A	0	0		
			7	14
B	1	7		
			...........**6**	**12**
C	**2**	13		
			5	10
D	3	18		
			4	8
E	4	22		
			3	6
F	5	25		

The value of the marginal product of labor equals the price of the product multiplied by marginal product of labor. If Angelo's hires 2 workers, the marginal product of the second worker is 6 loaves an hour (in the third column). The price of a loaf is $2, so the value of the marginal product of the second worker is $2 a loaf multiplied by 6 loaves an hour, which is $12 an hour (in fourth column).

one more worker. If the wage rate exceeds the value of marginal product of labor, a firm can increase its profit by firing one worker. But if the wage rate equals the value of the marginal product of labor, the firm cannot increase its profit by changing the number of workers it employs. The firm is making the maximum possible profit.

So the quantity of labor demanded by a firm is the quantity at which the value of the marginal product of labor equals the wage rate.

A Firm's Demand for Labor Curve

A firm's demand for labor curve is derived from its value of marginal product curve. Figure 18.1 shows these two curves. Figure 18.1(a) shows the value of marginal product curve at Angelo's Bakery. The blue bars graph the numbers in Table 18.1. The curve labeled *VMP* is Angelo's value of marginal product curve.

If the wage rate falls and other things remain the same, a firm hires more workers. Figure 18.1(b) shows Angelo's demand for labor curve.

Suppose the wage rate is $10 an hour. You can see in Fig.18.1(a) that if Angelo hires 2 workers, the value of the marginal product of labor is $12 an hour. At a wage rate of $10 an hour, Angelo makes a profit of $2 an hour on the second worker. If Angelo hires a third worker, the value of the marginal product of the that worker is $10 an hour. So on this third worker, Angelo breaks even.

If Angelo hired 4 workers, his profit would fall. The fourth worker generates a value of marginal product of only $8 an hour but costs $10 an hour, so Angelo does not hire 4 workers. When the wage rate is $10 an hour, the quantity of labor demanded by Angelo is 3 workers, which is a point on Angelo's demand for labor curve, *D*, in Fig. 18.2(b).

If the wage rate increased to $12 an hour, Angelo would decrease the quantity of labor demanded to 2 workers. If the wage rate decreased to $8 an hour, Angelo would increase the quantity of labor demanded to 4 workers.

A change in the wage rate brings a change in the quantity of labor demanded and a movement along the demand for labor curve.

A change in any other influence on a firm's labor-hiring plans changes the demand for labor and shifts the demand for labor curve.

FIGURE 18.1   The Demand for Labor at Angelo's Bakery

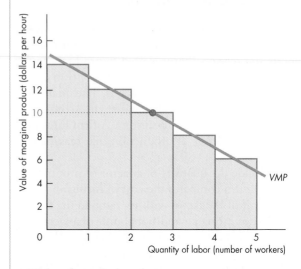

(a) Value of marginal product

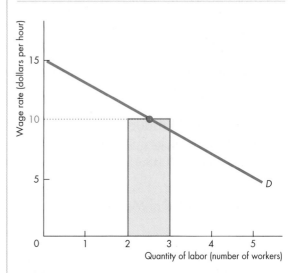

(b) Demand for labor

Angelo's Bakery can sell any quantity of bread at $2 a loaf. The blue bars in part (a) represent the firm's value of marginal product of labor (based on Table 18.1). The orange line is the firm's value of marginal product curve. Part (b) shows Angelo's demand for labor curve. Angelo hires the quantity of labor that makes the value of marginal product equal to the wage rate. The demand for labor curve slopes downward because the value of marginal product diminishes as the quantity of labor employed increases.

Changes in a Firm's Demand for Labor

A firm's demand for labor depends on

- The price of the firm's output
- The prices of other factors of production
- Technology

The Price of the Firm's Output The higher the price of a firm's output, the greater is the firm's demand for labor. The price of output affects the demand for labor through its influence on the value of marginal product of labor. A higher price for the firm's output increases the value of the marginal product of labor. A change in the price of a firm's output leads to a shift in the firm's demand for labor curve. If the price of the firm's output increases, the demand for labor increases and the demand for labor curve shifts rightward.

For example, if the price of bread increased to $3 a loaf, the value of the marginal product of Angelo's fourth worker would increase from $8 an hour to $12 an hour. At a wage rate of $10 an hour, Angelo would now hire 4 workers instead of 3.

The Prices of Other Factors of Production If the price of using capital decreases relative to the wage rate, a firm substitutes capital for labor and increases the quantity of capital it uses. Usually, the demand for labor will decrease when the price of using capital falls. For example, if the price of a bread-making machine falls, Angelo might decide to install one machine and lay off a worker. But the demand for labor could increase if the lower price of capital led to a sufficiently large increase in the scale of production. For example, with cheaper machines available, Angelo might install a machine and hire more labor to operate it. This type of factor substitution occurs in the long run when the firm can change the size of its plant.

Technology New technologies decrease the demand for some types of labor and increase the demand for other types. For example, if a new automated bread-making machine becomes available, Angelo might install one of these machines and fire most of his workforce—a decrease in the demand for bakery workers. But the firms that manufacture and service automated bread-making machines hire more labor, so there is an increase in the demand for this type of labor. An example occurred during the 1990s when electronic telephone exchanges decreased the demand for telephone operators and increased the demand for computer programmers and electronics engineers.

Table 18.2 summarizes the influences on a firm's demand for labor.

TABLE 18.2 A Firm's Demand for Labor

The Law of Demand
(Movements along the demand curve for labor)
The quantity of labor demanded by a firm

Decreases if:	Increases if:
■ The wage rate increases	■ The wage rate decreases

Changes in Demand
(Shifts in the demand curve for labor)
A firm's demand for labor

Decreases if:	Increases if:
■ The price of the firm's output decreases	■ The price of the firm's output increases
■ The price of a substitute for labor falls.	■ The price of a substitute for labor rises.
■ The price of a complement of labor rises.	■ The price of a complement of labor falls.
■ A new technology or new capital decreases the marginal product of labor	■ A new technology or new capital increases the marginal product of labor

---

Review Quiz

1 What is the value of marginal product of labor?
2 What is the relationship between the value of marginal product of labor and the marginal product of labor?
3 How is the demand for labor derived from the value of marginal product of labor?
4 What are the influences on the demand for labor?

myeconlab Work Study Plan 18.2 and get instant feedback.

Labor Markets

Labor services are traded in many different labor markets. Examples are markets for bakery workers, van drivers, crane operators, computer support specialists, air traffic controllers, surgeons, and economists. Some of these markets, such as the market for bakery workers, are local. They operate in a given urban area. Some labor markets, such as the market for air traffic controllers, are national. Firms and workers search across the nation for the right match of worker and job. And some labor markets are global, such as the market for super star hockey, basketball, and soccer players.

We'll look at a local market for bakery workers as an example. First, we'll look at a *competitive* labor market. Then, we'll see how monopoly elements can influence a labor market.

A Competitive Labor Market

A competitive labor market is one in which many firms demand labor and many households supply labor.

Market Demand for Labor Earlier in the chapter, you saw how an individual firm decides how much labor to hire. The market demand for labor is derived from the demand for labor by individual firms. We determine the market demand for labor by adding together the quantities of labor demanded by all the firms in the market at each wage rate. (The market demand for a good or service is derived in a similar way—see p. 110.)

Because each firm's demand for labor curve slopes downward, the market demand for labor curve also slopes downward.

The Market Supply of Labor The market supply of labor is derived from the supply of labor decisions made by individual households.

Individual's Labor Supply Decision People can allocate their time to two broad activities: labor supply and leisure. (Leisure is a catch-all term. It includes all activities other than supplying labor.) For most people, leisure is more fun than work so to induced them to work they must be offered a wage.

Think about the labor supply decision of Jill, one of the workers at Angelo's Bakery. Let's see how the wage rate influences the quantity of labor she is willing to supply.

Reservation Wage Rate Jill enjoys her leisure time, and she would be pleased if she didn't have to spend her time working at Angelo's Bakery. But Jill wants to earn an income, and as long as she can earn a wage rate of at least $5 an hour, she's willing to work. This wage is called her *reservation wage*. At any wage rate above her reservation wage, Jill supplies some labor.

The wage rate at Angelo's is $10 an hour, and at that wage rate, Jill chooses to work 30 hours a week. At a wage rate of $10 an hour, Jill regards this use of her time as the best available. Figure18.2 illustrates.

Backward-Bending Labor Supply Curve If Jill were offered a wage rate between $5 and $10 an hour, she would want to work fewer hours. If she were offered a wage rate above $10 an hour, she would want to work more hours, but only up to a point. If Jill could

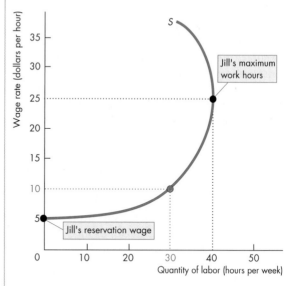

FIGURE 18.2 Jill's Labor Supply Curve

Jill's labor supply curve is *S*. Jill supplies no labor at wage rates below her reservation wage of $5 an hour. As the wage rate rises above $5 an hour, the quantity of labor that Jill supplies increases to a maximum of 40 hours a week at a wage rate of $25 an hour. As the wage rate rises above $25 an hour, Jill supplies a decreasing quantity of labor: her labor supply curve bends backward. The income effect on the demand for leisure dominates the substitution effect.

earn $25 an hour, she would be willing to work 40 hours a week (and earn $1,000 a week). But at a wage rate above $25 an hour, with the goods and services that Jill can buy for $1,000, her priority would be a bit more leisure time. So if the wage rate increased above $25 an hour, Jill would cut back on her work hours and take more leisure. Jill's labor supply curve eventually bends backward.

Jill's labor supply decisions are influenced by a substitution effect and an income effect.

Substitution Effect At wage rates below $25 an hour, the higher the wage rate Jill is offered, the greater is the quantity of labor that she supplies. Jill's wage rate is her *opportunity cost of leisure*. If she quits work an hour early to catch a movie, the cost of that extra hour of leisure is the wage rate that Jill forgoes. The higher the wage rate, the less willing Jill is to forgo the income and take the extra leisure time. This tendency for a higher wage rate to induce Jill to work longer hours is a *substitution effect*.

Income Effect The higher Jill's wage rate, the higher is her income. A higher income, other things remaining the same, induces Jill to increase her demand for most goods and services. Leisure is one of those goods. Because an increase in income creates an increase in the demand for leisure, it also creates a decrease in the quantity of labor supplied.

Market Supply Curve Jill's supply curve shows the quantity of labor supplied by Jill as her wage rate changes. Most people behave like Jill and have a backward bending labor supply curve, but they have different reservation wage rates and wage rates at which their labor supply curves bend backward.

A market supply curve shows the quantity of labor supplied by all households in a particular job market. It is found by adding together the quantities of labor supplied by all households to a given job market at each wage rate.

Also, along a supply curve in a particular job market, the wage rates available in other job markets remain the same. For example, along the supply curve of car-wash workers, the wage rates of car salespeople, mechanics, and all other labor are constant.

Despite the fact that an individual's labor supply curve eventually bends backward, the market supply curve of labor slopes upward. The higher the wage rate for car-wash workers, the greater is the quantity of labor supplied in that labor market.

Let's now look at labor market equilibrium.

Competitive Labor Market Equilibrium Labor market equilibrium determines the wage rate and employment. In Fig. 18.3, the market demand curve for bakery workers is D and the market supply curve of bakery workers is S. The equilibrium wage rate is $10 an hour, and the equilibrium quantity is 300 bakery workers. If the wage rate exceeded $10 an hour, there would be a surplus of bakery workers. More people would be looking for jobs in bakeries than firms were willing to hire. In such a situation, the wage rate would fall as firms found it easy to hire people at a lower wage rate. If the wage rate were less than $10 an hour, there would be a shortage of bakery workers. Firms would not be able to fill all the positions they had available. In this situation, the wage rate would rise as firms found it necessary to offer higher wages to attract labor. Only at a wage rate of $10 an hour are there no forces operating to change the wage rate.

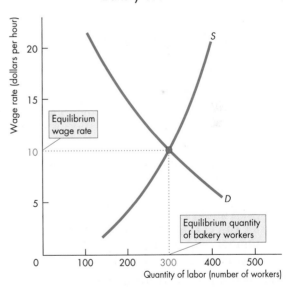

FIGURE 18.3   The Market for Bakery Workers

A competitive labor market coordinates firms' and households' plans. The market is in equilibrium—the quantity of labor demanded equals the quantity supplied at a wage rate of $10 an hour when 300 workers are employed. If the wage rate exceeds $10 an hour, the quantity supplied exceeds the quantity demanded and the wage rate will fall. If the wage rate is below $10 an hour, the quantity demanded exceeds the quantity supplied and the wage rate will rise.

A Labor Market with a Union

A **labor union** is an organized group of workers that aims to increase the wage rate and influence other job conditions. Let's see what happens when a union enters a competitive labor market.

Influences on Labor Supply One way of raising the wage rate is to decrease the supply of labor. In some labor markets, a union can restrict supply by controlling entry into apprenticeship programs or by influencing job qualification standards. Markets for skilled workers, doctors, dentists, and lawyers are the easiest ones to control in this way.

If there is an abundant supply of nonunion labor, a union can't decrease supply. For example, in the market for farm labor in southern California, the flow of nonunion labor from Mexico makes it difficult for a union to control the supply.

On the demand-side of the labor market, the union faces a tradeoff: The demand for labor curve slopes downward, so restricting supply to raise the wage rate costs jobs. For this reason, unions also try to influence the demand for union labor.

Influences on Labor Demand A union tries to increase the demand for the labor of its members in four main ways:

1. Increasing the value of marginal product of its members by organizing and sponsoring training schemes and apprenticeship programs, and by professional certification.
2. Lobbying for imports restrictions and encouraging people to buy goods made by unionized workers.
3. Supporting minimum wage laws, which increase the cost of employing low-skilled labor and lead firms to substitute high-skilled union labor for low-skilled nonunion labor.
4. Lobbying for restrictive immigration laws to decrease the supply of foreign workers.

Labor Market Equilibrium with a Union Figure 18.4 illustrates what happens to the wage rate and employment when a union successfully enters a competitive labor market. With no union, the demand curve is D_C, the supply curve is S_C, the wage rate is $10 an hour, and 300 workers have jobs.

Now a union enters this labor market. First, look at what happens if the union has sufficient control

FIGURE 18.4 A Union Enters a Competitive Labor Market

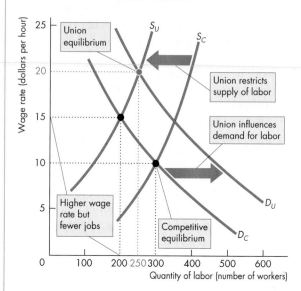

In a competitive labor market, the demand curve is D_C and the supply curve is S_C. The wage rate is $10 an hour and 300 workers are employed. If a union decreases the supply of labor and the supply of labor shifts to S_U, the wage rate rises to $15 an hour and employment decreases to 200 workers. If the union can also increase the demand for labor and shift the demand curve to D_U, the wage rate rises to $20 an hour and 250 workers are employed.

myeconlab animation

over the supply of labor to be able to restrict supply below its competitive level—to S_U. If that is all the union is able to do, employment falls to 200 workers and the wage rate rises to $15 an hour.

Suppose now that the union is also able to increase the demand for labor to D_U. The union can get an even bigger increase in the wage rate and with a smaller fall in employment. By maintaining the restricted labor supply at S_U, the union increases the wage rate to $20 an hour and achieves an employment level of 250 workers.

Because a union restricts the supply of labor in the market in which it operates, the union's actions spill over into nonunion markets. Workers who can't get union jobs must look elsewhere for work. This action increases the supply of labor in nonunion markets and lowers the wage rate in those markets. This spillover effect further widens the gap between union and nonunion wages.

Monopsony in the Labor Market Not all labor markets in which unions operate are competitive. Rather, they are labor markets in which the employer possesses market power and the union enters to try to counteract that power.

A market in which there is a single buyer is called a **monopsony**. A monopsony labor market has one employer. In some parts of the country, managed health-care organizations are the major employer of health-care professionals. In some communities, Wal-Mart is the main employer of sales clerks. These firms have monopsony power.

A monopsony acts on the buying side of a market in a similar way to a monopoly on the selling side. The firm maximizes profit by hiring the quantity of labor that makes the marginal cost of labor equal to the value of marginal product of labor and by paying the lowest wage rate at which it can attract this quantity of labor.

Figure 18.5 illustrates a monopsony labor market. Like all firms, a monopsony faces a downward-sloping value of marginal product curve, *VMP,* which is its demand for labor curve, *D*—the curve *VMP = D* in the figure.

What is special about monopsony is the marginal cost of labor. For a firm in a competitive labor market, the marginal cost of labor is the wage rate. For a monopsony, the marginal cost of labor exceeds the wage rate. The reason is that being the only buyer in the market, the firm faces an upward-sloping labor supply curve—the curve *S* in the figure.

To attract one more worker, the monopsony must offer a higher wage rate. But it must pay this higher wage rate to all its workers, so the marginal cost of a worker is the wage rate plus the increased wage bill that arises from paying all the workers the higher wage rate.

The supply curve is now the average cost of labor curve and the relationship between the supply curve and the marginal cost of labor curve, *MCL,* is similar to that between a monopoly's demand curve and marginal revenue curve (see p. 302). The relationship between the supply curve and the *MCL* curve is also similar to that between a firm's average cost curve and marginal cost curve (see pp. 258–259).

To find the profit-maximizing quantity of labor to hire, the monopsony sets the marginal cost of labor equal to the value of marginal product of labor. In Fig. 18.5, this outcome occurs when the firm employs 100 workers.

To hire 100 workers, the firm must pay $10 an hour (on the supply of labor curve). Each worker is paid $10 an hour, but the value of marginal product of labor is $20 an hour, so the firm makes an economic profit of $10 an hour on the marginal worker.

If the labor market in Fig. 18.5 were competitive, equilibrium wage rate and employment would be determined by the demand and supply curves. The wage rate would be $15 an hour, and 150 workers would be employed. So compared with a competitive labor market, a monopsony pays a lower wage rate and employs fewer workers.

A Union and a Monopsony A union is like a monopoly. If the union (monopoly seller) faces a monopsony buyer, the situation is called **bilateral monopoly**. The Writers Guild of America that represents film, television, and radio writers, and an alliance that represents CBS, MGM, NBC, and other entertainment

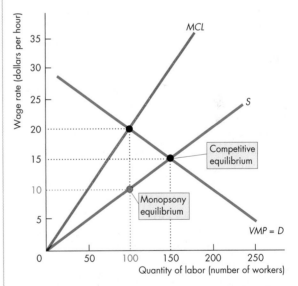

FIGURE 18.5   A Monopsony Labor Market

A monopsony is a market structure in which there is a single buyer. A monopsony in the labor market has a value of marginal product curve *VMP* and faces a labor supply curve *S.* The marginal cost of labor curve is *MCL.* Making the marginal cost of labor equal to value of marginal product maximizes profit. The monopsony hires 100 hours of labor and pays the lowest wage rate for which that quantity of labor will work, which is $10 an hour.

companies is an example of bilateral monopoly. Every three years, the Writers Guild and the alliance negotiate a pay deal.

The outcome of bargaining depends on the costs that each party can inflict on the other. The firm can shut down the plant and lock out its workers, and the workers can shut down the plant by striking. Each party estimates the other's strength and what it will lose if it does not agree to the other's demands.

Usually, an agreement is reached without a strike or a lockout. The threat is usually enough to bring the bargaining parties to an agreement. When a strike or lockout does occur, it is because one party has misjudged the costs each party can inflict on the other. Such an event occurred in November 2007 when the writers and entertainment producers failed to agree on a compensation deal. A 100-day strike followed that ended up costing the entertainment industry an estimated $2 billion.

In the example in Fig. 18.5, if the union and employer are equally strong, and each party knows the strength of the other, they will agree to split the gap between $10 (the wage rate on the supply curve) and $20 (the wage rate on the demand curve) and agree to a wage rate of $15 an hour.

You've now seen that in a monopsony, a union can bargain for a higher wage rate without sacrificing jobs. A similar outcome can arise in a monopsony labor market when a minimum wage law is enforced. Let's look at the effect of a minimum wage.

Monopsony and the Minimum Wage In a competitive labor market, a minimum wage that exceeds the equilibrium wage decreases employment (see pp. 133–134). In a monopsony labor market, a minimum wage can increase both the wage rate and employment. Let's see how.

Figure 18.6 shows a monopsony labor market without a union. The wage rate is $10 an hour and 100 workers are employed.

A minimum wage law is passed that requires employers to pay at least $15 an hour. The monopsony now faces a perfectly elastic supply of labor at $15 an hour up to 150 workers (along the minimum wage line). To hire more than 150 workers, a wage rate above $15 an hour must be paid (along the supply curve). Because the wage rate is $15 an hour up to 150 workers, so is the marginal cost of labor $15 an hour up to 150 workers. To maximize profit, the monopsony sets the marginal cost of labor equal to the value of marginal product of

FIGURE 18.6 Minimum Wage Law in Monopsony

In a monopsony labor market, the wage rate is $10 an hour and 100 workers are hired. If a minimum wage law increases the wage rate to $15 an hour, the wage rate rises to this level and employment increases to 150 workers.

myeconlab   animation

labor (on the demand curve). That is, the monopsony hires 150 workers and pays $15 an hour. The minimum wage law has succeeded in raising the wage rate and increasing the amount of labor employed.

The Scale of the Union–Nonunion Wage Gap

You've seen how a union can influence the wage rate, but how much of a difference to wage rates do unions actually make? This question is difficult to answer. To measure the difference in wages attributable to unions, economists have looked at the wages of unionized and nonunionized workers who do similar work and have similar skills.

The evidence based on these comparisons is that the union–nonunion wage gap lies between 10 and 25 percent of the wage. For example, unionized airline pilots earn about 25 percent more than nonunion pilots with the same level of skill. In markets that have only a union wage rate, we might presume that the wage rate is 10 to 25 percent higher than it would be in the absence of a union.

Wage Rates in the United States
How School Pays

In 2007, the average wage rate in the United States was a bit less than $20 an hour. The figure shows the *average hourly wage rates* for twenty jobs selected from the more than 700 jobs for which the Bureau of Labor Statistics reports wage rate data.

You can see that a surgeon, on average, earns more than 11 times as much per hour as a fast-food worker and more than twice as much as an economist. Remember that these numbers are averages. Individual surgeons earn much more or much less than the average surgeon.

Many more occupations earn a wage rate below the national average than above it. And most of the occupations that earn more than the national average require a college degree and postgraduate training.

Earning differences are explained by differences in the value of the marginal product of the skills in the various occupations and in market power.

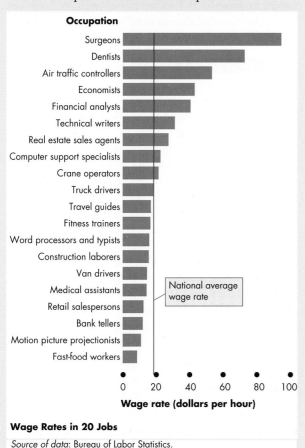

Wage Rates in 20 Jobs

Source of data: Bureau of Labor Statistics.

Trends and Differences in Wage Rates

You can use what you've learned about labor markets to explain the trends and differences in wage rates.

Wage rates increase over time—trend upward. The reason is that the value of marginal product of labor trends upward. Technological change and the new types of capital that it brings make workers more productive. With greater labor productivity, the demand for labor increases and so does the average wage rate. Even jobs in which productivity doesn't increase experience an increase in the *value* of marginal product. Child care is an example. A child-care worker can't care for an increasing number of children, but an increasing number of parents who earn high wages are willing to hire child-care workers. The *value* of marginal product of these workers increases.

Wage rates are unequal, and in recent years, they have become increasingly unequal. High wage rates have increased rapidly while low wage rates have stagnated or even fallen. The reasons are complex and not fully understood.

One reason is that the new technologies of the 1990s and 2000s made skilled workers more productive and destroyed some low-skilled jobs. An example is the ATM, which took the jobs and lowered the wage rate of bank tellers and created the jobs and increased the wage rates of computer programmers and electronic engineers. Another reason is that globalization has brought increased competition for low-skilled workers and opened global markets for high-skilled workers.

Review Quiz

1 What determines the amount of labor that households plan to supply?
2 How is the wage rate and employment determined in a competitive labor market?
3 How do labor unions influence wage rates?
4 What is a monopsony and why is a monopsony able to pay a lower wage rate than a firm in a competitive labor market?
5 How is the wage rate determined when a union faces a monopsony?
6 What is the effect of a minimum wage law in a monopsony labor market?

 Work Study Plan 18.3 and get instant feedback.

Capital and Natural Resource Markets

The markets for capital and land can be understood by using the same basic ideas that you've seen when studying a competitive labor market. But markets for nonrenewable natural resources are different. We'll now examine three groups of factor markets:

- Capital rental markets
- Land rental markets
- Nonrenewable natural resource markets

Capital Rental Markets

The demand for capital is derived from the *value of marginal product of capital*. Profit-maximizing firms hire the quantity of capital services that makes the value of marginal product of capital equal to the *rental rate of capital*. The *lower* the rental rate of capital, other things remaining the same, the *greater* is the quantity of capital demanded. The supply of capital responds in the opposite way to the rental rate. The *higher* the rental rate, other things remaining the same, the *greater* is the quantity of capital supplied. The equilibrium rental rate makes the quantity of capital demanded equal to the quantity supplied.

Figure 18.7 illustrates the rental market for tower cranes—capital used to construct high-rise buildings. The value of marginal product and the demand curve is *VMP = D*. The supply curve is *S*. The equilibrium rental rate is $1,000 per day and 100 tower cranes are rented.

Rent-Versus-Buy Decision Some capital services are obtained in a rental market like the market for tower cranes. And like tower cranes, many of the world's large airlines rent their airplanes. But not all capital services are obtained in a rental market. Instead, firms buy the capital equipment that they use. You saw in Chapter 10 (pp. 228–229) that the cost of the services of the capital that a firm owns and operates itself is an implicit rental rate that arises from depreciation and interest costs. Firms that buy capital *implicitly* rent the capital to themselves.

The decision to obtain capital services in a rental market rather than buy capital and rent it implicitly is made to minimize cost. The firm compares the cost of explicitly renting the capital and the cost of buying and implicitly renting it. This decision is the same as

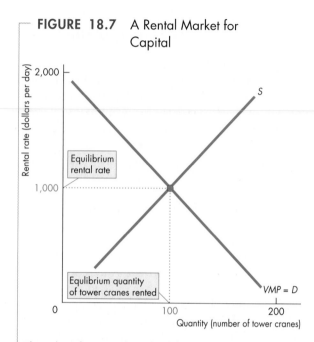

FIGURE 18.7 A Rental Market for Capital

The value of marginal product of tower cranes, *VMP*, determines the demand, *D*, for tower crane rentals. With the supply curve, *S*, the equilibrium rental rate is $1,000 a day and 100 cranes are rented.

myeconlab   animation

the one that a household makes in deciding whether to rent or buy a home.

To make a rent-versus-buy decision, a firm must compare a cost incurred in the *present* with a stream of rental costs incurred over some *future* period. The Mathematical Note (pp. 434–435) explains how to make this comparison by calculating the *present value* of a future amount of money. If the *present value* of the future rental payments of an item of capital equipment exceeds the cost of buying the capital, the firm will buy the equipment. If the *present value* of the future rental payments of an item of capital equipment is less than the cost of buying the capital, the firm will rent (or lease) the equipment.

Land Rental Markets

The demand for land is based on the same factors as the demand for labor and the demand for capital—the *value of marginal product of land*. Profit-maximizing firms rent the quantity of land at which the value of marginal product of land is equal to the *rental rate of land*. The *lower* the rental rate, other things remaining the same, the *greater* is the quantity of land demanded.

But the supply of land is special: Its quantity is fixed, so the quantity supplied cannot be changed by people's decisions. The supply of each particular block of land is perfectly inelastic.

The equilibrium rental rate makes the quantity of land demanded equal to the quantity available. Figure 18.8 illustrates the market for a 10-acre block of land on 42nd Street in New York City. The quantity supplied is fixed and the supply curve is *S*. The value of marginal product and the demand curve is *VMP* = *D*. The equilibrium rental rate is $1,000 an acre per day.

The rental rate of land is high in New York because the willingness to pay for the services produced by that land is high, which makes the *VMP* of land high. A Big Mac costs more at McDonald's on 42nd Street, New York, than at McDonald's on Jefferson Avenue, St. Louis, but not because the rental rate of land is higher in New York. The rental rate of land is higher in New York because of the greater willingness to pay for a Big Mac (and other goods and services) in New York.

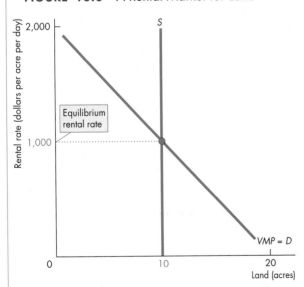

FIGURE 18.8 A Rental Market for Land

The value of marginal product of a 10-acre block, *VMP*, determines the rental demand, *D*, for this land. With the supply curve, *S*, the block rents for $10,000 a day.

Nonrenewable Natural Resource Markets

The nonrenewable natural resources are oil, gas, and coal. Burning one of these fuels converts it to energy and other by-products, and the used resource cannot be re-used. The natural resources that we use to make metals are also nonrenewable, but they can be used again, at some cost, by recycling them.

Oil, gas, and coal are traded in global commodity markets. The price of a given grade of crude oil is the same in New York, London, and Singapore. Traders, linked by telephone and the Internet, operate these markets around the clock every day of the year.

Demand and supply determine the prices and the quantities traded in these commodity markets. We'll look at the influences on demand and supply by considering the global market for crude oil.

The Demand for Oil The two key influences on the demand for oil are

1. The *value of marginal product* of oil
2. The expected future price of oil

The value of marginal product of oil is the *fundamental* influence on demand. It works in exactly the same way for a nonrenewable resource as it does for any other factor of production. The greater the quantity of oil used, the smaller is the value of marginal product of oil. Diminishing value of marginal product makes the demand curve slope downward. The lower the price, the greater is the quantity demanded.

The higher the expected future price of oil, the greater is the present demand for oil. The expected future price is a *speculative* influence on demand. Oil in the ground and oil in storage tanks are inventories that can be held or sold. A trader might plan to buy oil to hold now and to sell it later for a profit. Instead of buying oil to hold and sell later, the trader could buy a bond and earn interest. The forgone interest is the opportunity cost of holding the oil. If the price of oil is expected to rise by a bigger percentage than the interest rate, a trader will hold oil and incur the opportunity cost. In this case, the return from holding oil exceeds the return from holding bonds.

The Supply of Oil The three key influences on the supply of oil are

1. The known oil reserves
2. The scale of current oil production facilities
3. The expected future price of oil

Known oil reserves are the oil that has been discovered and can be extracted with today's technology. This quantity increases over time because advances in technology enable ever less accessible sources to be discovered. The greater the size of known reserves, the greater is the supply of oil. But this influence on supply is small and indirect. It operates by changing the expected distant future price of oil. Even a major new discovery of oil would have a negligible effect on current supply.

The scale of current oil production facilities is the *fundamental* influence on supply. Producing oil is like any production activity: it is subject to increasing marginal cost. The increasing marginal cost of extracting oil means that the supply curve of oil slopes upward. The higher the price of oil, the greater is the quantity supplied. When new oil wells are sunk or when new faster pumps are installed, the supply of oil increases. When existing wells run dry, the supply of oil decreases. Over time, the factors that increase supply are more powerful than those that decrease supply, so changes in the fundamental influence increase the supply of oil.

Speculative forces based on expectations about the future price also influence the supply of oil. The *higher* the expected future price of oil, the *smaller* is the present supply of oil. A trader with an oil inventory might plan to sell now or to hold and sell later. You've seen that forgone interest is the opportunity cost of holding the oil. If the price of oil is expected to rise by a bigger percentage than the interest rate, it is profitable to incur the opportunity cost of holding oil rather than selling it immediately.

The Equilibrium Price of Oil The demand for oil and the supply of oil determine the equilibrium price and quantity traded. Figure 18.9 illustrates the market equilibrium.

The value of marginal product of oil, *VMP*, is the *fundamental determinant of demand*, and the marginal cost of extraction, *MC*, is the *fundamental determinant of supply*. Together, they determine the *market fundamentals price*.

If expectations about the future price are also based on fundamentals, the equilibrium price is the market fundamentals price. But if expectations about the future price of oil depart from what the market fundamentals imply, *speculation* can drive a wedge between the equilibrium price and the market fundamentals price.

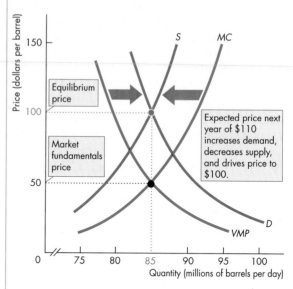

FIGURE 18.9 A Nonrenewable Natural Resource Market

The value of marginal product of a natural resource, *VMP*, and the marginal cost of extraction, *MC*, determine the *market fundamentals* price. Demand, *D*, and supply, *S*, which determine the equilibrium price, are influenced by the expected future price. Speculation can bring a gap between the market fundamentals price and the equilibrium price.

myeconlab   animation

The Hotelling Principle Harold Hotelling, an economist at Columbia University, had an incredible idea: Traders expect the price of a nonrenewable natural resource to rise at a rate equal to the interest rate. We call this idea the **Hotelling Principle.** Let's see why it is correct.

You've seen that the interest rate is the opportunity cost of holding an oil inventory. If the price of oil is expected to rise at a rate that exceeds the interest rate, it is profitable to hold a bigger inventory. Demand increases, supply decreases, and the price rises. If the interest rate exceeds the rate at which the price of oil is expected to rise, it is not profitable to hold an oil inventory. Demand decreases, supply increases, and the price falls. But if the price of oil is expected to rise at a rate equal to the interest rate, holding an inventory of oil is just as good as holding bonds. Demand and supply don't change and the price does not change. Only when the price of oil is expected to rise at a rate equal to the interest rate is the price at its equilibrium.

The World and U.S. Markets for Oil
Diverse Sources and Wild Prices

The world produced about 31 billion barrels of oil in 2008 and the price shot upward from $85 in January to $135 in June. The high price of oil and dependence on foreign supplies became major political issues.

Although the United States imports almost three quarters of its oil from other countries, much of it comes from close to home. Figure 1 provides the details: Only 14 percent of the U.S. oil supply comes from the Middle East and more than one third comes from Canada, Mexico, and other Western Hemisphere nations.

Even if the United States produced all its own oil, it would still face a fluctuating global price. U.S. producers would not willingly sell to U.S. buyers for a price below the world price. So energy independence doesn't mean an independent oil price.

The Hotelling Principle tells us that we must expect the price of oil to rise at a rate equal to the interest rate. But expecting the price to rise at a rate equal to the interest rate doesn't mean that the price will rise at this rate. As you can see in Fig. 2, the price of oil over the past 50 or so years has not followed the path predicted by the Hotelling Principle.

The future is unpredictable and expectations about future prices keep changing. The forces that influence expectations are not well understood. The expected future price of oil depends on its expected future rate of use and the rate of discovery of new sources of supply. One person's expectation about a future price also depends on guesses about other

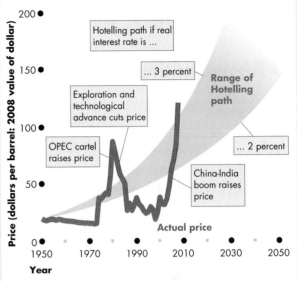

Figure 2 The Price of Oil and Its Hotelling Path

people's expectations. These guesses can change abruptly and become self-reinforcing. When the expected future price of oil changes for whatever reason, demand and supply change, and so does the price. Prices in speculative markets are always volatile.

Review Quiz

1 What determines demand and supply in rental markets for capital and land?
2 What determines the demand for a nonrenewable natural resource?
3 What determines the supply of a nonrenewable natural resource?
4 What is the market fundamentals price and how might it differ from the equilibrium price?
5 Explain the Hotelling Principle.

myeconlab Work Study Plan 18.4 and get instant feedback.

◆ *Reading Between the Lines* on pp. 432–433 focuses on the market for oil and the political debate about increasing U.S. domestic production.

The next chapter looks at how the market economy distributes income and explains the trends in the distribution of income. The chapter also looks at the efforts by governments to redistribute income and modify the market outcome.

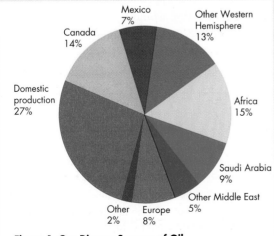

Figure 1 Our Diverse Sources of Oil

The Oil Market in Action

Offshore Drilling Backed as Remedy for Oil Prices

http://www.washingtonpost.com
July 14, 2008

… Polls show that Americans, pressed by high gasoline prices, may be open to offshore drilling. In a May Gallup poll, 57 percent of people surveyed were willing to allow drilling in coastal and wilderness areas currently off limits, if it had the potential to reduce high gas prices. …

The debate over offshore drilling has been muddied by a variety of claims about how much oil and gas might lie under the sea, what it would take to get hold of it and what the impact would be.

… [T]he U.S. Geological Survey estimates that there are "undiscovered conventionally recoverable resources" of 17.8 billion barrels. That's not the same thing as "reserves." In the oil business, "reserves" refers to oil that has been found and "proven," whereas "resources" refers to promising geological structures where the presence of oil remains uncertain.

In the eastern Gulf of Mexico, those "resources" are likely to represent actual oil because the geology is an extension of the western Gulf of Mexico, where oil has been drilled for years. There is less certainty about what may lie off the Atlantic coast.

If, in fact, there are 17.8 billion barrels of oil offshore, that would equal half the reserves of Nigeria or about 60 percent of proven U.S. reserves. It could substantially reduce U.S. imports for a decade or two or sustain U.S. production when other fields decline.

But developing those resources would take time. A report last year by the Energy Department's Energy Information Administration said that "access to the Pacific, Atlantic, and eastern Gulf regions would not have a significant impact on domestic crude oil and natural gas production or prices before 2030. Leasing would begin no sooner than 2012, and production would not be expected to start before 2017." It added, "Because oil prices are determined on the international market, however, any impact on average wellhead prices is expected to be insignificant." …

Essence of the Story

- 57 percent of respondents in a Gallup poll want to allow drilling for oil and gas in U.S. coastal waters and wilderness if it would lower the price of gasoline.

- The U.S. Geological Survey estimates "undiscovered conventionally recoverable resources" of 17.8 billion barrels.

- Proven reserves will likely equal half the 17.8 billion barrels of offshore oil—equivalent to half the reserves of Nigeria or 60 percent of proven U.S. reserves.

- The first oil and gas would flow in 2017.

- Full-scale production and an impact on price would become significant only after 2030.

Economic Analysis

- The market for oil is a global market, and demand and supply in the global oil market determine the price.

- Both demand and supply depend on expectations of the future price of oil.

- An expected future increase in production increases the expected future supply and lowers the expected future price. A lower expected future price immediately decreases demand, increases supply, and lowers the current price.

- The amount by which the current price falls depends on (1) the number of years in the future when the change in supply is expected to occur, (2) the expected increase in supply, and (3) the elasticity of demand.

- Using the ideas just reviewed, we can work out the likely effect of a decision by Congress to authorize off-shore oil production in the United States.

- Based on the information provided in the news article, production would be expected to increase somewhat in 2017 and be in full operation by 2030.

- The quantity of oil likely to be found is guessed at 50 percent of the quantity in Nigeria. If we assume that production will also be 50 percent of Nigerian production, then U.S. oil production and global oil production, other things remaining the same, will increase by 1 million barrels per day.

- The demand for oil is inelastic, and we will assume that the elasticity is 0.1.

- An elasticity of demand equal to 0.1 means that a 10 percent rise in price brings a 1 percent decrease in the quantity demanded, other things remaining the same.

- It also means that a 1 percent increase in the quantity brings a 10 percent decrease in price, other things remaining the same.

- World oil production in 2009 was approximately 85 million barrels a day. So an increase of 1 million barrels is an increase of a bit more than 1 percent (1.18 percent).

- This percentage increase in the quantity would lower the price by 11.8 percent (10 times the percentage change in the quantity).

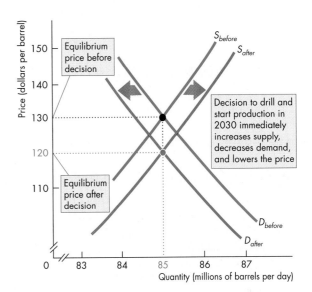

Figure 1 The global market for crude oil

- This percentage fall in the price is expected to occur when production is in full operation in 2030.

- To translate the price fall to its effects in 2009, we use the Hotelling Principle and the concept of present value (see Mathematical Note).

- The Hotelling Principle tells us that the price is expected to rise at a rate equal to the interest rate.

- Assume an interest rate of 2 percent a year. Then the price in 2030 is expected to be just over 50 percent higher than the price in 2009. ($1.02^{21} = 1.52$)

- Because the price in 2030 is expected to fall by 11.8 percent, the price today will fall by 11.8/1.52, or 7.8 percent.

- The figure illustrates what happens in 2009 if a decision is made to produce offshore oil. Demand decreases and supply increases immediately to reflect the lower expected future price and the price falls immediately.

- In the figure, the price in 2009 is assumed to be $130 a barrel. So a 7.8 percent fall in the price means price will fall by $10 to $120 (rounding to the nearest dollar).

MATHEMATICAL NOTE

Present Value and Discounting

Rent-Versus-Buy Decision

To decide whether to rent an item of capital equipment or to buy the capital and implicitly rent it, a firm must compare the present expenditure on the capital with the future rental cost of the capital.

Comparing Current and Future Dollars

To compare a present expenditure with a future expenditure, we convert the future expenditure to its "present value."

The **present value** of a future amount of money is the amount that, if invested today, will grow to be as large as that future amount when the interest that it will earn is taken into account.

So the present value of a future amount of money is smaller than the future amount. The calculation that we use to convert a future amount of money to its present value is called **discounting**.

The easiest way to understand discounting and present value is to first consider its opposite: How a present value grows to a future amount of money because of *compound interest*.

Compound Interest

Compound interest is the interest on an initial investment plus the interest on the interest that the investment has previously earned. Because of compound interest, a present amount of money (a present value) grows into a larger future amount. The future amount is equal to the present amount (present value) plus the interest it will earn in the future. That is,

Future amount = Present value + Interest income.

The interest in the first year is equal to the present value multiplied by the interest rate, r, so

Amount after 1 year = Present value +
$\qquad\qquad\qquad\quad$ (r × Present value).

or

Amount after 1 year = Present value × $(1 + r)$.

If you invest $100 today and the interest rate is 10 percent a year ($r = 0.1$), one year from today you will have $110—the original $100 plus $10 interest.

Check that the above formula delivers that answer: $100 × 1.1 = $110.

If you leave this $110 invested to earn 10 percent during a second year, at the end of that year you will have

Amount after 2 years = Present value × $(1 + r)^2$.

With the numbers of the previous example, you invest $100 today at an interest rate of 10 percent a year ($r = 0.1$). After one year you will have $110—the original $100 plus $10 interest. And after the second year, you will have $121. In the second year, you earned $10 on your initial $100 plus $1 on the $10 interest that you earned in the first year.

Check that the above formula delivers that answer: $100 × (1.1)^2 = $100 × 1.21 = $121.

If you leave your $100 invested for n years, it will grow to

Amount after n years = Present value × $(1 + r)^n$.

With an interest rate of 10 percent a year, your $100 will grow to $195 after 7 years ($n = 7$)—almost double the present value of $100.

Discounting a Future Amount

We have just calculated future amounts one year, two years, and n years in the future, knowing the present value and the interest rate. To calculate the present value of these future amounts, we just work backward.

To find the present value of an amount one year in the future, we divide the future amount by $(1 + r)$.

That is,

$$\text{Present value} = \frac{\text{Amount of money one year in future}}{(1 + r)}.$$

Let's check that we can use the present value formula by calculating the present value of $110 one year from now when the interest rate is 10 percent a year. You'll be able to guess that the answer is $100 because we just calculated that $100 invested today at 10 percent a year becomes $110 in one year. So the present value of $110 one year from today is $100. But let's use the formula. Putting the numbers into the above formula, we have

$$\text{Present value} = \frac{\$110}{(1 + 0.1)}$$

$$= \frac{\$110}{1.1} = \$100.$$

To calculate the present value of an amount of money two years in the future, we use the formula:

$$\text{Present value} = \frac{\text{Amount of money two years in future}}{(1 + r)^2}.$$

Use this formula to calculate the present value of $121 two years from now at an interest rate of 10 percent a year. With these numbers, the formula gives

$$\text{Present value} = \frac{\$121}{(1 + 0.1)^2}$$

$$= \frac{\$121}{(1.1)^2}$$

$$= \frac{\$121}{1.21}$$

$$= \$100$$

We can calculate the present value of an amount of money n years in the future by using the general formula

$$\text{Present value} = \frac{\text{Amount of money } n \text{ years in future}}{(1 + r)^n}.$$

For example, if the interest rate is 10 percent a year, $100 to be received 10 years from now has a present value of $38.55. That is, if $38.55 is invested today at 10 percent a year it will accumulate to $100 in 10 years.

Present Value of a Sequence of Future Amounts

You've seen how to calculate the present value of an amount of money one year, two years, and n years in the future. Most practical applications of present value calculate the present value of a sequence of future amounts of money that are spread over several years. An airline's payment of rent for the lease of airplanes is an example.

To calculate the present value of a sequence of amounts over several years, we use the formula you have learned and apply it to each year. We then sum the present values for all the years to find the present value of the sequence of amounts.

For example, suppose that a firm expects to pay $100 a year for each of the next five years and the interest rate is 10 percent a year ($r = 0.1$). The present value (PV) of these five payments of $100 each is calculated by using the following formula:

$$PV = \frac{\$100}{1.1} + \frac{\$100}{1.1^2} + \frac{\$100}{1.1^3} + \frac{\$100}{1.1^4} + \frac{\$100}{1.1^5},$$

which equals

$$PV = \$90.91 + \$82.64 + \$75.13 + \$68.30 + \$62.09$$
$$= \$379.07.$$

You can see that the firm pays $500 over five years. But because the money is paid in the future, it is not worth $500 today. Its present value is only $379.07. And the farther in the future the money is paid, the smaller is its present value. The $100 paid one year in the future is worth $90.91 today, but the $100 paid five years in the future is worth only $62.09 today.

The Decision

If this firm could lease a machine for five years at $100 a year or buy the machine for $500, it would jump at leasing. Only if the firm could buy the machine for less than $379.07 would it want to buy.

Many personal and business decisions turn on calculations like the one you've just made. A decision to buy or rent an apartment, to lease or rent a car, to pay off a student loan or let the loan run another year can all be made using the above calculation.

SUMMARY

Key Points

The Anatomy of Factor Markets (p. 418)

- The factor markets are: job markets for labor; rental markets (often implicit rental markets) for capital and land; and global commodity markets for nonrenewable natural resources.
- The services of entrepreneurs are not traded on a factor market.

The Demand for a Factor of Production (pp. 419–421)

- The value of marginal product determines the demand for a factor of production.
- The value of marginal product decreases as the quantity of the factor employed increases.
- The firm employs the quantity of each factor of production that makes the value of marginal product equal to the factor price.

Labor Markets (pp. 422–427)

- The value of marginal product of labor determines the demand for labor. A rise in the wage rate brings a decrease in the quantity demanded.
- The quantity of labor supplied depends on the wage rate. At low wage rates, a rise in the wage rate increases the quantity supplied. Beyond a high enough wage rate, a rise in the wage rate decreases the quantity supplied—the supply curve eventually bends backward.
- Demand and supply determine the wage rate in a competitive labor market.
- A labor union can raise the wage rate by restricting the supply or increasing the demand for labor.
- A monopsony can lower the wage rate below the competitive level.
- A union or a minimum wage in monopsony labor market can raise the wage rate without a fall in employment.

Capital and Natural Resource Markets (pp. 428–431)

- The value of marginal product of capital (and land) determines the demand for capital (and land).
- Firms make a rent-versus-buy decision by choosing the option that minimizes cost.
- The supply of land is inelastic and the demand for land determines the rental rate.
- The demand for a nonrenewable natural resource depends on the value of marginal product and on the expected future price.
- The supply of a nonrenewable natural resource depends on the known reserves, the cost of extraction, and the expected future price.
- The price of nonrenewable natural resources can differ from the market fundamentals price because of speculation based on expectations about the future price.
- The price of a nonrenewable natural resource is expected to rise at a rate equal to the interest rate.

Key Figures and Tables

Key Terms

PROBLEMS and APPLICATIONS

 Work problems 1–10 in Chapter 18 Study Plan and get instant feedback.
Work problems 11–19 as Homework, a Quiz, or a Test if assigned by your instructor.

1. Wanda owns a fish shop. She employs students to sort and pack the fish. Students can pack the following amounts of fish in an hour:

Number of students	Quantity of fish (pounds)
1	20
2	50
3	90
4	120
5	145
6	165
7	180
8	190

The fish market is competitive and Wanda can sell her fish for 50¢ a pound. The market for packers is competitive and their market wage rate is $7.50 an hour.
   a. Calculate the marginal product of the students and draw the marginal product curve.
   b. Calculate the value of marginal product of labor and draw the value of marginal product curve.
   c. Find Wanda's demand for labor curve.
   d. How many students does Wanda employ?

2. Back at Wanda's fish shop described in problem 1, the market price of fish falls to 33.33¢ a pound but the wage rate of fish packers remains at $7.50 an hour.
   a. How does the students' marginal product change?
   b. How does the value of marginal product of labor change?
   c. How does Wanda's demand for labor change?
   d. What happens to the number of students that Wanda employs?

3. Back at Wanda's fish shop described in problem 1, packers' wages increase to $10 an hour but the price of fish remains at 50¢ a pound.
   a. What happens to the value of marginal product of labor?
   b. What happens to Wanda's demand for labor curve?
   c. How many students does Wanda employ?

4. **In Modern Rarity, Workers Form Union at Small Chain**
   Among the thousands of stores in New York's low-income neighborhoods, labor unions have virtually no presence, except in a few supermarkets. But in a remarkable culmination to a yearlong struggle, 95 workers at a chain of 10 sneaker stores have formed a union. ... On Jan. 18, after three months of negotiations, the two sides signed a contract. The three-year accord sets wages at $7.25 an hour, rising to $7.50 on July 1.
   The New York Times, February 5, 2006
   a. Why are labor unions scarce in New York's low-income neighborhoods?
   b. Who wins from this new union contract? Who loses?
   c. How can this union try to change the demand for labor?

5. Which of the following items are nonrenewable natural resources, which are renewable natural resources, and which are not natural resources? Explain your answers.
   a. Trump Tower
   b. Lake Michigan
   c. Coal in a West Virginia coal mine
   d. The Internet
   e. Yosemite National Park
   f. Power generated by wind turbines

6. **Trump Group Selling Parcel For $1.8 Billion**
   A consortium of Hong Kong investors and Donald J. Trump are selling a stretch of riverfront land and three buildings on the Upper West Side for about $1.8 billion in the largest residential sale in city history. ... If it is completed, ... the deal should be a windfall for the investors and Mr. Trump, who acquired the land for less than $100 million a decade ago during a real estate recession. ...
   The New York Times, June 1, 2005
   a. Why has the price of land on the Upper West Side of New York City increased over the last decade? Include in your answer a discussion of the demand for land and the supply of land.
   b. Use a graph to show why the price of land on

the Upper West Side of New York City increased over the last decade.

   c. Is the supply of land on the Upper West Side perfectly inelastic?

7. Keshia operates a bookkeeping service. She is considering buying or leasing some new laptop computers. The purchase price of a laptop is $1,500 and after three years it is worthless. The annual lease rate is $550 per laptop. The value of marginal product of one laptop is $700 a year. The value of marginal product of a second laptop is $625 a year. The value of marginal product of a third laptop is $575 a year. And the value of marginal product of a fourth laptop is $500 a year.

   a. How many laptops will Keshia lease or buy?

   b. If the interest rate is 4 percent a year, will Keshia lease or buy her laptops?

   c. If the interest rate is 6 percent a year, will Keshia lease or buy her laptops?

8. **British Construction Activity Falls**

Construction activity in Britain declined in June at the fastest rate in 11 years ... and a major home builder said it had been unable to raise more capital—both signs of worsening conditions in the battered housing industry. ... Construction employment declined in June after 23 months of growth. ... The housing market has been hit by falling prices. ... Average house prices in the United Kingdom fell 0.9 percent in June, the eighth consecutive month of declines, leaving the average 6.3 percent below June 2007.

Forbes, July 2, 2008

   a. Explain how a fall in house prices influences the market for construction labor.

   b. Draw a graph to illustrate the effect of a fall in house prices in the market for construction labor.

   c. Explain how a fall in house prices influences the market for construction equipment leases.

   d. Draw a graph to illustrate the effect of a fall in house prices in the market for construction equipment leases.

9. **Fixing Farming**

Backyard vegetable gardens are fine. So are organics, slow food and locavores—people who eat produce grown nearby. But solutions to the global food crisis will come from big business, genetically engineered crops and large-scale farms. ... The problem they face has made headlines lately. Demand for farm products—food, fiber and fuel—will keep growing, as the population grows and as hundreds of millions of people move into the middle class and consume more meat and dairy. Global per capita meat consumption has increased by 60 percent in the last 40 years—that's 60 percent per person. Meanwhile, the supply of farmland is limited. Agriculture already uses 55 percent of the habitable land on the planet ... . The answer is for farmers to become more productive—generating more output from fewer inputs.

Fortune, May 22, 2008

   a. Is farmland a renewable or nonrenewable resource?

   b. Explain how the growing demand for farm products will affect the market for land.

   c. Draw a graph to illustrate how the growing demand for farm products will affect the market for land.

   d. How might farmers meet the growing demand for farm products without having to use a greater quantity of farmland?

10. **Copter Crisis**

Helicopters are in short supply these days. You could blame a rise in military spending, a jump in disaster relief, even crowded airports pushing executives into private travel. But the fastest growth is coming from the offshore oil-and-gas industry, where helicopters—affectionately known as "the pickups of the Gulf Coast"—are the only way to ferry crews to and from rigs and platforms. ... Hundred-dollar oil has pushed producers to work existing fields harder than ever and open new frontiers like the coasts of Brazil, India, and Alaska. That has led the number of rigs and platforms to grow by 800, or 13%, over the past decade. ... [Oil] companies are [facing] ... a two-year backlog in orders for the Sikorsky S92, a favorite of the oil industry, and a 40% rise in prices for used models.

Fortune, May 12, 2008

   a. Explain how high oil prices influence the market for helicopter leases and services (such as the Sikorsky S92).

   b. What happens to the value of marginal product of helicopters as a firm leases or buys additional helicopters?

11. Kaiser's Ice Cream Parlor hires workers to produce smoothies. The market for smoothies is perfectly competitive, and the price of a smoothie is $4. The labor market is competitive, and the wage rate is $40 a day. The table shows the workers' total product schedule.

Number of workers	Quantity produced (smoothies per day)
1	7
2	21
3	33
4	43
5	51
6	55

   a. Calculate the marginal product of hiring the fourth worker and the value of the marginal product of the fourth worker.
   b. How many workers will Kaiser's hire to maximize its profit and how many smoothies a day will Kaiser's produce?
   c. If the price rises to $5 a smoothie, how many workers will Kaiser's hire?

12. Kaiser's installs a new soda fountain that increases the productivity of workers by 50 percent. If the price of a smoothie remains at $4 and the wage rises to $48 a day, how many workers does Kaiser's hire?

13. **Detroit Oil Refinery Expansion Approved**

   Marathon Oil Saturday started work on a $1.9 billion expansion of its gasoline refinery in Detroit. ... Marathon said the company will employ 800 construction workers and add 135 permanent jobs to the existing 480 workers at the refinery.

   United Press International, June 21, 2008

   a. Explain how rising gasoline prices influence the market for refinery labor.
   b. Draw a graph to illustrate the effects of rising gasoline prices on the market for refinery labor.
   c. How do rising gasoline prices affect a firm's demand for refineries and how does the implicit rental rate of refineries change?

14. **You May be Paid More (or Less) than You Think**

   It's so hard to put a price on happiness, isn't it? But if you've ever had to choose between a job you like and a better-paying one that you like

less, you probably wished some economist would get on the stick and tell you how much job satisfaction is worth. ...

Economists John Helliwell and Haifang Huang at the University of British Columbia have done just that. Their estimates are based on an analysis of life satisfaction surveys that consider four key factors of job satisfaction. Trust in management is ... like getting a 36 percent pay raise. ... Having a job that offers a lot of variety in projects ... is the equivalent of a 21 percent hike in pay. Having a position that requires a high level of skill is the equivalent of a 19 percent raise. And having enough time to finish your work is the equivalent of an 11 percent boost in pay. ...

   CNN, March 29, 2006

   a. How might the job characteristics described here affect the supply of labor for different types of jobs?
   b. How might this influence on supply result in different wage rates that reflect the attractiveness of a job's characteristics?

15. **The New War over Wal-Mart**

   Today, Wal-Mart employs more people—1.7 million—than any other private employer, and by this measure is not just the largest company in the world but the largest company in the history of the world. With size comes power. ... The Wal-Mart effect drives down consumer prices ... and, some argue, it also drives down wages and benefits. ...

   One of the major forces opposing Wal-Mart is organized labor. The United Food and Commercial Workers International Union has long wanted to organize Wal-Mart's stores. Last year, it succeeded at a Canadian Wal-Mart, which the company immediately shut down. ... What the war against Wal-Mart tends to gloss over is that it's not at all clear that the company behaves any worse than its competitors. When it comes to payroll and benefits, Wal-Mart's median hourly wage pretty much tracks the national median wage for general merchandise retail jobs. And its health-care benefits are a good deal more accessible ... than those of many of its competitors.

   The Atlantic, June 2006

   a. Assuming that Wal-Mart has market power in a labor market, explain how the firm could use that market power in setting wages.

b. Draw a graph to illustrate how Wal-Mart might use labor market power to set wages.

c. Explain how a union of Wal-Mart's employees would attempt to counteract Wal-Mart's wage offers (a bilateral monopoly).

d. Explain the response by the Canadian Wal-Mart to the unionization of employees.

e. Based upon evidence presented in this article, does Wal-Mart function as a monopsony in labor markets, or is the market for retail labor more competitive? Explain.

f. If the market for retail labor is competitive, explain the potential effect of a union on the wage rates.

g. Draw a graph to illustrate the potential effect of a union on the wage rates in a competitive labor market.

16. **Gas Prices Create Land Rush**

There is a land rush going on across Pennsylvania, but buyers aren't interested in the land itself. Buyers are interested in what lies beneath the earth's surface—mineral rights to natural gas deposits. Record high crude oil and natural gas prices have already pushed up drilling activity in northwestern Pennsylvania and other areas of the state. But now that already heightened interest is spreading. The reason is the Marcellus Formation—a hardly tapped formation of deep gas-bearing shale that drilling companies have only recently found a way to exploit. Development companies, drilling companies and speculators have been crisscrossing the state, trying to lease mineral rights from landowners. … Horizontal drilling techniques developed in Texas and Oklahoma might conservatively recover about 10 percent of those reserves, and that would ring up at a value of $1 trillion. …

Erie Times-News, June 15, 2008

a. Is natural gas a renewable or nonrenewable resource? Explain.

b. Explain why the demand for land in Pennsylvania has increased.

c. If companies are responding to the higher prices for natural gas by drilling right now wherever they can, what does that imply about their assumptions about the future price of natural gas in relation to current interest rates?

d. What could cause the price of natural gas to fall in the future?

17. New technology has allowed oil to be pumped from much deeper offshore oil fields than before. For example, 28 deep ocean rigs operate in the deep waters of the Gulf of Mexico.

a. What effect do you think deep ocean sources have had on the world oil price?

b. Who will benefit from drilling for oil in the Gulf of Mexico? Explain your answer.

18. Water is a natural resource that is plentiful in Canada but not plentiful in Arizona and southern California.

a. If Canadians start to export bulk water to Arizona and southern California, what do you predict will be the effect on the price of bulk water?

b. Will Canada eventually run out of water?

c. Do you think the Hotelling Principle applies to Canada's water? Explain why or why not.

19. Study *Reading Between the Lines* on pp. 432–433 and answer the following questions:

a. What determines the demand for oil? In your answer, distinguish between the market fundamentals and speculative influences on demand.

b. What determines the supply of oil? In your answer, distinguish between the market fundamentals and speculative influences on supply.

c. What is the Hotelling Principle and why is it correct?

d. How does the Hotelling Principle tell us that a change in oil production in 2030 will change the price of oil today?

e. Suppose that the elasticity of demand for oil turns out to be close to 1 rather than approximately 0.1. Will the fall in today's price of oil resulting from an increase in oil production in 2030 exceed $10 a barrel? Explain your answer.

f. If the interest rate is 4 percent a year rather than the 2 percent a year assumed in the analysis on p. 433, does that make the effect on today's price of a change in production in 2030 greater or smaller? Explain your answer with reference to the Hotelling Principle.

20 Uncertainty and Information

Life is like a lottery. You work hard in school, but will the payoff be worth it? Will you get an interesting, high-paying job or a miserable, low-paying one? You set up a summer business and work hard at it. But will you make enough income to keep you in school next year or will you get wiped out? How do people make a decision when they don't know what its consequences will be?

As you drive across an intersection on a green light, you see a car on your left that's still moving. Will it stop or will it run the red light? You buy insurance against such a risk, and insurance companies gain from your business. Why are we willing to buy insurance at prices that leave insurance companies with a gain?

Buying a new car—or a used car—is fun, but it's also scary. You could get stuck with a lemon. Just about every complicated product you buy could be defective. How do car dealers and retailers induce us to buy goods that might turn out to be lemons?

Although markets do a good job in helping people to use scarce resources efficiently, there are impediments to efficiency. Can markets lead to an efficient outcome when there is uncertainty and incomplete information? In this chapter, we answer questions such as these. And in *Reading Between the Lines* at the end of the chapter, you will see how accurate grading by high schools, colleges, and universities helps students get the right jobs and the problem that arises in job markets if grades are inflated.

Decisions in the Face of Uncertainty

Tania, a student, is trying to decide which of two summer jobs to take. She can work as a house painter and earn enough for her to save $2,000 by the end of the summer. There is no uncertainty about the income from this job. If Tania takes it, she will definitely have $2,000 in her bank account at the end of the summer. The other job, working as a telemarketer selling subscriptions to a magazine, is risky. If Tania takes this job, her bank balance at the end of the summer will depend on her success at selling. She will earn enough to save $5,000 if she is successful but only $1,000 if she turns out to be a poor salesperson. Tania has never tried selling, so she doesn't know how successful she'll be. But some of her friends have done this job, and 50 percent of them do well and 50 percent do poorly. Basing her expectations on this experience, Tania thinks there is a 50 percent chance that she will earn $5,000 and a 50 percent chance that she will earn $1,000.

Tania is equally as happy to paint as she is to make phone calls. She cares only about the money. Which job does she prefer: the one that provides her with $2,000 for sure or the one that offers her a 50 percent chance of making $5,000 but a 50 percent risk of making only $1,000?

To answer this question, we need a way of comparing the two outcomes. One comparison is the expected wealth that each job creates.

Expected Wealth

Expected wealth is the money value of what a person expects to own at a given point in time. An expectation is an average calculated by using a formula that weights each possible outcome with the probability (chance) that it will occur.

For Tania, the probability that she will have $5,000 is 0.5 (a 50 percent chance). The probability that she will have $1,000 is also 0.5. Notice that the probabilities sum to 1. Using these numbers, we can calculate Tania's expected wealth, *EW*, which is

$$EW = (\$5,000 \times 0.5) + (\$1,000 \times 0.5) = \$3,000.$$

Notice that expected wealth decreases if the risk of a poor outcome increases. For example, if Tania has a

20 percent chance of success (and 80 percent chance of failure), her expected wealth falls to $1,800— ($5,000 × 0.2) + ($1,000 × 0.8) = $1,800.

Tania can now compare the expected wealth from each job—$3,000 for the risky job and $2,000 for the non-risky job.

So does Tania prefer the risky job because it gives her a greater expected wealth? The answer is we don't know because we don't know how much Tania dislikes risk.

Risk Aversion

Risk aversion is the dislike of risk. Almost everyone is risk averse but some more than others. In football, running is less risky than passing. Coach Mike Holmgren of the Seattle Seahawks, who favors a cautious running game, is risk averse. Indianapolis quarterback Peyton Manning, who favors a risky passing game, is less risk averse. But almost everyone is risk averse to some degree.

We can measure the degree of risk aversion by the compensation needed to make a given amount of risk acceptable. Returning to Tania: If she needs to be paid more than $1,000 to take on the risk arising from the telemarketing job, she will choose the safe painting job and take the $2,000 non-risky income. But if she thinks that the extra $1,000 of expected income is enough to compensate her for the risk, she will take the risky job.

To make this idea concrete, we need a way of thinking about how a person values different levels of wealth. The concept that we use is *utility*. We apply the same idea that explains how people make expenditure decisions (see Chapter 8) to explain risk aversion and decisions in the face of risk.

Utility of Wealth

Wealth (money in the bank and other assets of value) is like all good things. It yields utility. The more wealth a person has, the greater is that person's total utility. But each additional dollar of wealth brings a diminishing increment in total utility—the marginal utility of wealth diminishes as wealth increases.

Diminishing marginal utility of wealth means that the gain in utility from an increase in wealth is smaller than the loss in utility from an equal decrease in wealth. Stated differently, *the pain from a loss is greater than the pleasure from a gain of equal size.*

Figure 20.1 illustrates Tania's utility of wealth. Each point *A* through *F* on Tania's utility of wealth curve corresponds to the value identified by the same letter in the table. For example, at point *C*, Tania's wealth is $2,000, and her total utility is 70 units. As Tania's wealth increases, her total utility increases and her marginal utility decreases. Her marginal utility is 25 units when wealth increases from $1,000 to $2,000, but only 13 units when wealth increases from $2,000 to $3,000.

We can use a person's utility of wealth curve to calculate expected utility and the cost of risk.

Expected Utility

Expected utility is the utility value of what a person expects to own at a given point in time. Like expected wealth, it is calculated by using a formula that weights each possible outcome with the probability that it will occur. But it is the utility outcome, not the money outcome, that is used to calculate expected utility.

Figure 20.2 illustrates the calculation for Tania. Wealth of $5,000 gives 95 units of utility and wealth of $1,000 gives 45 units of utility. Each outcome has a probability of is 0.5 (a 50 percent chance). Using these numbers, we can calculate Tania's expected utility, *EU*, which is

$$EU = (95 \times 0.5) + (45 \times 0.5) = 70.$$

FIGURE 20.1 The Utility of Wealth

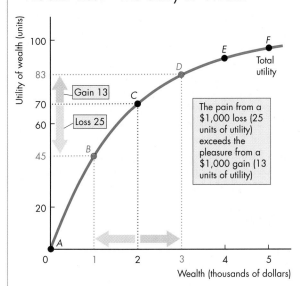

	Wealth (thousands of dollars)	Total utility (units)	Marginal utility (units)
A	0	0	
			45
B	1	45	
			25
C	**2**	**70**	
			13
D	3	83	
			8
E	4	91	
			4
F	5	95	

The table shows Tania's utility of wealth schedule, and the figure shows her utility of wealth curve. Utility increases as wealth increases, but the marginal utility of wealth diminishes.

FIGURE 20.2 Expected Utility

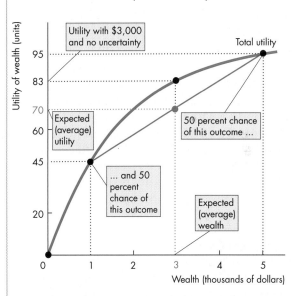

Tania has a 50 percent chance of having $5,000 of wealth and a total utility of 95 units. She also has a 50 percent chance of having $1,000 of wealth and a total utility of 45 units. Tania's expected wealth is $3,000 (the average of $5,000 and $1,000) and her expected utility is 70 units (the average of 95 and 45). With a wealth of $3,000 and no uncertainty, Tania's total utility is 83 units. For a given expected wealth, the greater the range of uncertainty, the smaller is expected utility.

Expected utility decreases if the risk of a poor outcome increases. For example, if Tania has a 20 percent chance of success (and an 80 percent chance of failure), her expected utility is 55 units—
$(95 \times 0.2) + (45 \times 0.8) = 55$.

Notice how the range of uncertainty affects expected utility. Figure 20.2 shows that with $3,000 of wealth and no uncertainty, total utility is 83 units. But with the same expected wealth and Tania's uncertainty—a 50 percent chance of having $5,000 and a 50 percent chance of having $1,000—expected utility is only 70 units. Tania's uncertainty lowers her expected utility by 13 units.

Expected utility combines expected wealth and risk into a single index.

Making a Choice with Uncertainty

Faced with uncertainty, a person chooses the action that maximizes expected utility. To select the job that gives her the maximum expected utility, Tania must:

1. Calculate the expected utility from the risky telemarketing job
2. Calculate the expected utility from the safe painting job
3. Compare the two expected utilities

Figure 20.3 illustrates the calculations. You've just seen that the risky telemarketing job gives Tania an expected utility of 70 units. The safe painting job also gives Tania a utility of 70. That is, the total utility of $2,000 with no risk is 70 units. So with either job, Tania has an expected utility of 70 units. She is indifferent between these two jobs.

If Tania had only a 20 percent chance of success and an 80 percent chance of failure in the telemarketing job, her expected utility would be 55 (calculated above). In this case, she would take the painting job and get 70 units of utility. But if the probabilities were reversed and she had an 80 percent chance of success and only a 20 percent chance of failure in the telemarketing job, her expected utility would be 85 units—$(95 \times 0.8) + (45 \times 0.2) = 85$. In this case, she would take the risky telemarketing job.

We can calculate the cost of risk by comparing the expected wealth in a given risky situation with the wealth that gives the same total utility but no risk. Using this principle, we can find Tania's cost of bearing the risk that arises from the telemarketing job. That cost, highlighted in Figure 20.3, is $1,000.

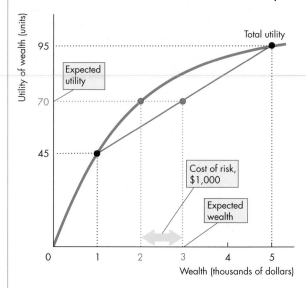

FIGURE 20.3   Choice Under Uncertainty

With a 50 percent chance of having $5,000 of wealth and a 50 percent chance of having $1,000 of wealth, Tania's expected wealth is $3,000 and her expected utility is 70 units. Tania would have the same 70 units of total utility with wealth of $2,000 and no risk, so Tania's cost of bearing this risk is $1,000. Tania is indifferent between the job that pays $2,000 with no risk and the job that offers an equal chance of $5,000 and $1,000.

myeconlab animation

Review Quiz

1 What is the distinction between expected wealth and expected utility?
2 How does the concept of utility of wealth capture the idea that pain of loss exceeds the pleasure of gain?
3 What do people try to achieve when they make a decision under uncertainty?
4 How is the cost of the risk calculated when making a decision with an uncertain outcome.

myeconlab Work Study Plan 20.1 and get instant feedback.

You've now seen how a person makes a risky decision. In the next section, we'll see how markets enable people to reduce the risks they face.

Buying and Selling Risk

You've seen at many points in your study of markets how both buyers and sellers gain from trade. Buyers gain because they value what they buy more highly than the price they must pay—they receive a *consumer surplus*. And sellers gain because they face costs that are less than the price at which they can sell—they receive a *producer surplus*.

Just as buyers and sellers gain from trading goods and services, so they can also gain by trading risk. But risk is a bad, not a good. The good that is traded is risk avoidance. A buyer of risk avoidance can gain because the value of avoiding risk is greater than the price that must be paid to someone else to get them to bear the risk. The seller of risk avoidance faces a lower cost of risk than the price that people are willing to pay to avoid the risk.

We're going to put some flesh on the bare bones of this brief account of how people can gain from trading risk by looking at insurance markets.

Insurance Markets

Insurance plays a huge role in our economic lives. We'll explain

- How insurance reduces risk
- Why people buy insurance
- How insurance companies earn a profit

How Insurance Reduces Risk Insurance reduces the risk that people face by sharing or pooling the risks. When people buy insurance against the risk of an unwanted event, they pay an insurance company a *premium*. If the unwanted event occurs, the insurance company pays out the amount of the insured loss.

Think about auto collision insurance. The probability that any one person will have a serious auto accident is small. But a person who does have an auto accident incurs a large loss. For a large population, the probability of one person having an accident is the proportion of the population that has an accident. But this proportion is known, so the probability of an accident occurring and the total cost of accidents can be predicted. An insurance company can pool the risks of a large population and enable everyone to share the costs. It does so by collecting premiums from everyone and paying out benefits to those who suffer a loss. An insurance company that remains in business collects at least as much in premiums as it pays out in benefits.

Why People Buy Insurance People buy insurance and insurance companies earn a profit by selling insurance because people are risk averse. To see why people buy insurance and why it is profitable, let's consider an example. Dan owns a car worth $10,000, and that is his only wealth. There is a 10 percent chance that Dan will have a serious accident that makes his car worth nothing. So there is a 90 percent chance that Dan's wealth will remain at $10,000 and a 10 percent chance that his wealth will be zero. Dan's expected wealth is $9,000—($10,000 × 0.9) + ($0 × 0.1).

Dan is risk averse (just like Tania in the previous example). Because Dan is risk averse, he will be better off by buying insurance to avoid the risk that he faces, if the insurance premium isn't too high.

Without knowing some details about just how risk averse Dan is, we don't know the most that he would be willing to pay to avoid this risk. But we do know that he would pay more than $1,000. If Dan did pay $1,000 to avoid the risk, he would have $9,000 of wealth and face no uncertainty about his wealth. If he does not have an accident, his wealth is the $10,000 value of his car minus the $1,000 he pays the insurance company. If he does lose his car, the insurance company pays him $10,000, so he still has $9,000. Being risk averse, Dan's expected utility from $9,000 with no risk is greater than his expected utility from an expected $9,000 with risk. So Dan would be willing to pay more than $1,000 to avoid this risk.

How Insurance Companies Earn a Profit For the insurance company, $1,000 is the minimum amount at which it would be willing to insure Dan and other people like him. With say 50,000 customers all like Dan, 5,000 customers (50,000 × 0.1) lose their cars and 45,000 don't. Premiums of $1,000 give the insurance company a total revenue of $50,000,000. With 5,000 claims of $10,000, the insurance company pays out $50,000,000. So a premium of $1,000 enables the insurance company to break even (make zero economic profit) on this business.

But Dan (and everyone else) is willing to pay more than $1,000, so insurance is a profitable business and there is a gain from trading risk.

The gain from trading risk is shared by Dan (and the other people who buy insurance) and the insurance company. The exact share of the gain depends on the state of competition in the market for insurance.

If the insurance market is a monopoly, the insurance company can take all the gains from trading risk. But if the insurance market is competitive, economic profit will induce entry and profits will be competed away. In this case, Dan (and the other buyers of insurance) get the gain.

A Graphical Analysis of Insurance

We can illustrate the gains from insurance by using a graph of Dan's utility of wealth curve. We begin, in Figure 20.4, with the situation if Dan doesn't buy insurance and decides to bear the risk he faces.

Risk-Taking Without Insurance With no accident, Dan's wealth is $10,000 and his total utility is 100 units. If Dan has an accident, his car is worthless, he has no wealth and no utility. Because the chance of an accident is 10 percent (or 0.1), the chance of not having an accident is 90 percent (or 0.9). Dan's expected wealth is $9,000—($10,000 × 0.9) + ($0 × 0.1)—and his expected utility is 90 units—(100 × 0.9) + (0 × 0.1).

You've just seen that without insurance, Dan gets 90 units of utility. But Dan also gets 90 units of utility if he faces no uncertainty with a smaller amount of wealth.

We're now going to see how much Dan will pay to avoid uncertainty.

The Value and Cost of Insurance Figure 20.5 shows the situation when Dan buys insurance. You can see that for Dan, having $7,000 with no risk is just as good as facing a 90 percent chance of having $10,000 and a 10 percent chance of having no wealth. So if Dan pays $3,000 for insurance, he has $7,000 of wealth, faces no uncertainty, and gets 90 units of utility. The amount of $3,000 is the maximum that Dan is willing to pay for insurance. It is the value of insurance to Dan.

Figure 20.5 also shows the cost of insurance. With a large number of customers each of whom has a 10 percent chance of making a $10,000 claim for the loss of a vehicle, the insurance company can provide insurance at a cost of $1,000 (10 percent of

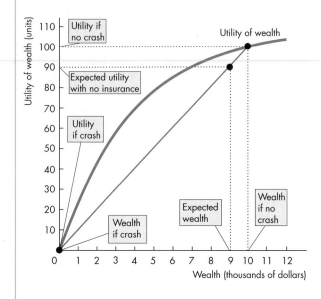

FIGURE 20.4   Taking a Risk Without Insurance

Dan's wealth (the value of his car) is $10,000, which gives him 100 units of utility.

With no insurance, if Dan has a crash, he has no wealth and no utility.

With a 10 percent chance of a crash, Dan's expected wealth is $9,000 and his expected utility is 90 units.

$10,000). If Dan pays only $1,000 for insurance, his wealth is $9,000 (the $10,000 value of his car minus the $1,000 he pays for insurance), and his utility from $9,000 of wealth with no uncertainty is about 98 units.

Gains From Trade Because Dan is willing to pay up to $3,000 for insurance that costs the insurance company $1,000, there is a gain from trading risk of $2,000 per insured person. How the gains are shared depends on the nature of the market. If the insurance market is competitive, entry will increase supply and lower the price to $1,000 (plus normal profit and operating costs). Dan (and the other buyers of insurance) enjoy a consumer surplus. If the insurance market is a monopoly, the insurance company takes the $2,000 per insured person as economic profit.

FIGURE 20.5 The Gains from Insurance

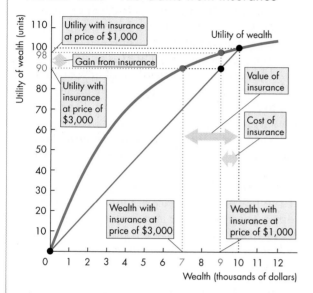

If Dan pays $3,000 for insurance, his wealth is $7,000 and his utility is 90 units—the same utility as with no insurance—so $3,000 is the value of insurance for Dan.

If Dan pays $1,000 for insurance, which is the insurance company's cost of providing insurance, his wealth is $9,000 and his utility is about 98 units.

Dan and the insurance company share the gain from insurance.

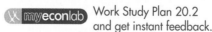 animation

Risk That Can't Be Insured

The gains from auto collision insurance that we've studied here apply to all types of insurance. Examples are property and casualty insurance, life insurance, and health care insurance. One person's risks associated with driving, life, and health are independent of other person's. That's why insurance is possible. The risks are spread across a population.

But not all risks can be insured. To be insurable, risks must be independent. If an event causes everyone to be a loser, it isn't possible to spread and pool the risks. For example, flood insurance is often not available for people who live on a floodplain because if one person incurs a loss, most likely all do.

Also, to be insurable, a risky event must be observable to both the buyer and seller of insurance. But much of the uncertainty that we face arises

Insurance in the United States
A Big Budget Item

We spend 7 percent of our income on private insurance. That's more than we spend on cars or food. In addition, we buy Social Security and unemployment insurance through our taxes. The figure shows the relative sizes of the four main types of private insurance. More than 80 percent of Americans have life insurance, and 85 percent have health insurance. The United States is the only rich country that does not have compulsory health insurance.

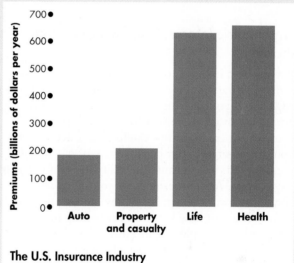

The U.S. Insurance Industry

Source of data: U.S. Bureau of the Census, *Statistical Abstract of the United States 2007*, Tables 121, 1206, and 1207.

Review Quiz

1 How does insurance reduce risk?
2 How do we determine the value (willingness to pay) for insurance?
3 How can an insurance company offer people a deal worth taking? Why do both the buyers and the sellers of insurance gain?
4 What kinds of risks can't be insured?

myeconlab Work Study Plan 20.2 and get instant feedback.

because we know less (or more) than others with whom we do business. In the next section, we look at the way markets cope when buyers and sellers have different information.

Private Information

In all the markets that you've studied so far, the buyers and the sellers are well informed about the good, service, or factor of production being traded. But in some markets, either the buyers or the sellers—usually the sellers—are better informed about the value of the item being traded than the person on the other side of the market. Information about the value of the item being traded that is possessed by only buyers or sellers is called **private information**. And a market in which the buyers or sellers have private information has **asymmetric information**.

Asymmetric Information: Examples and Problems

Asymmetric information affects many of your own economic transactions. One example is your knowledge about your driving skills and temperament. You know much more than your auto insurance company does about how carefully and defensively you drive—about your personal risk of having an accident that would cause the insurance company to pay a claim. Another example is your knowledge about your work effort. You know more than your employer about how hard you are willing to work. Yet another example is your knowledge about the quality of your car. You know whether it's a lemon, but the person to whom you are about to sell it does not know and can't find out until after he or she has bought it.

Asymmetric information creates two problems:

- Adverse selection
- Moral hazard

Adverse Selection **Adverse selection** is the tendency for people to *enter into agreements* in which they can use their private information to their own advantage and to the disadvantage of the uninformed party.

For example, if Jackie offers her salespeople a fixed wage, she will attract lazy salespeople. Hardworking salespeople will prefer not to work for Jackie because they can earn more by working for someone who pays by results. The fixed-wage contract adversely selects those with private information (knowledge about their work habits) who can use that knowledge to their own advantage and to the disadvantage of the other party.

Moral Hazard **Moral hazard** is the tendency for people with private information, *after entering into an agreement*, to use that information for their own benefit and at the cost of the less-informed party. For example, Jackie hires Mitch as a salesperson and pays him a fixed wage regardless of how much he sells. Mitch faces a moral hazard. He has an incentive to put in the least possible effort, benefiting himself and lowering Jackie's profits. For this reason, salespeople are usually paid by a formula that makes their income higher, the greater is the volume (or value) of their sales.

A variety of devices have evolved that enable markets to function in the face of moral hazard and adverse selection. We've just seen one, the use of incentive payments for salespeople. We're going to look at how three markets cope with adverse selection and moral hazard. They are

- The market for used cars
- The market for loans
- The market for insurance

The Market for Used Cars

When a person buys a car, it might turn out to be a lemon. If the car is a lemon, it is worth less to the buyer than if it has no defects. Does the used car market have two prices reflecting these two values— a low price for lemons and a higher price for cars without defects? It turns out that it does. But it needs some help to do so and to overcome what is called the **lemon problem**—the problem that in a market in which it is not possible to distinguish reliable products from lemons, there are too many lemons and too few reliable products traded.

To see how the used car market overcomes the lemon problem, we'll first look at a used car market that has a lemon problem.

The Lemon Problem in a Used Car Market

To explain the lemon problem as clearly as possible, we'll assume that there are only two kinds of cars: defective cars—lemons—and cars without defects that we'll call good cars. Whether or not a car is a lemon is private information that is available only to the current owner. The buyer of a used car can't tell whether he is buying a lemon until after he has bought the car and learned as much about it as its current owner knows.

Some people with low incomes and the time and ability to fix cars are willing to buy lemons as long as they know what they're buying and pay an appropriately low price. Suppose that a lemon is worth $5,000 to a buyer. More people want to buy a good car and we'll assume that a good car is worth $25,000 to a buyer.

But the buyer can't tell the difference between a lemon and a good car. Only the seller has this information. And telling the buyer that a car is not a lemon does not help. The seller has no incentive to tell the truth.

So the most that the buyer knows is the probability of buying a lemon. If half of the used cars sold turn out to be lemons, the buyer know that he has a 50 percent chance of getting a good car and a 50 percent chance of getting a lemon.

The price that a buyer is willing to pay for a car of unknown quality is more than the value of a lemon because the car might be a good one. But the price is less than the value of a good car because it might turn out to be a lemon.

Now think about the sellers of used cars, who know the quality of their cars. Someone who owns a good car is going to be offered a price that is less than the value of that car to the buyer. Many owners will be reluctant to sell for such a low price. So the quan-

tity of good used cars supplied will not be as large as it would be if people paid the price they are worth.

In contrast, someone who owns a lemon is going to be offered a price that is greater than the value of that car to the buyer. So owners of lemons will be eager to sell and the quantity of lemons supplied will be greater than it would be if people paid the price that a lemon is worth.

Figure 20.6 illustrates the used car market that we've just described. Part (a) shows the demand for used cars, D, and the supply of used cars, S. Equilibrium occurs at a price of $10,000 per car with 400 cars traded each month.

Some cars are good ones and some are lemons, but buyers can't tell the difference until it is too late to influence their decision to buy. But buyers do know what a good car and a lemon are worth to them, and sellers know the quality of the cars they are offering for sale. Figure 20.6(b) shows the demand curve for good cars, D_G, and the supply curve of good cars, S_G. Figure 20.6(c) shows the demand curve for lemons, D_L, and the supply curve of lemons, S_L.

At the market price of $10,000, owners of good cars supply 200 cars a month for sale. Owners of lemons also supply 200 cars a month for sale. The used car market is inefficient because there are too

FIGURE 20.6   The Lemon Problem

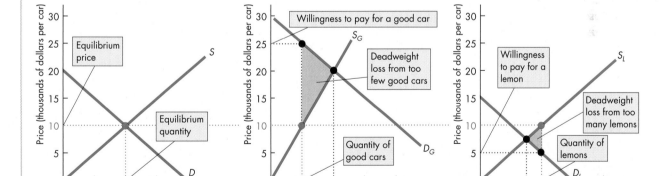

(a) All cars   **(b) Good cars**   **(c) Lemons**

Buyers can't tell a good used car from a lemon. Demand and supply determine the price and quantity of used cars traded in part (a). In part (b), D_G is the demand for good used cars and S_G is the supply. At the market price, too few

good cars are available, which brings a deadweight loss. In part (c), D_L is the demand for lemons and S_L is the supply. At the market price, too many lemons are available, which brings a deadweight loss.

many lemons and not enough good cars. Figure 20.6 makes this inefficiency clear by using the concept of deadweight loss (see Chapter 5, pp. 115–116).

At the quantity of good cars supplied, buyers are willing to pay $25,000 for a good car. They are willing to pay more than a good car is worth to its current owner for all good cars up to 400 cars a month. The gray triangle shows the deadweight loss that results from there being too few good used cars.

At the quantity of lemons supplied, buyers are willing to pay $5,000 for a lemon. They are willing to pay less than a lemon is worth to its current owner for all lemons above 150 cars a month. The gray triangle shows the deadweight loss that results from there being too many lemons.

You can see *adverse selection* in this used car market because there is a greater incentive to offer a lemon for sale. You can also see *moral hazard* because the owner of a lemon has little incentive to take good care of the car, so it is likely to become an even worse lemon. The market for used cars is not working well. Too many lemons and too few good used cars are traded.

A Used Car Market with Dealers' Warranties

How can used car dealers convince buyers that a car isn't a lemon? The answer is by giving a guarantee in the form of a warranty. By providing warranties only on good cars, dealers signal which cars are good ones and which are lemons.

Signaling occurs when an informed person takes actions that send information to uninformed persons. The grades and degrees that a university awards students are signals. They inform potential (uninformed) employers about the ability of the people they are considering hiring.

In the market for used cars, dealers send signals by giving warranties on the used cars they offer for sale. The message in the signal is that the dealer agrees to pay the costs of repairing the car if it turns out to have a defect.

Buyers believe the signal because the cost of sending a false signal is high. A dealer who gives a warranty on a lemon ends up bearing a high cost of repairs—and gains a bad reputation. A dealer who gives a warranty only on good cars has no repair costs and a reputation that gets better and better. It pays

FIGURE 20.7   Warranties Make the Used Car Market Efficient

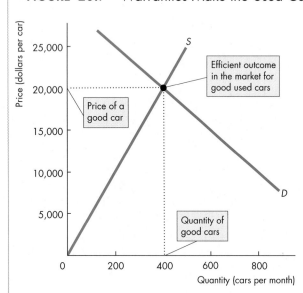

(a) Good cars

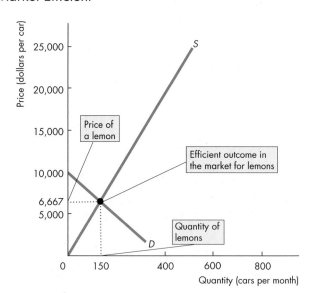

(b) Lemons

With dealers' warranties as signals, the equilibrium price of a good used car is $20,000 and 400 cars are traded. The market for good used cars is efficient. Because the signal

enables buyers to spot a lemon, the price of a lemon is $6,667 and 150 lemons are traded. The market for lemons is efficient.

dealers to send an accurate signal, and it is rational for buyers to believe the signal.

So a car with a warranty is a good car; a car without a warranty is a lemon. Warranties solve the lemon problem and enable the used car market to function efficiently with two prices: one for lemons and one for good cars.

Figure 20.7 illustrates this outcome. In part (a) the demand for and supply of good cars determine the price of a good car. In part (b), the demand for and supply of lemons determine the price of a lemon. Both markets are efficient.

Pooling Equilibrium and Separating Equilibrium

You've seen two outcomes in the market for used cars. Without warranties, there is only one message visible to the buyer: All cars look the same. So there is one price regardless of whether the car is a good car or a lemon. We call the equilibrium in a market when only one message is available and an uninformed person cannot determine quality a **pooling equilibrium**.

But in a used-car market with warranties, there are two messages. Good cars have warranties and lemons don't. So there are two car prices for the two types of cars. We call the equilibrium in a market when signaling provides full information to a previously uninformed person a **separating equilibrium**.

The Market for Loans

When you buy a tank of gasoline and swipe your credit card, you are taking a loan from the bank that issued your card. You demand and your bank supplies a loan. Have you noticed the interest rate on an unpaid credit card balance? In 2007, it ranged between 7 percent a year and 36 percent a year. Why are these interest rates so high? And why is there such a huge range?

The answer is that when banks make loans, they face the risk that the loan will not be repaid. The risk that a borrower, also known as a creditor, might not repay a loan is called **credit risk** or **default risk**. For credit card borrowing, the credit risk is high and it varies among borrowers. The highest-risk borrowers pay the highest interest rate.

Interest rates and the price of credit risk are determined in the market for loans. The lower the interest rate, the greater is the quantity of loans demanded and for a given level of credit risk, the higher the interest rate, the greater is the quantity of loans supplied. Demand and supply determine the interest rate and the price of credit risk.

If lenders were unable to charge different interest rates to reflect different degrees of credit risk, there would be a pooling equilibrium and an inefficient loans market.

Inefficient Pooling Equilibrium To see why a pooling equilibrium would be inefficient, suppose that banks can't identify the individual credit risk of their borrowers: they have no way of knowing how likely it is that a given loan will be repaid. In this situation, every borrower pays the same interest rate and the market is in a pooling equilibrium.

If all borrowers pay the same interest rate, the market for loans has the same problem as the used car market. Low-risk customers borrow less than they would if they were offered the low interest rate appropriate for their low credit risk. High-risk customers borrow more than they would if they faced the high interest rate appropriate for their high credit risk. So banks face an *adverse selection* problem. Too many borrowers are high risk and too few are low risk.

Signaling and Screening in the Market for Loans Lenders don't know how likely it is that a given loan will be repaid, but the borrower does know. Low-risk borrowers have an incentive to signal their risk by providing lenders with relevant information. Signals might include information about the length of time a person has been in the current job or has lived at the current address, home ownership, marital status, age, and business record.

High-risk borrowers might be identified simply as those who have failed to signal low risk. These borrowers have an incentive to mislead lenders; and lenders have an incentive to induce high-risk borrowers to reveal their risk level. Inducing an informed party to reveal private information is called **screening**.

By not lending to people who refuse to reveal relevant information, banks are able to screen as well as receive signals that help them to separate their borrowers into a number of credit-risk categories. If lenders succeed, the market for loans comes to a separating equilibrium with a high interest rate for high-risk borrowers and a low interest rate for low-risk borrowers. Signaling and screening in the market for loans works like warranties in the used car market and avoids the deadweight loss of a pooling equilibrium.

The Sub-Prime Credit Crisis

Too Much Risk-Taking

A sub-prime mortgage is a loan to a home buyer who has a high risk of default. Figure 1 shows that between 2001 and 2005, the price of risk was low. Figure 2 shows why: The supply of credit, S_0, was large and so was the amount of risk taking. After 2005, the supply of credit decreased to S_1. The price of risk jumped and, faced with a higher interest rate, many sub-prime borrowers defaulted. Defaults in the sub-prime mortgage market spread to other markets that supplied the funds that financed mortgages.

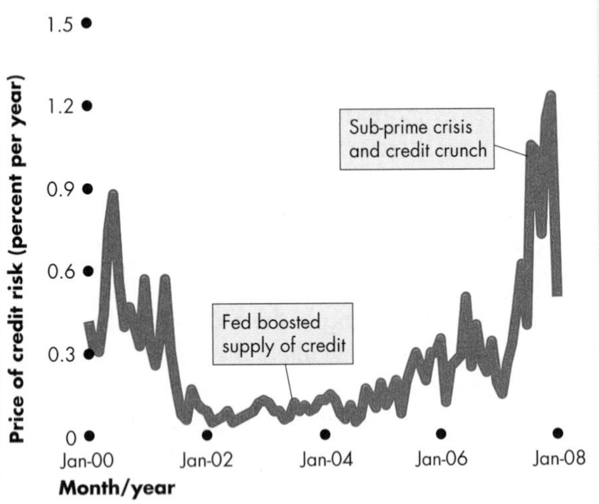

Figure 1 The Price of Commercial Credit Risk

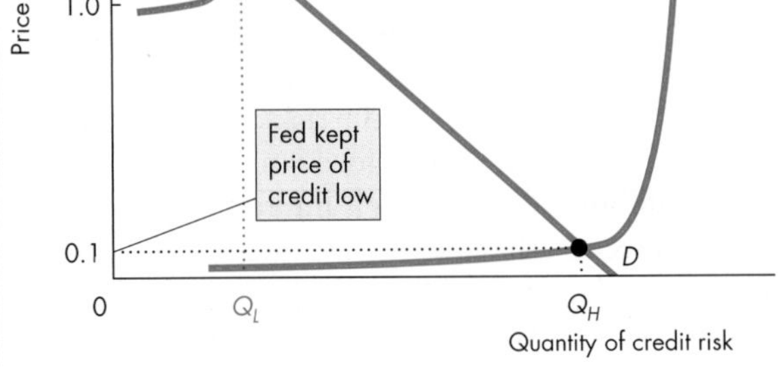

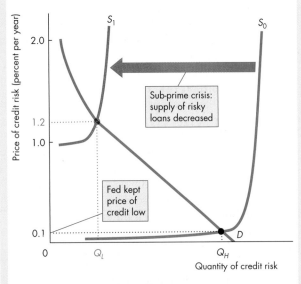

Figure 2 The Market for Risky Loans

The Market for Insurance

People who buy insurance face moral hazard, and insurance companies face adverse selection. Moral hazard arises because a person with insurance against a loss has less incentive than an uninsured person to avoid the loss. For example, a business with fire insurance has less incentive to install a fire alarm or sprinkler system than a business with no fire insurance does. Adverse selection arises because people who create greater risks are more likely to buy insurance. For example, a person with a family history of serious illness is more likely to buy health insurance than is a person with a family history of good health. Insurance companies have an incentive to find ways around the moral hazard and adverse selection problems. By doing so, they can lower premiums for low-risk people and raise premiums for high-risk people. One way in which auto insurance companies separate high-risk and low-risk customers is with a "no-claim" bonus. A driver accumulates a no-claim bonus by driving safely and avoiding accidents. The greater the bonus, the greater is the incentive to drive carefully. Insurance companies also use a deductible. A deductible is the amount of a loss that the insured person agrees to bear. The premium is smaller, the larger is the deductible, and the decrease in the premium is more than proportionate to the increase in the deductible. By offering insurance with full coverage—no deductible—on terms that are attractive only to the high-risk people and by offering coverage with a deductible on more favorable terms that are attractive to low-risk people, insurance companies can do profitable business with everyone. High-risk people choose policies with a low deductible and a high premium; low-risk people choose policies with a high deductible and a low premium.

Review Quiz

1. How does private information create adverse selection and moral hazard?
2. How do markets for cars use warranties to cope with private information?
3. How do markets for loans use signaling and screening to cope with private information?
4. How do markets for insurance use no-claim bonuses to cope with private information?

myeconlab Work Study Plan 20.3 and get instant feedback.

◆ Uncertainty, Information, and the Invisible Hand

A recurring theme throughout microeconomics is the big question: When do choices made in the pursuit of *self-interest* also promote the *social interest?* When does the invisible hand work well and when does it fail us? You've learned about the concept of efficiency, a major component of what we mean by the social interest. And you've seen that while competitive markets generally do a good job in helping to achieve efficiency, impediments such as monopoly and the absence of well-defined property rights can prevent the attainment of an efficient use of resources.

How do uncertainty and incomplete information affect the ability of self-interested choices to lead to a social interest outcome? Are these features of economic life another reason why markets fail and why some type of government intervention is required to achieve efficiency?

These are hard questions, and there are no definitive answers. But there are some useful things that we can say about the effects of uncertainty and a lack of complete information on the efficiency of resource use. We'll begin our brief review of this issue by thinking about information as just another good.

Information as a Good

More information is generally useful, and less uncertainty about the future is generally useful. Think about information as one of the goods that we want more of.

The most basic lesson about efficiency that you learned in Chapter 2 can be applied to information. Along our production possibilities frontier, we face a tradeoff between information and all other goods and services. Information, like everything else, can be produced at an increasing opportunity cost—an increasing marginal cost. For example, we could get more accurate weather forecasts, but only at increasing marginal cost, as we increased the amount of information that we gather from the atmosphere and the amount of money that we spend on supercomputers to process the data.

The principle of decreasing marginal benefit also applies to information. More information is valuable, but the more you know, the less you value another increment of information. For example, knowing that it will rain tomorrow is valuable information.

Knowing the amount of rain to within an inch is even more useful. But knowing the amount of rain to within a millimeter probably isn't worth much more.

Because the marginal cost of information is increasing and the marginal benefit is decreasing, there is an efficient amount of information. It would be inefficient to be overinformed.

In principle, competitive markets in information might deliver this efficient quantity. Whether they actually do so is hard to determine.

Monopoly in Markets that Cope with Uncertainty

There are probably large economies of scale in providing services that cope with uncertainty and incomplete information. The insurance industry, for example, is highly concentrated. Where monopoly elements exist, exactly the same inefficiency issues arise as occur in markets where uncertainty and incomplete information are not big issues. So it is likely that in some information markets, including insurance markets, there is underproduction arising from the attempt to maximize monopoly profit.

Review Quiz ◆

1 Thinking about information as a good, what determines the information that people are willing to pay for?
2 Why is it inefficient to be overinformed?
3 Why are some of the markets that provide information likely to be dominated by monopolies?

 Work Study Plan 20.4 and get instant feedback.

◆ You've seen how people make decisions when faced with uncertainty and how markets work when there is asymmetric information. *Reading Between the Lines* on pages 476–477 looks at the way markets in human capital and labor use grades as signals that sort students by ability so that employers can hire the type of labor they seek. You'll see why grade deflation can be efficient and grade inflation is inefficient. Discriminating grades are in the social interest and in the self-interest of universities and students.

Grades as Signals

Princeton Leads in Grade Deflation

http://www.usatoday.com
28 March, 2007

Jennifer Mickel, a Princeton University senior, can't help but look around a class of 10 students and think, "Just three of us can get A's."

Since Princeton took the lead among Ivy League schools to formally adopt a grade-deflation policy three years ago—limiting A's to an average 35% across departments—students say the pressure to score the scarcer A has intensified. Students say they now eye competitive classmates warily and shy away from classes perceived as difficult. …

There is no quota in individual courses, despite what students think, says Dean of the College Nancy Malkiel. …

Though a typical Princeton overachiever might blanch at the mere mention of a B, the university is sticking by its policy, Malkiel says. Students' employment and graduate school placements actually have improved the past two years, she says.

Grade inflation, well documented at many schools, is most pronounced in the Ivy League, according to an American Academy of Arts and Sciences 2002 study. For example, in 1966, 22% of all grades given to Harvard undergraduates were A's. That grew to 46% in 1996, the study found.

Princeton's grade spike became alarming in the last decade, Malkiel says. The policy, supported by a faculty vote, returns grades to early 1990s levels. "By grading in a more discriminating fashion, faculty members are able to give clearer signals about whether a student's work is inadequate, ordinary, good or excellent," Malkiel says. …

Princeton undergrads may take heart from Merrill Lynch's director of campus recruiting, Connie Thanasoulis. "I'm not in the least bit concerned about the chances for those at Princeton in comparison with any other Ivy League student," she says.

"I have never seen the quality of students that I've seen this year," she says. "I'm impressed."

Essence of the Story

- Princeton was the first Ivy League school to formally adopt a grade-deflation policy.
- The school limits A's to an average 35 percent across departments but has no quota in individual courses.
- Graduate school placements have improved since the policy was adopted.
- At Harvard, A's increased from 22 percent in 1966 to 46 percent in 1996.

- Princeton's grade inflation became alarming in the 1990s.
- More discriminating grades give clearer signals about students says Dean Malkiel.
- Merrill Lynch's director of campus recruiting is impressed with the high quality of Princeton students.

Economic Analysis

- Accurate grades provide valuable information to students and potential employers about a student's ability.

- Princeton University wants to provide accurate information and avoid grade inflation—awarding a high grade to most students—because this practice fails to provide information about a student's true ability.

- The labor market for new college graduates works badly with grade inflation and works well with accurate grading.

- Figure 1 shows a labor market for new college graduates when there is grade inflation.

- Students with high ability are not distinguished from other students, and the supply curve represents the supply of students of all ability levels.

- The demand curve shows the employers' willingness to hire new workers without knowledge of their true ability.

- Students get hired for a low wage rate. Eventually, they get sorted by ability as employers discover the true ability of their workers from on-the-job performance.

- Figures 2 and 3 show the outcome with accurate grading.

- In Fig. 2, students with high grades get high-wage jobs and in Fig. 3, students with low grades get low-wage jobs.

- The outcomes in Figs. 2 and 3 that arise immediately with accurate grading occur eventually with grade inflation as information about ability accumulates.

- But the cost to the student and the employer of discovering true ability is greater with grade inflation than with accurate grading.

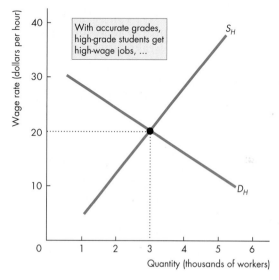

Figure 2 The market for A students

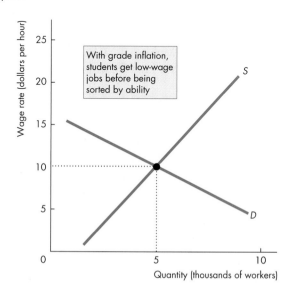

Figure 1 Market with grade inflation

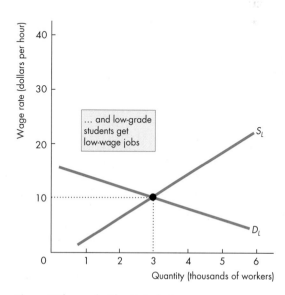

Figure 3 The market for D students

SUMMARY

Key Points

Decisions in the Face of Uncertainty (pp. 464–466)

- To make a rational choice under uncertainty, people choose the action that maximizes the expected utility of wealth.
- A decreasing marginal utility of wealth makes people risk averse. A sure outcome with a given expected wealth is preferred to a risky outcome with the same expected wealth—risk is costly.
- The cost of risk is found by comparing the expected wealth in a given risky situation with the wealth that gives the same utility but with no risk.

Buying and Selling Risk (pp. 467–469)

- People trade risk in markets for insurance.
- By pooling risks, insurance companies can reduce the risks people face (from insured activities) at a lower cost than the value placed on the lower risk.

Private Information (pp. 470–474)

- Asymmetric information creates an adverse selection and a moral hazard problem.

- When it is not possible to distinguish good-quality products from lemons, too many lemons and too few good-quality products are traded in a pooling equilibrium.
- Signaling can overcome the lemon problem.
- In the market for used cars, warranties signal good cars and enable an efficient separating equilibrium.
- Private information about credit risk is overcome by using signals and screening based on personal characteristics.
- Private information about risk in insurance markets is overcome by using the no-claim bonus and deductibles.

Uncertainty, Information, and the Invisible Hand (p. 475)

- Less uncertainty and more information can be viewed as a good that has increasing marginal cost and decreasing marginal benefit.
- Competitive information markets might be efficient, but economies of scale might bring inefficient underproduction of information and insurance.

Key Figures

Key Terms

PROBLEMS and APPLICATIONS

 Work problems 1–10 in Chapter 20 Study Plan and get instant feedback.
Work problems 11–19 as Homework, a Quiz, or a Test if assigned by your instructor.

1. The figure shows Lee's utility of wealth curve.

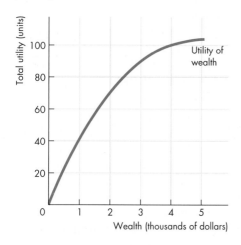

Lee is offered a job as a salesperson in which there is a 50 percent chance that she will make $4,000 a month and a 50 percent chance that she will make nothing.

a. What is Lee's expected income from taking this job?

b. What is Lee's expected utility from taking this job?

c. How much would another firm have to offer Lee with certainty to persuade her not to take the risky sales job?

d. What is Lee's cost of risk?

2. Lee in problem 1 has built a small weekend shack on a steep, unstable hillside. She spent all her wealth, which is $5,000, on this project. There is a 75 percent chance that the house will be washed down the hill and be worthless. How much is Lee willing to pay for an insurance policy that pays her $5,000 if the house is washed away?

3. Zaneb is a high-school teacher and is well known in her community for her honesty and integrity. She is shopping for a used car and plans to borrow the money from her local bank to pay for the car.

a. Does Zaneb create any moral hazard or ad-verse selection problems either for the bank or the car dealer? Explain your answer.

b. Do either the bank or the car dealer create any moral hazard or adverse selection problems for Zaneb? Explain your answer.

c. What arrangements is Zaneb likely to encounter that are designed to help cope with the moral hazard and adverse selection problems she encounters in her car buying and bank loan transactions?

4. Suppose that there are three national football leagues: Time League, Goal Difference League, and Bonus for Win League. The leagues are of equal quality, but the players are paid differently. In the Time League, they are paid by the hour for time spent practicing and time spent playing. In the Goal Difference league, they are paid an amount that depends on the points that the team scores minus the points scored against it. In the Bonus for Win League, the players are paid one wage for a loss, a higher wage for a tie, and the highest wage of all for a win.

a. Briefly describe the predicted differences in the quality of the games played by each of the leagues.

b. Which league is the most attractive to players?

c. Which league will generate the largest profits?

5. **Phillies Hamstrung by Burrell's No-Trade Clause**
Phillies general manager Pat Gillick, … who previously built winners in Toronto, Baltimore and Seattle, is no fan of blanket no-trade clauses. Gillick is so averse to giving out complete no-trade provisions that he says it could be a "deal breaker" when the Phillies negotiate with big free agents this winter.

ESPN.com, November 8, 2006

a. Provide an example of private information that a baseball player who wants a no-trade clause possesses.

b. Does a baseball player with a no-trade clause present a moral hazard to his baseball team?

c. Does a baseball player with a no-trade clause present adverse selection problems to his base-ball team?

6. **Larry Page on How to Change the World**

As president of Google, Larry Page has pushed his people to take risks that have led to hot new applications like Gmail and Google Maps. ... But he also sees a world of timidity; not enough people, he worries, are willing to place the big bets that could make a difference in meeting humanity's biggest challenges. ... "In our [Google's] first founders' letter in 2004, we talked about the risk profile with respect to doing new innovations. We said we would do some things that would have only a 10 percent chance of making $1 billion over the long term. But we don't put many people on those things; 90 percent work on everything else. So that's not a big risk. And if you look at where many of our new features come from, it's from these riskier investments. Even when we started Google, we thought, 'Oh, we might fail,' and we almost didn't do it. The reason we started is that Stanford said, 'You guys can come back and finish your Ph.D.s if you don't succeed.' Probably that one decision caused Google to be created."

Fortune, May 12, 2008

a. If much of Google's success has come from "riskier investments," then why doesn't Google dedicate all of their resources towards these riskier innovations?

b. In spite of the many risks that Larry Page has taken with Google, what evidence does this article provide that he is risk averse?

7. **We All Pay for the Uninsured**

When buying health care, most of us don't behave like regular consumers. Seven out of eight dollars we spend is somebody else's money, and we don't have very good information about doctors or hospitals. ... At Aetna [a health insurance company], in 35 markets, you can go online and know what your physician will charge you before you see that physician. That's helpful for a routine service, but when it comes to, say, a serious cardiac condition, what you really want to know is whether this is a high-quality physician. ... Important efforts are on the way, with the collaboration of physicians, to agree on quality standards. There's collaboration in the industry for all health plans to pool their data to create very rich data sets. So consumers could look at a set of performance indicators that physicians think are appropriate, and be able to judge how their physicians fare.

Fortune, May 12, 2008

a. Explain how the adverse selection problem applies to health care.

b. How does the moral hazard problem apply to health insurance?

c. What role can better information play in the health care market?

d. Is it possible for there to be too much information in this market?

8. **Show Us Our Money**

I have no clue what my colleagues make. I suspect some earn more than I do and others take home less. Like most American workers, I consider my salary my own damn business. Turns out that could be a huge mistake. ... What if employers made all employee salaries known? If you think about it, who is served by all the secrecy? Not you. It may irk you to learn that the junior analyst in the next cube really can afford his Bora Bora honeymoon—but that's all the more ammunition to gun for a raise.

Time, May 12, 2008

a. How might employers use their private information regarding worker wages to their own advantage and to the disadvantage of workers?

b. How might adverse selection discourage firms from underpaying their workers?

c. How might moral hazard discourage firms from offering workers a fixed wage?

d. Explain why a worker might be willing to pay for the salary information of other workers.

9. You can't buy insurance against the risk of being sold a lemon. Why isn't there a market in insurance against being sold a lemon? How does the market provide a buyer with some protection against being sold a lemon? What are the main ways in which markets overcome the lemon problem?

10. Larry is a safe driver and Harry is a reckless driver. Each knows what type of driver he is, but no one else knows. As the owner of an automobile insurance company, what might you do to get Larry to signal that he is a safe driver so that you can offer him insurance at a lower premium than you offer to Harry?

11. Jimmy and Zenda have the following utility of wealth schedules:

Wealth	Jimmy's utility	Zenda's utility
0	0	0
100	200	512
200	300	640
300	350	672
400	375	678
500	387	681
600	393	683
700	396	684

a. What are Jimmy's and Zenda's expected utilities from a bet that gives them a 50 percent chance of having a wealth of $600 and a 50 percent chance of having nothing?

b. Calculate Jimmy's and Zenda's marginal utility of wealth schedules.

c. Who is more risk averse, Jimmy or Zenda? How do you know?

d. Who is more likely to buy insurance, Jimmy or Zenda?

12. Suppose that Jimmy and Zenda in problem 11 each have $400, and each sees a business opportunity that involves committing the entire $400 to the project. They reckon that the project could return $600 (a profit of $200) with a probability of 0.85 or $200 (a loss of $200) with a probability of 0.15. Who goes for the project and who hangs on to the initial $400?

13. **Genetic Nondiscrimination Bill Deserves a Double Helix of Applause**

As our understanding of human genes has improved, so too has the ability to screen for various genetic traits. This has primarily been seen in tests that determine genetic predisposition to various afflictions. The Genetic Information Nondiscrimination Act … will prevent employers and health-insurance companies from discriminating based on a person's genetic information. … As one would expect, the motivation for such testing comes down to cost savings. … As a matter of economics, health-insurance companies seek out genetic information in their attempts to reduce a phenomenon known as adverse selection. … If genetic testing is permitted, those afflicted by—or prone to become afflicted by—certain diseases are essentially red-flagged as a result of their high-risk status. … True enough, health-insurance companies will once again be subjected to the same uncertainty that plagues insurance carriers of all sorts, imposing greater costs on the average client.

The Daily Iowan, May 8, 2008

a. How does adverse selection apply to the market for health insurance?

b. How might genetic testing be used to reduce adverse selection?

c. Explain the arguments that could be made in favor of and in opposition to The Genetic Information Nondiscrimination Act.

14. **Why We Worry About the Things We Shouldn't … and Ignore the Things We Should**

We agonize over avian flu, which to date has killed precisely no one in the U.S., but have to be cajoled into getting vaccinated for the common flu, which contributes to the deaths of 36,000 Americans each year. We wring our hands over the mad cow pathogen that might be (but almost certainly isn't) in our hamburger and worry far less about the cholesterol that contributes to the heart disease that kills 700,000 of us annually. We pride ourselves on being the only species that understands the concept of risk, yet we have a confounding habit of worrying about mere possibilities while ignoring probabilities, building barricades against perceived dangers while leaving ourselves exposed to real ones. … 20% of all adults still smoke; nearly 20% of drivers and more than 30% of backseat passengers don't use seat belts; two-thirds of us are overweight or obese. We dash across the street against the light and build our homes in hurricane-prone areas—and when they're demolished by a storm, we rebuild in the same spot.

Time, December 4, 2006

a. Explain how "worrying about mere possibilities while ignoring probabilities" can result in people making decisions that not only fail to satisfy social interest, but also fail to satisfy self-interest.

b. How can information be used to improve people's decision making?

c. How does health insurance and flood insurance result in both a moral hazard and adverse selection?

d. How do insurance companies use premiums and deductibles in an attempt to resolve these problems?

15. **The Appeal of Gold**

It's 2008. Inflation is on the rise ... energy prices are high, unemployment is going up, and political instability is an ongoing source of anxiety. Concurrently, survivalism is enjoying a revival, and after a horrendous performance during most of the '80s and '90s (dropping to around $264 an ounce in 2000), gold has once again shot up, reaching a record high of $1,030.80. ... [T]he value of the dollar is a perpetual concern ... while the dollar is unlikely to fall into total worthlessness, it's getting a bit more worthless day by day. ... To guard against this ... [people] buy gold on the assumption that gold is a store of value. Conventional wisdom holds that an ounce of gold can generally buy the same goods over time regardless of how expensive things get, making it a good hedge against inflation. ... Investment advisors have long suggested that gold in small doses helps protect an overall portfolio. It tends to move independently of other asset classes, and unlike any type of security, it doesn't run the risk of going to absolute zero.

Fortune, April 17, 2008

a. Explain how the concept of risk aversion can be used to explain the dramatically increased price of gold.
b. Why don't investment advisors suggest that people convert all of their assets into gold?

16. **Are You Paid What You're Worth?**

In calendar year 2004, the profit-per-employee at U.S. companies was $68,655, up 55 percent from the year before. ... Of course, not all employees contribute to a company's profits equally. ... So how do you know if your pay adequately reflects your contributions to your employer's profits? In many instances, you don't. If there's one thing that can be said about being an employee, it's that you're at a huge disadvantage when it comes to compensation issues. ... Your employer has far more and far better information than you do about how your salary and bonus compare to others in your field, to others in your office, and relative to the company's profits in any given year. You can narrow the information gap a bit if you're willing to buy salary reports from compensation sources. ... At $200, though, a quick-call salary report from ERI [Economic Research Institute] is hardly cheap. But it includes specific salary and bonus information that is updated quarterly and is derived from a host of surveys that are filled out by companies' human resource departments. ... The quick-call report will offer you compensation data for your position based on your years of experience, your industry and the place where your company is located.

CNN, April 3, 2006

a. Explain the role that asymmetric information can play in worker wages.
b. What adverse selection problem exists if a firm offers lower wages to existing workers?
c. What will determine how much a worker should actually pay for a detailed salary report?

17. After you have studied *Reading Between the Lines* on pp. 476–477, answer the following questions:
a. What information do accurate grades provide that grade inflation hides?
b. If grade inflation became widespread in high schools, colleges, and universities, what new arrangements do you predict would emerge to provide better information about student ability?
c. Do you think grade inflation is in anyone's self-interest? Explain who benefits and how they benefit from grade inflation.
d. How do you think grade inflation might be controlled?

18. Why do you think it is not possible to buy insurance against having to put up with a low-paying, miserable job? Explain why a market in insurance of this type would be valuable to workers buy unprofitable for an insurance provider and so would not work.

19. Explain to your softest-subject teacher why her/his grades are too generous.

Measuring GDP and Economic Growth

After studying this chapter, you will be able to:

- Define GDP and use the circular flow model to explain why GDP equals aggregate expenditure and aggregate income

- Explain how the Bureau of Economic Analysis measures U.S. GDP and real GDP

- Describe how real GDP is used to measure economic growth and fluctuations and explain the limitations of real GDP as a measure of economic well-being

Will our economy remain weak through 2009 or will it begin to expand more rapidly? Will it sink into recession, or worse, depression? Many U.S. corporations wanted to know the answers to these questions at the beginning of 2009. Google wanted to know whether to expand its server network and introduce new services or hold off on any new launches. Amazon.com wanted to know whether to increase its warehousing facilities. To assess the state of the economy and to make big decisions about business expansion, firms such as Google and Amazon use forecasts of GDP. What exactly is GDP and what does it tell us about the state of the economy?

To reveal the rate of growth or shrinkage of production, we must remove the effects of inflation and assess how production is *really* changing. How do we remove the effects of inflation to reveal *real* production?

Some countries are rich while others are poor. How do we compare economic well-being in one country with that in another? How can we make international comparisons of production?

In this chapter, you will find out how economic statisticians at the Bureau of Economic Analysis measure GDP and the economic growth rate. You will also learn about the uses and the limitations of these measures. In *Reading Between the Lines* at the end of the chapter, we'll look at the U.S. economy during the slowdown that began in 2008.

487

Gross Domestic Product

What exactly is GDP, how is it calculated, what does it mean, and why do we care about it? You are going to discover the answers to these questions in this chapter. First, what *is* GDP?

GDP Defined

GDP, or **gross domestic product**, is the market value of the final goods and services produced within a country in a given time period. This definition has four parts:

- Market value
- Final goods and services
- Produced within a country
- In a given time period

We'll examine each in turn.

Market Value To measure total production, we must add together the production of apples and oranges, computers and popcorn. Just counting the items doesn't get us very far. For example, which is the greater total production: 100 apples and 50 oranges or 50 apples and 100 oranges?

GDP answers this question by valuing items at their *market values*—the prices at which items are traded in markets. If the price of an apple is 10 cents, then the market value of 50 apples is $5. If the price of an orange is 20 cents, then the market value of 100 oranges is $20. By using market prices to value production, we can add the apples and oranges together. The market value of 50 apples and 100 oranges is $5 plus $20, or $25.

Final Goods and Services To calculate GDP, we value the *final goods and services* produced. A **final good** (or service) is an item that is bought by its final user during a specified time period. It contrasts with an **intermediate good** (or service), which is an item that is produced by one firm, bought by another firm, and used as a component of a final good or service.

For example, a Ford truck is a final good, but a Firestone tire on the truck is an intermediate good. A Dell computer is a final good, but an Intel Pentium chip inside it is an intermediate good.

If we were to add the value of intermediate goods and services produced to the value of final goods and services, we would count the same thing many times—a problem called *double counting*. The value of a truck already includes the value of the tires, and the value of a Dell PC already includes the value of the Pentium chip inside it.

Some goods can be an intermediate good in some situations and a final good in other situations. For example, the ice cream that you buy on a hot summer day is a final good, but the ice cream that a restaurant buys and uses to make sundaes is an intermediate good. The sundae is the final good. So whether a good is an intermediate good or a final good depends on what it is used for, not what it is.

Some items that people buy are neither final goods nor intermediate goods and they are not part of GDP. Examples of such items include financial assets—stocks and bonds—and secondhand goods—used cars or existing homes. A secondhand good was part of GDP in the year in which it was produced, but not in GDP this year.

Produced Within a Country Only goods and services that are produced *within a country* count as part of that country's GDP. Nike Corporation, a U.S. firm, produces sneakers in Vietnam, and the market value of those shoes is part of Vietnam's GDP, not part of U.S. GDP. Toyota, a Japanese firm, produces automobiles in Georgetown, Kentucky, and the value of this production is part of U.S. GDP, not part of Japan's GDP.

In a Given Time Period GDP measures the value of production *in a given time period*—normally either a quarter of a year—called the quarterly GDP data—or a year—called the annual GDP data.

GDP measures not only the value of total production but also total income and total expenditure. The equality between the value of total production and total income is important because it shows the direct link between productivity and living standards. Our standard of living rises when our incomes rise and we can afford to buy more goods and services. But we must produce more goods and services if we are to be able to buy more goods and services.

Rising incomes and a rising value of production go together. They are two aspects of the same phenomenon: increasing productivity. To see why, we study the circular flow of expenditure and income.

GDP and the Circular Flow of Expenditure and Income

Figure 21.1 illustrates the circular flow of expenditure and income. The economy consists of households, firms, governments, and the rest of the world (the rectangles), which trade in factor markets and goods (and services) markets. We focus first on households and firms.

Households and Firms Households sell and firms buy the services of labor, capital, and land in factor markets. For these factor services, firms pay income to households: wages for labor services, interest for the use of capital, and rent for the use of land. A fourth factor of production, entrepreneurship, receives profit.

Firms' retained earnings—profits that are not distributed to households—are part of the household sector's income. You can think of retained earnings as being income that households save and lend back to firms. Figure 21.1 shows the total income—*aggregate income*—received by households, including retained earnings, by the blue flow labeled *Y*.

Firms sell and households buy consumer goods and services—such as inline skates and haircuts—in the goods market. The total payment for these goods and services is **consumption expenditure**, shown by the red flow labeled *C*.

Firms buy and sell new capital equipment—such as computer systems, airplanes, trucks, and assembly line equipment—in the goods market. Some of what firms produce is not sold but is added to inventory. For example, if GM produces 1,000 cars and sells 950 of them, the other 50 cars remain in GM's inventory of unsold cars, which increases by 50 cars. When a firm adds unsold output to inventory, we can think of the firm as buying goods from itself. The

FIGURE 21.1   The Circular Flow of Expenditure and Income

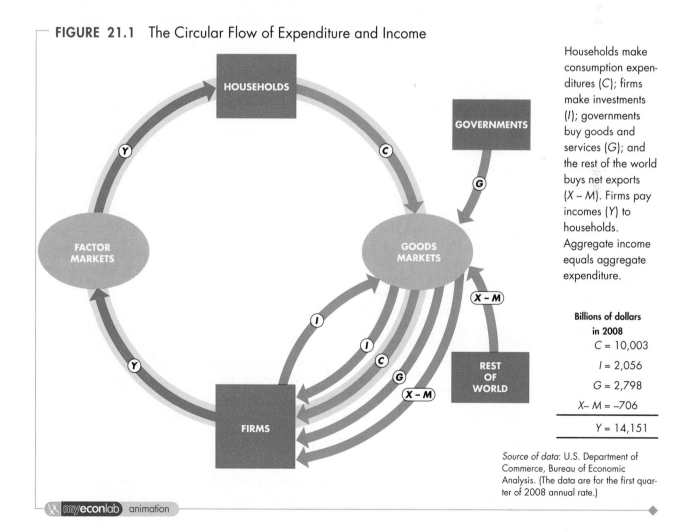

Households make consumption expenditures (*C*); firms make investments (*I*); governments buy goods and services (*G*); and the rest of the world buys net exports (*X* – *M*). Firms pay incomes (*Y*) to households. Aggregate income equals aggregate expenditure.

Billions of dollars in 2008

C =	10,003
I =	2,056
G =	2,798
X– *M* =	–706
Y =	14,151

Source of data: U.S. Department of Commerce, Bureau of Economic Analysis. (The data are for the first quarter of 2008 annual rate.)

myeconlab   animation

purchase of new plant, equipment, and buildings and the additions to inventories are **investment**, shown by the red flow labeled *I*.

Governments Governments buy goods and services from firms and their expenditure on goods and services is called **government expenditure**. In Fig. 21.1, government expenditure is shown as the red flow *G*.

Governments finance their expenditure with taxes. But taxes are not part of the circular flow of expenditure and income. Governments also make financial transfers to households, such as Social Security benefits and unemployment benefits, and pay subsidies to firms. These financial transfers, like taxes, are not part of the circular flow of expenditure and income.

Rest of the World Firms in the United States sell goods and services to the rest of the world— **exports**—and buy goods and services from the rest of the world—**imports**. The value of exports (*X*) minus the value of imports (*M*) is called **net exports**, the red flow *X − M* in Fig 21.1. If net exports are positive, the net flow of goods and services is from U.S. firms to the rest of the world. If net exports are negative, the net flow of goods and services is from the rest of the world to U.S. firms.

GDP Equals Expenditure Equals Income Gross domestic product can be measured in two ways: By the total expenditure on goods and services or by the total income earned producing goods and services.

The total expenditure—*aggregate expenditure*—is the sum of the red flows in Fig. 21.1. Aggregate expenditure equals consumption expenditure plus investment plus government expenditure plus net exports.

Aggregate income is equal to the total amount paid for the services of the factors of production used to produce final goods and services—wages, interest, rent, and profit. The blue flow in Fig. 21.1 shows aggregate income. Because firms pay out as incomes (including retained profits) everything they receive from the sale of their output, aggregate income (the blue flow) equals aggregate expenditure (the sum of the red flows). That is,

$$Y = C + I + G + X - M.$$

The table in Fig. 21.1 shows the numbers for 2008. You can see that the sum of the expenditures is $14,151 billion, which also equals aggregate income.

Because aggregate expenditure equals aggregate income, the two methods of measuring GDP give the same answer. So

GDP equals aggregate expenditure and equals aggregate income.

The circular flow model is the foundation on which the national economic accounts are built.

Why Is Domestic Product "Gross"?

"Gross" means before subtracting the depreciation of capital. The opposite of "gross" is "net," which means after subtracting the depreciation of capital.

Depreciation is the decrease in the value of a firm's capital that results from wear and tear and obsolescence. The total amount spent both buying new capital and replacing depreciated capital is called **gross investment**. The amount by which the value of capital increases is called **net investment**. Net investment equals gross investment minus depreciation.

For example if an airline buys 5 new airplanes and retires 2 old airplanes from service, its gross investment is the value of the 5 new airplanes, depreciation is the value of the 2 old airplanes retired, and net investment is the value of 3 new airplanes.

Gross investment is one of the expenditures included in the expenditure approach to measuring GDP. So the resulting value of total product is a gross measure.

Gross profit, which is a firm's profit before subtracting depreciation, is one of the incomes included in the income approach to measuring GDP. So again, the resulting value of total product is a gross measure.

Review Quiz

1 Define GDP and distinguish between a final good and an intermediate good. Provide examples.
2 Why does GDP equal aggregate income and also equal aggregate expenditure?
3 What is the distinction between gross and net?

myeconlab Work Study Plan 21.1 and get instant feedback.

Let's now see how the ideas that you've just studied are used in practice. We'll see how GDP and its components are measured in the United States today.

Measuring U.S. GDP

The Bureau of Economic Analysis (BEA) uses the concepts in the circular flow model to measure GDP and its components in the *National Income and Product Accounts*. Because the value of aggregate production equals aggregate expenditure and aggregate income, there are two approaches available for measuring GDP, and both are used. They are

- The expenditure approach
- The income approach

The Expenditure Approach

The *expenditure approach* measures GDP as the sum of consumption expenditure (*C*), investment (*I*), government expenditure on goods and services (*G*), and net exports of goods and services (*X* – *M*), corresponding to the red flows in the circular flow model in Fig. 21.1. Table 21.1 shows the result of this approach for 2008. The table uses the terms in the *National Income and Product Accounts*.

Personal consumption expenditures are the expenditures by U.S. households on goods and services produced in the United States and in the rest of the world. They include goods such as soda and books and services such as banking and legal advice. They also include the purchase of consumer durable goods, such as TVs and microwave ovens. But they do *not* include the purchase of new homes, which the BEA counts as part of investment.

Gross private domestic investment is expenditure on capital equipment and buildings by firms and the additions to business inventories. It also includes expenditure on new homes by households.

Government expenditure on goods and services is the expenditure by all levels of government on goods and services, such as national defense and garbage collection. It does *not* include *transfer payments*, such as unemployment benefits, because they are not expenditures on goods and services.

Net exports of goods and services are the value of exports minus the value of imports. This item includes airplanes that Boeing sells to British Airways (a U.S. export), and Japanese DVD players that Circuit City buys from Sony (a U.S. import).

Table 21.1 shows the relative magnitudes of the four items of aggregate expenditure.

TABLE 21.1 GDP: The Expenditure Approach

Item	Symbol	Amount in 2008 (billions of dollars)	Percentage of GDP
Personal consumption expenditures	C	10,003	70.7
Gross private domestic investment	I	2,056	14.5
Government expenditure on goods and services	G	2,798	19.8
Net exports of goods and services	X– M	–706	–5.0
Gross domestic product	**Y**	**14,151**	**100.0**

The expenditure approach measures GDP as the sum of personal consumption expenditures (C), gross private domestic investment (I), government expenditure on goods and services (G), and net exports (X – M). In 2008, GDP measured by the expenditure approach was $14,151 billion. More than two thirds of aggregate expenditure is on personal consumption goods and services.

Source of data: U.S. Department of Commerce, Bureau of Economic Analysis.

The Income Approach

The *income approach* measures GDP by summing the incomes that firms pay households for the factors of production they hire—wages for labor, interest for capital, rent for land, and profit for entrepreneurship. The *National Income and Product Accounts* divide incomes into five categories:

1. Compensation of employees
2. Net interest
3. Rental income
4. Corporate profits
5. Proprietors' income

Compensation of employees is the payment for labor services. It includes net wages and salaries (called "take-home pay") that workers receive plus taxes withheld on earnings plus fringe benefits such as Social Security and pension fund contributions.

Net interest is the interest households receive on loans they make minus the interest households pay on their own borrowing.

Rental income is the payment for the use of land and other rented resources.

Corporate profits are the profits of corporations, some of which are paid to households in the form of dividends and some of which are retained by corporations as undistributed profits. They are all income.

Proprietors' income is the income earned by the owner-operator of a business, which includes compensation for the owner's labor, the use of the owner's capital, and profit.

Table 21.2 shows these five incomes and their relative magnitudes. They sum to *net domestic income at factor cost*. The term "factor cost" is used because it is the cost of the factors of production used to produce final goods. When we sum the expenditures on final goods, we arrive at a total called *domestic product at market prices*. Market prices and factor cost diverge because of indirect taxes and subsidies.

An *indirect tax* is a tax paid by consumers when they buy goods and services. (In contrast, a *direct tax* is a tax on income.) State sales taxes and taxes on alcohol, gasoline, and tobacco products are indirect taxes. Because of indirect taxes, consumers pay more for some goods and services than producers receive. Market price exceeds factor cost. For example, if the sales tax is 7 percent, you pay $1.07 when you buy a $1 chocolate bar. The factor cost of the chocolate bar including profit is $1. The market price is $1.07.

A *subsidy* is a payment by the government to a producer. Payments made to grain growers and dairy farmers are subsidies. Because of subsidies, consumers pay less for some goods and services than producers receive. Factor cost exceeds market price.

To get from factor cost to market price, we add indirect taxes and subtract subsidies. Making this adjustment brings us to *net domestic income at market prices*. We still must get from a *net* to a *gross* measure.

Total expenditure is a *gross* number because it includes *gross* investment. Net domestic income at market prices is a net income measure because corporate profits are measured *after deducting depreciation*. They are a *net* income measure. To get from net income to gross income, we must *add depreciation*.

We've now arrived at GDP using the income approach. This number is not exactly the same as GDP using the expenditure approach. If a waiter doesn't report all his tips when he fills out his income

TABLE 21.2   GDP: The Income Approach

Item	Amount in 2008 (billions of dollars)	Percentage of GDP
Compensation of employees	8,037	56.8
Net interest	915	6.5
Rental income	39	0.3
Corporate profits	1,195	8.4
Proprietors' income	1,072	7.6
Net domestic income at factor cost	11,258	79.6
Indirect taxes *less* subsidies	1,071	7.6
Net domestic income at market prices	12,329	87.2
Depreciation	1,778	12.6
GDP (income approach)	**14,107**	**99.7**
Statistical discrepancy	44	0.3
GDP (expenditure approach)	**14,151**	**100.0**

The sum of all incomes equals *net domestic income at factor cost*. GDP equals net domestic income at factor cost plus indirect taxes less subsidies plus depreciation. In 2008, GDP measured by the income approach was $14,107 billion. This amount is $44 billion less than GDP measured by the expenditure approach—a statistical discrepancy of $44 billion or 0.3 percent of GDP. Compensation of employees—labor income—is by far the largest part of aggregate income.

Source of data: U.S. Department of Commerce, Bureau of Economic Analysis.

tax return, they get missed in the income approach but they show up in the expenditure approach when he spends his income. So the sum of expenditures might exceed the sum of incomes. The sum of expenditures might exceed the sum of incomes because some expenditure items are estimated rather than directly measured.

The gap between the expenditure approach and the income approach is called the **statistical discrepancy** and it is calculated as the GDP expenditure total minus the GDP income total. The discrepancy is never large. In 2008, it was 0.3 percent of GDP.

Nominal GDP and Real GDP

Often, we want to *compare* GDP in two periods, say 2000 and 2008. In 2000, GDP was $9,817 billion and in 2008, it was $14,151 billion—44 percent higher than in 2000. This increase in GDP is a combination of an increase in production and a rise in prices. To isolate the increase in production from the rise in prices, we distinguish between *real* GDP and *nominal* GDP.

Real GDP is the value of final goods and services produced in a given year when *valued at the prices of a reference base year*. By comparing the value of production in the two years at the same prices, we reveal the change in production.

Currently, the reference base year is 2000 and we describe real GDP as measured in 2000 dollars—in terms of what the dollar would by in 2000.

Nominal GDP is the value of final goods and services produced in a given year valued at the prices of that year. Nominal GDP is just a more precise name for GDP.

Economists at the Bureau of Economic Analysis calculate real GDP using the method described in the Mathematical Note on pp. 502–503. Here, we'll explain the basic idea but not the technical details.

Calculating Real GDP

We'll calculate real GDP for an economy that produces one consumption good, one capital good, and one government service. Net exports are zero.

Table 21.3 shows the quantities produced and the prices in 2000 (the base year) and in 2009. In part (a), we calculate nominal GDP in 2000. For each item, we multiply the quantity produced by its price to find the total expenditure on the item. We then sum the expenditures to find nominal GDP, which in 2000 is $100 million. Because 2000 is the base year, real GDP and nominal GDP both equal $100 million.

In Table 21.3(b), we calculate nominal GDP in 2009, which is $300 million. Nominal GDP in 2009 is three times its value in 2000. But by how much has production increased? Real GDP will tell us.

In Table 21.3(c), we calculate real GDP in 2009. The quantities of the goods and services produced are those of 2009, as in part (b). The prices are those in the reference base year—2000, as in part (a).

For each item, we multiply the quantity produced in 2009 by its price in 2000. We then sum these expenditures to find real GDP in 2009, which is

TABLE 21.3   Calculating Nominal GDP and Real GDP

	Item	Quantity (millions)	Price (dollars)	Expenditure (millions of dollars)
(a) In 2000				
C	T-shirts	10	5	50
I	Computer chips	3	10	30
G	Security services	1	20	20
Y	Real and Nominal GDP in 2000			100
(b) In 2009				
C	T-shirts	4	5	20
I	Computer chips	2	20	40
G	Security services	6	40	240
Y	Nominal GDP in 2009			300
(c) Quantities of 2009 valued at prices of 2000				
C	T-shirts	4	5	20
I	Computer chips	2	10	20
G	Security services	6	20	120
Y	Real GDP in 2009			160

In 2000, the reference base year, real GDP equals nominal GDP and was $100 million. In 2009, nominal GDP increased to $300 million. But real GDP in 2009 in part (c), which is calculated by using the quantities of 2009 in part (b) and the prices of 2000 in part (a) was only $160 million—a 60 percent increase from 2000.

$160 million. This number is what total expenditure would have been in 2009 if prices had remained the same as they were in 2000.

Nominal GDP in 2009 is three times its value in 2000, but real GDP in 2009 is only 1.6 times its 2000 value—a 60 percent increase in production.

Review Quiz

1 What is the expenditure approach to measuring GDP?
2 What is the income approach to measuring GDP?
3 What adjustments must be made to total income to make it equal GDP?
4 What is the distinction between nominal GDP and real GDP?
5 How is real GDP calculated?

myeconlab Work Study Plan 21.2 and get instant feedback.

The Uses and Limitations of Real GDP

Economists use estimates of real GDP for two main purposes:

- To compare the standard of living over time
- To compare the standard of living across countries

The Standard of Living Over Time

One method of comparing the standard of living over time is to calculate real GDP per person in different years. **Real GDP per person** is real GDP divided by the population. Real GDP per person tells us the value of goods and services that the average person can enjoy. By using *real* GDP, we remove any influence that rising prices and a rising cost of living might have had on our comparison.

We're interested in both the long-term trends and the shorter-term cycles in the standard of living.

Long-Term Trend A handy way of comparing real GDP per person over time is to express it as a ratio of some reference year. For example, in 1958, real GDP per person was $12,883 and in 2008, it was $38,422. So real GDP per person in 2008 was 3 times its 1958 level—that is, $38,422 ÷ $12,883 = 3. To the extent that real GDP per person measures the standard of living, people were three times as well off in 2008 as their grandparents had been in 1958.

Figure 21.2 shows the path of U.S. real GDP per person for the 50 years from 1958 to 2008 and highlights two features of our expanding living standard:

- The growth of potential GDP per person
- Fluctuations of real GDP per person

The Growth of Potential GDP When all the economy's labor, capital, land, and entrepreneurial ability are fully employed, the value of real GDP is called **potential GDP**. Potential GDP per person, the smoother black line in Fig. 21.2, grows at a steady pace because the quantities of the factors of production and their productivity grow at a steady pace.

But potential GDP per person doesn't grow at a *constant* pace. During the 1960s, it grew at 2.7 percent per year, but then its growth rate slowed and growth after 1970 averaged only 2 percent per year. This slowdown might seem small, but it had big consequences, as you'll soon see.

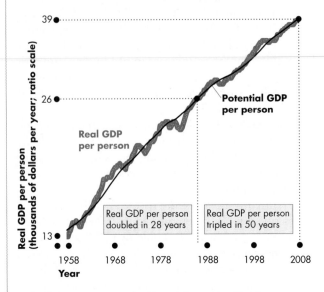

FIGURE 21.2 Rising Standard of Living in the United States

Real GDP per person in the United States doubled between 1958 and 1986 and tripled between 1958 and 2008. Real GDP per person, the red line, fluctuates around potential GDP per person, the black line.

Sources of data: Bureau of Economic Analysis and Congressional Budget Office.

myeconlab animation

Fluctuations of Real GDP You can see that real GDP shown by the red line in Fig. 21.2 fluctuates around potential GDP. Sometimes, real GDP is above potential; sometimes, it is below potential; and sometimes, real GDP shrinks.

Let's take a closer look at the two features of our expanding living standard that we've just outlined.

Productivity Growth Slowdown You've just seen that the growth rate of real GDP per person slowed after 1970. How costly was that slowdown? The answer is provided by a number that we'll call the **Lucas wedge**, which is the dollar value of the accumulated gap between what real GDP per person would have been if the 1960s growth rate had persisted and what real GDP per person turned out to be.

University of Chicago economist and Nobel Laureate Robert E. Lucas Jr., who drew attention to this measure, remarked that once he began to think about the benefits of faster economic growth, he found it hard to think about anything else.

Figure 21.3 illustrates the Lucas wedge. The red line is actual real GDP per person and the thin black line is the trend that real GDP per person would have followed if the 1960s growth rate of potential GDP had persisted through the years to 2008.

You can see in the figure that the gap—the wedge—had accumulated to an astonishing $153,000 per person by 2008. The gap started out small during the 1970s but in 2008, real GDP per person was $12,400 per year lower than it would have been with no growth slowdown.

Real GDP Fluctuations We call the fluctuations in the pace of expansion of real GDP the business cycle. A **business cycle** is a periodic but irregular up-and-down movement of total production and other measures of economic activity. The business cycle isn't a regular, predictable, and repeating cycle like the phases of the moon. The timing and the intensity of the business cycle vary a lot, but every cycle has two phases:

1. Expansion
2. Recession

and two turning points:
1. Peak
2. Trough

Figure 21.4 shows these features of the most recent U.S. business cycle.

An **expansion** is a period during which real GDP increases. In the early stage of an expansion real GDP returns to potential GDP and as the expansion progresses, potential GDP grows and real GDP eventually exceeds potential GDP.

A common definition of **recession** is a period during which real GDP decreases—its growth rate is negative—for at least two successive quarters. But the National Bureau of Economic Research, which dates the U.S. business cycle phases and turning points, defines a recession more broadly as "a period of significant decline in total output, income, employment, and trade, usually lasting from six months to a

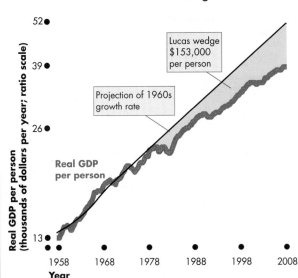

FIGURE 21.3 The Cost of Slower Growth: The Lucas Wedge

The black line projects the 1960s growth rate of real GDP per person to 2008. The Lucas wedge arises from the slowdown of productivity growth that began during the 1970s. The cost of the slowdown is $153,000 per person.

Sources of data: Bureau of Economic Analysis, Congressional Budget Office, and author's calculations.

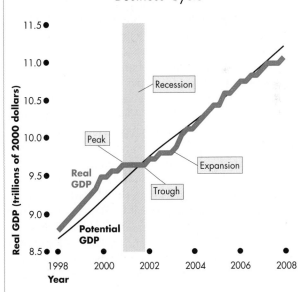

FIGURE 21.4 The Most Recent U.S. Business Cycle

The most recent business cycle peak was in the fourth quarter of 2000. A recession ran from the first quarter through the third quarter of 2001. An expansion began in the fourth quarter of 2001.

Sources of data: Bureau of Economic Analysis, Congressional Budget Office, and National Bureau of Economic Research.

 myeconlab animation

year, and marked by contractions in many sectors of the economy." This definition means that sometimes a recession is declared even though real GDP has not decreased for two successive quarters. The most recent recession, in 2001, was such a recession.

An expansion ends and recession begins at a business cycle peak. A *peak* is the highest level of real GDP that has been attained up to that time.

A recession ends at a *trough*, when real GDP reaches a temporary low point and from which the next expansion begins.

Let's now leave comparisons of the standard of living over time and look at those across countries.

The Standard of Living Across Countries

Two problems arise in using real GDP to compare living standards across countries. First, the real GDP of one country must be converted into the same currency units as the real GDP of the other country. Second, the goods and services in both countries must be valued at the same prices. We'll look at these two problems by using a striking example: a comparison of the United States and China.

China and the United States Compared In 2008, real GDP per person in the United States was $38,422. The official Chinese statistics published in the International Monetary Fund's *World Economic Outlook* says that real GDP per person in China in 2008 was 16,400 yuan. (The yuan is the currency of China.) On average, during 2008, $1 U.S. was worth 8.3 yuan. If we use this exchange rate to convert 16,400 yuan into U.S. dollars, we get $1,976. This comparison of real GDP per person in China and the United States makes China look extremely poor. In 2008, real GDP per person in the United States was 19 times that in China, or real GDP person in China was less than 4 percent of that in the United States.

The red line in Fig. 21.5 shows real GDP per person in China from 1980 to 2008 when the market exchange rate is used to convert yuan to U.S. dollars.

Purchasing Power Parity Comparison Figure 21.5 shows a second estimate of China's real GDP per person that is much larger than the one we've just calculated. Let's see how this alternative measurement is made.

U.S. real GDP is measured by using prices that prevail in the United States. China's real GDP is measured by using prices that prevail in China. But the *relative prices* in these countries are very different.

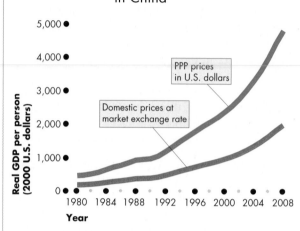

FIGURE 21.5   Two Views of Real GDP in China

Real GDP per person in China has grown rapidly. But how rapidly it has grown and to what level depends on how real GDP is valued. When GDP is valued at the market exchange rate, China is a poor developing country in which income per person in 2008 is less than 4 percent of the U.S. level. But when GDP is valued at purchasing power parity prices, China seems to be much less poor with real GDP per person in 2008 at 20 percent of the U.S. level.

Sources of data: International Monetary Fund, *World Economic Outlook database,* April 2008 and Alan Heston, Robert Summers, and Bettina Aten, Penn World Table Version 6.1 Center for International Comparisons at the University of Pennsylvania (CICUP), October 2002.

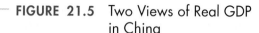

The prices of some goods are higher in the United States than in China, so these items get a smaller weight in China's real GDP than they get in U.S. real GDP. For example, a Big Mac that costs $3.57 in Chicago costs 12.5 yuan, which is the equivalent of $1.83, in Shanghai. So in China's real GDP, a Big Mac gets about half the weight that it gets in U.S. real GDP.

At the same time, the prices of some goods are higher in China than in the United States, so these items get a bigger weight in China's real GDP than they get in U.S. real GDP. For example, a Buick LaCrosse that costs $25,000 in Chicago costs 239,800 yuan, which is the equivalent of $35,000, in Shanghai. So a Buick LaCrosse made in China gets about 40 percent more weight than the same car made in Detroit gets in U.S. real GDP.

More prices are lower in China than in the United States, so Chinese prices put a lower value on China's production than do U.S. prices.

To avoid putting a lower value on China's production, we use **purchasing power parity** or **PPP** prices, which are the same for both countries when converted at the market exchange rate. By using PPP prices, we make a more valid comparison of real GDP in China and the United States.

Alan Heston, Robert Summers, and Bettina Aten, economists in the Center for International Comparisons at the University of Pennsylvania, have used PPP prices to construct real GDP data for more than 100 countries. The IMF now uses a method similar to that of Heston, Summers, and Aten to calculate PPP estimates of real GDP in all countries. The PPP comparisons tell a remarkable story.

Figure 21.5 shows the PPP view of China's real GDP, the green line. According to the PPP comparisons, real GDP per person in the United States in 2008 was 8 times that of China, or real GDP per person in China was 20 percent of that in the United States.

You've seen how real GDP is used to make standard of living comparisons over time and across countries. But real GDP isn't a perfect measure of the standard of living and we'll now examine its limitations.

Limitations of Real GDP

Real GDP measures the value of goods and services that are bought in markets. Some of the factors that influence the standard of living and that are not part of GDP are

- Household production
- Underground economic activity
- Health and life expectancy
- Leisure time
- Environmental quality
- Political freedom and social justice

Household Production An enormous amount of production takes place every day in our homes. Preparing meals, cleaning the kitchen, changing a light bulb, cutting the grass, washing the car, and caring for a child are all examples of household production. Because these productive activities are not traded in markets, they are not included in GDP.

The omission of household production from GDP means that GDP *underestimates* total production. But

it also means that the growth rate of GDP *overestimates* the growth rate of total production. The reason is that some of the growth rate of market production (included in GDP) is a replacement for home production. So part of the increase in GDP arises from a decrease in home production.

Two trends point in this direction. One is the number of women who have jobs, which has increased from 54 percent in 1970 to 62 percent in 2008. The other is the trend in the market purchase of traditionally home-produced goods and services. For example, more and more families now eat in fast-food restaurants—one of the fastest-growing industries in the United States—and use day-care services. This trend means that an increasing proportion of food preparation and child care that were part of household production are now measured as part of GDP. So real GDP grows more rapidly than does real GDP plus home production.

Underground Economic Activity The *underground economy* is the part of the economy that is purposely hidden from the view of the government to avoid taxes and regulations or because the goods and services being produced are illegal. Because underground economic activity is unreported, it is omitted from GDP.

The underground economy is easy to describe, even if it is hard to measure. It includes the production and distribution of illegal drugs, production that uses illegal labor that is paid less than the minimum wage, and jobs done for cash to avoid paying income taxes. This last category might be quite large and includes tips earned by cab drivers, hairdressers, and hotel and restaurant workers.

Estimates of the scale of the underground economy in the United States range between 9 and 30 percent of GDP ($1,200 billion to almost $4,000 billion). Provided that the underground economy is a reasonably stable proportion of the total economy, the growth rate of real GDP still gives a useful estimate of changes in economic well-being and the standard of living. But sometimes production shifts from the underground economy to the rest of the economy, and sometimes it shifts the other way. The underground economy expands relative to the rest of the economy if taxes become especially high or if regulations become especially restrictive. And the underground economy shrinks relative to the rest of the economy if the burdens of taxes and regulations are eased. During the 1980s, when tax rates were cut, there was an increase in the reporting of previously hidden income and tax revenues increased. So some part (but probably a very small part) of the expansion of real GDP during the 1980s represented a shift from the underground economy rather than an increase in production.

Health and Life Expectancy Good health and a long life—the hopes of everyone—do not show up in real GDP, at least not directly. A higher real GDP enables us to spend more on medical research, health care, a good diet, and exercise equipment. And as real GDP has increased, our life expectancy has lengthened— from 70 years at the end of World War II to approaching 80 years today. Infant deaths and death in childbirth, two fearful scourges of the nineteenth century, have been greatly reduced.

But we face new health and life expectancy problems every year. AIDS and drug abuse are taking young lives at a rate that causes serious concern. When we take these negative influences into account, we see that real GDP growth overstates the improvements in the standard of living.

Leisure Time Leisure time is an economic good that adds to our economic well-being and the standard of living. Other things remaining the same, the more leisure we have, the better off we are. Our working time is valued as part of GDP, but our leisure time is not. Yet that leisure time must be at least as valuable to us as the wage that we earn for the last hour worked. If it were not, we would work instead of taking leisure. Over the years, leisure time has steadily increased. The workweek has become shorter, more people take early retirement, and the number of vacation days has increased. These improvements in economic well-being are not reflected in real GDP.

Environmental Quality Economic activity directly influences the quality of the environment. The burning of hydrocarbon fuels is the most visible activity that damages our environment. But it is not the only example. The depletion of nonrenewable natural resources, the mass clearing of forests, and the pollution of lakes and rivers are other major environmental consequences of industrial production.

Resources that are used to protect the environment are valued as part of GDP. For example, the value of catalytic converters that help to protect the atmosphere from automobile emissions is part of GDP. But if we did not use such pieces of equipment and instead polluted the atmosphere, we would not count the deteriorating air that we were breathing as a negative part of GDP.

An industrial society possibly produces more atmospheric pollution than an agricultural society does. But pollution does not always increase as we become wealthier. Wealthy people value a clean environment and are willing to pay for one. Compare the pollution in China today with pollution in the United States. China, a poor country, pollutes its rivers, lakes, and atmosphere in a way that is unimaginable in the United States.

Political Freedom and Social Justice Most people in the Western world value political freedoms such as those provided by the U.S. Constitution. And they value social justice—equality of opportunity and of access to social security safety nets that protect people from the extremes of misfortune.

A country might have a very large real GDP per person but have limited political freedom and social justice. For example, a small elite might enjoy political liberty and extreme wealth while the vast majority are effectively enslaved and live in abject poverty. Such an economy would generally be regarded as having a lower standard of living than one that had the same amount of real GDP but in which political freedoms were enjoyed by everyone. Today, China has rapid real GDP growth but limited political freedoms, while Poland and Ukraine have moderate real GDP growth but democratic political systems. Economists have no easy way to determine which of these countries is better off.

The Bottom Line Do we get the wrong message about the growth in economic well-being and the standard of living by looking at the growth of real GDP? The influences that are omitted from real GDP are probably important and could be large. Developing countries have a larger underground economy and a larger amount of household production than do developed countries. So as an economy develops and grows, part of the apparent growth of real GDP might reflect a switch from underground to regular production and from home production to market production. This measurement error overstates the growth in economic well-being and the improvement in the standard of living.

A Broader Indicator of Economic Well-Being

The Human Development Index

The limitations of real GDP reviewed in this chapter affects the standard of living and general well-being of every country. So to make international comparisons of the general state of economic well-being, we must look at real GDP and other indicators.

The United Nations has constructed a broader measure called the Human Development Index (HDI), which combines real GDP, life expectancy and health, and education. Real GDP per person (measured on the PPP basis) is a major component of the HDI

The dots in the figure show the relationship between real GDP per person and the HDI. The United States has the highest real GDP per person (with Norway and Luxembourg) but the twelfth highest HDI. (The countries with higher HDIs are named in the figure).

The HDI of the United States is lower than that of the 11 countries because the people of those countries live longer and have better access to health care and education than do Americans.

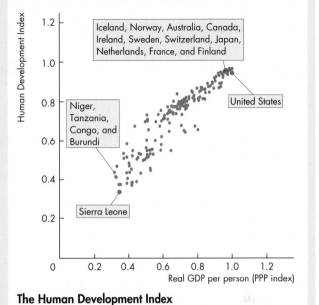

The Human Development Index

Source of data: United nations hdr.undp.org/en/statistics/data

Five African nations have the lowest real GDP per person and Sierra Leone has the lowest HDI.

Other influences on the standard of living include the amount of leisure time available, the quality of the environment, the security of jobs and homes, and the safety of city streets.

It is possible to construct broader measures that combine the many influences that contribute to human happiness. Real GDP will be one element in those broader measures, but it will by no means be the whole of those measures.

The United Nations Development Index (HDI) is one example of attempts to provide broader measures of economic well-being and the standard of living. But this measure places a good deal of weight on real GDP.

Dozens of other measures have been proposed. One includes resource depletion and emissions in a Green GDP measure. Another emphasizes the enjoyment of life rather than the production of goods in a "genuine progress index" or GPI.

Despite all the alternatives, real GDP per person remains the most widely used indicator of economic well-being.

Review Quiz

1 Distinguish between real GDP and potential GDP and describe how each grows over time.

2 How does the growth rate of real GDP contribute to an improved standard of living?

3 What is a business cycle and what are its phases and turning points?

4 What is PPP and how does it help us to make valid international comparisons of real GDP?

5 Explain why real GDP might be an unreliable indicator of the standard of living?

 Work Study Plan 21.3 and get instant feedback.

You've now studied the methods used to measure GDP and real GDP. *Reading Between the Lines* on pp. 500–501 looks at U.S. real GDP in 2008.

Real GDP in the Slowing Economy of 2008

More Arrows Seen Pointing to a Recession

http://www.nytimes.com
August 1, 2008

The American economy expanded more slowly than expected from April to June, the government reported Thursday, while numbers for the last three months of 2007 were revised downward to show a contraction—the first official slide backward since the last recession in 2001.

Economists construed the tepid growth in the second quarter, combined with a surge in claims for unemployment benefits, as a clear indication that the economy remains mired in the weeds of a downturn. Many said the data increased the likelihood that a recession began late last year. ...

President Bush zeroed in on the positive growth in the second quarter—a 1.9 percent annual rate of expansion, compared with an anticipated 2.3 percent rate. That follows growth of 0.9 percent in the first quarter. He claimed success for the $100 billion in tax rebates sent out by the government this year in a bid to spur spending, along with $52 billion in tax cuts for businesses. ...

That the economy grew at all this spring is a testament to two bright spots—increased consumer spending fueled by the tax rebates, and the continuing expansion of American exports.

Consumer spending, which amounts to 70 percent of the economy, grew at a 1.5 percent annual rate between April and June, after growing at a meager 0.9 percent clip in the previous quarter. ...

Exports expanded at a 9.2 percent annual pace in the second quarter, up from 5.1 percent in the first three months of the year. Foreign sales have been lubricated by the weak dollar, which makes American-made goods cheaper on world markets.

Adding to the improving trade picture, imports dropped by 6.6 percent, as Americans tightened their spending. Imports are subtracted from economic growth, so the effect was positive.

Over all, trade added 2.42 percentage points to the growth rate from April to June. Without that contribution, the economy would have contracted. ...

Essence of the Story

- Real GDP grew at an annual rate of 1.9 percent from April through June 2008.

- This growth was slower than anticipated but faster than the previous quarter.

- Economists feared that the slow growth might mean that the economy entered a recession in late 2007.

- Consumer spending, fueled by tax rebates, grew at an annual rate of 1.5 percent.

- Net exports, helped by a weak dollar, added 2.42 percentage points to the growth rate.

Economic Analysis

- This news article reports real GDP numbers for the second quarter of 2008.

- The data for this quarter show slower than average growth but not the negative growth that signals recession.

- Figure 1 shows the real GDP growth rate (annualized) quarter to quarter from the first quarter of 2000 to the second quarter of 2008.

- The quarter to quarter growth rate fluctuated between a high of 7.3 percent in 2003 and a low of −1.4 percent in 2001.

- You can see slow growth in 2001, 2002, and into 2003 then more rapid growth in 2004 through 2006.

- The slow growth rate in 2007 started out at zero in the first quarter, jumped to 4.7 percent in the two middle quarters, and then fell back to being slightly negative in the final quarter.

- The 2008 growth rates increased each quarter but are well below the average since 2000, shown by the red line at 2.3 percent per year.

- Figure 2 shows the growth rates of the components of real GDP. The green bars are average growth rates from 2000 through 2007 and the orange bars are the growth rates for the second quarter of 2008.

- You can see that in the second quarter of 2008, as reported in the news article, consumption expenditure (*C*) grew at 1.5 percent. You can also see that net exports (*X − M*) made the main contribution to the growth of real GDP.

- Figure 2 shows that government expenditure increased and also contributed to the real GDP growth rate.

- Figure 2 shows a sign of possible recession: the large 15.7 percent decrease in investment (*I*).

- If exports stop growing, the decrease in investment and the slow growth of consumption expenditure will push real GDP growth negative, and a recession will occur.

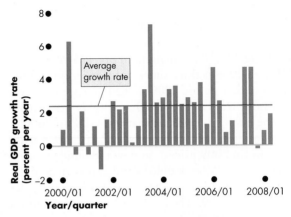

Figure 1 Real GDP growth rates: 2000–2006

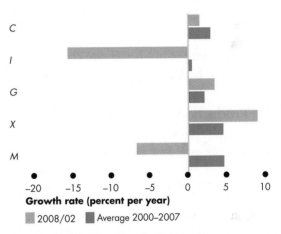

Figure 2 Growth rates of real GDP components

501

MATHEMATICAL NOTE

Chained-Dollar Real GDP

In the real GDP calculation on pp. 493–494, real GDP in 2009 is three times its value in 2000. But suppose that we use 2009 as the reference base year and value real GDP in 2000 at 2009 prices. If you do the math, you will see that real GDP in 2000 is $150 million at 2009 prices. GDP in 2009 is $300 million (in 2009 prices), so now the numbers say that real GDP has doubled. Which is correct: did real GDP double or triple? Should we use the prices of 2000 or 2009? The answer is that we need to use *both* sets of prices.

The Bureau of Economic Analysis uses a measure of real GDP called **chained-dollar real GDP**. Three steps are needed to calculate this measure:

- Value production in the prices of adjacent years
- Find the average of two percentage changes
- Link (chain) back to the reference base year

Value Production in Prices of Adjacent Years

The first step is to value production in *adjacent* years at the prices of *both* years. We'll make these calculations for 2009 and its preceding year, 2008.

Table 1 shows the quantities produced and prices in the two years. Part (a) shows the nominal GDP calculation for 2008—the quantities produced in 2008 valued at the prices of 2008. Nominal GDP in 2008 is $145 million. Part (b) shows the nominal GDP calculation for 2009—the quantities produced in 2009 valued at the prices of 2009. Nominal GDP in 2009 is $172 million. Part (c) shows the value of the quantities produced in 2009 at the prices of 2008. This total is $160 million. Finally, part (d) shows the value of the quantities produced in 2008 at the prices of 2009. This total is $158 million.

Find the Average of Two Percentage Changes

The second step is to find the percentage change in the value of production based on the prices in the two adjacent years. Table 2 summarizes these calculations.

Part (a) shows that, valued at the prices of 2008, production increased from $145 million in 2008 to $160 million in 2009, an increase of 10.3 percent.

TABLE 1   Real GDP Calculation Step 1: Value Production in Adjacent Years at Prices of Both Years

Item		Quantity (millions)	Price (dollars)	Expenditure (millions of dollars)
(a) In 2008				
C	T-shirts	3	5	15
I	Computer chips	3	10	30
G	Security services	5	20	100
Y	Real and Nominal GDP in 2008			**145**
(b) In 2009				
C	T-shirts	4	4	16
I	Computer chips	2	12	24
G	Security services	6	22	132
Y	Nominal GDP in 2009			**172**
(c) Quantities of 2009 valued at prices of 2008				
C	T-shirts	4	5	20
I	Computer chips	2	10	20
G	Security services	6	20	120
Y	2009 production at 2008 prices			**160**
(d) Quantities of 2008 valued at prices of 2009				
C	T-shirts	3	4	12
I	Computer chips	3	12	36
G	Security services	5	22	110
Y	2008 production at 2009 prices			**158**

Step 1 is to value the production of adjacent years at the prices of both years. Here, we value the production of 2008 and 2009 at the prices of both 2008 and 2009. The value of 2008 production at 2008 prices, in part (a), is nominal GDP in 2008. The value of 2009 production at 2009 prices, in part (b), is nominal GDP in 2009. Part (c) calculates the value of 2009 production at 2008 prices, and part (d) calculates the value of 2008 production at 2009 prices. We use these numbers in Step 2.

Part (b) shows that, valued at the prices of 2009, production increased from $158 million in 2008 to $172 million in 2009, an increase of 8.9 percent. Part (c) shows that the average of these two percentage changes in the value of production is 9.6. That is, $(10.3 + 8.9) \div 2 = 9.6$.

By applying this average percentage change to real GDP, we can find the value of real GDP in 2009. Real GDP in 2008 is $145 million, so a 9.6 percent increase is $14 million, so real GDP in 2009 is $145

TABLE 2 Real GDP Calculation Step 2: Find Average of Two Percentage Changes

Value of Production	Millions of dollars	
(a) At 2008 prices		
Nominal GDP in 2008	145	
2009 production at 2008 prices	160	
Percentage change in production at 2008 prices		10.3
(b) At 2009 prices		
2008 production at 2009 prices	158	
Nominal GDP in 2009	172	
Percentage change in production at 2009 prices		8.9
(c) Average of percentage change		**9.6**

Using the numbers calculated in Step 1, the percentage change in production from 2008 to 2009 valued at 2008 prices is 10.3 percent, in part (a). The percentage change in production from 2008 to 2009 valued at 2009 prices is 8.9 percent, in part (b). The average of these two percentage changes is 9.6 percent, in part (c). ◆

million plus $14 million, which equals $159 million. Because real GDP in 2008 is in 2008 dollars, real GDP in 2009 is also in 2008 dollars.

Although the real GDP of $159 million is expressed in 2008 dollars, the calculation uses the average of the prices of the final goods and services that make up GDP in 2008 and 2009.

Link (Chain) Back to the Base Year

Today, the BEA uses 2000 as the reference base year. The third step in calculating real GDP is to express it in the prices of the reference base year. To do this, the BEA performs calculations like the ones that you've just worked through to find the percentage change in real GDP in each pair of years going back to 2000.

We start with nominal GDP in 2000, which equals real GDP in 2000. We then use the calculated percentage change for 2001 to find real GDP in 2001 expressed in the prices of 2000. We repeat this calculation for each year. In this way, real GDP in 2009 is linked (chained) to the base-year real GDP.

Figure 1 shows an example. Starting with real GDP in 2000 (assumed to be $100 million), we apply the calculated percentage changes to obtain

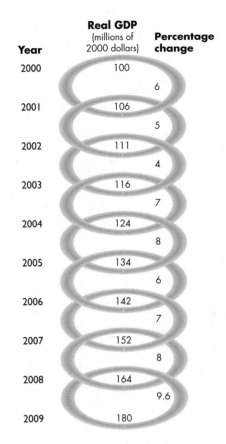

Figure 1 Real GDP calculation step 3: link (chain) back to base year

chained-dollar real GDP in 2000 dollars. By 2008, real GDP was $164 million (in 2000 dollars). In 2009, real GDP grew by 9.6 percent of $164 million, which is $16 million, so real GDP in 2009 was $180 million (in 2000 dollars).

Exercise

The table provides data on the economy of Tropical Republic that produces only bananas and coconuts.

Quantities	2008	2009
Bananas	1,000 bunches	1,100 bunches
Coconuts	500 bunches	525 bunches
Prices		
Bananas	$2 a bunch	$3 a bunch
Coconuts	$10 a bunch	$8 a bunch

Calculate Tropical Republic's nominal GDP in 2008 and 2009 and its chained-dollar real GDP in 2009 expressed in 2008 dollars.

SUMMARY

Key Points

Gross Domestic Product (pp. 488–490)

- GDP, or gross domestic product, is the market value of all the final goods and services produced in a country during a given period.
- A final good is an item that is bought by its final user, and it contrasts with an intermediate good, which is a component of a final good.
- GDP is calculated by using either the expenditure or income totals in the circular flow model.
- Aggregate expenditure on goods and services equals aggregate income and GDP.

Measuring U.S. GDP (pp. 491–493)

- Because aggregate expenditure, aggregate income, and the value of aggregate production are equal, we can measure GDP by using the expenditure approach or the income approach.
- The expenditure approach sums consumption expenditure, investment, government expenditure on goods and services, and net exports.

- The income approach sums wages, interest, rent, and profit (and indirect taxes less subsidies and depreciation).
- Real GDP is measured using a common set of prices to remove the effects of inflation from GDP.

The Uses and Limitations of Real GDP (pp. 494–499)

- Real GDP is used to compare the standard of living over time and across countries.
- Real GDP per person grows and fluctuates around the more smoothly growing potential GDP.
- A slowing of the growth rate of real GDP per person during the 1970s has lowered incomes by a large amount.
- International real GDP comparisons use PPP prices.
- Real GDP is not a perfect measure of the standard of living because it excludes household production, the underground economy, health and life expectancy, leisure time, environmental quality, and political freedom and social justice.

Key Figures and Tables

Key Terms

PROBLEMS and APPLICATIONS

 Work problems 1–11 in Chapter 21 Study Plan and get instant feedback.
Work problems 12–18 as Homework, a Quiz, or a Test if assigned by your instructor.

1. The figure below shows the flows of expenditure and income in the United States. During the second quarter of 2007, B was $9,658 billion, C was $2,147 billion, D was $2,656 billion, and E was –$723 billion. Name the flows and then calculate

   a. Aggregate expenditure.
   b. Aggregate income.
   c. GDP.

2. In the figure below, during the second quarter of 2008, B was $10,144 billion, C was $1,980 billion, D was $2,869 billion, and E was –$737 billion.

   Calculate the quantities in problem 1 during the second quarter of 2008.

3. In figure below, during the second quarter of 2006, A was $13,134 billion, B was $9,162 billion, D was $3,340 billion, and E was –$777 billion. Calculate

   a. Aggregate expenditure.
   b. Aggregate income.
   c. GDP.
   d. Government expenditure.

4. The firm that printed this textbook bought the paper from XYZ Paper Mills. Was this purchase of paper part of GDP? If not, how does the value of the paper get counted in GDP?

5. In the United Kingdom in 2005,

Item	Billions of pounds
Wages paid to labor	685
Consumption expenditure	791
Taxes	394
Transfer payments	267
Profits	273
Investment	209
Government expenditure	267
Exports	322
Saving	38
Imports	366

   a. Calculate GDP in the United Kingdom.
   b. Explain the approach (expenditure or income) that you used to calculate GDP.

6. Tropical Republic produces only bananas and coconuts. The base year is 2008, and the tables give the quantities produced and the prices.

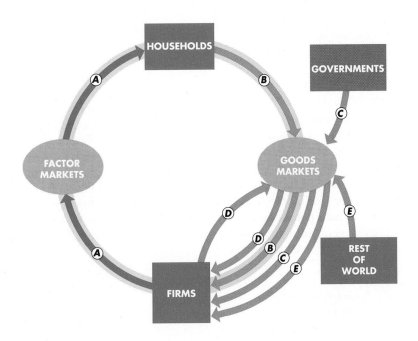

Quantities	2008	2009
Bananas	800 bunches	900 bunches
Coconuts	400 bunches	500 bunches
Prices		
Bananas	$2 a bunch	$4 a bunch
Coconuts	$10 a bunch	$5 a bunch

a. Calculate Tropical Republic's nominal GDP in 2008 and 2009.

b. Calculate real GDP in 2009 in terms of the base-year prices.

7. Use the Data Grapher in MyEconLab to answer the following questions. In which country, in 2007 was

a. The growth rate of real GDP highest: Canada, Japan, or the United States?

b. The growth rate of real GDP lowest: France, China, or the United States?

8. **Toyota to Shift U.S. Manufacturing Efforts**

Toyota Motor Corp. will start producing the hybrid Prius in the U.S. for the first time as the Japanese automaker adjusts its U.S. manufacturing operations to meet customer demands for smaller, more fuel-efficient vehicles. The company said Thursday it will start producing the Prius in 2010 at a plant it is building in Blue Springs, Mississippi. ... This will be the first time the Prius, which has been on sale for more than a decade, will be built outside of Asia. ...

CNN, July 10, 2008

a. Explain how this change by Toyota will influence U.S. GDP and the components of aggregate expenditure.

b. Explain how this change by Toyota will influence the factor incomes that make up U.S. GDP.

9. **Toting Katrina's Severe Distortions**

Hurricane Katrina could wind up being the most devastating storm to hit the U.S. Early forecasts of insured losses run as much as $26 billion. ... As far as damage to the economy, the storm is likely to drop third-quarter gross domestic product (GDP) growth by 50 basis points, figures Beth Ann Bovino, senior economist at Standard & Poor's. She also expects consumer sentiment and production to be hurt. ... However, likely repairs from hurricane-related damage should boost GDP in the following three quarters. This is largely because of rebuilding. ...

BusinessWeek, August 31, 2005

a. Explain how a devastating storm can initially decrease GDP.

b. How can a devastating storm then contribute to an increase in GDP?

c. Does the increase in GDP indicate a rise in the standard of living as a result of the storm?

10. **Poor India makes millionaires at fastest pace**

India, with the world's largest population of poor people living on less than a dollar a day, also paradoxically created millionaires at the fastest pace in the world in 2007. ... Growing them at a blistering pace of 22.7 per cent, India added another 23,000 more millionaires in 2007 to its 2006 tally of 100,000 millionaires measured in dollars. ... In contrast, developmental agencies put the number of subsistence level Indians living on less than a dollar a day at 350 million and those living on less than $2 a day at 700 million. In other words, for every millionaire, India has about 7,000 impoverished people. ...

The Times of India, June 25, 2008

a. Why might a measurement of real GDP per person misrepresent the standard of living of the average Indian?

b. Why might $1 a day and $2 a day under estimate the standard of living of the poorest Indians?

11. **Canada Agency Says 2nd Quarter GDP Dip Won't Prove Recession**

Statistics Canada may not conclude the economy is in a recession even if gross domestic product contracts for a second straight quarter, according to one of the agency's top economists. ... Defining a recession as two consecutive quarterly drops in GDP "is a silly, simplistic, simplification," Cross said by telephone. ... The National Bureau of Economic Research, which chronicles business cycles in the U.S., defines a recession as "a significant decline in economic activity spread across the economy, lasting more than a few months, normally visible in real GDP, real income, employment, industrial production, and wholesale-retail sales."

Bloomberg, June 18, 2008

a. Why might defining a recession as "two consecutive quarterly drops in GDP" be too "simplistic"?

b. Why might people still be feeling the pain of recession after an expansion begins?

12. **GDP Expands 11.4 Percent, Fastest in 13 Years**

China's economy expanded at its fastest pace in 13 years in 2007. … The country's Gross Domestic Product (GDP) grew 11.4 percent last year from 2006, to 24.66 trillion yuan ($3.42 trillion). … That marked a fifth year of double-digit growth for the world's fourth largest economy after the U.S., Japan, and Germany. The increase was especially remarkable given the fact that the United States is experiencing a slowdown due to the sub-prime crisis and housing slump. … According to Citigroup estimates, each one percent drop in the U.S. economy will shave 1.3 percent off China's growth, as Americans are heavy users of Chinese products. In spite of the uncertainties, the country's economy is widely expected to post its sixth year of double-digit growth in 2008 on investment and exports.

The China Daily, January 24, 2008

a. Use the expenditure approach for calculating China's GDP to explain why "each one percent drop in the U.S. economy will shave 1.3 percent off China's growth."

b. Why might China's recent double-digit GDP growth rates overstate the actual increase in the level of production taking place in China?

c. Explain the complications involved with attempting to compare the economic welfare in China and the United States by using the GDP for each country.

13. **Consumers Can't Save the Economy**

Consumers are too tapped out to lead the economy out of its troubles, according to a report on household credit released Wednesday. And even after things turn around, consumers weighed down by debt won't be able to spend as they did in the past.

Americans have little money on hand and banks aren't eager to lend anymore, said Scott Hoyt, senior director of consumer economics at Moody's Economy.com. … Sluggish consumer spending power means that the recovery may be a little slower and less vigorous, leaving it to corporations to spur the economy. It will also take years for consumers to straighten out their household budgets since their debt bur-

dens are near record highs. Americans put 14.3 percent of their disposable income toward debt in the first quarter, near the record 14.5 percent reached at the end of 2006. By comparison, the rate was 12.3 percent in 2000. … Before the 1980s, consumer spending made up about 63 percent of the nation's gross domestic product, a key measure of the economy. Since then, it has grown to about 70 percent as Americans took on more debt to fuel their buying habits. Going forward, consumer spending will likely drift back to about 67 percent of GDP, Hoyt said. Americans simply can't sustain a near-zero savings rate and an ever-growing debt load.

CNN, May 22, 2008

a. How has the influence of consumer spending on GDP changed over the past three decades in the United States? What has allowed this change to take place?

b. Why does Hoyt predict that consumer spending will shrink as a percentage of GDP?

14. **Consumer Spending a Big Factor: NBS**

When the [Chinese] National Bureau of Statistics (NBS) in October released its consumption figures for the first three quarters, people were surprised to discover that consumers are playing an ever-important role in the growth of the economy. … Consumption contributed 37 percent of gross domestic product while foreign demand, or net exports, accounted for 21.4 percent. … The remaining 41.6 percent was made by investment. …

While exports are growing, imports are increasing at a faster pace, narrowing the gap and leading to shrinking net exports. … But challenges lie ahead. Consumption will continue to grow, but only slowly, analysts said, because the public are still bothered by spending pressures like Social Security, health, education and housing. With those uncertainties, they prefer to save rather than spend.

China remains a developing country with a relatively low level of income, which cannot provide a strong back-up for consumption. … The government has yet to provide adequate public services, such as education and health, and people prefer to save more in anticipation of rising future expenditure. … In 2006, rural residents earned about one third of the income earned by urban residents.

The China Daily, December 11, 2007

a. Compare the relative magnitudes of consumption expenditure, net exports, and investment in China with those in the United States.

b. Why is consumption expenditure in China so low?

15. **Totally Gross**

… Over the years, GNP and GDP have proved spectacularly useful in tracking economic change—both short-term fluctuations and long-run growth. Which isn't to say GDP doesn't miss some things. … [Amartya] Sen, a development economist at Harvard, has long argued that health is a big part of living standards—and in 1990 he helped create the United Nations' Human Development Index, which combines health and education data with per capita GDP to give a more complete view of the wealth of nations (the United States currently comes in 12th, while on per capita GDP alone, it ranks second). [Joseph] Stiglitz, a Columbia professor and former World Bank chief economist, advocates a "green net national product" that takes into account the depletion of natural resources. Also sure to come up … is the currently fashionable idea of trying to include happiness in the equation. The issue with these alternative benchmarks is not whether they have merit (most do) but whether they can be measured with anything like the frequency, reliability and impartiality of GDP. …

Time, April 21, 2008

a. Explain the factors identified here that limit the usefulness of using GDP to measure economic welfare.

b. What are the challenges involved in trying to incorporate measurements of those factors in an effort to better measure economic welfare?

c. What does the ranking of the United States in the Human Development Index (12th) imply about the levels of health and education relative to other nations?

16. **Boeing Bets the House**

Boeing plans to produce some components of its new 787 Dreamliner in Japan. The aircraft will be assembled in the United States, and much of the

first year's production will be sold to ANA (All Nippon Airways), a Japanese airline.

The New York Times, May 7, 2006

a. Explain how Boeing's activities and its transactions affect U.S. and Japanese GDP.

b. Explain how ANA's activities and its transactions affect U.S. and Japanese GDP.

c. Use a circular flow diagram to illustrate your answers to a and b.

17. The United Nations' Human Development Index (HDI) is based on real GDP per person, life expectancy at birth, and indicators of the quality and quantity of education.

a. Explain why the HDI might be better than real GDP as a measure of economic welfare.

b. Which items in the HDI are part of real GDP and which items are not in real GDP?

c. Do you think the HDI should be expanded to include items such as pollution, resource depletion, and political freedom? Explain.

d. What other influences on economic welfare should be included in a comprehensive measure?

18. Study *Reading Between the Lines* on pp. 500–501 and then answer the following questions:

a. Which components of aggregate expenditure increased at the fastest rate in the second quarter of 2008?

b. Which components of aggregate expenditure increased at the slowest rate (or decreased at the fastest rate) in the second quarter of 2008?

c. For how long has the U.S. economy been expanding since the last business cycle trough?

d. Argue the case that the economy was in recession in 2007 and 2008.

e. Argue the case that the economy was not in recession in 2007 and 2008.

19. Use the link on MyEconLab (Chapter Resources, Chapter 21, Web links) to find the available data from the BEA on GDP and the components of aggregate expenditure and aggregate income. The data are in current prices (nominal GDP) and constant prices (real GDP).

a. What are the levels of nominal GDP and real (chained-dollar) GDP in the current quarter?

b. What was the level of real GDP in the same quarter of the previous year?

c. By what percentage has real GDP changed over the past year?

22 ◆ Monitoring Jobs and Inflation

After studying this chapter, you will be able to:

- Explain why unemployment is a problem, define the unemployment rate, the employment-to-population ratio, and the labor force participation rate, and describe the trends and cycles in these labor market indicators

- Explain why unemployment is an imperfect measure of underutilized labor, why it is present even at full employment, and how unemployment and real GDP fluctuate together over a business cycle

- Explain why inflation is a problem, how we measure the price level and the inflation rate, and why the CPI measure of inflation might be biased

Each month, we chart the course of employment

and unemployment as measures of U.S. economic health. How do we count the number of people working and the number unemployed? What do the level of employment and the unemployment rate tell us? Are they reliable vital signs for the economy?

We always have some unemployment—we never get to a point at which no one is unemployed. So what is full employment? How many people are unemployed when there is full employment?

Having a good job that pays a decent wage is only half of the equation that translates into a good standard of living. The other half is the cost of living. We track the cost of the items that we buy with another number that is published every month, the Consumer Price Index, or CPI. What is the CPI?

How is it calculated? And does it provide a reliable guide to the changes in our cost of living?

As the U.S. economy expanded after a recession in 2001, job growth was weak and questions about the health of the labor market became of vital importance to millions of American families. *Reading Between the Lines*, at the end of this chapter, puts the spotlight on the labor market during the expansion of the past few years and the slowdown of 2008.

We begin by looking at unemployment: what it is, why it matters, and how we measure it.

◆ Employment and Unemployment

What kind of job market will you enter when you graduate? Will there be plenty of good jobs to choose among, or will jobs be so hard to find that you end up taking one that doesn't use your education and pays a low wage? The answer depends, to a large degree, on the total number of jobs available and on the number of people competing for them.

The U.S. economy is an incredible job-creating machine. In 2008, 146 million people had jobs, which was 15 million more than in 1998 and 31 million more than in 1988. But not everyone who wants a job can find one. On a typical day, 7 million people are unemployed. That's equivalent to the population of Los Angeles. During a recession, this number rises and during a boom year it falls. At its worst, during the Great Depression, one in every four workers was unemployed.

Why Unemployment Is a Problem

Unemployment is a serious personal and social economic problem for two main reasons. It results in

- Lost production and incomes
- Lost human capital

Lost Production and Incomes The loss of a job brings a loss of income for the unemployed worker and a loss of production. The loss of income is devastating for the people who bear it and makes unemployment a frightening prospect for everyone. Today, employment benefits create a safety net, but they don't fully replace lost earnings and not every person who becomes unemployed receives benefits.

Lost Human Capital Prolonged unemployment permanently damages a person's job prospects by destroying human capital.

The Great Depression
What Keeps Ben Bernanke Awake at Night

The Great Depression began in October 1929, when the U.S. stock market crashed. It reached it deepest point in 1933, when 25 percent of the labor force was unemployed, and lasted until 1941, when the United States entered World War II. It was a depression that quickly spread globally to envelop most nations.

The 1930s were and remain the longest and worst period of high unemployment in history. Failed banks, shops, farms, and factories left millions of Americans without jobs, homes, and food. Without the support of government and charities, millions would have starved.

The Great Depression was an enormous political event: It fostered the rise of the German and Japanese militarism that were to bring the most devastating war humans have ever fought. It also led to President Franklin D. Roosevelt's "New Deal" which enhanced the role of government in economic life and made government intervention in markets popular and the market economy unpopular.

The Great Depression also brought a revolution in economics. British economist John Maynard Keynes published his *General Theory of Employment, Interest, and Money*, that created what we now call macroeconomics.

Many economists have studied the Great Depression and tried to determine why what started out as an ordinary recession became so devastating. Among them are Ben Bernanke, the Chairman of the Federal Reserve.

One of the reasons why the Fed has been so aggressive in cutting interest rates, saving Bear Sterns, and propping up Fannie Mae and Freddie Mac is because Ben Bernanke is so vividly aware of the horrors of total economic collapse and determined to avoid any risk of a repeat of the Great Depression.

Think about a manager who loses his job when his employer downsizes. The only work he can find is driving a taxi. After a year in this work, he discovers that he can't compete with new MBA graduates. Eventually, he gets hired as a manager but in a small firm and at a lower wage than before. He has lost some of his human capital.

The cost of unemployment is spread unequally, which makes it a highly charged political problem as well as a serious economic problem.

Governments make strenuous efforts to measure unemployment accurately and to adopt policies to moderate its level and ease its pain. Here, we'll learn how the U.S. government monitors unemployment.

Current Population Survey

Every month, the U.S. Census Bureau surveys 60,000 households and asks a series of questions about the age and job market status of the members of each household. This survey is called the Current Population Survey. The Census Bureau uses the answers to describe the anatomy of the labor force.

Figure 22.1 shows the population categories used by the Census Bureau and the relationships among the categories.

The population divides into two broad groups: the working-age population and others who are too young to work or who live in institutions and are unable to work. The **working-age population** is the total number of people aged 16 years and over who are not in jail, hospital, or some other form of institutional care.

The Census Bureau divides the working-age population into two groups: those in the labor force and those not in the labor force. It also divides the labor force into two groups: the employed and the unemployed. So the **labor force** is the sum of the employed and the unemployed.

To be counted as employed in the Current Population Survey, a person must have either a full-time job or a part-time job. To be counted as *un*employed, a person must be available for work and must be in one of three categories:

1. Without work but has made specific efforts to find a job within the previous four weeks

2. Waiting to be called back to a job from which he or she has been laid off

3. Waiting to start a new job within 30 days

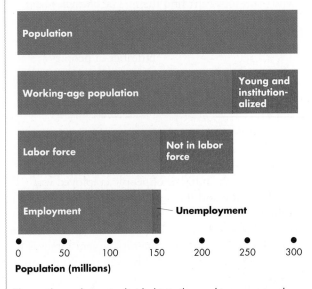

FIGURE 22.1   Population Labor Force Categories

The total population is divided into the working-age population and the young and institutionalized. The working-age population is divided into those in the labor force and those not in the labor force. The labor force is divided into the employed and the unemployed.

Source of data: Bureau of Labor Statistics.

Anyone surveyed who satisfies one of these three criteria is counted as unemployed. People in the working-age population who are neither employed nor unemployed are classified as not in the labor force.

In 2008, the population of the United States was 304.5 million; the working-age population was 233.8 million. Of this number, 79.2 million were not in the labor force. Most of these people were in school full time or had retired from work. The remaining 154.6 million people made up the U.S. labor force. Of these, 145.8 million were employed and 8.8 million were unemployed.

Three Labor Market Indicators

The Census Bureau calculates three indicators of the state of the labor market. They are

- The unemployment rate
- The employment-to-population ratio
- The labor force participation rate

The Unemployment Rate The amount of unemployment is an indicator of the extent to which people who want jobs can't find them. The **unemployment rate** is the percentage of the people in the labor force who are unemployed. That is,

$$\text{Unemployment rate} = \frac{\text{Number of people unemployed}}{\text{Labor force}} \times 100$$

and

$$\text{Labor force} = \text{Number of people employed} + \text{Number of people unemployed}.$$

In 2008, the number of people employed was 145.8 million and the number unemployed was 8.8 million. By using the above equations, you can verify that the labor force was 154.6 million (145.8 million plus 8.8 million) and the unemployment rate was 5.7 percent (8.8 million divided by 154.6 million, multiplied by 100).

Figure 22.2 shows the unemployment rate from 1961 to 2008. The average unemployment rate during this period was 5.8 percent. As a percentage of the labor force in 2008, that represents 9 million people.

The unemployment rate fluctuates over the business cycle and reached a peak value after the recession ends.

The unemployment rate was lower during the 1960s than the 1970s and 1980s. The average rate fell during the 1990s and remained low during the 2000s, but not as low as it had been during the 1960s.

The Employment-to-Population Ratio The number of people of working age who have jobs is an indicator of both the availability of jobs and the degree of match between people's skills and jobs. The **employment-to-population ratio** is the percentage of people of working age who have jobs. That is,

$$\text{Employment-to-population ratio} = \frac{\text{Number of people employed}}{\text{Working-age population}} \times 100.$$

In 2008, the number of people employed was 145.8 million and the working-age population was 233.8 million. By using the above equation, you can calculate the employment-to-population ratio. It was 62.4 percent (145.8 million divided by 233.8 million, multiplied by 100).

Figure 22.3 shows the employment-to-population ratio. This indicator follows an upward trend before 2000 and then flattens off after 2000. The increase before 2000 means that the U.S. economy created

FIGURE 22.2   The Unemployment Rate: 1960–2008

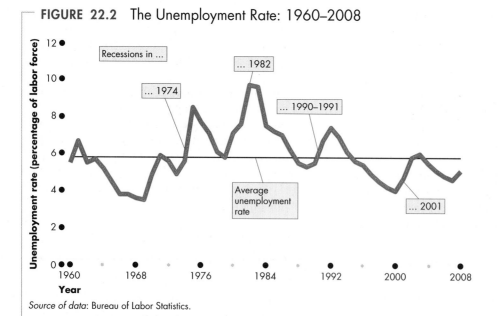

The average unemployment rate from 1960 to 2008 was 5.8 percent. The unemployment rate increases in a recession, peaks after the recession ends, and decreases in an expansion. The unemployment rate fell to an unusually low point during the expansion of the 1990s and increased during the 2001 recession. As the economy expanded in 2003 through 2007, the unemployment rate fell below the average. It remained below the average in 2008 in spite of a slowing economy.

Source of data: Bureau of Labor Statistics.

myeconlab   animation

FIGURE 22.3 Labor Force Participation and Employment: 1960–2008

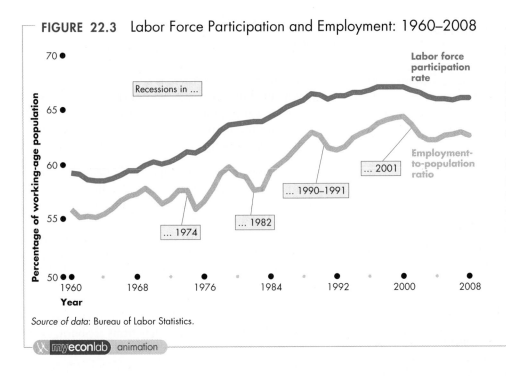

The labor force participation rate and the employment-to-population ratio have upward trends before 2000 and no trend after 2000. They fluctuate with the business cycle.

The employment-to-population ratio fluctuates more than the labor force participation rate and reflects cyclical fluctuations in the unemployment rate.

Source of data: Bureau of Labor Statistics.

 animation

jobs at a faster rate than the working-age population grew. This indicator also fluctuates: It falls during a recession and increases during an expansion.

The Labor Force Participation Rate The number of people in the labor force is an indicator of the willingness of people of working age to take jobs. The **labor force participation rate** is the percentage of the working-age population who are members of the labor force. That is,

$$\text{Labor force participation rate} = \frac{\text{Labor force}}{\text{Working-age population}} \times 100.$$

In 2008, the labor force was 154.6 million and the working-age population was 233.8 million. By using the above equation, you can calculate the labor force participation rate. It was 66.1 percent (154.6 million divided by 233.8 million, multiplied by 100).

Figure 22.3 shows the labor force participation rate. Like the employment-to-population ratio, this indicator has an upward trend before 2000 and then flattens off. It also has mild fluctuations around the trend. These fluctuations result from unsuccessful job seekers who are available and willing to work but have not made specific efforts to find a job within the previous four weeks. These

workers temporarily leave the labor force during a recession and reenter during an expansion and become active job seekers.

Review Quiz

1 What determines whether a person is in the labor force?

2 What distinguishes an unemployed person from a person who is not in the labor force?

3 Describe the trends and fluctuations in the U.S. unemployment rate between 1960 and 2008.

4 Describe the trends and fluctuations in the U.S. employment-to-population ratio and the labor force participation rate between 1960 and 2008.

myeconlab Work Study Plan 22.1 and get instant feedback.

You've seen how we measure employment and unemployment. Your next task is to see what the unemployment numbers tell us and what we mean by full employment.

Unemployment and Full Employment

What does the unemployment rate seek to measure and does it provide an accurate measure?

The purpose of the unemployment rate is to measure the underutilization of labor resources, but it is an imperfect measure for two sets of reasons.

- It excludes some underutilized labor
- Some unemployment is unavoidable—is "natural."

Underutilized Labor Excluded

Two types of underutilized labor are excluded from the official unemployment measure. They are

- Marginally attached workers
- Part-time workers who want full-time jobs

Marginally attached workers A **marginally attached worker** is a person who currently is neither working nor looking for work but has indicated that he or she wants and is available for a job and has looked for work sometime in the recent past. A subset of marginally attached workers is a group called discouraged workers.

A **discouraged worker** is a marginally attached worker who has stopped looking for a job because of repeated failure to find one. The numbers of marginally attached and discouraged workers is small. In August 2008, when the official unemployment rate was 6.1 percent, adding the marginally attached raised the rate to 7.0 percent of the labor force.

Part-Time Workers Who Want Full-Time Jobs Many part-time workers want to work part time. This arrangement fits in with the other demands on their time. But some part-time workers would like full-time jobs and can't find them. In the official statistics, these workers are called *economic part-time workers* and they are partly unemployed.

A large number of workers fall into this group, and the rate fluctuates with the overall unemployment rate. In August 2008, when the official unemployment rate was 6.1 percent, the economic part-time unemployment rate was 3.7 percent, which means that the overall unemployment rate including marginally attached workers was 10.7 percent of the labor force.

"Natural" Unemployment

Unemployment arises from job search activity. There is always someone without a job who is searching for one, so there is always some unemployment. The key reason why there is always someone who is searching for a job is that the economy is a complex mechanism that is always changing—it is a churning economy.

The Churning Economy Some of the change in the churning economy comes from the transitions that people make through the stages of life—from being in school to finding a job, to working, perhaps to becoming unhappy with a job and looking for a new one, and finally, to retiring from full-time work.

In the United States in 2008, more than 3 million new workers entered the labor force and more than 2.5 million workers retired.

Other change comes from the transitions that businesses make. Every day, new firms are born, existing firms grow or shrink, and firms fail and go out of business. This process of business creation, expansion, contraction, and failure creates and destroys jobs.

Both of these transition processes—of people and businesses—create frictions and dislocations that make unemployment unavoidable.

The Sources of Unemployment In the churning economy that we've just described, people become unemployed if they

1. Lose their jobs and search for another job.
2. Leave their jobs and search for another job.
3. Enter or reenter the labor force to search for a job.

And people end a spell of unemployment if they

1. Are hired or recalled.
2. Withdraw from the labor force.

People who are laid off, either permanently or temporarily, from their jobs are called *job losers*. Some job losers become unemployed, but some immediately withdraw from the labor force. People who voluntarily quit their jobs are called *job leavers*. Like job losers, some job leavers become unemployed and search for a better job while others either withdraw from the labor force temporarily or permanently retire from work. People who enter or reenter the labor force are called *entrants* and *reentrants*. Entrants are mainly people who have just left school. Some entrants get a job right away and are never unemployed, but many spend time searching for their first job, and during this period, they are unemployed. Reentrants are people who have previously withdrawn from the labor force. Most of these people are formerly discouraged workers.

Figure 22.4 shows unemployment by reason for becoming unemployed. Job losers are the biggest source of unemployment. On the average, they account for around half of total unemployment. Also, their number fluctuates a great deal. At the trough of the recession of 1990–1991, on any given day, more than 5 million of the 9.4 million unemployed were job losers. In contrast, at the business cycle peak in March 2001, only 3.3 million of the 6 million unemployed were job losers.

FIGURE 22.4   Unemployment by Reason

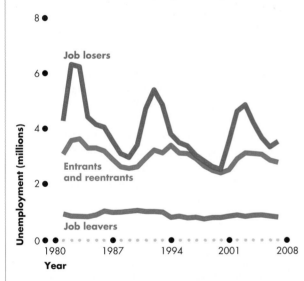

Everyone who is unemployed is a job loser, a job leaver, or an entrant or reentrant into the labor force. Most unemployment results from job loss. The number of job losers fluctuates more closely with the business cycle than do the numbers of job leavers and entrants and reentrants. Entrants and reentrants are the second most common type of unemployed people. Their number fluctuates with the business cycle because of discouraged workers. Job leavers are the least common type of unemployed people.

Source of data: Bureau of Labor Statistics.

myeconlab animation

Entrants and reentrants also make up a large component of the unemployed. Their number fluctuates but more mildly than the fluctuations in the number of job losers.

Job leavers are the smallest and most stable source of unemployment. On any given day, fewer than 1 million people are unemployed because they are job leavers. The number of job leavers is remarkably constant. To the extent that this number fluctuates, it does so in line with the business cycle: A slightly larger number of people leave their jobs in good times than in bad times.

Frictions, Structural Change, and Cycles The unemployment that arises from normal labor turnover—from people entering and leaving the labor force and from the ongoing creation and destruction of jobs—is **frictional unemployment**. Frictional unemployment is a permanent and healthy phenomenon in a dynamic, growing economy.

The unending flow of people into and out of the labor force and the processes of job creation and job destruction create the need for people to search for jobs and for businesses to search for workers. There are always businesses with unfilled jobs and people seeking jobs. Businesses don't usually hire the first person who applies for a job, and unemployed people don't usually take the first job that comes their way. Instead, both firms and workers spend time searching out what they believe will be the best match available. By this process of search, people can match their own skills and interests with the available jobs and find a satisfying job and a good income. While these unemployed people are searching, they are frictionally unemployed.

The unemployment that arises when changes in technology or international competition change the skills needed to perform jobs or change the locations of jobs is called **structural unemployment**. Structural unemployment usually lasts longer than frictional unemployment because workers must usually retrain and possibly relocate to find a job. When a steel plant in Gary, Indiana, is automated, some jobs in that city disappear. Meanwhile, new jobs for security guards, retail clerks, and life-insurance salespeople are created in Chicago, Indianapolis, and other cities. The unemployed former steelworkers remain unemployed for several months until they move, retrain, and get one of these jobs. Structural unemployment is painful, especially for older workers for whom the best available option might be to retire early or take a lower-skilled, lower-paying job. At some times, the amount of structural unemployment is modest. At other times, it is large, and at such times, structural unemployment can become a serious long-term problem. It was especially large during the late 1970s and early 1980s. During those years, oil price hikes and an increasingly competitive international environment destroyed jobs in traditional U.S. industries, such as auto and steel, and created jobs in new industries, such as electronics and bioengineering, as well as in banking and insurance. Structural unemployment was also present during the early 1990s as many businesses and governments "downsized."

Two other structural sources of higher unemployment are a *minimum wage* and an *efficiency wage*. Chapter 6 (see pp. 133–135) explains how the minimum wage creates unemployment.

An **efficiency wage** is a wage set above the going market wage and it creates unemployment just like the minimum wage does.

A firm might choose to pay an efficiency wage for four reasons. First, it enables the firm to face a steady stream of available new workers. Second, it attracts the most productive workers. Third, the fear of losing a well-paid job stimulates greater work effort. Fourth, workers are less likely to quit their jobs, so the firm has a lower rate of labor turnover and lower recruiting and training costs.

The firm balances these benefits against the cost of a higher wage and offers the wage rate that maximizes its profit.

The higher than normal unemployment that arises at a business cycle trough and the unusually low unemployment that exists at a business cycle peak is called **cyclical unemployment**. A worker who is laid off because the economy is in a recession and who gets rehired some months later when the expansion begins has experienced cyclical unemployment.

What is "Natural" Unemployment? Natural unemployment is the unemployment that arises from normal frictions and structural change when there is no cyclical unemployment—when all the unemployment is frictional and structural. Natural unemployment as a percentage of the labor force is called the **natural unemployment rate**.

Full employment is defined as a situation in which the unemployment rate equals the natural unemployment rate.

There can be a lot of unemployment at full employment, and the term "full employment" is an example of a technical economic term that does not correspond with everyday language. The term "natural unemployment rate" is another technical economic term whose meaning does not correspond with everyday language. For most people—especially for unemployed workers—there is nothing natural about unemployment. But if you think for a moment, you will come up with many other natural phenomena that are unpleasant. Floods, hurricanes, and the feeding frenzy of sharks are just three examples.

So when economists call a situation with a lot of unemployment one of "full employment" and describe the unemployment rate at full employment as the "natural rate," they are talking about the unemployment that results from natural physical constraints on the ease with which the labor market can match workers with jobs.

There is not much controversy about the existence of a natural unemployment rate. Nor is there much disagreement that it changes. The natural unemployment rate arises from the existence of labor market frictions and structural change, and it fluctuates because the frictions and the amount of structural change fluctuate. But economists don't agree about the size of the natural unemployment rate and the extent to which it fluctuates. Some economists believe that the natural unemployment rate fluctuates frequently and that at times of rapid demographic and technological change, the natural unemployment rate can be high. Others think that the natural unemployment rate changes slowly.

Real GDP and Unemployment Over the Cycle

The quantity of real GDP at full employment is *potential GDP* (p. 494). Over the business cycle, real GDP fluctuates around potential GDP. The gap between real GDP and potential GDP is called the **output gap**. As the output gap fluctuates over the business cycle, the unemployment rate fluctuates around the natural unemployment rate.

Figure 22.5 illustrates these fluctuations in the United States between 1981 and 2008—the output gap in part (a) and the unemployment rate and natural unemployment rate in part (b).

When the economy is at full employment, the unemployment rate equals the natural unemploy-

FIGURE 22.5 The Output Gap and the Unemployment Rate

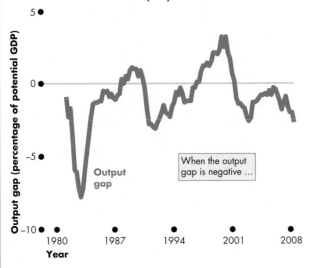

(a) Output gap

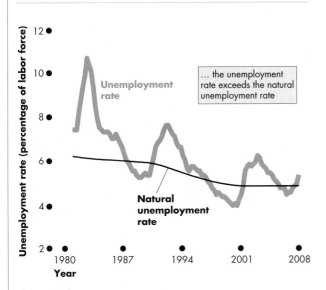

(b) Unemployment rate

As real GDP fluctuates around potential GDP in part (a), the unemployment rate fluctuates around the natural unemployment rate in part (b). At the end of the deep 1982 recession, the unemployment rate reached almost 11 percent. At the end of the milder 1990–1991 and 2001 recessions, unemployment peaked at lower rates. The natural unemployment rate decreased somewhat during the 1980s and 1990s.

Sources of data: Bureau of Economic Analysis, Bureau of Labor Statistics, and Congressional Budget Office.

 animation

ment rate and real GDP equals potential GDP so the output gap is zero. When the unemployment rate is less than the natural unemployment rate, real GDP is greater than potential GDP and the output gap is positive. And when the unemployment rate is greater than the natural unemployment rate, real GDP is less than potential GDP and the output gap is negative.

Figure 22.5(b) shows one view of the natural unemployment rate—the view of the Congressional Budget Office. Economists do not know the magnitude of the natural unemployment rate and that shown in the figure is only one estimate. It shows that the natural unemployment rate was 6.2 percent in 1981 and that it fell steadily through the 1980s and 1990s to 4.8 percent by 2000. This estimate of the natural unemployment rate in the United States is one that many, but not all, economists agree with.

Review Quiz

1 What is the unemployment rate supposed to measure and why is it an imperfect measure?
2 Why might the official unemployment rate underestimate the underutilization of labor resources?
3 Why does unemployment arise and what makes some unemployment unavoidable?
4 Define frictional unemployment, structural unemployment, and cyclical unemployment. Give examples of each type of unemployment.
5 What is the natural unemployment rate?
6 How does the natural unemployment rate change and what factors might make it change?
7 How does the unemployment rate fluctuate over the business cycle?

myeconlab Work Study Plan 22.2 and get instant feedback.

Your next task in this chapter is to see how we monitor the price level and the inflation rate. You will learn about the Consumer Price Index (CPI), which is monitored every month. You will also learn about other measures of the price level and the inflation rate.

The Price Level and Inflation

What will it *really* cost you to pay off your student loan? What will your parent's life savings buy when they retire? The answers depend on what happens to the **price level**, the average level of prices, and the value of money.

We are interested in the price level for two main reasons. First, we want to measure the **inflation rate**, which is the annual percentage change of the price level. Second, we want to distinguish between the money values and real values of economic variables such as your student loan and your parent's savings.

We will begin by explaining why we're interested in the inflation rate—why inflation is a problem. We'll then look at the ways in which we measure the price level and the inflation rate. Finally, we'll return to the task of separating real values from money values of economic variables.

Why Inflation Is a Problem

Inflation is a problem for several reasons, but the main one is that once it takes hold, its rate is unpredictable. Unpredictable inflation brings serious social and personal problems because it

- Redistributes income and wealth
- Diverts resources from production

Redistributes Income and Wealth Inflation makes the economy behave like a casino in which some people gain and some lose and no one can predict where the gains and losses will fall. Gains and losses occur because of unpredictable changes in the value of money. Money is used as a measuring rod of value in the transactions that we undertake. Borrowers and lenders, workers and employers, all make contracts in terms of money. If the value of money varies unpredictably over time, then the amounts *really* paid and received—the quantities of goods that the money will buy—also fluctuate unpredictably. Measuring value with a measuring rod whose units vary is a bit like trying to measure a piece of cloth with an elastic tape measure. The size of the cloth depends on how tightly the elastic is stretched.

Diverts Resources from Production In a period of rapid, unpredictable inflation, resources get diverted from productive activities to forecasting inflation. It can even become more profitable to forecast the infla-

tion rate correctly than to invent a new product. Doctors, lawyers, accountants, farmers—just about everyone—can make themselves better off, not by specializing in the profession for which they have been trained but by spending more of their time dabbling as amateur economists and inflation forecasters and managing their investments.

From a social perspective, the diversion of talent that results from rapid inflation is like throwing scarce resources onto the garbage heap. This waste of resources is a cost of inflation.

At its worst, inflation becomes **hyperinflation**, an inflation rate so rapid that workers are paid twice a day because money loses its value so quickly. As soon as workers are paid, they rush out to spend their wages before the money loses too much value. In this situation, the economy grinds to a halt and society collapses. Hyperinflation is rare, but Zimbabwe has it today and several European and Latin American countries have experienced it.

It is to avoid the consequences of inflation that we pay close attention to it, even when its rate is low. We monitor inflation every month and devote considerable resources to measuring it accurately. You're now going to see how we do this.

The Consumer Price Index

Every month, the Bureau of Labor Statistics (BLS) measures the price level by calculating the **Consumer Price Index (CPI)**, which is a measure of the average of the prices paid by urban consumers for a fixed basket of consumer goods and services. What you learn here will help you to make sense of the CPI and relate it to your own economic life. The CPI tells you what has happened to the value of the money in your pocket.

Reading the CPI Numbers

The CPI is defined to equal 100 for a period called the **reference base period**. Currently, the reference base period is 1982–1984. That is, for the average of the 36 months from January 1982 through December 1984, the CPI equals 100.

In July 2008, the CPI was 220. This number tells us that the average of the prices paid by urban consumers for a fixed market basket of consumer goods and services was 120 percent higher in 2008 than it was on the average during 1982–1984.

Constructing the CPI

Constructing the CPI is a huge operation that involves three stages:

- Selecting the CPI basket
- Conducting the monthly price survey
- Calculating the CPI

The CPI Basket The first stage in constructing the CPI is to select what is called the *CPI basket*. This basket contains the goods and services represented in the index and the relative importance attached to each of them. The idea is to make the relative importance of the items in the CPI basket the same as that in the budget of an average urban household. For example, because people spend more on housing than on bus rides, the CPI places more weight on the price of housing than on the price of a bus ride.

To determine the CPI basket, the BLS conducts a Consumer Expenditure Survey. Today's CPI basket is based on data gathered in the Consumer Expenditure Survey of 2004.

Figure 22.6 shows the CPI basket at the end of 2007. The basket contains around 80,000 goods and services arranged in the eight large groups shown in the figure. The most important item in a household's budget is housing, which accounts for 42 percent of total expenditure. Transportation comes next at 18 percent. Third in relative importance are food and beverages at 15 percent. These three groups account for three quarters of the average household budget. Medical care, recreation, and education and communication take 6 percent each. Another 4 percent is spent on apparel (clothing and footwear) and 3 percent is spent on other goods and services.

The BLS breaks down each of these categories into smaller ones. For example, the education and communication category breaks down into textbooks and supplies, tuition, telephone services, and personal computer services.

As you look at the relative importance of the items in the CPI basket, remember that they apply to the *average* household. *Individual* households are spread around the average. Think about your own expenditure and compare the basket of goods and services you buy with the CPI basket.

The Monthly Price Survey Each month, BLS employees check the prices of the 80,000 goods and services in the CPI basket in 30 metropolitan areas. Because the CPI aims to measure price *changes*, it is

FIGURE 22.6 The CPI Basket

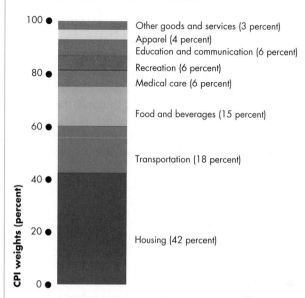

The CPI basket consists of the items that an average urban household buys. It consists mainly of housing (42 percent), transportation (18 percent), and food and beverages (15 percent). All other items add up to 25 percent of the total.

Sources of data: United States Census Bureau and Bureau of Labor Statistics.

myeconlab animation

important that the prices recorded each month refer to exactly the same item. For example, suppose the price of a box of jelly beans has increased but a box now contains more beans. Has the price of jelly beans increased? The BLS employee must record the details of changes in quality or packaging so that price changes can be isolated from other changes.

Once the raw price data are in hand, the next task is to calculate the CPI.

Calculating the CPI To calculate the CPI, we

1. Find the cost of the CPI basket at base-period prices.
2. Find the cost of the CPI basket at current-period prices.
3. Calculate the CPI for the base period and the current period.

We'll work through these three steps for a simple example. Suppose the CPI basket contains only two goods and services: oranges and haircuts. We'll construct an annual CPI rather than a monthly CPI with the reference base period 2008 and the current period 2009.

Table 22.1 shows the quantities in the CPI basket and the prices in the base period and current period.

Part (a) contains the data for the base period. In that period, consumers bought 10 oranges at $1 each and 5 haircuts at $8 each. To find the cost of the CPI basket in the base-period prices, multiply the quantities in the CPI basket by the base-period prices. The cost of oranges is $10 (10 at $1 each), and the cost of haircuts is $40 (5 at $8 each). So total cost in the base period of the CPI basket is $50 ($10 + $40).

Part (b) contains the price data for the current period. The price of an orange increased from $1 to $2, which is a 100 percent increase—($1 ÷ $1) × 100 = 100. The price of a haircut increased from $8 to $10, which is a 25 percent increase—($2 ÷ $8) × 100 = 25.

The CPI provides a way of averaging these price increases by comparing the cost of the basket rather than the price of each item. To find the cost of the CPI basket in the current period, 2009, multiply the quantities in the basket by their 2009 prices. The cost of

oranges is $20 (10 at $2 each), and the cost of haircuts is $50 (5 at $10 each). So total cost of the fixed CPI basket at current-period prices is $70 ($20 + $50).

You've now taken the first two steps toward calculating the CPI: calculating the cost of the CPI basket in the base period and the current period. The third step uses the numbers you've just calculated to find the CPI for 2008 and 2009.

The formula for the CPI is

$$CPI = \frac{\text{Cost of CPI basket at current prices}}{\text{Cost of CPI basket at base-period prices}} \times 100.$$

In Table 22.1, you established that in 2008 (the base period), the cost of the CPI basket was $50 and in 2009, it was $70. If we use these numbers in the CPI formula, we can find the CPI for 2008 and 2009. For 2008, the CPI is

$$CPI \text{ in } 2008 = \frac{\$50}{\$50} \times 100 = 100.$$

For 2009, the CPI is

$$CPI \text{ in } 2009 = \frac{\$70}{\$50} \times 100 = 140.$$

The principles that you've applied in this simplified CPI calculation apply to the more complex calculations performed every month by the BLS.

Measuring the Inflation Rate

A major purpose of the CPI is to measure changes in the cost of living and in the value of money. To measure these changes, we calculate the *inflation rate* as the annual percentage change in the CPI. To calculate the inflation rate, we use the formula:

$$\text{Inflation rate} = \frac{\text{CPI this year} - \text{CPI last year}}{\text{CPI last year}} \times 100.$$

We can use this formula to calculate the inflation rate in 2008. The CPI in July 2008 was 220, and the CPI in July 2007 was 208.3. So the inflation rate during the twelve months to July 2008 was

$$\text{Inflation rate} = \frac{(220 - 208.3)}{208.3} \times 100 = 5.6\%.$$

TABLE 22.1 The CPI: A Simplified Calculation

(a) The cost of the CPI basket at base-period prices: 2008

Item	Quantity	Price	Cost of CPI Basket
Oranges	10	$1.00	$10
Haircuts	5	$8.00	$40
Cost of CPI basket at base-period prices			$50

(b) The cost of the CPI basket at current-period prices: 2009

Item	Quantity	Price	Cost of CPI Basket
Oranges	10	$2.00	$20
Haircuts	5	$10.00	$50
Cost of CPI basket at current-period prices			$70

Distinguishing High Inflation from a High Price Level

Figure 22.7 shows the CPI and the inflation rate in the United States during the 37 years between 1971 and 2008. The two parts of the figure are related and emphasize the distinction between high inflation and high prices.

Figure 22.7 shows that when the price level in part (a) *rises rapidly*, as it did during the 1970s and through 1982, the inflation rate in part (b) is *high*. When the price level in part (a) *rises slowly*, as it did after 1982, the inflation rate in part (b) is *low*.

A high inflation rate means that the price level is rising rapidly. A high price level means that there has been a sustained period of rising prices like that shown in Fig 22.7(a).

The CPI is not a perfect measure of the price level and changes in the CPI probably overstate the inflation rate. Let's look at the sources of bias.

The Biased CPI

The main sources of bias in the CPI are

- New goods bias
- Quality change bias
- Commodity substitution bias
- Outlet substitution bias

New Goods Bias If you want to compare the price level in 2009 with that in 1969, you must somehow compare the price of a computer today with that of a typewriter in 1969. Because a PC is more expensive than a typewriter was, the arrival of the PC puts an upward bias into the CPI and its inflation rate.

Quality Change Bias Cars, CD players, and many other items get better every year. Part of the rise in the prices of these items is a payment for improved quality and is not inflation. But the CPI counts the entire price rise as inflation and so overstates inflation.

Commodity Substitution Bias Changes in relative prices lead consumers to change the items they buy. For example, if the price of beef rises and the price of chicken remains unchanged, people buy more chicken and less beef. This switch from beef to chicken might provides the same amount of protein and the same enjoyment as before and expenditure is the same as before. The price of protein has not changed. But because the CPI ignores the substitution of chicken for beef, it says the price of protein has increased.

FIGURE 22.7 The CPI and the Inflation Rate

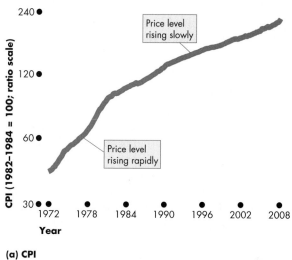

(a) CPI

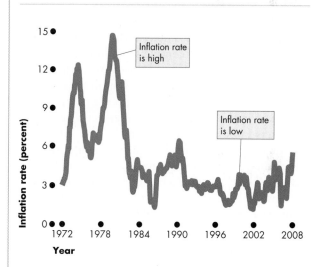

(b) Inflation rate

When the price level rises rapidly, the inflation rate is high, and when the price level rises slowly, the inflation rate is low. During the 1970s and through 1982, the price level increased rapidly in part (a) and the inflation rate was high in part (b). The inflation rate averaged 8 percent a year and sometimes exceeded 14 percent a year.

After 1982, the price level rose slowly in part (a) and the inflation rate was low in part (b). The inflation rate averaged 3.2 percent a year.

Source of data: Bureau of Labor Statistics.

Outlet Substitution Bias When confronted with higher prices, people use discount stores more frequently and convenience stores less frequently. This phenomenon is called *outlet substitution*. The CPI surveys do not monitor outlet substitutions.

The Magnitude of the Bias

You've reviewed the sources of bias in the CPI. But how big is the bias? This question was tackled in 1996 by a Congressional Advisory Commission on the Consumer Price Index chaired by Michael Boskin, an economics professor at Stanford University. This commission said that the CPI overstates inflation by 1.1 percentage points a year. That is, if the CPI reports that inflation is 3.1 percent a year, most likely inflation is actually 2 percent a year.

Some Consequences of the Bias

The bias in the CPI distorts private contracts and increases government outlays. Many private agreements, such as wage contracts, are linked to the CPI. For example, a firm and its workers might agree to a three-year wage deal that increases the wage rate by 2 percent a year *plus* the percentage increase in the CPI. Such a deal ends up giving the workers more real income than the firm intended.

Close to a third of federal government outlays, including Social Security checks, are linked directly to the CPI. And while a bias of 1 percent a year seems small, accumulated over a decade it adds up to almost a trillion dollars of additional expenditures.

Alternative Price Indexes

The CPI is just one of many alternative price level index numbers and because of the bias in the CPI, other measures are used for some purposes. We'll describe three alternatives to the CPI and explain when and why they might be preferred to the CPI. The alternatives are

- Chained CPI
- Personal consumption expenditure deflator
- GDP deflator

Chained CPI The *chained CPI* is a price index that is calculated using a similar method to that used to calculate *chained-dollar real GDP* described in Chapter 21 (see pp. 502–503).

The *chained* CPI overcomes the sources of bias in the CPI. It incorporates substitutions and new goods bias by using current and previous period quantities rather than fixed quantities from an earlier period.

The practical difference made by the chained CPI is small. This index has been calculated since 2000 and the average inflation rate since then as measured by the chained CPI is only 0.3 percentage points lower than the standard CPI—2.5 percent versus 2.8 percent per year.

Personal Consumption Expenditure Deflator The *personal consumption expenditure deflator* (or *PCE deflator*) is calculated from data in the national income accounts that you studied in Chapter 21. When the Bureau of Economic Analysis calculates *real GDP*, it also calculates the real values of its expenditure components: real consumption expenditure, real investment, real government expenditure, and real net exports. These calculations are done in the same way as that for real GDP described in simplified terms on p. 493 and more technically on pp. 502–503.

To calculate the PCE deflator, we use the formula:

$$\text{PCE deflator} = (\text{Nominal } C \div \text{Real } C) \times 100,$$

where C is personal consumption expenditure.

The basket of goods and services included in the PCE deflator is broader than that in the CPI because it includes all consumption expenditure, not only the items bought by a typical urban family.

Again, the difference between the PCE deflator and the CPI is small. Since 2000, the inflation rate measured by the PCE deflator is 2.4 percent per year, 0.4 percentage points lower than the CPI inflation rate.

GDP Deflator The *GDP deflator* is a bit like the PCE deflator except that it includes all the goods and services that are counted as part of GDP. So it is an index of the prices of the items in consumption, investment, government expenditure, and net exports.

This broader price index is appropriate for macroeconomics because, like GDP itself, it is a comprehensive measure of the cost of the real GDP basket of goods and services.

Since 2000, the GDP deflator has increased at an average rate of 2.6 percent per year, only 0.2 percentage points below the CPI inflation rate.

Core CPI Inflation No matter whether we calculate the inflation rate using the CPI, the chained CPI, the personal consumption expenditure deflator, or the GDP deflator, the number bounces around a good deal from month to month or quarter to quarter. To determine whether the inflation rate is trending upward or downward, we need to strip the raw numbers of their volatility. The **core CPI inflation rate**, which is the CPI inflation rate excluding volatile elements, attempts to do just that and reveal the underlying inflation trend.

As a practical matter, the core CPI inflation rate is calculated as the percentage change in the CPI (or other price index) excluding food and fuel. The prices of these two items are among the most volatile.

While the core CPI inflation rate removes the volatile elements in inflation, it can give a misleading view of the true underlying inflation rate. If the relative prices of the excluded items are changing, the core CPI inflation rate will give a biased measure of the true underlying inflation rate.

Such a misleading account was given during the years between 2003 and 2008 when the relative prices of food and fuel were rising. The result was a core CPI inflation rate that was systematically below the CPI inflation rate. Figure 22.8 shows the two series since 2001. More refined measures of core inflation have been suggested that eliminate the bias.

The Real Variables in Macroeconomics

You saw in Chapter 21 how we measure real GDP. And you've seen in this chapter how we can use nominal GDP and real GDP to provide another measure of the price level—the GDP deflator. But viewing real GDP as nominal GDP deflated, opens up the idea of other real variables. By using the GDP deflator, we can deflate other nominal variables to find their real values. For example, the *real wage rate* is the nominal wage rate divided by the GDP deflator.

We can adjust any nominal quantity or price variable for inflation by deflating it—by dividing it by the price level.

There is one variable that is a bit different—an interest rate. A real interest rate is *not* a nominal interest rate divided by the price level. You'll learn how to adjust the nominal interest rate for inflation to find the real interest rate in Chapter 24. But all the other real variables of macroeconomics are calculated by dividing a nominal variable by the price level.

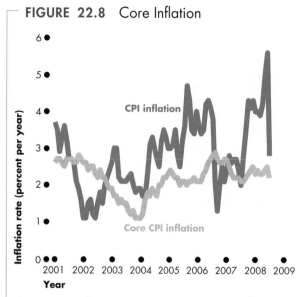

FIGURE 22.8 Core Inflation

The core CPI inflation rate excludes volatile price changes of food and fuel. Since 2003, the core CPI inflation rate has mostly been below the CPI inflation rate because the relative prices of food and fuel have been rising.

Source of data: Bureau of Labor Statistics.

myeconlab animation

Review Quiz

1 What is the price level?
2 What is the CPI and how is it calculated?
3 How do we calculate the inflation rate and what is the relationship between the CPI and the inflation rate?
4 What are the four main ways in which the CPI is an upward-biased measure of the price level?
5 What problems arise from the CPI bias?
6 What are the alternative measures of the price level and how do they address the problem of bias in the CPI?

myeconlab Work Study Plan 22.3 and get instant feedback.

◆ You've now completed your study of the measurement of macroeconomic performance. Your task in the following chapters is to learn what determines that performance and how policy actions might improve it. But first, take a close-up look at the labor market in the slowdown of 2008 in *Reading Between the Lines* on pp. 524–525.

Jobs in the Slowdown of 2008

Jobless Rate Soars to 6.1%

http://money.cnn.com
September 5, 2008

The unemployment rate soared to a nearly five-year high in August as employers trimmed jobs for the eighth straight month, the government reported Friday.

The unemployment rate rose to 6.1%, the highest level since September 2003. That's up from 5.7% in July and 4.7% a year ago.

In addition, the economy suffered a net loss of 84,000 jobs in August, according to the U.S. Department of Labor, compared to a revised reading of a 60,000 job loss in July.

The U.S. economy has lost 605,000 jobs so far this year.

The jobs report immediately drew comment from the presidential candidates as well as the Bush administration.

The White House pointed to other economic readings, including last week's gross domestic product report. It showed second quarter growth jumping to a 3.3% annual rate, helped by economic stimulus checks and strong exports.

"While these (jobs) numbers are disappointing, what is most important is the overall direction the economy is headed," said the White House statement.

But the campaign of Democratic presidential candidate Barack Obama said the report points out the failure of Republican policies.

…

The unemployment rate doesn't tell the whole picture about how difficult the job market has become. It only counts those who looked for work during the month; it excludes the unemployed who want jobs but have stopped looking for work. And it also doesn't count those who want full-time jobs but can only find part-time positions.

The so-called underemployment rate, which includes those two other groups, rose to 10.7% —the highest reading since 1994.

Essence of the Story

- The unemployment rate increased to 6.1 percent in August 2008, the highest level since September 2003.
- The unemployment rate was 5.7 percent in July and 4.7 percent in August 2007.
- Employment decreased by 84,000 in August and by 605,000 since January 2008.
- In contrast, second quarter real GDP increased at a 3.3 percent annual rate.
- The broader underemployment rate, which includes those who stopped looking for work and part-time workers who want full-time work increased to 10.7 percent, its highest rate since 1994.

Economic Analysis

- This news article reports some labor market data for August 2008: the rise in the unemployment rate and the number of jobs lost.

- This weak labor market performance comes at the end of an unusually weak expansion from a recession in 2001.

- The figures show the job creation performance of the U.S. economy during the expansion that began in 2002 and place that expansion in a longer-term historical perspective.

- In Fig. 1, the *y*-axis shows the level of employment as a percentage of its level at the business cycle trough and the *x*-axis shows the number of months since the business cycle trough.

- By August 2008, the expansion had been running for 79 months (6 years and 7 months).

- The blue line in the figure shows the growth of employment during the 2002–2008 expansion.

- Employment peaked at the beginning of 2008 and then flattened off.

- The shaded area in the graph enables you to compare the 2002–2008 expansion with the previous U.S. business cycle expansions. That shaded area shows the range of employment over the first 54 months (4½ years) of those previous expansions.

- You can see that the current expansion runs along the bottom of the range of previous experience.

- Figure 2 shows a similar comparison for the unemployment rate.

- In an average expansion, the unemployment rate falls after 54 months to 70 percent of its trough level.

- In the current expansion, the unemployment rate actually increased and after 18 months stood at 10 percent above its trough level.

- As measured by the unemployment rate, the current expansion was similar to the weakest of the previous ones.

- The unemployment rate began to rise at the beginning of 2007, when the pace of job growth came to a standstill.

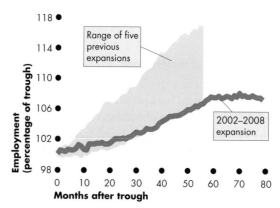

Figure 1 Employment during the 2002–2008 expansion

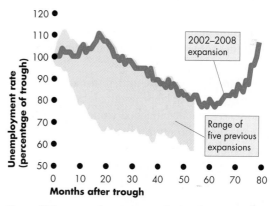

Figure 2 The unemployment rate during the 2002–2008 expansion

SUMMARY

Key Points

Employment and Unemployment (pp. 510–513)

- Unemployment is a serious personal, social, and economic problem because it results in lost output and income and a loss of human capital.
- The unemployment rate averaged 5.8 percent between 1961 and 2008. It increases in recessions and decreases in expansions.
- The labor force participation rate and the employment-to-population ratio have an upward trend and fluctuate with the business cycle.

Unemployment and Full Employment (pp. 514–517)

- The unemployment rate is an imperfect measure of the underutilization of labor resources because it excludes some underutilized labor and some unemployment is unavoidable.
- The unemployment rate underestimates the underutilization of labor resources because it excludes marginally attached workers and part-time workers who want full-time jobs.
- Some unemployment is unavoidable because people are constantly entering and leaving the labor force and losing or quitting jobs; also firms that create jobs are constantly being borne, expanding, contracting, and dying.
- Unemployment can be frictional, structural, or cyclical.
- When all unemployment is frictional and structural, the unemployment rate equals the natural unemployment rate, the economy is at full employment, and real GDP equals potential GDP.
- Over the business cycle, real GDP fluctuates around potential GDP and the unemployment rate fluctuates around the natural unemployment rate.

The Price Level and Inflation (pp. 518–523)

- Inflation is a problem because it redistributes income and wealth and diverts resources from production.
- The Consumer Price Index (CPI) is a measure of the average of the prices paid by urban consumers for a fixed basket of consumer goods and services.
- The CPI is defined to equal 100 for a reference base period—currently 1982–1984.
- The inflation rate is the percentage change in the CPI from one period to the next.
- Changes in the CPI probably overstate the inflation rate because of the bias that arises from new goods, quality changes, commodity substitution, and outlet substitution.
- The bias in the CPI distorts private contracts and increases government outlays.
- Alternative price level measures avoid the bias of the CPI but do not make a large difference to the measured inflation rate.
- Real economic variables are calculated by dividing nominal variables by the price level.

Key Figures

Key Terms

PROBLEMS and APPLICATIONS

 Work problems 1–9 in Chapter 22 Study Plan and get instant feedback.
Work problems 10–18 as Homework, a Quiz, or a Test if assigned by your instructor.

1. The Bureau of Labor Statistics reported the following data for the second quarter of 2008:
   Labor force: 154,294,000
   Employment: 146,089,000
   Working-age population: 233,410,000
   Calculate for that quarter the
   a. Unemployment rate.
   b. Labor force participation rate.
   c. Employment-to-population ratio.

2. In March 2007, the U.S. unemployment rate was 4.4 percent. In August 2008, the unemployment rate was 6.1 percent. Use this information to predict what happened between March 2007 and August 2008 to the numbers of
   a. Job losers and job leavers.
   b. Entrants and reentrants into the labor force.

3. In July 2009, in the economy of Sandy Island, 10,000 people were employed, 1,000 were unemployed, and 5,000 were not in the labor force. During August 2009, 80 people lost their jobs and didn't look for new ones, 20 people quit their jobs and retired, 150 people were hired or recalled, 50 people withdrew from the labor force, and 40 people entered or reentered the labor force to look for work. Calculate for July 2009
   a. The unemployment rate.
   b. The employment-to-population ratio.

   And calculate for the end of August 2009
   c. The number of people unemployed.
   d. The number of people employed.
   e. The unemployment rate.

4. The Bureau of Labor Statistics reported the following CPI data:
   June 2006   201.9
   June 2007   207.2
   June 2008   217.4
   a. What do these numbers tell you about the price level in these three years?
   b. Calculate the inflation rates for the years ended June 2007 and June 2008.
   c. How did the inflation rate change in 2008?
   d. Why might these CPI numbers be biased?

   e. How do alternative price indexes help to avoid the bias in the CPI numbers?

5. The IMF *World Economic Outlook* reports the following price level data (2000 = 100):

Region	2006	2007	2008
United States	117.1	120.4	124.0
Euro area	113.6	117.1	119.6
Japan	98.1	98.1	98.8

   a. Which region had the highest inflation rate in 2007 and which had the highest inflation rate in 2008?
   b. Describe the path of the price level in Japan.

6. **Nation's Economic Pain Deepens**
   A spike in the unemployment rate—the biggest in more than two decades—raised new concerns Friday that a weak labor outlook, high oil prices and continuing woes in the housing and credit markets are leading the U.S. economy into a painful recession. The government said Friday that the unemployment rate soared to 5.5% in May from 5% in April—much higher than economists had forecast. The surge marked the biggest one-month jump in unemployment since February 1986, and the 5.5% rate is the highest level seen since October 2004. Unemployment is now a full percentage point higher than it was a year ago. ...
   CNN, June 6, 2008
   a. How does the unemployment rate in May compare to the unemployment rate during the past few recessions?
   b. Why might the unemployment rate tend to actually underestimate the unemployment problem, especially during a recession?
   c. How does the unemployment rate in May compare to the estimated natural unemployment rate? What does this imply about the relationship between real GDP and potential GDP at this time?

7. **Michigan: Epicenter of Unemployment**
   Michigan, once the center of America's industrial heartland, now holds a more dubious distinction: It leads the U.S. in joblessness. The state's

unemployment rate hit 8.5% in May … and compares with a figure of 5.5% for the whole U.S. in May. There's little mystery as to the cause. Detroit's bet on big trucks and sport-utility vehicles has turned snake-eyes. … Overall U.S. vehicle sales are expected to drop below 15 million this year. Three years ago, the industry sold 17 million cars and trucks. But bad as those unemployment figures look, the reality is actually worse. The official number is arrived at by surveying households and learning how many family members are unemployed but seeking work. So it does not reflect those who have given up finding a job, or those who are not yet looking but soon will be. … One of the bright spots, if you can call it that, for Michigan is the health-care industry. With baby boomers aging and their parents living longer, hospitals, nursing homes, clinics, and medical laboratories have the most jobs to offer in Michigan today. But the cruel irony is that there is a shortage of trained professionals. … Registered nurses and lab technicians are in big demand, with not enough applicants.

BusinessWeek, June 24, 2008

a. Why is the reality of the unemployment problem in Michigan actually worse than the 8.5% unemployment rate statistic?

b. Is this higher unemployment rate in Michigan frictional, structural, or cyclical? Explain.

8. **Inflation Getting "Uglier and Uglier"**

The Consumer Price Index, a key inflation reading, rose 4.2% through the 12 months ending in May, according to the Labor Department. … For the month of May, overall CPI rose 0.6% … the biggest increase since last November, when the overall CPI surged 0.9%. … The dramatic increases in energy costs were largely responsible for the overall inflation. Energy costs rose 4.4% in May, and surged 17.4% over the 12 months ending in May … transportation costs increased 2% in May, and jumped 8.1% over the 12 months ending in May. The index for household energy costs climbed 2.8% in May, its fourth consecutive jump, the Labor Department said. The price of food also pushed up overall costs. Food costs increased 0.3% in May, and jumped 5.1% during the 12 months ending in May. The price of milk was a big influence on the overall

price, increasing 10.2% over the 12 months. … The cost of clothing was the one area where consumers got some relief. Apparel costs deflated 0.2% in May, and decreased 0.4% over the 12 months. The core CPI, which excludes the cost of food and energy, rose 0.2% in May. … The core CPI rose 2.3% during the 12 months ending in May.

CNN, June 13, 2008

a. How do the inflation rates described in this article compare to average inflation since 1983? How do they compare to average inflation during the 1970s and early 1980s?

b. Which components of the CPI basket are experiencing price increases faster than the average and which have price increases below the average?

c. What is the difference between the CPI and the core CPI? Why might the core CPI be a useful measurement and why might it be misleading?

9. **Dress for Less**

Since 1998, the price of a "Speedy" handbag — the entry-level style at Louis Vuitton—has more than doubled, to $685, indicative of a precipitous price increase throughout the luxury goods market. The price of Joe Boxer's "licky face" underwear, meanwhile, has dropped by nearly half, to $8.99, representing just as seismic a shift at the other end of the fashion continuum, where the majority of American consumers do their shopping.

As luxury fashion has become more expensive, mainstream apparel has become markedly less so. … Clothing is one of the few categories in the federal Consumer Price Index in which overall prices have declined—about 10 percent—since 1998 (the cost of communication is another). That news may be of solace to anyone whose budget has been stretched just to drive to work or to stop at the supermarket; in fashion, at least, there are still deals to be had. …

The New York Times, May 29, 2008

a. What percentage of the CPI basket does apparel comprise?

b. If luxury clothing prices have increased dramatically since the late 1990s, why has the clothing category of the CPI actually declined by about 10 percent?

10. In the New Orleans metropolitan area in August 2005, the labor force was 634,512 and 35,222 people were unemployed. In September 2005 following Hurricane Katrina, the labor force fell by 156,518 and the number employed fell by 206,024. Calculate the unemployment rate in August 2005 and in September 2005.

11. The IMF *World Economic Outlook* reports the following unemployment rates:

Region	2007	2008
United States	4.6	5.4
Euro area	7.4	7.3
Japan	3.9	3.9

   a. What do these numbers tell you about the phase of the business cycle in the United States, Euro area, and Japan in 2008?
   b. What do you think these numbers tell us about the relative size of the natural unemployment rates in the United States, the Euro area, and Japan?
   c. Do these numbers tell us anything about the relative size of the labor force participation rates and employment-to-population ratios in the three regions?
   d. Why might these unemployment numbers understate or overstate the true amount of unemployment?

12. A typical family on Sandy Island consumes only juice and cloth. Last year, which was the base year, the family spent $40 on juice and $25 on cloth. In the base year, juice was $4 a bottle and cloth was $5 a length. This year, juice is $4 a bottle and cloth is $6 a length. Calculate
   a. The CPI basket.
   b. The CPI in the current year.
   c. The inflation rate in the current year.

13. **A Half-Year of Job Losses**
   Employers trimmed jobs from their payrolls in June for the sixth straight month, as the government's closely watched report Thursday showed continued weakness in the labor market. ... The June number brought to 438,000 the number of jobs lost by the U.S. economy so far this year. ... The job losses in the monthly report were concentrated in manufacturing and construction, two sectors that have been badly battered in the current economic downturn. ...
   CNN, July 3, 2008

   a. How do the job losses for the first half of 2008 compare to the total number of people employed?
   b. Based on the news clip, what might be the main source of increased unemployment?
   c. Based on the news clip, what might be the main type of increased unemployment?

14. **Out of a Job and Out of Luck at 54**
   Too young to retire, too old to get a new job. That's how many older workers are feeling these days. ... Older job seekers are discovering the search is even rougher as many employers shy away from hiring those closer to retirement than to the start of their careers. ... After they get the pink slip, older workers spend more time on the unemployment line. Many lack the skills to search for jobs in today's online world and to craft resumes and cover letters, experts say. ... It took those age 55 and older an average of 21.1 weeks to land a new job in 2007, about five weeks longer than their younger counterparts, according to AARP. "Clearly older workers will be more adversely affected because of the time it takes to transition into another job," said Deborah Russell, AARP's director of workforce issues.
   CNN, May 21, 2008

   a. What type of unemployment might older workers be more prone to experience?
   b. Explain how the unemployment rate of older workers would be influenced by the business cycle.
   c. Why might older unemployed workers become marginally attached or discouraged workers during a recession?

15. **Governor Plans to Boost Economy with Eco-friendly Jobs**
   Oregon's 5.6 percent unemployment rate hovers close to the national average of 5.5 percent. ... Less than four years ago, the state had one of the highest unemployment rates in the nation. [Oregon Governor] Kulongoski hopes to avoid a repeat of those days. When the 2009 Legislature meets, he'll present a package of proposals he thinks will keep the jobs picture bright, despite what may be going on elsewhere. The cornerstone, he says, is making sure public schools and universities get enough state dollars to meet growing demand for skilled workers. Those range

from high school seniors looking to go straight into a vocation, such as welding or electrical wiring, to college grads armed with advanced marketing or engineering degrees. Beyond that, Kulongoski wants to … use state and federal money for bridges, roads and buildings to stimulate more construction jobs.

The Oregonian, July 8, 2008

a. What is the main type of unemployment that Governor Kulongoski is using policies to avoid? Explain.

b. How might these policies impact Oregon's natural unemployment rate? Explain.

16. **Economic "Misery" More Widespread**

Unemployment and inflation are typically added together to come up with a so-called "Misery Index." The "Misery Index" was often cited during periods of high unemployment and inflation, such as the mid 1970s and late 1970s to early 1980s.

And some fear the economy may be approaching those levels again. The official numbers produce a current Misery Index of only 8.9—inflation of 3.9% plus unemployment of 5%. That's not far from the Misery Index's low of 6.1 seen in 1998. … Some worry it could even approach the post-World War II record of 20.6 in 1980. …

CNN, May 13, 2008

a. Explain how the "Misery Index" might serve as a gauge of how the economy is performing.

b. How does the most current "Misery Index" compare to the high and low given in this article? (You may find it useful to use the link of MyEconLab—Chapter Resources, Chapter 22, Web links—to visit the Bureau of Labor Statistics Website for the current unemployment rate and the most recent 12-month change in the CPI.)

17. **The Great Inflation Cover-Up**

The 1996 Boskin Commission … was established to determine the accuracy of the CPI. The commission concluded that the CPI overstated inflation by 1.1%, and methodologies were adjusted to reflect that. Critics of the Boskin Commission suggest that the basis upon which the CPI was revised doesn't account for the way people actually purchase and consume products. The commission pointed to four biases inherent in the way the CPI was determined that suppos-

edly contribute to overstatement. … But the Boskin critics note several reasonable exceptions to those biases. The Boskin Commission suggests that when customers substitute one good for another, the CPI should treat those goods equally. If [someone] orders a hanger steak instead of his beloved filet mignon because the hanger steak is cheaper, Boskin argues that the hanger steak prices should be compared with previous filet mignon prices. It's all beef, right? But critics of the Boskin report point to areas where substitution is so price-driven that consumers are pushed out of the category altogether. What happens when the consumer gives up steak entirely and switches to chicken? (Or to use a scarier example, goes from some health insurance to no health insurance?) Boskin also says that whatever you're paying in price increases is offset by the additional pleasure you get from better goods. To put it another way, you adjust for improvement in quality over time. … So, for example, energy price increases due to federally mandated environmental measures are offset by how much we all sit around enjoying the cleaner environment.

Fortune, April 3, 2008

a. What are the main sources of bias that are generally believed to make the CPI overstate the inflation rate? By how much did Boskin estimate the CPI overstates the inflation rate?

b. Do the substitutions among different kinds of meat make the CPI biased up or down?

c. Why does it matter if the CPI overstates or understates the inflation rate?

18. Study *Reading Between the Lines* on pp. 524–525 and then answer the following questions:

a. When did the unemployment rate peak after the 2001 recession?

b. When did the unemployment rate reach its lowest point in the 2002–2008 expansion?

c. Did the expansion of 2002–2008 create jobs at an unusually fast rate, an unusually slow rate, or an average rate?

d. Provide reasons why the first two years of the expansion didn't create many jobs.

e. Is the slow job growth and rise in unemployment after mid-2007 most likely cyclical, structural, or frictional? Explain.

f. Suggest some actions that the U.S. government might take if it wants to create more jobs.

24 Finance, Saving, and Investment

After studying this chapter, you will be able to:

■ Describe and define the flows of funds through financial markets and the financial institutions

■ Explain how investment and saving along with borrowing and lending decisions are made and how these decisions interact in the market for loanable funds

■ Explain how a government deficit (or surplus) influences the real interest rate, saving, and investment in the market for loanable funds

■ Explain how international borrowing or lending influences the real interest rate, saving, and investment in the global market for loanable funds

During September 2008, Wall Street put on a spectacular show. To prevent the collapse of Fannie Mae and Freddie Mac, the two largest lenders to home buyers, the U.S. government took over their risky debts. When Lehman Brothers, a venerable Wall Street investment bank, was on the verge of bankruptcy, secure phone lines and limousines worked overtime as the Federal Reserve Bank of New York, the U.S. Treasury, and senior officials of Bank of America and Barclays Bank (a British bank) tried to find ways to save the bank. The effort failed. On the same weekend, Bank of America bought Merrill Lynch, another big Wall Street investment bank. And a

few days later, the U.S. government bought insurance giant AIG and tried to get Congress to provide $700 billion to buy just about every risky debt that anyone wanted to unload.

Behind such drama, Wall Street plays a crucial unseen role funneling funds from savers and lenders to investors and borrowers. This chapter explains how financial markets work and their place in the economy.

In *Reading Between the Lines* at the end of the chapter, we'll return to the events of September 2008 and apply what you've learned to better understand what was happening in those crucial days.

◆ Financial Institutions and Financial Markets

The financial institutions and markets that we study in this chapter play a crucial role in the economy. They provide the channels through which saving flows to finance the investment in new capital that makes the economy grow.

In studying the economics of financial institutions and markets, we distinguish between:

- Finance and money
- Physical capital and financial capital

Finance and Money

In economics, we use the term *finance* to describe the activity of providing the funds that finance expenditures on capital. The study of finance looks at how households and firms obtain and use financial resources and how they cope with the risks that arise in this activity.

Money is what we use to pay for goods and services and factors of production and to make financial transactions. The study of money looks at how households and firms use it, how much of it they hold, how banks create and manage it, and how its quantity influences the economy.

In the economic lives of individuals and businesses, finance and money are closely interrelated. And some of the main financial institutions, such as banks, provide both financial services and monetary services. Nevertheless, by distinguishing between *finance* and *money* and studying them separately, we will better understand our financial and monetary markets and institutions.

For the rest of this chapter, we study finance. Money is the topic of the next chapter.

Physical Capital and Financial Capital

Economists distinguish between physical capital and financial capital. *Physical capital* is the tools, instruments, machines, buildings, and other items that have been produced in the past and that are used today to produce goods and services. Inventories of raw materials, semifinished goods, and components are part of physical capital. When economists use the term capital, they mean *physical* capital. The funds that firms use to buy physical capital are called **financial capital**.

Along the *aggregate production function* in Chapter 23, the quantity of capital is fixed. An increase in the quantity of capital increases production possibilities and shifts the aggregate production function upward. You're going to see, in this chapter, how investment, saving, borrowing, and lending decisions influence the quantity of capital and make it grow, and as a consequence, make real GDP grow.

We begin by describing the links between capital and investment and between wealth and saving.

Capital and Investment

The quantity of capital changes because of investment and depreciation. *Investment* (Chapter 21, p. 535) increases the quantity of capital and *depreciation* (Chapter 21, p. 542) decreases it. The total amount spent on new capital is called **gross investment**. The change in the value of capital is called **net investment**. Net investment equals gross investment minus depreciation.

Figure 24.1 illustrates these terms. On January 1, 2008, Ace Bottling Inc. had machines worth $30,000—Ace's initial capital. During 2008, the market value of Ace's machines fell by 67 percent—$20,000. After this depreciation, Ace's machines were valued at $10,000. During 2008, Ace spent $30,000 on new machines. This amount is Ace's gross investment. By December 31, 2008, Ace Bottling had capital valued at $40,000, so its capital had increased by $10,000. This amount is Ace's net investment. Ace's net investment equals its gross investment of $30,000 minus depreciation of its initial capital of $20,000.

Wealth and Saving

Wealth is the value of all the things that people own. What people own is related to what they earn, but it is not the same thing. People earn an *income*, which is the amount they receive during a given time period from supplying the services of the resources they own. **Saving** is the amount of income that is not paid in taxes or spent on consumption goods and services. Saving increases wealth. Wealth also increases when the market value of assets rises—called *capital gains*—and decreases when the market value of assets falls—called *capital losses*.

For example, at the end of the school year you have $250 in the bank and a coin collection worth $300, so your wealth is $550. During the summer,

FIGURE 24.1   Capital and Investment

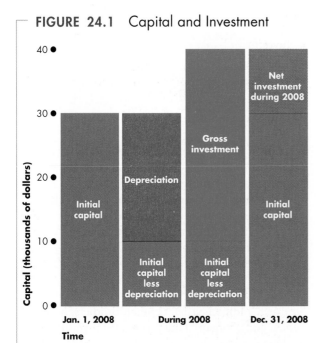

On January 1, 2008, Ace Bottling had capital worth $30,000. During the year, the value of Ace's capital fell by $20,000—depreciation—and it spent $30,000 on new capital—gross investment. Ace's net investment was $10,000 ($30,000 gross investment minus $20,000 depreciation) so that at the end of 2008, Ace had capital worth $40,000.

myeconlab   animation

you earn $5,000 (net of taxes) and spend $1,000 on consumption goods and services so your saving is $4,000. Your bank account increases to $4,250 and your wealth becomes $4,550. The $4,000 increase in wealth equals saving. If coins rise in value and your coin collection is now worth $500, you have a capital gain of $200, which is also added to your wealth.

National wealth and national saving work like this personal example. The wealth of a nation at the end of a year equals its wealth at the start of the year plus its saving during the year, which equals income minus consumption expenditure.

To make real GDP grow, saving and wealth must be transformed into investment and capital. This transformation takes place in the markets for financial capital and through the activities of financial institutions. We're now going to describe these markets and institutions.

Markets for Financial Capital

Saving is the source of the funds that are used to finance investment, and these funds are supplied and demanded in three types of financial markets:

- Loan markets
- Bond markets
- Stock markets

Loan Markets Businesses often want short-term finance to buy inventories or to extend credit to their customers. Sometimes they get this finance in the form of a loan from a bank. Households often want finance to purchase big ticket items, such as automobiles or household furnishings and appliances. They get this finance as bank loans, often in the form of outstanding credit card balances.

Households also get finance to buy new homes. (Expenditure on new homes is counted as part of investment.) These funds are usually obtained as a loan that is secured by a **mortgage**—a legal contract that gives ownership of a home to the lender in the event that the borrower fails to meet the agreed loan payments (repayments and interest). Mortgage loans were at the center of the U.S. credit crisis of 2007–2008.

All of these types of financing take place in loan markets.

Bond Markets When Wal-Mart expands its business and opens new stores, it gets the finance it needs by selling bonds. Governments—federal, state, and municipal—also raise finance by issuing bonds.

A **bond** is a promise to make specified payments on specified dates. For example, you can buy a Wal-Mart bond that promises to pay $3.4375 every May and October until 2009 and then to make a final payment of $100 in October 2009.

The buyer of a bond from Wal-Mart makes a loan to the company and is entitled to the payments promised by the bond. When a person buys a newly issued bond, he or she may hold the bond until the borrower has repaid the amount borrowed or sell it to someone else. Bonds issued by firms and governments are traded in the **bond market**.

The term of a bond might be long (decades) or short (just a month or two). Firms often issue very short-term bonds as a way of getting paid for their sales before the buyer is able to pay. For example, when GM sells $100 million of railway locomotives to Union Pacific, GM wants to be paid when the items are shipped. But Union Pacific doesn't want to pay until the locomotives are earning an income. In this situation, Union Pacific might promise to pay GM $101 million three months in the future. A bank would be willing to buy this promise for (say) $100 million. GM gets $100 million immediately and the bank gets $101 million in three months when Union Pacific honors its promise. The U.S. Treasury issues promises of this type, called Treasury bills.

Another type of bond is a **mortgage-backed security**, which entitles its holder to the income from a package of mortgages. Mortgage lenders create mortgage-backed securities. They make mortgage loans to home buyers and then create securities that they sell to obtain more funds to make more mortgage loans. The holder of a mortgage-backed security is entitled to receive payments that derive from the payments received by the mortgage lender from the home-buyer–borrower.

Mortgage-backed securities were at the center of the storm in the financial markets in 2007–2008.

Stock Markets When Boeing wants finance to expand its airplane building business, it issues stock. A **stock** is a certificate of ownership and claim to the firm's profits. Boeing has issued about 900 million shares of its stock. So if you owned 900 Boeing shares, you would own one millionth of Boeing and be entitled to receive one millionth of its profits.

Unlike a stockholder, a bondholder does not own part the firm that issued the bond.

A **stock market** is a financial market in which shares of stocks of corporations are traded. The New York Stock Exchange, the London Stock Exchange (in England), the Frankfurt Stock Exchange (in Germany), and the Tokyo Stock Exchange (in Japan) are all examples of stock markets.

Financial Institutions

Financial markets are highly competitive because of the role played by financial institutions in those markets. A **financial institution** is a firm that operates on both sides of the markets for financial capital. It is a borrower in one market and a lender in another.

Financial institutions also stand ready to trade so that households with funds to lend and firms or households seeking funds can always find someone on the other side of the market with whom to trade.

The key financial institutions are

- Investment banks
- Commercial banks
- Government-sponsored mortgage lenders
- Pension funds
- Insurance companies

Investment Banks Investment banks are firms that help other financial institutions and governments raise finance by issuing and selling bonds and stocks, as well as providing advice on transactions such as mergers and acquisitions. Until the late 1980s, the United States maintained a sharp separation between investment banking and commercial banking—a separation that was imposed by the *Glass-Steagall Act of 1933.*

Until 2008, five big Wall Street firms, Bear Stearns, Goldman Sachs, Lehman Brothers, Merrill Lynch, and Morgan Stanley, provided investment banking services. But in the financial meltdown of 2008, all of these firms disappeared and were absorbed into larger financial institutions that provide both investment banking and commercial banking services.

Commercial Banks The bank that you use for your own banking services and that issues your credit card is a commercial bank. We'll return to these banks and explain their role in Chapter 25 where we study the role of money in our economy.

Government-Sponsored Mortgage Lenders Two large financial institutions, the Federal National Mortgage Association, or Fannie Mae, and the Federal Home Loan Mortgage Corporation, or Freddie Mac, were government-sponsored enterprises that bought mortgages from banks, packaged them into mortgage-backed securities, and sold them. On September 7, 2008, Fannie Mae and Freddie Mac owned or guaranteed $6 trillion worth of mortgages (half of the U.S $12 trillion of mortgages) and were taken over by the federal government.

Pension Funds Pension funds are financial institutions that use the pension contributions of firms and workers to buy bonds and stocks. The mortgage-backed securities of Fannie Mae and Freddie Mac are among the assets of pension funds. Some pension funds are very large and play an active role in the firms whose stock they hold.

Financial Failures
The Institutions at the Center of the Storm

Bear Stearns: absorbed by JPMorgan Chase with help from the Federal Reserve. Lehman Brothers: gone. Fannie Mae and Freddie Mac: taken into government oversight with U.S. taxpayer guarantees. Merrill Lynch: absorbed by Bank of America. AIG: given an $85 billion lifeline by the Federal Reserve and sold off in parcels to financial institutions around the world. Wachovia: taken over by Wells Fargo. Washington Mutual: taken over by JPMorgan Chase. Morgan Stanley: 20 percent bought by Mitsubishi, a large Japanese bank. These are some of the events in the financial crisis of 2008. What is going on?

Between 2002 and 2005, mortgage lending exploded and home prices rose. Mortgage lenders bundled their loans into *mortgage-backed securities* and sold them to eager buyers around the world.

In 2006, interest rates began to rise and the values of financial assets fell. With lower asset values, financial institutions took big losses. Some losses of some institutions were too big to bear and these institutions became insolvent.

Insurance Companies   Insurance companies provide risk-sharing services. They enter into agreements with households and firms to provide compensation in the event of accident, theft, fire, ill-health, and a host of other misfortunes. They receive premiums from their customers and make payments against claims.

Insurance companies use the funds they have received but not paid out as claims to buy bonds and stocks on which they earn an interest income.

Some insurance companies also insure bonds and other risky financial assets. In effect, they provide insurance that pays out if a firm fails and cannot meet its bond obligations. Some insurance companies insure other insurers in a complex network of reinsurance.

In normal times, insurance companies have a steady flow of funds coming in from premiums and interest on the financial assets they hold and a steady, but smaller, flow of funds paying claims. Their profit is the gap between the two flows. But in unusual times, when large and widespread losses are being incurred, insurance companies can run into difficulty in meeting their obligations. Such a situation arose in 2008 for one of the biggest insurers, AIG, and the firm was taken into public ownership.

Insolvency and Illiquidity

A financial institution's **net worth** is the total market value of what it has lent minus the market value of what it has borrowed. If net worth is positive, the institution is *solvent* and can remain in business. But if net worth is negative, the institution is *insolvent* and go out of business. The owners of an insolvent financial institution—usually its stockholders—bear the loss when the assets are sold and debts paid.

A financial institution both borrows and lends, so it is exposed to the risk that its net worth might become negative. To limit that risk, financial institutions are regulated and a minimum amount of their lending must be backed by their net worth.

Sometimes, a financial institution is solvent but illiquid. A firm is *illiquid* if it has made long-term loans with borrowed funds and is faced with a sudden demand to repay more of what it has borrowed than its available cash. In normal times, a financial institution that is illiquid can borrow from another institution. But if the all financial institutions are short of cash, the market for loans among financial institutions dries up.

Insolvency and illiquidity were at the core of the financial meltdown of 2007–2008.

Interest Rates and Asset Prices

Stocks, bonds, short-term securities, and loans are collectively called *financial assets*. The interest rate on a financial asset is the interest received expressed as a percentage of the price of the asset.

Because the interest rate is a percentage of the price of an asset, if the asset price rises, other things remaining the same, the interest rate falls. Conversely, if the asset price falls, other things remaining the same, the interest rate rises.

To see this inverse relationship between an asset price and the interest rate, look at the example of a Microsoft share. In October 2008, the price of a Microsoft share was $26 and each share entitled its owner to 48 cents of Microsoft profit. The interest rate on a Microsoft share was

Interest rate = ($0.48 ÷ $26) × 100 = 1.85 percent.

If the price of a Microsoft share increased to $30 and each share still entitled its owner to 48 cents of Microsoft profit, the interest rate on a Microsoft share would become

Interest rate = ($0.48 ÷ $30) × 100 = 1.6 percent.

This relationship means that the price of an asset and the interest rate on that asset are determined simultaneously—one implies the other.

This relationship also means that if the interest rate on the asset rises, the price of the asset falls, debts become harder to pay, and the net worth of the financial institution falls. Insolvency can arise from previously unexpected large rises in the interest rate.

In the next part of this chapter, we learn how interest rates and asset prices are determined in the financial markets.

Review Quiz

1 Distinguish between physical capital and financial capital and give two examples of each.
2 What is the distinction between gross investment and net investment?
3 What are the three main types of markets for financial capital?
4 Explain the connection between the price of a financial asset and its interest rate.

 Work Study Plan 24.1 and get instant feedback.

The Market for Loanable Funds

In macroeconomics, we group all the financial markets that we described in the previous section into a single market for loanable funds. The **market for loanable funds** is the aggregate of all the individual financial markets.

The circular flow model of Chapter 21 (see p. 489) can be extended to include flows in the market for loanable funds that finance investment.

Funds that Finance Investment

Figure 24.2 shows the flows of funds that finance investment. They come from three sources:

1. Household saving
2. Government budget surplus
3. Borrowing from the rest of the world

Households' income, Y, is spent on consumption goods and services, C, saved, S, or paid in net taxes, T. **Net taxes** are the taxes paid to governments minus the cash transfers received from governments (such as Social Security and unemployment benefits). So income is equal to the sum of consumption expenditure, saving, and net taxes:

$$Y = C + S + T.$$

You saw in Chapter 21 (p. 490) that Y also equals the sum of the items of aggregate expenditure: consumption expenditure, C, investment, I, government expenditure, G, and exports, X, minus imports, M. That is:

$$Y = C + I + G + X - M.$$

By using these two equations, you can see that

$$I + G + X = M + S + T.$$

Subtract G and X from both sides of the last equation to obtain

$$I = S + (T - G) + (M - X).$$

This equation tells us that investment, I, is financed by household saving, S, the government budget surplus, $(T - G)$, and borrowing from the rest of the world, $(M - X)$.

A government budget surplus $(T > G)$ contributes funds to finance investment, but a government budget deficit $(T < G)$, competes with investment for funds.

FIGURE 24.2   Financial Flows and the Circular Flow of Expenditure and Income

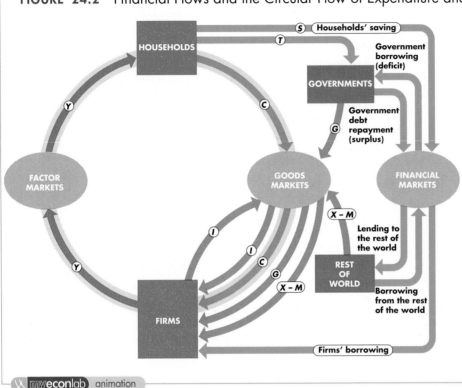

Households use their income for consumption expenditure (*C*), saving (*S*), and net taxes (*T*). Firms borrow to finance their investment expenditure. Governments borrow to finance a budget deficit or repay debt if they have a budget surplus. The rest of the world borrows to finance its deficit or lends its surplus.

myeconlab animation

If we export less than we import, we borrow (*M* – *X*) from the rest of the world to finance some of our investment. If we export more than we import, we lend (*X* – *M*) to the rest of the world and part of U.S. saving finances investment in other countries.

The sum of private saving, *S*, and government saving, (*T* – *G*), is called **national saving**. National saving and foreign borrowing finance investment.

In 2008, U.S. investment was $2,056 billion. Governments (federal, state, and local combined) had a deficit of $707 billion. This total of $2,763 billion was financed by private saving of $2,045 billion and borrowing from the rest of the world (negative net exports) of $718 billion.

You're going to see how investment and saving and the flows of loanable funds—all measured in constant 2000 dollars—are determined. The price in the market for loanable funds that achieves equilibrium is an interest rate, which we also measure in real terms as the *real* interest rate. In the market for loanable funds, there is just one interest rate, which is an average of the interest rates on all the different types of financial securities that we described earlier. Let's see what we mean by the real interest rate.

The Real Interest Rate

The **nominal interest rate** is the number of dollars that a borrower pays and a lender receives in interest in a year expressed as a percentage of the number of dollars borrowed and lent. For example, if the annual interest paid on a $500 loan is $25, the nominal interest rate is 5 percent per year: $25 ÷ $500 × 100 or 5 percent.

The **real interest rate** is the nominal interest rate adjusted to remove the effects of inflation on the buying power of money. The real interest rate is approximately equal to the nominal interest rate minus the inflation rate.

You can see why if you suppose that you have put $500 in a savings account that earns 5 percent a year. At the end of a year, you have $525 in your savings account. Suppose that the inflation rate is 2 percent per year—during the year, all prices increased by 2 percent. You need $510 to buy what a year earlier cost $500. So you can buy $15 worth more of goods and services than you could have bought a year earlier. You've earned goods and services worth $15, which is a real interest rate of 3 percent a year. And the bank has paid a real interest rate of 3 percent a year. So the real interest rate is the 5 percent nominal interest rate minus the 2 percent inflation rate[1].

The real interest rate is the opportunity cost of loanable funds. The real interest *paid* on borrowed funds is the opportunity cost of borrowing. And the real interest rate *forgone* when funds are used either to buy consumption goods and services or to invest in new capital goods is the opportunity cost of not saving or not lending those funds.

We're now going to see how the loanable funds market determines the real interest rate, the quantity of funds loaned, saving, and investment. In the rest of this section, we will ignore the government and the rest of the world and focus on households and firms in the market for loanable funds. We will study

- The demand for loanable funds
- The supply of loanable funds
- Equilibrium in the market for loanable funds

The Demand for Loanable Funds

The *quantity of loanable funds demanded* is the total quantity of funds demanded to finance investment, the government budget deficit, and international investment or lending during a given period. Our focus here is on investment. We'll bring the other two items into the picture in later sections of this chapter.

What determines investment and the demand for loanable funds to finance it? Many details influence this decision, but we can summarize them in two factors:

1. The real interest rate
2. Expected profit

Firms invest in capital only if they expect to earn a profit and fewer projects are profitable at a high real interest rate than at a low real interest rate, so:

Other things remaining the same, the higher the real interest rate, the smaller is the quantity of loanable funds demanded; and the lower the real interest rate, the greater is the quantity of loanable funds demanded.

---

[1]The *exact* real interest rate formula, which allows for the change in the purchasing power of both the interest and the loan is: Real interest rate = (Nominal interest rate − Inflation rate) ÷ (1 + Inflation rate/100). If the nominal interest rate is 5 percent a year and the inflation rate is 2 percent a year, the real interest rate is (5 − 2) ÷ (1 + 0.02) = 2.94 percent a year.

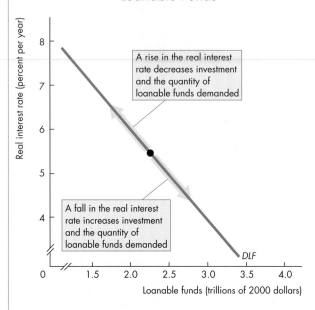

FIGURE 24.3   The Demand for Loanable Funds

A rise in the real interest rate decreases investment and the quantity of loanable funds demanded

A fall in the real interest rate increases investment and the quantity of loanable funds demanded

A change in the real interest rate changes the quantity of loanable funds demanded and brings a movement along the demand curve.

myeconlab   animation

Demand for Loanable Funds Curve   The **demand for loanable funds** is the relationship between the quantity of loanable funds demanded and the real interest rate, when all other influences on borrowing plans remain the same. The demand curve *DLF* in Fig. 24.3 is a demand for loanable funds curve.

To understand the demand for loanable funds, think about Amazon.com's decision to borrow $100 million to build some new warehouses. If Amazon expects to get a return of $5 million a year from this investment before paying interest costs and the interest rate is less than 5 percent a year, Amazon would make a profit, so it builds the warehouses. But if the interest rate is more than 5 percent a year, Amazon would incur a loss, so it doesn't build the warehouses. The quantity of loanable funds demanded is greater the lower is the real interest rate.

Changes in the Demand for Loanable Funds   When the expected profit changes, the demand for loanable funds changes. Other things remaining the same, the greater the expected profit from new capital, the greater is the amount of investment and the greater the demand for loanable funds.

Expected profit rises during a business cycle expansion and falls during a recession; rises when technological change creates profitable new products; rises as a growing population brings increased demand for goods and services; and fluctuates with contagious swings of optimism and pessimism, called "animal spirits" by Keynes and "irrational exuberance" by Alan Greenspan.

When expected profit changes, the demand for loanable funds curve shifts.

The Supply of Loanable Funds

The *quantity of loanable funds supplied* is the total funds available from private saving, the government budget surplus, and international borrowing during a given period. Our focus here is on saving. We'll bring the other two items into the picture later.

How do you decide how much of your income to save and supply in the market for loanable funds? Your decision is influenced by many factors, but chief among them are

1. The real interest rate
2. Disposable income
3. Expected future income
4. Wealth
5. Default risk

We begin by focusing on the real interest rate.

Other things remaining the same, the higher the real interest rate, the greater is the quantity of loanable funds supplied; and the lower the real interest rate, the smaller is the quantity of loanable funds supplied.

The Supply of Loanable Funds Curve The **supply of loanable funds** is the relationship between the quantity of loanable funds supplied and the real interest rate when all other influences on lending plans remain the same. The curve *SLF* in Fig. 24.4 is a supply of loanable funds curve.

Think about a student's decision to save some of what she earns from her summer job. With a real interest rate of 2 percent a year, she decides that it is not worth saving much—better to spend the income and take a student loan if funds run out during the semester. But if the real interest rate jumped to 10 percent a year, the payoff from saving would be high enough to encourage her to cut back on spending and increase the amount she saves.

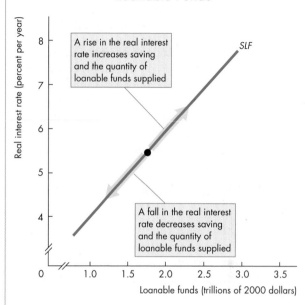

FIGURE 24.4 The Supply of Loanable Funds

A rise in the real interest rate increases saving and the quantity of loanable funds supplied

A fall in the real interest rate decreases saving and the quantity of loanable funds supplied

A change in the real interest rate changes the quantity of loanable funds supplied and brings a movement along the supply curve.

myeconlab animation

Changes in the Supply of Loanable Funds A change in disposable income, expected future income, wealth, or default risk changes the supply of loanable funds.

Disposable Income A household's *disposable income* is the income earned minus net taxes. When disposable income increases, other things remaining the same, consumption expenditure increases but by less than the increase in income. Some of the increase in income is saved. So the greater a household's disposable income, other things remaining the same, the greater is its saving.

Expected Future Income The higher a household's expected future income, other things remaining the same, the smaller is its saving today.

Wealth The higher a household's wealth, other things remaining the same, the smaller is its saving. If a person's wealth increases because of a capital gain, the person sees less need to save. For example, from 2002 through 2006, when house prices were rising rapidly, wealth increased despite the fact that personal saving dropped close to zero.

Default Risk Default risk is the risk that a loan will not be repaid. The greater that risk, the higher is the interest rate needed to induce a person to lend and the smaller is the supply of loanable funds.

Shifts of the Supply of Loanable Funds Curve When any of the four influences on the supply of loanable funds changes, the supply of loanable funds changes and the supply curve shifts. An increase in disposable income, a decrease in expected future income, a decrease in wealth, or a fall in default risk increases saving and increases the supply of loanable funds.

Equilibrium in the Market for Loanable Funds

You've seen that other things remaining the same, the higher the real interest rate, the greater is the quantity of loanable funds supplied and the smaller is the quantity of loanable funds demanded. There is one real interest rate at which the quantities of loanable funds demanded and supplied are equal, and that interest rate is the equilibrium real interest rate.

Figure 24.5 shows how the demand for and supply of loanable funds determine the real interest rate. The *DLF* curve is the demand curve and the *SLF* curve is the supply curve. If the real interest rate exceeds 6 percent a year, the quantity of loanable funds supplied exceeds the quantity demanded. Borrowers find it easy to get funds, but lenders are unable to lend all the funds they have available. The real interest rate falls until the quantity of funds supplied equals the quantity of funds demanded.

If the real interest rate is less than 6 percent a year, the quantity of loanable funds supplied is less than the quantity demanded. Borrowers can't get the funds they want, but lenders are able to lend all the funds they have available. So the real interest rate rises and continues to rise until the quantity of funds supplied equals the quantity demanded.

Regardless of whether there is a surplus or a shortage of loanable funds, the real interest rate changes and is pulled toward an equilibrium level. In Fig. 24.5, the equilibrium real interest rate is 6 percent a year. At this interest rate, there is neither a surplus nor a shortage of loanable funds. Borrowers can get the funds they want, and lenders can lend all the funds they have available. The investment plans of borrowers and the saving plans of lenders are consistent with each other.

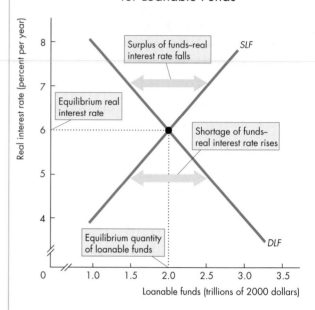

FIGURE 24.5 Equilibrium in the Market for Loanable Funds

A surplus of funds lowers the real interest rate and a shortage of funds raises it. At an interest rate of 6 percent a year, the quantity of funds demanded equals the quantity supplied and the market is in equilibrium.

 myeconlab animation

Changes in Demand and Supply

Financial markets are highly volatile in the short run but remarkably stable in the long run. Volatility in the market comes from fluctuations in either the demand for loanable funds or the supply of loanable funds. These fluctuations bring fluctuations in the real interest rate and in the equilibrium quantity of funds lent and borrowed. They also bring fluctuations in asset prices.

Here we'll illustrate the effects of *increases* in demand and supply in the market for loanable funds.

An Increase in Demand If the profits that firms expect to earn increase, they increase their planned investment and increase their demand for loanable funds to finance that investment. With an increase in the demand for loanable funds, but no change in the supply of loanable funds, there is a shortage of funds. As borrowers compete for funds, the interest rate rises and lenders increase the quantity of funds supplied.

Figure 24.6(a) illustrates these changes. An increase in the demand for loanable funds shifts the demand curve rightward from DLF_0 to DLF_1. With

FIGURE 24.6 Changes in Demand and Supply

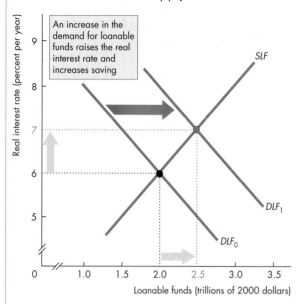

An increase in the demand for loanable funds raises the real interest rate and increases saving

(a) An increase in demand

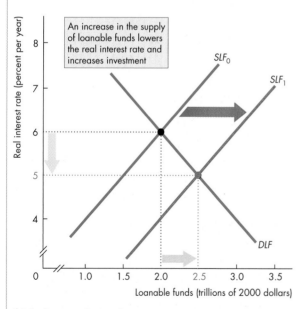

An increase in the supply of loanable funds lowers the real interest rate and increases investment

(b) An increase in supply

In part (a), the demand for loanable funds increases and supply doesn't change. The real interest rate rises (financial asset prices fall) and the quantity of funds increases.
In part (b), the supply of loanable funds increases and demand doesn't change. The real interest rate falls (financial asset prices rise) and the quantity of funds increases.

〔ＸＭ〕myeconlab animation

no change in the supply of loanable funds, there is a shortage of funds at a real interest rate of 6 percent a year. The real interest rate rises until it is 7 percent a year. Equilibrium is restored and the equilibrium quantity of funds has increased.

An Increase in Supply If one of the influences on saving plans changes and increases saving, the supply of loanable funds increases. With no change in the demand for loanable funds, the market is flush with loanable funds. Borrowers find bargains and lenders find themselves accepting a lower interest rate. At the lower interest rate, borrowers find additional investment projects profitable and increase the quantity of loanable funds that they borrow.

Figure 24.6(b) illustrates these changes. An increase in supply shifts the supply curve rightward from SLF_0 to SLF_1. With no change in demand, there is a surplus of funds at a real interest rate of 6 percent a year. The real interest rate falls until it is 5 percent a year. Equilibrium is restored and the equilibrium quantity of funds has increased.

Long-Run Growth of Demand and Supply Over time, both demand and supply in the market for loanable funds fluctuate and the real interest rate rises and falls. Both the supply of loanable funds and the demand for loanable funds tend to increase over time. On the average, they increase at a similar pace, so although demand and supply trend upward, the real interest rate has no trend. It fluctuates around a constant average level.

Review Quiz

1 What is the market for loanable funds?
2 Why is the real interest rate the opportunity cost of loanable funds?
3 How do firms make investment decisions?
4 What determines the demand for loanable funds and what makes it change?
5 How do households make saving decisions?
6 What determines the supply of loanable funds and what makes it change?
7 How do changes in the demand for and supply of loanable funds change the real interest rate and quantity of loanable funds?

〔ＸＭ〕myeconlab Work Study Plan 24.2 and get instant feedback.

The Origins of the 2007–2008 Financial Crisis

Loanable Funds Fuel Home Price Bubble

The financial crisis that gripped the U.S. and global economies in 2007 and cascaded through the financial markets in 2008 had its origins much earlier in events taking place in the market for loanable funds.

Between 2001 and 2005, a massive injection of loanable funds occurred. Some funds came from the rest of the world, but that source of supply has been stable. The Federal Reserve provided funds to keep interest rates low and that was a major source of the increase in the supply of funds. (The next chapter explains how the Fed does this.)

Figure 1 illustrates the loanable funds market starting in 2001. In that year, the demand for loanable funds was DLF_{01} and the supply of loanable funds was SLF_{01}. The equilibrium real interest rate was 4 percent a year and the equilibrium quantity of loanable funds was $29 trillion (in 2000 dollars).

During the ensuing four years, a massive increase in the supply of loanable funds shifted the supply curve rightward to SLF_{05}. A smaller increase in demand shifted the demand for loanable funds curve to DLF_{05}. The real interest rate fell to 1 percent a year and the quantity of loanable funds increased to $36 trillion—a 24 percent increase in just four years.

With this large increase in available funds, much of it in the form of mortgage loans to home buyers, the demand for homes increased by more than the increase in the supply of homes. Home prices rose and the expectation of further increases fueled the demand for loanable funds.

By 2006, the expectation of continued rapidly rising home prices brought a very large increase in the demand for loanable funds. At the same time, the Federal Reserve began to tighten credit. (Again, you'll learn how this is done in the next chapter). The result of the Fed's tighter credit policy was a slowdown in the pace of increase in the supply of loanable funds.

Figure 2 illustrates these events. In 2006, the demand for loanable funds increased from DLF_{05} to DLF_{06} and the supply of loanable funds increased by a smaller amount from SLF_{05} to SLF_{06}. The real interest rate increased to 3 percent.

The rise in the real interest rate (and a much higher rise in the nominal interest rate) put many home owners in financial difficulty. Mortgage repayments increased and some borrowers stopped repaying their loans.

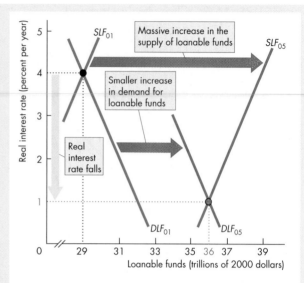

Figure 1   The Foundation of the Crisis: 2001–2005

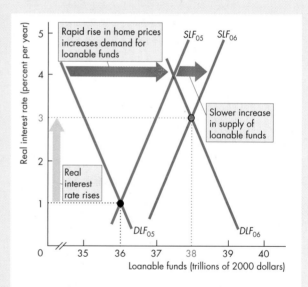

Figure 2   The Start of the Crisis: 2005-2006

By August 2007, the damage from mortgage default and foreclosure was so large that the credit market began to dry up. A large decrease in both demand and supply kept interest rates roughly constant but decreased the quantity of new business.

The total quantity of loanable funds didn't decrease, but the rate of increase slowed to a snail's pace and financial institutions most exposed to the bad mortgage debts and the securities that they backed (described on p. 566) began to fail.

These events illustrate the crucial role played by the loanable funds market in our economy.

Government in the Market for Loanable Funds

Government enters the market for loanable funds when it has a budget surplus or budget deficit. A government budget surplus increases the supply of loanable funds and contributes to financing investment; a government budget deficit increases the demand for loanable funds and competes with businesses for funds. Let's study the effects of government on the market for loanable funds.

A Government Budget Surplus

A government budget surplus increases the supply of loanable funds. The real interest rate falls, which decreases household saving and decreases the quantity of private funds supplied. The lower real interest rate increases the quantity of loanable funds demanded, and increases investment.

Figure 24.7 shows these effects of a government budget surplus. The private supply of loanable

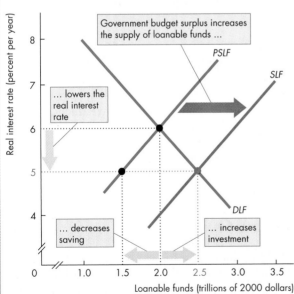

FIGURE 24.7   A Government Budget Surplus

A government budget surplus of $1 trillion is added to private saving and the private supply of loanable funds (*PSLF*) to determine the supply of loanable funds, *SLF*. The real interest rate falls to 5 percent a year, private saving decreases, but investment increases to $2.5 trillion.

funds curve is *PSLF*. The supply of loanable funds curve, *SLF*, shows the sum of private supply and the government budget surplus. Here, the government budget surplus is $1 trillion, so at each real interest rate the *SLF* curve lies $1 trillion to the right of the *PSLF* curve. That is, the horizontal distance between the *PSLF* curve and the *SLF* curve equals the government budget surplus.

With no government surplus, the real interest rate is 6 percent a year, the quantity of loanable funds is $2 trillion a year and investment is $2 trillion a year. But with the government surplus of $1 trillion a year, the equilibrium real interest rate falls to 5 percent a year and the quantity of loanable funds increases to $2.5 trillion a year.

The fall in the interest rate decreases private saving to $1.5 trillion, but investment increases to $2.5 trillion, which is financed by private saving plus the government budget surplus (government saving).

A Government Budget Deficit

A government budget deficit increases the demand for loanable funds. The real interest rate rises, which increases household saving and increases the quantity of private funds supplied. But the higher real interest rate decreases investment and the quantity of loanable funds demanded by firms to finance investment.

Figure 24.8 shows these effects of a government budget deficit. The private demand for loanable funds curve is *PDLF*. The demand for loanable funds curve, *DLF*, shows the sum of private demand and the government budget deficit. Here, the government budget deficit is $1 trillion, so at each real interest rate the *DLF* curve lies $1 trillion to the right of the *PDLF* curve. That is, the horizontal distance between the *PDLF* curve and the *DLF* curve equals the government budget deficit.

With no government deficit, the real interest rate is 6 percent a year, the quantity of loanable funds is $2 trillion a year and investment is $2 trillion a year. But with the government budget deficit of $1 trillion a year, the equilibrium real interest rate rises to 7 percent a year and the quantity of loanable funds increases to $2.5 trillion a year.

The rise in the real interest rate increases private saving to $2.5 trillion, but investment decreases to $1.5 trillion because $1 trillion of private saving must finance the government budget deficit.

FIGURE 24.8   A Government Budget Deficit

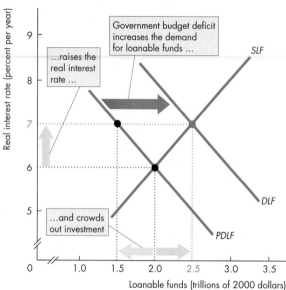

A government budget deficit adds to the private demand for loanable funds (*PDLF*) to determine the demand for loanable funds, *DLF*. The real interest rate rises, saving increases, but investment decreases—a crowding-out effect.

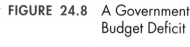 animation ◆

FIGURE 24.9   The Ricardo-Barro Effect

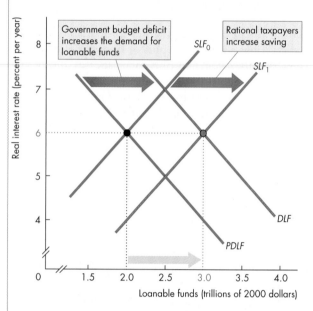

A budget deficit increases the demand for loanable funds to *DLF*. Rational taxpayers increase saving, which increases the supply of loanable funds from *SLF*$_0$ to *SLF*$_1$. Crowding out is avoided: Increased saving finances the budget deficit.

myeconlab animation ◆

The Crowding-Out Effect The tendency for a government budget deficit to raise the real interest rate and decrease investment is called the **crowding-out effect**. The budget deficit crowds out investment by competing with businesses for scarce financial capital.

The crowding-out effect does not decrease investment by the full amount of the government budget deficit because the higher real interest rate induces an increase in private saving that partly contributes toward financing the deficit.

The Ricardo-Barro Effect First suggested by the English economist David Ricardo in the eighteenth century and refined by Robert J. Barro of Harvard University, the Ricardo-Barro effect holds that both of the effects we've just shown are wrong and the government budget, whether in surplus or deficit, has no effect on either the real interest rate or investment.

Barro says that taxpayers are rational. They can see that a budget deficit today means that future taxes will be higher and future disposable incomes will be smaller. With smaller expected future disposable

incomes, saving increases today. Private saving and the private supply of loanable funds increase to match the quantity of loanable funds demanded by the government. So the budget deficit has no effect on either the real interest rate or investment. Figure 24.9 shows this outcome.

Most economists regard the Ricardo-Barro view as extreme. But there might be some change in private saving that goes in the direction suggested by the Ricardo-Barro effect that lessens the crowding-out effect.

Review Quiz

1 How does a government budget surplus or deficit influence the market for loanable funds?

2 What is the crowding-out effect and how does it work?

3 What is the Ricardo-Barro effect and how does it modify the crowding-out effect?

myeconlab   Work Study Plan 24.3 and get instant feedback.

The Global Loanable Funds Market

The loanable funds market is global, not national. Lenders on the supply side of the market want to earn the highest possible real interest rate and they will seek it by looking everywhere in the world. Borrowers on the demand side of the market want to pay the lowest possible real interest rate and they will seek it by looking everywhere in the world. Financial capital is mobile: It moves to the best advantage of lenders and borrowers.

International Capital Mobility

If a U.S. supplier of loanable funds can earn a higher interest rate in Tokyo than in New York, funds supplied in Japan will increase and funds supplied in the United States will decrease—funds will flow from the United States to Japan.

If a U.S. demander of loanable funds can pay a lower interest rate in Paris than in New York, the demand for funds in France will increase and the demand for funds in the United States will decrease —funds will flow from France to the United States.

Because lenders are free to seek the highest real interest rate and borrowers are free to seek the lowest real interest rate, the loanable funds market is a single, integrated, global market. Funds flow into the country in which the interest rate is highest and out of the country in which the interest rate is lowest.

When funds leave the country with the lowest interest rate, a shortage of funds raises the real interest rate. When funds move into the country with the highest interest rate, a surplus of funds lowers the real interest rate. The free international mobility of financial capital pulls real interest rates around the world toward equality.

Only when the real interest rates in New York, Tokyo, and Paris are equal does the incentive to move funds from one country to another stop.

Equality of real interest rates does not mean that if you calculate the average real interest rate in New York, Tokyo, and Paris, you'll get the same number. To compare real interest rates, we must compare financial assets of equal risk.

Lending is risky. A loan might not be repaid. Or the price of a stock or bond might fall. Interest rates include a risk premium—the riskier the loan, other things remaining the same, the higher is the interest

rate. The interest rate on a risky loan minus that on a safe loan is called the *risk premium*.

International capital mobility brings *real* interest rates in all parts of the world to equality except for differences that reflect differences in risk—differences in the risk premium.

International Borrowing and Lending

A country's loanable funds market connects with the global market through net exports. If a country's net exports are negative $(X < M)$, the rest of the world supplies funds to that country and the quantity of loanable funds in that country is greater than national saving. If a country's net exports are positive $(X > M)$, the country is a net supplier of funds to the rest of the world and the quantity of loanable funds in that country is less than national saving.

Demand and Supply in the Global and National Markets

The demand for and supply of funds in the global loanable funds market determines the world equilibrium real interest rate. This interest rate makes the quantity of loanable funds demanded equal the quantity supplied in the world economy. But it does not make the quantity of funds demanded and supplied equal in each national economy. The demand for and supply of funds in a national economy determine whether the country is a lender to or a borrower from the rest of the world.

The Global Loanable Funds Market Figure 24.10(a) illustrates the global market. The demand for loanable funds, DLF_W is the sum of the demands in all countries. Similarly, the supply of loanable funds, SLF_W is the sum of the supplies in all countries. The world equilibrium real interest rate makes the quantity of funds supplied in the world as a whole equal to the quantity demanded. In this example, the equilibrium real interest rate is 5 percent a year and the quantity of funds is $10 trillion.

An International Borrower Figure 24.10(b) shows the market for loanable funds in a country that borrows from the rest of the world. The country's demand for loanable funds, DLF, is part of the world demand in Fig. 24.10(a). The country's supply of loanable funds, SLF_D, is part of the world supply.

FIGURE 24.10   Borrowing and Lending in the Global Loanable Funds Market

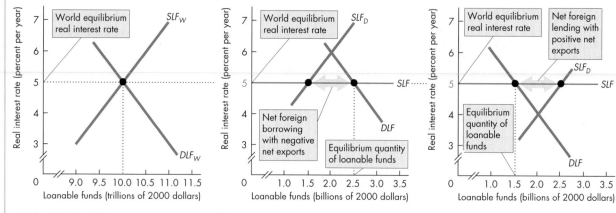

(a) The global market　　　**(b) An international borrower**　　　**(c) An international lender**

In part (a), the demand for loanable funds, *DLF*, and the supply of funds, *SLF*, determine the equilibrium real interest rate in the global loanable funds market.

The country in part (b) has a shortage of funds at the world equilibrium real interest rate and the country bor-

rows from the rest of the world. The country has negative net exports.

The country in part (c) has a surplus of funds at the world equilibrium real interest rate and the country lends to the rest of the world. The country has positive net exports.

myeconlab animation

If this country were isolated from the global market, the real interest rate would be 6 percent a year (where the *DLF* and *SLF_D* curves intersect). But if the country is integrated into the global economy, with an interest rate of 6 percent a year, funds would flood into it. With a real interest rate of 5 percent a year in the rest of the world, suppliers of loanable funds would seek the higher return in this country. In effect, the country faces the supply of loanable funds curve *SLF*, which is horizontal at the world equilibrium real interest rate.

The country's demand for loanable funds and the world interest rate determine the equilibrium quantity of loanable funds—$2.5 billion in Fig. 24.10(b).

An International Lender Figure 24.10(c) shows the situation in a country that lends to the rest of the world. As before, the country's demand for loanable funds, *DLF*, is part of the world demand and the country's supply of loanable funds, *SLF_D*, is part of the world supply in Fig. 24.10(a).

If this country were isolated from the global economy, the real interest rate would be 4 percent a year (where the *DLF* and *SLF_D* curves intersect). But if this country is integrated into the global economy, with an interest rate of 4 percent a year, funds would

quickly flow out of it. With a real interest rate of 5 percent a year in the rest of the world, suppliers of loanable funds would seek the higher return in other countries. Again, the country faces the supply of loanable funds curve *SLF*, which is horizontal at the world equilibrium real interest rate.

The country's demand for loanable funds and the world interest rate determine the equilibrium quantity of loanable funds—$1.5 billion in Fig. 24.10(c).

Changes in Demand and Supply A change in the demand or supply in the global market of loanable funds changes the real interest rate in the way shown in Fig. 24.6 (see p. 573). The effect of a change in demand or supply in a national market depends on the size of the country. A change in demand or supply in a small country has no significant effect on global demand or supply, so it leaves the world real interest rate unchanged and changes only the country's net exports and international borrowing or lending. A change in demand or supply in a large country has a significant effect on global demand or supply, so it changes the world real interest rate as well as the country's net exports and international borrowing or lending. Every country feels some of the effect of a large country's change in demand or supply.

Greenspan's Interest Rate Puzzle
The Role of the Global Market

The real interest rate paid by big corporations in the United States fell from 5.5 percent a year in 2001 to 2.5 percent a year in 2005. Alan Greenspan, then the Chairman of the Federal Reserve, said he was puzzled that the real interest rate was falling at a time when the U.S. government budget deficit was increasing.

Why did the real interest rate fall?

The answer lies in the global loanable funds market. Rapid economic growth in Asia and Europe brought a large increase in global saving, which in turn increased the global supply of loanable funds. The supply of loanable funds increased because Asian and European saving increased strongly.

The U.S. government budget deficit increased the U.S. and global demand for loanable funds. But this increase was very small compared to the increase in supply.

The result of a large increase in supply and a small increase in demand was a fall in the world average real interest rate and an increase in the equilibrium quantity of loanable funds.

The figure illustrates these events. The supply of loanable funds increased from SLF_{01} in 2001 to SLF_{05} in 2005. (In the figure, we ignore the change in the global demand for loanable funds because it was small relative to the increase in supply.)

With the increase in supply, the real interest rate fell from 5.5 percent to 2.5 percent a year and the

quantity of loanable funds increased.

In the United States, borrowing from the rest of the world increased to finance the increased government budget deficit.

The interest rate puzzle illustrates the important fact that the loanable funds market is a global market, not a national market.

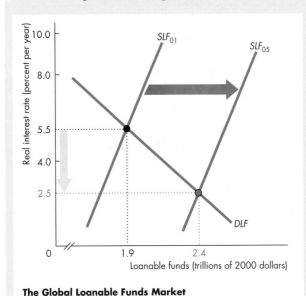

The Global Loanable Funds Market

Review Quiz

1 Why do loanable funds flow among countries?
2 What determines the demand for and supply of loanable funds in an individual economy?
3 What happens if a country has a shortage of loanable funds at the world real interest rate?
4 What happens if a country has a surplus of loanable funds at the world real interest rate?
5 How is a government budget deficit financed in an open economy?

 Work Study Plan 24.4 and get instant feedback.

To complete your study of financial markets, take a look at *Reading Between the Lines* on pp. 580–581 and see how you can use the model of the loanable funds market to understand the events in the financial market crisis of 2008.

Bailing Out Financial Markets

Bailout Plan Wins Approval

http://www.nytimes.com
October 3, 2008

After the House reversed course and gave final approval to the $700 billion economic bailout package, President Bush quickly signed it into law on Friday, authorizing the Treasury to undertake what could become the most expensive government intervention in history.

But even as Mr. Bush declared that the measure would "help prevent the crisis on Wall Street from becoming a crisis in communities across our country," Congressional Democrats said that it was only a first step and pledged to carry out a sweeping overhaul of the nation's financial regulatory system. ...

Some measures of the credit markets improved after the bill was approved, but only modestly. Analysts said it was too soon to tell whether borrowing rates—the interest rates banks charge each other for loans, and a key indicator of the flow of credit—would fall. ...

Supporters said the bailout was needed to prevent economic collapse; opponents said it was hasty, ill conceived and risked too much taxpayer money to help Wall Street tycoons, while providing no guarantees of success. The rescue plan allows the Treasury to buy troubled securities from financial firms in an effort to ease a deepening credit crisis that is choking off business and consumer loans, the lifeblood of the economy, and contributing to a string of bank failures. ...

Essence of the Story

- In October 2008, Congress passed a $700 billion economic bailout package for troubled financial institutions.

- The plan allows the Treasury to buy troubled securities from financial firms.

- The goal was to unfreeze credit and make loan markets work normally.

- Analysts said it was too soon to tell whether interest rates would fall.

- Supporters of the bailout said it was needed to prevent economic collapse.

- Opponents of the bailout said it risked too much tax-payer money and provided no guarantees of success.

Economic Analysis

- In the fall of 2008, the U.S. loanable funds market was in a distressed state.

- The spread in interest rates between safe U.S. government Treasury bills and risky commercial loans was unusually high and the quantity of loans was unusually low.

- Banks and other financial institutions were holding financial assets that they could sell only at a large loss— referred to as *toxic assets*.

- The financial markets were operating at an equilibrium that was hampering continued economic growth.

- The Congress and the Bush Administration hoped to inject some life into the markets by creating a $700 billion fund to buy up the toxic assets and enable financial institutions to start lending again.

- It was feared that without the $700 billion of funds, financial institutions would not only fail to provide the funds required to make the economy grow but also slide into a deeper state of stress with the quantity of funds available decreasing further.

- The figures illustrate the hope and the fear.

- In 2008 (both figures), the demand for loanable funds was DLF_{08} and the supply is SLF_{08}. The real interest rate was 3 percent a year and quantity of funds was $40 trillion (2000 dollars).

- Figure 1 shows the hope. A rescue package increases the supply of loanable funds and increases optimism about the future. Increased optimism increases profit expectations and increases the demand for funds. The demand and supply curves shift rightward to DLF_{09} and SLF_{09}. The quantity of funds increases and the economy begins to expand again.

- Figure 2 shows the fear. With no rescue package, the supply of loanable funds decreases and increases pessimism about the future. The increased pessimism decreases profit expectations and decreases the demand for funds. The demand and supply curves shift leftward to DLF_{09} and SLF_{09}. The quantity of funds decreases and the economy goes into recession or worse.

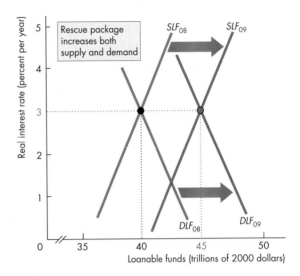

Figure 1 The hope

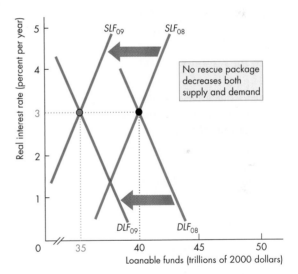

Figure 2 The fear

- Whether a rescue would work as hoped or whether the dire consequences of no rescue would occur as feared is not known. We have no direct experience of events like the ones described here on which to base solid predictions.

SUMMARY

Key Points

Financial Institutions and Financial Markets
(pp. 564–568)

- Capital (*physical capital*) is a real productive resource; financial capital is the funds used to buy capital.
- Gross investment increases the quantity of capital and depreciation decreases it. Saving increases wealth.
- The markets for financial capital are the markets for loans, bonds, and stocks.
- Financial institutions ensure that borrowers and lenders can always find someone with whom to trade.

The Market for Loanable Funds (pp. 568–574)

- Investment in capital is financed by household saving, a government budget surplus, and funds from the rest of the world.
- The quantity of loanable funds demanded depends negatively on the real interest rate and the demand for loanable funds changes when profit expectations change.
- The quantity of loanable funds supplied depends positively on the real interest rate and the supply of loanable funds changes when disposable income, expected future income, wealth, and default risk change.
- Equilibrium in the loanable funds market determines the real interest rate and quantity of funds.

Government in the Market for Loanable Funds
(pp. 575–576)

- A government budget surplus increases the supply of loanable funds, lowers the real interest rate, and increases investment and the equilibrium quantity of loanable funds.
- A government budget deficit increases the demand for loanable funds, raises the real interest rate, decreases investment in a crowding-out effect, and decreases the equilibrium quantity of loanable funds.
- The Ricardo-Barro effect is the response of rational taxpayers to a budget deficit: private saving increases to finance the budget deficit. The real interest rate remains constant and the crowding-out effect is avoided.

The Global Loanable Funds Market (pp. 577–579)

- The loanable funds market is a global market.
- The equilibrium real interest rate is determined in the global loanable funds market and national demand and supply determine the quantity of international borrowing or lending.

Key Figures

Key Terms

PROBLEMS and APPLICATIONS

Work problems 1–10 in Chapter 24 Study Plan and get instant feedback.
Work problems 11–19 as Homework, a Quiz, or a Test if assigned by your instructor.

1. Michael is an Internet service provider. On December 31, 2007, he bought an existing business with servers and a building worth $400,000. During his first year of operation, his business grew and he bought new servers for $500,000. The market value of some of his older servers fell by $100,000.
   a. What was Michael's gross investment, depreciation, and net investment during 2008?
   b. What is the value of Michael's capital at the end of 2008?

2. Lori is a student who teaches golf on the weekend and in a year earns $20,000 after paying her taxes. At the beginning of 2007, Lori owned $1,000 worth of books, CDs, and golf clubs and she had $5,000 in a savings account at the bank. During 2007, the interest on her savings account was $300 and she spent a total of $15,300 on consumption goods and services. There was no change in the market values of her books, CDs, and golf clubs.
   a. How much did Lori save in 2007?
   b. What was her wealth at the end of 2007?

3. First Call, Inc., is a cellular phone company. It plans to build an assembly plant that costs $10 million if the real interest rate is 6 percent a year. If the real interest rate is 5 percent a year, First Call will build a larger plant that costs $12 million. And if the real interest rate is 7 percent a year, First Call will build a smaller plant that costs $8 million.
   a. Draw a graph of First Call's demand for loanable funds curve.
   b. First Call expects its profit from the sale of cellular phones to double next year. If other things remain the same, explain how this increase in expected profit influences First Call's demand for loanable funds.

4. Draw a graph to illustrate how an increase in the supply of loanable funds and a decrease in the demand for loanable funds can lower the real interest rate and leave the equilibrium quantity of loanable funds unchanged.

5. The table at the top of the next column shows an economy's demand for loanable funds and the

Real interest rate (percent per year)	Loanable funds demanded	Loanable funds supplied
	(trillions of 2000 dollars)	
4	8.5	5.5
5	8.0	6.0
6	7.5	6.5
7	7.0	7.0
8	6.5	7.5
9	6.0	8.0
10	5.5	8.5

supply of loanable funds schedules, when the government's budget is balanced.
   a. If the government has a budget surplus of $1 trillion, what are the real interest rate, the quantity of investment, and the quantity of private saving? Is there any crowding out in this situation?
   b. If the government has a budget deficit of $1 trillion, what are the real interest rate, the quantity of investment, and the quantity of private saving? Is there any crowding out in this situation?
   c. If the government has a budget deficit of $1 trillion and the Ricardo-Barro effect occurs, what are the real interest rate and the quantity of investment?

6. In the loanable funds market in problem 5, the quantity of loanable funds demanded increases by $1 trillion at each real interest rate and the quantity of loanable funds supplied increases by $2 trillion at each interest rate.
   a. If the government budget is balanced, what are the real interest rate, the quantity of loanable funds, investment, and private saving? Does any crowding out occur?
   b. If the government budget becomes a deficit of $1 trillion, what are the real interest rate, the quantity of loanable funds, investment, and private saving? Does any crowding out occur?
   c. If governments wants to stimulate the quantity of investment and increase it to $9 trillion, what must they do?

7. In a speech at the CFA Society of Nebraska in February 2007, William Poole, former Chairman of the St. Louis Federal Reserve said:

Over most of the post-World War II period, the personal saving rate averaged about 6 percent, with some higher years from the mid 1970s to mid 1980s. The negative trend in the … saving rate started in the mid 1990s, about the same time the stock market boom started. Thus it is hard to dismiss the hypothesis that the decline in the measured saving rate in the late 1990s reflected the response of consumption to large capital gains from corporate equity [stock]. Evidence from panel data of households also supports the conclusion that the decline in the personal saving rate since 1984 is largely a consequence of capital gains on corporate equities [stocks].

   a. Is the purchase of corporate equities part of household consumption or saving? Explain your answer.
   b. Equities reap a capital gain in the same way that houses reap a capital gain. Does this mean that the purchase of equities is investment? If not, explain why it is not.
   c. U.S. household income has grown considerably since 1984. Has U.S. saving been on a downward trend because Americans feel wealthier?
   d. Explain why households preferred to buy corporate equities rather than bonds.

8. **The Global Saving Glut and the U.S. Current Account,** remarks by Ben Bernanke (when a governor of the Federal Reserve) on March 10, 2005:

On most dimensions the U.S. economy appears to be performing well. Output growth has returned to healthy levels, the labor market is firming, and inflation appears to be well controlled. However, one aspect of U.S. economic performance still evokes concern among economists and policymakers: the nation's large and growing current account deficit [negative net exports]. … Most forecasters expect the nation's current account imbalance to decline slowly at best, implying a continued need for foreign credit and a concomitant decline in the U.S. net foreign asset position.

Bernanke went on to ask the following questions. What are *your* answers to his questions:

   a. Why is the United States, with the world's largest economy, borrowing heavily on international capital markets—rather than lending, as would seem more natural?
   b. What implications do the U.S. current account deficit (negative net exports) and our consequent reliance on foreign credit have for economic performance in the United States?
   c. What policies, if any, should be used to address this situation?

9. **The New New World Order**
   … While gross domestic product growth is cooling a bit in emerging markets, the results are still tremendous compared with the United States and much of Western Europe. The 54 developing markets surveyed by Global Insight will post a 6.7% jump in real GDP this year, down from 7.5% last year. The 31 developed countries will grow an estimated 1.6%. The difference in growth rates represents the largest spread between developed and developing markets in the 37-year history of the survey.
   Fortune, July 14, 2008
   a. Do growth rates of real GDP over the past few decades indicate that world saving is shrinking, growing, or staying the same? Explain.
   b. If the world demand for loanable funds remains the same, will the world real interest rate rise, fall, or remain the same? Explain.

10. **IMF Warning Over Slowing Growth**
    The global economy may face a marked slowdown next year as a result of the turmoil in financial markets, the International Monetary Fund has warned. The IMF said the global credit squeeze would test the ability of the economy to continue expanding at recent rates. While future economic stability could not be taken for granted, there was plenty of evidence that the global economy remained durable, it added.
    BBC News, October 10, 2007
    a. Explain how turmoil in global financial markets might affect the demand for loanable funds, investment, and global economic growth in the future.
    b. What might be the evidence that the global economy will continue to grow?

11. Annie runs a fitness center. On December 31, 2008, she bought an existing business with exercise equipment and a building worth $300,000. During 2009, business improved and she bought some new equipment for $50,000. At the end of 2009, her equipment and buildings were worth $325,000. Calculate Annie's gross investment, depreciation, and net investment during 2009.

12. Karrie is a golf pro, and after she paid taxes, her income from golf and interest from financial assets was $1,500,000 in 2008. At the beginning of 2008, she owned $900,000 worth of financial assets. At the end of 2008, Karrie's financial assets were worth $1,900,000.
    a. How much did Karrie save during 2008?
    b. How much did she spend on consumption goods and services?

13. In 2008, the Lee family had disposable income of $80,000, wealth of $140,000, and an expected future income of $80,000 a year. At a real interest rate of 4 percent a year, the Lee family saves $15,000 a year; at a real interest rate of 6 percent a year, they save $20,000 a year; and at a real interest rate of 8 percent, they save $25,000 a year.
    a. Draw a graph of the Lee family's supply of loanable funds curve.
    b. In 2009, suppose that the stock market crashes and the default risk increases. Explain how this increase in default risk influences the Lee family's supply of loanable funds curve.

14. Draw a graph to illustrate the effect of an increase in the demand for loanable funds and an even larger increase in the supply of loanable funds on the real interest rate and the equilibrium quantity of loanable funds.

15. **India's Economy Hits the Wall**

    Just six months ago, India was looking good. Annual growth was 9%, corporate profits were surging 20%, the stock market had risen 50% in 2007, consumer demand was huge, local companies were making ambitious international acquisitions, and foreign investment was growing. Nothing, it seemed, could stop the forward march of this Asian nation. But stop it has. ... The country is reeling from 11.4% inflation, large government deficits, and rising interest rates. ... Most economic forecasts expect growth to slow to 7%—a big drop for a country that needs to accelerate growth, not reduce it. ... A June 16 report by Goldman Sachs' Jim O'Neill and Tushar Poddar ... urges India to improve governance, raise educational achievement, and control inflation. It also advises ... liberalizing its financial markets. ...

    BusinessWeek, July 1, 2008
    a. Suppose that the Indian government reduces its deficit and returns to a balanced budget. If other things remain the same, how will the demand or supply of loanable funds in India change?
    b. With economic growth forecasted to slow, future incomes are expected to fall. If other things remain the same, how will the demand or supply of loanable funds in India change?

16. **The Global Savings Glut and Its Consequences**

    The world is experiencing an unprecedented glut of savings, driving down real interest rates. It is a good time to borrow rather than lend. ... Several developing countries are running large current account surpluses (representing an excess of savings over investment). ... China has the biggest surplus of $1.2 trillion, but other developing countries put together have accumulated almost as much. ... Rapid growth leads to high saving rates: people save a large fraction of additional income. In India, GDP growth has accelerated from 6% to 9%, lifting the saving rate from 23% a decade ago to 33% today. China's saving rate is a dizzy 55%. Not even the investment boom in Asia can absorb these huge savings, which are therefore put into U.S. bonds. When a poor country buys U.S. bonds, it is in effect lending to the United States.

    The Cato Institute, June 8, 2007
    a. Graphically illustrate and explain the impact of the "unprecedented glut of savings" on the real interest rate and the quantity of loanable funds.
    b. How do the high saving rates in China and India impact investment in the United States? How does this investment influence the production function and potential GDP in the United States?

17. ... Most economists agree that the problems we are witnessing today developed over a long period of time. For more than a decade, a massive amount of money flowed into the United

States from investors abroad, because our country is an attractive and secure place to do business. This large influx of money to U.S. banks and financial institutions—along with low interest rates—made it easier for Americans to get credit. These developments allowed more families to borrow money for cars and homes and college tuition—some for the first time. They allowed more entrepreneurs to get loans to start new businesses and create jobs.

President George W. Bush, *Address to the Nation*, September 24, 2008

a. Explain why, for more than a decade, a massive amount of money flowed into the United States and compare and contrast your explanation with that of the President.

b. Explain why interest rates were low using the loanable funds analysis.

c. Provide a graphical analysis of the reasons why the interest rate was low.

d. Funds have been flowing into the United States since the early 1980s. Why might they have created problems in 2008 but not earlier?

e. Could the United States stop funds from flowing in from other countries? How?

18. **Greenspan's Conundrum Spells Confusion for Us All**

… At the beginning of the year, the consensus was that … bond yields would rise. … Gradually, over February, the consensus has started to reassert itself. … Ten-year Treasury bond yields were hovering below 4 percent in the early part of the month but now they are around 4.3 percent.

Because the consensus was that bond yields should be 5 percent by the end of the year, most commentators have focused, not on why bond yields have suddenly risen, but on why they were so low before.

A number of explanations for this "conundrum" have been advanced. First, bond yields are being held artificially low by unusual buying. … Another [is] … bond yields reflect investors' expectations for an economic slowdown in 2005.

Financial Times, February 26, 2005

a. Explain how "unusual buying" might lead to a low real interest rate.

b. Explain how "investors' expectations for an economic slowdown" might lead to a lower real interest rate.

19. Study *Reading Between the Lines* on pp. 580–581 and then answer the following questions.

a. What was the financial rescue package proposed by the Administration and what was it supposed to do?

b. What did the government hope would occur after the rescue package was passed?

c. Based on what happened in the stock market, do you think we can conclude that suppliers of loanable funds believed that the rescue package was needed and would work? Explain your answer.

d. What did the government fear would occur if the rescue package was not passed?

e. Again, based on what happened in the stock market, do you think we can conclude that suppliers of loanable funds shared the government's fears? Explain your answer.

f. What other measures might the government take if it wants to boost supply and demand in the market for loanable funds?

g. How do you think the global nature of the loanable funds markets influences how the U.S. market would have responded to no rescue package?

25 ◆ Money, the Price Level, and Inflation

After studying this chapter, you will be able to:

- Define money and describe its functions

- Explain the economic functions of banks and other depository institutions

- Describe the structure and functions of the Federal Reserve System (the Fed)

- Explain how the banking system creates money

- Explain what determines the demand for money, the supply of money, and the nominal interest rate

- Explain how the quantity of money influences the price level and the inflation rate in the long run

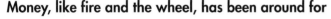

Money, like fire and the wheel, has been around for a long time, and it has taken many forms. Money was wampum (beads made from shells) for North American Indians, whale's teeth for Fijians, and tobacco for early American colonists. Cakes of salt served as money in Ethiopia and Tibet. Today, when we want to buy something, we use coins or dollar bills, write a check, or swipe a debit card or a credit card. Soon, we'll be using a "smart card" that keeps track of spending and that our pocket computer can read. Are all these things money?

When we deposit some coins or notes into a bank, is that still money? And what happens when the bank lends the money we've deposited to someone else? How can we get our money back if it has been lent out?

The quantity of money in our economy is regulated by the Federal Reserve—the Fed. How does the Fed influence the quantity of money? And what happens if the Fed creates too much money or too little money?

In this chapter, we study the functions of money, the banks that create it, the Federal Reserve and its influence on the quantity of money, and the long-run consequences of changes in the quantity of money. In *Reading Between the Lines* at the end of the chapter, we look at a spectacular example of money and inflation in action in the African nation Zimbabwe.

What Is Money?

What do wampum, tobacco, and nickels and dimes have in common? They are all examples of **money**, which is defined as any commodity or token that is generally acceptable as a means of payment.
A **means of payment** is a method of settling a debt. When a payment has been made, there is no remaining obligation between the parties to a transaction. So what wampum, tobacco, and nickels and dimes have in common is that they have served (or still do serve) as the means of payment. Money serves three other functions:

- Medium of exchange
- Unit of account
- Store of value

Medium of Exchange

A *medium of exchange* is any object that is generally accepted in exchange for goods and services. Without a medium of exchange, goods and services must be exchanged directly for other goods and services—an exchange called **barter**. Barter requires a *double coincidence of wants*, a situation that rarely occurs. For example, if you want a hamburger, you might offer a CD in exchange for it. But you must find someone who is selling hamburgers and wants your CD.

A medium of exchange overcomes the need for a double coincidence of wants. Money acts as a medium of exchange because people with something to sell will always accept money in exchange for it. But money isn't the only medium of exchange. You can buy with a credit card, but a credit card isn't money. It doesn't make a final payment, and the debt it creates must eventually be settled by using money.

Unit of Account

A *unit of account* is an agreed measure for stating the prices of goods and services. To get the most out of your budget, you have to figure out whether seeing one more movie is worth its opportunity cost. But that cost is not dollars and cents. It is the number of ice-cream cones, sodas, or cups of coffee that you must give up. It's easy to do such calculations when all these goods have prices in terms of dollars and cents (see Table 25.1). If the price of a movie is $8 and the price of a case of soda is $4, you know

TABLE 25.1   The Unit of Account Function of Money Simplifies Price Comparisons

Good	Price in money units	Price in units of another good
Movie	$8.00 each	2 cases of soda
Soda	$4.00 per case	2 ice-cream cones
Ice cream	$2 per cone	4 packs of jelly beans
Jelly beans	$0.50 per pack	2 sticks of gum
Gum	$0.25 per stick	

Money as a unit of account: The price of a movie is $8 and the price of a stick of gum is 25¢, so the opportunity cost of a movie is 32 sticks of gum ($8.00 ÷ 25¢ = 32).
No unit of account: You go to a movie theater and learn that the price of a movie is 2 cases of soda. You go to a candy store and learn that a pack of jelly beans costs 2 sticks of gum. But how many sticks of gum does seeing a movie cost you? To answer that question, you go to the convenience store and find that a case of soda costs 2 ice-cream cones. Now you head for the ice-cream shop, where an ice-cream cone costs 4 packs of jelly beans. Now you get out your pocket calculator: 1 movie costs 2 cases of soda, or 4 ice-cream cones, or 16 packs of jelly beans, or 32 sticks of gum!

right away that seeing one movie costs you 2 cases of soda. If jelly beans are 50¢ a pack, one movie costs 16 packs of jelly beans. You need only one calculation to figure out the opportunity cost of any pair of goods and services.

Imagine how troublesome it would be if your local movie theater posted its price as 2 cases of soda, the convenience store posted the price of a case of soda as 2 ice-cream cones, the ice-cream shop posted the price of an ice-cream cone as 4 packs of jelly beans, and the candy store priced a pack of jelly beans as 2 sticks of gum! Now how much running around and calculating will you have to do to find out how much that movie is going to cost you in terms of the soda, ice cream, jelly beans, or gum that you must give up to see it? You get the answer for soda right away from the sign posted on the movie theater. But for all the other goods, you're going to have to visit many different stores to establish the price of each commodity in terms of another and then calculate the prices in units that are relevant for your own decision. The hassle of doing all this research might be enough to make a person swear off movies! You can see how much simpler it is if all the prices are expressed in dollars and cents.

Store of Value

Money is a *store of value* in the sense that it can be held and exchanged later for goods and services. If money were not a store of value, it could not serve as a means of payment.

Money is not alone in acting as a store of value. A house, a car, and a work of art are other examples.

The more stable the value of a commodity or token, the better it can act as a store of value and the more useful it is as money. No store of value has a completely stable value. The value of a house, a car, or a work of art fluctuates over time. The value of the commodities and tokens that are used as money also fluctuate over time.

Inflation lowers the value of money and the values of other commodities and tokens that are used as money. To make money as useful as possible as a store of value, a low inflation rate is needed.

Money in the United States Today

In the United States today, money consists of

- Currency
- Deposits at banks and other depository institutions

Currency The notes and coins held by individuals and businesses are known as **currency**. Notes are money because the government declares them so with the words "This note is legal tender for all debts, public and private." You can see these words on every dollar bill. Notes and coins *inside* banks are not counted as currency because they are not held by individuals and businesses.

Deposits Deposits of individuals and businesses at banks and other depository institutions, such as savings and loan associations, are also counted as money. Deposits are money because the owners of the deposits can use them to make payments.

Official Measures of Money Two official measures of money in the United States today are known as M1 and M2. **M1** consists of currency and traveler's checks plus checking deposits owned by individuals and businesses. M1 does *not* include currency held by banks, and it does not include currency and checking deposits owned by the U.S. government. **M2** consists of M1 plus time deposits, savings deposits, and money market mutual funds and other deposits.

Official Measures of U.S. Money
Currency a Small Part of the Total

The figure shows the relative magnitudes of the items that make up M1 and M2. Notice that M2 is almost five times as large as M1 and that currency is a small part of our money.

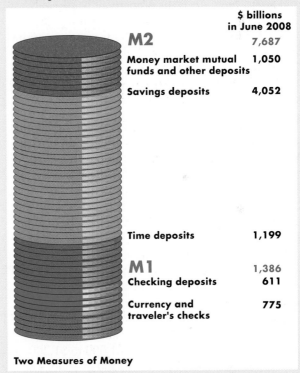

	$ billions in June 2008
M2	7,687
Money market mutual funds and other deposits	1,050
Savings deposits	4,052
Time deposits	1,199
M1	1,386
Checking deposits	611
Currency and traveler's checks	775

Two Measures of Money

M1
- Currency and traveler's checks
- Checking deposits at commercial banks, savings and loan associations, savings banks, and credit unions

M2
- M1
- Time deposits
- Savings deposits
- Money market mutual funds and other deposits

Source of data: The Federal Reserve Board.

Are M1 and M2 Really Money? Money is the means of payment. So the test of whether an asset is money is whether it serves as a means of payment. Currency passes the test. But what about deposits? Checking deposits are money because they can be transferred from one person to another by writing a check or using a debit card. Such a transfer of ownership is equivalent to handing over currency. Because M1 consists of currency plus checking deposits and each of these is a means of payment, *M1 is money.*

But what about M2? Some of the savings deposits in M2 are just as much a means of payment as the checking deposits in M1. You can use the ATM at the grocery store checkout or gas station and transfer funds directly from your savings account to pay for your purchase. But some savings deposits are not means of payment. These deposits are known as liquid assets. *Liquidity* is the property of being easily convertible into a means of payment without loss in value. Because the deposits in M2 that are not means of payment are quickly and easily converted into a means of payment—into currency or checking deposits—they are counted as money.

Deposits Are Money but Checks Are Not In defining money, we include, along with currency, deposits at banks and other depository institutions. But we do not count the checks that people write as money. Why are deposits money and checks not?

To see why deposits are money but checks are not, think about what happens when Colleen buys some roller-blades for $200 from Rocky's Rollers. When Colleen goes to Rocky's shop, she has $500 in her deposit account at the Laser Bank. Rocky has $1,000 in his deposit account—at the same bank, as it happens. The total deposits of these two people are $1,500. Colleen writes a check for $200. Rocky takes the check to the bank right away and deposits it. Rocky's bank balance rises from $1,000 to $1,200, and Colleen's balance falls from $500 to $300. The total deposits of Colleen and Rocky are still the same as before: $1,500. Rocky now has $200 more than before, and Colleen has $200 less.

This transaction has transferred money from Colleen to Rocky, but the check itself was never money. There wasn't an extra $200 of money while the check was in circulation. The check instructs the bank to transfer money from Colleen to Rocky.

If Colleen and Rocky use different banks, there is an extra step. Rocky's bank credits $200 to Rocky's

account and then takes the check to a check-clearing center. The check is then sent to Colleen's bank, which pays Rocky's bank $200 and then debits Colleen's account $200. This process can take a few days, but the principles are the same as when two people use the same bank.

Credit Cards Are Not Money You've just seen that checks are not money. What about credit cards? Isn't having a credit card in your wallet and presenting the card to pay for your roller-blades the same thing as using money? Why aren't credit cards somehow valued and counted as part of the quantity of money?

When you pay by check, you are frequently asked to prove your identity by showing your driver's license. It would never occur to you to think of your driver's license as money. It's just an ID card. A credit card is also an ID card, but one that lets you take out a loan at the instant you buy something. When you sign a credit card sales slip, you are saying, "I agree to pay for these goods when the credit card company bills me." Once you get your statement from the credit card company, you must make at least the minimum payment due. To make that payment, you need money—you need to have currency or a checking deposit to pay the credit card company. So although you use a credit card when you buy something, the credit card is not the *means of payment* and it is not money.

Review Quiz

1 What makes something money? What functions does money perform? Why do you think packs of chewing gum don't serve as money?

2 What are the problems that arise when a commodity is used as money?

3 What are the main components of money in the United States today?

4 What are the official measures of money? Are all the measures really money?

5 Why are checks and credit cards not money?

myeconlab Work Study Plan 25.1 and get instant feedback.

We've seen that the main component of money in the United States is deposits at banks and other depository institutions. Let's take a closer look at these institutions.

Depository Institutions

A **depository institution** is a financial firm that takes deposits from households and firms. These deposits are components of M1 and M2. You will learn what these institutions are, what they do, the economic benefits they bring, how they are regulated, and how they have innovated to create new financial products.

Types of Depository Institution

The deposits of three types of financial firm make up the nation's money. They are

- Commercial banks
- Thrift institutions
- Money market mutual funds

Commercial Banks A *commercial bank* is a firm that is licensed to receive deposits and make loans. In 2008, about 7,000 commercial banks operated in the United States but mergers make this number fall each year as small banks disappear and big banks expand.

A few very large commercial banks offer a wide range of banking services and have extensive international operations. The largest of these banks are Bank of America, Citigroup, and JPMorgan Chase. Most commercial banks are small and serve their regional and local communities.

The deposits of commercial banks represent 37 percent of M1 and 61 percent of M2.

Thrift Institutions Savings and loan associations, savings banks, and credit unions are *thrift institutions*.

Savings and Loan Association A *savings and loan association* (S&L) is a depository institution that receives deposits and makes personal, commercial, and home-purchase loans.

Savings Bank A *savings bank* is a depository institution that accepts savings deposits and makes mostly home-purchase loans.

Credit Union A *credit union* is a depository institution owned by a social or economic group, such as a firm's employees, that accepts savings deposits and makes mostly personal loans.

The deposits of the thrift institutions represent 10 percent of M1 and 18 percent of M2.

Money Market Mutual Funds A *money market mutual fund* is a fund operated by a financial institution that sells shares in the fund and holds assets such as U.S. Treasury bills and short-term commercial bills.

Money market mutual fund shares act like bank deposits. Shareholders can write checks on their money market mutual fund accounts, but there are restrictions on most of these accounts. For example, the minimum deposit accepted might be $2,500, and the smallest check a depositor is permitted to write might be $500.

Money market mutual funds do not feature in M1 and represent 13 percent of M2

What Depository Institutions Do

Depository institutions provide services such as check clearing, account management, credit cards, and Internet banking, all of which provide an income from service fees.

But depository institutions earn most of their income by using the funds they receive from depositors to make loans and buy securities that earn a higher interest rate than that paid to depositors. In this activity, a depository institution must perform a balancing act weighing return against risk. To see this balancing act, we'll focus on the commercial banks.

A commercial bank puts the funds it receives from depositors and other funds that it borrows into four types of assets:

1. *Reserves* are notes and coins in a bank's vault or in a deposit account at the Federal Reserve. (We'll study the Federal Reserve later in this chapter.) These funds are used to meet depositors' currency withdrawals (such as when you use an ATM to get cash to buy your midnight pizza) and to make payments to other banks. In normal times, a bank keeps about a half of one percent of deposits as reserves.

2. *Liquid assets* are U.S. government Treasury bills and commercial bills. These assets are the banks' first line of defense if they need reserves. Liquid assets can be sold and instantly converted into reserves with virtually no risk of loss. Because they have a low risk, they also earn a low interest rate.

3. *Securities* are U.S. government bonds and other bonds such as mortgage-backed securities. These assets can be sold and converted into reserves but at prices that fluctuate. Because their prices

fluctuate, these assets are riskier than liquid assets, but they also have a higher interest rate.

4. *Loans* are commitments of funds for an agreed-upon period of time. Banks make loans to corporations to finance the purchase of capital. They also make mortgage loans to finance the purchase of homes, and personal loans to finance consumer durable goods, such as cars or boats. The outstanding balances on credit card accounts are also bank loans. Loans are the riskiest assets of a bank. They cannot be converted into reserves until they are due to be repaid. And some borrowers default and never repay. These riskiest of a bank's assets earn the highest interest rate.

Table 25.2 provides a snapshot of the sources and uses of funds of all the commercial banks in June 2008 that serves as a summary of the above account.

Economic Benefits Provided by Depository Institutions

You've seen that a depository institution earns part of its profit because it pays a lower interest rate on deposits than what it earns on loans. What benefits do these institutions provide that make depositors willing to put up with a low interest rate and borrowers willing to pay a higher one?

TABLE 25.2   Commercial Banks: Sources and Uses of Funds

	$ billion June 2008	Percentage of deposits
Total funds	10,371	150.1
Sources		
Deposits	6,911	100.0
Borrowing	2,322	33.6
Own capital and other	1,138	16.5
Uses		
Reserves	44	0.6
Liquid assets	256	3.7
Securities and other assets	3,168	45.8
Loans	6,903	99.9

Commercial banks get two thirds of their funds from depositors and use a similar amount to make loans. In normal times (and the data here are for such a time) banks hold about a half of one percent as reserves and only a further almost 4 percent as liquid assets.

Source of data: The Federal Reserve Board.

Depository institutions provide four benefits:

- Create liquidity
- Pool risk
- Lower the cost of borrowing
- Lower the cost of monitoring borrowers

Create Liquidity   Depository institutions create liquidity by *borrowing short and lending long*—taking deposits and standing ready to repay them on short notice or on demand and making loan commitments that run for terms of many years.

Pool Risk   A loan might not be repaid—a default. If you lend to one person who defaults, you lose the entire amount loaned. If you lend to 1,000 people (through a bank) and one person defaults, you lose almost nothing. Depository institutions pool risk.

Lower the Cost of Borrowing   Imagine there are no depository institutions and a firm is looking for $1 million to buy a new factory. It hunts around for several dozen people from whom to borrow the funds. Depository institutions lower the cost of this search. The firm gets its $1 million from a single institution that gets deposits from a large number of people but spreads the cost of this activity over many borrowers.

Lower the Cost of Monitoring Borrowers   By monitoring borrowers, a lender can encourage good decisions that prevent defaults. But this activity is costly. Imagine how costly it would be if each household that lent money to a firm incurred the costs of monitoring that firm directly. Depository institutions can perform this task at a much lower cost.

How Depository Institutions Are Regulated

Depository institutions are engaged in a risky business. And a failure, especially of a large bank, would have damaging effects on the entire financial system and economy. To make the risk of failure small, depository institutions are required to hold levels of reserves and owners' capital that equal or surpass ratios laid down by regulation. If a depository institution fails, its deposits are guaranteed up to $250,000 per depositor per bank by the *Federal Deposit Insurance Corporation* or FDIC. The FDIC can take over management of a bank that appears to be heading toward failure.

Financial Innovation

Depository institutions are constantly seeking ways to improve their products and make larger profits. The process of developing new financial products is called *financial innovation*. Two influences on financial innovation are

- Economic environment
- Technology

The pace of financial innovation was remarkable during the 1980s and 1990s, and both of these forces played a role.

Economic Environment During the late 1970s and early 1980s, a high inflation rate brought high interest rates—the interest rate on home-purchase loans was as high as 15 percent a year. Traditional fixed interest rate mortgages became unprofitable and variable interest rate mortgages were introduced.

During the 2000s, when interest rates were extremely low and depository institutions were flush with funds, sub-prime mortgages were developed. These mortgages often exceeded the value of the home that secured the loan and usually had a low starter interest that escalated in later years.

To avoid the risk of carrying sub-prime mortgages, mortgage-backed securities were developed. The original lending institution sold these securities, lowered their own exposure to risk, and obtained funds to make more mortgage loans.

Technology The major technological influence on financial innovation is the development of low-cost computing and communication. Some examples of financial innovation that resulted from these technologies are the widespread use of credit cards and the spread of daily interest deposit accounts.

Financial Innovation and Money

Financial innovation has brought changes in the composition of money. Checking deposits at thrift institutions—at S&Ls, savings banks, and credit unions—have become an increasing percentage of M1 while checking deposits at commercial banks have become a decreasing percentage. The composition of M2 has also changed as savings deposits have decreased, while time deposits and money market mutual funds have expanded. Surprisingly, the use of currency has not fallen much.

Commercial Banks Under Stress
The 2008 Credit Crisis

When Lehman Brothers (a New York investment bank) failed, panic spread through financial markets. Banks that are normally happy to lend to each other overnight for an interest rate barely above the rate they can earn on safe Treasury bills suddenly lost confidence and the interest rate in this market shot up to 3 percentage points above the Treasury bill rate. Banks wanted to be safe and to hold cash. Reserves increased to an unheard of level: They jumped to 2.6 percent and liquid assets to 4.1 percent of deposits.

But despite the credit crisis, bank deposits and bank lending kept expanding as you can see by comparing October 2008 in the table below with June 2008 in Table 25.2.

Commercial Banks in October 2008		
	$ billion October 2008	Percentage of deposits
Total funds	10,869	152.6
Sources		
Deposits	7,124	100.0
Borrowing	2,521	35.4
Own capital and other	1,224	17.2
Uses		
Reserves	184	2.6
Liquid assets	294	4.1
Securities and other assets	3,178	44.6
Loans	7,213	101.2

Source of data: The Federal Reserve Board.

Review Quiz

1 What are depository institutions?
2 What are the functions of depository institutions?
3 How do depository institutions balance risk and return?
4 How do depository institutions create liquidity, pool risks, and lower the cost of borrowing?
5 How have depository institutions made innovations that have influenced the composition of money?

 Work Study Plan 25.2 and get instant feedback.

You now know what money is. Your next task is to learn about the Federal Reserve System and the ways in which it can influence the quantity of money.

The Federal Reserve System

The central bank of the United States is the **Federal Reserve System** (usually called the **Fed**). A **central bank** is a bank's bank and a public authority that regulates a nation's depository institutions and controls the quantity of money. As the banks' bank, the Fed provides banking services to commercial banks such as Citibank. A central bank is not a citizens' bank. That is, the Fed does not provide general banking services for businesses and individual citizens.

The Fed's Goals and Targets

The Fed conducts the nation's *monetary policy*, which means that it adjusts the quantity of money in circulation. The Fed's goals are to keep inflation in check, maintain full employment, moderate the business cycle, and contribute toward achieving long-term growth. Complete success in the pursuit of these goals is impossible, and the Fed's more modest aim is to improve the performance of the economy and to get closer to the goals than a hands-off approach would achieve. Whether the Fed succeeds in improving economic performance is a matter on which there is a range of opinion.

In pursuit of its ultimate goals, the Fed pays close attention to interest rates and pays special attention to one interest rate, the **federal funds rate**, which is the interest rate that the banks charge each other on overnight loans of reserves. The Fed sets a target for the federal funds rate that is consistent with its ultimate goals and then takes actions to achieve its target.

This section examines the Fed's policy tools. Later in this chapter, we look at the long-run effects of the Fed's actions, and in Chapter 31, we look at the short-run context in which the Fed conducts monetary policy. We begin by describing the structure of the Fed.

The Structure of the Fed

The key elements in the structure of the Federal Reserve System are

- The Board of Governors
- The regional Federal Reserve banks
- The Federal Open Market Committee

The Board of Governors The Board of Governors has seven members, who are appointed by the President of the United States and confirmed by the Senate, each for a 14-year term. The terms are staggered so that one seat on the board becomes vacant every two years. The President appoints one of the board members as chairman for a term of four years, which is renewable.

The Federal Reserve Banks There are 12 Federal Reserve banks, one for each of the 12 Federal Reserve districts shown in Fig. 25.1. These Federal Reserve banks provide check-clearing services to commercial banks and other depository institutions, hold the reserve accounts of commercial banks, lend reserves to banks, and issue the bank notes that circulate as currency.

One of the district banks, the Federal Reserve Bank of New York (known as the New York Fed), occupies a special place in the Federal Reserve System because it implements the policy decisions of the Federal Open Market Committee.

The Federal Open Market Committee The **Federal Open Market Committee** (FOMC) is the main policy-making organ of the Federal Reserve System. The FOMC consists of the following voting members:

- The chairman and the other six members of the Board of Governors
- The president of the Federal Reserve Bank of New York
- The presidents of the other regional Federal Reserve banks (of whom, on a yearly rotating basis, only four vote)

The FOMC meets approximately every six weeks to review the state of the economy and to decide the actions to be carried out by the New York Fed.

The Fed's Power Center

A description of the formal structure of the Fed gives the impression that power in the Fed resides with the Board of Governors. In practice, it is the chairman of the Board of Governors who has the largest influence on the Fed's monetary policy actions, and some remarkable individuals have held this position. The current chairman is Ben Bernanke, a former eco-

FIGURE 25.1   The Federal Reserve System

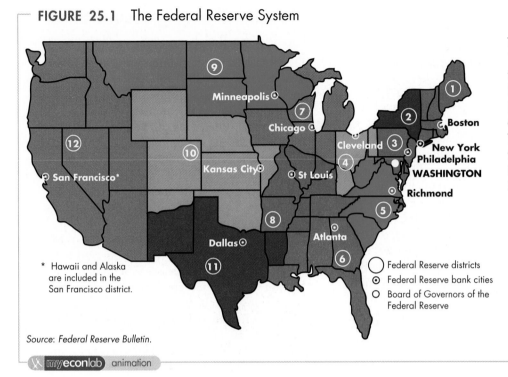

The nation is divided into 12 Federal Reserve districts, each having a Federal Reserve bank. (Some of the larger districts also have branch banks.) The Board of Governors of the Federal Reserve System is located in Washington, D.C.

* Hawaii and Alaska are included in the San Francisco district.

○ Federal Reserve districts
◉ Federal Reserve bank cities
○ Board of Governors of the Federal Reserve

Source: *Federal Reserve Bulletin.*

myeconlab animation

nomics professor at Princeton University, who was appointed by President George W. Bush in 2006. Bernanke followed Alan Greenspan (1987–2006) and Paul Volker (1979–1987).

The chairman's power and influence stem from three sources. First, it is the chairman who controls the agenda and who dominates the meetings of the FOMC. Second, day-to-day contact with a large staff of economists and other technical experts provides the chairman with detailed background briefings on monetary policy issues. Third, the chairman is the spokesperson for the Fed and the main liaison between the Fed, the President, and the U.S. government and with foreign central banks and governments.

The Fed's Balance Sheet

The Fed influences the economy through the size and composition of its balance sheet—the assets that the Fed owns and the liabilities that it owes. You will learn *how* the Fed influences the economy in stages in the rest of this chapter and in Chapter 31. Here, you will learn about the items in the Fed's balance sheet.

The Fed's Assets The Fed has two main assets:

1. U.S. government securities
2. Loans to depository institutions

The Fed holds U.S. securities—Treasury bills and Treasury bonds—that it buys in the bond market. When the Fed buys or sells bonds, it participates in the *market for loanable funds* (see pp. 568–574).

The Fed makes loans to depository institutions. When these institutions in aggregate are short of reserves, they can borrow from the Fed. In normal times this item is small, but during 2007 and 2008, it grew as the Fed provided increasing amounts of relief from the sub-prime mortgage crisis. By October 2008, loans to depository institutions exceeded government securities in the Fed's balance sheet.

The Fed's Liabilities The Fed has two liabilities:

1. Federal Reserve notes
2. Depository institution deposits

Federal Reserve notes are the dollar bills that we use in our daily transactions. Some of these notes are held by individuals and businesses; others are in the tills and vaults of banks and other depository institutions.

Depository institution deposits at the Fed are part of the reserves of these institutions (see p. 591).

The Monetary Base The Fed's liabilities together with coins issued by the Treasury (coins are not liabilities of the Fed) make up the monetary base. That is, the **monetary base** is the sum of Federal Reserve notes, coins, and depository institution deposits at the Fed. The monetary base is so named because it acts like a base that supports the nation's money. Table 25.3 provides a snapshot of the sources and uses of the monetary base in October 2008.

When the Fed changes the monetary base, the quantity of money changes, as you will soon see. But first, we'll look at the policy tools available to the Fed for changing the monetary base and then, in the next section of this chapter, we'll see how banks create money and how the Fed can regulate its quantity.

The Fed's Policy Tools

The Federal Reserve System has many responsibilities, but we'll examine its single most important one: regulating the amount of money floating around in the United States. How does the Fed control the quantity of money? It does so by adjusting the monetary base. Also, it is by adjusting the monetary base and by standing ready to make loans to banks that the Fed is able to prevent bank failures. The Fed uses three main policy tools to achieve its objectives.

These tools are

TABLE 25.3 The Sources and Uses of the Monetary Base

Sources (billions of dollars)		Uses (billions of dollars)	
U.S. government securities	491	Currency	805
Loans to depository institutions	543	Reserves of depository institutions	180
Other items (net)	–49		
Monetary base	985	Monetary base	985

Source of data: Federal Reserve Board: The data are for October 8, 2008.

The Fed's Changing Balance Sheet
Bearing the Risks

The Fed's balance sheet underwent some remarkable changes from mid-2007 to October 2008. The figure shows the effects of these changes on the size and composition of the monetary base.

In normal times, the Fed's holdings of U.S. government securities are almost as large as the monetary base (currency and depository institution reserves). But during the 2007–2008 sub-prime crisis, the Fed swapped a large volume of government securities for riskier loans to depository institutions. Holdings of government securities almost halved from close to $800 billion to less than $500 billion. Loans to depository institutions increased from zero to $1,000 billion. Some of this increase, $150 billion, was Term Auction Credit, a new credit facility that enables financial institutions to obtain high quality government securities in exchange for hard-to-sell risky private securities.

On the liabilities side of the Fed's balance sheet, reserves of depository institutions are usually a very small item. But during the sub-prime crisis, these institutions wanted to keep larger reserves and this item grew from $44 billion to $650 billion.

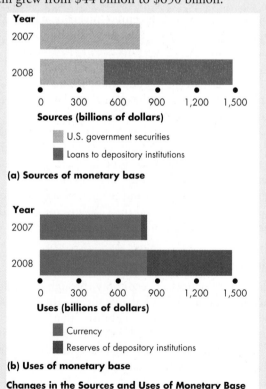

(a) Sources of monetary base

(b) Uses of monetary base

Changes in the Sources and Uses of Monetary Base

- Required reserve ratio
- Last resort loans
- Open market operations

Required Reserve Ratio Depository institutions are required to hold a minimum percentage of deposits as reserves, which is known as a **required reserve ratio**. In 2008, the Fed required banks to hold minimum reserves equal to 3 percent of checking deposits between $10.3 million and $44.4 million and 10 percent of these deposits in excess of $44.4 million. The required reserves on other types of deposits are zero.

Last Resort Loans The Fed is the **lender of last resort**, which means that if depository institutions are short of reserves, they can borrow from the Fed. But the Fed sets the interest rate on last resort loans and this interest rate is called the **discount rate**.

During the period since August 2007 when the first effects of the sub-prime mortgage crisis started to be felt, the Fed has been especially active as lender of last resort and has created, with the U.S. Treasury, a number of new lending facilities and initiatives to prevent banks from failing.

Open Market Operations An **open market operation** is the purchase or sale of government securities—U.S. Treasury bills and bonds—by the Federal Reserve System in the open market. When the Fed conducts an open market operation, it makes a transaction with a bank or some other business but it does not transact with the federal government.

Review Quiz

1 What is the central bank of the United States and what functions does it perform?
2 What is the monetary base and how does it relate to the Fed's balance sheet?
3 What are the Fed's three policy tools?
4 What is the Federal Open Market Committee and what are its main functions?

 Work Study Plan 25.3 and get instant feedback.

Next, we're going to see how the banking system—the banks and the Fed—creates money.

How Banks Create Money

Banks create money. But this doesn't mean that they have smoke-filled back rooms in which counterfeiters are busily working. Remember, most money is bank deposits, not currency. What banks create is deposits, and they do so by making loans.

Creating Deposits by Making Loans

The easiest way to see that banks create deposits is to think about what happens when Andy, who has a Visa card issued by Citibank, uses his card to buy a tank of gas from Chevron. When Andy signs the card sales slip, he takes a loan from Citibank and obligates himself to repay the loan at a later date. At the end of the business day, a Chevron clerk takes a pile of signed credit card sales slips, including Andy's, to Chevron's bank. For now, let's assume that Chevron also banks at Citibank. The bank immediately credits Chevron's account with the value of the slips (minus the bank's commission).

You can see that these transactions have created a bank deposit and a loan. Andy has increased the size of his loan (his credit card balance), and Chevron has increased the size of its bank deposit. Because bank deposits are money, Citibank has created money.

If, as we've just assumed, Andy and Chevron use the same bank, no further transactions take place. But the outcome is essentially the same when two banks are involved. If Chevron's bank is Bank of America, then Citibank uses its reserves to pay Bank of America. Citibank has an increase in loans and a decrease in reserves; Bank of America has an increase in reserves and an increase in deposits. The banking system as a whole has an increase in loans and deposits but no change in reserves.

If Andy had swiped his card at an automatic payment pump, all these transactions would have occurred at the time he filled his tank, and the quantity of money would have increased by the amount of his purchase (minus the bank's commission for conducting the transactions).

The quantity of deposits that the banking system can create is limited by three factors:

- The monetary base
- Desired reserves
- Desired currency holdings

The Monetary Base You've seen that the *monetary base* is the sum of Federal Reserve notes, coins, and banks' deposits at the Fed. The size of the monetary base limits the total quantity of money that the banking system can create. The reason is that banks have a desired level of reserves, households and firms have a desired holding of currency, and both of these desired holdings of the monetary base depend on the quantity of money.

Desired Reserves A bank's *actual* **reserves** consist of the notes and coins in its vaults and its deposit at the Federal Reserve. A bank uses its reserves to meet depositors' demand for currency and to make payments to other banks.

You've also seen that banks don't have $100 of reserves for every $100 that people have deposited with them. If the banks did behave that way, they wouldn't make a profit.

In September 2008, banks had reserves of $7.50 for every $100 of M1 deposits and $1.36 for every $100 of M2 deposits. Most of these reserves are currency. You saw in the previous section that reserves in the form of deposits at the Federal Reserve are tiny. But there's no need for panic. Banks hold the quantity of reserves that are adequate for their ordinary business needs.

The fraction of a bank's total deposits that are held in reserves is called the **reserve ratio**. So with reserves of $7.50 for every $100 of M1 deposits, the M1 reserve ratio is 0.075 or 7.5 percent, and with reserves of $1.36 for every $100 of M2 deposits, the M2 reserve ratio is 0.0136 or 1.36 percent.

A bank's desired reserves are the reserves that it wishes to hold. Banks are *required* to hold a quantity of reserves that does not fall below a specified percentage of total deposits. This percentage is the *required reserve ratio*.

The fraction of a bank's total deposits that it *wants* to hold in reserves is called the **desired reserve ratio**. This ratio exceeds the required reserve ratio by an amount that the banks determine to be prudent on the basis of their daily business requirements.

A bank's reserve ratio changes when its customers make a deposit or a withdrawal. If a bank's customer makes a deposit, reserves and deposits increase by the same amount, so the bank's reserve ratio increases. Similarly, if a bank's customer makes a withdrawal, reserves and deposits decrease by the same amount, so the bank's reserve ratio decreases.

A bank's **excess reserves** are its actual reserves minus its desired reserves. When a bank has excess reserves, it makes loans and creates money; and when it is short of reserves—when desired reserves exceed actual reserves—its loans and deposits shrink.

When the entire banking system has excess reserves, loans and deposits increase and when the banking system is short of reserves, loans and deposits decrease.

The greater the desired reserve ratio, the smaller is the quantity of money that the banking system can create from a given monetary base.

Desired Currency Holding We hold our money in the form of currency and bank deposits. The proportion of money held as currency isn't constant but at any given time, people have a definite view as to how much they want to hold in each form of money.

In 2008, for every dollar of M1 deposits held, we held $1.27 of currency and for every dollar of M2 deposits, we held 11¢ of currency.

Because households and firms want to hold some proportion of their money in the form of currency, when the total quantity of bank deposits increases, so does the quantity of currency that they want to hold. Because desired currency holding increases when deposits increase, currency leaves the banks when loans are made and deposits increase. We call the leakage of currency from the banking system the *currency drain*, and we call the ratio of currency to deposits the **currency drain ratio**.

The greater the currency drain ratio, the smaller is the quantity of deposits and money that the banking system can create from a given amount of monetary base.

The Money Creation Process

The money creation process begins when the monetary base increases and the banking system has excess reserves. These excess reserves come from a purchase of securities by the Fed from a bank. (Chapter 31, pp. 759–760, explains exactly how the Fed conducts such a purchase—what is called an open market operation.)

When the Fed buys securities from a bank, the bank's reserves increase but its deposits do not change. So the bank has excess reserves. It lends those excess reserves and a sequence of events then plays out.

The sequence, which keeps repeating until all the

reserves held are desired and banks have no excess reserves, has eight steps:

1. Banks have excess reserves.
2. Banks lend excess reserves.
3. The quantity of money increases.
4. New money is used to make payments.
5. Some of the new money remains on deposit.
6. Some of the new money is a *currency drain*.
7. Desired reserves increase because deposits have increased.
8. Excess reserves decrease but remain positive.

The sequence repeats in a series of rounds, but each round begins with a smaller quantity of excess reserves than the quantity at the start of the previous one. The process of money creation continues until excess reserves have been eliminated. Figure 25.2 illustrates the first round in this process.

The Money Multiplier

The **money multiplier** is the ratio of the change in the quantity of money to the change in monetary base. For example, if an increase in the monetary base by $100,000 increases the quantity of money by $250,000, then the money multiplier is 2.5.

The Mathematical Note on pp. 608–609 explains how the magnitude of the money multiplier depends on the reserve ratio and the currency drain ratio.

Review Quiz

1 How do banks create money?
2 What limits the quantity of money that the banking system can create?
3 A bank manager tells you that she doesn't create money. She just lends the money that people deposit. Explain why she's wrong.

 Work Study Plan 25.4 and get instant feedback.

FIGURE 25.2   How the Banking System Creates Money by Making Loans

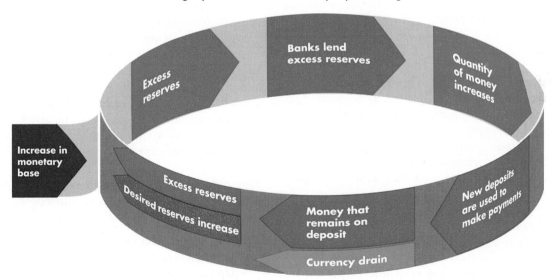

The Federal Reserve increases the monetary base which increases bank reserves and creates excess reserves. Banks lend the excess reserves and create new deposits. The quantity of money increases. New deposits are used to make payments. Some of the new money remains on deposit at banks and some leaves the banks in a currency drain. The increase in bank deposits increases banks' desired reserves. But the banks still have excess reserves, though less than before. The process repeats until excess reserves have been eliminated.

myeconlab animation

The Market for Money

There is no limit to the amount of money we would like to *receive* in payment for our labor or as interest on our savings. But there *is* a limit to how big an inventory of money we would like to *hold* and neither spend nor use to buy assets that generate an income. The *quantity of money demanded* is the inventory of money that people plan to hold on any given day. It is the quantity of money in our wallets and in our deposit accounts at banks. The quantity of money held must equal the quantity supplied, and the forces that bring about this equality in the money market have powerful effects on the economy, as you will see in the rest of this chapter.

But first, we need to explain what determines the amount of money that people plan to hold.

The Influences on Money Holding

The quantity of money that people plan to hold depends on four main factors:

- The price level
- The *nominal* interest rate
- Real GDP
- Financial innovation

The Price Level The quantity of money measured in dollars is *nominal money*. The quantity of nominal money demanded is proportional to the price level, other things remaining the same. If the price level rises by 10 percent, people hold 10 percent more nominal money than before, other things remaining the same. If you hold $20 to buy your weekly movies and soda, you will increase your money holding to $22 if the prices of movies and soda—and your wage rate—increase by 10 percent.

The quantity of money measured in constant dollars (for example, in 2000 dollars) is real money. *Real money* is equal to nominal money divided by the price level and is the quantity of money measured in terms of what it will buy. In the above example, when the price level rises by 10 percent and you increase your money holding by 10 percent, your *real* money holding is constant. Your $22 at the new price level buys the same quantity of goods and is the same quantity of *real money* as your $20 at the original price level. The quantity of real money demanded is independent of the price level.

The *Nominal* Interest Rate A fundamental principle of economics is that as the opportunity cost of something increases, people try to find substitutes for it. Money is no exception. The higher the opportunity cost of holding money, other things remaining the same, the smaller is the quantity of real money demanded. The nominal interest rate on other assets minus the nominal interest rate on money is the opportunity cost of holding money.

The interest rate that you earn on currency and checking deposits is zero. So the opportunity cost of holding these items is the nominal interest rate on other assets such as a savings bond or Treasury bill. By holding money instead, you forgo the interest that you otherwise would have received.

Money loses value because of inflation, so why isn't the inflation rate part of the cost of holding money? It is. Other things remaining the same, the higher the expected inflation rate, the higher is the nominal interest rate.

Real GDP The quantity of money that households and firms plan to hold depends on the amount they are spending, and the quantity of money demanded in the economy as a whole depends on aggregate expenditure—real GDP.

Again, suppose that you hold an average of $20 to finance your weekly purchases of movies and soda. Now imagine that the prices of these goods and of all other goods remain constant but that your income increases. As a consequence, you now buy more goods and services and you also keep a larger amount of money on hand to finance your higher volume of expenditure.

Financial Innovation Technological change and the arrival of new financial products influence the quantity of money held. Financial innovations include

1. Daily interest checking deposits
2. Automatic transfers between checking and saving deposits
3. Automatic teller machines
4. Credit cards and debit cards
5. Internet banking and bill paying

These innovations have occurred because of the development of computing power that has lowered the cost of calculations and record keeping.

We summarize the effects of the influences on money holding by using a demand for money curve.

The Demand for Money

The **demand for money** is the relationship between the quantity of real money demanded and the nominal interest rate when all other influences on the amount of money that people wish to hold remain the same.

Figure 25.3 shows a demand for money curve, *MD*. When the interest rate rises, other things remaining the same, the opportunity cost of holding money rises and the quantity of real money demanded decreases—there is a movement up along the demand for money curve. Similarly, when the interest rate falls, the opportunity cost of holding money falls, and the quantity of real money demanded increases—there is a movement down along the demand for money curve.

When any influence on money holding other than the interest rate changes, there is a change in the demand for money and the demand for money curve shifts. Let's study these shifts.

Shifts in the Demand for Money Curve

A change in real GDP or financial innovation changes the demand for money and shifts the demand for money curve.

Figure 25.4 illustrates the change in the demand for money. A decrease in real GDP decreases the demand for money and shifts the demand for money curve leftward from MD_0 to MD_1. An increase in real GDP has the opposite effect: It increases the demand for money and shifts the demand for money curve rightward from MD_0 to MD_2.

The influence of financial innovation on the demand for money curve is more complicated. It decreases the demand for currency and might increase the demand for some types of deposits and decrease the demand for others. But generally, financial innovation decreases the demand for money.

You can see the effects of changes in real GDP and financial innovation by looking at the demand for money in the United States on the next page.

FIGURE 25.3 The Demand for Money

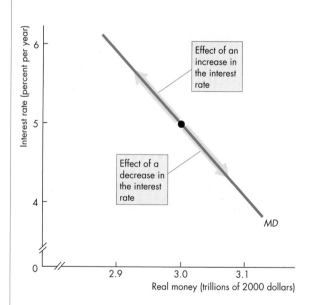

The demand for money curve, *MD*, shows the relationship between the quantity of real money that people plan to hold and the nominal interest rate, other things remaining the same. The interest rate is the opportunity cost of holding money. A change in the interest rate brings a movement along the demand for money curve.

myeconlab animation

FIGURE 25.4 Changes in the Demand for Money

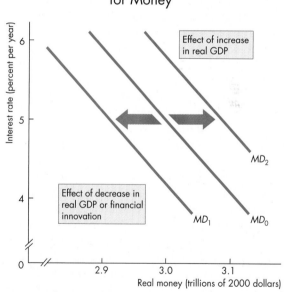

A decrease in real GDP decreases the demand for money. The demand for money curve shifts leftward from MD_0 to MD_1. An increase in real GDP increases the demand for money. The demand for money curve shifts rightward from MD_0 to MD_2. Financial innovation generally decreases the demand for money.

myeconlab animation

Demand for Money in the United States
How Money Holding Bounces Around

The growth of real GDP brings sustained growth in the demand for money. If real GDP were the only influence on the demand for money, the demand for money curve would shift rightward whenever real GDP increased, which is most of the time.

But financial innovation also influences the demand for money. During the early 1970s, the spread of credit cards decreased the demand for currency and checking deposits (M1).

A continued increase in the use of credit cards and the spread of ATMs further decreased the demand for M1 during the 1990s and 2000s.

Similarly, financial innovation has changed the demand for the savings deposits and money market funds that make up M2. New interest-bearing deposits increased the demand for M2 from 1970 through 1989. But between 1989 and 1994, innovations in financial products that compete with deposits of all kinds occurred and the demand for M2 decreased.

The figures illustrate the effects of the growth of real GDP and financial innovation on the demand for M1 in part (a) and M2 in part (b).

Each dot represents the quantity of real money and the interest rate in each year between 1970 and 2008. In 1970, the demand for M1 curve was MD_0 in part (a). The demand for M1 decreased during the early 1970s because of financial innovation, and the demand curve shifted leftward to MD_1. But real GDP growth increases the demand for M1, and by 1994, the demand curve had shifted rightward to MD_2. Further financial innovation decreased the demand for M1 during the 1990s and 2000s and shifted the demand curve leftward again to MD_3.

In 1970, the demand for M2 curve was MD_0 in part (b). The growth of real GDP increased the demand for M2, and by 1989, the demand curve had shifted rightward to MD_1. During the early 1990s, new substitutes for M2 decreased the demand for M2 and the demand curve shifted leftward to MD_2. But during the late 1990s, rapid growth of real GDP increased the demand for M2. By 2005, the demand curve had shifted rightward to MD_3.

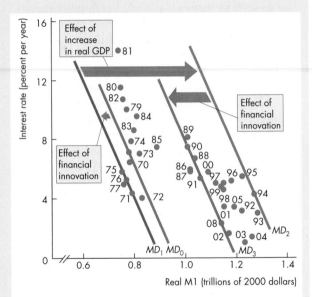

(a) M1 demand

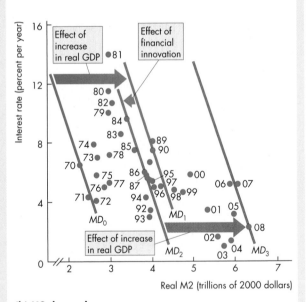

(b) M2 demand

The U.S. Demand for Money

Sources of data: Bureau of Economic Analysis and Federal Reserve Board.

You now know what determines the demand for money, and you've seen how the banking system cre-

ates money. Let's now see how the money market reaches an equilibrium.

Money Market Equilibrium

Money market equilibrium occurs when the quantity of money demanded equals the quantity of money supplied. The adjustments that occur to bring money market equilibrium are fundamentally different in the short run and the long run. Our primary focus here is the long run. (We explore short-run issues in Chapters 27–31.) But we need to say a little bit about the short run so that you can appreciate how the long-run equilibrium comes about.

Short-Run Equilibrium The quantity of money supplied is determined by the actions of the banks and the Fed. Each day, the Fed adjusts the quantity of money to hit its interest rate target. In Fig. 25.5, with the demand for money curve *MD*, if the Fed wants the interest rate to be 5 percent a year, the Fed adjusts

the quantity of money so that the quantity of real money supplied is $3.0 trillion and the supply of money curve is *MS*.

The equilibrium interest rate is 5 percent a year. If the interest rate were 4 percent a year, people would want to hold more money than is available. They would sell bonds, bid down their price, and the interest rate would rise. If the interest rate were 6 percent a year, people would want to hold less money than is available. They would buy bonds, bid up their price, and the interest rate would fall.

Long-Run Equilibrium In the long run, supply and demand in the loanable funds market determines the real interest rate. The nominal interest rate equals the equilibrium real interest rate plus the expected inflation rate. Real GDP, which influences the demand for money, equals potential GDP. So the *only* variable that is left to adjust in the long run is the price level. The price level adjusts to make the quantity of real money supplied equal to the quantity demanded. If the Fed changes the nominal quantity of money, the price level changes (in the long run) by a percentage equal to the percentage change in the quantity of nominal money. In the long run, the change in the price level is proportional to the change in the quantity of money.

FIGURE 25.5 Money Market Equilibrium

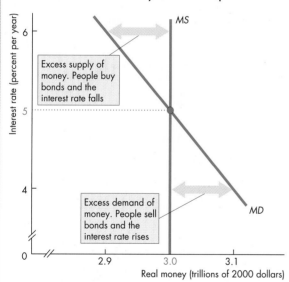

Money market equilibrium occurs when the quantity of money demanded equals the quantity supplied.

   Short run: In the short run, the quantity of real money and real GDP are given and the interest rate adjusts to achieve equilibrium, here 5 percent a year.

   Long run: In the long run, supply and demand in the loanable funds market determines the interest rate, real GDP equals potential GDP, and the price level adjusts to make the quantity of real money supplied equal the quantity demanded, here $3 trillion.

myeconlab animation

Review Quiz

1 What are the main influences on the quantity of real money that people and businesses plan to hold?

2 How does a change in the nominal interest rate change the quantity of money demanded? Illustrate the effect by using the demand for money curve.

3 How does a change in real GDP change the demand for money? Illustrate the effect by using the demand for money curve.

4 How has financial innovation changed the demand for M1 and the demand for M2?

5 How is money market equilibrium determined in the short run and in the long run?

myeconlab Work Study Plan 25.5 and get instant feedback.

Let's explore the long-run link between money and the price level a bit more thoroughly.

The Quantity Theory of Money

In the long run, the price level adjusts to make the quantity of real money demanded equal the quantity supplied. A special theory of the price level and inflation—the quantity theory of money—explains this long-run adjustment of the price level.

The **quantity theory of money** is the proposition that in the long run, an increase in the quantity of money brings an equal percentage increase in the price level. To explain the quantity theory of money, we first need to define *the velocity of circulation*.

The **velocity of circulation** is the average number of times a dollar of money is used annually to buy the goods and services that make up GDP. But GDP equals the price level (P) multiplied by *real* GDP (Y). That is,

$$GDP = PY.$$

Call the quantity of money M. The velocity of circulation, V, is determined by the equation

$$V = PY/M.$$

For example, if GDP is $1,000 billion ($PY = $1,000 billion) and the quantity of money is $250 billion, then the velocity of circulation is 4.

From the definition of the velocity of circulation, the *equation of exchange* tells us how M, V, P, and Y are connected. This equation is

$$MV = PY.$$

Given the definition of the velocity of circulation, the equation of exchange is always true—it is true by definition. It becomes the quantity theory of money if the quantity of money does not influence the velocity of circulation or real GDP. In this case, the equation of exchange tells us that in the long run, the price level is determined by the quantity of money. That is,

$$P = M(V/Y),$$

where (V/Y) is independent of M. So a change in M brings a proportional change in P.

We can also express the equation of exchange in growth rates,[1] in which form it states that

$$\text{Money growth rate} + \text{Rate of velocity change} = \text{Inflation rate} + \text{Real GDP growth rate}$$

Does the Quantity Theory Work?
Yes, on Average

On average, as predicted by the quantity theory of money, the inflation rate fluctuates in line with fluctuations in the money growth rate minus the real GDP growth rate. Figure 1 shows the relationship between money growth (M2 definition) and inflation in the United States. You can see a clear relationship between the two variables.

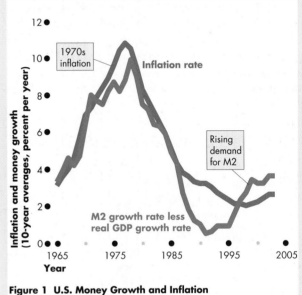

Figure 1 U.S. Money Growth and Inflation

Source of data: Federal Reserve and Bureau of Labor Statistics.

Solving this equation for the inflation rate gives

$$\text{Inflation rate} = \text{Money growth rate} + \text{Rate of velocity change} - \text{Real GDP growth rate}$$

In the long run, the rate of velocity change is not influenced by the money growth rate. More strongly, in the long run, the rate of velocity change is approxi-

---

[1] To obtain this equation, begin with
$$MV = PY.$$
and then changes in these variables are related by the equation
$$\Delta MV + M\Delta V = \Delta PY + P\Delta Y.$$
Divide this equation by the equation of exchange to obtain
$$\Delta M/M + \Delta V/V = \Delta P/P + \Delta Y/Y.$$
The term $\Delta M/M$ is the money growth rate, $\Delta V/V$ is the rate of velocity change, $\Delta P/P$ is the inflation rate, and $\Delta Y/Y$ is the real GDP growth rate.

International data also support the quantity theory. Figure 2 shows a scatter diagram of the inflation rate and the money growth rate in 134 countries and Fig. 3 shows the inflation rate and money growth rate in countries with inflation rates below 20 percent a year. You can see a general tendency for money growth and inflation to be correlated but the quantity theory (the red line) does not predict inflation precisely.

The correlation between money growth and inflation isn't perfect, and the correlation does not tell us that money growth *causes* inflation. Money growth might cause inflation; inflation might cause money growth; or some third variable might cause both inflation and money growth. Other evidence does confirm, though, that causation runs from money growth to inflation.

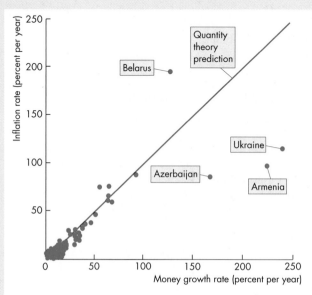

Figure 2 134 Countries: 1990–2005

Figure 3 104 Lower-inflation countries: 1990–2005

Sources of data: International Financial Statistics Yearbook, 2008 and International Monetary Fund, *World Economic Outlook*, October, 2008.

mately zero. With this assumption, the inflation rate in the long run is determined as

$$\text{Inflation rate} = \text{Money growth rate} - \text{Real GDP growth rate}.$$

In the long run, fluctuations in the money growth rate minus the real GDP growth rate bring equal fluctuations in the inflation rate.

Also, in the long run, with the economy at full employment, real GDP equals potential GDP, so the real GDP growth rate equals the potential GDP growth rate. This growth rate might be influenced by inflation, but the influence is most likely small and the quantity theory assumes that it is zero. So the real GDP growth rate is given and doesn't change when the money growth rate changes—inflation is correlated with money growth.

Review Quiz

1 What is the quantity theory of money?
2 How is the velocity of circulation calculated?
3 What is the equation of exchange? Can it be wrong?
4 Does the quantity theory correctly predict the effects of money growth on inflation?

 Work Study Plan 25.6 and get instant feedback.

You now know what money is, how the banks create it, and how the quantity of money influences the nominal interest rate in the short-run and the price level in the long run. *Reading Between the Lines* rounds out the chapter by looking at the quantity theory of money in action in Zimbabwe today.

The Quantity Theory of Money in Zimbabwe

Life in Zimbabwe: Wait for Useless Money, Then Scour for Food

http://www.nytimes.com
October 2, 2008

Harare, Zimbabwe—Long before the rooster in their dirt yard crowed, Rose Moyo and her husband rolled out of bed … and took their daily moonlit stroll to the bank … hoping for a chance to withdraw the maximum amount of Zimbabwean currency the government allowed last month—the equivalent of just a dollar or two.

Zimbabwe is in the grip of one of the great hyperinflations in world history. The people of this once proud capital have been plunged into a Darwinian struggle to get by. Many have been reduced to peddlers and paupers, hawkers and black-market hustlers, eating just a meal or two a day, their hollowed cheeks a testament to their hunger.

… Mrs. Moyo has calculate the price of goods by the number of days she had to spend in line at the bank to withdraw cash to buy them: a day for a bar of soap; another for a bag of salt; and four for a sack of cornmeal.

The withdrawal limit rose on Monday, but with inflation surpassing what independent economists say is an almost unimaginable 40 million percent, she said the value of the new amount would quickly be a pittance, too.

"It's survival of the fittest," said Mrs. Moyo, 29, a hair braider who sells the greens she grows in her yard for a dime a bunch. "If you're not fit, you will starve."

Economists here and abroad say Zimbabwe's economic collapse is gaining velocity, radiating instability into the heart of southern Africa. As the bankrupt government prints ever more money, inflation has gone wild, rising from 1,000 percent in 2006 to 12,000 percent in 2007 to a figure so high the government had to lop 10 zeros off the currency in August to keep the nation's calculators from being overwhelmed. (Had it left the currency alone, $1 would now be worth about 10 trillion Zimbabwean dollars.) …

Essence of the Story

- Hyperinflation in Zimbabwe is the worst in world history— 40 million percent a year.

- $1 U.S. was heading toward $10 trillion Zimbabwean before 10 zeros were lopped off the currency unit.

- People get up in the middle of the night to stand in line for cash at the bank because the government limits cash withdrawals.

- Prices of goods are measured in the number of days spent in line to withdraw the cash to buy them: a day for a bar of soap or a bag of salt; four days for a sack of cornmeal.

- The people of Harare (the capital city) are on the edge of survival.

- The government fuels the inflation by printing ever more money.

Economic Analysis

- Zimbabwe has the highest inflation rate in world history, so it provides a good example of the quantity theory of money in action.

- The quantity theory predicts that a low growth rate of the quantity of money keeps inflation low and a rapid growth rate of the quantity of money brings a high inflation rate.

- During 2008, the inflation rate in Zimbabwe was so high, it could not be measured accurately but it was reputed to be 231 million percent a year.

- To appreciate an inflation rate of 231 million percent a year, translate it to a monthly inflation rate. Every month, on average, prices rise by 239 percent. A cup of coffee that costs $3 in January costs $10 in February, $117 in April and $4,560 in July!

- Figure 1 shows Zimbabwe's reported inflation rate and ~~money growth rate record from 2000 to 2007.~~

- The money growth rate increased from 52 percent a year in 2000 to 66,700 percent a year in 2007.

- The reported inflation rate increased slowly at first, from 56 percent a year in 2000 to 303 percent a year in 2005. In 2006, the inflation rate took off and climbed to a reported 1,100 percent in 2006 and 24,000 percent in 2007.

- The quantity theory predicts that inflation will outpace the money growth rate, not fall behind it as these reported inflation rates show.

- The reported inflation rate is almost certainly far lower than the true inflation rate.

- When people expect rapid inflation, they expect the money they hold to lose value rapidly, so they spend and hold goods rather than money.

- The velocity of circulation rises. The velocity of circulation is independent of the quantity of money but not independent of the money growth rate.

- We can measure the velocity of circulation in Zimbabwe by using the equation of exchange,

$$MV = PY$$

along with data on M, P, and Y.

- Real GDP, Y, has fallen every year since 2000, and in 2007 it stood at 70 percent of its 2000 level.

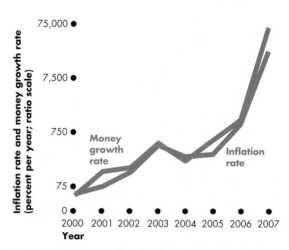

Figure 1 Money growth and inflation

- The velocity of circulation, based on the reported data, *fell* from 6.7 in 2000 to 0.6 in 2007.

- The true velocity of circulation could not have fallen. A lower velocity implies that people are hoarding more money.

- The explanation for the fall in the calculated velocity of circulation is that the true inflation rate is much higher than the reported rate.

- The unofficial reported inflation of 40 million percent a year in 2008 might be close to the truth. The inflation rate during the years 2003 through 2007 was almost certainly greater than the money growth rate.

- The reported change in the currency unit, lopping off 10 zeroes, has no effect on the inflation rate. It only changes the units in which prices are measured.

- To lower its inflation rate, the government of Zimbabwe must stop printing money to finance its expenditures.

MATHEMATICAL NOTE

The Money Multiplier

This note explains the basic math of the money multiplier and shows how the value of the multiplier depends on the banks' reserve ratio and the currency drain ratio.

To make the process of money creation concrete, we work through an example for a banking system in which each bank has a desired reserve ratio of 10 percent of deposits and the currency drain ratio is 50 percent of deposits or 0.5. (Although these ratios are larger than the ones in the U.S. economy, they make the process end more quickly and enable you to see more clearly the principles at work.)

The figure keeps track of the numbers. Before the process begins, the banks have no excess reserves. Then the monetary base increases by $100,000 and a bank has excess reserves of this amount.

The bank lends the $100,000 of excess reserves. When this loan is made, new money increases by $100,000.

With a currency drain ratio of 50 percent of

deposits, $33,333 drains out of the banks as currency and $66,667 remains in the banks as deposits. The quantity of money has increased by $100,000—the increase in deposits plus the increase in currency holdings.

The increased bank deposits of $66,667 generate an increase in desired reserves of 10 percent of that amount, which is $6,667. Actual reserves have increased by the same amount as the increase in deposits: $66,667. So the banks now have excess reserves of $60,000.

The process we've just described repeats but begins with excess reserves of $60,000. The figure shows the next two rounds. At the end of the process, the quantity of money has increased by a multiple of the increase in the monetary base. In this case, the increase is $250,000, which is 2.5 times the increase in the monetary base.

The sequence in the figure is the first stages of the process that finally reaches the total shown in the final row of the "money" column.

To calculate what happens at the later stages in the process and the final increase in the quantity of money, look closely at the numbers in the figure. The

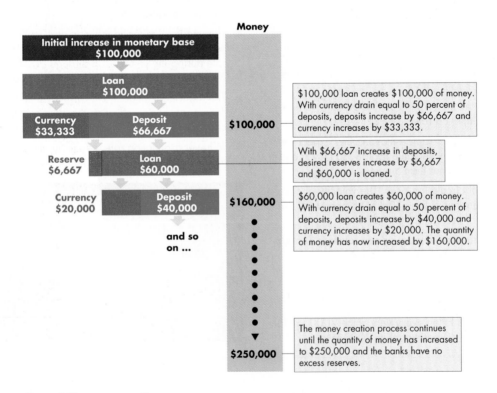

Figure 1 The money creation process

initial increase in reserves is $100,000 (call it A). At each stage, the loan is 60 percent (0.6) of the previous loan and the quantity of money increases by 0.6 of the previous increase. Call that proportion L ($L = 0.6$). We can write down the complete sequence for the increase in the quantity of money as

$$A + AL + AL^2 + AL^3 + AL^4 + AL^5 + \dots .$$

Remember, L is a fraction, so at each stage in this sequence, the amount of new loans and new money gets smaller. The total value of loans made and money created at the end of the process is the sum of the sequence, which is[1]

$$A/(1 - L).$$

If we use the numbers from the example, the total increase in the quantity of money is

$100,000 + 60,000 + 36,000 + \dots$

$= \$100,000 \, (1 + 0.6 + 0.36 + \dots)$

$= \$100,000 \, (1 + 0.6 + 0.6^2 + \dots)$

$= \$100,000 \times 1/(1 - 0.6)$

$= \$100,000 \times 1/(0.4)$

$= \$100,000 \times 2.5$

$= \$250,000.$

The magnitude of the money multiplier depends on the desired reserve ratio and the currency drain ratio. Call the monetary base MB and the quantity of money M. When there are no excess reserves,

MB = Desired currency holding + Desired reserves.

---

[1] The sequence of values is called a convergent geometric series. To find the sum of a series such as this, begin by calling the sum S. Then write the sum as

$$S = A + AL + AL^2 + AL^3 + AL^4 + AL^5 + \dots .$$

Multiply by L to get

$$LS = AL + AL^2 + AL^3 + AL^4 + AL^5 + \dots$$

and then subtract the second equation from the first to get

$$S(1 - L) = A$$

or

$$S = A/(1 - L).$$

M = Deposits + Desired currency holding.

Call the currency drain ratio a and the desired reserve ratio b. Then

Desired currency holding = $a \times$ Deposits

Desired reserves = $b \times$ Deposits

$MB = (a + b) \times$ Deposits

$M = (1 + a) \times$ Deposits.

Call the change in monetary base ΔMB and the change in the quantity of money ΔM. Then

$\Delta MB = (a + b) \times$ Change in deposits

$\Delta M = (1 + a) \times$ Change in deposits.

The money multiplier is the ratio of ΔM to ΔMB, so divide the above equation for ΔM by the one for ΔMB. That is,

Money multiplier = $(1 + a)/(a + b)$.

If we use the values of the example summarized in the figure, $a = 0.5$ and $b = 0.1$, the

Money multiplier = $(1 + 0.5)/(0.5 + 0.1)$.

$= 1.5/0.6 = 2.5.$

The U.S. Money Multiplier

The money multiplier in the United States can be found by using the formula above along with the values of a and b in the U.S. economy.

Because we have two definitions of money, M1 and M2, we have two money multipliers. The numbers for M1 in 2008 are $a = 1.24$ and $b = 0.28$. So

M1 multiplier = $(1 + 1.24)/(1.24 + 0.28)$

$= 2.24/1.52 = 1.47.$

For M2 in 2008, $a = 0.12$ and $b = 0.03$, so

M2 multiplier = $(1 + 0.12)/(0.12 + 0.03)$

$= 1.12/0.15 = 7.5$

SUMMARY

Key Points

What Is Money? (pp. 588–590)

- Money is the means of payment. It functions as a medium of exchange, a unit of account, and a store of value.
- Today, money consists of currency and deposits.

Depository Institutions (pp. 591–593)

- Commercial banks, S&Ls, savings banks, credit unions, and money market mutual funds are depository institutions whose deposits are money.
- Depository institutions provide four main economic services: They create liquidity, minimize the cost of obtaining funds, minimize the cost of monitoring borrowers, and pool risks.

The Federal Reserve System (pp. 594–597)

- The Federal Reserve System is the central bank of the United States.
- The Fed influences the quantity of money by setting the required reserve ratio, the discount rate, and by conducting open market operations.

How Banks Create Money (pp. 597–599)

- Banks create money by making loans.

- The total quantity of money that can be created depends on the monetary base, the desired reserve ratio, and the currency drain ratio.

The Market for Money (pp. 600–603)

- The quantity of money demanded is the amount of money that people plan to hold.
- The quantity of real money equals the quantity of nominal money divided by the price level.
- The quantity of real money demanded depends on the nominal interest rate, real GDP, and financial innovation. A rise in the nominal interest rate brings a decrease in the quantity of real money demanded.
- In the short run, the Fed sets the quantity of money to hit a target nominal interest rate.
- In the long run, the loanable funds market determines the real interest rate and money market equilibrium determines the price level.

The Quantity Theory of Money (pp. 604–605)

- The quantity theory of money is the proposition that money growth and inflation move up and down together in the long run.
- The U.S. and international evidence is consistent with the quantity theory, on average.

Key Figures

Figure 25.2   How the Banking System Creates Money by Making Loans, 599
Figure 25.3   The Demand for Money, 601

Figure 25.5   Money Market Equilibrium, 603

Key Terms

Barter, 588
Central bank, 594
Currency, 589
Currency drain ratio, 598
Demand for money, 601
Depository institution, 591
Desired reserve ratio, 598
Discount rate, 597
Excess reserves, 598
Federal funds rate, 594

Federal Open Market
    Committee, 594
Federal Reserve System
    (the Fed), 594
Lender of last resort, 597
M1, 589
M2, 589
Means of payment, 588
Monetary base, 596
Money, 588

Money multiplier, 599
Open market operation, 597
Quantity theory of money, 604
Required reserve ratio, 597
Reserve ratio, 598
Reserves, 598
Velocity of circulation, 604

PROBLEMS and APPLICATIONS ◆

 Work problems 1–12 in Chapter 25 Study Plan and get instant feedback.
Work problems 13–22 as Homework, a Quiz, or a Test if assigned by your instructor.

1. In the United States today, money includes which of the following items?
   a. Federal Reserve bank notes in Citibank's cash machines
   b. Your Visa card
   c. Coins inside a vending machine
   d. U.S. dollar bills in your wallet
   e. The check you have just written to pay for your rent
   f. The loan you took out last August to pay for your school fees

2. The commercial banks in Zap have

Reserves	$250 million
Loans	$1,000 million
Deposits	$2,000 million
Total assets	$2,500 million

   If banks have no excess reserves, calculate the banks' desired reserve ratio.

3. You are given the following information about the economy of Nocoin: The banks have deposits of $300 billion. Their reserves are $15 billion, two thirds of which is in deposits with the central bank. Households and firms hold $30 billion in bank notes. There are no coins! Calculate
   a. The monetary base.
   b. The quantity of money.
   c. The banks' reserve ratio (as a percentage).
   d. The currency drain ratio (as a percentage).

4. [Study the Mathematical Note on pp. 608–609 to work this problem.] In problem 3, the banks have no excess reserves. Suppose that the Bank of Nocoin, the central bank, increases bank reserves by $0.5 billion.
   a. What happens to the quantity of money?
   b. Explain why the change in the quantity of money is not equal to the change in the monetary base.
   c. Calculate the money multiplier.

5. In problem 3, the banks have no excess reserves. Suppose that the Bank of Nocoin, the central bank, decreases bank reserves by $0.5 billion.
   a. Calculate the money multiplier.
   b. What happens to the quantity of money?

   c. What happens to the quantity of deposits?
   d. What happens to the quantity of currency?

6. The spreadsheet provides information about the demand for money in Minland. Column A is the nominal interest rate, r.

	A	B	C
1	r	Y_0	Y_1
2	7	1.0	1.5
3	6	1.5	2.0
4	5	2.0	2.5
5	4	2.5	3.0
6	3	3.0	3.5
7	2	3.5	4.0
8	1	4.0	4.5

   Columns B and C show the quantity of money demanded at two different levels of real GDP: Y_0 is $10 billion and Y_1 is $20 billion. The quantity of money is $3 billion. Initially, real GDP is $20 billion. What happens in Minland if the interest rate
   a. Exceeds 4 percent a year?
   b. Is less than 4 percent a year?
   c. Equals 4 percent a year?

7. The Minland economy in problem 6 experiences a severe recession. Real GDP decreases to $10 billion. If the quantity of money supplied does not change,
   a. What happens in Minland if the interest rate is 4 percent a year?
   b. Do people buy bonds or sell bonds?
   c. Will the interest rate rise or fall? Why?

8. Quantecon is a country in which the quantity theory of money operates. The country has a constant population, capital stock, and technology. In year 1, real GDP was $400 million, the price level was 200, and the velocity of circulation was 20. In year 2, the quantity of money was 20 percent higher than in year 1. What was
   a. The quantity of money in year 1?
   b. The quantity of money in year 2?
   c. The price level in year 2?
   d. The level of real GDP in year 2?
   e. The velocity of circulation in year 2?

9. In Quantecon described in problem 8, in year 3, the quantity of money falls to one fifth of its level in year 2.
   a. What is the quantity of money in year 3?
   b. What is the price level in year 3?
   c. What is the level of real GDP in year 3?
   d. What is the velocity of circulation in year 3?
   e. If it takes more than one year for the full quantity theory effect to occur, what do you predict happens to real GDP in Quantecon in year 3? Why?

10. **Regulators Give Bleak Forecast for Banks**

   … Federal Reserve Vice Chairman Donald Kohn, [told Congress] that banks have not allocated enough money to keep up with the growth of their problem assets. As a result, they may have to boost their skyrocketing loan loss reserves even further. … Regulators added that they were bracing for an uptick in the number of bank failures, at least in the near term. Kohn declined to comment on the health of specific companies but said that Wall Street firms have learned a great deal from Bear Stearns and have reduced leverage and built up their liquidity. "I think we have a stronger set of investment banks than we had a month-and-a-half ago," said Kohn.

   CNN, June 5, 2008

   a. Explain a bank's "balancing act" and how the over-pursuit of profit or underestimation of risk can lead to a bank failure.
   b. During a time of uncertainty, why might it be necessary for a bank to build up its liquidity?

11. **Firms, Banks Using Fewer Emergency Loans**

   In a sign of some improvement in the credit crisis, Wall Street [investment] firms for the first time didn't borrow from the Federal Reserve's emergency lending program and commercial banks also scaled back. … In the broadest use of the central bank's lending power since the 1930s, the Fed in March scrambled to avert a market meltdown by giving investment houses a place to go for emergency overnight loans. … Commercial banks and investment companies now pay 2.25 percent in interest for the loans. Separately, as part of efforts to relieve credit strains, the Fed auctioned $21.3 billion in Treasury securities to investment companies Thursday. The auction drew bids for less than the $25 billion the Fed was making available, which was viewed as possible sign of some improvements in credit conditions. In exchange for the 28-day loans of Treasury securities, bidding companies can put up as collateral more risky investments. These include certain mortgage-backed securities and bonds secured by federally guaranteed student loans. The auction program, which began March 27, is intended to make investment companies more inclined to lend to each other. A second goal is providing relief to the distressed market for mortgage-linked securities and for student loans.

   Time, July 11, 2008

   a. What is the rationale behind allowing the Federal Reserve to make loans to banks?
   b. How might the Federal Reserve offering these "emergency loans" create a moral hazard problem in banking?

12. **Banks Drop on Higher Reserve Requirement**

   China's central bank will raise its reserve ratio requirement by a percentage point to a record 17.5 percent by June 25, stepping up a battle to contain lending growth. … The increase will freeze up about 422 billion yuan of funds, equivalent to 91 percent of the value of new yuan-denominated loans extended in April. … The latest move adds to the 614.7 billion yuan removed from the financial system through reserve ratio increases since January. China's banks had an average excess reserve deposit ratio of 2 percent as of March 31, down from 3.3 percent in December. The rate that banks charge each other for seven-day loans … rose to 4.93 percent in Shanghai, the highest since Jan 24, according to China Bond Interbank Market. The gain suggests banks are hoarding cash in anticipation of further reserve ratio requirement increases. … Every half-point increase in the reserve ratio requirement cuts banks' profits by as much as 1.5 percent, assuming they reduce lending to comply with it, said Li Qing, an analyst at CSC Securities HK Ltd.

   People's Daily Online, June 11, 2008

   a. Compare the required reserve ratio in China and in the United States.
   b. Explain how increasing the required reserve ratio can impact money creation in China's banking system.
   c. Why might higher required reserve ratios decrease bank profits?
   d. Explain how raising the required reserve ratio changes the interest rate in the short run and draw a graph to illustrate the change.

13. Sara withdraws $1,000 from her savings account at the Lucky S&L, keeps $50 in cash, and deposits the balance in her checking account at the Bank of Illinois. What is the immediate change in M1 and M2?

14. Banks in New Transylvania have a desired reserve ratio of 10 percent and no excess reserves. The currency drain ratio is 50 percent. Then the central bank increases bank reserves by $1,200.
   a. What is the initial increase in the monetary base?
   b. How much do the banks lend in the first round of the money creation process?
   c. How much of the amount initially lent does not return to the banks but is held as currency?
   d. Set out the transactions that take place and calculate the amount of deposits created and the increase in the amount of currency held after the second round of the money creation process.

15. [Study the Mathematical Note on pp. 608–609 to work this problem.] In the United Kingdom, the currency drain ratio is 0.38 of deposits and the desired reserve ratio is 0.002. In Australia, the quantity of money is $150 billion, the currency drain ratio is 33 percent of deposits and the desired reserve ratio is 8 percent.
   a. Calculate the U.K. money multiplier.
   b. Calculate the monetary base in Australia.

16. The table provides some data for the United States in the first decade following the Civil War.

	1869	1879
Quantity of money	$1.3 billion	$1.7 billion
Real GDP (1929 dollars)	$7.4 billion	Z
Price level (1929 = 100)	X	54
Velocity of circulation	4.50	4.61

Source: Milton Friedman and Anna J. Schwartz, *A Monetary History of the United States 1867-1960*

   a. Calculate the value of X in 1869.
   b. Calculate the value of Z in 1879.
   c. Are the data consistent with the quantity theory of money? Explain your answer.

17. **Fed to Curb Shady Lending Practices**
The Federal Reserve will issue new rules next week aimed at protecting future home buyers from dubious lending practices, its most sweeping response to a housing crisis that has pro-

pelled foreclosures to record highs. ... To prevent a repeat of the current mortgage mess, [Chairman Ben] Bernanke said the Fed will adopt rules cracking down on a range of shady lending practices that have burned many of the nation's riskiest "sub-prime" borrowers—those with spotty credit or low incomes—who were hardest hit by the housing and credit debacles. ... Under the proposal unveiled last December, the rules would restrict lenders from penalizing risky borrowers who pay loans off early, require lenders to make sure these borrowers set aside money to pay for taxes and insurance and bar lenders from making loans without proof of a borrower's income. It also would prohibit lenders from engaging in a pattern or practice of lending without considering a borrower's ability to repay a home loan from sources other than the home's value.

Time, July 9, 2008

How are the proposed changes consistent with the overall purpose of the Federal Reserve System?

18. **What Bad Banking Means to You**
Bad news about the banking industry may have you wondering about the safety of your hard earned cash at your own bank. In the past year there have been four bank failures. And the chairman of the Federal Deposit Insurance Corp and banking industry experts foresee many bank failures down the road. "Regulators are bracing for 100–200 bank failures over the next 12–24 months," says Jaret Seiberg, an analyst with the financial services firm, the Stanford Group. Expected loan losses, the deteriorating housing market and the credit squeeze are blamed for the drop in bank profits. ... The number of institutions categorized as "problem" institutions by the FDIC has also grown from 50 at the end of 2006 to 76 at the end of last year. But to put that in perspective—by the end of 1992—at the tail end of the banking crisis—there were 1,063 banks on that "trouble" list. ... Banking experts say there is one thing that will save your money if your bank goes under. That's FDIC insurance. "It's the gold standard," says banking consultant Bert Ely. "The FDIC has ample resources. It's never been an issue," he says. The FDIC insures deposits in banks and thrift institutions. The federal agency was created during the Great Depression in

response to thousands of bank failures. The FDIC maintains that not one depositor has lost a single cent of insured funds since 1934 as a result of a bank failure. ...

CNN, February 28, 2008

a. Explain how bank attempts to maximize profits can sometimes lead to bank failures.

b. How does FDIC insurance help minimize bank failures and bring more stability to the banking system?

c. How might FDIC insurance create a moral hazard situation for banks?

19. **Fed at Odds with ECB over Value of Policy Tool**

Financial innovation and the spread of U.S. currency throughout the world has broken down relationships between money, inflation and growth, making monetary gauges a less useful tool for policy makers, the U.S. Federal Reserve chairman, Ben Bernanke, said. ... The European Central Bank, Bank of Japan and Bank of England all use growth in the supply of money in formulating policy. "Heavy reliance on monetary aggregates as a guide to policy would seem to be unwise in the U.S. context," Bernanke said. ... "The empirical relationship between money growth and variables such as inflation and nominal output growth has continued to be unstable. ... " He said the Fed had "philosophical" and economic differences with European central bankers regarding the role of money and that debate between institutions was healthy. ... "Unfortunately, forecast errors for money growth are often significant," reducing their effectiveness as a tool for policy, Bernanke said. "There are differences between the U.S. and Europe in terms of the stability of money demand and financial innovation," Bernanke said. ... [Ultimately,] the risk of bad policy through a devoted following of money growth led the Fed to downgrade the importance of money measures.

International Herald Tribune, November 10, 2006

a. Explain how the debate surrounding the quantity theory of money could make "monetary gauges a less useful tool for policy makers."

b. What do Bernanke's statements reveal about his stance on the accuracy of the quantity theory of money?

20. Rapid inflation in Brazil in the early 1990s caused the cruzeiro to lose its ability to function as money. Which of the following commodities do you think would most likely have taken the place of the cruzeiro in the Brazilian economy? Explain why.

a. Tractor parts
b. Packs of cigarettes
c. Loaves of bread
d. Impressionist paintings
e. Baseball trading cards

21. **From Paper-Clip to House, in 14 Trades**

A 26-year-old Montreal man appears to have succeeded in his quest to barter a single, red paper-clip all the way up to a house. It took almost a year and 14 trades. ...

CBC News, 7 July 2006

a. Is barter a means of payment?

b. Is barter just as efficient as money when trading on e-Bay? Explain.

22. Study *Reading Between the Lines* on pp. 606–607 and then

a. Describe the money growth rate and the inflation rate in Zimbabwe since 2000.

b. How do we know that Zimbabwe's reported inflation between 2003 and 2007 is almost certainly below the true inflation rate?

c. What feature of Zimbabwe's economy provides a view of the cost of hyperinflation?

d. What must be done to stop Zimbabwe's inflation?

e. Why will knocking ten zeroes off all prices not stop Zimbabwe's inflation?

23. Use the link on MyEconLab (Textbook Resources, Chapter 25, Web links) to visit "Money—Past, Present, and Future" and study the section on e-money:

a. What is e-money and what are the alternative forms that it takes?

b. Do you think that the widespread use of e-money will limit the ability of the Federal Reserve to control the quantity of money? Why or why not?

c. When you buy an item on the Internet and pay for it using PayPal, are you using money? Explain why or why not.

d. Why might e-money be superior to cash as a means of payment?

27

Aggregate Supply and Aggregate Demand

After studying this chapter, you will be able to:

■ Explain what determines aggregate supply in the long run and in the short run

■ Explain what determines aggregate demand

■ Explain how real GDP and the price level are determined and how changes in aggregate supply and aggregate demand bring economic growth, inflation, and the business cycle

■ Describe the main schools of thought in macroeconomics today

Production grows and prices rise. But the pace at which production grows and prices rise is uneven. In 2005, real GDP grew by 3 percent, but in 2008, growth slowed to less than 2 percent and was expected to stop growing or even shrink in 2009.

Similarly, during recent years, prices have increased at rates ranging from a barely perceptible 1 percent to a disturbing 5 percent a year.

The uneven pace of economic growth and inflation—the business cycle—is the subject of this chapter and the two that follow it. Here, you will discover the forces that bring fluctuations in the pace of real GDP growth and inflation and the associated fluctuations in employment and unemployment.

This chapter explains a model of real GDP and the price level—the *aggregate supply–aggregate demand model* or *AS-AD model*. This model represents the consensus view of macroeconomists on how real GDP and the price level are determined. The model provides a framework for understanding the forces that make our economy expand, that bring inflation, and that cause business cycle fluctuations. The *AS-AD* model also provides a framework within which we can see the range of views of macroeconomists in different schools of thought.

In *Reading Between the Lines* at the end of the chapter, we use the *AS-AD* model to interpret the course of U.S. real GDP and the price level in 2008.

Aggregate Supply

The purpose of the aggregate supply–aggregate demand model that you study in this chapter is to explain how real GDP and the price level are determined and how they interact. The model uses similar ideas to those that you encountered in Chapter 3 when you learned how the quantity and price in a competitive market are determined. But the *aggregate* supply-*aggregate* demand model (*AS-AD* model) isn't just an application of the competitive market model. Some differences arise because the *AS-AD* model is a model of an imaginary market for the total of all the final goods and services that make up real GDP. The quantity in this "market" is real GDP and the price is the price level measured by the GDP deflator.

One thing that the *AS-AD* model shares with the competitive market model is that both distinguish between *supply* and the *quantity supplied*. We begin by explaining what we mean by the quantity of real GDP supplied.

Quantity Supplied and Supply

The *quantity of real GDP supplied* is the total quantity of goods and services, valued in constant base-year (2000) dollars, that firms plan to produce during a given period. This quantity depends on the quantity of labor employed, the quantity of physical and human capital, and the state of technology.

At any given time, the quantity of capital and the state of technology are fixed. They depend on decisions that were made in the past. The population is also fixed. But the quantity of labor is not fixed. It depends on decisions made by households and firms about the supply of and demand for labor.

The labor market can be in any one of three states: at full employment, above full employment, or below full employment. At full employment, the quantity of real GDP supplied is *potential GDP*, which depends on the full-employment quantity of labor (see Chapter 23, pp. 541–543). Over the business cycle, employment fluctuates around full employment and the quantity of real GDP supplied fluctuates around potential GDP.

Aggregate supply is the relationship between the quantity of real GDP supplied and the price level. This relationship is different in the long run than in the short run and to study aggregate supply, we distinguish between two time frames:

- Long-run aggregate supply
- Short-run aggregate supply

Long-Run Aggregate Supply

Long-run aggregate supply is the relationship between the quantity of real GDP supplied and the price level when the money wage rate changes in step with the price level to achieve full employment. The quantity of real GDP supplied at full employment equals potential GDP and this quantity is the same regardless of the price level.

The long-run aggregate supply curve in Fig. 27.1 illustrates long-run aggregate supply as the vertical line at potential GDP labeled *LAS*. Along the long-run aggregate supply curve, as the price level changes, the money wage rate also changes so the real wage rate is constant and real GDP remains at potential GDP. The long-run aggregate supply curve is always vertical and is always located at potential GDP.

The long-run aggregate supply curve is vertical because potential GDP is independent of the price level. The reason for this independence is that a movement along the *LAS* curve is accompanied by a change in *two* sets of prices: the prices of goods and services—the price level—and the prices of the factors of production, most notably, the money wage rate. A 10 percent increase in the prices of goods and services is matched by a 10 percent increase in the money wage rate. Because the price level and the money wage rate change by the same percentage, the *real wage rate* remains constant at its full-employment equilibrium level. So when the price level changes and the real wage rate remains constant, employment remains constant and real GDP remains constant at potential GDP.

Production at a Pepsi Plant You can see more clearly why real GDP remains constant when all prices change by the same percentage by thinking about production decisions at a Pepsi bottling plant. How does the quantity of Pepsi supplied change if the price of Pepsi changes and the wage rate of the workers and prices of all the other resources used vary by the same percentage? The answer is that the quantity supplied doesn't change. The firm produces the quantity that maximizes profit. That quantity depends on the price of Pepsi relative to the cost of producing it. With no change in price *relative to cost*, production doesn't change.

Short-Run Aggregate Supply

Short-run aggregate supply is the relationship between the quantity of real GDP supplied and the price level *when the money wage rate, the prices of other resources, and potential GDP remain constant.* Figure 27.1 illustrates this relationship as the short-run aggregate supply curve *SAS* and the short-run aggregate supply schedule. Each point on the *SAS* curve corresponds to a row of the short-run aggregate supply schedule. For example, point *A* on the *SAS* curve and row *A* of the schedule tell us that if the price level is 105, the quantity of real GDP supplied is $11 trillion. In the short run, a rise in the price level brings an increase in the quantity of real GDP supplied. The short-run aggregate supply curve slopes upward.

With a given money wage rate, there is one price level at which the real wage rate is at its full-employment equilibrium level. At this price level, the quantity of real GDP supplied equals potential GDP and the *SAS* curve intersects the *LAS* curve. In this example, that price level is 115. If the price level rises above 115, the quantity of real GDP supplied increases along the *SAS* curve and exceeds potential GDP; if the price level falls below 115, the quantity of real GDP supplied decreases along the *SAS* curve and is less than potential GDP.

Back at the Pepsi Plant You can see why the short-run aggregate supply curve slopes upward by returning to the Pepsi bottling plant. If production increases, marginal cost rises and if production decreases, marginal cost falls (see Chapter 2, p. 35).

If the price of Pepsi rises with no change in the money wage rate and other costs, Pepsi can increase profit by increasing production. Pepsi is in business to maximize its profit, so it increases production.

Similarly, if the price of Pepsi falls while the money wage rate and other costs remain constant, Pepsi can avoid a loss by decreasing production. The lower price weakens the incentive to produce, so Pepsi decreases production.

What's true for Pepsi bottlers is true for the producers of all goods and services. When all prices rise, the *price level rises.* If the price level rises and the money wage rate and other factor prices remain constant, all firms increase production and the quantity of real GDP supplied increases. A fall in the price level has the opposite effect and decreases the quantity of real GDP supplied.

FIGURE 27.1 Long-Run and Short-Run Aggregate Supply

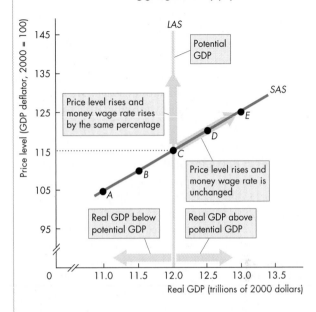

	Price level (GDP deflator)	Real GDP supplied (trillions of 2000 dollars)
A	105	11.0
B	110	11.5
C	**115**	**12.0**
D	120	12.5
E	125	13.0

In the long run, the quantity of real GDP supplied is potential GDP and the *LAS* curve is vertical at potential GDP.

In the short-run, the quantity of real GDP supplied increases if the price level rises, while all other influences on supply plans remain the same.

The short-run aggregate supply curve, *SAS*, slopes upward. The short-run aggregate supply curve is based on the aggregate supply schedule in the table. Each point *A* through *E* on the curve corresponds to the row in the table identified by the same letter.

When the price level is 115, the quantity of real GDP supplied is $12 trillion, which is potential GDP. If the price level rises above 115, the quantity of real GDP supplied increases and exceeds potential GDP; if the price level falls below 115, the quantity of real GDP supplied decreases below potential GDP.

Changes in Aggregate Supply

You've just seen that a change in the price level brings a movement along the aggregate supply curves but it does not change aggregate supply. Aggregate supply changes when an influence on production plans other than the price level changes. These other influences include a change in potential GDP and changes in the money wage rate and other factor prices. Let's begin by looking at factors that change potential GDP.

Changes in Potential GDP   When potential GDP changes, aggregate supply changes. An increase in potential GDP increases both long-run aggregate supply and short-run aggregate supply.

Figure 27.2 shows the effects of an increase in potential GDP. Initially, the long-run aggregate supply curve is LAS_0 and the short-run aggregate supply curve is SAS_0. If potential GDP increases to $13 trillion, long-run aggregate supply increases and the long-run aggregate supply curve shifts rightward to LAS_1. Short-run aggregate supply also increases, and the short-run aggregate supply curve shifts rightward to SAS_1. The two supply curves shift by the same amount only if the full-employment price level remains constant, which we will assume to be the case.

Potential GDP can increase for any of three reasons:

- An increase in the full-employment quantity of labor
- An increase in the quantity of capital
- An advance in technology

Let's look at these influences on potential GDP and the aggregate supply curves.

An Increase in the Full-Employment Quantity of Labor   A Pepsi bottling plant that employs 100 workers bottles more Pepsi than does an otherwise identical plant that employs 10 workers. The same is true for the economy as a whole. The larger the quantity of labor employed, the greater is real GDP.

Over time, potential GDP increases because the labor force increases. But (with constant capital and technology) *potential* GDP increases only if the full-employment quantity of labor increases. Fluctuations in employment over the business cycle bring fluctuations in real GDP. But these changes in real GDP are fluctua-

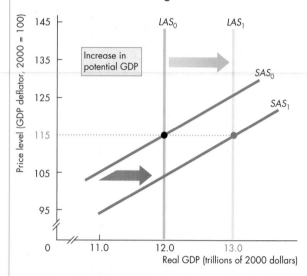

FIGURE 27.2 A Change in Potential GDP

An increase in potential GDP increases both long-run aggregate supply and short-run aggregate supply and shifts both aggregate supply curves rightward from LAS_0 to LAS_1 and from SAS_0 to SAS_1.

myeconlab   animation

tions around potential GDP. They are not changes in potential GDP and long-run aggregate supply.

An Increase in the Quantity of Capital   A Pepsi bottling plant with two production lines bottles more Pepsi than does an otherwise identical plant that has only one production line. For the economy, the larger the quantity of capital, the more productive is the labor force and the greater is its potential GDP. Potential GDP per person in the capital-rich United States is vastly greater than that in capital-poor China and Russia.

Capital includes *human capital*. One Pepsi plant is managed by an economics major with an MBA and has a labor force with an average of 10 years of experience. This plant produces a larger output than does an otherwise identical plant that is managed by someone with no business training or experience and that has a young labor force that is new to bottling. The first plant has a greater amount of human capital than the second. For the economy as a whole, the larger the quantity of *human capital*—the skills that people have acquired in school and through on-the-job training—the greater is potential GDP.

An Advance in Technology A Pepsi plant that has pre-computer age machines produces less than one that uses the latest robot technology. Technological change enables firms to produce more from any given amount of factors of production. So even with fixed quantities of labor and capital, improvements in technology increase potential GDP.

Technological advances are by far the most important source of increased production over the past two centuries. As a result of technological advances, one farmer in the United States today can feed 100 people and in a year one autoworker can produce almost 14 cars and trucks.

Let's now look at the effects of changes in the money wage rate.

Changes in the Money Wage Rate and Other Factor Prices

When the money wage rate (or the money price of any other factor of production such as oil) changes, short-run aggregate supply changes but long-run aggregate supply does not change.

Figure 27.3 shows the effect of an increase in the money wage rate. Initially, the short-run aggregate supply curve is SAS_0. A rise in the money wage rate *decreases* short-run aggregate supply and shifts the short-run aggregate supply curve leftward to SAS_2.

A rise in the money wage rate decreases short-run aggregate supply because it increases firms' costs. With increased costs, the quantity that firms are willing to supply at each price level decreases, which is shown by a leftward shift of the SAS curve.

A change in the money wage rate does not change long-run aggregate supply because on the LAS curve, the change in the money wage rate is accompanied by an equal percentage change in the price level. With no change in *relative* prices, firms have no incentive to change production and real GDP remains constant at potential GDP. With no change in potential GDP, the long-run aggregate supply curve LAS does not shift.

What Makes the Money Wage Rate Change?

The money wage rate can change for two reasons: departures from full employment and expectations about inflation. Unemployment above the natural rate puts downward pressure on the money wage rate, and unemployment below the natural rate puts upward pressure on it. An expected rise in the inflation rate makes the money wage rate rise faster, and an expected fall in the inflation rate slows the rate at which the money wage rate rises.

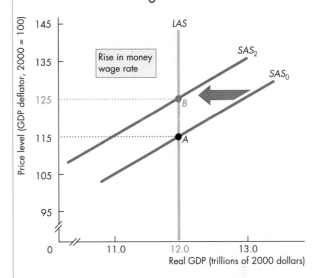

FIGURE 27.3 A Change in the Money Wage Rate

A rise in the money wage rate decreases short-run aggregate supply and shifts the short-run aggregate supply curve leftward from SAS_0 to SAS_2. A rise in the money wage rate does not change potential GDP, so the long-run aggregate supply curve does not shift.

myeconlab animation

Review Quiz

1 If the price level and the money wage rate rise by the same percentage, what happens to the quantity of real GDP supplied? Along which aggregate supply curve does the economy move?

2 If the price level rises and the money wage rate remains constant, what happens to the quantity of real GDP supplied? Along which aggregate supply curve does the economy move?

3 If potential GDP increases, what happens to aggregate supply? Does the LAS curve shift or is there a movement along the LAS curve? Does the SAS curve shift or is there a movement along the SAS curve?

4 If the money wage rate rises and potential GDP remains the same, does the LAS curve or the SAS curve shift or is there a movement along the LAS curve or the SAS curve?

myeconlab Work Study Plan 27.1 and get instant feedback.

Aggregate Demand

The quantity of real GDP demanded (Y) is the sum of real consumption expenditure (C), investment (I), government expenditure (G), and exports (X) minus imports (M). That is,

$$Y = C + I + G + X - M.$$

The *quantity of real GDP demanded* is the total amount of final goods and services produced in the United States that people, businesses, governments, and foreigners plan to buy.

These buying plans depend on many factors. Some of the main ones are

- The price level
- Expectations
- Fiscal policy and monetary policy
- The world economy

We first focus on the relationship between the quantity of real GDP demanded and the price level. To study this relationship, we keep all other influences on buying plans the same and ask: How does the quantity of real GDP demanded vary as the price level varies?

The Aggregate Demand Curve

Other things remaining the same, the higher the price level, the smaller is the quantity of real GDP demanded. This relationship between the quantity of real GDP demanded and the price level is called **aggregate demand**. Aggregate demand is described by an *aggregate demand schedule* and an *aggregate demand curve*.

Figure 27.4 shows an aggregate demand curve (*AD*) and an aggregate demand schedule. Each point on the *AD* curve corresponds to a row of the schedule. For example, point C' on the *AD* curve and row C' of the schedule tell us that if the price level is 115, the quantity of real GDP demanded is $12 trillion.

The aggregate demand curve slopes downward for two reasons:

- Wealth effect
- Substitution effects

Wealth Effect When the price level rises but other things remain the same, *real* wealth decreases. Real

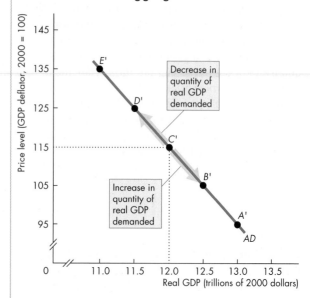

FIGURE 27.4 Aggregate Demand

	Price level (GDP deflator)	Real GDP demanded (trillions of 2000 dollars)
A'	95	13.0
B'	105	12.5
C'	**115**	**12.0**
D'	125	11.5
E'	135	11.0

The aggregate demand curve (*AD*) shows the relationship between the quantity of real GDP demanded and the price level. The aggregate demand curve is based on the aggregate demand schedule in the table. Each point A' through E' on the curve corresponds to the row in the table identified by the same letter. When the price level is 115, the quantity of real GDP demanded is $12 trillion, as shown by point C' in the figure. A change in the price level, when all other influences on aggregate buying plans remain the same, brings a change in the quantity of real GDP demanded and a movement along the *AD* curve.

 animation

wealth is the amount of money in the bank, bonds, stocks, and other assets that people own, measured not in dollars but in terms of the goods and services that the money, bonds, and stocks will buy.

People save and hold money, bonds, and stocks for many reasons. One reason is to build up funds for education expenses. Another reason is to build up enough funds to meet possible medical expenses or other big bills. But the biggest reason is to build up enough funds to provide a retirement income.

If the price level rises, real wealth decreases. People then try to restore their wealth. To do so, they must increase saving and, equivalently, decrease current consumption. Such a decrease in consumption is a decrease in aggregate demand.

Maria's Wealth Effect You can see how the wealth effect works by thinking about Maria's buying plans. Maria lives in Moscow, Russia. She has worked hard all summer and saved 20,000 rubles (the ruble is the currency of Russia), which she plans to spend attending graduate school when she has finished her economics degree. So Maria's wealth is 20,000 rubles. Maria has a part-time job, and her income from this job pays her current expenses. The price level in Russia rises by 100 percent, and now Maria needs 40,000 rubles to buy what 20,000 once bought. To try to make up some of the fall in value of her savings, Maria saves even more and cuts her current spending to the bare minimum.

Substitution Effects When the price level rises and other things remain the same, interest rates rise. The reason is related to the wealth effect that you've just studied. A rise in the price level decreases the real value of the money in people's pockets and bank accounts. With a smaller amount of real money around, banks and other lenders can get a higher interest rate on loans. But faced with a higher interest rate, people and businesses delay plans to buy new capital and consumer durable goods and cut back on spending.

This substitution effect involves substituting goods in the future for goods in the present and is called an *intertemporal* substitution effect—a substitution across time. Saving increases to increase future consumption.

To see this intertemporal substitution effect more clearly, think about your own plan to buy a new computer. At an interest rate of 5 percent a year, you might borrow $1,000 and buy the new computer. But at an interest rate of 10 percent a year, you might decide that the payments would be too high. You don't abandon your plan to buy the computer, but you decide to delay your purchase.

A second substitution effect works through international prices. When the U.S. price level rises and other things remain the same, U.S.-made goods and services become more expensive relative to foreign-made goods and services. This change in *relative prices* encourages people to spend less on U.S.-made items and more on foreign-made items. For example, if the U.S. price level rises relative to the Japanese price level, Japanese buy fewer U.S.-made cars (U.S. exports decrease) and Americans buy more Japanese-made cars (U.S. imports increase). U.S. GDP decreases.

Maria's Substitution Effects In Moscow, Russia, Maria makes some substitutions. She was planning to trade in her old motor scooter and get a new one. But with a higher price level and a higher interest rate, she decides to make her old scooter last one more year. Also, with the prices of Russian goods sharply increasing, Maria substitutes a low-cost dress made in Malaysia for the Russian-made dress she had originally planned to buy.

Changes in the Quantity of Real GDP Demanded
When the price level rises and other things remain the same, the quantity of real GDP demanded decreases—a movement up along the *AD* curve as shown by the arrow in Fig. 27.4. When the price level falls and other things remain the same, the quantity of real GDP demanded increases—a movement down along the *AD* curve.

We've now seen how the quantity of real GDP demanded changes when the price level changes. How do other influences on buying plans affect aggregate demand?

Changes in Aggregate Demand
A change in any factor that influences buying plans other than the price level brings a change in aggregate demand. The main factors are

- Expectations
- Fiscal policy and monetary policy
- The world economy

Expectations An increase in expected future income increases the amount of consumption goods (especially big-ticket items such as cars) that people plan to buy today and increases aggregate demand.

An increase in the expected future inflation rate increases aggregate demand today because people decide to buy more goods and services at today's relatively lower prices.

An increase in expected future profits increases the investment that firms plan to undertake today and increases aggregate demand.

Fiscal Policy and Monetary Policy The government's attempt to influence the economy by setting and changing taxes, making transfer payments, and purchasing goods and services is called **fiscal policy**. A tax cut or an increase in transfer payments—for example, unemployment benefits or welfare payments—increases aggregate demand. Both of these influences operate by increasing households' *disposable* income. **Disposable income** is aggregate income minus taxes plus transfer payments. The greater the disposable income, the greater is the quantity of consumption goods and services that households plan to buy and the greater is aggregate demand.

Government expenditure on goods and services is one component of aggregate demand. So if the government spends more on spy satellites, schools, and highways, aggregate demand increases.

Monetary policy consists of changes in the interest rate and in the quantity of money in the economy. The quantity of money is determined by the Federal Reserve (the Fed) and the banks (in a process described in Chapters 25 and 31). An increase in the quantity of money in the economy increases aggregate demand. To see why money affects aggregate demand, imagine that the Fed borrows the army's helicopters, loads them with millions of new $10 bills, and sprinkles them like confetti across the nation. People gather the newly available money and plan to spend some of it. So the quantity of goods and services demanded increases. But people don't plan to spend all the new money. They plan to save some of it and lend it to others through the banks. The interest rate falls, and with a lower interest rate, people plan to buy more consumer durables and firms plan to increase their investment.

The World Economy Two main influences that the world economy has on aggregate demand are the exchange rate and foreign income. The *exchange rate* is the amount of a foreign currency that you can buy with a U.S. dollar. Other things remaining the same, a rise in the exchange rate decreases aggregate

Fiscal Policy to Fight Recession
The 2008 Fiscal Stimulus Package

In February 2008, Congress passed legislation that gave $168 billion to businesses and low- and middle-income Americans—$600 to a single person and $1,200 to a couple with an additional $300 for each child. The benefit was scaled back for individuals with incomes above $75,000 a year and for families with incomes greater than $150,000 a year.

The idea of the package was to stimulate business investment and consumption expenditure and increase aggregate demand.

Deal makers Senators Harry Reid and Mitch McConnell

Monetary Policy to Fight Recession
Concerted Interest Rate Cuts

In October 2008, the Federal Reserve, in concert with the European Central Bank, the Bank of Canada, and the Bank of England, cut the interest rate and took other measures to ease credit and encourage banks and others to increase their lending. The U.S. interest rate was the lowest (see below).

Like the earlier fiscal stimulus package, the idea of these interest rate cuts and easier credit was to stimulate business investment and consumption expenditure and increase aggregate demand.

 1.5%

Ben Bernake
Federal Reserve

 3.75%

Jean-Claude Trichet
ECB

 4.5%

Marvyn King
Bank of England

 2.5%

Mark Carrey
Bank of Canada

FIGURE 27.5 Changes in Aggregate Demand

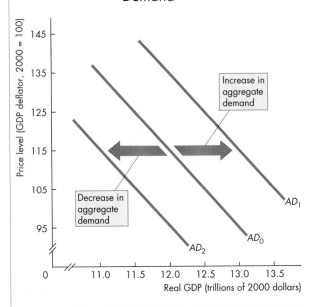

Aggregate demand

Decreases if:

- Expected future income, inflation, or profits decrease
- Fiscal policy decreases government expenditure, increases taxes, or decreases transfer payments
- Monetary policy decreases the quantity of money and increases interest rates
- The exchange rate increases or foreign income decreases

Increases if:

- Expected future income, inflation, or profits increase
- Fiscal policy increases government expenditure, decreases taxes, or increases transfer payments
- Monetary policy increases the quantity of money and decreases interest rates
- The exchange rate decreases or foreign income increases

myeconlab animation

demand. To see how the exchange rate influences aggregate demand, suppose that the exchange rate is 1.20 euros per U.S. dollar. A Nokia cell phone made in Finland costs 120 euros, and an equivalent Motorola phone made in the United States costs $110. In U.S. dollars, the Nokia phone costs $100, so people around the world buy the cheaper phone from Finland. Now suppose the exchange rate falls to 1 euro per U.S. dollar. The Nokia phone now costs $120 and is more expensive than the Motorola phone. People will switch from the Nokia phone to the Motorola phone. U.S. exports will increase and U.S. imports will decrease, so U.S. aggregate demand will increase.

An increase in foreign income increases U.S. exports and increases U.S. aggregate demand. For example, an increase in income in Japan and Germany increases Japanese and German consumers' and producers' planned expenditures on U.S.-produced goods and services.

Shifts of the Aggregate Demand Curve When aggregate demand changes, the aggregate demand curve shifts. Figure 27.5 shows two changes in aggregate demand and summarizes the factors that bring about such changes.

Aggregate demand increases and the *AD* curve shifts rightward from AD_0 to AD_1 when expected future income, inflation, or profit increases; government expenditure on goods and services increases; taxes are cut; transfer payments increase; the quantity of money increases and the interest rate falls; the exchange rate falls; or foreign income increases.

Aggregate demand decreases and the *AD* curve shifts leftward from AD_0 to AD_2 when expected future income, inflation, or profit decreases; government expenditure on goods and services decreases; taxes increase; transfer payments decrease; the quantity of money decreases and the interest rate rises; the exchange rate rises; or foreign income decreases.

Review Quiz

1. What does the aggregate demand curve show? What factors change and what factors remain the same when there is a movement along the aggregate demand curve?
2. Why does the aggregate demand curve slope downward?
3. How do changes in expectations, fiscal policy and monetary policy, and the world economy change aggregate demand and the aggregate demand curve?

myeconlab Work Study Plan 27.2 and get instant feedback.

Explaining Macroeconomic Fluctuations

The purpose of the *AS-AD* model is to explain changes in real GDP and the price level. The model's main purpose is to explain business cycle fluctuations in these variables. But the model also aids our understanding of economic growth and inflation trends. We begin by combining aggregate supply and aggregate demand to determine real GDP and the price level in equilibrium. Just as there are two time frames for aggregate supply, there are two time frames for macroeconomic equilibrium: a long-run equilibrium and a short-run equilibrium. We'll first look at short-run equilibrium.

Short-Run Macroeconomic Equilibrium

The aggregate demand curve tells us the quantity of real GDP demanded at each price level, and the short-run aggregate supply curve tells us the quantity of real GDP supplied at each price level. **Short-run macroeconomic equilibrium** occurs when the quantity of real GDP demanded equals the quantity of real GDP supplied. That is, short-run macroeconomic equilibrium occurs at the point of intersection of the *AD* curve and the *SAS* curve. Figure 27.6 shows such an equilibrium at a price level of 115 and real GDP of $12 trillion (points *C* and *C'*).

To see why this position is the equilibrium, think about what happens if the price level is something other than 115. Suppose, for example, that the price level is 125 and that real GDP is $13 trillion (at point *E* on the *SAS* curve). The quantity of real GDP demanded is less than $13 trillion, so firms are unable to sell all their output. Unwanted inventories pile up, and firms cut both production and prices. Production and prices are cut until firms can sell all their output. This situation occurs only when real GDP is $12 trillion and the price level is 115.

Now suppose the price level is 105 and real GDP is $11 trillion (at point *A* on the *SAS* curve). The quantity of real GDP demanded exceeds $11 trillion, so firms are unable to meet the demand for their output. Inventories decrease, and customers clamor for goods and services, so firms increase production and raise prices. Production and prices increase until firms can meet the demand for their

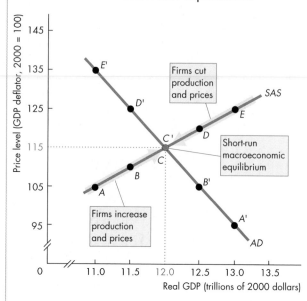

FIGURE 27.6   Short-Run Equilibrium

Short-run macroeconomic equilibrium occurs when real GDP demanded equals real GDP supplied—at the intersection of the aggregate demand curve (*AD*) and the short-run aggregate supply curve (*SAS*). Here, such an equilibrium occurs at points *C* and *C'*, where the price level is 115 and real GDP is $12 trillion.

If the price level is 125 and real GDP is $13 trillion (point *E*), firms will not be able to sell all their output. They will decrease production and cut prices. If the price level is 105 and real GDP is $11 trillion (point *A*), people will not be able to buy all the goods and services they demand. Firms will increase production and raise their prices.

Only when the price level is 115 and real GDP is $12 trillion can firms sell all that they produce and can people buy all the goods and services they demand. This is the short-run macroeconomic equilibrium.

myeconlab   animation

output. This situation occurs only when real GDP is $12 trillion and the price level is 115.

In the short run, the money wage rate is fixed. It does not adjust to move the economy to full employment. So in the short run, real GDP can be greater than or less than potential GDP. But in the long run, the money wage rate does adjust and real GDP moves toward potential GDP. We are going to study this adjustment process. But first, let's look at the economy in long-run equilibrium.

Long-Run Macroeconomic Equilibrium

Long-run macroeconomic equilibrium occurs when real GDP equals potential GDP—equivalently, when the economy is on its *LAS* curve. Figure 27.7 shows the long-run macroeconomic equilibrium, which occurs at the intersection of the *AD* curve and the *LAS* curve (the blue curves). Long-run macroeconomic equilibrium comes about because the money wage rate adjusts. Potential GDP and aggregate demand determine the price level, and the price level influences the money wage rate. In long-run equilibrium, the money wage rate has adjusted to put the *SAS* curve through the long-run equilibrium point.

We'll look at this money wage adjustment process later in this chapter. But first, let's see how the *AS-AD* model helps us to understand economic growth and inflation.

Economic Growth in the *AS-AD* Model

Economic growth occurs because, the quantity of labor and labor productivity grow. Population growth is the source of labor growth, and capital accumulation and technological change are the sources of labor productivity growth. Chapter 23 explains and illustrates the effects of population growth as an increase in the supply of labor. That chapter also explains and illustrates the effects of labor productivity growth as an upward shift in the aggregate production function and an increase in the demand for labor. These changes increase potential GDP.

The *AS-AD* model explains and illustrates potential GDP growth as a rightward shift of the *LAS* curve. For example, in Fig. 27.8, potential GDP grows from $12 trillion to $13 trillion and the *LAS* curve shifts rightward from LAS_0 to LAS_1.

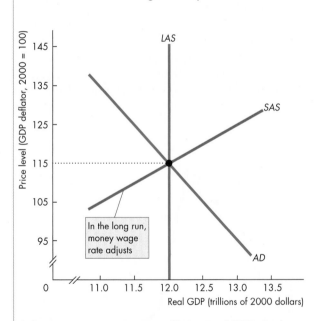

FIGURE 27.7   Long-Run Equilibrium

In long-run macroeconomic equilibrium, real GDP equals potential GDP. So long-run equilibrium occurs where the aggregate demand curve, *AD*, intersects the long-run aggregate supply curve, *LAS*. In the long run, aggregate demand determines the price level and has no effect on real GDP. The money wage rate adjusts in the long run, so that the *SAS* curve intersects the *LAS* curve at the long-run equilibrium price level.

myeconlab animation

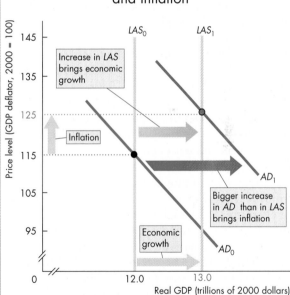

FIGURE 27.8   Economic Growth and Inflation

Economic growth is the persistent increase in potential GDP. Economic growth is shown as an ongoing rightward shift of the *LAS* curve. The pace at which the *LAS* curve shifts rightward depends on the growth rate of the labor force and the growth rate of labor productivity.

Inflation is a persistently rising price level and it occurs when the quantity of money grows to make the *AD* curve shift rightward at a faster pace than that of the *LAS* curve.

myeconlab animation

Inflation in the *AS-AD* Model

Inflation occurs because the quantity of money grows more rapidly than potential GDP. In Chapter 25, the quantity theory of money, derived from the equation of exchange, explains inflation. With a constant velocity of circulation of money, the inflation rate equals the growth rate of the quantity of money minus the growth rate of real GDP. At full employment (in the macroeconomic long run), real GDP grows at the growth rate of potential GDP. So the inflation rate equals the growth rate of the quantity of money minus the growth rate of potential GDP.

We can explain and illustrate this inflation process using the *AS-AD* model. Inflation occurs when aggregate demand increases at a faster rate than the growth rate of potential GDP. That is, inflation occurs if the *AD* curve shifts rightward at a faster rate than the rate of rightward shift of the *LAS* curve. Figure 27.8 shows shifts of the *AD* and *LAS* curves that bring inflation.

If aggregate demand increases at the same rate as long-run aggregate supply, we experience real GDP growth with no inflation.

You've seen that the growth rate of potential GDP doesn't change much, but the inflation rate varies a great deal. During the 1970s, it reached a double-digit level and then during the 1980s, its rate fell to the low levels maintained through the 1990s and into the 2000s. Changes in the growth rate of aggregate demand explain the changes in the inflation rate.

Any of the influences on aggregate demand can change its growth rate. Using the ideas from the quantity theory of money, we can summarize those influences as the quantity of money and the velocity of circulation. Although either one can change, only the growth rate of the quantity of money can change by enough to explain the large and persistent changes in the inflation rate that we experience. When the quantity of money grows rapidly, aggregate demand grows rapidly and the inflation rate is high. When the growth rate of the quantity of money slows, the inflation rate eventually slows.

Our economy experiences periods of growth and inflation, like those shown in Fig. 27.8, but it does not experience *steady* growth and *steady* inflation. Real GDP fluctuates around potential GDP in a business cycle, and inflation fluctuates. When we study the business cycle, we ignore economic growth. By doing so, we see the business cycle more clearly.

The Business Cycle in the *AS-AD* Model

The business cycle occurs because aggregate demand and short-run aggregate supply fluctuate but the money wage rate does not adjust quickly enough to keep real GDP at potential GDP. Figure 27.9 shows three types of short-run equilibrium.

Figure 27.9(a) shows an above full-employment equilibrium. An **above full-employment equilibrium** is an equilibrium in which real GDP exceeds potential GDP. The gap between real GDP and potential GDP is the **output gap.** When real GDP exceeds potential GDP, the output gap is called an **inflationary gap.**

The above full-employment equilibrium shown in Fig. 27.9(a) occurs where the aggregate demand curve AD_0 intersects the short-run aggregate supply curve SAS_0 at a real GDP of $12.2 trillion. There is an inflationary gap of $0.2 trillion.

The Business Cycle in the U.S. Economy
The Fluctuating Output Gap

The U.S. economy had an inflationary gap in 2000 (at *A* in the figure), full employment in 2001 (at *B*), and a recessionary gap in 2003 (at *C*). The fluctuating output gap in the figure is the real-world version of Fig. 27.9(d) and is generated by fluctuations in aggregate demand and short-run aggregate supply.

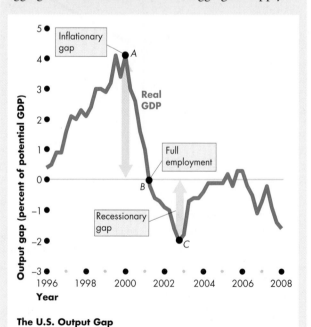

The U.S. Output Gap

Sources of data: Bureau of Economic Analysis and Congressional Budget Office.

Figure 27.9(b) is an example of **full-employment equilibrium,** in which real GDP equals potential GDP. In this example, the equilibrium occurs where the aggregate demand curve AD_1 intersects the short-run aggregate supply curve SAS_1 at an actual and potential GDP of $12 trillion.

In part (c), there is a below full-employment equilibrium. A **below full-employment equilibrium** is an equilibrium in which potential GDP exceeds real GDP. When potential GDP exceeds real GDP, the output gap is called a **recessionary gap**.

The below full-employment equilibrium shown in

Fig. 27.9(c) occurs where the aggregate demand curve AD_2 intersects the short-run aggregate supply curve SAS_2 at a real GDP of $11.8 trillion. Potential GDP is $12 trillion, so the recessionary gap is $0.2 trillion.

The economy moves from one type of macroeconomic equilibrium to another as a result of fluctuations in aggregate demand and in short-run aggregate supply. These fluctuations produce fluctuations in real GDP. Figure 27.9(d) shows how real GDP fluctuates around potential GDP.

Let's now look at some of the sources of these fluctuations around potential GDP.

FIGURE 27.9   The Business Cycle

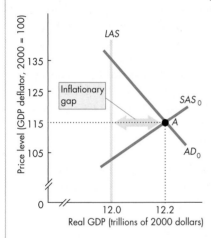

(a) Above full-employment equilibrium

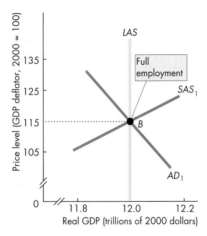

(b) Full-employment equilibrium

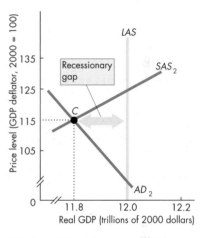

(c) Below full-employment equilibrium

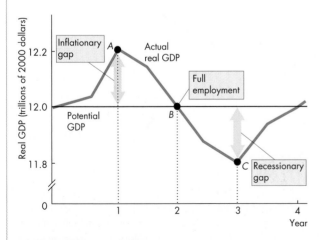

(d) Fluctuations in real GDP

Part (a) shows an above full-employment equilibrium in year 1; part (b) shows a full-employment equilibrium in year 2; and part (c) shows a below full-employment equilibrium in year 3. Part (d) shows how real GDP fluctuates around potential GDP in a business cycle.

In year 1, an inflationary gap exists and the economy is at point A in parts (a) and (d). In year 2, the economy is at full employment and the economy is at point B in parts (b) and (d). In year 3, a recessionary gap exists and the economy is at point C in parts (c) and (d).

myeconlab animation

Fluctuations in Aggregate Demand

One reason real GDP fluctuates around potential GDP is that aggregate demand fluctuates. Let's see what happens when aggregate demand increases.

Figure 27.10(a) shows an economy at full employment. The aggregate demand curve is AD_0, the short-run aggregate supply curve is SAS_0, and the long-run aggregate supply curve is LAS. Real GDP equals potential GDP at $12 trillion, and the price level is 115.

Now suppose that the world economy expands and that the demand for U.S.-produced goods increases in Asia and Europe. The increase in U.S. exports increases aggregate demand in the United States, and the aggregate demand curve shifts rightward from AD_0 to AD_1 in Fig. 27.10(a).

Faced with an increase in demand, firms increase production and raise prices. Real GDP increases to $12.5 trillion, and the price level rises to 120. The economy is now in an above full-employment equilibrium. Real GDP exceeds potential GDP, and there is an inflationary gap.

The increase in aggregate demand has increased the prices of all goods and services. Faced with higher prices, firms have increased their output rates. At this stage, prices of goods and services have increased but the money wage rate has not changed. (Recall that as we move along the SAS curve, the money wage rate is constant.)

The economy cannot produce in excess of potential GDP forever. Why not? What are the forces at work that bring real GDP back to potential GDP?

Because the price level has increased and the money wage rate is unchanged, workers have experienced a fall in the buying power of their wages and firms' profits have increased. Under these circumstances, workers demand higher wages and firms, anxious to maintain their employment and output levels, meet those demands. If firms do not raise the money wage rate, they will either lose workers or have to hire less productive ones.

As the money wage rate rises, the short-run aggregate supply begins to decrease. In Fig. 27.10(b), the short-run aggregate supply curve begins to shift from

FIGURE 27.10 An Increase in Aggregate Demand

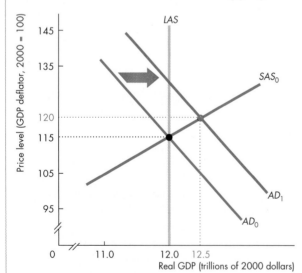

(a) Short-run effect

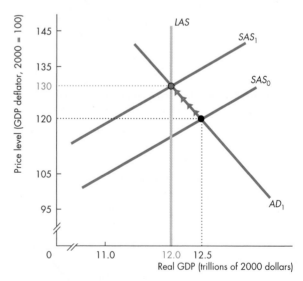

(b) Long-run effect

An increase in aggregate demand shifts the aggregate demand curve from AD_0 to AD_1. In short-run equilibrium, real GDP increases to $12.5 trillion and the price level rises to 120. In this situation, an inflationary gap exists. In the long run in part (b), the money wage rate rises and the short-run aggre-

gate supply curve shifts leftward. As short-run aggregate supply decreases, the SAS curve shifts from SAS_0 to SAS_1 and intersects the aggregate demand curve AD_1 at higher price levels and real GDP decreases. Eventually, the price level rises to 130 and real GDP decreases to $12 trillion—potential GDP.

SAS_0 toward SAS_1. The rise in the money wage rate and the shift in the SAS curve produce a sequence of new equilibrium positions. Along the adjustment path, real GDP decreases and the price level rises. The economy moves up along its aggregate demand curve as shown by the arrows in the figure.

Eventually, the money wage rate rises by the same percentage as the price level. At this time, the aggregate demand curve AD_1 intersects SAS_1 at a new full-employment equilibrium. The price level has risen to 130, and real GDP is back where it started, at potential GDP.

A decrease in aggregate demand has effects similar but opposite to those of an increase in aggregate demand. That is, a decrease in aggregate demand shifts the aggregate demand curve leftward. Real GDP decreases to less than potential GDP, and a recessionary gap emerges. Firms cut prices. The lower price level increases the purchasing power of wages and increases firms' costs relative to their output prices because the money wage rate is unchanged. Eventually, the money wage rate falls and the short-run aggregate supply increases.

Let's now work out how real GDP and the price level change when aggregate supply changes.

Fluctuations in Aggregate Supply

Fluctuations in short-run aggregate supply can bring fluctuations in real GDP around potential GDP. Suppose that initially real GDP equals potential GDP. Then there is a large but temporary rise in the price of oil. What happens to real GDP and the price level?

Figure 27.11 answers this question. The aggregate demand curve is AD_0, the short-run aggregate supply curve is SAS_0, and the long-run aggregate supply curve is LAS. Real GDP is $12 trillion, which equals potential GDP, and the price level is 115. Then the price of oil rises. Faced with higher energy and transportation costs, firms decrease production. Short-run aggregate supply decreases, and the short-run aggregate supply curve shifts leftward to SAS_1. The price level rises to 125, and real GDP decreases to $11.5 trillion. Because real GDP decreases, the economy experiences recession. Because the price level increases, the economy experiences inflation. A combination of recession and inflation, called **stagflation**, actually occurred in the United States in the mid-1970s and early 1980s, but events like this are not common.

When the price of oil returns to its original level, the economy returns to full employment.

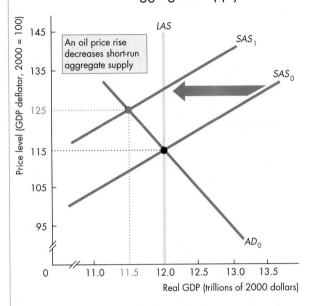

FIGURE 27.11   A Decrease in Aggregate Supply

An increase in the price of oil decreases short-run aggregate supply and shifts the short-run aggregate supply curve from SAS_0 to SAS_1. Real GDP falls from $12 trillion to $11.5 trillion, and the price level rises from 115 to 125. The economy experiences stagflation.

myeconlab   animation

Review Quiz

1   Does economic growth result from increases in aggregate demand, short-run aggregate supply, or long-run aggregate supply?

2   Does inflation result from increases in aggregate demand, short-run aggregate supply, or long-run aggregate supply?

3   Describe three types of short-run macroeconomic equilibrium.

4   How do fluctuations in aggregate demand and short-run aggregate supply bring fluctuations in real GDP around potential GDP?

myeconlab   Work Study Plan 27.3 and get instant feedback.

We can use the *AS-AD* model to explain and illustrate the views of the alternative schools of thought in macroeconomics. That is your next task.

Macroeconomic Schools of Thought

Macroeconomics is an active field of research, and much remains to be learned about the forces that make our economy grow and fluctuate. There is a greater degree of consensus and certainty about economic growth and inflation—the longer-term trends in real GDP and the price level—than there is about the business cycle—the short-term fluctuations in these variables. Here, we'll look only at differences of view about short-term fluctuations.

The *AS-AD* model that you've studied in this chapter provides a good foundation for understanding the range of views that macroeconomists hold about this topic. But what you will learn here is just a first glimpse at the scientific controversy and debate. We'll return to these issues at various points later in the text and deepen your appreciation of the alternative views.

Classification usually requires simplification, and classifying macroeconomists is no exception to this general rule. The classification that we'll use here is simple, but it is not misleading. We're going to divide macroeconomists into three broad schools of thought and examine the views of each group in turn. The groups are

- Classical
- Keynesian
- Monetarist

The Classical View

A **classical** macroeconomist believes that the economy is self-regulating and always at full employment. The term "classical" derives from the name of the founding school of economics that includes Adam Smith, David Ricardo, and John Stuart Mill.

A **new classical** view is that business cycle fluctuations are the efficient responses of a well-functioning market economy that is bombarded by shocks that arise from the uneven pace of technological change.

The classical view can be understood in terms of beliefs about aggregate demand and aggregate supply.

Aggregate Demand Fluctuations In the classical view, technological change is the most significant influence on both aggregate demand and aggregate supply. For

this reason, classical macroeconomists don't use the *AS-AD* framework. But their views can be interpreted in this framework. A technological change that increases the productivity of capital brings an increase in aggregate demand because firms increase their expenditure on new plant and equipment. A technological change that lengthens the useful life of existing capital decreases the demand for new capital, which decreases aggregate demand.

Aggregate Supply Response In the classical view, the money wage rate that lies behind the short-run aggregate supply curve is instantly and completely flexible. The money wage rate adjusts so quickly to maintain equilibrium in the labor market that real GDP always adjusts to equal potential GDP.

Potential GDP itself fluctuates for the same reasons that aggregate demand fluctuates: technological change. When the pace of technological change is rapid, potential GDP increases quickly and so does real GDP. And when the pace of technological change slows, so does the growth rate of potential GDP.

Classical Policy The classical view of policy emphasizes the potential for taxes to stunt incentives and create inefficiency. By minimizing the disincentive effects of taxes, employment, investment, and technological advance are at their efficient levels and the economy expands at an appropriate and rapid pace.

The Keynesian View

A **Keynesian** macroeconomist believes that left alone, the economy would rarely operate at full employment and that to achieve and maintain full employment, active help from fiscal policy and monetary policy is required.

The term "Keynesian" derives from the name of one of the twentieth century's most famous economists, John Maynard Keynes (see p. 723).

The Keynesian view is based on beliefs about the forces that determine aggregate demand and short-run aggregate supply.

Aggregate Demand Fluctuations In the Keynesian view, *expectations* are the most significant influence on aggregate demand. Those expectations are based on herd instinct, or what Keynes himself called "animal spirits." A wave of pessimism about future profit prospects can lead to a fall in aggregate demand and plunge the economy into recession.

Aggregate Supply Response In the Keynesian view, the money wage rate that lies behind the short-run aggregate supply curve is extremely sticky in the downward direction. Basically, the money wage rate doesn't fall. So if there is a recessionary gap, there is no automatic mechanism for getting rid of it. If it were to happen, a fall in the money wage rate would increase short-run aggregate supply and restore full employment. But the money wage rate doesn't fall, so the economy remains stuck in recession.

A modern version of the Keynesian view, known as the **new Keynesian** view, holds not only that the money wage rate is sticky but also that prices of goods and services are sticky. With a sticky price level, the short-run aggregate supply curve is horizontal at a fixed price level.

Policy Response Needed The Keynesian view calls for fiscal policy and monetary policy to actively offset changes in aggregate demand that bring recession.

By stimulating aggregate demand in a recession, full employment can be restored.

The Monetarist View

A **monetarist** is a macroeconomist who believes that the economy is self-regulating and that it will normally operate at full employment, provided that monetary policy is not erratic and that the pace of money growth is kept steady.

The term "monetarist" was coined by an outstanding twentieth-century economist, Karl Brunner, to describe his own views and those of Milton Friedman (see p. 781).

The monetarist view can be interpreted in terms of beliefs about the forces that determine aggregate demand and short-run aggregate supply.

Aggregate Demand Fluctuations In the monetarist view, *the quantity of money* is the most significant influence on aggregate demand. The quantity of money is determined by the Federal Reserve (the Fed). If the Fed keeps money growing at a steady pace, aggregate demand fluctuations will be minimized and the economy will operate close to full employment. But if the Fed decreases the quantity of money or even just slows its growth rate too abruptly, the economy will go into recession. In the monetarist view, all recessions result from inappropriate monetary policy.

Aggregate Supply Response The monetarist view of short-run aggregate supply is the same as the Keynesian view: the money wage rate is sticky. If the economy is in recession, it will take an unnecessarily long time for it to return unaided to full employment.

Monetarist Policy The monetarist view of policy is the same as the classical view on fiscal policy. Taxes should be kept low to avoid disincentive effects that decrease potential GDP. Provided that the quantity of money is kept on a steady growth path, no active stabilization is needed to offset changes in aggregate demand.

The Way Ahead

In the chapters that follow, you're going to encounter Keynesian, classical, and monetarist views again. In the next chapter, we study the original Keynesian model of aggregate demand. This model remains useful today because it explains how expenditure fluctuations are magnified and bring changes in aggregate demand that are larger than the changes in expenditure. We then go on to apply the *AS-AD* model to a deeper look at U.S. inflation and business cycles.

Our attention then turns to short-run macroeconomic policy—the fiscal policy of the Administration and Congress and the monetary policy of the Fed.

Review Quiz

1 What are the defining features of classical macroeconomics and what policies do classical macroeconomists recommend?
2 What are the defining features of Keynesian macroeconomics and what policies do Keynesian macroeconomists recommend?
3 What are the defining features of monetarist macroeconomics and what policies do monetarist macroeconomists recommend?

 Work Study Plan 27.4 and get instant feedback.

◆ To complete your study of the *AS-AD* model, take a look at the U.S. economy in 2008 through the eyes of this model in *Reading Between the Lines* on pp. 664–665.

Aggregate Supply and Aggregate Demand in Action

GDP Figures Revised Downward

http://www.nytimes.com
September 26, 2008

Looks as if that brief burst of economic growth we saw wasn't as strong as it seemed.

Friday morning, the government said the economy grew at a rate of just 2.8 percent in the second quarter. That was less than forecasters had expected—and less than the government had previously estimated.

That doesn't bode well for future growth. As Joshua Shapiro, the chief United States economist for MFR Inc., put it in a note Friday, "The outlook remains grim."

Morgan Stanley said that it continued to expect no growth—0 percent—in the current quarter, which ends next week.

You can think of the economy as being made up of five parts: consumer spending, business spending on new factories and equipment, home building, government spending and trade. Trade is lifting growth right now, and home building activity, of course, is plunging. But as Goldman Sachs economists noted, the major reason for Friday's disappointing number was weaker-than-expected spending by consumers.

In the coming months, economists say, consumer spending is likely to weaken further. The spring coincided with the $100 billion in tax rebates the government sent out. And yet consumer spending still wasn't all that strong.

©2008 The New York Times Company. Reprinted with permission. Further reproduction prohibited.

Essence of the Story

- Real GDP grew at an annual rate of 2.8 percent in the second quarter of 2008.

- The growth rate was less than forecasters had expected and less than the previous estimate.

- Only exports lifted the growth rate in the second quarter. Consumer expenditure was less than expected despite a $100 billion tax rebate during the quarter.

- Economists expected consumer expenditure to decrease further and forecast zero growth in the third quarter of 2008.

Economic Analysis

- U.S. real GDP grew at a 2.8 percent annual rate during the second quarter of 2008—a slower than average growth rate and slower than the original estimate a month earlier.

- In September 2008, most forecasters expected that real GDP growth would be zero in the third quarter and many forecasted a recession—falling real GDP—in the fourth quarter and the first half of 2009.

- The Congressional Budget Office (CBO) estimate of potential GDP implied a widening recessionary gap.

- Figure 1 illustrates the path of real GDP and the CBO estimate of potential GDP as well as the implied recessionary gap through 2007 and in the first half of 2008.

- Real GDP grew faster than potential GDP during 2007, so the recessionary gap narrowed, but it didn't disappear. In 2008, it widened.

- Another number estimated by the CBO places a question mark on the output gap estimate.

- The CBO estimate of the natural unemployment rate suggests that during 2007, the economy was above full employment and there was an inflationary gap.

- Figure 2 shows the actual unemployment rate and the CBO estimate of the natural rate.

- Whatever the true state of the output gap in 2007, by 2008 both the unemployment and real GDP data agreed that the output gap was a recessionary gap.

- In the second quarter of 2008, real GDP was $11.7 trillion and the price level (GDP deflator) was 122. In the third quarter of 2008, real GDP was expected to remain constant.

- Figure 3 illustrates the forecasted state of the economy in the fourth quarter of 2008.

- The CBO estimate of potential GDP was $12.1 trillion, which provides the location of the *LAS* curve.

- Aggregate demand, *AD*, and short-run aggregate supply, *SAS*, were expected to make real GDP decrease. In the outcome shown in Fig. 3, real GDP decreases to $11.5 trillion and the price level rises to 125. (These are assumptions.)

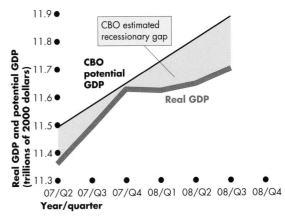

Figure 1 Actual and potential real GDP

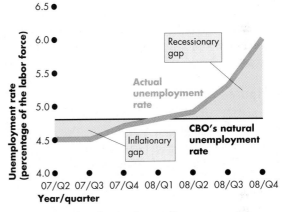

Figure 2 Actual and natural unemployment rate

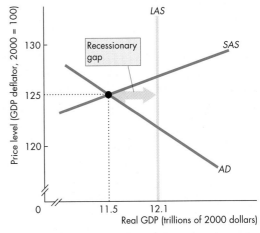

Figure 3 Aggregate supply and aggregate demand in 2008

SUMMARY

Key Points

Aggregate Supply (pp. 648–651)

- In the long run, the quantity of real GDP supplied is potential GDP.
- In the short run, a rise in the price level increases the quantity of real GDP supplied.
- A change in potential GDP changes long-run and short-run aggregate supply. A change in the money wage rate changes only short-run aggregate supply.

Aggregate Demand (pp. 652–655)

- A rise in the price level decreases the quantity of real GDP demanded.
- Changes in expected future income, inflation, and profits; in fiscal policy and monetary policy; and in foreign income and the exchange rate change aggregate demand.

Explaining Macroeconomic Fluctuations (pp. 656–661)

- Aggregate demand and short-run aggregate supply determine real GDP and the price level.
- In the long run, real GDP equals potential GDP and aggregate demand determines the price level.
- The business cycle occurs because aggregate demand and aggregate supply fluctuate.

Macroeconomic Schools of Thought (pp. 662–663)

- Classical economists believe that the economy is self-regulating and always at full employment.
- Keynesian economists believe that full employment can be achieved only with active policy.
- Monetarist economists believe that recessions result from inappropriate monetary policy.

Key Figures

Key Terms

PROBLEMS and APPLICATIONS

 Work problems 1–7 in Chapter 27 Study Plan and get instant feedback.
Work problems 8–15 as Homework, a Quiz, or a Test if assigned by your instructor.

1. The following events have occurred at times in the history of the United States:
   - A deep recession hits the world economy.
   - The world oil price rises sharply.
   - U.S. businesses expect future profits to fall.
   a. Explain for each event whether it changes short-run aggregate supply, long-run aggregate supply, aggregate demand, or some combination of them.
   b. Explain the separate effects of each event on U.S. real GDP and the price level, starting from a position of long-run equilibrium.
   c. Explain the combined effects of these events on U.S. real GDP and the price level, starting from a position of long-run equilibrium.
   d. Describe what a classical macroeconomist, a Keynesian, and a monetarist would want to do in response to each of the above events.

2. In the United Kingdom, potential GDP is 1,050 billion pounds and the table shows the aggregate demand and short-run aggregate supply schedules.

Price level	Real GDP demanded	Real GDP supplied in the short run
	(billions of 2001 pounds)	
100	1,150	1,050
110	1,100	1,100
120	1,050	1,150
130	1,000	1,200
140	950	1,250
150	900	1,300
160	850	1,350

   a. What is the short-run equilibrium real GDP and price level?
   b. Does the United Kingdom have an inflationary gap or a recessionary gap and what is its magnitude?

3. In September 2008, the Bureau of Economic Analysis reported that real GDP during the second quarter of 2008 was $11,727 billion compared to $11,491 billion in the same quarter of 2007. The GDP deflator was 121.9, up from 119.5 in the second quarter of 2007. The Congressional Budget Office estimated potential GDP to be $11,888 billion in the second quarter of 2008 and $11,568 billion a year earlier.
   a. Draw a graph of the aggregate demand curve, the short-run aggregate supply curve, and the long-run aggregate supply curve in 2007 that is consistent with these numbers.
   b. On the graph, show how the aggregate demand curve, the short-run aggregate supply curve, and the long-run aggregate supply curve shifted during the year to the second quarter of 2008.

4. Initially, the short-run aggregate supply curve is SAS_0 and the aggregate demand curve is AD_0. Some events change aggregate demand, and later, some other events change aggregate supply.

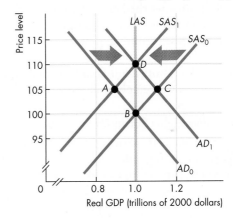

   a. What is the equilibrium after the change in aggregate demand?
   b. What is the equilibrium after the change in aggregate supply?
   c. Describe two events that could have changed aggregate demand from AD_0 to AD_1.
   d. Describe two events that could have changed aggregate supply from SAS_0 to SAS_1.

5. **It's a Recession—75 Percent of Americans Say**
   In a telephone poll of over 1,000 adult Americans, 75 percent said they believe the nation is now in a recession. ... "From a consumers's perspective, the economy is bad, and the environment is going to be tough for a while," said Wachovia economist Mark Vitner. ... Though growth was sluggish in the last quarter

of 2007 and the first quarter of 2008, the U.S. economy has not yet shown retraction in the current slowdown. ... "Whether the economy technically meets the definition of a recession matters more for economists and policy makers than it does for consumers," said Vitner. ... Of those who think the economy is in a recession, 27 percent said they believe we are in a serious recession. ... Americans are less confident in the future of the economy than they were in March. The poll showed that 23 percent believe the downturn will last more than two years, up from 19 percent in March. ...

CNN, July 7, 2008

a. Explain the effects of a decrease in consumer confidence on the short-run macroeconomic equilibrium and draw a graph to illustrate the effects.
b. If the economy had been operating at a full-employment equilibrium, describe the state of equilibrium after the fall in consumer confidence. In what way might consumer expectations have a self-fulfilling prophecy?
c. Explain how the economy can adjust in the long run to restore a full-employment equilibrium and draw a graph to illustrate this adjustment process.

6. **Weak Dollar Helps Shrink Trade Deficit**

The United States trade deficit narrowed in May as exports, including industrial supplies and consumer goods, climbed to records. ... Exports of American-made goods and services totaled $157.6 billion in May, a 0.9 percent increase from April. The declining value of the dollar relative to other currencies, especially the euro, is helping to make American exports cheaper and thus more attractive to foreign buyers. Growth in exports has been one of the few bright spots for the economy, which has been pounded by housing, credit and financial crises. ... The stronger export figures should help bolster overall economic growth during the April-to-June quarter, which is already shaping up to be better than the grim projections made at the start of the year, when many feared the economy might contract. Tax rebates also are energizing shoppers, which should help second-quarter activity. "The narrowing trade deficit may be enough to keep second-quarter growth in the black," said Joel L.

Naroff, president of Naroff Economic Advisors. The economy could grow to more than 2 percent, from 1 percent, in the second quarter. ...

The New York Times, July 12, 2008

a. Explain and draw a graph to illustrate how depreciation of the dollar changes the short-run equilibrium real GDP and price level.
b. Explain the competing forces on aggregate demand in the second quarter that are identified in this article.
c. What will determine if aggregate demand increases or decreases as a result of the forces identified in the article? What prediction is made in the article concerning whether aggregate demand will increase or decrease?
d. Why would a recessionary gap eventually emerge even if aggregate demand remained constant?

7. **Adding Up the Cost of Obama's Agenda**

In more than a year of campaigning, Barack Obama has made a long list of promises for new federal programs costing tens of billions of dollars, many of them aimed at protecting people from the pain of a souring economy. ... Obama has said he would strengthen the nation's bridges and dams ($6 billion a year) ... extend health insurance to more people (part of a $65-billion-a-year health plan), develop cleaner energy sources ($15 billion a year), curb home foreclosures ($10 billion in one-time spending) and add $18 billion a year to education spending. ... His $10-billion fund to reduce home foreclosures ... is part of a $50-billion plan to stimulate the economy through increased government spending. ... It is a far different blueprint than [John] McCain is offering. The senator from Arizona has proposed relatively little new spending, arguing that tax cuts and private business are more effective means of solving problems. ... Unlike McCain, Obama [advocates] ... rolling back the Bush tax cuts for families earning more than $250,000 annually.

Los Angeles Times, July 8, 2008

a. Based upon this news clip, explain what macroeconomic school of thought Barack Obama most likely follows.
b. Based upon this news clip, explain what macroeconomic school of thought John McCain most likely follows.

8. The following events have occurred at times in the history of the United States:
   - The world economy goes into an expansion.
   - U.S. businesses expect future profits to rise.
   - The government increases its expenditure on goods and services in a time of war or increased international tension.
   a. Explain for each event whether it changes short-run aggregate supply, long-run aggregate supply, aggregate demand, or some combination of them.
   b. Explain the separate effects of each event on U.S. real GDP and the price level, starting from a position of long-run equilibrium.
   c. Explain the combined effects of these events on U.S. real GDP and the price level, starting from a position of long-run equilibrium.

9. In Japan, potential GDP is 600 trillion yen and the table shows the aggregate demand and short-run aggregate supply schedules.

Price level	Real GDP demanded	Real GDP supplied in the short run
	(trillions of 2000 yen)	
75	600	400
85	550	450
95	500	500
105	450	550
115	400	600
125	350	650
135	300	700

   a. Draw a graph of the aggregate demand curve and the short-run aggregate supply curve.
   b. What is the short-run equilibrium real GDP and price level?
   c. Does Japan have an inflationary gap or a recessionary gap and what is its magnitude?

10. **Low Spending Is Taking Toll on Economy**

   For months, beleaguered American consumers have defied expert forecasts that they would soon succumb to the pressures of falling home prices, fewer jobs and shrinking paychecks. Now, they appear to have given in. On Wednesday, the Commerce Department reported that the economy continued to stagnate during the first three months of the year, with a sharp pullback in consumer spending the primary factor at play. ... Americans cut back on a wide variety of discretionary purchases. ... As real estate prices plunge, so does the ability of homeowners to borrow against the value of their homes, crimping a major artery of spending. As banks grow tighter with their dollars in a period of uncertainty, families are running up against credit limits, forcing many to live within their incomes. And as companies lay off employees and cut working hours, paychecks are effectively shrinking. ... Consumer spending fell for a broad range of goods and services, including cars, auto parts, furniture, food and recreation, reflecting a growing inclination toward thrift. ...

   The New York Times, May 1, 2008
   a. Explain and draw a graph to illustrate the effect of a fall in consumption expenditure on real GDP and the price level in the short run.
   b. If the economy had been operating at a full-employment equilibrium, describe the type of equilibrium after the fall in consumer spending in a.
   c. Why do changes in consumer spending play such a large role in the business cycle?
   d. Explain and draw a graph to illustrate how the economy can adjust in the long run to restore a full-employment equilibrium.

11. **It's Pinching Everyone**

   The rate of inflation [in India] has now touched a mind-boggling 11 per cent. ... No one can predict when the process of spiraling prices will come to an end. ... [T]he current inflationary process is a global phenomenon and practically every country is suffering. ...

   Emerging and developing countries have been growing significantly faster than the rest of the world, and there has been a steep surge in demand in these countries. ... Since there is no reason to believe that world production will rise miraculously at least in the immediate future, many people expect that prices will keep on rising. These expectations in turn exacerbate the inflationary process. Households buy more of non-perishable goods than they need for their immediate consumption because they expect prices to go up even further. What is worse is that traders withhold stocks from the market in the hope of being able to sell these at higher prices later on. In other words, expectations of higher prices become self-fulfilling.

   The Times of India, June 24, 2008

Explain and draw a graph to illustrate how inflation and inflation expectations "become self-fulfilling."

12. **Shoppers Stimulate Discount Stores**

Consumers sought the biggest bang for their economic stimulus bucks in June, sending the sales of discount merchants such as Wal-Mart and Costco surging. ... As the economy remains weak ... shoppers—rich and poor—are flocking to discounters for low-cost goods. ... Wal-Mart Stores Inc. trounced analyst expectations Thursday with a 5.8 percent jump in June sales, ... attributing the increase to the government's economic stimulus payments. ... The retailer said sales jumped across the board. But the most dramatic increases were in entertainment, particularly for flat-screen televisions, and apparel, especially in swimwear and sportswear. ... Another major retailer, the warehouse club Costco Wholesale, beat analyst expectations with a 9 percent increase in same-store sales for June. ... Target, a top competitor to Wal-Mart, said that its same-store sales edged up 0.4 percent, well above the 0.5 percent decline projected by analyst consensus. ...

CNN, July 10, 2008

a. Explain and draw a graph to illustrate the effect of the fiscal stimulus payments on real GDP and the price level in the short run.

b. At which type of short-run equilibrium would the government want to use this policy?

c. Which macroeconomic school of thought would justify this policy?

d. If the government used this policy when the economy was at full employment, explain what would happen in the long run.

e. Draw a graph to illustrate your answer to d.

13. The International Monetary Fund's World Economic Outlook database provides the following data for India in 2004, 2005, and 2006.

	2004	2005	2006
Real GDP growth rate	8.1	8.3	7.3
Inflation rate	4.2	4.7	4.6

a. What changes in long-run and short-run aggregate supply and aggregate demand are consistent with these numbers?

b. Draw a graph to illustrate your answer to a.

c. List the main factors that might have produced the changes in aggregate supply and aggregate demand that you have described in your answer to a.

d. From the above data, do you think India has an inflationary gap, a recessionary gap, or is at full employment?

14. **That '70s Look: Stagflation**

Lately, many people are hearing an echo—faintly perhaps but distinctly audible—of the stagflation of the 1970s. Even as economic growth sags, oil and gasoline prices are surging to new heights. Gold is on the rise, along with the prices of such basic commodities as wheat and steel. And on Wednesday, with the latest government report on consumer prices, there are signs that overall inflation, after years of only modest increases, may be breaking out of its box.

The New York Times, February 21, 2008

a. What is stagflation?

b. Explain how the increase in the price of oil, gasoline, wheat, and steel can cause stagflation and draw a graph to illustrate this outcome.

15. After you have studied the account of the U.S. economy in 2008 in *Reading Between the Lines* on pp. 664–665,

a. Describe the main features of the U.S. economy in the second quarter of 2008.

b. Did the United States have a recessionary gap or an inflationary gap in 2008? How do you know?

c. Use the *AS-AD* model to show the changes in aggregate demand and aggregate supply that brought the slow increase in real GDP and rise in the price level between the first and second quarters of 2008.

d. Use the *AS-AD* model to show the changes in aggregate demand and aggregate supply that would occur if monetary policy cut the interest rate and increased the quantity of money.

e. Use the *AS-AD* model to show the changes in aggregate demand and aggregate supply that would occur if the federal government increased its expenditure on goods and services or cut taxes further.

Fiscal Policy

After studying this chapter,
you will be able to:

- Describe the federal budget process and the recent history of outlays, tax revenues, deficits, and debt

- Explain the supply-side effects of fiscal policy

- Explain how fiscal policy choices redistribute benefits and costs across generations

- Explain how fiscal policy is used to stabilize the business cycle

In 2009, the federal government planned to collect taxes of 20 cents on every dollar Americans earned and spend 23 cents of every dollar that Americans earned. So the government planned a deficit of 3 cents on every dollar earned—a total deficit of $393 billion. Federal government deficits are not new. Aside from the four years 1998–2001, the government's budget has been in deficit every year since 1970. Deficits bring debts, and your share of the federal government's debt is around $30,000.

What are the effects of taxes on the economy? Do they harm employment and production?

Does it matter if the government doesn't balance its books? What are the effects of an ongoing government deficit and accumulating debt? Do they slow economic growth? Do they

impose a burden on future generations—on you and your children?

What are the effects of government spending on the economy? Does a dollar spent by the government on goods and services have the same effect as a dollar spent by someone else? Does it create jobs, or does it destroy them?

These are the fiscal policy issues that you will study in this chapter. In *Reading Between the Lines* at the end of the chapter, we look at fiscal policy actions that the new president-elect Obama outlined in his first post-election news conference in November 2008.

The Federal Budget

The annual statement of the outlays and tax revenues of the government of the United States together with the laws and regulations that approve and support those outlays and tax revenues make up the **federal budget**. The federal budget has two purposes:

1. To finance the activities of the federal government
2. To achieve macroeconomic objectives

The first purpose of the federal budget was its only purpose before the Great Depression of the 1930s. The second purpose arose as a reaction to the Great Depression. The use of the federal budget to achieve macroeconomic objectives such as full employment, sustained economic growth, and price level stability is called **fiscal policy**. In this chapter, we focus on this second purpose—U.S. fiscal policy.

The Institutions and Laws

Fiscal policy is made by the president and Congress on an annual timeline that is shown in Fig. 30.1 for the 2009 budget.

The Roles of the President and Congress The president *proposes* a budget to Congress each February. Congress debates the proposed budget and passes the budget acts in September. The president either signs those acts into law or vetoes the *entire* budget bill. The president does not have the veto power to eliminate specific items in a budget bill and approve others—known as a *line-item veto*. Many state governors have long had line-item veto authority. Congress attempted to grant these powers to the president of the United States in 1996, but in a 1998 Supreme Court ruling, the line-item veto for the president was declared unconstitutional. Although the president proposes and ultimately approves the budget, the task of making the tough decisions on spending and taxes rests with Congress.

Congress begins its work on the budget with the president's proposal. The House of Representatives and the Senate develop their own budget ideas in their respective House and Senate Budget Committees. Formal conferences between the two houses eventually resolve differences of view, and a series of spending acts and an overall budget act are usually passed

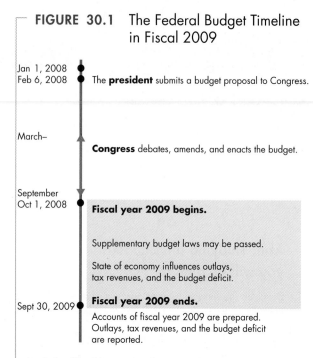

FIGURE 30.1   The Federal Budget Timeline in Fiscal 2009

Jan 1, 2008
Feb 6, 2008 — The **president** submits a budget proposal to Congress.

March– — **Congress** debates, amends, and enacts the budget.

September
Oct 1, 2008 — **Fiscal year 2009 begins.**

Supplementary budget laws may be passed.

State of economy influences outlays, tax revenues, and the budget deficit.

Sept 30, 2009 — **Fiscal year 2009 ends.**
Accounts of fiscal year 2009 are prepared. Outlays, tax revenues, and the budget deficit are reported.

The federal budget process begins with the president's proposals in February. Congress debates and amends these proposals and enacts a budget before the start of the fiscal year on October 1. The president signs the budget acts into law or vetoes the entire budget bill. Throughout the fiscal year, Congress might pass supplementary budget laws. The budget outcome is calculated after the end of the fiscal year.

myeconlab animation

by both houses before the start of the fiscal year. A *fiscal year* is a year that runs from October 1 to September 30 in the next calendar year. *Fiscal* 2009 is the fiscal year that *begins* on October 1, 2008.

During a fiscal year, Congress often passes supplementary budget laws, and the budget outcome is influenced by the evolving state of the economy. For example, if a recession begins, tax revenues fall and welfare payments increase.

The Employment Act of 1946 Fiscal policy operates within the framework of the landmark **Employment Act of 1946** in which Congress declared that

. . . it is the continuing policy and responsibility of the Federal Government to use all practicable means . . . to coordinate and utilize all its plans, functions, and resources . . . to promote maximum employment, production, and purchasing power.

This act recognized a role for government actions to keep unemployment low, the economy expanding, and inflation in check. The *Full Employment and Balanced Growth Act of 1978*, more commonly known as the *Humphrey-Hawkins Act*, went farther than the Employment Act of 1946 and set a specific target of 4 percent for the unemployment rate. But this target has never been treated as an unwavering policy goal. Under the 1946 act, the president must describe the current economic situation and the policies he believes are needed in the annual *Economic Report of the President*, which the Council of Economic Advisers writes.

The Council of Economic Advisers

The president's Council of Economic Advisers was established in the Employment Act of 1946. The Council consists of a chairperson and two other members, all of whom are economists on a one- or two-year leave from their regular university or public service jobs. In 2006, the chair of President Bush's Council of Economic Advisers was Edward P. Lazear of Stanford University. The **Council of Economic Advisers** monitors the economy and keeps the President and the public well informed about the current state of the economy and the best available forecasts of where it is heading. This economic intelligence activity is one source of data that informs the budget-making process.

Let's look at the most recent federal budget.

Highlights of the 2009 Budget

Table 30.1 shows the main items in the federal budget proposed by President Bush for 2009. The numbers are projected amounts for the fiscal year beginning on October 1, 2008—fiscal 2009. Notice the three main parts of the table: *Tax revenues* are the government's receipts, *outlays* are the government's payments, and the *deficit* is the amount by which the government's outlays exceed its tax revenues.

Tax Revenues Tax revenues were projected to be $2,805 billion in fiscal 2009. These revenues come from four sources:

1. Personal income taxes
2. Social Security taxes
3. Corporate income taxes
4. Indirect taxes

The largest source of revenue is *personal income taxes*, which in 2009 are expected to be $1,234 billion. These taxes are paid by individuals on their incomes. The second largest source is *Social Security taxes*. These taxes are paid by workers and their employers to finance the government's Social Security programs. Third in size are *corporate income taxes*. These taxes are paid by companies on their profits. Finally, the smallest source of federal revenue is what are called *indirect taxes*. These taxes are on the sale of gasoline, alcoholic beverages, and a few other items.

Outlays Outlays are classified into three categories:

1. Transfer payments
2. Expenditure on goods and services
3. Debt interest

The largest item of outlays, *transfer payments*, are payments to individuals, businesses, other levels of government, and the rest of the world. In 2009, this item is expected to be $1,855 billion. It includes Social Security benefits, Medicare and Medicaid, unemployment checks, welfare payments, farm subsidies, grants to state and local governments, aid to developing countries, and dues to international organizations such as the United Nations. Transfer

TABLE 30.1 Federal Budget in Fiscal 2009

Item	Projections (billions of dollars)	
Tax Revenues	**2,805**	
Personal income taxes		1,234
Social security taxes		1,033
Corporate income taxes		352
Indirect taxes		186
Outlays	**3,198**	
Transfer payments		1,854
Expenditure on goods and services		1,006
Debt interest		338
Deficit	**393**	

Source of data: Budget of the United States Government, Fiscal Year 2009, Table 14.1.

payments, especially those for Medicare and Medicaid, are sources of persistent growth in government expenditures and are a major source of concern and political debate.

Expenditure on goods and services is the expenditure on final goods and services, and in 2009, it is expected to total $1,006 billion. This expenditure, which includes that on national defense, homeland security, research on cures for AIDS, computers for the Internal Revenue Service, government cars and trucks, federal highways, and dams, has decreased in recent years. This component of the federal budget is the *government expenditure on goods and services* that appears in the circular flow of expenditure and income and in the National Income and Product Accounts (see Chapter 21, pp. 489–490).

Debt interest is the interest on the government debt. In 2009, this item is expected to be $338 billion—about 10 percent of total expenditure. This interest payment is large because the government has a debt of more than $4.4 trillion, which has arisen from many years of budget deficits during the 1970s, 1980s, 1990s, and 2000s.

Surplus or Deficit The government's budget balance is equal to tax revenues minus outlays.

Budget balance = Tax revenues – Outlays.

If tax revenues exceed outlays, the government has a **budget surplus**. If outlays exceed tax revenues, the government has a **budget deficit**. If tax revenues equal outlays, the government has a **balanced budget**. For fiscal 2009, with projected outlays of $3,198 billion and tax revenues of $2,805 billion, the government projected a budget deficit of $393 billion.

Big numbers like these are hard to visualize and hard to compare over time. To get a better sense of the magnitude of tax revenues, outlays, and the deficit, we often express them as percentages of GDP. Expressing them in this way lets us see how large government is relative to the size of the economy and also helps us to study *changes* in the scale of government over time.

How typical is the federal budget of 2009? Let's look at the recent history of the budget.

The Budget in Historical Perspective

Figure 30.2 shows the government's tax revenues, outlays, and budget surplus or deficit since 1980. Through 1997, there was a budget deficit. The federal government began running a deficit in 1970, and the 1983 deficit shown in the figure was the highest on record at 5.2 percent of GDP. The deficit declined through 1989 but climbed again during the 1990–1991 recession. During the 1990s expansion,

FIGURE 30.2 The Budget Surplus and Deficit

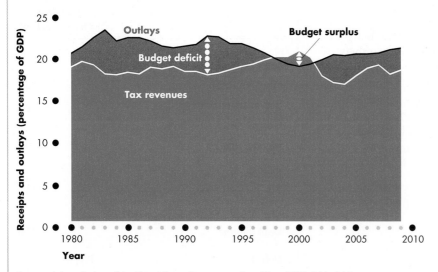

The figure records the federal government's outlays, tax revenues, and budget balance from 1980 to 2009. During the 1980s, a large and persistent budget deficit arose from the combination of falling tax revenues and rising outlays. In 1998, rising tax revenues and falling outlays (as percentages of GDP) created a budget surplus, but a deficit emerged again in 2002 as expenditure on security increased and taxes were cut.

Source of data: Budget of the United States Government, Fiscal Year 2009, Table 14.2.

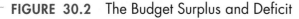

the deficit gradually shrank, and in 1998, the first budget surplus since 1969 emerged. But by 2002, the budget was again in deficit.

Why did the budget deficit grow during the 1980s and vanish in the late 1990s? The answer lies in the changes in outlays and tax revenues. But which components of outlays and tax revenues changed to swell and then shrink the deficit? Let's look at tax revenues and outlays in a bit more detail.

Tax Revenues Figure 30.3(a) shows the components of tax revenues as percentages of GDP from 1980 to 2009. Cuts in corporate and personal income taxes lowered total tax revenues between 1983 and 1986. The decline resulted from tax cuts that had been passed during 1981. From 1986 through 1991, tax revenues did not change much as a percentage of GDP. Personal income tax payments increased through the 1990s but fell after 2000.

FIGURE 30.3 Federal Government Tax Revenues and Outlays

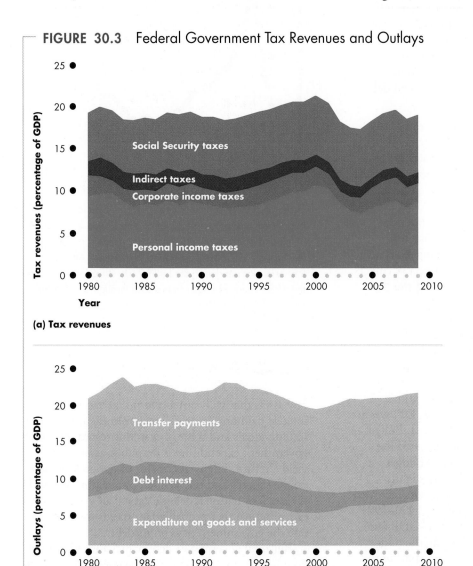

(a) Tax revenues

(b) Outlays

In part (a), revenues from personal and corporate income taxes as a percentage of GDP were approximately constant during the 1980s, increased during the 1990s, and decreased sharply from 2000 to 2004 but then increased again. The other components of tax revenues remained steady.

In part (b), expenditure on goods and services as a percentage of GDP decreased through 2001 but then increased because expenditure on security-related goods and services increased sharply after 2001. Transfer payments increased over the entire period. Debt interest held steady during the 1980s and decreased during the 1990s and 2000s, helped by a shrinking budget deficit during the 1990s and low interest rates during 2002 and 2003.

Source of data: Budget of the United States Government, Fiscal Year 2009 Table 14.2.

myeconlab animation

Outlays Figure 30.3(b) shows the components of government outlays as percentages of GDP from 1980 to 2009. Total outlays decreased slightly through 1989, increased during the early 1990s, decreased steadily until 2000, and then increased again. Expenditure on goods and services decreased through 2001. It increased when expenditure on security-related goods and services increased sharply in 2002 in the wake of the attacks that occurred on September 11, 2001. Transfer payments increased over the entire period. Debt interest was a constant percentage of GDP during the 1980s and fell slightly during the late 1990s and 2000s. To understand the role of debt interest, we need to see the connection between the government's budget balance and debt.

Budget Balance and Debt The government borrows when it has a budget deficit and makes repayments when it has a budget surplus. **Government debt** is the total amount that the government has borrowed. It is the sum of past budget deficits minus the sum of past budget surpluses. A government budget deficit increases government debt. A persistent budget deficit feeds itself: The budget deficit leads to increased borrowing; increased borrowing leads to larger interest payments; and larger interest payments lead to a larger deficit. That is the story of the increasing budget deficit during the 1970s and 1980s.

Figure 30.4 shows two measures of government debt since 1940. Gross debt includes the amounts that the government owes to future generations in Social Security payments. Net debt is the debt held by the public, and it excludes social security obligations.

Government debt (as a percentage of GDP) was at an all-time high at the end of World War II. Budget surpluses and rapid economic growth lowered the debt-to-GDP ratio through 1974. Small budget deficits increased the debt-to-GDP ratio slightly through the 1970s, and large budget deficits increased it dramatically during the 1980s and the 1990–1991 recession. The growth rate of the debt-to-GDP ratio slowed as the economy expanded during the mid-1990s, fell when the budget went into surplus in the late 1990s and early 2000s, and began to rise again as the budget turned in to a deficit.

Debt and Capital Businesses and individuals incur debts to buy capital—assets that yield a return. In fact, the main point of debt is to enable people to

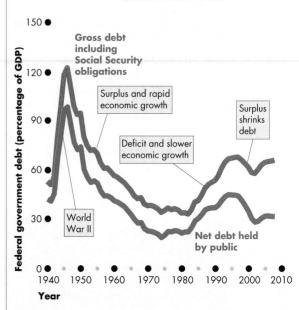

FIGURE 30.4 The Federal Government Debt

Gross and net government debt (the accumulation of past budget deficits less past budget surpluses) was at its highest at the end of World War II. Debt as a percentage of GDP fell through 1974 but then started to increase. After a further brief decline during the late 1970s, it exploded during the 1980s and continued to increase through 1995, after which it fell. After 2002, it began to rise again.

Source of data: Budget of the United States Government, Fiscal Year 2009, Table 7.1.

buy assets that will earn a return that exceeds the interest paid on the debt. The government is similar to individuals and businesses in this regard. Much government expenditure is on public assets that yield a return. Highways, major irrigation schemes, public schools and universities, public libraries, and the stock of national defense capital all yield a social rate of return that probably far exceeds the interest rate the government pays on its debt.

But total government debt, which exceeds $4 trillion, is four times the value of the government's capital stock. So some government debt has been incurred to finance public consumption expenditure and transfer payments, which do not have a social return. Future generations bear the cost of this debt.

How does the U.S. government budget balance compare with those in other countries?

The U.S. Government Budget in Global Perspective

More Deficits than Surpluses

The U.S. government budget deficit in Fiscal 2009 was projected to be almost $400 billion, or close to 3 percent of GDP. How does this U.S. budget deficit compare with the deficits of other countries?

To compare the deficits of governments across countries, we must take into account the differences in local and regional government arrangements. Some countries, and the United States is one of them, have large state and local governments. Other countries, and the United Kingdom is one, have larger central government and small local governments. These differences make the international comparison more valid at the level of total government. The figure shows the budget balances of all levels of government in the United States and other countries.

Of the countries shown here, the United States has the largest deficit, as a percentage of GDP. Japan, the United Kingdom, France, and Italy come next, followed by the European Union as a whole and Germany.

Canada, the newly industrialized economies of Asia (Hong Kong, South Korea, Singapore, and Taiwan), and other advanced economies as a group, had projected surpluses in 2009. One country, Norway, which has substantial oil wealth, dominates the other advanced countries surplus.

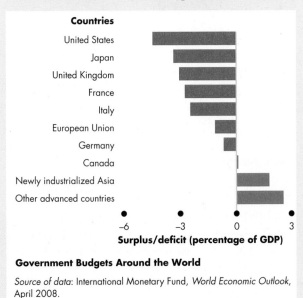

Government Budgets Around the World

Source of data: International Monetary Fund, *World Economic Outlook*, April 2008.

State and Local Budgets

The *total government* sector of the United States includes state and local governments as well as the federal government. In 2008, when federal government outlays were $3,200 billion, state and local outlays were a further $2,000 billion. Most of these expenditures were on public schools, colleges, and universities ($550 billion); local police and fire services; and roads.

It is the combination of federal, state, and local government tax revenues, outlays, and budget deficits that influences the economy. But state and local budgets are not designed to stabilize the aggregate economy. So sometimes, when the federal government cuts taxes or outlays, state and local governments do the reverse and, to a degree, cancel out the effects of the federal actions. For example, since 2000, federal taxes decreased as a percentage of GDP, but state and local taxes and total government taxes increased.

Review Quiz

1 What is fiscal policy, who makes it, and what is it designed to influence?
2 What special role does the president play in creating fiscal policy?
3 What special roles do the Budget Committees of the House of Representatives and the Senate play in creating fiscal policy?
4 What is the timeline for the U.S. federal budget each year? When does a fiscal year begin and end?
5 Is the federal government budget today in surplus or deficit?

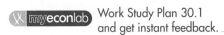 Work Study Plan 30.1 and get instant feedback.

Now that you know what the federal budget is and what the main components of tax revenues and outlays are, it is time to study the *effects* of fiscal policy. We'll begin by learning about the effects of taxes on employment, aggregate supply, and potential GDP. Then we'll study the effects of budget deficits and see how fiscal policy brings redistribution across generations. Finally, we'll look at the demand-side effects of fiscal policy and see how it provides a tool for stabilizing the business cycle.

Supply-Side Effects of Fiscal Policy

Fiscal policy has important effects on employment, potential GDP, and aggregate supply that we'll now examine. These effects are known as **supply-side effects**, and economists who believe these effects to be large ones are generally referred to as *supply-siders*. To study these effects, we'll begin with a refresher on how full employment and potential GDP are determined in the absence of taxes. Then we'll introduce an income tax and see how it changes the economic outcome.

Full Employment and Potential GDP

You learned in Chapter 23 (pp. 541–543) how the full-employment quantity of labor and potential GDP are determined. At full employment, the real wage rate adjusts to make the quantity of labor demanded equal the quantity of labor supplied. Potential GDP is the real GDP that the full-employment quantity of labor produces.

Figure 30.5 illustrates a full-employment situation. In part (a), the demand for labor curve is *LD*, and the supply of labor curve is *LS*. At a real wage rate of $30 an hour and 250 billion hours of labor a year employed, the economy is at full employment.

In Fig. 30.5(b), the production function is *PF*. When 250 billion hours of labor are employed, real GDP—which is also potential GDP—is $13 trillion.

Let's now see how an income tax changes potential GDP.

The Effects of the Income Tax

The tax on labor income influences potential GDP and aggregate supply by changing the full-employment quantity of labor. The income tax weakens the incentive to work and drives a wedge between the take-home wage of workers and the cost of labor to firms. The result is a smaller quantity of labor and a lower potential GDP.

Figure 30.5 shows this outcome. In the labor market, the income tax has no effect on the demand for labor, which remains at *LD*. The reason is that the quantity of labor that firms plan to hire depends only on how productive labor is and what it costs— its real wage rate.

FIGURE 30.5 The Effects of the Income Tax on Aggregate Supply

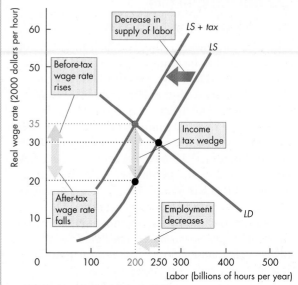

(a) Income tax and the labor market

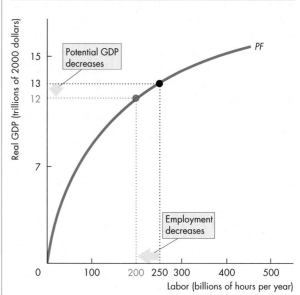

(b) Income tax and potential GDP

In part (a), with no income tax, the real wage rate is $30 an hour and employment is 250 billion hours. In part (b), potential GDP is $13 trillion. An income tax shifts the supply of labor curve leftward to *LS + tax*. The before-tax wage rate rises to $35 an hour, the after-tax wage rate falls to $20 an hour, and the quantity of labor employed decreases to 200 billion hours. With less labor, potential GDP decreases.

myeconlab animation

But the supply of labor *does* change. With no income tax, the real wage rate is $30 an hour and 250 billion hours of labor a year are employed. An income tax weakens the incentive to work and decreases the supply of labor. The reason is that for each dollar of before-tax earnings, workers must pay the government an amount determined by the income tax code. So workers look at the after-tax wage rate when they decide how much labor to supply. An income tax shifts the supply curve leftward to *LS + tax*. The vertical distance between the *LS* curve and the *LS + tax* curve measures the amount of income tax. With the smaller supply of labor, the *before-tax* wage rate rises to $35 an hour but the *after-tax* wage rate falls to $20 an hour. The gap created between the before-tax and after-tax wage rates is called the **tax wedge**.

The new equilibrium quantity of labor employed is 200 billion hours a year—less than in the no-tax case. Because the full-employment quantity of labor decreases, so does potential GDP. And a decrease in potential GDP decreases aggregate supply.

In this example, the tax rate is high—$15 tax on a $35 wage rate, about 43 percent. A lower tax rate would have a smaller effect on employment and potential GDP.

An increase in the tax rate to above 43 percent would decrease the supply of labor by more than the decrease shown in Fig. 30.5. Equilibrium employment and potential GDP would also decrease still further. A tax cut would increase the supply of labor, increase equilibrium employment, and increase potential GDP.

Taxes on Expenditure and the Tax Wedge

The tax wedge that we've just considered is only a part of the wedge that affects labor-supply decisions. Taxes on consumption expenditure add to the wedge. The reason is that a tax on consumption raises the prices paid for consumption goods and services and is equivalent to a cut in the real wage rate.

The incentive to supply labor depends on the goods and services that an hour of labor can buy. The higher the taxes on goods and services and the lower the after-tax wage rate, the less is the incentive to supply labor. If the income tax rate is 25 percent and the tax rate on consumption expenditure is 10 percent, a dollar earned buys only 65 cents worth of goods and services. The tax wedge is 35 percent.

Some Real World Tax Wedges
Why Americans Work Longer Hours than Europeans

Edward C. Prescott of Arizona State University, who shared the 2004 Nobel Prize for Economic Science, has estimated the tax wedges for a number of countries, among them the United States, the United Kingdom, and France.

The U.S. tax wedge is a combination of 13 percent tax on consumption and 32 percent tax on incomes. The income tax component of the U.S. tax wedge includes Social Security taxes and is the *marginal* tax rate—the tax rate paid on the marginal dollar earned.

Prescott estimates that in France, taxes on consumption are 33 percent and taxes on incomes are 49 percent.

The estimates for the United Kingdom fall between those for the United States and France. The figure shows these components of the tax wedges in the three countries.

Does the Tax Wedge Matter?

According to Prescott's estimates, the tax wedge has a powerful effect on employment and potential GDP. Potential GDP in France is 14 percent below that of the United States (per person), and the entire difference can be attributed to the difference in the tax wedge in the two countries.

Potential GDP in the United Kingdom is 41 percent below that of the United States (per person), and about a third of the difference arises from the different tax wedges. (The rest is due to different productivities.)

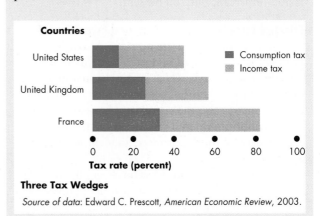

Three Tax Wedges

Source of data: Edward C. Prescott, *American Economic Review*, 2003.

Taxes and the Incentive to Save

A tax on interest income weakens the incentive to save and drives a wedge between the after-tax interest rate earned by savers and the interest rate paid by firms. These effects are analogous to those of a tax on labor income. But they are more serious for two reasons.

First, a tax on labor income lowers the quantity of labor employed and lowers potential GDP, while a tax on capital income lowers the quantity of saving and investment and *slows the growth rate of real GDP.*

Second, the true tax rate on interest income is much higher than that on labor income because of the way in which inflation and taxes on interest income interact. Let's examine this interaction.

Effect of Tax Rate on Real Interest Rate

The interest rate that influences investment and saving plans is the *real after-tax interest rate.* The real *after-tax* interest rate subtracts the income tax rate paid on interest income from the real interest rate. But the taxes depend on the nominal interest rate, not the real interest rate. So the higher the inflation rate, the higher is the true tax rate on interest income. Here is an example. Suppose the real interest rate is 4 percent a year and the tax rate is 40 percent.

If there is no inflation, the nominal interest rate equals the real interest rate. The tax on 4 percent interest is 1.6 percent (40 percent of 4 percent), so the real after-tax interest rate is 4 percent minus 1.6 percent, which equals 2.4 percent.

If the inflation rate is 6 percent a year, the nominal interest rate is 10 percent. The tax on 10 percent interest is 4 percent (40 percent of 10 percent), so the real after-tax interest rate is 4 percent minus 4 percent, which equals zero. The true tax rate in this case is not 40 percent but 100 percent!

Effect of Income Tax on Saving and Investment

In Fig. 30.6, initially there are no taxes. Also, the government has a balanced budget. The demand for loanable funds curve, which is also the investment demand curve, is *DLF.* The supply of loanable funds curve, which is also the saving supply curve, is *SLF.* The equilibrium interest rate is 3 percent a year, and the quantity of funds borrowed and lent is $2 trillion a year.

A tax on interest income has no effect on the demand for loanable funds. The quantity of investment and borrowing that firms plan to undertake depends only on how productive capital is and what it costs—its

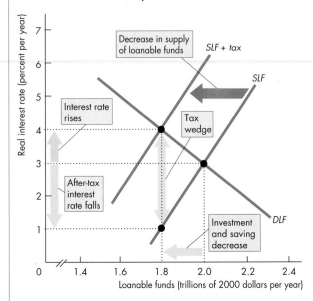

FIGURE 30.6   The Effects of a Tax on Capital Income

The demand for loanable funds and investment demand curve is *DLF,* and the supply of loanable funds and saving supply curve is *SLF.* With no income tax, the real interest rate is 3 percent a year and investment is $2 trillion. An income tax shifts the supply curve leftward to *SLF + tax.* The interest rate rises to 4 percent a year, the after-tax interest rate falls to 1 percent a year, and investment decreases to $1.8 trillion. With less investment, the real GDP growth rate decreases.

myeconlab   animation

real interest rate. But a tax on interest income weakens the incentive to save and lend and decreases the supply of loanable funds. For each dollar of before-tax interest, savers must pay the government an amount determined by the tax code. So savers look at the after-tax real interest rate when they decide how much to save.

When a tax is imposed, saving decreases and the supply of loanable funds curve shifts leftward to *SLF + tax.* The amount of tax payable is measured by the vertical distance between the *SLF* curve and the *SLF + tax* curve. With this smaller supply of loanable funds, the interest rate rises to 4 percent a year but the *after-tax* interest rate falls to 1 percent a year. A tax wedge is driven between the interest rate and the after-tax interest rate, and the equilibrium quantity of loanable funds decreases. Saving and investment also decrease.

Tax Revenues and the Laffer Curve

An interesting consequence of the effect of taxes on employment and saving is that a higher tax *rate* does not always bring greater tax *revenue*. A higher tax rate brings in more revenue per dollar earned. But because a higher tax rate decreases the number of dollars earned, two forces operate in opposite directions on the tax revenue collected.

The relationship between the tax rate and the amount of tax revenue collected is called the **Laffer curve**. The curve is so named because Arthur B. Laffer, a member of President Reagan's Economic Policy Advisory Board, drew such a curve on a table napkin and launched the idea that tax *cuts* could *increase* tax revenue.

Figure 30.7 shows a Laffer curve. The tax *rate* is on the *x*-axis, and total tax *revenue* is on the *y*-axis. For tax rates below T^*, an increase in the tax rate increases tax revenue; at T^*, tax revenue is maximized; and a tax rate increase above T^* decreases tax revenue.

Most people think that the United States is on the upward-sloping part of the Laffer curve; so is the United Kingdom. But France might be close to the maximum point or perhaps even beyond it.

The Supply-Side Debate

Before 1980, few economists paid attention to the supply-side effects of taxes on employment and potential GDP. Then, when Ronald Reagan took office as president, a group of supply-siders began to argue the virtues of cutting taxes. Arthur Laffer was one of them. Laffer and his supporters were not held in high esteem among mainstream economists, but they were influential for a period. They correctly argued that tax cuts would increase employment and increase output. But they incorrectly argued that tax cuts would increase tax revenues and decrease the budget deficit. For this prediction to be correct, the United States would have had to be on the "wrong" side of the Laffer curve. Given that U.S. tax rates are among the lowest in the industrial world, it is unlikely that this condition was met. And when the Reagan administration did cut taxes, the budget deficit increased, a fact that reinforces this view.

Supply-side economics became tarnished because of its association with Laffer and came to be called "voodoo economics." But mainstream economists, including Martin Feldstein, a Harvard professor who was Reagan's chief economic advisor, recognized the

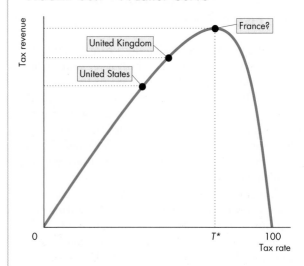

FIGURE 30.7   A Laffer Curve

A Laffer curve shows the relationship between the tax rate and tax revenues. For tax rates below T^*, an increase in the tax rate increases tax revenue. At the tax rate T^*, tax revenue is maximized. For tax rates above T^*, an increase in the tax rate decreases tax revenue.

myeconlab   animation

power of tax cuts as incentives but took the standard view that tax cuts without spending cuts would swell the budget deficit and bring serious further problems. This view is now widely accepted by economists of all political persuasions.

Review Quiz

1 How does a tax on labor income influence the equilibrium quantity of employment?
2 How does the tax wedge influence potential GDP?
3 Why are consumption taxes relevant for measuring the tax wedge?
4 Why are income taxes on capital income more powerful than those on labor income?
5 What is the Laffer curve and why is it unlikely that the United States is on the "wrong" side of it?

myeconlab   Work Study Plan 30.2
and get instant feedback.

You now know how taxes influence potential GDP and saving and investment. Next we look at the intergenerational effects of fiscal policy.

Generational Effects of Fiscal Policy

Is a budget deficit a burden on future generations? If it is, how will the burden be borne? And is the budget deficit the only burden on future generations? What about the deficit in the Social Security fund? Does it matter who owns the bonds that the government sells to finance its deficit? What about the bonds owned by foreigners? Won't repaying those bonds impose a bigger burden than repaying bonds owned by Americans?

To answer questions like these, we use a tool called **generational accounting**—an accounting system that measures the lifetime tax burden and benefits of each generation. This accounting system was developed by Alan Auerbach of the University of Pennsylvania and Laurence Kotlikoff of Boston University. Generational accounts for the United States have been prepared by Jagadeesh Gokhale of the Federal Reserve Bank of Cleveland and Kent Smetters of the University of Pennsylvania.

Generational Accounting and Present Value

Income taxes and Social Security taxes are paid by people who have jobs. Social Security benefits are paid to people after they retire. So to compare taxes and benefits, we must compare the value of taxes paid by people during their working years with the benefits received in their retirement years. To compare the value of an amount of money at one date with that at a later date, we use the concept of present value. A **present value** is an amount of money that, if invested today, will grow to equal a given future amount when the interest that it earns is taken into account. We can compare dollars today with dollars in 2030 or any other future year by using present values.

For example, if the interest rate is 5 percent a year, $1,000 invested today will grow, with interest, to $11,467 after 50 years. So the present value (in 2008) of $11,467 in 2058 is $1,000.

By using present values, we can assess the magnitude of the government's debts to older Americans in the form of pensions and medical benefits.

But the assumed interest rate and growth rate of taxes and benefits critically influence the answers we get. For example, at an interest rate of 3 percent a

year, the present value (in 2008) of $11,467 in 2058 is $2,616. The lower the interest rate, the greater is the present value of a given future amount.

Because there is uncertainty about the proper interest rate to use to calculate present values, plausible alternative numbers are used to estimate a range of present values.

Using generational accounting and present values, economists have studied the situation facing the federal government arising from its Social Security obligations, and they have found a time bomb!

The Social Security Time Bomb

When Social Security was introduced in the New Deal of the 1930s, today's demographic situation was not envisaged. The age distribution of the U.S. population today is dominated by the surge in the birth rate after World War II that created what is called the "baby boom generation." There are 77 million "baby boomers."

In 2008, the first of the baby boomers will start collecting Social Security pensions and in 2011, they will become eligible for Medicare benefits. By 2030, all the baby boomers will have retired and, compared to 2008, the population supported by social security will have doubled.

Under the existing Social Security laws, the federal government has an obligation to these citizens to pay pensions and Medicare benefits on an already declared scale. These obligations are a debt owed by the government and are just as real as the bonds that the government issues to finance its current budget deficit.

To assess the full extent of the government's obligations, economists use the concept of fiscal imbalance. **Fiscal imbalance** is the present value of the government's commitments to pay benefits minus the present value of its tax revenues. Fiscal imbalance is an attempt to measure the scale of the government's true liabilities.

Gokhale and Smetters estimated that the fiscal imbalance was $45 trillion in 2003. (Using alternative assumptions about interest rates and growth rates, the number might be as low as $29 trillion or as high as $65 trillion.) To put the $45 trillion in perspective, note that U.S. GDP in 2003 was $11 trillion. So the fiscal imbalance was four times the value of one year's production.

How can the federal government meet its social security obligations? Gokhale and Smetters consider four alternative fiscal policy changes that might be made:

- Raise income taxes
- Raise Social Security taxes
- Cut Social Security benefits
- Cut federal government discretionary spending

They estimated that starting in 2003 and making only one of these changes, income taxes would need to be raised by 69 percent, or Social Security taxes raised by 95 percent, or Social Security benefits cut by 56 percent. Even if the government stopped all its discretionary spending, including that on national defense, it would not be able to pay its bills.

Of course, by combining the four measures, the pain from each could be lessened. But the pain would still be severe. And worse, delay makes all these numbers rise. With no action, the fiscal imbalance climbs from the $45 trillion of 2003 to $54 trillion in 2008.

Generational Imbalance

A fiscal imbalance must eventually be corrected and when it is, people either pay higher taxes or receive lower benefits. The concept of generational imbalance tells us who will pay. **Generational imbalance** is the division of the fiscal imbalance between the current and future generations, assuming that the current generation will enjoy the existing levels of taxes and benefits.

Figure 30.8 shows an estimate of how the fiscal imbalance is distributed across the current (born before 1988) and future (born in or after 1988) generations. It also shows that the major source of the imbalances is Medicare. Social Security pension benefits create a fiscal imbalance, but these benefits will be more than fully paid for by the current generation. But the current generation will pay less than 50 percent of its Medicare costs, and the balance will fall on future generations. If we sum all the items, the current generation will pay 43 percent and future generations will pay 57 percent of the fiscal imbalance.

Because the estimated fiscal imbalance is so large, it is not possible to predict how it will be resolved. But we can predict that the outcome will involve both lower benefits and higher taxes. One of these taxes could be the inflation tax—paying bills with new money and creating inflation. But the Fed will resist inflation being used to deal with the imbalance, as you will see in the next chapter.

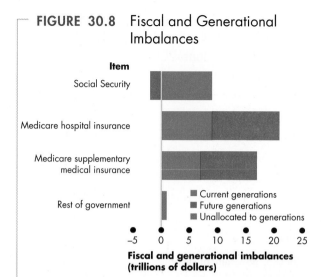

FIGURE 30.8 Fiscal and Generational Imbalances

The bars show the scale of the fiscal imbalance. The largest component is the more than $20 trillion of Medicare benefits. These benefits are also the main component of the generational imbalance. Social Security pensions are paid for entirely by the current generation.

Source of data: Jagadeesh Gokhale and Kent Smetters, *Fiscal and Generational Imbalances: New Budget Measures for New Budget Priorities*, Washington, D.C.: The AEI Press, April 2003.

myeconlab animation

International Debt

So far in our discussion of government deficits and debts, we've ignored the role played by the rest of the world. We'll conclude this discussion by considering the role and magnitude of international debt.

You've seen that borrowing from the rest of the world is one source of investment finance. And you've also seen that this source of investment finance became larger during the late 1990s and 2000s.

How large is the contribution of the rest of the world? How much investment have we paid for by borrowing from the rest of the world? And how much U.S. government debt is held abroad?

Table 30.2 answers these questions. In June 2008, the United States had a net debt to the rest of the world of $8.1 trillion. Of that debt, $4.7 trillion was U.S. government debt. U.S. corporations had used $5.9 trillion of foreign funds ($3.1 trillion in bonds and $2.8 trillion in equities). Almost 90 percent of government debt is held by foreigners.

The international debt of the United States is important because, when that debt is repaid, the United States will transfer real resources to the rest of

TABLE 30.2   What the United States Owed the Rest of the World in June 2008

	$ trillions
(a) U.S. Liabilities	
Deposits in U.S. banks	1.5
U.S. government securities	4.7
U.S. corporate bonds	3.1
U.S. corporate equities	2.8
Other (net)	–4.0
Total	8.1
(b) U.S. government securities	
Held by rest of world	4.7
Held in the United States	0.6
Total	5.3

Source of data: Federal Reserve Board.

the world. Instead of running a large net exports deficit, the United States will need a surplus of exports over imports. To make a surplus possible, U.S. saving must increase and consumption must decrease. Some tough choices lie ahead.

Review Quiz

1 What is a present value?
2 Distinguish between fiscal imbalance and generational imbalance.
3 How large was the estimated U.S. fiscal imbalance in 2003 and how did it divide between current and future generations?
4 What is the source of the U.S. fiscal imbalance and what are the painful choices that face current and future generations?
5 How much of U.S. government debt is held by the rest of the world?

myeconlab   Work Study Plan 30.3 and get instant feedback.

You now know how economists assess fiscal imbalance and how they divide the cost of covering an imbalance across generations. And you've seen the extent and implication of U.S. debt held in the rest of the world. We conclude this chapter by looking at fiscal policy as a tool for stabilizing the business cycle.

Stabilizing the Business Cycle

Fiscal policy actions that seek to stabilize the business cycle work by changing aggregate demand and are either

- Discretionary or
- Automatic

A fiscal action initiated by an act of Congress is called **discretionary fiscal policy**. It requires a change in a spending program or in a tax law. For example, an increase in defense spending or a cut in the income tax rate is a discretionary fiscal policy.

A fiscal action that is triggered by the state of the economy is called **automatic fiscal policy**. For example, an increase in unemployment induces an increase in payments to the unemployed. A fall in incomes induces a decrease in tax revenues.

Changes in government expenditure and changes in taxes have multiplier effects on aggregate demand. Chapter 28 explains the basic idea of the multiplier and the Mathematical Note on pp. 692–695 shows the algebra of the fiscal policy multipliers that we'll now study.

Government Expenditure Multiplier

The **government expenditure multiplier** is the magnification effect of a change in government expenditure on goods and services on aggregate demand. Government expenditure is a component of aggregate expenditure, so when government expenditure changes, aggregate demand changes. Real GDP changes and induces a change in consumption expenditure, which brings a further change in aggregate expenditure. A multiplier process ensues.

A Homeland Security Multiplier The terrorist attacks of September 11, 2001, brought a reappraisal of the nation's homeland security requirements and an increase in government expenditure. This increase initially increased the incomes of producers of airport and border security equipment and security workers. Better-off security workers increased their consumption expenditure. With rising revenues, other businesses in all parts of the nation boomed and expanded their payrolls. A second round of increased consumption expenditure increased incomes yet further. This multiplier effect helped to end the 2001 recession.

The Autonomous Tax Multiplier

The **autonomous tax multiplier** is the magnification effect of a change in autonomous taxes on aggregate demand. A *decrease* in taxes *increases* disposable income, which increases consumption expenditure. A decrease in taxes works like an increase in government expenditure. But the magnitude of the autonomous tax multiplier is smaller than the government expenditure multiplier. The reason is that a $1 tax cut generates *less than* $1 of additional expenditure. The marginal propensity to consume determines the increase in consumption expenditure induced by a tax cut. For example, if the marginal propensity to consume is 0.75, then a $1 tax cut increases consumption expenditure by only 75 cents. In this case, the tax multiplier is 0.75 times the magnitude of the government expenditure multiplier.

A Bush Tax Cut Multiplier Congress enacted the Bush tax cut package that lowered taxes starting in 2002. These tax cuts had a multiplier effect. With more disposable income, people increased consumption expenditure. This spending increased other people's incomes, which spurred yet more consumption expenditure. Like the increase in security expenditures, the tax cut and its multiplier effect helped to end the 2001 recession.

The Balanced Budget Multiplier

The **balanced budget multiplier** is the magnification effect on aggregate demand of a *simultaneous* change in government expenditure and taxes that leaves the budget balance unchanged. The balanced budget multiplier is positive because a $1 increase in government expenditure increases aggregate demand by more than a $1 increase in taxes decreases aggregate demand. So when both government expenditure and taxes increase by $1, aggregate demand increases.

Discretionary Fiscal Stabilization

If real GDP is below potential GDP, discretionary fiscal policy might be used in an attempt to restore full employment. The government might increase its expenditure on goods and services, cut taxes, or do some of both. These actions would increase aggregate demand. If they were timed correctly and were of the correct magnitude, they could restore full employment. Figure 30.9 shows how. Potential GDP is $12 trillion, but real GDP is below potential at $11 trillion

and there is a $1 trillion *recessionary gap* (see Chapter 27, p. 659). To restore full employment, the government takes a discretionary fiscal policy action. An increase in government expenditure or a tax cut increases aggregate expenditure by ΔE. If this were the only change in spending plans, the *AD* curve would become $AD_0 + \Delta E$ in Fig. 30.9. But the fiscal policy action sets off a multiplier process, which increases consumption expenditure. As the multiplier process plays out, aggregate demand increases further and the *AD* curve shifts rightward to AD_1.

With no change in the price level, the economy would move from point *A* to point *B* on AD_1. But the increase in aggregate demand combined with the upward-sloping *SAS* curve brings a rise in the price level. The economy moves to point *C*, and the economy returns to full employment.

Figure 30.10 illustrates the opposite case in which discretionary fiscal policy is used to eliminate inflationary pressure. The government decreases its expenditure on goods and services or raises taxes to

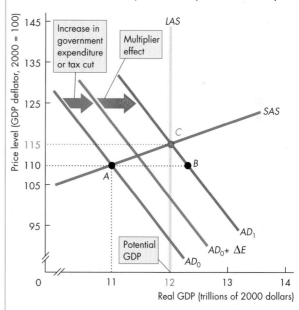

FIGURE 30.9   Expansionary Fiscal Policy

Potential GDP is $12 trillion, real GDP is $11 trillion, and there is a $1 trillion recessionary gap. An increase in government expenditure or a tax cut increases expenditure by ΔE. The multiplier increases induced expenditure. The *AD* curve shifts rightward to AD_1, the price level rises to 115, real GDP increases to $12 trillion, and the recessionary gap is eliminated.

decrease aggregate demand. In the figure, the fiscal policy action decreases aggregate expenditure by ΔE and the *AD* curve shifts to $AD_0 - \Delta E$. The initial decrease in aggregate expenditure sets off a multiplier process, which decreases consumption expenditure. The multiplier process decreases aggregate demand further and the *AD* curve shifts leftward to AD_1.

With no change in the price level, the economy would move from point *A* to point *B* on AD_1 in Fig. 30.10. But the decrease in aggregate demand combined with the upward-sloping *SAS* curve brings a fall in the price level. So the economy moves to point *C*, where the inflationary gap has been eliminated, inflation has been avoided, and the economy is back at full employment.

Figures 30.9 and 30.10 make fiscal policy look easy: Calculate the recessionary gap or the inflationary gap and the multiplier, change government expenditure or taxes, and eliminate the gap. In reality, things are not that easy.

FIGURE 30.10 Contractionary Fiscal Policy

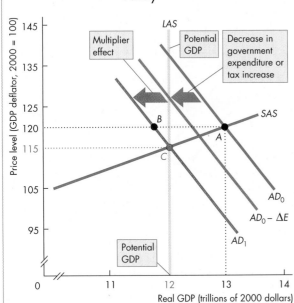

Potential GDP is $12 trillion, real GDP is $13 trillion, and there is a $1 trillion inflationary gap. A decrease in government expenditure or a rise in taxes decreases expenditure by ΔE. The multiplier decreases induced expenditure. The *AD* curve shifts leftward to AD_1, the price level falls to 115, real GDP decreases to $12 trillion, and the inflationary gap is eliminated.

myeconlab animation

Limitations of Discretionary Fiscal Policy

The use of discretionary fiscal policy is seriously hampered by three time lags:

- Recognition lag
- Law-making lag
- Impact lag

Recognition Lag The *recognition lag* is the time it takes to figure out that fiscal policy actions are needed. This process has two aspects: assessing the current state of the economy and forecasting its future state.

Law-Making Lag The *law-making lag* is the time it takes Congress to pass the laws needed to change taxes or spending. This process takes time because each member of Congress has a different idea about what is the best tax or spending program to change, so long debates and committee meetings are needed to reconcile conflicting views. The economy might benefit from fiscal stimulation today, but by the time Congress acts, a different fiscal medicine is needed.

Impact Lag The *impact lag* is the time it takes from passing a tax or spending change to its effects on real GDP being felt. This lag depends partly on the speed with which government agencies can act and partly on the timing of changes in spending plans by households and businesses.

Economic forecasting has improved in recent years, but it remains inexact and subject to error. So because of these three time lags, discretionary fiscal action might end up moving real GDP *away* from potential GDP and creating the problem it seeks to correct.

Let's now look at automatic fiscal policy.

Automatic Stabilizers

Automatic fiscal policy is a consequence of tax revenues and outlays that fluctuate with real GDP. These features of fiscal policy are called **automatic stabilizers** because they work to stabilize real GDP without explicit action by the government. Their name is borrowed from engineering and conjures up images of shock absorbers, thermostats, and sophisticated devices that keep airplanes and ships steady in turbulent air and seas.

The 2008 Fiscal Stimulus Package
Congress Aims to Close the Output Gap

As recession fears grew in the wake of the sub-prime mortgage crisis, Congress passed the *Economic Stimulus Act of 2008*. This act of *discretionary fiscal policy* was designed to increase aggregate demand and close a recessionary gap.

Tax rebates were the key component of the package and their effect on aggregate demand depends on the extent to which they are spent and saved.

The last time the federal government boosted aggregate demand with a tax rebate was in 2001 and a statistical investigation of the effects estimated that 70 percent of the rebates were spent within six months of being received.

The rebates in the 2008 fiscal package were targeted predominantly at low-income individuals and families, so the experience of 2001 would be likely to apply: Most of the rebates would be spent.

The cost of the package in 2008 was about $160 billion, so aggregate demand would be expected to increase by close to this amount and then by a multiplier as the initial spending became someone else's income and so boosted their spending.

The figure illustrates the effects of the package. Before the rebates, aggregate demand was AD_0 and real GDP was $11.7 trillion. The rebates increased aggregate demand to $AD_0 + \Delta E$, and a multiplier increased it to AD_1. Real GDP and the price level increased and the recessionary gap narrowed.

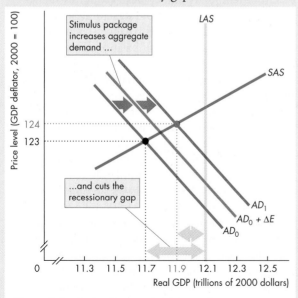

Effects of Fiscal Stimulus Act of 2008

Induced Taxes On the revenues side of the budget, tax laws define tax *rates*, not tax *dollars*. Tax dollars paid depend on tax rates and incomes. But incomes vary with real GDP, so tax revenues depend on real GDP. Taxes that vary with real GDP are called **induced taxes**. When real GDP increases in an expansion, wages and profits rise, so the taxes on these incomes—induced taxes—rise. When real GDP decreases in a recession, wages and profits fall, so the induced taxes on these incomes fall.

Needs-Tested Spending On the outlays side of the budget, the government creates programs that pay benefits to suitably qualified people and businesses. The spending on such programs is called **needs-tested spending**, and it results in transfer payments that depend on the economic state of individual citizens and businesses. When the economy is in a recession, unemployment is high and the number of people experiencing economic hardship increases, and needs-tested spending on unemployment benefits and food stamps also increases. When the economy expands, unemployment falls, the number of people experiencing economic hardship decreases, and needs-tested spending decreases.

Induced taxes and needs-tested spending decrease the multiplier effects of changes in autonomous expenditure (such as investment and exports). So they moderate both expansions and recessions and make real GDP more stable. They achieve this outcome by weakening the link between real GDP and disposable income and so reduce the effect of a change in real GDP on consumption expenditure. When real GDP increases, induced taxes increase and needs-tested spending decreases, so disposable income does not increase by as much as the increase in real GDP. As a result, consumption expenditure does not increase by as much as it otherwise would and the multiplier effect is reduced.

We can see the effects of automatic stabilizers by looking at the way in which the government budget deficit fluctuates over the business cycle.

Budget Deficit Over the Business Cycle Figure 30.11 shows the business cycle in part (a) and fluctuations in the budget deficit in part (b) between 1998 and 2008. Both parts highlight recessions by shading those periods. By comparing the two parts of the figure, you can see the relationship between the business cycle and the budget deficit. When the economy is in

FIGURE 30.11   The Business Cycle and the Budget Deficit

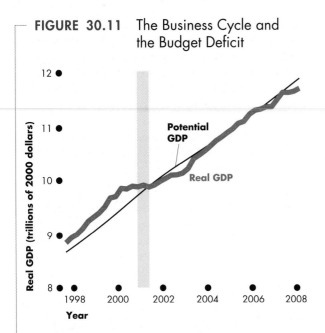

(a) Growth and recessions

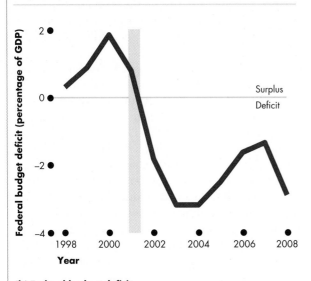

(b) Federal budget deficit

As real GDP fluctuates around potential GDP (part a), the budget deficit fluctuates (part b). During a recession (shaded years), tax revenues decrease, transfer payments increase, and the budget deficit increases. The deficit also increases before a recession as real GDP growth slows and after a recession before real GDP growth speeds up.

Sources of data: Bureau of Economic Analysis, Congressional Budget Office, and Office of Management and Budget.

myeconlab animation

an expansion, the budget deficit declines. (In the figure, a declining deficit means a deficit that is getting closer to zero.) As the expansion slows before the recession begins, the budget deficit increases. It continues to increase during the recession and for a period after the recession is over. Then, when the expansion is well under way, the budget deficit declines again.

The budget deficit fluctuates with the business cycle because both tax revenues and outlays fluctuate with real GDP. As real GDP increases during an expansion, tax revenues increase and transfer payments decrease, so the budget deficit automatically decreases. As real GDP decreases during a recession, tax revenues decrease and transfer payments increase, so the budget deficit automatically increases. Fluctuations in investment and exports have a multiplier effect on real GDP. But fluctuations in the budget deficit decrease the swings in disposable income and make the multiplier effect smaller. They dampen both expansions and recessions.

Cyclical and Structural Balances Because the government budget balance fluctuates with the business cycle, we need a method of measuring the balance that tells us whether it is a temporary cyclical phenomenon or a persistent phenomenon. A temporary cyclical surplus or deficit vanishes when full employment returns. A persistent surplus or deficit requires government action to remove it.

To determine whether the budget balance is persistent or temporary and cyclical, economists have developed the concepts of the structural budget balance and the cyclical budget balance. The **structural surplus or deficit** is the budget balance that would occur if the economy were at full employment and real GDP were equal to potential GDP. The **cyclical surplus or deficit** is the actual surplus or deficit minus the structural surplus or deficit. That is, the cyclical surplus or deficit is the part of the budget balance that arises purely because real GDP does not equal potential GDP. For example, suppose that the budget deficit is $100 billion, and that economists have determined that there is a structural deficit of $25 billion. In that case, there is a cyclical deficit of $75 billion.

Figure 30.12 illustrates the concepts of the cyclical surplus or deficit and the structural surplus or deficit. The blue curve shows government outlays. The outlays curve slopes downward because transfer payments, a component of government outlays, decreases as real GDP increases. The green curve

FIGURE 30.12   Cyclical and Structural Surpluses and Deficits

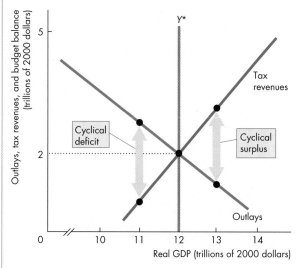

(a) Cyclical deficit and cyclical surplus

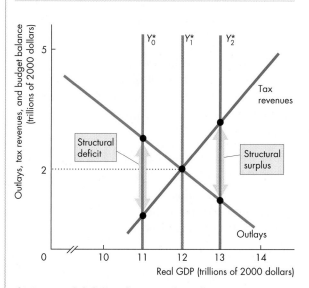

(b) Structural deficit and structural surplus

In part (a), potential GDP is $12 trillion. When real GDP is less than potential GDP, the budget is in a *cyclical deficit*. When real GDP exceeds potential GDP, the budget is in a *cyclical surplus*. The government has a *balanced budget* when real GDP equals potential GDP. In part (b), if real GDP and potential GDP are $11 trillion, there is a *structural deficit*. But if real GDP and potential GDP are $13 trillion, there is a *structural surplus*.

myeconlab   animation

shows tax revenues. The tax revenues curve slopes upward because most components of tax revenues increase as incomes and real GDP increase.

In Fig. 30.12(a), potential GDP is $12 trillion. If real GDP equals potential GDP, the government has a *balanced budget*. Outlays and tax revenues each equal $2 trillion. If real GDP is less than potential GDP, outlays exceed tax revenues and there is a *cyclical deficit*. If real GDP is greater than potential GDP, outlays are less than tax revenues and there is a *cyclical surplus*.

In Fig. 30.12(b), if both real GDP and potential GDP are $11 trillion ($Y^*_0$), the government has a budget deficit and it is a *structural deficit*. If both real GDP and potential GDP are $12 trillion ($Y^*_1$), the budget is balanced—a *structural balance* of zero. If both real GDP and potential GDP are $13 trillion ($Y^*_2$), the government has a budget surplus and it is a *structural surplus*.

The U.S. federal budget is a structural deficit and has been in that state since the early 1970s. The structural deficit decreased from 1992 to 2000 and was almost eliminated in 2000. But since 2000, the structural deficit has increased. The cyclical deficit is estimated to be small relative to the structural deficit.

The federal government faces some tough fiscal policy challenges.

Review Quiz

1 How can the federal government use fiscal policy to stabilize the business cycle?
2 Why is the government expenditure multiplier larger than the autonomous tax multiplier?
3 Why does a balanced budget increase in spending and taxes increase aggregate demand?
4 How do induced taxes and needs-tested spending programs work as automatic stabilizers to dampen the business cycle?
5 How do we tell whether a budget deficit needs government action to remove it?

myeconlab   Work Study Plan 30.4 and get instant feedback.

◆ You've seen how fiscal policy influences potential GDP, the growth rate of real GDP, and real GDP fluctuations. *Reading Between the Lines* on pp. 746–747 looks further at the fiscal policy actions proposed by President Obama.

Obama Fiscal Policy

"I'm going to confront this economic crisis," Obama says

http://www.cnn.com
November 7, 2008

Sen. Barack Obama spoke at his first news conference as president-elect Friday afternoon. The following is a transcript of the conference:

President-elect Barack Obama emphasized the economy in a news conference in Chicago, Illinois, on Friday.

Obama: Thank you very much, everybody. Thank you very much.

This morning, we woke up to more sobering news about the state of our economy. The 240,000 jobs lost in October marks the 10th consecutive month that our economy has shed jobs. In total, we've lost nearly 1.2 million jobs this year, and more than 10 million Americans are now unemployed. ...

First of all, we need a rescue plan for the middle class that invests in immediate efforts to create jobs and provide relief to families that are watching their paychecks shrink and their life savings disappear.

A particularly urgent priority is a further extension of unemployment insurance benefits for workers who cannot find work in the increasingly weak economy.

A fiscal stimulus plan that will jump-start economic growth is long overdue. I've talked about it throughout this—the last few months of the campaign. We should get it done.

Second, we have to address the spreading impact of the financial crisis on the other sectors of our economy: small businesses that are struggling to meet their payrolls and finance their holiday inventories; and state and municipal governments facing devastating budget cuts and tax increases. ...

Essence of the Story

- Barack Obama gave his first news conference as president-elect November 7, 2008.

- The economy lost 240,000 jobs in October and nearly 1.2 million jobs in 2008.

- More than 10 million Americans are unemployed.

- We need a rescue plan for the middle class that creates jobs and provides income to families.

- A further extension of unemployment insurance benefits is an urgent priority.

- A fiscal stimulus plan that will jump-start economic growth is overdue.

- Small businesses are struggling to meet payrolls.

- State and municipal governments are facing devastating budget cuts and tax increases.

Economic Analysis

- The transcript of president-elect Obama's first post-election news conference included a preview of the new president's fiscal policy priorities.

- Two urgent changes are described: (1) an extension of unemployment insurance benefits, and (2) a fiscal stimulus package.

- In November 2008, the economy had not yet entered the worst of the predicted recession of 2009, but the labor market was already showing serious weakness and real GDP had just begun to shrink.

- With no further policy action, most likely real GDP would shrink further during 2009 and an output gap of as much as $800 billion (more than 6 percent of potential GDP) would emerge.

- The new president wanted to avoid this bleak outcome.

- Figure 1 shows what might happen in the labor market with an extension of unemployment insurance benefits.

- Extended benefits increase the incentive to spend longer in job search looking for the best available job. The supply of labor decreases, the labor supply curve shifts leftward from LS_0 to LS_1. Equilibrium employment decreases.

- Figure 2 shows the effects of both an extension of unemployment insurance benefits and a fiscal stimulus package.

- The extension of unemployment benefits decreases aggregate supply and the SAS curve shifts leftward from SAS_0 to SAS_1.

- When people spend their increased unemployment benefits, aggregate demand increases. Also the other components of the fiscal stimulus package ($100 billion to $200 billion were the numbers considered) increase aggregate demand. The AD curve shifts rightward from AD_0 to AD_1.

- The demand-side effects are (most likely) more powerful than the supply-side effects, so real GDP increases (and the price level rises).

- But the change in real GDP that results from the two policy actions is small compared to the size of the output gap, so a large output gap remains through 2009.

- Either a larger fiscal stimulus package or an expansionary monetary policy (see Chapter 31) would be need-

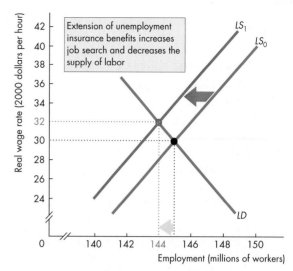

Figure 1 The labor market and unemployment insurance benefits

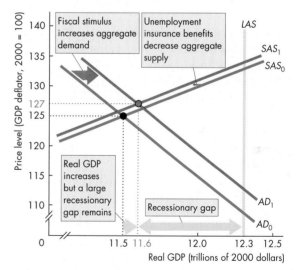

Figure 2 Aggregate supply and aggregate demand in 2009

ed to eliminate a recessionary gap of the size emerging in 2009.

- Greater fiscal stimulus (or monetary stimulus) risks putting upward pressure on the price level, so the inflation rate would likely rise.

SUMMARY

Key Points

The Federal Budget (pp. 728–733)

- The federal budget is used to achieve macroeconomic objectives.
- Tax revenues can exceed, equal, or fall short of outlays—the budget can be in surplus, balanced, or in deficit.
- Budget deficits create government debt.

Supply-Side Effects of Fiscal Policy
(pp. 734–737)

- Fiscal policy has supply-side effects because taxes weaken the incentive to work and decrease employment and potential GDP.
- The U.S. labor market tax wedge is large but it is small compared to those of other industrial countries.
- Fiscal policy has supply-side effects because taxes weaken the incentive to save and invest, which lowers the growth rate of real GDP.
- The Laffer curve shows the relationship between the tax rate and the amount of tax revenue collected.

Generational Effects of Fiscal Policy (pp. 738–740)

- Generational accounting measures the lifetime tax burden and benefits of each generation.
- A major 2003 study estimated the U.S. fiscal imbalance to be $45 trillion—4 times the value of one year's production.
- Future generations will pay for 57 percent of the benefits of the current generation.
- About half of U.S. government debt is held by the rest of the world.

Stabilizing the Business Cycle (pp. 740–745)

- Fiscal stabilization can be discretionary or automatic.
- Discretionary changes in government expenditure or taxes can change aggregate demand but are hampered by law-making lags and the difficulty of correctly diagnosing and forecasting the state of the economy.
- Automatic changes in fiscal policy moderate the business cycle.

Key Figures

Figure 30.5   The Effects of the Income Tax on Aggregate Supply, 734
Figure 30.6   The Effects of a Tax on Capital Income, 736

Figure 30.9   Expansionary Fiscal Policy, 741
Figure 30.10 Contractionary Fiscal Policy, 742

Key Terms

Automatic fiscal policy, 740
Automatic stabilizers, 742
Autonomous tax multiplier, 741
Balanced budget, 730
Balanced budget multiplier, 741
Budget deficit, 730
Budget surplus, 730
Council of Economic Advisers, 729

Cyclical surplus or deficit, 744
Discretionary fiscal policy, 740
Employment Act of 1946, 728
Federal budget, 728
Fiscal imbalance, 738
Fiscal policy, 728
Generational accounting, 738
Generational imbalance, 739
Government debt, 732

Government expenditure multiplier, 740
Induced taxes, 743
Laffer curve, 737
Needs-tested spending, 743
Present value, 738
Structural surplus or deficit, 744
Supply-side effects, 734
Tax wedge, 735

PROBLEMS and APPLICATIONS ◆

 Work problems 1–10 in Chapter 30 Study Plan and get instant feedback.
Work problems 11–20 as Homework, a Quiz, or a Test if assigned by your instructor.

1. The government is proposing to increase the tax rate on labor income and asks you to report on the supply-side effects of such an action. Answer the following questions using appropriate diagrams. You are being asked about directions of change, not exact magnitudes.
   a. What will happen to the supply of labor and why?
   b. What will happen to the demand for labor and why?
   c. How will the equilibrium level of employment change and why?
   d. How will the equilibrium before-tax wage rate change and why?
   e. How will the equilibrium after-tax wage rate change and why?
   f. What will happen to potential GDP?
   g. How would your answers to the above questions change if at the same time as raising the tax rate on labor income, the government cut the rate of sales tax to keep the amount of tax collected constant?
   h. What evidence would you present to the government to support the view that a lower tax on labor income will increase employment, potential GDP, and aggregate supply?

2. Suppose that in China, investment is $400 billion, saving is $400 billion, tax revenues are $500 billion, exports are $300 billion, and imports are $200 billion.
   a. Calculate government expenditure.
   b. What is the government budget balance?
   c. Is the government exerting a positive or negative impact on investment?
   d. What fiscal policy action might increase investment and speed economic growth? Explain how the policy action would work.

3. Suppose that instead of taxing nominal capital income, the government changed the tax code so that the inflation rate is subtracted from the interest rate before the taxable income from capital is calculated. Use appropriate diagrams to explain and illustrate the effect that this change would have on
   a. The tax rate on capital income.

   b. The supply of loanable funds.
   c. The demand for loanable funds.
   d. Investment and the real interest rate.

4. The economy is in a recession, and the recessionary gap is large.
   a. Describe the discretionary and automatic fiscal policy actions that might occur.
   b. Describe a discretionary fiscal stimulation package that could be used that would *not* bring a budget deficit.
   c. Explain the risks of discretionary fiscal policy in this situation.

5. The economy is in a recession, the recessionary gap is large, and there is a budget deficit.
   a. Do we know whether the budget deficit is structural or cyclical? Explain your answer.
   b. Do we know whether automatic stabilizers are increasing or decreasing aggregate demand? Explain your answer.
   c. If a discretionary increase in government expenditure occurs, what happens to the structural deficit or surplus? Explain.

6. **Comprehensive Tax Code Overhaul Is Overdue**

   Some right-wingers in Congress claim that … tax cuts pay for themselves. Despite their insistence, there is ample evidence and general expert agreement that they do not. …
   Washington Post, April 24, 2006
   a. Explain what is meant by tax cuts paying for themselves. What does this statement imply about the tax multiplier?
   b. Why would tax cuts not pay for themselves?

7. **How the Next President Should Fix the Economy**

   The message many Republicans took from Reagan's successes of the early 1980s, and still preach today, is that tax cuts pay for themselves. That's nonsense—Reagan's rate cuts for the rich may have paid for themselves, but the 1981 tax package as a whole (which included cuts for the poor, the middle class and corporations) clearly did not. The real lesson of the 1980s was that the U.S. can get away with running far bigger deficits than anyone thought possible while still enjoying strong growth and low inflation ... but it can't go on forever. There comes a point at which government debts grow so large that they start to weigh down on the economy, through higher interest rates, bigger debt payments, a weaker currency, etc.

Time, May 26, 2008

a. Explain under what circumstances it is possible that "tax cuts pay for themselves" and draw a Laffer curve to illustrate this outcome.
b. Explain why Reagan's tax rate cuts for high-income taxpayers may have paid for themselves, but cuts for lower-income and middle-income taxpayers did not.
c. Explain the negative consequences of running persistently large budget deficits.

8. **Stimulus Debate Turns on Rebates**

As pressure builds on Washington to juice the economy, a one-time consumer rebate has emerged as the likely centerpiece of a $150 billion stimulus program. ... But ... Democrats and Republicans still disagree on who should actually get rebates. Bush has said he wants rebates for those who pay income taxes. ... Democrats contend such an approach would mean tens of millions of households would get only a partial rebate or none at all. ... Proponents of the rebate-for-all assert that more of lower- and middle-income households should be included in any rebate plan because they are more likely to spend a bigger chunk of their rebate than are higher-income households ... and targeted to people most likely to spend it quickly, every dollar spent on stimulus could generate a dollar in gross domestic product.

CNN, January 22, 2008

a. Explain the intended effect of the $150 billion fiscal stimulus package and draw a graph to illustrate the effect.
b. Explain why the effect of this fiscal policy depends on who receives the tax rebates.
c. What would have a larger effect on aggregate demand: $150 billion worth of tax rebates or $150 billion worth of government spending?
d. Explain whether a stimulus package centered around a one-time consumer tax rebate is likely to have a small or a large supply-side effect.

9. **What Obama Means for Business**

The core of Obama's economic plan is (a) more government spending: $65 billion a year for universal health insurance, $15 billion a year on alternative energy, $20 billion to help homeowners avoid default, $60 billion to bolster the nation's infrastructure, $10 billion annually to give students college tuition in exchange for public service, and on and on; and (b) shifting the tax burden upward: ending the Bush tax cuts on families making more than $250,000 and raising payroll taxes on those same higher-income earners. ... Middle-class earners would receive tax cuts, and low-income seniors would pay no income tax. ... Obama also wants to raise a range of other taxes on business and investment. He would increase the 15 percent capital gains tax rate—probably to 25 percent, according to advisors. ... He would raise the dividends tax, reinstate a 45 percent tax on estates worth more than $3.5 million, and close $1.3 trillion in "corporate tax loopholes."

Fortune, June 23, 2008

a. Explain the potential supply-side effects of the various components of Obama's economic plan. How might these policies change potential GDP and its growth rate?
b. What would be the impact on aggregate demand of a same-sized increase in taxes and government expenditure?

10. **2008 U.S. Budget Deficit Bleeding Red Ink**

The Bush administration sent its final budget request to Congress last week, projecting that the deficit for all of 2008 will total $410 billion. ... For 2007, the budget deficit totaled $162 billion. ... [T]he slowing economy is expected to stunt the growth of tax revenues while the $168 billion economic stimulus plan passed by Congress last week will swell the deficit. It is hoped the stimulus plan will keep the economy out of a recession or at least make the downturn milder and shorter than it otherwise would have been. ...

CBS News, February 12, 2008

a. Explain why the business cycle increased the federal budget deficit in 2008.
b. Explain how the fiscal stimulus package might lead to a smaller budget deficit.

11. Suppose that in the United States, investment is $1,600 billion, saving is $1,400 billion, government expenditure on goods and services is $1,500 billion, exports are $2,000 billion, and imports are $2,500 billion.
    a. What is the amount of tax revenue?
    b. What is the government budget balance?
    c. Is the government exerting a positive or negative impact on investment?
    d. What fiscal policy action might increase investment and speed economic growth? Explain how the policy action would work.

12. Suppose that capital income taxes are based (as they are in the United States and most countries) on nominal interest rates. And suppose that the inflation rate increases by 5 percent. Use appropriate diagrams to explain and illustrate the effect that this change would have on
    a. The tax rate on capital income.
    b. The supply of loanable funds.
    c. The demand for loanable funds.
    d. Equilibrium investment.
    e. The equilibrium real interest rate.

13. The economy is in a boom and the inflationary gap is large.
    a. Describe the discretionary and automatic fiscal policy actions that might occur.
    b. Describe a discretionary fiscal restraint package that could be used that would not produce serious negative supply-side effects.
    c. Explain the risks of discretionary fiscal policy in this situation.

14. The economy is in a boom, the inflationary gap is large, and there is a budget deficit.
    a. Do we know whether the budget deficit is structural or cyclical? Explain your answer.
    b. Do we know whether automatic stabilizers are increasing or decreasing aggregate demand? Explain your answer.
    c. If a discretionary decrease in government expenditure occurs, what happens to the structural balance? Explain your answer.

15. **Juicing the Economy Will Come at a Cost**
    Within weeks, lawmakers hope to pass a package of measures intended to minimize the effects of a recession. ... President Bush and leading Democrats have indicated they envisioned stimulus measures—cash rebates, business breaks and other proposals—worth roughly $150 billion. ... Even if the stimulus package proves wildly suc-

cessful, however, it won't pay for itself in full, at least not in the near term. The Congressional Budget Office estimated Wednesday that the federal budget deficit this year will increase to $219 billion or 1.5 percent of gross domestic product. ... And that doesn't count the cost of a stimulus plan. Stimulus will bump that deficit up, but not necessarily dollar for dollar. Here's why: If the stimulus effort works, the increased economic activity will generate federal tax revenue. ... Some lawmakers want the cost of any stimulus measures to be offset by other revenue-raising steps, such as raising taxes. But proponents of the stimulus package note that it would defeat the purpose to spend money to stimulate the economy and at the same time replace it. ... Of course, there's another way to view cost in the stimulus debate: How much will it cost the country if the economy continues to slide and Congress takes no action? ... What's not clear is the cost to the economy if a stimulus package comes too late—a real concern since legislation could get bogged down by politics.

CNN, January 23, 2008

    a. Explain the intended effect of this fiscal stimulus package and draw a graph to illustrate it.
    b. Why might the stimulus package come "too late?" What are the potential consequences of the stimulus package coming "too late?"
    c. Explain why $150 billion of tax cuts won't increase the budget deficit by $150 billion.
    d. Explain why the government doesn't just raise taxes to cover the cost of the stimulus package so that it does not add to the budget deficit.
    e. Will the total budget deficit for 2008 be only the result of a structural deficit, a cyclical deficit, or a combination of the two? Explain.

16. **Hair of the Dog**
    Here we are, plunging into a recession. The proximate cause is irresponsible mortgage loans made to people who can't pay the money back. The deeper cause is, at least in part, years of too much borrowing and spending by Americans, both as individuals and collectively through the government. ... Although quibbling over the details, everyone—Republicans and Democrats, the White House and Congress, all the presidential candidates—agrees that what we need is a "fiscal stimulus." In other words, the government should go out and borrow even more money and

pass it around for us to spend. The experts caution that for maximum stimulus effect, we must be sure to spend it immediately. No squirreling it away for a rainy day. In drinking circles, they call this hair of the dog: to cure a hangover, you have another drink. … My gripe is that telling Americans they need to borrow and spend just a little bit more to get us past this recession—and then reform their ways—is like telling an alcoholic he needs one more drink before sobering up. I think we should sober up first. …

Time, January 24, 2008

a. Explain the argument made that "too much borrowing" by individuals and the federal government can contribute to a recession.

b. Why does effective fiscal stimulus require less saving (or even dissaving) by both the government and households?

c. How does fiscal stimulus reflect the "hair of the dog" mentality?

17. **Obama: Give Economy $50 Billion Boost**

Barack Obama said Monday that lawmakers should inject another $50 billion immediately into the sluggish U.S. economy. … "Such relief can't wait until the next president takes office." … He said that he supports the expansion and extension of unemployment benefits. … One bill, expected to go to the House floor for consideration this week, calls for an additional 13 weeks of benefits to be added to what is typically a 26-week cap on federal payments. In addition, it calls for 13 weeks on top of that for workers in states with very high unemployment rates. … Obama in his speech criticized his Republican rival, John McCain, for proposing to extend all of President Bush's 2001 and 2003 tax cuts. …

CNN, June 9, 2008

a. Explain the potential demand-side effect of extending unemployment benefits.

b. Explain the potential supply-side effect of extending unemployment benefits.

c. Draw a graph to illustrate the combined demand-side and supply-side effect of extending unemployment benefits.

d. Compare the supply-side effect of Obama's proposal to extend unemployment benefits with McCain's policy to extend Bush's 2001 and 2003 tax cuts.

18. **The Evolution of John McCain**

McCain wants to make the Bush tax cuts permanent; then he wants to keep going. He would repeal the alternative minimum tax, slash the corporate tax, double the child-care tax credit, and … allow businesses to write off the full cost of capital investments in one year. It'll be expensive … but McCain insists that he can balance the budget in four years with promised savings from running a tighter ship and increased tax revenues as the economy expands. … [H]e's in favor of tax cuts … because he'll insist on linking them to spending cuts.

Fortune, July 7, 2008

a. Explain the potential supply-side effects of the various components of McCain's economic plan.

b. Explain McCain's argument that a balanced budget is possible within four years, even with tax cuts.

19. **U.S. Budget Deficit Will Climb to $250 Billion as Economy Weakens**

The U.S. deficit for the current budget year will jump to about $250 billion … as a weaker economy and lower corporate profits weigh on the government's fiscal ledger.

International Herald Tribune, January 23, 2008

a. How did the business cycle influence the U.S. federal budget in 2008?

b. Explain why the federal budget deficit was larger in 2008 than in 2007.

c. How did automatic stabilizers influence the budget deficit in 2008? Did they change the structural deficit?

20. Study *Reading Between the Lines* on pp. 746–747.

a. Describe the key proposals to help middle income families and boost the economy outlined by president-elect Obama in November 2008.

b. Explain why extending unemployment insurance benefits has both a supply-side and demand-side effect on real GDP and the price level.

c. Going forward in 2009 and 2010, do you think the federal budget should be brought back into balance or do you think a large and perhaps even larger deficit should be maintained? Explain and illustrate your answer.

31 ◆ Monetary Policy

After studying this chapter, you will be able to:

- Describe the objectives of U.S. monetary policy and the framework for setting and achieving them

- Explain how the Federal Reserve makes its interest rate decision and achieves its interest rate target

- Explain the transmission channels through which the Federal Reserve influences the inflation rate

- Explain and compare alternative monetary policy strategies

At eight regularly scheduled meetings a year, and in an emergency between regular meetings, the Federal Reserve decides whether to change its interest rate target. And every business day, the Federal Reserve Bank of New York operates in financial markets to implement the Fed's decision and ensure that its target interest rate is achieved. Financial market traders, economic journalists, and pundits watch the economy for clues about what the Fed will decide at its next meeting.

How does the Fed make its interest rate decision? What exactly does the New York Fed do every day to keep the interest rate where it wants it? And how do the Fed's interest rate changes influence the economy? Can the Fed speed up economic growth and lower unemployment by lowering the interest rate and keep inflation in check by raising the interest rate?

The Fed's monetary policy strategy isn't the only one that might be used. Is the Fed's current monetary policy strategy the

best one? What are the benefits and what are the risks associated with the alternative monetary policy strategies?

What special measures can the Fed take in a financial crisis like the one that engulfed the U.S. and global economies in 2008?

You learned about the functions of the Fed and its long-run effects on the price level and inflation rate in Chapter 25. In this chapter, you will learn about the Fed's monetary policy in both the long run and the short run. You will learn how the Fed influences the interest rate and how the interest rate influences the economy. You will also review the alternative ways in which monetary policy might be conducted. In *Reading Between the Lines* at the end of the chapter, you will see the Fed in an aggressive move against recession and deflation in 2008 and 2009.

Monetary Policy Objectives and Framework

A nation's monetary policy objectives and the framework for setting and achieving those objectives stem from the relationship between the central bank and the government.

We'll describe the objectives of U.S. monetary policy and the framework and assignment of responsibility for achieving those objectives.

Monetary Policy Objectives

The objectives of monetary policy are ultimately political. The objectives of U.S. monetary policy are set out in the mandate of the Board of Governors of the Federal Reserve System, which is defined by the Federal Reserve Act of 1913 and its subsequent amendments.

Federal Reserve Act The Fed's mandate was most recently clarified in amendments to the Federal Reserve Act passed by Congress in 2000. The 2000 law states that mandate in the following words:

> The Board of Governors of the Federal Reserve System and the Federal Open Market Committee shall maintain long-run growth of the monetary and credit aggregates commensurate with the economy's long-run potential to increase production, so as to promote effectively the goals of maximum employment, stable prices, and moderate long-term interest rates.

Goals and Means This description of the Fed's monetary policy objectives has two distinct parts: a statement of the goals, or ultimate objectives, and a prescription of the means by which the Fed should pursue its goals.

Goals of Monetary Policy The goals are "maximum employment, stable prices, and moderate long-term interest rates." In the long run, these goals are in harmony and reinforce each other. But in the short run, these goals might come into conflict. Let's examine these goals a bit more closely.

Achieving the goal of "maximum employment" means attaining the maximum sustainable growth rate of potential GDP and keeping real GDP close to potential GDP. It also means keeping the unemployment rate close to the natural unemployment rate.

Achieving the goal of "stable prices" means keeping the inflation rate low (and perhaps close to zero).

Achieving the goal of "moderate long-term interest rates" means keeping long-term *nominal* interest rates close to (or even equal to) long-term *real* interest rates.

Price stability is the key goal. It is the source of maximum employment and moderate long-term interest rates. Price stability provides the best available environment for households and firms to make the saving and investment decisions that bring economic growth. So price stability encourages the maximum sustainable growth rate of potential GDP.

Price stability delivers moderate long-term interest rates because the nominal interest rate reflects the inflation rate. The nominal interest rate equals the real interest rate plus the inflation rate. With stable prices, the nominal interest rate is close to the real interest rate, and most of the time, this rate is likely to be moderate.

In the short run, the Fed faces a tradeoff between inflation and interest rates and between inflation and real GDP, employment, and unemployment. Taking an action that is designed to lower the inflation rate and achieve stable prices might mean raising interest rates, which lowers employment and real GDP and increases the unemployment rate in the short run.

Means for Achieving the Goals The 2000 law instructs the Fed to pursue its goals by "maintain[ing] long-run growth of the monetary and credit aggregates commensurate with the economy's long-run potential to increase production." You can perhaps recognize this statement as being consistent with the quantity theory of money that you studied in Chapter 25 (see pp. 604–605). The "economy's long-run potential to increase production" is the growth rate of potential GDP. The "monetary and credit aggregates" are the quantities of money and loans. By keeping the growth rate of the quantity of money in line with the growth rate of potential GDP, the Fed is expected to be able to maintain full employment and keep the price level stable.

To pursue the goals of monetary policy, the Fed must make the general concepts of price stability and maximum employment precise and operational.

Operational "Stable Prices" Goal

The Fed pays attention to two measures of inflation: the Consumer Price Index (CPI) and the personal consumption expenditure (PCE) deflator. But the *core PCE deflator,* which excludes food and fuel prices, is the Fed's operational guide and the Fed defines the rate of increase in the core PCE deflator as the **core inflation rate.**

The Fed focuses on the core inflation rate because it is less volatile than the total CPI inflation rate and the Fed believes that it provides a better indication of whether price stability is being achieved.

Figure 31.1 shows the core inflation rate alongside the total CPI inflation rate since 1992. You can see why the Fed says that the core rate is a better indicator. Its fluctuations are smoother and represent a sort of trend through the wider fluctuations in total CPI inflation.

The Fed has not defined price stability, but the Fed almost certainly doesn't regard price stability as meaning a core inflation rate equal to zero. Former Fed Chairman Alan Greenspan suggests that "price stability is best thought of as an environment in which inflation is so low and stable over time that it does not materially enter into the decisions of households and firms." He also believes that a "specific numerical inflation target would represent an unhelpful and false precision."[1]

Ben Bernanke, Alan Greenspan's successor, has been more precise and suggested that a core inflation rate of between 1 and 2 percent a year is the equivalent of price stability. This inflation range might be thought of as the Fed's comfort zone for the inflation rate.

Operational "Maximum Employment" Goal

The Fed regards stable prices (a core inflation rate of 1 to 2 percent a year) as the primary goal of monetary policy and as a means to achieving the other two goals. But the Fed also pays attention to the business cycle and tries to steer a steady course between inflation and recession. To gauge the state of output and employment relative to full employment, the Fed looks at a large number of indicators that include the labor force participation rate, the unemployment rate, measures of capacity utiliza-

FIGURE 31.1   Operational Price Stability Goal: Core Inflation

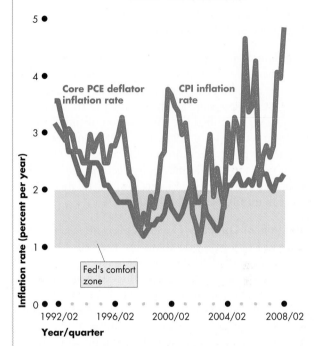

The CPI inflation rate fluctuates more than the core inflation rate. If a 1 to 2 percent core inflation rate is price stability, then the Fed achieved stable prices between 1996 and 2004. In all the other years, the inflation rate was above the level consistent with price stability.

Source of data: Bureau of Labor Statistics.

myeconlab animation

tion, activity in the housing market, the stock market, and regional information gathered by the regional Federal Reserve Banks. All these data are summarized in the Fed's *Beige Book.*

While the Fed considers a vast range of data, one number stands out as a summary of the overall state of aggregate demand relative to potential GDP. That number is the *output gap*—the percentage deviation of real GDP from potential GDP.

When the output gap is positive, it is an inflationary gap that brings an increase in the inflation rate. And when the output gap is negative, it is a recessionary gap that results in lost output and in employment being below its full-employment equilibrium level. So the Fed tries to minimize the output gap.

[1] Alan Greenspan, "Transparency in Monetary Policy," *Federal Reserve of St. Louis Review*, 84(4), 5–6, July/August 2002.

Responsibility for Monetary Policy

Who is responsible for monetary policy in the United States? What are the roles of the Fed, Congress, and the president?

The Role of the Fed The Federal Reserve Act makes the Board of Governors of the Federal Reserve System and the Federal Open Market Committee (FOMC) responsible for the conduct of monetary policy. We described the composition of the FOMC in Chapter 25 (see p. 594). The FOMC makes a monetary policy decision at eight scheduled meetings each year and communicates its decision with a brief explanation. Three weeks after an FOMC meeting, the full minutes are published.

The Role of Congress Congress plays no role in making monetary policy decisions but the Federal Reserve Act requires the Board of Governors to report on monetary policy to Congress. The Fed makes two reports each year, one in February and another in July. These reports and the Fed chairman's testimony before Congress along with the minutes of the FOMC communicate the Fed's thinking on monetary policy to lawmakers and the public.

The Role of the President The formal role of the president of the United States is limited to appointing the members and the chairman of the Board of Governors. But some presidents—Richard Nixon was one—have tried to influence Fed decisions.

You now know the objectives of monetary policy and can describe the framework and assignment of responsibility for achieving those objectives. Your next task is to see how the Federal Reserve conducts its monetary policy.

Review Quiz

1 What are the objectives of monetary policy?
2 Are the goals of monetary policy in harmony or in conflict (a) in the long run and (b) in the short run?
3 What is the core inflation rate and how does it differ from the overall CPI inflation rate?
4 Who is responsible for U.S. monetary policy?

 Work Study Plan 31.1 and get instant feedback.

◗ The Conduct of Monetary Policy

In this section, we describe the way in which the Federal Reserve conducts its monetary policy and we explain the Fed's monetary policy strategy. We evaluate the Fed's strategy in the final section of this chapter, where we describe and compare alternative monetary policy strategies.

Choosing a Policy Instrument

A **monetary policy instrument** is a variable that the Fed can directly control or closely target. As the sole issuer of the monetary base, the Fed is a monopoly. Like all monopolies, it can fix the quantity of its product and leave the market to determine the price; or it can fix the price of its product and leave the market to choose the quantity.

The first decision is whether to fix the price of U.S. money on the foreign exchange market—the exchange rate. A country that operates a fixed exchange rate cannot pursue an independent monetary policy. The United States has a flexible exchange rate and pursues an independent monetary policy. (Chapter 26 explains the foreign exchange market and the factors that influence the exchange rate.)

Even with a flexible exchange rate, the Fed still has a choice of policy instrument. It can decide to target the monetary base or a short-term interest rate. While the Fed can set either of these two variables, it cannot set both. The value of one is the consequence of the other. If the Fed decided to decrease the monetary base, the interest rate would rise. If the Fed decided to raise the interest rate, the monetary base would decrease. So the Fed must decide which of these two variables to target.

The Federal Funds Rate

The Fed's choice of monetary policy instrument, which is the same choice as that made by most other major central banks, is a short-term interest rate. Given this choice, the Fed permits the exchange rate and the quantity of money to find their own equilibrium values and has no preset views about what those values should be.

The interest rate that the Fed targets is the **federal funds rate**, which is the interest rate on overnight loans that banks make to each other.

Figure 31.2 shows the federal funds rate since 1992. You can see that the federal funds rate ranges between a high of 6.5 percent and a low of 1 percent. In 1992 and again in 2000, when the federal funds rate was high (6.5 percent), the Fed's actions were aimed at lowering the inflation rate.

Between 2002 and 2004 the federal funds rate was set at historically low levels. During these years, inflation was well anchored at close to 2 percent a year, and the Fed was less concerned about inflation than it was about recession. So the Fed set a low interest rate to limit the risk of recession.

Although the Fed can change the federal funds rate by any (reasonable) amount that it chooses, it normally changes the federal funds rate by only a quarter of a percentage point.[2]

FIGURE 31.2   The Federal Funds Rate

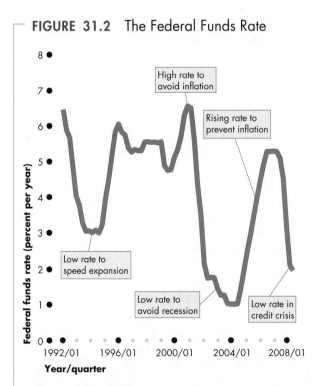

The Fed sets a target for the federal funds rate and then takes actions to keep the rate close to its target. When the Fed wants to slow inflation, it takes actions that raise the federal funds rate. When inflation is low and the Fed wants to avoid recession, it takes actions that lower the federal funds rate.

Source of data: Board of Governors of the Federal Reserve System.

myeconlab   animation

How does the Fed decide the appropriate level for the federal funds rate? And how, having made that decision, does the Fed move the federal funds rate to its target level? We'll now answer these two questions.

The Fed's Decision-Making Strategy

Two alternative decision-making strategies might be used. They are summarized by the terms:

- Instrument rule
- Targeting rule

Instrument Rule   An **instrument rule** is a decision rule for monetary policy that sets the policy instrument at a level that is based on the current state of the economy. The best-known instrument rule is the **Taylor rule**, in which the instrument is the federal funds rate and the rule is to make the federal funds rate respond by formula to the inflation rate and the output gap. (We compare the Fed's decisions with the Taylor rule on the next page.)

To implement the Taylor instrument rule, the FOMC would simply get the best estimates available of the current inflation rate and output gap and then mechanically calculate the level at which to set the federal funds rate.

Targeting Rule   A **targeting rule** is a decision rule for monetary policy that sets the policy instrument at a level that makes the forecast of the ultimate policy goal equal to its target. If the ultimate policy goal is a 2 percent inflation rate and the instrument is the federal funds rate, the targeting rule sets the federal funds rate at a level that makes the forecast of the inflation rate equal to 2 percent.

To implement such a targeting rule, the FOMC must gather and process a large amount of information about the economy, the way it responds to shocks, and the way it responds to policy. The FOMC must then process all these data and come to a judgment about the best level for the policy instrument.

The FOMC minutes suggest that the Fed follows a targeting rule strategy. But some economists think the interest rate settings decided by the FOMC are too responsive to the output gap and outlook for the real economy.

---

[2] A quarter of a percentage point is also called 25 *basis points*. A basis point is one hundredth of one percentage point.

Influences on the Federal Funds Rate
Does the Fed Overreact to Output Fluctuations?

Stanford economist John B. Taylor has suggested a rule for the federal funds that he says would perform better than the FOMC's historical performance.

The *Taylor rule* sets the federal funds rate (*FFR*) at the equilibrium real interest rate (which Taylor says is 2 percent a year) plus amounts based on the inflation rate (*INF*), and the output gap (*GAP*) according to the following formula (all the values are percentages):

$$FFR = 2 + INF + 0.5(INF - 2) + 0.5GAP$$

In words, the Taylor rule sets the federal funds rate at 2 percent plus the inflation rate plus one half of the deviation of inflation from its implicit target of 2 percent, plus one half of the output gap.

The figure shows how the Fed has deviated from the Taylor rule. Part (a) shows the extent to which the inflation rate has exceeded 2 percent a year—the extent to which the Fed has missed the goal of price stability. This variable had a downward trend through mid-1998 and then an upward trend.

Part (b) shows the output gap—the extent to which the Fed missed its maximum employment goal. This variable cycles.

Part (c) shows the federal funds rate (the green line labeled FOMC decision) alongside the federal funds rate that would have been set based on parts (a) and (b) if the Taylor rule had been followed (the blue line labeled Taylor rule).

You can see that the Fed moves the federal funds rate in the same general directions as the Taylor rule, but in swings that have much greater amplitude.

Between 1992 and 1994 and again between 2002 and 2006, the Fed set the federal funds rate at a lower level than what the Taylor rule would have achieved. Between 1994 and 2001 and again between 2007 and 2008, the Fed set the interest rate higher than what the Taylor rule would have set.

One reason for the Fed's deviation from the Taylor rule is that the Fed places a greater weight on achieving the goal of "maximum employment" and a lower weight on the inflation rate than the Taylor rule's equal weights. Notice the similarity in the cycles of the output gap in part (b) and the federal funds rate in part (c).

Another reason for the deviation is that the Fed uses more information than just the output gap and inflation rate. For example, after 9/11, the Fed low-

ered the federal funds rate to ensure that financial markets did not collapse during a period of increased political uncertainty and pessimism. But interestingly, the Taylor rule and the Fed's decision delivered the same level of the federal funds rate during the sub-prime credit crisis of 2008.

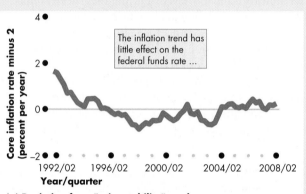

(a) Deviation from "price stability" goal

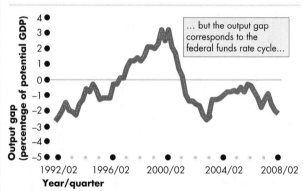

(b) Deviation from "maximum employment" goal

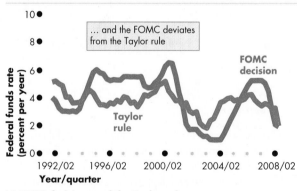

(c) FOMC decisions and the Taylor rule

Influences on the Federal Funds Rate

Sources of data: Board of Governors of the Federal Reserve System, Congressional Budget Office, and Bureau of Labor Statistics.

Hitting the Federal Funds Rate Target: Open Market Operations

Once an interest rate decision has been made, the Fed achieves its target by instructing the New York Fed to make *open market operations*—to purchase or sell government securities from or to a commercial bank or the public. When the Fed buys securities, it pays for them with newly created reserves held by banks. When the Fed sells securities, it is paid for them with reserves held by banks. So open market operations directly influence the reserves of banks.

An Open Market Purchase To see how an open market operation changes bank reserves, suppose the Fed buys $100 million of government securities from the Bank of America. When the Fed makes this transaction, two things happen:

1. The Bank of America has $100 million less securities, and the Fed has $100 million more securities.

2. The Fed pays for the securities by placing $100 million in the Bank of America's deposit account at the Fed.

Figure 31.3 shows the effects of these actions on

the balance sheets of the Fed and the Bank of America. Ownership of the securities passes from the Bank of America to the Fed, so the Bank of America's assets decrease by $100 million and the Fed's assets increase by $100 million, as shown by the blue arrow running from the Bank of America to the Fed.

The Fed pays for the securities by placing $100 million in the Bank of America's reserve account at the Fed, as shown by the green arrow running from the Fed to the Bank of America.

The Fed's assets and liabilities increase by $100 million. The Bank of America's total assets are unchanged: It sold securities to increase its reserves.

An Open Market Sale If the Fed *sells* $100 million of government securities in the open market:

1. The Bank of America has $100 million more securities, and the Fed has $100 million less securities.

2. The Bank of America pays for the securities by using $100 million of its reserves deposit account at the Fed.

Figure 31.4 shows the effects of these actions on the balance sheets of the Fed and the Bank of

FIGURE 31.3 The Fed Buys Securities in the Open Market

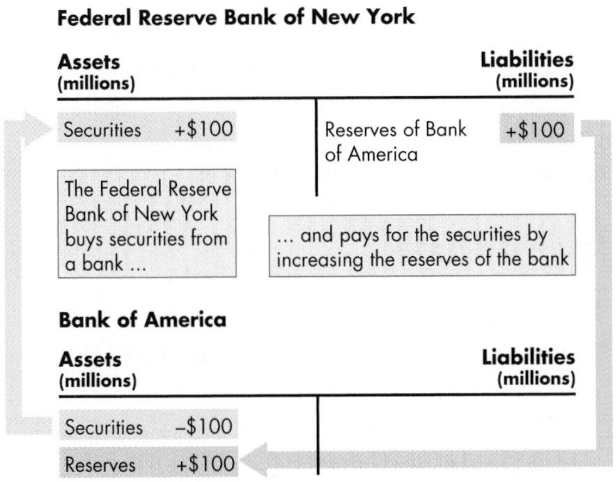

Federal Reserve Bank of New York

Assets (millions)	Liabilities (millions)
Securities +$100	Reserves of Bank of America +$100

The Federal Reserve Bank of New York buys securities from a bank ...

... and pays for the securities by increasing the reserves of the bank

Bank of America

Assets (millions)	Liabilities (millions)
Securities −$100	
Reserves +$100	

When the Fed buys securities in the open market, it creates bank reserves. Fed assets and liabilities increase, and the selling bank exchanges securities for reserves.

myeconlab animation

FIGURE 31.4 The Fed Sells Securities in the Open Market

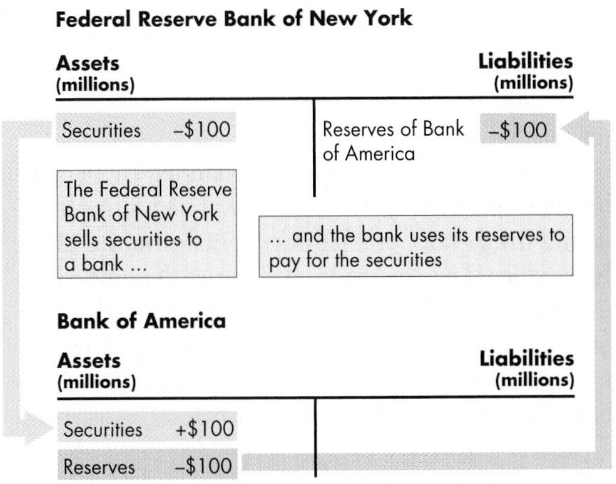

Federal Reserve Bank of New York

Assets (millions)	Liabilities (millions)
Securities −$100	Reserves of Bank of America −$100

The Federal Reserve Bank of New York sells securities to a bank ...

... and the bank uses its reserves to pay for the securities

Bank of America

Assets (millions)	Liabilities (millions)
Securities +$100	
Reserves −$100	

When the Fed sells securities in the open market, it reduces bank reserves. Fed assets and liabilities decrease, and the buying bank exchanges reserves for securities.

myeconlab animation

America. Ownership of the securities passes from the Fed to the Bank of America, so the Fed's assets decrease by $100 million and the Bank of America's assets increase by $100 million, as shown by the blue arrow running from the Fed to the Bank of America.

The Bank of America uses $100 million of its reserves to pay for the securities, as the green arrow running from the Bank of America to the Fed shows.

Both the Fed's assets and liabilities decrease by $100 million. The Bank of America's total assets are unchanged: It has used reserves to buy securities.

Equilibrium in the Market for Reserves

To see how an open market operation changes the federal funds rate, we must see what happens in the federal funds market—the market in which banks lend to and borrow from each other overnight—and in the market for bank reserves.

The higher the federal funds rate, the greater is the quantity of overnight loans supplied and the smaller is the quantity of overnight loans demanded in the federal funds market. The equilibrium federal funds rate balances the quantities demanded and supplied.

An equivalent way of looking at the forces that determine the federal funds rate is to consider the demand for and supply of bank reserves. Banks hold reserves to meet the required reserve ratio and so that they can make payments. But reserves are costly to hold. The alternative to holding reserves is to lend them in the federal funds market and earn the federal funds rate. The higher the federal funds rate, the higher is the opportunity cost of holding reserves and the greater is the incentive to economize on the quantity of reserves held.

So the quantity of reserves demanded by banks depends on the federal funds rate. The higher the federal funds rate, other things remaining the same, the smaller is the quantity of reserves demanded.

Figure 31.5 illustrates the market for bank reserves. The *x*-axis measures the quantity of reserves on deposit at the Fed, and the *y*-axis measures the federal funds rate. The demand for reserves is the curve labeled *RD*.

The Fed's open market operations determine the supply of reserves, which is shown by the supply curve *RS*. To decrease reserves, the Fed conducts an open market sale. To increase reserves, the Fed conducts an open market purchase.

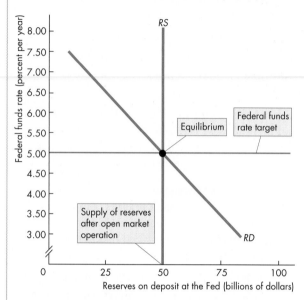

FIGURE 31.5   The Market for Reserves

The demand curve for reserves is *RD*. The quantity of reserves demanded decreases as the federal funds rate rises because the federal funds rate is the opportunity cost of holding reserves. The supply curve of reserves is *RS*. The Fed uses open market operations to make the quantity of reserves supplied equal the quantity of reserves demanded ($50 billion in this case) at the federal funds rate target (5 percent a year in this case).

 animation

Equilibrium in the market for bank reserves determines the federal funds rate where the quantity of reserves demanded by the banks equals the quantity of reserves supplied by the Fed. By using open market operations, the Fed adjusts the supply of reserves to keep the federal funds rate on target.

Review Quiz

1 What is the Fed's monetary policy instrument?
2 What are the main influences on the FOMC federal funds rate decision?
3 What happens when the Fed buys or sells securities in the open market?
4 How is the federal funds rate determined in the market for reserves?

myeconlab   Work Study Plan 31.2 and get instant feedback.

Monetary Policy Transmission

You've seen that the Fed's goal is to keep the price level stable (keep the inflation rate around 2 percent a year) and to achieve maximum employment (keep the output gap close to zero). And you've seen how the Fed can use its power to set the federal funds rate at its desired level. We're now going to trace the events that follow a change in the federal funds rate and see how those events lead to the ultimate policy goal. We'll begin with a quick overview of the transmission process and then look at each step a bit more closely.

Quick Overview

When the Fed lowers the federal funds rate, other short-term interest rates and the exchange rate also fall. The quantity of money and the supply of loanable funds increase. The long-term real interest rate falls. The lower real interest rate increases consumption expenditure and investment. And the lower exchange rate makes U.S. exports cheaper and imports more costly, so net exports increase. Easier bank loans reinforce the effect of lower interest rates on aggregate expenditure. Aggregate demand increases, which increases real GDP and the price level relative to what they would have been. Real GDP growth and inflation speed up.

When the Fed raises the federal funds rate, as the sequence of events that we've just reviewed plays out, the effects are in the opposite directions.

Figure 31.6 provides a schematic summary of these ripple effects for both a cut and a rise in the federal funds rate.

These ripple effects stretch out over a period of between one and two years. The interest rate and exchange rate effects are immediate. The effects on money and bank loans follow in a few weeks and run for a few months. Real long-term interest rates change quickly and often in anticipation of the short-term interest rate changes. Spending plans change and real GDP growth changes after about one year. The inflation rate changes between one year and two years after the change in the federal funds rate. But these time lags are not entirely predictable and can be longer or shorter.

We're going to look at each stage in the transmission process, starting with the interest rate effects.

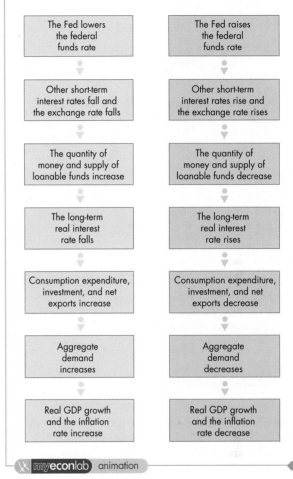

FIGURE 31.6 The Ripple Effects of a Change in the Federal Funds Rate

The Fed lowers the federal funds rate	The Fed raises the federal funds rate
Other short-term interest rates fall and the exchange rate falls	Other short-term interest rates rise and the exchange rate rises
The quantity of money and supply of loanable funds increase	The quantity of money and supply of loanable funds decrease
The long-term real interest rate falls	The long-term real interest rate rises
Consumption expenditure, investment, and net exports increase	Consumption expenditure, investment, and net exports decrease
Aggregate demand increases	Aggregate demand decreases
Real GDP growth and the inflation rate increase	Real GDP growth and the inflation rate decrease

myeconlab animation

Interest Rate Changes

The first effect of a monetary policy decision by the FOMC is a change in the federal funds rate. Other interest rates then change. These interest rate effects occur quickly and relatively predictably.

Figure 31.7 shows the fluctuations in three interest rates: the federal funds rate, the short-term bill rate, and the long-term bond rate.

Federal Funds Rate As soon as the FOMC announces a new setting for the federal funds rate, the New York Fed undertakes the necessary open market operations to hit the target. There is no doubt about where the interest rate changes shown in Fig. 31.7 are generated. They are driven by the Fed's monetary policy.

FIGURE 31.7   Three Interest Rates

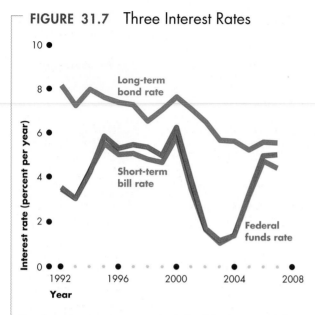

The short-term interest rates—the federal funds rate and the short-term bill rate—move closely together. The long-term bond rate is higher than the short-term rates, and it fluctuates less than the short-term rates.

Source of data: Board of Governors of the Federal Reserve System.

myeconlab animation

Short-Term Bill Rate The short-term bill rate is the interest rate paid by the U.S. government on 3-month Treasury bills. It is similar to the interest rate paid by U.S. businesses on short-term loans. Notice how closely the short-term bill rate follows the federal funds rate. The two rates are almost identical.

A powerful substitution effect keeps these two interest rates close. Commercial banks have a choice about how to hold their short-term liquid assets, and an overnight loan to another bank is a close substitute for short-term securities such as Treasury bills. If the interest rate on Treasury bills is higher than the federal funds rate, the quantity of overnight loans supplied decreases and the demand for Treasury bills increases. The price of Treasury bills rises and the interest rate falls.

Similarly, if the interest rate on Treasury bills is lower than the federal funds rate, the quantity of overnight loans supplied increases and the demand for Treasury bills decreases. The price of Treasury bills falls, and the interest rate rises.

When the interest rate on Treasury bills is close to the federal funds rate, there is no incentive for a bank to switch between making an overnight loan and buying Treasury bills. Both the Treasury bill market and the federal funds market are in equilibrium.

The Long-Term Bond Rate The long-term bond rate is the interest rate paid on bonds issued by large corporations. It is this interest rate that businesses pay on the loans that finance their purchase of new capital and that influences their investment decisions.

Two features of the long-term bond rate stand out: It is higher than the short-term rates, and it fluctuates less than the short-term rates.

The long-term interest rate is higher than the two short-term rates because long-term loans are riskier than short-term loans. To provide the incentive that brings forth a supply of long-term loans, lenders must be compensated for the additional risk. Without compensation for the additional risk, only short-term loans would be supplied.

The long-term interest rate fluctuates less than the short-term rates because it is influenced by expectations about future short-term interest rates as well as current short-term interest rates. The alternative to borrowing or lending long term is to borrow or lend using a sequence of short-term securities. If the long-term interest rate exceeds the expected average of future short-term interest rates, people will lend long term and borrow short term. The long-term interest rate will fall. And if the long-term interest rate is below the expected average of future short-term interest rates, people will borrow long term and lend short term. The long-term interest rate will rise.

These market forces keep the long-term interest rate close to the expected average of future short-term interest rates (plus a premium for the extra risk associated with long-term loans). The expected average future short-term interest rate fluctuates less than the current short-term interest rate.

Exchange Rate Fluctuations

The exchange rate responds to changes in the interest rate in the United States relative to the interest rates in other countries—*the U.S. interest rate differential*. We explain this influence in Chapter 26 (see p. 623).

When the Fed raises the federal funds rate, the U.S. interest rate differential rises and, other things remaining the same, the U.S. dollar appreciates, and when the Fed lowers the federal funds rate, the U.S. interest rate differential falls and, other things remaining the same, the U.S. dollar depreciates.

Many factors other than the U.S. interest rate differential influence the exchange rate, so when the Fed changes the federal funds rate, the exchange rate does not usually change in exactly the way it would with other things remaining the same. So while monetary policy influences the exchange rate, many other factors also make the exchange rate change.

Money and Bank Loans

The quantity of money and bank loans change when the Fed changes the federal funds rate target. A rise in the federal funds rate decreases the quantity of money and bank loans, and a fall in the federal funds rate increases the quantity of money and bank loans. These changes occur for two reasons: The quantity of deposits and loans created by the banking system changes and the quantity of money demanded changes.

You've seen that to change the federal funds rate, the Fed must change the quantity of bank reserves. A change in the quantity of bank reserves changes the monetary base, which in turn changes the quantity of deposits and loans that the banking system can create. A rise in the federal funds rate decreases reserves and decreases the quantity of deposits and bank loans created; and a fall in the federal funds rate increases reserves and increases the quantity of deposits and bank loans created.

The quantity of money created by the banking system must be held by households and firms. The change in the interest rate changes the quantity of money demanded. A fall in the interest rate increases the quantity of money demanded, and a rise in the interest rate decreases the quantity of money demanded.

A change in the quantity of money and the supply of bank loans directly affects consumption and investment plans. With more money and easier access to loans, consumers and firms spend more. With less money and loans harder to get, consumers and firms spend less.

The Long-Term Real Interest Rate

Demand and supply in the market for loanable funds determine the long-term *real interest rate*,

which equals the long-term *nominal* interest rate minus the expected inflation rate. The long-term real interest rate influences expenditure decisions.

In the long run, demand and supply in the loanable funds market depend only on real forces—on saving and investment decisions. But in the short run, when the price level is not fully flexible, the supply of loanable funds is influenced by the supply of bank loans. Changes in the federal funds rate change the supply of bank loans, which changes the supply of loanable funds and changes the interest rate in the loanable funds market.

A fall in the federal funds rate that increases the supply of bank loans increases the supply of loanable funds and lowers the equilibrium real interest rate. A rise in the federal funds rate that decreases the supply of bank loans decreases the supply of loanable funds and raises the equilibrium real interest rate.

These changes in the real interest rate, along with the other factors we've just described, change expenditure plans.

Expenditure Plans

The ripple effects that follow a change in the federal funds rate change three components of aggregate expenditure:

- Consumption expenditure
- Investment
- Net exports

Consumption Expenditure Other things remaining the same, the lower the real interest rate, the greater is the amount of consumption expenditure and the smaller is the amount of saving.

Investment Other things remaining the same, the lower the real interest rate, the greater is the amount of investment.

Net Exports Other things remaining the same, the lower the interest rate, the lower is the exchange rate and the greater are exports and the smaller are imports.

So eventually, a cut in the federal funds rate increases aggregate expenditure and a rise in the federal funds rate curtails aggregate expenditure. These changes in aggregate expenditure plans change aggregate demand, real GDP, and the price level.

The Change in Aggregate Demand, Real GDP, and the Price Level

The final link in the transmission chain is a change in aggregate demand and a resulting change in real GDP and the price level. By changing real GDP and the price level relative to what they would have been without a change in the federal funds rate, the Fed influences its ultimate goals: the inflation rate and the output gap.

The Fed Fights Recession

If inflation is low and real GDP is below potential GDP, the Fed takes actions that are designed to restore full employment. Figure 31.8 shows the effects of the Fed's actions, starting in the market for bank reserves and ending in the market for real GDP.

Market for Bank Reserves In Fig. 31.8(a), which shows the market for bank reserves, the FOMC lowers the target federal funds rate from 5 percent to 4

percent a year. To achieve the new target, the New York Fed buys securities and increases the supply of reserves of the banking system from RS_0 to RS_1.

Money Market With increased reserves, the banks create deposits by making loans and the supply of money increases. The short-term interest rate falls and the quantity of money demanded increases. In Fig. 31.8(b), the supply of money increases from MS_0 to MS_1, the interest rate falls from 5 percent to 4 percent a year and the quantity of money increases from $3 trillion to $3.1 trillion. The interest rate in the money market and the federal funds rate are kept close to each other by the powerful substitution effect described on p. 762.

Loanable Funds Market Banks create money by making loans. In the long run, an increase in the supply of bank loans is matched by a rise in the price level and the quantity of *real* loans is unchanged. But in the short run, with a sticky price level, an increase in the supply of bank loans increases the supply of (real) loanable funds.

FIGURE 31.8   The Fed Fights Recession

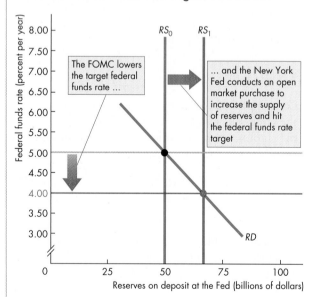

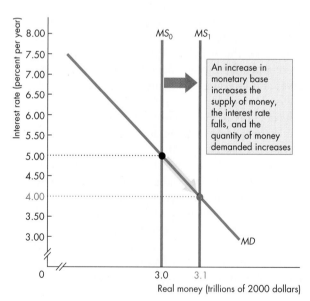

(a) The market for bank reserves

(b) Money market

In part (a), the FOMC lowers the federal funds rate target from 5 percent to 4 percent. The New York Fed buys securities in an open market operation and increases the supply of reserves from RS_0 to RS_1 to hit the new federal funds rate target.

In part (b), the supply of money increases from MS_0 to MS_1, the short-term interest rate falls, and the quantity of money demanded increases. The short-term interest rate and the federal funds rate change by similar amounts.

In Fig. 31.8(c), the supply of loanable funds curve shifts rightward from SLF_0 to SLF_1. With the demand for loanable funds at DLF, the real interest rate falls from 6 percent to 5.5 percent a year. (We're assuming a zero inflation rate so that the real interest rate equals the nominal interest rate.) The long-term interest rate changes by a smaller amount than the change in the short-term interest rate for the reason explained on p. 762.

The Market for Real GDP Figure 31.8(d) shows aggregate demand and aggregate supply—the demand for and supply of real GDP. Potential GDP is $12 trillion, where LAS is located. The short-run aggregate supply curve is SAS, and initially, the aggregate demand curve is AD_0. Real GDP is $11.8 trillion, which is less than potential GDP, so there is a recessionary gap. The Fed is reacting to this recessionary gap.

The increase in the supply of loans and the decrease in the real interest rate increase aggregate planned expenditure. (Not shown in the figure, a fall in the interest rate lowers the exchange rate, which increases net exports and aggregate planned expenditure.) The increase in aggregate expenditure, ΔE, increases aggregate demand and shifts the aggregate demand curve rightward to $AD_0 + \Delta E$. A multiplier process begins. The increase in expenditure increases income, which induces an increase in consumption expenditure. Aggregate demand increases further, and the aggregate demand curve eventually shifts rightward to AD_1.

The new equilibrium is at full employment. Real GDP is equal to potential GDP. The price level rises to 120 and then becomes stable at that level. So after a one-time adjustment, there is price stability.

In this example, we have given the Fed a perfect hit at achieving full employment and keeping the price level stable. It is unlikely that the Fed would be able to achieve the precision of this example. If the Fed stimulated demand by too little and too late, the economy would experience a recession. And if the Fed hit the gas pedal too hard, it would push the economy from recession to inflation.

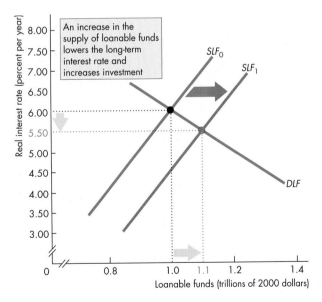

(c) The market for loanable funds

In part (c), an increase in the supply of bank loans increases the supply of loanable funds from SLF_0 to SLF_1 and the real interest rate falls. Investment increases.

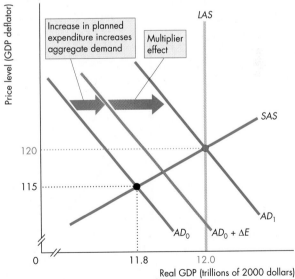

(d) Real GDP and the price level

In part (d), aggregate planned expenditure increases. The aggregate demand curve shifts to $AD_0 + \Delta E$ and eventually it shifts rightward to AD_1. Real GDP increases to potential GDP, and the price level rises.

The Fed Fights Inflation

If the inflation rate is too high and real GDP is above potential GDP, the Fed takes actions that are designed to lower the inflation rate and restore price stability. Figure 31.9 shows the effects of the Fed's actions starting in the market for reserves and ending in the market for real GDP.

Market for Bank Reserves In Fig. 31.9(a), which shows the market for bank reserves, the FOMC raises the target federal funds rate from 5 percent to 6 percent a year. To achieve the new target, the New York Fed sells securities and decreases the supply of reserves of the banking system from RS_0 to RS_1.

Money Market With decreased reserves, the banks shrink deposits by decreasing loans and the supply of money decreases. The short-term interest rate rises and the quantity of money demanded decreases. In Fig. 31.9(b), the supply of money decreases from MS_0 to MS_1, the interest rate rises from 5 percent to

6 percent a year and the quantity of money decreases from $3 trillion to $2.9 trillion.

Loanable Funds Market With a decrease in reserves, banks must decrease the supply of loans. The supply of (real) loanable funds decreases, and the supply of loanable funds curve shifts leftward in Fig. 31.9(c) from SLF_0 to SLF_1. With the demand for loanable funds at DLF, the real interest rate rises from 6 percent to 6.5 percent a year. (Again, we're assuming a zero inflation rate so that the real interest rate equals the nominal interest rate.)

The Market for Real GDP Figure 31.9(d) shows aggregate demand and aggregate supply in the market for real GDP. Potential GDP is $12 trillion where LAS is located. The short-run aggregate supply curve is SAS and initially the aggregate demand is AD_0. Now, real GDP is $12.2 trillion, which is greater than potential GDP, so there is an inflationary gap. The Fed is reacting to this inflationary gap.

FIGURE 31.9   The Fed Fights Inflation

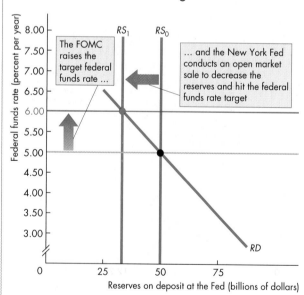

(a) The market for bank reserves

In part (a), the FOMC raises the federal funds rate from 5 percent to 6 percent. The New York Fed sells securities in an open market operation to decrease the supply of reserves from RS_0 to RS_1 and hit the new federal funds rate target.

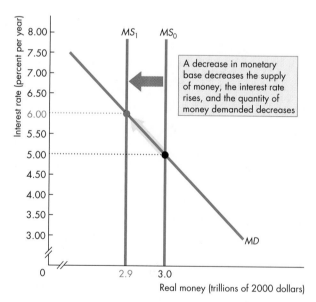

(b) Money market

In part (b), the supply of money decreases from MS_0 to MS_1, the short-term interest rate rises, and the quantity of money demanded decreases. The short-term interest rate and the federal funds rate change by similar amounts.

The increase in the short-term interest rate, the decrease in the supply of bank loans, and the increase in the real interest rate decrease aggregate planned expenditure. (Not shown in the figures, a rise in the interest rate raises the exchange rate, which decreases net exports and aggregate planned expenditure.)

The decrease in aggregate expenditure, ΔE, decreases aggregate demand and shifts the aggregate demand curve to $AD_0 - \Delta E$. A multiplier process begins. The decrease in expenditure decreases income, which induces a decrease in consumption expenditure. Aggregate demand decreases further, and the aggregate demand curve eventually shifts leftward to AD_1.

The economy returns to full employment. Real GDP is equal to potential GDP. The price level falls to 120 and then becomes stable at that level. So after a one-time adjustment, there is price stability.

Again, in this example, we have given the Fed a perfect hit at achieving full employment and keeping the price level stable. If the Fed decreased aggregate demand by too little and too late, the economy would have remained with an inflationary gap and the inflation rate would have moved above the rate that is consistent with price stability. And if the Fed hit the brakes too hard, it would push the economy from inflation to recession.

Loose Links and Long and Variable Lags

The ripple effects of monetary policy that we've just analyzed with the precision of an economic model are, in reality, very hard to predict and anticipate.

To achieve price stability and full employment, the Fed needs a combination of good judgment and good luck. Too large an interest rate cut in an underemployed economy can bring inflation, as it did during the 1970s. And too large an interest rate rise in an inflationary economy can create unemployment, as it did in 1981 and 1991. Loose links between the federal funds rate and the ultimate policy goals make unwanted outcomes inevitable and long and variable time lags add to the Fed's challenges.

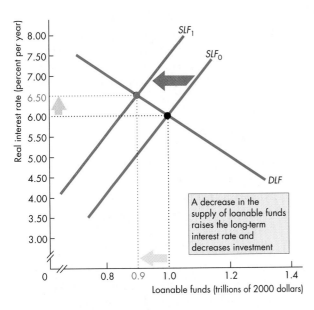

(c) The market for loanable funds

In part (c), a decrease in the supply of bank loans decreases the supply of loanable funds from SLF_0 to SLF_1 and the real interest rate rises. Investment decreases.

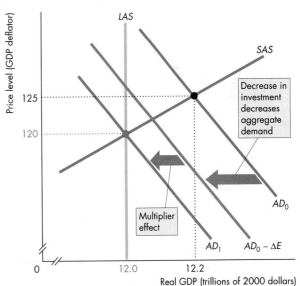

(d) Real GDP and the price level

In part (d), aggregate planned expenditure decreases. Aggregate demand decreases and the AD curve shifts leftward from AD_0 to AD_1. Real GDP decreases to potential GDP, and the price level falls.

A Reality Check
A View of the Long and Variable Lag

You've studied the theory of monetary policy. Does it really work in the way we've described? It does, and the figure opposite provides some evidence to support this claim.

The blue line in the figure is the federal funds rate that the Fed targets *minus* the long-term bond rate. (When the long-term bond rate exceeds the federal funds rate, this gap is negative.)

We can view the gap between the federal funds rate and the long-term bond rate as a measure of how hard the Fed is trying to steer a change in course.

When the Fed is more concerned about recession than inflation and is trying to stimulate real GDP growth, it cuts the federal funds rate target and the gap between the long-term bond rate and the federal funds rate widens.

When the Fed is more concerned about inflation than recession and is trying to restrain real GDP growth, it raises the federal funds rate target and the gap between the long-term bond rate and the federal funds rate narrows.

The red line in the figure is the real GDP growth rate *one year later*. You can see that when the FOMC raises the federal funds rate, the real GDP growth rate slows one year later. And when the Fed lowers the federal funds rate, the real GDP growth rate

speeds up one year later.

Not shown in the figure, the inflation rate increases and decreases corresponding to the fluctuations in the real GDP growth rate. But the effects on the inflation rate take even longer and are not as strong as the effects on the real GDP growth rate.

Interest Rates and Real GDP Growth

Sources of data: Interest rates, see Fig. 31.7; real GDP growth, Bureau of Economic Analysis.

Loose Link from Federal Funds Rate to Spending

The real long-term interest rate that influences spending plans is linked only loosely to the federal funds rate. Also, the response of the *real* long-term interest rate to a change in the nominal interest rate depends on how inflation expectations change. And the response of expenditure plans to changes in the real interest rate depend on many factors that make the response hard to predict.

Time Lags in the Adjustment Process The Fed is especially handicapped by the fact that the monetary policy transmission process is long and drawn out. Also, the economy does not always respond in exactly the same way to a policy change. Further, many factors other than policy are constantly changing and bringing new situations to which policy must respond.

Review Quiz

1 Describe the channels by which monetary policy ripples through the economy and explain why each channel operates.
2 Do interest rates fluctuate in response to the Fed's actions?
3 How do the Fed's actions change the exchange rate?
4 How do the Fed's actions influence real GDP and how long does it take for real GDP to respond to the Fed's policy changes?
5 How do the Fed's actions influence the inflation rate and how long does it take for inflation to respond to the Fed's policy changes?

 Work Study Plan 31.3 and get instant feedback.

Alternative Monetary Policy Strategies

So far in this chapter, we've described and analyzed the Fed's method of conducting monetary policy. But the Fed does have choices among alternative monetary policy strategies. We're going to end our discussion of monetary policy by examining the alternatives and explaining why the Fed has rejected them in favor of the interest rate strategy that we've described.

You've seen that we can summarize monetary policy strategies in two broad categories: *instrument rules* and *targeting rules*. And you've seen that the Fed uses a *targeting rule* strategy but one that comes close to being the same as the Taylor rule, an instrument rule for the federal funds rate. So the Fed has rejected a pure or simple instrument rule. It has also rejected some other possible instrument and targeting rules.

The Fed might have chosen any of four alternative monetary policy strategies: One of them is an instrument rule, and three are alternative targeting rules. The four alternatives are

- Monetary base instrument rule
- Money targeting rule
- Exchange rate targeting rule
- Inflation rate targeting rule

Monetary Base Instrument Rule

Although the Fed uses open market operations to hit its federal funds rate target, it could instead shoot for a target level of the monetary base.

The idea of using a rule to set the monetary base has been suggested by Carnegie-Mellon University economist Bennet T. McCallum, and a monetary base rule bears his name.

The **McCallum rule** makes the growth rate of the monetary base respond to the long-term average growth rate of real GDP and medium-term changes in the velocity of circulation of the monetary base.

The rule is based on the *quantity theory of money* (see Chapter 25, p. 604). McCallum's idea is to make the monetary base grow at a rate equal to the target inflation rate plus the long-term real GDP growth rate minus the medium-term growth rate of the velocity of circulation of the monetary base. This rule for the monetary base growth rate keeps the inflation

rate close to target and the economy close to full employment.

The McCallum rule has some advantages over the Taylor rule. To target the interest rate using the Taylor rule, the Fed must estimate the long-run equilibrium real interest rate and the output gap.

In the Taylor rule, which we described on p. 758, the long-run equilibrium real interest rate is 2 percent a year. The federal funds rate is set at this level if the inflation rate and output gap are zero. But if the long-run equilibrium real interest rate is not 2 percent a year, the Taylor rule would set the interest rate either too high on the average and bring persistent recession or too low on the average and bring persistent and accelerating inflation.

Similarly, if the Fed overestimated the output gap, it would set the federal funds rate too high on the average and bring persistent recession. And if the Fed underestimated the output gap, it would set the federal funds rate too low on the average and bring persistent inflation.

Because the McCallum rule doesn't react to either the real interest rate or the output gap, the McCallum rule doesn't suffer from the problems of the Taylor rule.

A disadvantage of the McCallum rule compared to the Taylor rule is that it relies on the demand for money and demand for monetary base being reasonably stable.

The Fed believes that shifts in the demand for money and the demand for monetary base would bring large fluctuations in the interest rate, which in turn would bring large fluctuations in aggregate demand.

Money Targeting Rule

As long ago as 1948, Nobel Laureate Milton Friedman proposed a targeting rule for the quantity of money. Friedman's **k-percent rule** makes the quantity of money grow at a rate of k percent a year, where k equals the growth rate of potential GDP.

Like the McCallum rule, Friedman's k-percent rule relies on a stable demand for money, which translates to a stable velocity of circulation. Friedman had examined data on money and nominal GDP and argued that the velocity of circulation of money was one of the most stable macroeconomic variables and that it could be exploited to deliver a stable price level and small business cycle fluctuations.

Friedman's idea remained just that until the 1970s, when inflation increased to more than 10 percent a year in the United States and to much higher rates in some other major countries.

During the mid-1970s, in a bid to end the inflation, the central banks of most major countries adopted the *k*-percent rule for the growth rate of the quantity of money. The Fed, too, began to pay close attention to the growth rates of money aggregates, including M1 and M2.

Inflation rates fell during the early 1980s in the countries that had adopted a *k*-percent rule. But one by one, these countries abandoned the *k*-percent rule.

Money targeting works when the demand for money is stable and predictable—when the velocity of circulation is stable. But in the world of the 1980s, and possibly in the world of today, technological change in the banking system leads to large and unpredictable fluctuations in the demand for money, which make the use of monetary targeting unreliable. With monetary targeting, aggregate demand fluctuates because the demand for money fluctuates. With interest rate targeting, aggregate demand is insulated from fluctuations in the demand for money (and the velocity of circulation).

Exchange Rate Targeting Rule

The Fed could, if it wished to do so, intervene in the foreign exchange market to target the exchange rate. A fixed exchange rate is one possible exchange rate target. The Fed could fix the value of the U.S. dollar against a basket of other currencies such as the *trade-weighted index* (see Chapter 26, p. 606).

But with a fixed exchange rate, a country has no control over its inflation rate. The reason is that for internationally traded goods, *purchasing power parity* (see p. 626) moves domestic prices in line with foreign prices. If a computer chip costs $100 in Los Angeles and if the exchange rate is 120 yen per $1.00, then the computer chip will sell for 12,000 yen (ignoring local tax differences) in Tokyo. If this purchasing power parity didn't prevail, it would be possible to earn a profit by buying at the lower price and selling at the higher price. This trading would compete away the profit and price difference.

So prices of traded goods (and in the long run the prices of all goods and services) must rise at the same rate in the United States as they do on the average in the other countries against which the value of the U.S. dollar is fixed.

The Fed could avoid a direct inflation link by using a *crawling peg exchange rate* (see Chapter 26, p. 634) as a means of achieving an inflation target. To do so, the Fed would make the exchange rate change at a rate equal to the U.S. inflation rate minus the target inflation rate. If other countries have an average inflation rate of 3 percent a year and the United States wants an inflation rate of 2 percent a year, the Fed would make the U.S. dollar appreciate at a rate of 1 percent a year against the trade-weighted index of other currencies.

Some developing countries that have an inflation problem use this monetary policy strategy to lower the inflation rate. The main reason for choosing this method is that these countries don't have well-functioning markets for bonds and overnight loans, so they cannot use the policy approach that relies on these features of a banking system.

A major disadvantage of a crawling peg to target the inflation rate is that the real exchange rate often changes in unpredictable ways. The **real exchange rate** between the United States and its trading partners is the relative price of the GDP basket of goods and services in the United States with respect to that in other countries. U.S. GDP contains a larger proportion of high-technology products and services than GDP in other countries contain. So when the relative prices of these items change, our real exchange rate changes. With a crawling peg targeting the inflation rate, we would need to be able to identify changes in the real exchange rate and offset them. This task is difficult to accomplish.

Inflation Rate Targeting Rule

Inflation rate targeting is a monetary policy strategy in which the central bank makes a public commitment

1. To achieve an explicit inflation target
2. To explain how its policy actions will achieve that target

Of the alternatives to the Fed's current strategy, inflation targeting is the most likely to be considered. In fact, some economists see it as a small step from what the Fed currently does. For these reasons, we'll explain this policy strategy in a bit of detail. Which countries practice inflation targeting, how do they do it, and what does it achieve?

Inflation Targeters Several major central banks practice inflation targeting and have done so since the mid-1990s. The best examples of central banks that use inflation targeting are the Bank of England, Bank of Canada, the Reserve Bank of New Zealand, and the Swedish Riksbank. The European Central Bank also practices inflation targeting. Japan and the United States are the most prominent major industrial economies that do not use this monetary policy strategy. But it is interesting to note that when the chairman of the Board of Governors of the Federal Reserve System, Ben Bernanke, and a member of the Board of Governors, Frederic S. Mishkin, were economics professors (at Princeton University and Columbia University, respectively), they did research together and wrote important articles and books on this topic. And their general conclusion was that inflation targeting is a sensible way in which to conduct monetary policy.

How Inflation Targeting is Conducted Inflation targets are specified in terms of a range for the CPI inflation rate. This range is typically between 1 percent and 3 percent a year, with an aim to achieve an average inflation rate of 2 percent per year. Because the lags in the operation of monetary policy are long, if the inflation rate falls outside the target range, the expectation is that the central bank will move the inflation rate back on target over the next two years.

All the inflation-targeting central banks use an overnight interest rate (the equivalent of the federal funds rate) as the policy instrument. And they use open market operations as the tool for achieving the desired overnight rate.

To explain their policy actions, inflation targeters publish an inflation report that describes the current state of the economy and its expected evolution over the next two years. The report also explains the central bank's current policy and how and why the central bank expects that its policy will achieve the inflation target.

What Does Inflation Targeting Achieve? The goals of inflation targeting are to state clearly and publicly the goals of monetary policy, to establish a framework of accountability, and to keep the inflation rate low and stable while maintaining a high and stable level of employment.

There is wide agreement that inflation targeting achieves its first two goals. And the inflation reports of inflation targeters have raised the level of discussion and understanding of the monetary policy process.

It is less clear whether inflation targeting does better than the implicit targeting that the Fed currently pursues in achieving low and stable inflation. The Fed's own record, without a formal inflation target, has been impressive over the past several years.

But monetary policy is about managing inflation expectations. And it seems clear that an explicit inflation target that is taken seriously and toward which policy actions are aimed and explained is a sensible way to manage expectations.

It is when the going gets tough that inflation targeting has the greatest attraction. It is difficult to imagine a serious inflation-targeting central bank permitting inflation to take off in the way that it did during the 1970s. And it is difficult to imagine deflation and ongoing recession such as Japan has endured for the past 10 years if monetary policy is guided by an explicit inflation target.

The debate on inflation targeting will continue!

Why Rules?

You might be wondering why all monetary policy strategies involve rules. Why doesn't the Fed just do what seems best every day, month, and year, at its discretion? The answer lies in what you've just read. Monetary policy is about managing inflation expectations. In both financial markets and labor markets, people must make long-term commitments. So these markets work best when plans are based on correctly anticipated inflation outcomes. A well-understood monetary policy rule helps to create an environment in which inflation is easier to forecast and manage.

Review Quiz

1 What are the four main alternative strategies for conducting monetary policy (other than the one used by the Fed)?

2 Briefly, why does the Fed reject each of these alternatives?

 Work Study Plan 31.4 and get instant feedback.

◆ The next two pages provide a quick guide to the extraordinary financial crisis policy actions of the past two years and *Reading Between the Lines* on pages 774–775 examine the Fed's aggressive interest rate cuts in 2008.

Extraordinary Policies for Extraordinary Times
The Fed Acts in Concert with the U.S. Treasury

A financial crisis began in the United States in August 2007 and quickly spread though the global economy. You are now well-equipped to understand the key elements in this crisis and its spread to the broader economy.

You studied the market for loanable funds in Chapter 24, the U.S. money market in Chapter 25, and the foreign exchange market in Chapter 26. All of these markets interacted in the financial crisis. And the crisis quickly became a broader economic crisis through its influence on aggregate demand and aggregate supply, which you studied in Chapter 27.

The Key Elements of the Crisis

We can describe the key elements of the crisis by thinking about the events that changed the values of the assets and liabilities of banks and other financial institutions.

Figure 1 shows the stylized balance sheet of a bank: deposits plus equity equals reserves plus loans and securities (see p. 592). Deposits and equity are the bank's sources of funds (other borrowing by banks is ignored here). Deposits are the funds loaned to the bank by households and firms, and equity is the capital provided by the bank's stockholders. Equity includes the bank's undistributed profits (and losses). The bank's reserves are currency and its deposit at the Fed. The bank's loans and securities are the loans made by the bank and government bonds, private bonds, asset-backed bonds, and other securities that the bank holds.

Three main events can put a bank under stress:

1. Widespread fall in asset prices
2. A significant currency drain
3. A run on the bank

Figure 1 summarizes the problems that each event presents to a bank. A widespread fall in asset prices means that the bank suffers a *capital loss*. It must write down the value of its assets and the value of the bank's equity decreases by the same amount as the fall in the value of its securities. If the fall in asset prices is large enough, the bank's equity might fall to zero, in which case the bank is insolvent. It fails.

A significant currency drain means that depositors withdraw funds and the bank loses reserves. This event puts the bank in a liquidity crisis. It is short of cash reserves.

A run on the bank occurs when depositors lose confidence in the bank and massive withdrawals of deposits occur. The bank loses reserves and must call in loans and sell off securities at unfavorable prices. Its equity shrinks.

The red arrows in Fig. 1 summarize the effects of these events and the problems they brought in the 2007–2008 financial crisis. A widespread fall in asset prices was triggered by the bursting of a house-price bubble that saw house prices switch from rapidly rising to falling. With falling house prices, sub-prime mortgage defaults occurred and the prices of mortgage-backed securities and derivatives whose values are based on these securities began to fall.

People with money market mutual fund deposits began to withdraw them, which created a fear of a massive withdrawal of these funds analagous to a run on a bank. In the United Kingdom, one bank, Northern Rock, experienced a bank run.

With low reserves and even lower equity, banks turned their attention to securing their balance sheets and called in loans. The loanable funds market and money market dried up.

Because the loanable funds market is global, the same problems quickly spread to other economies, and foreign exchange markets became highly volatile.

Hard-to-get loans, market volatility, and increased uncertainty transmitted the financial and monetary crisis to real expenditure decisions.

Event	Deposits	+ Equity	= Reserves	+ Loans and securities	Problem
Widespread fall in asset prices		▼		▼	Solvency
Currency drain	▼		▼		Liquidity
Run on bank	▼	▼	▼	▼	Liquidity and solvency

Figure 1 The Ingredients of a Financial and Banking Crisis

The Policy Actions

Policy actions in response to the financial crisis dribbled out over a period of more than a year. But by November 2008, eight groups of policies designed to contain the crisis and minimize its impact on the real economy were in place. They are

1. Open market operation
2. Extension of deposit insurance
3. Term auction credit
4. Primary dealer and other broker credit
5. Asset-backed commercial paper money market mutual fund liquidity facility
6. Troubled Asset Relief Program (TARP 1)
7. Troubled Asset Relief Program (TARP 2)
8. Fair value accounting

Figure 2 summarizes these actions, their effects on a bank's balance sheet (red and blue arrows), and the problem that each action sought to address.

An open market operation is the classic policy (described on pp. 759–760) for providing liquidity and enabling the Fed to hit its interest rate target. With substantial interest rate cuts, heavy open market operations were used to keep the banks well supplied with reserves. This action lowered bank holdings of securities and increased their reserves.

By extending deposit insurance (see p. 592) people with bank and money market mutual fund deposits became more secure and had less incentive to withdraw deposits. This action increased both deposits and reserves.

Three actions by the Fed supplemented open market operations to provide additional liquidity in exchange for troubled assets. Term auction credit, primary dealer and broker credit, and the asset-backed commercial paper money market mutual fund liquidity facility enabled institutions to swap troubled assets for reserves or safer assets. All of these actions decreased bank holdings of securities and increased reserves.

The Troubled Asset Relief Program (TARP) was an action by the U.S. Treasury, so technically it isn't a monetary policy action, but it has a direct impact on banks and other financial institutions. The program is funded by $700 billion of national debt.

The original intent, (we'll call it TARP 1) was for the U.S. Treasury to buy troubled assets from banks and other holders and replace them with U.S. government securities. Implementing this program proved more difficult than initially anticipated and the benefits of the action came to be questioned.

So instead of buying troubled assets (we'll call it TARP 2), the Treasury decided to buy equity stakes in troubled institutions. This action directly increased the institutions reserves and equity.

The final action was neither monetary policy nor fiscal policy but a change in accounting standards. It relaxed the requirement for institutions to value their assets at current market value—called "mark-to-market"—and permitted them, in rare conditions, to use a model to assess "fair market value."

Taken as a whole, a huge amount of relief was thrown at this financial crisis. Events through 2009 will show whether enough was done.

Action	Deposits	+ Equity	= Reserves	+ Loans and securities	Problem addressed
Open market operation			▲	▼	Liquidity
Extension of deposit insurance	▲		▲		Liquidity
Term auction credit			▲	▼	Liquidity
Primary dealer and other broker credit			▲	▼	Liquidity
Asset-backed commercial paper money market mutual fund liquidity facility			▲	▼	Liquidity
Troubled Asset Relief Program (TARP 1)			▲	▼	Liquidity
Troubled Asset Relief Program (TARP 2)		▲	▲		Solvency
Fair value accounting		▲		▲	Solvency

Figure 2 Policy Actions in a Financial and Banking Crisis

Monetary Policy in Action

Concerned Fed Trims Key Rate by a Half Point

http://www.nytimes.com
October 30, 2008

The Federal Reserve lowered its benchmark interest rate by half a percentage point on Wednesday, its second big rate cut this month, as policy makers tried to fend off what could be the worst economic downturn in decades.

The move brought the target rate for federal funds ... to 1 percent, down to the near-record lows reached in 2003 and 2004, when the Fed was trying to encourage an economic recovery after the bursting of the Internet bubble. The central bank left open the possibility of going still lower, warning "downside risks to growth remain." ...

In a statement, the Fed acknowledged that the economy had lost steam on almost every front—consumer spending, business investment, financial markets and even exports, which had been the one bright spot recently. For the time being, inflation is of little concern.

"The pace of economic activity appears to have slowed markedly, owing importantly to a decline in consumer expenditures," the central bank said. Industrial production and investment in new equipment have also slowed, it said, and slumping growth around the world has reduced demand for American exports. ...

But analysts said lower interest rates were not likely to accomplish much at this point, because the economy's biggest problem is the fear among banks and financial institutions about lending money.

"The difference between 1.5 percent and 1 percent is really pretty insignificant, particularly when the banking system is as weak as it is," said Ethan Harris, a senior economist at Barclay's Capital. "You have a big uncertainty shock. It's not just that the markets have declined. People are uncertain about where the world is going." ...

Essence of the Story

- The Federal Reserve lowered the federal funds rate target to 1 percent on October 29, 2008 in a bid to avoid a deep and long recession.

- The Fed warned that "downside risks to growth remain," a hint that the interest rate might go even lower.

- The Fed said that consumer spending, business investment, and even exports were all down.

- Analysts said lower interest rates would have a small effect because banks and financial institutions were not lending.

Economic Analysis

- The first estimate of GDP for the third quarter of 2008 suggested that real GDP was falling slightly (at an annualized rate of 0.25 percent) and the price level was rising sharply (at an annualized rate of 4.1 percent).

- Despite these numbers, the Fed believed recession was a more serious risk than inflation.

- The Fed's goal in cutting the federal funds rate was to help stimulate aggregate demand and boost real GDP in the following quarters.

- But in 2008, credit markets were not working normally. The perception of risk was unusually high, and institutions normally willing to lend to each other were reluctant to do so. Without an increase in lending, the interest rate cut would not have its desired effect.

- The figures illustrate the economy in late 2008.

- In Fig. 1, the Fed cuts the federal funds rate target and hits its new target by increasing the supply of reserves from RS_0 to RS_1.

- In Fig. 2, the economy average real interest rate is 3 percent at the intersection of the supply of loanable funds curve SLF_0 and the demand for loanable funds curve DLF.

- Normally, when the Fed cuts the federal funds rate, the supply of loanable funds increases and the supply curve shifts rightward, like the shift to SLF_1.

- In Fig. 3, real GDP is $11.7 trillion and the price level is 123 at the intersection of AD_0 and SAS. Potential GDP is $12 trillion, so there is a recessionary gap.

- Normally, when the Fed cuts the federal funds rate, aggregate demand increases and the AD curve shifts rightward, like the shift to AD_1.

- At the time when the Fed took its actions, it was not clear whether these normal responses to an interest rate cut would occur. That is probably why the Fed cut by such a large amount and to such a low level.

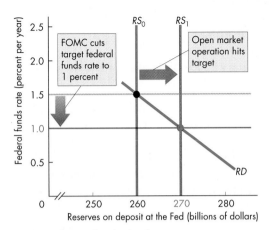

Figure 1 The market for bank reserves

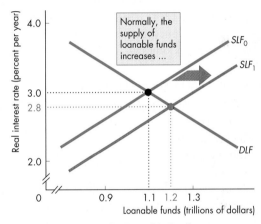

Figure 2 The market for loanable funds

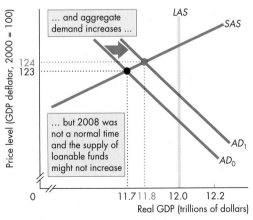

Figure 3 Real GDP and the price level

SUMMARY

Key Points

Monetary Policy Objectives and Framework
(pp. 754–756)

- The Federal Reserve Act requires the Fed to use monetary policy to achieve maximum employment, stable prices, and moderate long-term interest rates.
- The goal of stable prices delivers maximum employment and low interest rates in the long run but can conflict with the other goals in the short run.
- The Fed translates the goal of stable prices as an inflation rate of between 1 and 2 percent per year.
- The FOMC has the responsibility for the conduct of monetary policy, but the Fed reports to the public and to Congress.

The Conduct of Monetary Policy (pp. 756–760)

- The Fed's monetary policy instrument is the federal funds rate.
- The Fed sets the federal funds rate target and announces changes on eight dates each year.
- An *instrument rule* for monetary policy makes the instrument respond predictably to the state of the economy. The Fed does *not* use a mechanical instrument rule.

- A *targeting rule* for monetary policy sets the instrument to make the forecast of the inflation rate equal to the target inflation rate. The Fed *does* use such a rule, but its actions are similar to an instrument rule.
- The Fed hits its federal funds rate target by using open market operations.
- By buying or selling government securities in the open market, the Fed is able to change bank reserves and change the federal funds rate.

Monetary Policy Transmission (pp. 761–768)

- A change in the federal funds rate changes other interest rates, the exchange rate, the quantity of money and loans, aggregate demand, and eventually real GDP and the price level.
- Changes in the federal funds rate change real GDP about one year later and change the inflation rate with an even longer time lag.

Alternative Monetary Policy Strategies (pp. 769–773)

- The main alternatives to setting the federal funds rate are a monetary base instrument rule, a money targeting rule, an exchange rate targeting rule, or an inflation rate targeting rule.
- Rules trump discretion in monetary policy because they better enable the central bank to manage inflation expectations.

Key Figures

Key Terms

PROBLEMS and APPLICATIONS

myeconlab Work problems 1–8 in Chapter 31 Study Plan and get instant feedback.
Work problems 9–17 as Homework, a Quiz, or a Test if assigned by your instructor.

1. Suppose that the Fed is required to keep the inflation rate between 1 percent and 2 percent a year but with no requirement to keep trend inflation at the midpoint of this range. The Fed achieves its target.
   a. If initially the price level is 100,
      i. Calculate the highest price level that might occur after 10 years.
      ii. Calculate the lowest price level that might occur after 10 years.
      iii. What is the range of uncertainty about the price level after 10 years?
   b. Would this type of inflation goal serve the financial markets well and provide an anchor for inflation expectations?

2. Suppose that the Bank of England decides to follow the Taylor rule. In 2005, the United Kingdom has an inflation rate of 2.1 percent a year and its output gap is –0.3 percent. At what level does the Bank of England set the repo rate (the U.K. equivalent of the federal funds rate)?

3. Suppose that the Bank of Canada is following the McCallum rule. The Bank of Canada has an inflation target range of between 1 percent a year and 3 percent a year. The long-term real GDP growth rate in Canada is 2.4 percent a year. If the velocity of circulation of the monetary base is 2, what is the
   a. Highest growth rate of monetary base that will occur?
   b. Lowest growth rate of monetary base that will occur?

4. In Freezone, shown in the figure at the top of the next column, the aggregate demand curve is AD, potential GDP is $300 billion, and the short-run aggregate supply curve is SAS_B.
   a. What are the price level and real GDP?
   b. Does Freezone have an unemployment problem or an inflation problem? Why?
   c. What will happen in Freezone if the central bank takes no monetary policy actions?
   d. What monetary policy action would you advise the central bank to take and what do you predict will be the effect of that action?

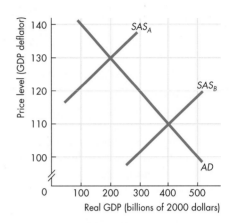

5. Suppose that in Freezone, shown in problem 4, the short-run aggregate supply curve is SAS_A and a drought decreases potential GDP to $250 billion.
   a. What happens in Freezone if the central bank lowers the federal funds rate and buys securities on the open market?
   b. What happens in Freezone if the central bank raises the federal funds rate and sells securities on the open market?
   c. Do you recommend that the central bank lower or raise the federal funds rate? Why?

6. **Fed Sees Both Unemployment, Prices on Rise**
   The Federal Reserve sees worse economic problems ahead. ... But even so, the Fed may be reluctant to cut interest rates any further than it already has. ... The Fed lowered its economic growth forecast for the year. At the same time, it raised its projections for inflation and unemployment. ... The Fed raised its unemployment forecast ... to between 5.5 percent and 5.7 percent ... [and] now expects personal consumption expenditures to rise between 3.1 percent and 3.4 percent in 2008 ... [and] expects steeper "core" inflation. ... In an effort to keep the country from falling into recession and to deal with the credit crisis, the Fed has cut its key federal funds rate seven times since September. This short-term interest rate is now 2 percent, down from 5.25 percent at the start of the Fed's easing campaign.

… Some believe the Fed cuts since last September helped fuel inflation, especially the sharp run-up in oil prices, because the rate cuts have led to a weakening of the dollar. Along those lines, the two Fed members who voted against the last rate cut … argued during the meeting that the Fed cuts were hurting the economy more than helping it.

CNN, May 21, 2008

a. Explain the intended effect of the Fed cutting the target federal funds rate from 5.25 percent to 2 percent and illustrate your explanation with an appropriate graphical analysis.
b. Explain how this monetary policy may have "helped fuel inflation, especially the sharp run-up in oil prices."
c. What is core inflation and why does the Fed tend to focus on that measurement of inflation more heavily than overall inflation?
d. Explain the dilemma that the Fed is facing when making decisions in the face of rising unemployment and rising inflation.

7. **Are Bernanke's Hands Tied on Inflation?**

Inflation has replaced the subprime meltdown and the possibility of recession as the hot-button economic issue. Bernanke's remarks in Spain signal that the central bank aims to keep the dollar … from sliding anew and further eroding consumers' purchasing power. … But with the U.S. economy slowing and the financial markets showing renewed signs of unrest, will the Fed actually follow through? That's another question altogether. … Indeed, the Fed has spent the past nine months cutting interest rates and lending freely to financial firms in a bid to prevent the financial system from seizing up. Those unusual actions have succeeded in staving off a calamity, but the economy remains weak. … So for now, the Fed simply wants to keep rates steady. … Doing so could maintain stability in the dollar and help arrest the rise in food and energy prices that have punished U.S. consumers. … Tough anti-inflation talk elsewhere in the world could also complicate the Fed's job. Jean-Claude Trichet, head of the European Central Bank, said Thursday the ECB hasn't ruled out raising interest rates next month. Many observers suspect the ECB is, like the Fed, trying to beat down inflation expectations by signaling that it is ready to

take action—while hoping it doesn't need to do so. But the mere suggestion the ECB could soon raise rates sent the dollar lower against the euro again Thursday.

Fortune, June 5, 2008

a. Explain how the Fed raising interest rates would "defend" the U.S. dollar. Is the Fed's stance reflecting an exchange rate targeting rule monetary policy strategy?
b. What adverse consequences might result if the Fed does actually increase rates?
c. Explain the argument made that the Fed is "trying to beat down inflation expectations by signaling that it is ready to take action—while hoping it doesn't need to do so."
d. Why do the monetary policy decisions of other central banks (such as the ECB) "complicate" the Fed's job?

8. **Politicians Urged to Leave the Economy to the Fed**

The U.S. economy is teetering on the edge. Many economists… put the risk of recession next year at about 50 percent. … The question on the minds of many in Congress and in the White House is this: What should they be doing now to keep the economy on track? The right answer: absolutely nothing. This advice isn't easy for politicians to follow. Because economic downturns mean fewer jobs and falling incomes, they are painful for many families. Voters can confuse inaction with nonchalance and send incumbents packing. … Congress made its most important contribution to taming the business cycle in 1913, when it created the Federal Reserve System. The Fed remains the first line of defense against recession. … Admittedly, monetary policy can sometimes use an assist from fiscal policy. If an economic downturn is deep, if a recovery is anemic or if the Fed is running out of ammunition, Congress can help raise aggregate demand for goods and services. …

International Herald Tribune, December 23, 2007

a. Explain and evaluate the rationale for using monetary policy as a "first line of defense" and reserving fiscal policy for "deep" downturns and when monetary policy has already been exhausted.
b. Why is this a difficult guideline for the president and Congress to follow?

9. Suppose the Fed is required to keep the inflation rate between 0 and 3 percent a year and is also required to keep trend inflation at the midpoint of the range. The Fed achieves its target.
   a. If initially the price level is 100, what is the likely price level after 10 years?
   b. Compare this economy with the economy in problem 1. Which economy has the greater certainty about inflation over the longer term? Which has the greater short-term certainty?

10. Suppose that the Reserve Bank of New Zealand is following the Taylor rule. In 2009, it sets the official cash rate (the N.Z. equivalent of the federal funds rate) at 4 percent a year. If the inflation rate in New Zealand is 2.0 percent a year, what is its output gap?

11. The figure shows the economy of Freezone. The aggregate demand curve is AD, and the short-run aggregate supply curve is SAS_A. Potential GDP is $300 billion.

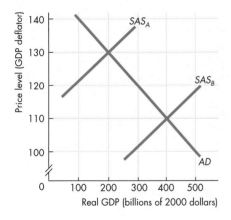

   a. What are the price level and real GDP?
   b. Does Freezone have an unemployment problem or an inflation problem? Why?
   c. What do you predict will happen in Freezone if the central bank takes no monetary policy actions?
   d. What monetary policy action would you advise the central bank to take and what do you predict will be the effect of that action?

12. Suppose that in Freezone, shown in problem 11, the short-run aggregate supply curve is SAS_B and potential GDP increases to $350 billion.
   a. What happens in Freezone if the central bank lowers the federal funds rate and buys securities on the open market?
   b. What happens in Freezone if the central bank raises the federal funds rate and sells securities on the open market?
   c. Do you recommend that the central bank lower or raise the federal funds rate? Why?

13. **The Fed Finds its Missing Link**
    Elizabeth "Betsy" Duke, the newest addition to the Federal Reserve's chief policy making group, is a lifelong commercial banker who many Fed watchers hope can balance out a board riven by inflation pressures, a weakened Wall Street, and a slowing economy. ...
    Duke is also the only member of the Federal Reserve Board with commercial-banking experience. ... Duke, a graduate of the University of North Carolina who majored in theater, has spent 32 years as a banker. ... Fed watchers expect her to play a key role in the Fed's ongoing examination of mortgage lending standards and bank regulations. As one of seven Fed board members, Duke will help set the country's monetary policy, which includes interest rates and banking standards. "The Federal Reserve's job is not only to tend to macroeconomic conditions, it must also ensure the integrity of borrowing and lending," said Lacy Hunt, a former Fed economist. ... "The regulatory process obviously broke down in a massive way; and one can't help but wonder whether we should have had more actual bankers on the board."
    CNN, July 8, 2008
   a. What are the primary functions of the Federal Reserve System?
   b. How is a member of the Board of Governors of the Federal Reserve System appointed?
   c. Explain the potential advantages and disadvantages of adding Duke, a theater major with 32 years of commercial banking experience, to the Board of Governors.
   d. Explain how, even if no members of the Board were bankers, monetary policy debates and decisions would still be influenced by individuals with banking experience.

14. **Fed Prepares to Hit Pause**
    Federal Reserve chairman Ben Bernanke all but closed the door on the chances of any more rate cuts during the next few months. ... Bernanke said that "for now, policy seems well positioned to promote moderate growth and price stability over time." Translation: Interest rates are going to

remain at 2 percent for a while. Get used to it. … The Fed cut its key federal funds rate to 1 percent following the 2001 recession and some market observers say that these low rates created the easy money environment that got banks and borrowers into the subprime mess that the Fed now has to clean up. It would appear that Bernanke would not want to make the same mistake. … What's more, Bernanke also seems to have gotten the message that more rate cuts may cause irreparable harm to the value of the dollar. The moribund greenback has been blamed by some economists for helping to lead to the surge in oil prices and other commodities, which in turn have led to rising prices of food and gas.

CNN, June 3, 2008

a. What are the potential consequences of the Fed cutting rates too much in the face of a recession?
b. Explain how rate cuts may have contributed to the "surge" in oil prices.

15. **Fed Rate Cuts and Your Wallet**

We've already had five interest rate cuts since September of last year. And we may be on the verge of yet another one. … It's hard to see the connection between what the Fed does and what the economy does. To some economists, the Fed has done its job. "The Fed has tried to stimulate bank lending. And to some extent, they've been successful," says Hugh Johnson of Illington Advisors. The bottom line here is that the Fed is fighting an uphill battle. There are serious drags on the economy, from housing and oil to unemployment and bad credit markets. … Keep in mind there is a limit to how much the Fed can cut rates before inflation becomes a real problem. … And it may be some time until we see exactly what the rate cuts do for the economy. "Rate cuts by the Fed are only effective with a lag," says Greg McBride of Bankrate.com. "That lag can be anywhere from 9–18 months. The five rate cuts so far … represent a lot of juice for the economy that's in the pipeline." … Fed rate cuts are not likely to help mortgage rates, because investors don't want to get locked into long-term investments with low interest rates in a high inflation rate environment. … Even if the Fed cuts rates, credit cards don't have to pass that reduced rate onto you. This is a turbulent time in the credit card industry.

CNN, March 17, 2008

a. Explain the intended effect of the Fed cutting the target for the federal funds rate and illustrate your explanation with an appropriate graphical analysis.
b. Explain what will limit the effectiveness of this monetary stimulus.

16. **Bernanke's Inflation Focus Boosts Rate Hike Odds**

Bernanke sent a fresh warning that the Fed will be on heightened alert against inflation dangers, especially any signs that investors, consumers and businesses think prices will keep going up and change their behavior in ways that will aggravate inflation. The Fed "will strongly resist an erosion of longer-term inflation expectations, as an unanchoring of those expectations would be destabilizing for growth as well as for inflation," Bernanke said. The Fed chief and his colleagues have been signaling that the Fed's rate-cutting campaign, started in September, is probably over given mounting concerns about inflation. And, little by little, Bernanke is preparing people for the prospects of higher rates down the road.

MSNBC, June 10, 2008

a. Explain why the Fed places so much emphasis on managing inflation expectations.
b. Why is Bernanke using public statements to prepare people "little by little" for future monetary policy decisions?
c. Graphically illustrate and explain the desired effect of the Fed raising the target for the federal funds rate.

17. Study *Reading Between the Lines* on pp. 774–775 and then answer the following questions.
a. How did the Fed's expectation about future real GDP growth and inflation differ from most recent actual changes in real GDP and the price level?
b. How would the market for loanable funds and aggregate demand normally respond to a large cut in the federal funds rate?
c. What made 2008 unusual and how would you analyze the special features of 2008 in the market for loanable funds?
d. If the Fed had not cut the federal funds rate, what might the consequences have been?

PHOTO CREDITS

College campus (p. 1) Image Source/Getty Images Inc-Image Source Royalty Free.

Ethenol plant (p. 31) Jim Parkin/Shutterstock.

Adam Smith (p. 53) Corbis-Bettmann.

Gas station price sign (p. 57) Anthony Berenyi/ Shutterstock.

SUVs (p. 85) Michael Shake/Shutterstock.

Drinking water (p. 107) Andrei Mihalcea/ Shutterstock.

Protesting high diesel prices (p. 129) DAMIAN DOVARGANES/AP Wide World Photos.

UPS cargo plane (p. 153) UPS/Bob Riha, Jr via Getty Images.

Alfred Marshall (p. 177) Stock Montage.

iPod (p. 181) AP Wide World Photos.

Digital reader (p. 203) Ruth Grimes/Alamy Images.

Kindle reader (p. 216) Wikipedia, The Free Encyclopedia.

Sony reader (p. 216) Newscom.

Jeremy Bentham (p. 223) Corbis-Bettmann.

Computer server room (p. 227) Getty Images/ Digital Vision.

Wheat field (p. 237) PhotoDisc, Inc.

Pizza dough (p. 237) Michael Newman/PhotoEdit.

Boeing and Airbus (p. 237) Alastair Miller/Bloomberg News/Landov LLC

Comcast truck (p. 237) AP Wide World Photos.

Google Search "SUV" (p. 245) © Google 2008.

Google homepage (p. 245) © Google 2008.

Yahoo! Homepage (p. 245) Copyright © 2008 Yahoo! Inc. All rights reserved.

Solar panels (p. 251) Adrian Matthiassen/ Shutterstock.

Automated car assembly (p. 265) Glowimages/ Getty Images-Creative Express Royalty Free.

Idle airplanes (p. 273) Adrian Britton/Shutterstock.

Harley-Davidson (p. 283) Rena Schild/Shutterstock.

Computer store shoppers (p. 285) Digital Vision/Getty Images/Digital Vision.

Tractor (p. 285) International Harvester Co.

Google headquarters (p. 299) AP Wide World Photos.

Chicago Pizza (p. 323) 360wichita.com.

iPhone (p. 334) Apple Computer, Inc.

Hewlett-Packard and Dell laptops (p. 341) AP Wide World Photos.

John von Neumann (p. 369) Stock Montage.

Oil Refinery (p. 373) Shutterstock.

Satellite (p. 393) National Oceanographic and Atmospheric Administration, NOAA.

Fish harvest (p. 393) MIXA/Getty Images Inc-Mixa.

Ronald H. Coase (p. 413) David Joel/David Joel Photography.

Caroline M. Hoxby (p. 414) E.S. Lee.

Offshore oil rig (p. 417) Yvan/Shutterstock.

Homeless person (p. 441) DON EMMERT/ AFP/Getty Images.

Lemon on wheels (p. 463) iStockPhoto.

Thomas Robert Malthus (p. 483) Corbis-Bettmann.

David Card (p. 484) Photo courtesy of Stuart Schwartz.

Man at computer (p. 487) Getty Images, Inc.-Blend Images.

Job interview (p. 509) OJO Images/Getty Images Royalty Free.

Great Depression (p. 510) Library of Congress.

David Hume (p. 531) Library of Congress.

Shanghai skyline (p. 535) Claudio Zaccherini/ Shutterstock.

Outdoor market (p. 549) Jose Silva Pinto/ AP Wide World Photos.

Wall Street (p. 563) Don Emmert/AFP/ Getty Images.

The Addison-Wesley Series in Economics

Abel/Bernanke/Croushore
Macroeconomics*

Bade/Parkin
Foundations of Economics*

Bierman/Fernandez
Game Theory with Economic Applications

Binger/Hoffman
Microeconomics with Calculus

Boyer
Principles of Transportation Economics

Branson
Macroeconomic Theory and Policy

Bruce
Public Finance and the American Economy

Byrns/Stone
Economics

Carlton/Perloff
Modern Industrial Organization

Caves/Frankel/Jones
World Trade and Payments: An Introduction

Chapman
Environmental Economics: Theory, Application, and Policy

Cooter/Ulen
Law & Economics

Downs
An Economic Theory of Democracy

Ehrenberg/Smith
Modern Labor Economics

Ekelund/Ressler/Tollison
Economics*

Fusfeld
The Age of the Economist

Gerber
International Economics

Ghiara
Learning Economics

Gordon
Macroeconomics

Gregory
Essentials of Economics

Gregory/Stuart
Russian and Soviet Economic Performance and Structure

Hartwick/Olewiler
The Economics of Natural Resource Use

Hoffman/Averett
Women and the Economy: Family, Work, and Pay

Holt
Markets, Games and Strategic Behavior

Hubbard
Money, the Financial System, and the Economy

Hughes/Cain
American Economic History

Husted/Melvin
International Economics

Jehle/Reny
Advanced Microeconomic Theory

Johnson-Lans
A Health Economics Primer

Klein
Mathematical Methods for Economics

Krugman/Obstfeld
International Economics: Theory and Policy*

Laidler
The Demand for Money

Leeds/von Allmen
The Economics of Sports

Leeds/von Allmen/Schiming
Economics*

Lipsey/Ragan/Storer
Economics*

Melvin
International Money and Finance

Miller
Economics Today*

Miller
Understanding Modern Economics

Miller/Benjamin
The Economics of Macro Issues

Miller/Benjamin/North
The Economics of Public Issues

Mills/Hamilton
Urban Economics

Mishkin
The Economics of Money, Banking, and Financial Markets*

Mishkin
The Economics of Money, Banking, and Financial Markets, Alternate Edition*

Murray
Econometrics: A Modern Introduction

Parkin
Economics*

Perloff
Microeconomics*

Perloff
Microeconomics: Theory and Applications with Calculus

Perman/Common/McGilvray/Ma
Natural Resources and Environmental Economics

Phelps
Health Economics

Riddell/Shackelford/Stamos/ Schneider
Economics: A Tool for Critically Understanding Society

Ritter/Silber/Udell
Principles of Money, Banking, and Financial Markets

Rohlf
Introduction to Economic Reasoning

Ruffin/Gregory
Principles of Economics

Sargent
Rational Expectations and Inflation

Scherer
Industry Structure, Strategy, and Public Policy

Sherman
Market Regulation

Stock/Watson
Introduction to Econometrics

Stock/Watson
Introduction to Econometrics, Brief Edition

Studenmund
Using Econometrics: A Practical Guide

Tietenberg
Environmental Economics and Policy

Tietenberg/Lewis
Environmental and Natural Resource Economics

Todaro/Smith
Economic Development

Waldman
Microeconomics

Waldman/Jensen
Industrial Organization: Theory and Practice

Weil
Economic Growth

Williamson
Macroeconomics